mended 4/24/07   BH

75   78   94
                        O
   75
      | | 85   95
74
   77

Also by Milton S. Eisenhower

THE WINE IS BITTER

THE
PRESIDENT
IS
CALLING

THE PRESIDENT IS CALLING

Milton S. Eisenhower

DOUBLEDAY & COMPANY, INC., GARDEN CITY, NEW YORK
1974

3-75   Pub   12⁵⁰

ISBN 0-385-01584-4
LIBRARY OF CONGRESS CATALOG CARD NUMBER: 73-9154
COPYRIGHT © 1974 BY MILTON S. EISENHOWER
ALL RIGHTS RESERVED
PRINTED IN THE UNITED STATES OF AMERICA
FIRST EDITION

At what point then is the approach of danger (to our American institutions) to be expected? I answer, if it is ever to reach us, it must spring up amongst us. It cannot come from abroad. If destruction be our lot, we must ourselves be its author and finisher. As a nation of freemen, we must live through all time, or die by suicide.

Abraham Lincoln
Springfield, Illinois
January 27, 1838

CONTENTS

* Italicized chapter headings denote recommendations for constitutional, legal,
or organizational changes in the federal government and in presidential-selection
processes.

FOREWORD

"Enter by the Basement Door"

FOR NEARLY HALF a century—forty-nine years to be exact—it was my good fortune to work for eight Presidents of the United States. I carried out significant policy and program assignments for six of these, four Democrats and two Republicans.

After serving full time in the federal establishment for nineteen years, I left the government to make higher education my major responsibility. Interestingly, however, assignments from Presidents of the United States thereafter, which I performed on a part-time basis, were usually more important and challenging than they had been when I was subordinate to a Cabinet member or to the President himself. At three different universities my office associates became familiar with the melodious voice of the White House operator, who would say, "The President is calling Dr. Eisenhower."

I testify with gratitude to the tolerance of three university boards of trustees, faculties, students, and alumni of these institutions who accepted my frequent absences as I carried out presidential chores in this country and in many nations of the world; indeed they often helped me and applauded the results beyond what I deserved.

At the age of seventy-four—the only remaining one of six Eisenhower brothers who have had varying influences in the American scene —I assume I have completed my work for the White House. After contemplating what I have done, and the toll the presidency exacted from the leaders I served, I now feel impelled to express my strong conviction that the responsibilities devolving upon the President of the United States by the Constitution, a myriad of laws, and tradition are more than any man, no matter how wise and physically robust he may be, can possibly redeem. Reorganization of executive agencies alone will not solve the problem. New laws, constitutional amendments, a break with some traditions, the creation of new supra-Cabinet positions, and other innovations are needed, and *needed now*.

This book, mainly chronological in development, is filled with personal narratives and anecdotes and is therefore a memoir, not an autobiography, for I have included nothing about twenty-five years as a university president, or about my industrial, financial, charitable, and other activities. It is a memoir with a theme: The purpose is to have the reader relive with me experiences which gradually offer an understanding of the presidency as it actually is—a post occupied by a normal human being who gets the same kind of stomach-aches and headaches that you and I do, a man overburdened with awesome responsibilities, sometimes the victim of misplaced confidences, a man often irritated and frustrated by unnecessary interruptions, thrilled by successes, and depressed by failures. The President is not a superman. He is not a computer. He is an individual who has the capacity to grow in stature and wisdom under responsibility but at the same time faces the danger of developing a monarchic complex and so reducing his effectiveness.

My hope is that a better understanding of the life any President must lead will stimulate widespread and thoughtful discussion. Perhaps debates may develop among some senators, congressmen, and officials of the executive establishment. Remedial actions, some perhaps deemed to be radical, will not be taken unless people generally realize the infinite dimensions and complexities of the problem.

I do not expect many persons to agree with the solutions I offer throughout this book. Theorists may be scornful. That will not bother me. Indeed, if criticism leads to constructive suggestions better than those I propose, I shall be grateful to the critics.

The President's official staff, minuscule when I entered the foreign service in 1924, and limited to four principal assistants under President Hoover, was greatly expanded during the long tenure of President Franklin D. Roosevelt. It increased under Truman, remained at that level under Eisenhower, expanded spectacularly under Kennedy and Johnson, and took another leap forward under Nixon, so that today in the Executive Office of the President there are 2,236 counselors, principal assistants, special assistants, assistants to assistants, administrators, lawyers, budget experts, economists, and supportive personnel. This number does not include a host of persons in several agencies, such as the Office of Economic Opportunity which, though normally part of the Executive Office, is in reality an independent agency as is, for example, the United States Information Agency. The present Executive Office staff could double in size and it would not help the President; it would exacerbate his problem.

The President's establishment is extensive. The central portion of the White House is the residence of the President and his family. The East and West wings contain presidential counselors and principal assistants. The President's own office (known as the oval room) is in the West Wing, but he also has a working office in the Executive Office Building, once the home of the State, War, and Navy departments, but now containing a substantial part of the Chief Executive's staff. Even this is not enough. Some who work for the President are in a large new brick building called the Executive Office Annex and in handsomely renovated houses in the same city square. The President's guest house, Blair House, sits snugly among this renovated complex.

Most official visitors who have appointments with the President or his principal assistants enter the northwest gate of the White House grounds and then the main door of the West Wing. Here they are seen by the corps of newspapermen assigned to cover this focal point of the United States Government.

Some who call on the President, however, are never seen by newspapermen, for they enter either from the south grounds or through the west basement door. The interior of the West Wing is such that from this lower entrance one may proceed to the President's office or offices of his assistants without being exposed to the press—and thus, too, escaping embarrassing demands for statements.

This west basement door became very familiar to me. I learned to know every guard and page who kept out the unauthorized but politely escorted the expected visitor to the proper office. It was President Franklin Roosevelt who first said to me, "Milton, I want to see you on a confidential matter, so enter by the basement door." That became habitual with me. The only exceptions occurred when I arrived by car; usually I then entered by the south grounds, walked through the ground floor of the residence and down the arcade to the Cabinet room and the President's office.

Had I had an inkling during my federal service that I would one day wish to write a book about my experiences with Presidents, I would have kept a detailed diary and logs of conversations. I did not. Neither has it been my habit to retain correspondence much beyond five years. So in preparing this book I have had to rely on memory, which is notoriously fallible. "Everyone complains of his memory, but no one complains of his judgment," said Rochefoucauld.

Fortunately, I have been able to check my recollections with the Presidents' official papers in the National Archives and several presidential libraries, books written by and about the Presidents, and a detailed set of memory books which my wife faithfully kept up to the time of her death.

I am deeply indebted to Ronald A. Wolk, an exceptionally talented former assistant of mine at The Johns Hopkins University, now vice-president of Brown University, who helped me with research and editorial matters; Francis O. Wilcox, eminent scholar, former Assistant Secretary of State, and until recently dean of the School of Advanced International Studies, who read the manuscript and suggested corrections; Michael McGrael, friend and former student at Johns Hopkins, who helped me with research; Mrs. Gertrude Holland, my secretary, who was properly critical when I used a careless word, and Wayne Anderson, Neil Grauer, and Mrs. Elizabeth Hughes, who nearly ruined their eyes reading newspapers for specific dates, events, and presidential messages. The tiny superior numbers appearing from time to time throughout the text are to indicate the books cited, listed at the back of the book.

From other duties that normally fill my days, I have stolen enough time to write this book in a period of a year and a half. More work would improve it. But as I wrote, dramatic developments, including the breakdown of the supportive-personnel system in the White House, scandals in high offices of government, and President Nixon's sudden advocacy of a single six-year term for the President, supported predictions I was making or views I was expressing, and these developments, far from changing my views, gave a sense of urgency to getting my manuscript to the publisher. These recent events, a major topic of conversation during much of 1972 and 1973, may stimulate the very kind of discussions about the presidency I am convinced are needed as we seek the best solution to what has become a gargantuan problem. So I have completed my work sooner than I had intended. There may therefore be errors here and there, inconsequential ones, I hope. If there are mistakes, they are mine. If the book as a whole merits serious thought, it is due in large part to some of the most intelligent individuals in our society, men and women, with whom it has been my rare privilege to work for a fairly long lifetime.

Milton S. Eisenhower

Baltimore
November 15, 1973

THE
PRESIDENT
IS
CALLING

CHAPTER 1

Considering the awful burdens he bears, I
have found it virtually impossible to say no
to the President of the United States.

ON THE EVENING of June 7, 1968, shortly before nine
o'clock, four of my undergraduate student friends came to my home
just across the street from The Johns Hopkins University. I had had
many such impromptu visits since my retirement from the university
presidency a year earlier, but this one was special. The four students
were in despair over the death of Senator Robert Kennedy the day before. The senator had been shot on the evening of the fifth and had
died in a Los Angeles hospital on the sixth without having regained
consciousness.

As I led the students into my study I was overcome by a feeling
of déjà vu. A few months earlier the murder of Martin Luther King
had stunned and saddened our campus community. Nearly five years
earlier I had seen in my students even more profoundly this same bewilderment and despair over the assassination of President Kennedy.

My visitors that June evening were intelligent young men, well informed on domestic and international problems. They were all personally involved in the 1968 presidential campaign. Originally they had
been supporters of Senator McCarthy for the Democratic nomination;
then the entry of Senator Robert Kennedy into the race had created
in them a kind of political schizophrenia.

Eugene McCarthy was part Don Quixote, part Pied Piper, and he
touched that deep strain of idealism in the young that makes tilting
at windmills a worthy enterprise. Bobby Kennedy was something else.
His idealism was rooted in a tough Boston Irish political pragmatism.
My young undergraduate friends admired him for his courage, his head-
on collision with President Johnson over the Vietnam War, his commitment to the poor and the blacks. And they saw in Bobby Kennedy,

1

or at least they wanted to see, the fulfillment of all the promises John Kennedy had been prevented from keeping.

The assassination of Robert Kennedy, like the murder of his brother and Martin Luther King, frightened and bewildered these young people. In common with all the rest of us, they found it difficult to believe that the will of the American people and the democratic process could be utterly nullified by the randomly insane act of one pitiful twisted human being. To them, these assassinations indicated a deep and infectious sickness in our society. Somehow these assassinations had to be related to a national malaise—to the growing disrespect for the law, the mounting tide of murder, rape, assault, and robbery. The racism in our land, the decay of our cities, the paralytic unresponsiveness of our social institutions, and the endless and devastating war in Southeast Asia were all both cause and symptom of some deeper and more profound malignancy. Those who recognized this and sought to lead the way to solutions, my student friends were convinced, were being cruelly snuffed out.

We sat in my study talking quietly about what had happened and what it would mean to the nation and to the presidential campaign. One of the students was expressing his deep concern about the "law and order" issue that had become so prominent in the campaign. It was a code phrase, he felt. He insisted that it really was used to mean silencing dissent and keeping the blacks under control. It implied that the proper way to deal with increasing lawlessness was to get tough, to improve the criminal justice system, whereas it was clear to him that the only lasting solution to American disorder was to attack its roots, to launch a massive attack on its social causes.

"People are calling for law and order," he said, "but too many of them really mean order, even at the expense of the law."

In this serious and somewhat gloomy atmosphere, the ringing of the telephone was a shrill interruption.

When I answered the phone and heard my name spoken, I immediately recognized the voice of the White House chief operator. I glanced at my watch. It was twenty-five minutes to ten.

After a brief greeting the operator said: "The President is calling."

I was not really surprised. Lyndon Johnson had telephoned me on many occasions over the long period of years that encompassed his service in the House of Representatives, the Senate, the vice-presidency, and

2

the White House. As President, he had at times sent a helicopter to the Johns Hopkins campus in order to hasten my trip from Baltimore to the White House.

Despite our differences in political philosophy, President Johnson and I were good friends. For years we had been on a first-name basis. Indeed, I had found it difficult to stop calling him Lyndon and to use only the formal "Mr. President." I had been rudely reminded of protocol years earlier when I called my brother "Ike" in front of his staff. Robert Cutler, his security assistant, had glared icily at me and snapped: "No one should refer to the President of the United States as Ike."

Usually President Johnson would make a bit of "small talk" before getting to the point of his call. He would pass along the regards of a mutual friend, or recall our last meeting, or relate a recent incident that he knew I would enjoy. That night, when he came on the phone, there was no chatty beginning.

"Milton, I very much need your help," he said quietly. "The assassination of Senator Kennedy is causing fear and anxiety to spread like wildfire across the country. It is a terrible, terrible tragedy." He paused.

"This has caused me to crystallize a thought that has been nagging at my mind for months. We need to make a deep study of the causes of violence in our society, and we must be wise enough to find solutions. I am creating a presidential commission to study the problem, beginning at once, and I want you to serve as chairman."

I was momentarily speechless. For years I had held the view that an American citizen does not have the right to decline a request made of him by the President, if he felt he had the ability to do the job. I had acted in this conviction over four decades in responding to the requests of Presidents of the United States.

Now I was torn. I am not a lawyer, sociologist, or criminologist. I felt I had no special competence to head a national commission which would attempt to analyze the manifold and complex causes of violence and to determine how to reduce substantially the crime and violence that were undermining the quality of American life. So I hedged. Only once before had I ever done so.

I told him his request had caught me unprepared and I asked for twenty-four hours to consider it.

"No, Milton," he replied, "I can't give you twenty-four hours—or one hour. In twenty minutes I am going on television to announce the appointment of the commission and to explain its task. I already have acceptances from Ambassador Patricia Harris, Judge Leon Higginbotham, Congressman McCulloch of Ohio, Congressman Boggs of Louisiana, Senator Hart of Michigan, Senator Hruska of Nebraska, Eric Hoffer of California, Archbishop Cooke of New York, and Albert Jenner of Chicago. Later, I hope to appoint Judge McFarland of the Supreme Court of Arizona, Leon Jaworski, a prominent attorney from Texas, and Dr. Walter Menninger of Kansas. As chairman, you will have an able group associated with you."

In desperation, I agreed to serve on the commission but urged him to select someone else as chairman, perhaps one of the two judges he had named.

As he answered, I knew that, had we been meeting face to face, he would have draped a long heavy arm over my shoulder and leaned into me. Even over the phone I could feel it coming—that special blend of cajolery and flattery, the irresistible Lyndon Johnson touch, dubbed by newspapermen as "the treatment."

"The chairman," he replied, "must be someone who has a national reputation for objectivity. Milton, you simply must see that I need your help and I need it now."

My misgivings, serious as they were, could not overcome the conditioned response of a lifetime. Almost inaudibly I agreed to do what he asked.

I glanced at my student friends. Their faces were comically curious. It was quite a change from the depression I had seen on their faces a few minutes before.

The President had me firmly in hand now and he hurried on:

"I want your approval of one appointment. You will need a top-flight executive director to help you form a staff and muster whatever other assistance you'll need. He can set up public hearings and do many other things to take some of the load off your shoulders. Do you know Lloyd Cutler? Here in Washington?"

I said I did not. The President quickly explained that Mr. Cutler, an eminent attorney, had long experience not only in the law but in carrying out a variety of federal tasks. He was respected on the Hill and the White House staff had confidence in him.

I agreed to the appointment (which proved to be superbly correct) and President Johnson said he would assemble the commission in the

4

White House within the next three days. Then I heard a click as the telephone connection was broken.

For what was only seconds but seemed to be many minutes, I said nothing to the students. I was confused and worried.

Only a year previously I had retired from the presidency of The Johns Hopkins University. A new program of diversified activity kept me busy, as of course I wished to be. But I no longer felt the strain of leadership and I no longer went through my days with that vague apprehension, wondering what the next emergency would be. I was delighted, at the age of sixty-nine, to be finally free of the frustration, sleeplessness, and sometime anguish which had been almost commonplace in my life.

I was now a director of thirteen corporations, continued to give such assistance to Johns Hopkins as my successor and the trustees asked of me, spent nearly a third of each day answering a flow of correspondence, and served on half a dozen charitable boards. My only federal assignment at the time was as a member of the five-man presidential commission studying the possibility of building a sea-level canal across the Central American isthmus. I was really enjoying retirement.

The students could contain themselves no longer.

"That was the President!" one of them exclaimed.

I acknowledged that it was, but felt strangely unwilling to explain the conversation that had just ended. I suggested that one of them turn on the television set, pointing out that in about ten minutes the President would be on the air and from his talk they could learn what had been discussed. We went to the kitchen for cold drinks and then returned to the library.

As the announcer intoned the traditional: "Ladies and gentlemen, the President of the United States," the students silently faced the television screen.

It was a solemn and deeply concerned Lyndon Johnson who appeared on the screen. He expressed the horror which all citizens felt about the assassination of Senator Kennedy and the earlier murder of Martin Luther King, and announced the creation of the National Commission on the Causes and Prevention of Violence. With emphasis, he said that I would serve as chairman.

I learned later that President Eisenhower had watched the telecast

5

from his hospital bed and had sympathized with me for having to accept this task. But he agreed that I could have made no other decision.

At the conclusion of President Johnson's talk, my friends shook hands with me and quietly left the house. They sensed that I wanted to be alone.

I returned to my favorite chair in the library and began to think back over the chores I had performed for Presidents of the United States. A fairly honorable record, spanning many years, was now possibly threatened.

Many of the assignments had been difficult, such as serving at President Truman's request on the first presidential fact-finding board in 1945–46, the task being to find a solution to the crippling strike against General Motors. That had been a grueling, time-consuming period, but the work was stimulating and, in the end, rewarding.

Some tasks had been sheer pleasure and exciting, especially my work as personal representative of the President and special ambassador to Latin America during the eight years of my brother's administration. My responsibility had been to develop a continental view of United States-Latin American relations, and to recommend to the President and the National Security Council changes in policies and programs. Occasionally I had felt compelled to accept unpopular and exhausting assignments. This had surely been the situation when President Roosevelt called me to his office and told me that one of my war tasks was to establish a War Relocation Authority and to move Japanese-Americans from the West Coast.

As I reflected on these experiences, I felt that in most cases I had been at least moderately helpful to the President and occasionally to the Congress; fortunately I had escaped the biting criticisms that so often were leveled at individuals on special presidential assignments.

Now, I honestly feared, the Johnson assignment could result in disaster for me and for the new commission. Presidential commissions were in disrepute. Columnists and television commentators had been charging that Presidents often appointed commissions when they did not know what else to do, that a commission was a stalling tactic and the reports submitted were put on the shelf to gather dust.

The Kerner Commission, which had studied urban riots, had done what seemed to me to be a commendable job; for several days after

6

the report reached President Johnson's desk the mass media gave prominent coverage to the commission's charge that the people of the United States were guilty of white racism and that we were rapidly becoming two societies—one white, the other black. No other aspect of the data-filled Kerner volumes was given similar public notice. Neither the President nor any member of his staff had commented on the report, and none of the recommendations submitted by the Kerner Commission had been transmitted by the President to the Congress.

The Katzenbach Commission, appointed to study the criminal justice system in the United States, had done a skillful and thorough job, but the only constructive consequence had been the creation of a new division in the Justice Department with funds sufficient to give only a modicum of assistance to law enforcement agencies in the states.

Earlier a report of a presidential commission which had studied the Selective Service system had been completely ignored. Indeed, one had to think back to the first Hoover Commission, in 1947, to find a commission that had been taken seriously and had had some impact. The Hoover Commission had made a massive study of the organization of the federal government over a period of years and many of its recommendations had been adopted. But it was a distinct exception. So the chances of still another study group's achieving success by persuading the President of the right course of action and by obtaining relevant legislation from Congress did not appear to be good. The chances of my staining the modest reputation I enjoyed seemed to be excellent.

These thoughts, though somewhat selfish, were tempered by a conviction that I had long held: namely, that the presidency of the United States had become an impossible job and that any help one could give was mandatory. Especially during the Eisenhower administration I had seen the President work fourteen hours a day, seven days a week, trying to meet his responsibilities as head of state, Chief Executive of government, Commander-in-Chief of the armed forces, constitutional director of foreign affairs, head of a political party, principal spokesman for the free world, advocate and architect of domestic programs, and the final authority on legislative enactments that were to be approved or vetoed.

I had seen these constitutional, legal, and traditional responsibilities of the President interrupted many times a day by a potpourri of comparatively trivial tasks: deciding whether an airline could fly the great

7

northern route to Tokyo or whether it must follow the 1,700-mile-longer route via Hawaii and Wake Island; approving or vetoing hundreds of private immigration and private relief bills; deciding whether a new drug was an opiate; appointing postmasters in all parts of the country; watching over the administration of the District of Columbia; settling quarrels about water resources between the Departments of Agriculture, Defense, and Interior; almost daily greeting groups in the Rose Garden and receiving a parade of visitors, many of whom had no serious purpose in taking the precious time of the Chief Executive.

When I entered the federal service in 1924 the duties of the President were not as time-consuming, seldom as far-reaching in their significance, as those of a single member of the Cabinet today. In 1924 total federal expenditures were less than three billion dollars; today, the Secretary of Agriculture oversees a farm program that in many years has cost twice that amount. Our government today is monumental in size, complex in structure, and more costly than were all the governments in the world in 1924.

The President is the executive head of a network that crisscrosses the globe; the truly great issues before him are peace or war, prosperity or depression, and the great social changes needed in the face of rapidly changing attitudes caused by burgeoning knowledge and a scientific and technological revolution.

Meeting such awesome challenges as these is surely all we should expect of any President. But he must also settle quarrels among federal departments and agencies; he must take to bed with him a volume of hundreds of pages and, having studied the conflicting evidence presented by five or six federal agencies, decide whether two airlines may compete in flying the same route abroad without causing a deficit that would have to be met by federal funds. Hundreds of federal laws, drawn over a period of many years, compel the President to do things and make judgments which, in our modern setting, ought to be handled by other responsible federal officials.

As I sat in the library late on the night of June 7, 1968, I was struck by the realization that my lifetime of nearly sixty-nine years spanned a third of the lifetime of our Republic. I realized, perhaps more vividly and poignantly than ever before, that American life had changed as significantly as the federal government during my forty-four years of intermittent federal service.

We had abandoned the predominantly rural society which Thomas Jefferson had felt was the indispensable bedrock of democracy. When I was a boy twenty-five per cent of our population was engaged in the task of providing food and fiber for the nation; today fewer than five per cent provide not only for the United States but for much of the world's population. The simple society I had known was gone. We were now coping with the complex, seemingly insoluble problems of urbanization. Science and technology had changed the ways we work, live, think, and relate to one another as human beings. Affluence had altered family life, and not all for the better. The concept of individualism which had characterized our life in the early twenties had been sacrificed, inevitably, to collective security and collective social action in solving human problems.

The county poorhouse, which terrified me as a youngster, had fallen into disuse, replaced by a more enlightened concept of Social Security and welfare. Organized labor, ignored and suppressed for so many years, had become the most powerful economic and political force in the country. The military establishment, once little more than a national peace-keeping force, was now a giant risen from the earth with men and deadly equipment stationed throughout the world and involving an annual cost of eighty billion dollars; we had discarded historic isolationism with the Japanese attack on Pearl Harbor and had been cast by world events in the role of Atlas bearing up the entire globe. Once we had differed politically among ourselves about such simple and comprehensible problems as free trade versus protectionism; now we struggled with problems that seemed hopelessly complex, almost beyond solution—environmental pollution, overpopulation, discrimination, inflation, an alarming growth in crime, unemployment, federal deficits, and serious imbalances in international payments. These problems and the overriding question of national priorities strained the comprehension of democratic citizens in whose hands the basic social power, in theory at least, still rested.

In this complex of social change and burgeoning government, I now had the unhappy task of heading a commission to study a social problem so critical that, in the words of a famous psychiatrist, it might well lead to the end of the grand experiment in democracy.

With effort, I cast off my reveries. In a few days I would be back in the White House, less well equipped than I had ever been to tackle a problem for the United States.

9

I pulled from the shelves of my library the reports of the Kerner and Katzenbach commissions. Before my meeting with the President in the next few days, I would immerse myself in the findings and recommendations of two presidential commissions which had dealt with some aspects of violence, hoping that I would not appear wholly naïve as I began this new and awesome assignment.

CHAPTER 2

When men are young, they are impatient to change the world; when they are old, they long for the world of their youth.

I RECALL VIVIDLY the streams of event and circumstance which caused me, prior to enrollment in college, to seek a career either in education or in the federal government, possibly in both. Two of these—a sense of insecurity and a determination to equal or surpass what in those years I deemed to be the rather remarkable achievements of my older brothers—were not especially commendable but nonetheless quite relevant. A third was the happy outcome of my association with several inspiring teachers. And the fourth, possibly the most impelling influence, was my admiration for Woodrow Wilson, whose every act as educator, governor of New Jersey, and President of the United States I followed in the press and often discussed with my father, who was less enthusiastic about Wilson than I was.

A series of events, none important in itself, cumulatively instilled in me a sense of fear, almost dread. At the age of three and a half an incident occurred early one morning which, humorous now as I think about it, appalled me. When I came downstairs for breakfast I noticed that my father was worried. He took my hand and led me to a door in the dining room that opened to the basement. Instead of stairs I saw only black water. The flood of 1903—involving Mud Creek and the Smoky Hill River—had risen during the night, filled the basement, and now was only a few inches below the dining-room floor. I was terrified. My older brothers scoffed at my crying and evidently determined to make it their responsibility to change me into a sturdier, less emotional youngster. As time went on I had to run several miles a day and also to practice baseball for hours, but I was butter-fingered and made a dismal showing. On several occasions I was taken to the smallest bedroom on the second floor where my head was pushed into the pitch-blackness of the attic; I was certain some horrible animal would spring at me. My screams would bring Mother to the rescue. Still later, when I was about eight, a playful accident occurred which enhanced and solidified my fears.

The main loft of our huge barn was filled with baled alfalfa. Off the loft was a low attic above a one-story section, the entrance to which was a square opening in the wall of the hayloft. As we romped from bale to bale I fell through the opening into a nightmare of darkness. Bales were quickly piled against the opening, by whom I could only guess. I was trapped in the heat and darkness for what seemed an hour, though probably it was only for a few moments. From then until I was through high school, dark places, even the open night of the elementary school grounds across the street from our house, became a threat. If high school or social activities kept me out late, I would run all the way home, keeping to open spaces as much as possible. Gradually I conquered this senseless fear, but the residue was a strong feeling of insecurity which impelled me toward career objectives that promised a minimum of risk.

By the time I was in my late twenties I could chuckle about this, for by then I had learned that if, with reasonable intelligence and serious application to duty, one did on an assignment more than was expected of him, opportunities multiplied. Throughout a long professional life I was never without attractive alternatives.

Since I was the youngest of six brothers, it was natural that my future should be shaped to some extent by my admiration of them. I early developed what later I realized was a premature pride in the achievements of the older members of the family. True, all eventually did well and thus justified my early view. But originally I was impressed by less consequential things. My brothers were star athletes in high school; I made only the third team in baseball and was water boy for football. Arthur left home to enter banking in Kansas City; Edgar went to the University of Michigan School of Law, and then Ike took off for West Point. To me, these were momentous achievements. I felt I had to earn their respect and I thought the only way I could do this was to become an outstanding student. Ike, before he left home, encouraged me in this, promising to give me a dollar for each A I brought home on my report card. I recall his amazement when I showed him a card with five A's—and later in life we often laughed about the fact that I never got paid.

This intense resolve to become a leading student was helped by another significant influence. Three teachers inspired and worked diligently with me. One, Miss Anna Hopkins, lived for a year in our house. Her only payment for her living costs was to see to it that I mastered my lessons. She was a skillful and persistent teacher. Her system was essentially the same as one now outlined in an excellent book, *How to Study*, by two eminent psychologists. She insisted that in studying mathematics, or history, or literature, or Latin I should first review quickly and comprehend the general scope and significance of the assignment. I then had to study the material in detail, often underlining sentences or making marginal notes. Finally I had to review the material before I was permitted to turn to the next lesson. Though foreign languages were difficult for me, she drilled me so completely that my Latin teacher once kept me after class and charged me with using a "pony"—a word that may be outdated; she thought I was using a book of translations, saying, "Your translations are too precise to be achieved any other way." After much discussion she accepted my explanation that Miss Hopkins had really taught me how to master a lesson.

Concurrently, Miss Ruth Hunt, an English teacher, insisted I had the capacity to change my pedestrian, uninspired, but grammatically correct writing into articles with acceptable style and some emotional content; what she taught me has always been an asset.

The third teacher was the daughter of the leading citizen and scholar of Abilene, Kansas. Mr. Charles Moreau Harger was a graduate of Harvard, editor of the daily newspaper, and a regular contributor to national magazines, such as *Harper's*. His daughter, who had tutored me in English literature, learning that I was about to lie about my age in order to join my friends who were entering the army, had her father hire me as a reporter on his newspaper. My association with Mr. Harger contributed greatly to my development. He taught me to be more objective, even critical, of statements I read in the press, even the glowing addresses of President Wilson, my idol. He gave me a host of books to read and talked with me at length about higher education; he was chairman of the Kansas Board of Regents, which had general supervision of all state colleges and universities in the state. He also helped me understand the operations of governments. Best of all, he quietly induced me to gain confidence in myself and to realize that I would have to obtain a breadth of knowledge and a disciplined mind that would make possible objective, critical, and creative thinking, which obviously were attributes needed in either of the lines of work that most appealed to me. Our close association continued, mainly by correspondence, after I left Abilene, went to Scotland for two years, and then began a fairly long tour of duty in Washington, D.C. I never ceased to absorb some of his wisdom, to learn from him up to the time of his death.

But it was, I think, my interest in Wilson that had the most profound influence on my career decision.

I had first become interested in Woodrow Wilson at the age of eleven. When he was inaugurated governor of New Jersey on January 17, 1911, my mother proudly commented that he had been born in Staunton, Virginia, only a few miles from her home village of Mount Sidney. I had romantic notions about Virginia, based on stories my mother had told me. That Woodrow Wilson had also experienced what I assumed to be an idyllic environment gave me, I felt, a special relationship with him. Nine months later, when Wilson sought out Edward Mandell House at the latter's apartment in New York City, presumably thinking even then of help he would need in seeking the Democratic nomination for the presidency of the United States, my parents spoke of Colonel House as a Texan; again I was intrigued, for my brother Ike had been born in Texas when my parents lived there for a year and a half. My interest in these two men became almost an obsession.

From the press I learned that Wilson had attended Davidson College, Princeton University, and the University of Virginia. One writer was so unkind, to my disgust, as to say that Wilson had done indifferently in his studies at these institutions. Later I learned that at Johns Hopkins University, where he obtained the doctor of philosophy degree, his dissertation on constitutional history and political science was published as a book which received favorable reviews.

Oratory was then in fashion, and Wilson no doubt was the nation's leading orator, rivaled only by William Jennings Bryan. I felt aggrieved when Republican elders in Abilene suggested that Wilson was infatuated with his ability as an orator, that he obviously was consumed with a conviction of future political greatness, and that, persuaded of his infallibility, the fawning Colonel House was the ideal man to serve him. This was shocking to me. My protests were countered with scoffing comments about Colonel House. This unknown confidant, they said, was obviously ambitious to help direct the destiny of the nation; he had an extraordinary ability to appear humble—to give Wilson the impression of always agreeing with him—and in doing so he met Wilson's need for reaffirmation of his political and philosophic superiority.

My first mild question about Woodrow Wilson developed when he abruptly changed from a political conservative to a liberal—a liberal ahead of his time. In his campaign for the gubernatorial nomination, Wilson had favored large trusts, opposed unionism, called federal regulation of business "socialism," and scorned the more liberal views of William Jennings Bryan, a fact which alienated the two men and required adroit work by Wilson and House to remedy the break at the next Democratic Convention.

Immediately following his inauguration as governor—already looking, I later realized, beyond New Jersey—Wilson began expressing liberal views. He cast aside the men who had originally projected him into politics, fought corruption, favored the regulation of utilities, pushed through a corrupt practices act, endorsed workmen's compensation, and demanded improved education in the state.

My father was conservative in political philosophy but did not actively engage in political affairs. Mother was aloof from public discussions, her interests being limited to her family, friends, religion, music, and help to neighbors. Despite my conservative background—though I'm sure I did not recognize it as such—I assumed Wilson's new program must be right; I did not, however, analyze or understand the reason for the sudden change in his views.

Radio and television were still developments of the future, so I was dependent on the Kansas City *Star*, the Topeka *Daily Capital*, and the Abilene (Kansas) *Reflector* for news of the 1912 Democratic Convention. Day after day I read of a stalemate. Then a truce with Bryan proved to be the turning point. With Bryan's help, Wilson was nominated on the forty-sixth ballot and I was elated.

In his inaugural speech Wilson dubbed his administration's program "The New Freedom," thus setting the stage for such euphonious phrases as "The New Deal," "The Fair Deal," "The New Frontier," and "The Great Society." I was fourteen years old when Wilson persuaded the Congress to create the Federal Reserve Board, which the Republicans of Abilene said would ruin the country. In that same year and the ensuing three years Wilson induced the Congress to submit to the states a constitutional amendment for a progressive income tax, to lower tariffs, adopt stronger anti-trust legislation, establish the Federal Trade Commission, create a Federal Farm Board to provide credit at reasonable rates for farmers, and establish an eight-hour day for railroad workers; later he would successfully urge Congress to institute a constitutional amendment establishing national prohibition and to pass a pure foods act to protect consumers. The record matched that of the Franklin Roosevelt one hundred days in which I would later be involved.

In the campaign of 1916 the slogan was "He kept us out of war" and on that pledge Wilson was re-elected, carrying California by a mere 4,000 votes. Before his second inauguration Germany resumed unrestricted submarine warfare, so on April 2, 1917, Wilson recommended and Congress declared war on Germany. It was at this time that Miss Ruth Harger persuaded me not to lie about my age in order to accompany friends into military service but instead to work for her father on his newspaper.

One of my assignments as a cub reporter was to interview William Jennings Bryan, a task that made me exceedingly nervous. Bryan was in Abilene to deliver an address in the annual Chautauqua program. Since he would speak from three to four in the afternoon, Mr. Harger directed that I see Mr. Bryan and get an advance on his speech, for our paper was put to bed at three. I went to the Union Pacific Hotel where Bryan was staying and the hotel clerk told me he was being shaved in the hotel barbershop. I peeked around the corner into the shop. That a barber could take the liberty of recklessly splashing soap on the great man's face gave me a modicum of courage, so I waited in the lobby for Bryan to appear. When he did so, I shuffled nervously toward him. He put his hand on my shoulder and asked what I wanted. I told him of our deadline and asked for a copy of his speech. He laughed and said he would speak extemporaneously and inquired whether I wrote shorthand. I did not, but told him I could write rapidly.

"Sit down," he said, "and I'll tell you what I'm going to say." He then proceeded to dictate a perfect newspaper story: summary lead, indirect and direct quotes, all in the best journalistic style. He gave me enough copy for two full columns in the newspaper and even went to his room and got for me a new photograph of himself. As I thanked him and prepared to leave, I asked him what he thought of President Wilson.

He motioned for me to sit down again. After a moment he said in words close to these: "I supported Wilson for the presidency because Tammany Hall was back of Champ Clark and Wilson supported many of the things I have long stood for. I became Secretary of State with high hopes, but I resigned after two years for several reasons. I thought his protest notes to Germany were stronger than was wise. Though these demands were bringing us closer to war, he did nothing to prepare the country militarily. Further, I did not approve of his imperialistic actions in Mexico, Central America, and the Caribbean. American naval forces should not have occupied Vera Cruz in 1914. The President should not have abrogated the historic policy of this and most other countries which proclaimed that recognition of other countries did not mean moral approval of their governments, but only that the nations concerned would live up to their foreign commitments and could maintain internal order. His change in policy—based on his insistence that a government should come to power only by democratic elective process —led to military intervention in Central America, Haiti, and elsewhere. We assumed a trusteeship over Haiti which we imposed upon that little country."

He indicated that the invasion of Mexico by troops under General Pershing may have been justified, for we were only trying to capture the bandit Francisco Villa, who had been making raids into Texas and causing loss of lives and property damage.

Bryan emphasized that our entry into the European war came at a time when our preparedness was catastrophically bad. It would take precious time to gear American industry to war production, to mobilize and train troops, to build ships, and eventually to send an American expeditionary force to Europe.

I would never have succeeded as a career newspaper reporter, for when I returned to my desk I did not write about our personal conversation; I felt that he had been speaking to me in confidence. I carefully typed out for the linotypist exactly, word for word, what Bryan had dictated to me. That weekend my pay envelope contained twelve dollars instead of the eight I had been receiving. I spoke to Mr. Harger about the error and he said, "Milton, that was a great story you wrote on the Bryan speech. You deserve the raise. You are learning quickly." All weekend I worried about that. Monday I explained to Mr. Harger that I had not really written the story. Bryan had done so. Mr. Harger leaned back in his chair, grinned, and said, "If you can get the real authority to do much of the work for you, you deserve whatever pay you get!"

I've always wondered what he would have done had he known that the big story—the one that surely would have made national headlines —was the one I didn't write.

It was years later, when I had been working in Washington for some time, that I viewed the Wilson administration in better perspective and understood the Wilson-House situation, the first of the presidential-confidant relationships that would be the subject of a plethora of analytical books.

From 1913 to 1917 President Wilson dominated the legislative situation as no President before him had done. None of the liberal enactments he pushed through the Congress has ever been repealed. His imperialistic activities abroad were a surprising departure from his normal democratic philosophy and will remain a stain upon his record; the same must be said of his indifference to the welfare of black citizens—as a Southerner, he felt "Negroes should stay in their place."[1]

Despite his success with the Congress in those first four years, his personal relationships with the senators and representatives were not good. He detested the idea of patronage, though he used it wisely. He remained socially aloof from the legislators. Indeed, in most human affairs, save with Colonel House, he was a cold man. Convinced of his infallibility, he scorned compromise, even creative compromise, which is the essence of effective political management.

It seems certain that the President's aloofness, his supreme confidence in the moral rightness of his position, and his refusal to compromise in achieving his purposes were constantly encouraged by Colonel House.

Some scholars have given House credit for developing some of the ideas incorporated in the Wilson program. Certainly there was a Machiavellian streak in House; under cover of his apparent subservience and constant flattery of the President, he cleverly added, one by one, significant suggestions to the President's own grand thoughts and designs. The President seemingly adopted these without actually being conscious of their having emanated outside his own fertile mind.

Shadowy evidence suggests that House, a man of moderate wealth inherited from his father, felt superior to the governors of Texas whom he advised, and to President Wilson. But this feeling was, as I have indicated, concealed in flattery which, as expressed in frequent letters to the President, had an effeminate quality. Certainly there can be no question that House induced Wilson to adopt the attitude and pursue the methods which finally brought Bryan to his support. He was influential in suggesting many Cabinet appointments. He declined such a post for himself and the President commented to friends that House was the most self-effacing man he knew. Except for his own family, President Wilson apparently had deep affection only for Colonel House.

Unlike many other Presidents, Wilson had no one who helped him regularly with his speeches and state documents. Of course he received the usual recommendations from Cabinet members for State of the Union addresses, but Wilson wrote his own speeches—speeches that were models of logical, clear, and expressive English, invariably interspersed with high moral phrases. He evidently believed the oft-quoted statement that "Reading maketh a full man, conference a ready man, and writing an exact man." House usually reviewed Wilson's drafts, praised them lavishly, and modestly suggested insertions or deletions.

The relationship of these two men may have been harmful to Wilson and thus to the United States. When Wilson insisted that the Central American and Caribbean countries had to employ acceptable democratic methods in selecting their leaders and began his imperialistic adventures, House approved, suggesting that this was evidence of the President's deep feeling of righteousness. The President, he implied, could not be wrong on such a moral question. It even seems to me possible, perhaps likely, that President Wilson might have had his fourteen points and the Treaty of Versailles accepted, had not House over a period of years contributed so steadily to Wilson's ego, and conviction of superiority and personal infallibility. A President is neither divine nor invariably right. Compromise at the right time can often salvage most that is good without sacrificing fundamental principle.

"It is true that House consciously tried to manipulate Wilson," wrote Alexander L. and Juliette L. George in their excellent book, *Woodrow Wilson and Colonel House*.[1] And to a considerable extent he succeeded until Wilson's first wife, Ellen, died and sixteen months later the President married Mrs. Edith Bolling Galt.

The new Mrs. Wilson disliked House. Whether this was mutual is not known. Nor is it clear whether Mrs. Wilson's opposition to House was due to jealousy or to suspicion of his motives. Though the relation-

19

ship between the two men now began to grow more formal, President Wilson nonetheless continued to confer with House and entrusted him with a good many specific responsibilities.

Then a highly important development occurred. Whenever House called to see the President, Mrs. Wilson was present. When the Paris Peace Conference was being planned two developments foreshadowed an end to the Wilson-House partnership. Mrs. Wilson approved the President's determination to head the American delegation himself, a move House cautiously opposed, one of the few times he ever ventured to differ with the President. Second, it was Mrs. Wilson who urged the President to make Colonel House a delegate and the one to be in charge in the President's absence; whether this was as devious as it now seems to have been no one knows, but it surely in time brought an end to the historic relationship. The other delegates were Secretary of State Robert Lansing, General Tasker Howard Bliss, and Henry White. Wilson, having become, in the words of George H. Reedy in his reference to Presidents generally, imbued with monarchic poise and wisdom, personally dominated the United States delegation. In Paris he refused to compromise in any meaningful way with the other conference participants. In the President's absence, however, House made reasonable and essential concessions. These changes angered Wilson, though he had to accept them. When the Treaty of Versailles was signed on June 28, 1919, Wilson and House parted and never saw one another again.

It was now Mrs. Wilson who became the sole confidante of the President, a relationship which made her President in all but legal authority during Wilson's serious illness. This illness followed his frantic tour of the country in an attempt to persuade the people to pressure the Senate for approval of our joining the League of Nations. The United States' failure to accept the League, Wilson's great dream for personal glory, was a crushing blow to him. Here was the final act of Wilson's inability to recognize his own fallibility and his stubborn refusal to compromise in order to achieve a major objective. He left the White House a broken man, moved to S Street in northwest Washington, just off Massachusetts Avenue, only three doors from a house my wife and I would occupy for several years.

The problems with which President Wilson had to deal were no more arduous than those faced daily by President Lincoln, who lived through the torment of the War between the States. No President has experienced a sinecure in the White House. But Lincoln and Wilson faced what all Presidents from Herbert Hoover onward would experience: national and international demands and responsibilities that call for more than one man can meet. If Lincoln had lived through his second term, struggling with the problems of reconstruction, he, too, might have lost his health. Certainly Wilson suffered a collapse that was the consequence of overwork and his rigid temperament. Had he completed his presidency in good health, I suspect he would have engaged in a good deal of revealing writing about the presidency.

When I left Abilene to begin college, first at the University of Kansas for a summer school period, and then at Kansas State University, I was able to pursue the type of broad program Mr. Harger and I had discussed as the best preparation for a career in education or government. It took me six years to earn a baccalaureate degree plus some graduate work, for I had to take time off to earn money. In any event, my first year had been largely wasted, for all of us freshmen were inducted into the Student Army Training Corps, my intention being to enter the aviation branch of the army. But the SATC was disbanded within a month after the Armistice in 1918 and it was clear to me that my academic progress while in uniform had been negligible. So I returned home to become editor of Mr. Harger's newspaper and then re-entered the university the following fall. My second absence from academe was mainly to earn money.

I had with youthful optimism started my higher education with only fifty dollars in my pocket, received no outside help, earned money while pursuing academic studies by serving as editor of the student daily newspaper, copyreading for numerous institutional publications, writing feature articles for magazines, and, in my final year, serving as student-teaching assistant in speech and journalism. So upon graduation I had accumulated $1,700 in the bank and felt comfortably rich.

Within weeks, I faced a dilemma, which called for an immediate and far-reaching decision. Upon graduation I was offered and accepted a position on the faculty of the Department of Journalism. I was a lowly instructor, with the privilege of pursuing graduate work toward the Ph.D.

Scarcely had I, with flourish and pride, settled myself at a desk in the department when a telegram came from the Secretary of State,

Charles Evans Hughes, offering me a post in the United States Consulate in Edinburgh, Scotland.

The Rogers Act, designed to regulate immigration into the United States, had recently been enacted, and the State Department was undergoing considerable expansion in personnel. The surprising offer from Secretary Hughes was the result of an action I had taken, partly seriously, partly as a lark, during my senior year. A young man who was working for the Republican National Committee had come to the campus and induced me to form a college Republican club. I did this, although with almost disastrous results. First, I called an organizational meeting. Four persons came. I was elected president, another vice-president, a third treasurer, and the fourth, secretary. Unfortunately an older student, a Democrat and correspondent for the St. Louis *Post Dispatch*, passed the room where we were meeting and saw what was happening. I learned from a friend that he intended to write a humorous article for his paper. So, frantically, I telephoned every friend I could locate in neighboring fraternities and early the next morning included in the college daily a list of one hundred members of the Republican Club, which of course had four officers, I being the president.

The young man from Washington remained on the campus for a few days and in a casual conversation suggested that I ought to apply for a post in the foreign service of the United States. I did so, filled up many papers, took an examination, and then forgot about the matter. When the telegram came from the Secretary of State I faced the first of many challenges. I was, I felt, at the parting of the ways. Which held the greater appeal, the most promise? Which would most completely absorb my allegiance: education or government?

I went to see the president of the university, Dr. William M. Jardine, an intelligent man of great heart, an intimate friend of students. As editor of the student daily newspaper I had become well acquainted with him.

I had scarcely given President Jardine an outline of my problem when he leaned back in his chair and said, "Milton, you're fired! There's no place at this institution for you for the next two years." He paused. "If you want to come back then, I'll see what I can do for you. Now go away and make up your own mind!"

Momentarily, I was stunned, not because he had violated the normal academic tradition in "firing" a faculty member (which required a year's notice), but because I had assumed he would plead with me to remain with the university. I stared at him. Then a trace of a smile touched his lips and I began to laugh, uproariously, I fear.

Within the next hour I had wired Secretary Hughes my acceptance, telephoned home for a steamer trunk, and visited a travel agency to get railroad tickets to New York and a reservation on the S.S. *United States*, sailing later in the month from New York to Plymouth.

Because I was not due at the consulate in Edinburgh for another week, I planned to spend a few days in London. On the ship I heard passengers say they would be staying at the Savoy. I knew nothing about London, and I decided that I, too, would go to the Savoy. The doorman was startled when the taxi drew up at the hotel, for my steamer trunk was on top of the car and my suitcases on the seat beside me. At the desk the clerk said he would assign me to the only remaining room. It proved to be mammoth in size, with a private bath across the hall overlooking the Thames. The opulence of the room and huge bath bothered me. So I went downstairs and asked the clerk about the room rate. When he informed me that in American currency it was fourteen dollars a day I decided to leave for Edinburgh the next morning.

In the compartment on the Edinburgh express I had only one companion, a public school lad about twelve years old. We tried to chat but the boy said he couldn't understand a word I said and my difficulty was as great as his.*

I arrived in Edinburgh on a comfortably warm evening and was astounded to see, in the North British Railroad station, Scotsmen dressed in normal business suits. Where were the kilts I had expected? My ignorance was abysmal. I would have to learn a great deal in a very short time.

A taxi driver heaved my steamer trunk and suitcases to the top of the car and took me to the Caledonian Hotel, at the far end of Princes Street. There were no vacancies. The North British Hotel was next, and the result the same. After several more attempts I was taken to an ob-

---

* In time I learned not only public school English but also Cockney and a miner's type of broad Scottish. In 1955 when I took my daughter to Scotland we had a car with a Cockney driver. We stopped a Scottish lorry driver to ask where we might find a good restaurant between Edinburgh and Glasgow, and I had to serve as interpreter. The Cockney and the Scot could not understand one another.

scure hotel, now nameless in memory, where a kind manager said he would put a bed in the hotel living room.

I went into the dining room for a late meal, doing my best to act like a native. Before I said a word to the waiter he asked, "Would you like ice in your water?" I wondered how he knew I was an American, so I examined my suit and compared it with others in the room. Obviously the quality of my clothing was inferior. At once I determined to invest some of my $1,700 in new tailor-made suits.

The United States Consulate was on George Street, just one square from Princes Street where I was temporarily located. When I introduced myself to Wilbert Bonney, the elderly, well-educated, and kindly consul who had recently arrived from Rosario, Argentina, he said at once to me, "I hope you are a specialist on the new Rogers Act." I was not. He expressed disappointment and turned me over to Thomas Maleady, a vice-consul whose place I would take in about two weeks.

Tom Maleady, before he left for his new post at Port-au-Prince, became a good friend, but my first meeting with him was a near calamity. In the room with him were two Scottish ladies, clerks of the consulate. They were in their mid-thirties, mildly attractive, but devoid of a sense of humor. When Maleady introduced them, one at once asked me, "What kind of a screw do women get in the United States?" I turned beet red. I blushed easily and I could feel the heat of my face. I looked imploringly at Maleady, and he merely grinned. There was an awful silence that seemed to me to last for a minute or more. Finally Maleady helped me. "She wants to know what salaries women receive in the United States."

It did not take long for me to realize that, though the Scottish people used the same words that we of the United States do, meanings could vary widely. I became careful of my speech but did not succeed in avoiding all embarrassment. Sir Joseph Dobby was then Lord Mayor of Edinburgh, and at his house one evening Lady Dobby, in the presence of her daughters and numerous guests, asked how I had enjoyed the rugby game that afternoon. I commented on the polite applause that greeted each good play and then added, "You don't root the way we do at a football game in the United States." The utter silence that ensued and my blushing shame when I suddenly realized the ambiguity of the word "root" were a punishment that caused me to work still harder in adapting my speech to the new environment.

The two years in Edinburgh surely contributed to my maturity. Mr. Bonney was a genuine scholar, his specialty English literature. He was a patient man with a genius for stimulating others. Under his guidance I was soon handling thousands of applications from individuals and families who wished to emigrate to the United States, making studies of Scottish industry, writing reports for the Commerce Department, settling an occasional dispute on an American ship that put in at Leith, traveling throughout the United Kingdom on a four-speed motorcycle, and taking part-time graduate work at the University of Edinburgh. When the consul at Dunfermline died, I was transferred there as acting consul; the post had been established in the Theodore Roosevelt administration and was still active even though in subsequent years the famous Firth of Forth bridge had brought Dunfermline within a thirty-minute train ride of Edinburgh. I recommended that the consulate be closed and when this was approved by the Secretary of State I moved the books and furniture to Edinburgh and returned as vice-consul in that exceptionally attractive city.

The post in Edinburgh was the first exposure I had to international affairs. While I had been in most of the states of the United States, I had never previously been abroad. My naïveté was monumental. This may have been a Midwestern artlessness, a simple belief in the unfailing rightness and righteousness of all the United States had done and stood for. I was rudely shaken when Scottish leaders with brutal candor attacked the United States on many matters, such as its failure to cancel the British war debt. I remember suggesting on one occasion that if the British government canceled its debt to its own citizens this might show good faith and thus induce the United States to become more charitable. This elicited a scornful discourse on the difference between an internal and an external debt.

My home in Edinburgh was in Ramsay Lodge, a university hostel, which nestled against the world-famous Edinburgh Castle. Some fifty students of the University of Edinburgh lived in the hostel. They came from all parts of the world, especially the Commonwealth nations associated with the United Kingdom. At first I was the object of joshing; as soon as I entered the common room of the mansion several students would shout at me in a nasal voice (they thought all Americans had a nasal quality in speech), "Say, guy, where did you get that hat?" It happened that I did not have a nasal twang, but that made no difference to my tormentors. So I decided to retaliate. Carefully I learned some of the broadest Scottish speech, which was scorned in Edinburgh where truly beautiful English is spoken. Later, when I entered the common room and the inevitable hat question was thrown at me, I said, "Hoot mon, ya dinna ken wha' you're a-talkin' aboot!" That solved the problem.

From Sunday evening to Friday evening the students applied themselves to their studies. Many were in the School of Medicine with its demanding curriculum. But on Saturday night the entire membership of the hostel went on a binge. Between Princes and George streets was a narrow alley, dignified with the name Row Street, which from the northern to the southern end had thirty-two pubs. The contest was to see which member, if any, could take one drink in each pub and come out of the thirty-second still standing. The group insisted that I accompany them but always sent me back to Ramsay Lodge after the second drink, saying that they did not want an international incident. They now affectionately referred to me as the FVC. This title was slightly embarrassing to a Kansan, imbued with Midwestern tabus. The last two initials obviously stood for vice-consul. The first is unmentionable, a seven-letter word that has become popular in the United States among yippies and hippies—a shock word which did, at that time, disturb me. Invariably on Sunday some of the members of the hostel gleefully would tell me of developments after my departure. Some would tear out the plumbing of a men's room in a pub. Others might break a mirror with a well-thrown beer bottle. They would be arrested, remain in jail overnight, pay a modest fine, and return to Ramsay Lodge late Sunday afternoon, ordered by the court to pay damages for the wreckage they had caused.

Sometimes on Saturday night the drinks were served at the Lodge in time for the entire group to go to the theater, which usually offered a variety program. Moderately but not disgustingly intoxicated, the students, if they disliked a particular act, would drive the entertainer off the stage by shuffling their feet and whistling loudly. This amused the audience, which apparently agreed with the students, and loud applause would follow the exit of the entertainer.

Only three Americans lived in Ramsay Lodge. One was a graduate student in political geography, a mountain of a man who weighed about two hundred and eighty-five pounds. Another was a law student, small, keenly intelligent, and skilled in parlor tricks. We three had many happy times together, including a motorcycle tour of Scotland and England. My heavy friend was a curiosity to the Scottish people. There were no fat people in that windy, sunless country; they tend to be sturdy, physically active, trim, handsome, and friendly. When my heavy colleague and I walked down Princes Street together, people would stare at us as we passed. One day my friend asked, "What are these people looking at us for?" I retorted, "What do you mean, *us?*" And he replied, "I am speaking in the royal singular!"

The budding lawyer, Everett Swing, and I became inseparable. A student from Wales was constantly pulling our legs about things in his country of which we were ignorant. We knew he was naïve, so we carefully planned a method of stopping his irritating habit. One evening the three of us gathered in my room. A cozy fire was burning. Everett began doing tricks with a large English penny, causing it to disappear with the snap of a finger and having it appear in a stated page of a book on the mantel. This dumfounded the Welshman, who suddenly said, "I'll bet you can't make the coin appear in the violin case under the bed!" "I'll bet you a shilling I can," Everett said. Quickly I took the bet, feigning confidence in his inability to do such a thing. The Welshman said he would bet thruppence, then insisted upon examining the violin case in advance. I did too. Our search was thorough. Just before I closed the case I dropped a single copper penny, dated 1920, in among the unused violin strings. I locked the case. Everett now showed the coin he would use, dated 1920. He waved his arms, intoned mumbo-jumbo nonsense, and then snapped his fingers, the coin disappearing. The Welshman started for the violin case. "Wait a minute," Everett protested, "it isn't there yet!" Finally he nodded. I let the Welshman open the case. There was the coin with the proper date.

Then Everett began to talk about hypnotism. I said no one could hypnotize me, for I knew all the tricks in the business. I began chatting at random as Everett stared at me. He was near the fireplace. I faced it. Our Welsh tormenter was to the side, watching me with care. I smoked a cigarette. Finally I dropped my head, closed my eyes, and let the cigarette fall on the hearth.

"Wind the clock," Everett ordered. I climbed up on my bed, reached to a shelf above, wound the alarm clock, and returned to my chair. He then ordered me to remove my tie and do a few other ridiculous things. Finally he snapped his fingers. I sat up, lighted another cigarette, and began the same frivolous conversation I had been carrying on when the travesty of hypnosis occurred.

"I thought you said you couldn't be hypnotized!" the Welshman shouted.

"I can't be," I said.

"You've been out for five minutes," he insisted. "What's the cigarette doing on the hearth? You dropped it when you passed out!"

I put my hand to my head and said I was feeling slightly faint. I asked the Welshman to go to the bathroom and get me a glass of water. The bathroom was far down the hall, so he was gone about one minute. In his absence I jumped on the bed and turned the alarm clock ahead two hours, while Everett rushed across the hall and asked a student from Suez, Jimmy Reid, to ask no questions, turn his clock up two hours, and have everyone on the floor do the same. When the Welshman returned with the water Everett and I began to laugh and said, "How does it feel to be hypnotized?"

"What do you mean?"

"You've been down in the bathroom running water into that glass for two hours!"

He glanced at my clock, rushed across the hall to Jimmy's room, and to one other room. All clocks showed that two hours had elapsed. His puzzlement was supreme. He never tormented us with his leg-pulling tales again.

Other than on Saturday nights, Ramsay Lodge was a place of learning for me. Students from England, Scotland, Wales, South Africa, Egypt, several cities of China, Hong Kong, Canada, India, and Southeast Asia would engage in serious conversations about world affairs, and I invariably participated. They occasionally criticized one another and the policies of their countries; nonetheless they were fiercely protective of the British Empire, and usually critical of the United States. The United States had been imperialistic in Latin America and the Caribbean they charged, citing the Monroe Doctrine, the Roosevelt corollary to that doctrine, the Platt Amendment to our peace treaty with Cuba, and President Wilson's use of marines in Central American and Caribbean countries. I insisted that Britain throughout its history had been the most imperialistic power in the world, mainly for financial gain.

They contended that His Majesty's Empire had maintained peace in the world—a peace that lasted longer than at any other period in history; further, if the Empire weakened, they thought wars would break out everywhere.

Usually, at the conclusion of a long discussion, we found a common ground in our views, each acknowledging that his government's policies were not perfect.

On one point they never yielded. The United States had made a terrible mistake—had placed its historic isolationism above world order —when it refused to join the League of Nations. I still retained my admiration for President Wilson, but for the sake of argument I derided the League as ineffective, citing G. K. Chesterton's famous comment, "The European nations found they couldn't govern themselves, so got together, formed the League of Nations, and tried to govern one another." This did not win any arguments.

And so I learned to compromise. My experience in Scotland sharpened my perspective on ône important aspect of human nature— namely, that man, individually and collectively, tends to act out of self-interest. Individuals and groups of individuals, from fraternities to nations, see facts, circumstances, actions, and consequences in the context of their own backgrounds, their own welfare, and their own goals.

What distinguishes individuals and organizations is how narrowly or broadly they construe self-interest. The human mind seems to have an unlimited capacity to absorb information (true and false) and ideas (valid and invalid) and to formulate from such information and ideas a viewpoint or perspective on the surrounding world. A trained intelligence and an intuition rooted in sound values enables an individual to sort out the information and ideas and to develop a clear and broad perspective.

Lacking a trained intelligence, minds are like rubber bands; confronted with facts, logic, and persuasive arguments, they are stretched to new insights but soon snap back to their original views. Others, even after a formal education, fail to develop a value system sound enough and durable enough to transform knowledge into wisdom; these minds, rigid and inflexible, can respond to new ideas, information, or challenges only with fear and dogmatism.

Individuals who define self-interest so narrowly and selfishly, even when associated with a cause or an organization, perceive the collective self-interest with a stubborn social selfishness. Individually and collectively, they assimilate only evidence that supports their narrow self-interest and reject—even fail to see—anything that is contrary to their preconceptions.

So long as there are such individuals in society our democratic system harbors the seeds of its own destruction. Our society is firmly based on the faith that individual citizens will act wisely. To them is entrusted the ultimate power to decide, to govern through their elected representatives. Our system has worked because enough individual citizens make right decisions most of the time. The mass judgment has been consistently sound in our society because the majority of citizens have been able to see beyond their own narrow self-interest and act for the greater good—either because they informed themselves on vital matters or because their value systems developed in them an intuition akin to wisdom.

I have always had faith in individuals—from the bricklayers and bankers to judges and janitors. In a lifetime of travel, I have found that now individuals everywhere wish to live in peace and to devote their energies to family welfare, better opportunities, and, borrowing Jefferson's famous phrase, "the pursuit of happiness." This universal personal aspiration, however, is never achieved. An organized society, the nation-state, is too often impervious to the simple aspirations of most of its citizens; instead it reflects narrow self-interest and too often resorts to coercive power. Theoretically, most of us would like to see observed the substance of the Kellogg Pact of the 1920s—a noble effort to outlaw war—but none abides by the theory when its own narrow interests are at stake.

Groups within nations have a similar tendency. It was not so long ago that capitalists essentially ruled our country and were contemptuous of the needs of labor and of the social responsibility of their industries and financial institutions. The national welfare, if understood, was subordinated to the group's welfare. Today organized labor is the most powerful segment of our society. Now labor's demands are often self-serving and threaten the economic stability of the nation.

Something seems to happen to the individual when he becomes a member of a group. Truck drivers in Pittsburgh, normally peaceful citizens, will resort to violent crime against those who oppose their strike demands. Organized students will bomb a bank to protest a war. A highly unified, well-financed group will thwart the wishes of a vast unorganized majority, for example, The National Rifle Association. In a country with a single race, common history, and common traditions, Catholics and Protestants will murder one another, unmindful of the cardinal religious concepts they share. In a country no larger than Maryland, Flemish-speaking people will be suspicious of and oppose most of the actions proposed by French-speaking fellow citizens. In a tiny island of the Caribbean, blacks will so discriminate against Indians and Chinese that life for the latter two groups becomes intolerable.

The true task of statesmanship, whether in domestic or international affairs, is to induce groups or nations to put the general welfare above their own selfishness. Compromise is often considered to be a morally feeble exercise; it is condemned with the phrase "wishy-washy." But compromise, domestically or internationally, is not only essential, it is also creative, a means of reaching constructive agreement on socially desirable actions.

Demosthenes observed cynically that "nothing is easier than self-deceit. For what each man wishes, that he also believes to be true." Edmund Burke, recognizing this tendency in individual and organized man, said: "All government—indeed every human benefit, every virtue, and every prudent act—is founded on compromise and barter."

CHAPTER 3

Calvin Coolidge was America's first energy
crisis.

PRESIDENT CALVIN COOLIDGE issued a directive
which caused me to leave the foreign service and begin many years of
hard work in the executive establishment, seventeen years on a full-time
basis in Washington and thirty as a part-time consultant to or personal
representative of the President.

The key figure in my departure from Edinburgh was the same Jardine who had made it possible for me to go there by "firing" me from
my academic post at Kansas State in 1924. He was now in the President's Cabinet. Coolidge had ascended to the presidency in 1923 upon
the death of Warren G. Harding, at a time when a major piece of controversial legislation before the Congress was the McNary-Haugen bill
for farm relief. The nation was worried about a serious economic depression in agriculture, caused by historic developments which many
did not understand, and the McNary-Haugen bill was intended to deal
with the problem. The background:

From the beginning of the Republic to 1878, the United States had
borrowed funds from Europe, mainly in the private sector of the economy, to build railroads, industries, communications, and other needs of
a rapidly growing nation.

The year 1878 was a turning point. The United States in that year
began exporting more in goods and services than it imported, thus initiating a gradual reduction of its foreign debt. In 1918 the United
States became for the first time a creditor country, but it was to be fifteen years before political thinking fully realized the significance of
this.

When we were a debtor country, the world, especially Europe, was
willing to accept our exports as partial payment of our debt, and the
largest single items in this trade were food and fiber from American

farms. In our debtor period, price-depressing surpluses were almost unknown. But after World War I, when farm production in Europe was restored to normal and foreign governments and businesses became aware of our creditor status, tariffs on the importation of some of our farm products were raised. The Italian tariff on American wheat, for example, was raised to thirty-two cents a bushel. Naturally, foreign demand for our wheat, cotton, and other farm products declined. Surpluses accumulated at home, causing agricultural prices to drop sharply. The parity of farm-industrial price relationships that had existed for half a century was rudely shaken.

President Coolidge took these developments rather calmly, but the farmers did not. For the first time, a real farm lobby was organized to press for federal relief through such organizations as the American Farm Bureau and the National Grange. Some analysts contended that the farm recession threatened to cause a general depression. President Coolidge blandly proposed the establishment of marketing co-operatives, increased information on market and crop conditions, and other sound measures. The farmers responded with the McNary-Haugen bill, which sought to sell agricultural surpluses abroad competitively at world prices while restoring a parity relationship of the prices of domestically consumed farm products to the prices farmers paid for industrial products, taxes, and services.

The McNary-Haugen bill was an ingenious measure. In the United States a crop could be sold on the market at the world price, plus a sum equal to the protective tariff. Abroad, the surplus would be dumped for whatever it would bring. This dumping would be handled by a federal agency. The bill did not provide for any reduction in production, and hence in the surpluses which were the main cause of the trouble.

President Coolidge, taciturn, imbued with a New England puritanism and conservatism, and deeply suspicious of governmental intervention in private enterprise, was firmly opposed to the McNary-Haugen bill. Although many farm organization leaders, agricultural economists, and, later, even Vice-President Charles G. Dawes, favored the legislation, one significant voice supported the President. That was Dr. William M. Jardine, president of Kansas State University, then called the Kansas State College of Agriculture and Applied Science. Jardine, an eminent agronomist and former dean of agriculture at Kansas State, wrote for a national magazine a long article which upheld President Coolidge's views.

So, when President Coolidge was re-elected in 1924 and began forming a new Cabinet, Secretary of Commerce Herbert Hoover urged him to appoint Dr. Jardine Secretary of Agriculture. Now President Coolidge did a very wise thing. He turned for advice to Kansas Senator Arthur Capper, spokesman for the farm bloc. As a matter of flattery and courtesy he first offered the job to Capper himself, but afterward presented two names for Capper's reaction: John Fields, president of the Farm Loan Bank in Wichita, and Dr. Jardine. Capper replied that both men were acceptable but indicated a preference. The following day Jardine's name went to the Senate for confirmation and, with Capper's support, the vote was quick and sure.

Dr. Jardine entered the Cabinet on March 5, 1925, and a few months later he wrote to me in Edinburgh suggesting that he would like very much for me to come to Washington as his assistant. As atonement for "firing" me, he now proposed to hire me for a highly responsible position. I had not yet reached my twenty-sixth birthday.

Although the residue of insecurity from my childhood was rapidly fading, I was still wary of accepting a political appointment with all its uncertainties. Moreover, I had been considering the foreign service as a permanent career.

Here was my second major career decision. The foreign service offered excitement, travel, prestige, reasonable security, and a growing knowledge of nations that rapidly were becoming more interdependent. On the other hand, the opportunity to work in Washington, in a position which would enable me to observe the functioning of every aspect of the federal government, was appealing. If I succeeded in the post of assistant to a Cabinet member, I would not necessarily be closing the door to a subsequent career in the foreign service, and I confess that by now I had developed the notion that an ambassadorship in later years was not beyond reach. After a week of indecision I wrote to Secretary Jardine and told him that although I was interested in his offer I did not wish a political appointment. I also pointed out that I wished to marry Helen Eakin, and I did not want to begin married life with serious career uncertainties.

Fortunately the Secretary was an understanding man. He looked over the department and found that it was necessary to add a person to the staff of the Office of Information, so he arranged with the Civil Service Commission to give a regular examination for the post. I applied to the Commission. Relevant papers were sent to the consul, Wilbert Bonney, under whose watchful eye I took the test in Edinburgh. Several months passed and then, early in 1926, a telegram came from Secretary Jardine informing me that I had ranked first in the examination and could proceed at once to Washington.

Then a new complication arose. Secretary of State Frank Kellogg, who had succeeded Charles Evans Hughes, objected to my transfer, obviously on the advice of his consular staff. By now I had become thoroughly informed on the legal aspects of my work in Edinburgh and was deemed to be essential to the consul, who was approaching retirement. The State Department had no one else prepared to take over my duties. Discouraged, I began planning a vacation to a remote village of Spain where only Spanish was spoken, for I wished to improve the language I had been studying in Edinburgh with a Berlitz instructor, a man who spoke pure Castilian.

The day before I was due to leave for Spain, a telegram came from Secretary Jardine informing me that Secretary Kellogg had changed his mind. At Secretary Jardine's urging, President Coolidge had intervened on my behalf. So I could proceed at once to Washington, providing only that I paid for my own transportation! I got my first taste of the Coolidge insistence on austere economy in government.

My salary as vice-consul had initially been one hundred and fifty dollars a month but was raised, upon my return from Dunfermline to Edinburgh, to the handsome sum of one hundred and seventy-five dollars a month. I had lived quite comfortably at Ramsay Lodge, high above beautiful Princes Street. I had accumulated a tailor-made wardrobe, at minimum cost and of a quality that elicited envious comments from Washington haberdashers when I finally arrived in the capital. Despite these costs, I had saved about fifty dollars a month, and my bank account had reached the astronomical sum of about $2,900. So, nursing a mild annoyance at the United States Government's parsimony, I bought a ticket to Washington.

I shall always remember with nostalgia and some embarrassment the farewell dinner given by the fifty university students who lived in Ramsay Lodge. I would carry with me always what I had learned from them about strange places in the world and the divergent attitudes of their peoples. I would also carry something else. In Kansas, I had never tasted liquor, not only because Kansas was constitutionally dry but also because of the fundamentalist upbringing of my parents. At Ramsay Lodge, however, I had learned to like moselle, a delightfully light white wine. So at the farewell dinner moselle was served. Unknown to me, however, my glass was repeatedly spiked with brandy. At the conclusion of the dinner, my speech must have been unintelligible; we then went to the common room where the heat from a massive fireplace and the spiked wine caused me to pass out. When I wakened the next morning, I had a hangover of historic proportions. I confess that I did not know what was wrong with me. I asked for a doctor. This elicited roars of laughter from Ramsay Lodge residents, who filled me with black coffee and aspirin. That afternoon they escorted me to the North British Railroad station and, as was the custom in Scotland when a friend departed, put me on the train through an open window. As the train began to pull out, my friends handed me a bottle of moselle and waved me laughingly on my way.

For three months I worked in the Office of Information of the Department of Agriculture. My duties enabled me to be busy twelve hours a day, seven days a week, not so much because the work required it as because I had nothing else to do. My fiancée had gone with her parents on a world tour and I had few friends in the capital. Then Secretary Jardine transferred me to his immediate office as his assistant. I was told that I was the first civil service assistant to a Cabinet member.

My new responsibilities were arduous but exciting. I controlled the Secretary's appointments calendar, drafted many of his addresses and much of his congressional testimony, instituted studies at his direction, and in time became involved in congressional matters as the McNary-Haugen bill began to progress through the House of Representatives.

Letters to the Secretary were so numerous that he could neither read them nor sign all of the replies. So he encouraged me to copy his signature and on less important correspondence to write and sign his name to letters. I had been doing this without difficulty for some months when I encountered a situation which reminds me of a comment we often made around the White House during President Eisenhower's administration referring to a rather obtuse member of the Cabinet: "The only thing he does worse than putting his foot in his mouth is taking it out again."

The difficulty arose when close friends of Secretary Jardine came to see me when he was out of the city. They explained that one of their colleagues, a man they said Jardine admired, was being considered for the presidency of a university in an intermountain state and a recommendation at once by the Secretary might tip the scales in his favor; the decision by the university trustees was to be made almost at once. To wait for the Secretary's return was not possible. So I wrote a persuasive letter, signed the Secretary's name, sent the message on its way, and promptly forgot about the matter.

About two months later the Secretary asked me to come into his office, where he had three visitors—the colleagues who had encouraged my letter writing. He told me that he had just bet a Stetson hat that he had not recommended the new president of the university in question. Innocently, I said that I thought he had and would get the carbon from the file. It clearly indicated that I was the sole author and signer. Fortunately for me, that was one of the Secretary's calm days. He was capable of displaying a huge temper. On this occasion he was charitable; he merely told me, after his visitors had left, that he would not have recommended his friend for the post: "Too pedestrian and not enough initiative," he said.

One of the pleasant experiences in my first year as assistant to Secretary Jardine was traveling with him throughout the country. On one trip, however, I was again embarrassed. We arrived in Butte, Montana, late at night. The temperature was forty degrees below zero. Even the hotel was cold. At the annual dinner of the National Wool Growers Association the next night, I was still shivering, not showing the composure that should characterize a Cabinet member's assistant. I found myself seated at the head table with the Secretary, a departure from protocol. To my amazement, the toastmaster, with no warning, asked me to say a few words before the Secretary spoke. I was so startled that I blurted out the first thing that came to mind: "I don't make speeches, I only write them!" The laughter was uproarious. I felt my face redden with embarrassment. Secretary Jardine smiled. When he rose to speak a few minutes later he said: "Anything good in what I have to say is mine; anything else I attribute to Milton Eisenhower."

37

By January 1927 I was at work with the Secretary and his executive assistant, Frank Russell, on a message President Coolidge might use in vetoing the McNary-Haugen bill, which was obviously headed for congressional approval. The document the Secretary took to the White House was, we thought, persuasive, but its tone must have been too mild for the President. He did not use it. Instead, on February 25, 1927, he sent a blistering veto message to the Congress.

"Government price fixing, once started, has alike no justice and no end," the President wrote. "It is an economic folly from which this country has every right to be spared." He contended that the granting of any such arbitrary power to a government agency would run counter to American traditions, the philosophy of our government, the spirit of our institutions, and all principles of equity. "Such action would establish bureaucracy on such a scale as to dominate not only the economic life, but the moral, social, and political future of our people," he said.

Almost as an afterthought, the President recognized that agriculture was at a disadvantage, but he offered it no federal help. "There is no thoughtful man who does not appreciate how vital a prosperous agriculture is to this nation," he conceded. "It must be helped and strengthened." He did not venture to say how this might be done. Instead, his final comment was negative: "To saddle it with unjust, unworkable schemes of governmental control is to invite disaster worse than any that has yet befallen our farmers."

Congress was unable to override the President's veto, but the movement for farm relief was not ended. Supporters of the bill went to great lengths to gain the President's favor, and, in drafting a new bill, Senator Charles McNary went to much trouble to accommodate administration objections in the hope that it would be signed when it passed the next session of Congress. However, Senator McNary wrote that what the President "doesn't know about 'sech' things would fill a great big library."

Fifteen months later the Surplus Control Act—a slightly amended version of the McNary-Haugen bill—passed both houses of Congress. It reached the President's desk in May 1928. This version was no longer constitutionally objectionable to the President, but he considered it "nonsense" and thus deserving of his veto.

This time the task of preparing a message for the President was assigned to me by the Secretary. I prepared a draft based on several of Secretary Jardine's speeches, memoranda to the President, and numerous letters he had written to congressmen. The message was that, though the farmers' plight for several years had been in sharp contrast to the prosperity of industrial groups, there was now genuine hope for improvement. Farm income had increased from nine billion dollars in 1921 to more than twelve billion in 1927, and improvement was continuing. Even so, the situation was unsatisfactory. To overcome the farm disadvantage many things should be done. State and local governments should lower the property tax on farm lands. Freight rates on agricultural commodities should be decreased. Tariffs on industrial goods might well be decreased, while those on farm products should be increased (there was severe competition in wheat from Canada). But the main attack should be made in the realization of the fact that farming was now a business, and had to operate like other businesses. When surpluses reduced prices, production should be contracted. This ought not to require the intervention of government. Farmers should organize wheat, corn, cotton, dairy, and other co-operatives in all parts of the nation; these farmer-controlled co-operatives could be powerful instruments for use in controlling production and moving products into consumption channels. We also ought to change our land policy. No longer should we sell or give away public lands. Indeed, we should begin taking submarginal land out of production. (Later, I would write for the Secretary an article for the *Saturday Evening Post* which advocated an appropriation of one billion dollars to take submarginal lands out of farm production and put most of them into forests, a proposal that was considered to be startling and radical. That was some years before we began spending as much as seven billion dollars a year on agriculture, some of it to buy submarginal lands.)

Secretary Jardine asked me to go with him to the White House to deliver the proposed veto message. This would be my first meeting with President Coolidge. I was uneasy. While I admired Secretary Jardine greatly, loved him as a friend and mentor, and on the whole felt he was mainly right in his analysis, I nonetheless wondered whether the President would not do better in a veto message if he offered specific amendments to the Congress and thus made the farm bill acceptable to him and probably to the farmers. Even as I drafted the veto message I had been troubled by it. Dependence on co-operative organizations of millions of farmers did not appear to me to be workable. Farmers were independent, and persuading millions of them to act in unison was probably an impossible task. Moreover, I was impressed with the critical writings of one or two agricultural economists who were beginning to suggest that a prolonged farm recession could lead to a serious collapse of the entire economy of the United States.

My misgivings were useless, for President Coolidge, grim and uncommunicative, hastily glanced through the document, nodded, and dismissed us.

My labors were also useless, for on May 23, 1928, President Coolidge issued his own veto message, filled with unrestrained ridicule. He described the bill and its provisions as "bureaucracy gone mad," "autocracy," "ponderously futile," "vicious devices," "delusive experiments," "fantastic promises," "futile sophistries," and a "system of wholesale commercial doles." "This plague of petty officialdom," the President wrote, "would set up an intolerable tyranny over the daily lives and operations of farmers and of every individual and firm engaged in the distribution of farm products, intruding into every detail of their affairs, setting up thousands of prohibitory restrictions and obnoxious inspections."

Again, Congress was unable to override the President's veto. A last-ditch effort was made to include a McNary-Haugen plan in the 1928 platform at the Republican Convention and 100,000 farmers were supposed to march on the Kansas City convention hall. But the demonstration failed to materialize and the loyal delegates upheld their retiring chief. McNary-Haugenism died, and no constructive farm legislation was enacted until President Hoover created the Federal Farm Board in an effort to overcome the agricultural depression by buying surplus commodities for sale when prices rose. Later, President Roosevelt put through Congress the Agricultural Adjustment Act, which paid farmers to reduce production. Neither program solved the problem. Farm prices were not restored to parity until World War II, when demand was greater than our enormous supplies.

In time my wife Helen and I became well acquainted with the Coolidge family, mostly on a social basis. My wife's parents, Secretary and Mrs. Jardine's closest friends, often joined the Jardines in White House affairs and my wife and I were included. In Helen's memory book, I still have four formal invitations to White House receptions and dinners during the Coolidge administration. This experience gave me my first close-up look at a real, live President.

Calvin Coolidge's election as Vice-President, elevation to the presidency in 1923, re-election in 1924, and refusal to run again in 1928 constitute one of the unique chapters in American politics.

He was as much an offspring of New England as the rocky hills of his native Vermont. At college, almost friendless, he practiced speech for hours and became recognized as an orator. Even so, one of his classmates recalled: "A drabber, more colorless boy I never knew than Calvin Coolidge when he was in Amherst. He was a perfect enigma to us all." After college he apprenticed himself to a prominent attorney in Northampton, Massachusetts, read law at night, and was admitted to the bar. This approach was then more practical and less expensive than law school. Coolidge set up his own practice in Northampton. He almost never got to court, feeling that a lawyer's highest duty was to settle to his client's advantage out of court. Although cold and aloof, the antithesis of the typical political candidate, he entered politics. In 1898 he was elected city councilman and was in one office or another for most of the rest of his life. (At dinner, when he was Vice-President, a dowager by his side said: "Mr. Coolidge, what is your hobby?" To which he replied laconically, "Holding public office.")

Coolidge's rise was rapid, albeit step by step: city solicitor, clerk of courts, state representative, mayor of Northampton, state senator, lieutenant governor of Massachusetts, then governor, Vice-President, and President.

It was while he was governor of Massachusetts that Calvin Coolidge became a national figure. The only noteworthy event to occur during his two terms in office thrust him into the national spotlight and ultimately put him in the White House: the 1919 Boston police strike, which began when the police were denied the right to form a union. Firmly and instinctively sensing the mood of the nation, he told AFL leader Samuel Gompers: "There is no right to organize against the public safety by anyone, anywhere, any time." National reaction was a landslide of support. The governor was on the front page of every newspaper in the nation and became a political hero overnight.

Coolidge's nomination for the vice-presidency was the result of a muddled situation and anger at Senator Henry Cabot Lodge in the 1920 Republican Convention. The Republican Party was so confident of victory in the presidential election against the party of the ill and politically rejected Woodrow Wilson that eighteen potential nominees were in the field, hoping to capitalize on the eclipse of the Democratic opposition. Among the contenders were General Leonard Wood, Senators Hiram Johnson of California and Frank O. Lowden of Illinois, Herbert Hoover, and Columbia University President Nicholas Murray Butler. Although Coolidge had skyrocketed into prominence, he remained a political dark horse, as did Ohio Senator Warren G. Harding.

By the eighth ballot, the Chicago convention was badly deadlocked with as many contending candidates and factions as the Italian Chamber of Deputies. This was the convention of the famous "smoke-filled room." Senator Lodge and his associates began dealing in earnest and on the tenth ballot Harding swept to victory.

The next order of business for the power brokers was to settle on an agreeable compromise vice-presidential nominee. Although Harding wanted Senator Johnson to run with him, Lodge's choice was Wisconsin Senator Irvine Lenroot.

Many of the delegates, thinking that the important business was over and the rest was cut and dried, were already leaving Chicago— probably to avoid an additional night's hotel charge. Many of those who remained were angry with Lodge and his cronies and were in the mood for a revolt. The nominating speech for Lenroot was interrupted by scattered shouts of "Coolidge!" from the delegates. As the seconding speeches for Lenroot went on, the sentiment for Coolidge grew. An otherwise unremembered delegate from Oregon, Wallace McCamant, succeeded in gaining recognition from the chair, in the belief that he was planning an additional seconding speech. Instead, McCamant placed Coolidge's name in nomination and stole the convention. (That was in the days before political conventions were so carefully scripted.) The stampede was on. Delegates, angered that the Harding nomination had been foisted on them, flocked to support the rebels. For the first time since 1880, when James Garfield was nominated, the delegates had taken control of a Republican National Convention. When the smoke cleared, Coolidge had received 674½ votes to 146½ votes for Lenroot.

Back in Boston, unconcerned with the doings in Chicago, the governor and his wife were preparing to go to dinner. The telephone rang in the hotel suite that served as their official residence.

Coolidge answered, listened, and hung up.

"Nominated for Vice-President," he said to Grace.

"You aren't going to take it, are you?" she asked.

"Suppose I'll have to."

When Coolidge entered Washington, following a Republican victory, he began, for reasons no one could fathom, to receive considerable publicity, despite his expressionless face, lack of color, and no newsworthy duties other than presiding over the Senate. His brittle and eccentric wit did seem to amuse the journalists.

Grace Coolidge was the exact opposite of her silent husband—lively, outgoing, graceful, poised, and socially adept. She was adored by many and loved by those who were privileged to know her well. Cal Coolidge was a thrifty man, managing to leave Washington at the end of his administration with more than $250,000 in assets. Grace was his one extravagance and he spared no expense in dressing her in the latest and most elegant fashions.

President Harding died in San Francisco on August 2, 1923. The Vice-President and his family were visiting his father in Plymouth Notch, Vermont—one of the last places in the country to receive the news, since there were no telephones. He was sworn into office by his father, a notary, at 2:47 A.M., August 3, and slept soundly for the rest of his first night as President of the United States.

President Coolidge's achievements during the remainder of the Harding term were few, a fact now scornfully referred to by historians. But his conservatism, his insistence upon economy, his opposition to government intrusion into private affairs appealed to the American people. So he was nominated and elected to a full term in 1924. As the time of the Republican National Convention approached, it was said around Washington that he had decided to offer the vice-presidency to the sharp-spoken, intelligent, arrogant, and highly independent Senator William Borah of Idaho. Newsmen who knew him fairly well insisted that he telephoned Senator Borah and said, "Senator, I'd like to have you on the ticket with me in the coming election." The senator is said to have replied, "In which position, Mr. President?" That disqualified Borah. Charles G. Dawes, who had been budget officer (and once issued a memo to all federal agencies admonishing them to save paper clips), became the vice-presidential nominee.

In nearly every presidency, Washington newspapermen have a genius for circulating amusing stories about the President. These passed all previous records during the Coolidge administration, perhaps in part because of his excellent relations with the press.

President Coolidge held more press conferences than any President before him. He was the first to put press conferences on a schedule—though he also often called special press conferences on a moment's notice—and to solicit support from the press for his administration in a systematic and effective fashion. The President was never quoted directly in a press conference. All of his comments were attributed to a "White House spokesman," a fictional character who did not disappear until Franklin D. Roosevelt became President. The "spokesman" was useful in protecting the President. If he had made a mistake or received an exceptionally unfavorable reaction to a comment by the "spokesman" he could then issue a direct quote correcting the situation.

Under these rules a personal interview was granted to the editor of the New York *Herald Tribune* who was, to the best of my knowledge, the only newspaperman outside a press conference whom President Coolidge ever saw. Just before the editor entered the large oval office, an assistant reminded him that he was not to ask any questions about domestic affairs. The editor was ushered to a chair across from the President, who said nothing.

Flustered, the editor plunged in with his first question:

"Mr. President, there is growing unrest in Panama about the perpetuity clause in the treaty which enabled the United States to build the lock canal. Do you care to comment on this?"

"Nope," said the President.

The next question had to do with the Haitian and Dominican situations, which had been bad since the imperialistic adventures of our government under Woodrow Wilson. Would the President give his views on this?

"Nope," again.

The editor asked three or four additional questions about foreign policy and the answer was the same. So, having received nothing but "nopes," the editor excused himself, rose from his chair, and started toward the door.

"Just a moment," President Coolidge said. "Remember the rules. Don't quote me."

When reporters entered the oval office, Coolidge, rising from his chair behind the big presidential desk, would carefully deposit his cigar in an ash tray. Then, the reporters would look on suspensefully while the President leafed through their written questions. He would read the questions silently and let the slips of paper flutter to the desk top without answering them. On one occasion, when the last question slip had fluttered into oblivion, President Coolidge looked the reporters squarely in the eye and said: "I have no questions today."

From 1924 to 1927, President and Mrs. Coolidge had spent their summers in Plymouth, Massachusetts, the White Court at Swampscott, Massachusetts, the White Pines Camp in the Adirondacks, and the Black Hills of South Dakota. In 1928 they chose the Cedar Island Lodge on the Pierce estate at Brule, Wisconsin. It was alleged that the lake was stocked each week with small-mouth bass and rainbow trout. Members of the official family considered it a rare privilege to be invited to stay a day or two at the summer White House, especially if they were asked by the President to join him in his daily fishing. My boss received such an invitation immediately following a visit there by Secretary of Commerce Herbert Hoover.

Secretary Jardine was a good fly fisherman and would have taken his own rod and flies, but his instructions were that equipment would be provided by the President. And so it was. The President provided Secretary Jardine with an ancient fly rod and two dry flies. He got into a new rowboat and waved Jardine toward an old, leaky one and said: "You go there."

On his first cast, Jardine's line caught in an overhanging branch. He threatened to maim the guide if he didn't succeed in freeing it without damage. Fortunately, the line was retrieved with fly intact and the Secretary went on to catch three sizable rainbows. The next day as he prepared to leave the temporary White House, the President walked with him to a car and commented: "You're a better fisherman than Hoover!" (Years later, at Frazier, Colorado, high in the Rockies, I fished with President Hoover, a purist using only dry flies, and found him to be skillful with a rod.)

One story about President Coolidge ran the gamut of the cocktail parties, hotel lounges, and official residences. I am certain it was true, for there were a good many witnesses. My version is shortened by omitting an oration delivered by Governor William Woodward Brandon of Alabama.

Southern Democrats were chagrined by the President's vacations in the North. So Governor Brandon of Alabama, accompanied by the Alabama members of the House and Senate, was ushered into the oval room of the White House one spring morning in 1927 to urge Coolidge to establish the summer White House in Alabama. The delegation remained standing as Governor Brandon, a noted orator, began to speak. The President rose, turned his back on the group, gazed out the window toward the Washington monument, placed his hands behind his back, and kept patting them together as the governor's pitch mounted in passion and eloquence. Brandon sang the praises of the sun-kissed hills of Alabama, the sparkling streams of pure water, the incomparable sailing and fishing, the famous hospitality of the people of the South, and on and on for fifteen minutes.

When the governor finished, the President turned slowly to face the delegation; he scanned their faces and said: "Can't go."

The amusing stories so prevalent in 1924 were lacking as 1928 approached. Late in 1927, President Coolidge, having consulted with nobody, not even his wife, handed newspapermen a curt written statement: "I do not choose to run in 1928." There was no elaboration.

Without exception, the press interpreted his statement as a final declaration that under no circumstances would he be a candidate. It was pointed out in numerous articles that the word "choose" had a special meaning in New England; the President's rhetoric always had a New England flavor. This special meaning was such that the public was led to believe that the President had said, in effect: "I have *determined* not to run for President in 1928."

I have always had a different view of his intention and I once possessed evidence to support my interpretation. My conviction was then and is now that he used the word "choose" in its normally accepted sense. He really was saying: "My *preference* is not to run."

The moment the President's statement was carried with banner headlines in the press, my boss, Secretary Jardine, went into action. He telephoned one or two close friends, all leading Republicans, in each of ten or twelve states, widely distributed geographically, and asked

46

what the reaction would be to Herbert Hoover as the Republican nominee. The responses were favorable, often enthusiastic. I don't recall that Jardine spoke to Hoover, his intimate friend. In any case, just two days after President Coolidge's precipitous statement, Secretary Jardine called a press conference and proposed that Secretary Hoover become the Republican nominee. He was the first to do so, and his statement made the front pages.

The next morning I reached my office in the Department of Agriculture about eight-fifteen. Shortly afterward, a messenger arrived from the White House and handed me an envelope, obviously addressed in the President's handwriting simply to: "Secretary Jardine."

Since I opened all of the Secretary's mail—and he had not yet arrived at the office—I had no hesitation in slitting open the President's letter. To my astonishment, I read:

Jardine,
Remember, you are working for me.
CALVIN COOLIDGE

My instant reaction was that the President believed that there would be an irresistible demand for him to run for a second full term, and his statement to the press had been intended to initiate a bandwagon movement in his behalf. There had been some discussion at the time as to whether a man who had occupied the office of President for five and a half years could be elected for another four-year term. The tradition of a maximum tour of duty of eight years was strong and had never been broken.

My abiding belief is that President Coolidge felt that if he responded to public demand and made the sacrifice of being a candidate again he could be elected. My view is slightly supported by comments made later by Arthur Krock and by some of the President's associates. They pointed out that persons who insisted the President could be drafted were thereafter frequently invited to social functions at the White House, but those who accepted the general interpretation of his "I do not choose to run" statement were not. Certainly my boss did not receive another invitation to White House social affairs.

The initiative taken by Jardine caught fire. Herbert Hoover, highly successful engineer, world famous for his humanitarian activities after World War I, and widely publicized as a successful Secretary of Commerce, was well known and liked in all states. He was a conservative. There was some doubt about his political affiliation, for in 1920 both Democrats and Republicans had considered him a possible nominee for the presidency. But the Hoover bandwagon was set rolling by the Republicans and it was quickly on the highways of the nation.

President Coolidge did not like Hoover, in part, I suppose, because the energetic Commerce Secretary seemed always to be pressing ideas or actions on him. The President once, referring to Hoover, snapped at Jardine: "That man has offered me unsolicited advice for six years, all of it bad!" The months remaining in Coolidge's term must have been awkward ones for Secretary Hoover, the candidate, and Secretary Jardine, the nominator, both continuing in the Cabinet of a President who now thoroughly disliked them. I would not have been surprised if, at this time, the President had found some excuse for removing the Secretary of Agriculture. Fortunately, he did not do so.*

President Coolidge was the last President of our country who was not overburdened with the responsibilities of the office. Had the conditions of his time continued, I would have little reason for writing this book, for it was the ever increasing responsibilities of the presidency that in time convinced me of the need for substantial changes in the White House—changes that would lighten the President's load without reducing his fundamental constitutional tasks.

Analysts who have studied the Coolidge administration do not agree with one another. Some have described him as a shrewd politician, steeped in history, suitable to the times, and painfully aware of his own prominence. Others have portrayed him as a sleepy, indolent man who paid little attention to the nation's business. They view his silence, his dry jokes, his apparent boredom, and his constant demands for thrift as sheer political posing.

President Coolidge was certainly not a stupid man, nor was he politically naïve. I would characterize him as a narrow and stubborn man who was woefully uninformed in some very important areas. Work

* Some weeks after the President's note came to Secretary Jardine, I asked if I might have it as a collector's item. The Secretary grinned and said he would prefer that it not be in the official files of the department. The letter has long since disappeared. I did not keep diaries, and I routinely destroyed obsolete correspondence. In those days we did not have Xerox machines in every other office, so there were no copies. And my search through the National Archives, the files of the Eisenhower Library, and the Jardine papers proved fruitless.

48

seemed to exhaust him, even though the burden he carried could not compare even to that of the head of a large business corporation today. He slept for at least ten hours every night and, according to Chief Usher "Ike" Hoover, he napped in the White House in the afternoon for as long as two to four hours.

I don't think the President was a procrastinator; it was just that he would not deal with a problem until it was literally forced upon him. He put things off in the belief (sometimes correct) that they would either go away or take care of themselves. When he did deal with a problem he dealt with it in his own way. He had a rigid conception of his role as President, and he treated the executive establishment as his personal fiefdom.

President Coolidge had almost no positive views of government. He felt that he had little constitutional role in the formulation of legislation, which is why he would flatly veto farm relief bills rather than suggest modifications that would make them mutually acceptable. He scrupulously avoided involvement with the independent agencies such as the Federal Reserve Board. His executive staff was very small, and most of what would now be considered the President's work was then handled in the Cabinet departments, especially the preparation of reports, speeches, policy statements, and so forth. Coolidge demanded loyalty from his Cabinet. In return he gave them remarkable latitude to formulate policy and he protected them, even though he might disagree with them. According to his limited vision of government, it was not his duty to exert a strong influence on its workings.

Nevertheless, when he moved into the White House he sought to become an effective leader—within his own conception of the job. He consolidated his authority over the Cabinet—most of whom had never really known him as Vice-President. His regular press conferences were a significant innovation. Regularly, members of Congress would be invited to take breakfast or an informal supper at the White House— not so much in an attempt to influence them as to get to know them. Coolidge showed almost no partisanship and was solicitous of Democrats as well as members of his own party. In addition to conferring with congressmen, he sought advice from a wide circle of experts in farm problems, labor, business, and foreign affairs.

Understandably, he was called "Silent Cal." He could sit through long and complicated meetings without ever uttering a syllable.

Frank Stearns, a Boston businessman and perhaps the closest friend and confidant Coolidge had, visited the President frequently in the White House. Apparently the two men would light cigars and sit smoking silently for an hour or more. Coolidge, shortly before leaving office, shared with Herbert Hoover his technique for dealing with talkative visitors: "You have to stand every day three or four hours of visitors. . . . If you keep dead still they will run down in three or four minutes. If you even cough or smile they will start up all over again."

President Coolidge had few intimate advisers, certainly no one like Colonel House in the Wilson administration or Bill Moyers in the Johnson administration. He did bring a man named C. Bascom Slemp to the White House. Mr. Slemp's only publicized activity was serving as liaison between the President and the Republicans in Congress and in the Republican National Committee. Coolidge was obviously satisfied with the appointment, for he adhered to it in the face of severe criticisms from many Republican leaders and even taunts by members of the press, who expressed dismay that the President should have appointed such a wholly partisan politician as his aide.

Coolidge did not rely on Slemp as an adviser or even as an intimate. He apparently felt he did not need advice, fancying himself to be a sagacious politician of keen insight who understood the mood of the people. Slemp did help the President to relax, apparently, which must not have been the most trying task. Coolidge generally left his office by 4:00 P.M. and Slemp usually accompanied him to the family rooms in the White House.

Bascom Slemp left the White House staff in 1925 and was succeeded by Everett Sanders, a former congressman from Indiana. Coolidge once referred to Sanders as the best secretary a President ever had. To Sanders, the President seems to have revealed—at least to some extent—the inner man and at times, it is reported, even became talkative with him.

Secretary Jardine often said to me that Coolidge was the most relaxed man who had ever occupied the White House. Theodore Roosevelt had been a man of perpetual motion, assertive and demanding, a dominant personality and a reformer, capable of such questionable decisions as his support of Panama in its move to secede from Colombia in 1903 and his imperialistic and unilateral promulgation of the Roosevelt corollary to the Monroe Doctrine which asserted our right to intervene in the internal affairs of Latin American countries. Taft had been a hard-working, good man, troubled, intellectual, but ineffective. Wilson, as I have related, had never known a moment of quiet and had literally worked and worried himself to death. Coolidge, never as affectionately regarded as were Franklin Roosevelt, or Eisenhower, or Kennedy, nonetheless seems to have been generally acceptable and thus could be complacent and maintain the dignity of the presidency.

Despite the general calm of the Coolidge period, his administration was not without difficulties. The Teapot Dome scandal that developed under Harding broke into the press under Coolidge. With the courage and action that he had displayed as governor of Massachusetts when he settled the Boston police strike, he fired Harding's Attorney General. In time he removed all but three of Harding's Cabinet members.

Even in the smallest matters, including my trip home from Scotland, Coolidge insisted parsimoniously on economy, at a time when federal appropriations in total were only two thirds the cost of our present space program. He favored lower taxes and higher tariffs, the latter an anachronism in view of the nation's creditor status, which had existed for nearly a decade. He vetoed a veterans' bonus bill, but that time he lost, for the Congress passed the measure over his veto. He was indifferent to the skyrocketing of the stock market, a prelude to the crash that would take place in the Hoover administration. The Kellogg-Briand Pact, which was designed to outlaw war, was acclaimed by Coolidge and Kellogg, but less than a score of nations signed it and even these eventually discarded it.

President Coolidge caused opposition politicians to emphasize anew that the Republican organization was a party of big business, a designation which persists, unfairly, to this day.

One of his most intelligent decisions was to appoint Dwight Morrow as ambassador to Mexico late in September 1927. Our relations with Mexico had been at a low ebb for many years, especially after Woodrow Wilson's blatant interference in that nation's internal affairs. Morrow, the type of intelligent, personable, and hard-working ambassador we ought to have in every nation, won the hearts of the Mexican people, gained the respect of Mexican officials, settled several aspects of an age-old quarrel regarding oil development, and laid the groundwork for a policy of non-intervention in the internal affairs of other nations which came into full flower as the Good Neighbor Policy under Franklin Roosevelt.

The Coolidge administration ended on March 4, 1929, and the President left Washington exhausted and anxious for a rest (but probably resentful that another man would occupy the spotlight he so enjoyed). Less than eight months later, on October 24, the New York Stock Market crashed, plunging this nation into the worst economic depression it has ever experienced. All of this was quite beyond the former President, who burned out like a candle. He died quietly of a sudden heart attack on January 5, 1933, and was buried near where he was born—in and among the rocky hills of Vermont, now one with them.

CHAPTER 4

In every tragedy, some unfortunate soul
must play the victim; Herbert Hoover had
all the qualifications to be an effective President except a magic wand.

IN THE SPRING of 1928, Nelson Antrim Crawford, a former
teacher of mine and director of information of the Department of
Agriculture, resigned, and I was appointed to his former position—a
career post which made me a member of what we called the Secretary's
cabinet.

Secretary Jardine obviously had confidence in me, but I knew that
he was nervous about naming a twenty-eight-year-old man to supervise
a major branch of the department. The director of information published hundreds of farm bulletins in millions of copies which were distributed free by members of Congress but were also sold by the
Superintendent of Documents; he controlled a large press service, operated a nationwide daily radio program on 134 stations of the National
Broadcasting Company "red network" (later changed to a television
network), and co-ordinated the information activities of the many
bureaus of one of the largest executive departments in government.
Fortunately for both of us, my promotion caused no criticism.

The 1928 Republican Convention was scheduled for Kansas City.
I took a week's leave so that my wife and I could accompany Secretary
and Mrs. Jardine to the convention. Our hotel rooms were one floor
above those of the Hoover family. My boss, anxious that everything
should proceed smoothly, asked me to keep an eye on Allan Hoover,
the younger son of Secretary and Mrs. Hoover. Allan was a handsome,
rosy-cheeked, socially active young man, and Jardine feared that the
exuberant youngster might get into some mischief that would embarrass his candidate. I made no effort to carry out the assignment, for I

could not have kept up with the young man even if I had tried, and so far as I knew his behavior was as flawless as that of his older brother, Herbert, Jr.*

Hoover was nominated without difficulty and handily won the November election, receiving 444 electoral votes against 87 for Governor Alfred E. Smith of New York. Since the Great War, Hoover had been one of the most highly respected and popular figures in America —a man who most people felt could provide genuine leadership. During the campaign Hoover stressed the certain growth of the American economy and made his fateful prediction of "two chickens in every pot and a car in every garage." Within a year after his election, the United States plunged into the worst and most profound depression in our history, and Hoover's promise became a humiliation that haunted him long thereafter.

Several weeks before he assumed office, President-elect Hoover, in a private conference at his home, indicated to Secretary Jardine that he wished to appoint Arthur M. Hyde, former governor of Missouri and a successful automobile dealer, as his Secretary of Agriculture. Jardine was disappointed. As one of Hoover's most intimate friends and the first national leader to promote him for the presidency, he had taken it for granted that he would continue in the President's Cabinet. Beyond that, he had been an effective and successful Secretary of Agriculture. In an attempt to sweeten the bitter pill, Hoover explained that the really important agricultural position in his administration would be that of head of a new Federal Farm Board which he intended to create to deal with the economic woes of the American farmer. He wanted Jardine to take this new post when it was established. After considering the offer for a week, Secretary Jardine declined. He became head of a large agricultural marketing co-operative, and a year later accepted the President's appointment as U.S. ambassador to Egypt. I regretted the break in an affectionate and helpful relationship that had existed between Jardine and me for a decade. As it turned out, however, our association was to be renewed in the 1940s.

President Hoover planned to summon a special session of Congress to deal with the worsening farm problem as soon as he took office. His

* I met the two sons from time to time during the convention and years later became a close friend of Herbert, Jr., when he served as Under Secretary of State in the Eisenhower administration.

major adviser was, of course, Secretary Hyde, a shrewd politician who knew little about American agriculture. A few days after the inauguration, I accompanied Secretary Hyde to the White House to review the message on which Hoover had been working since his election. Secretary Hyde and I sat in the Cabinet room, each of us with a draft of the message.

It called for the creation of a Federal Farm Board which would assist in establishing and financing farmer-owned and -operated co-operatives. With the use of federal funds, the co-operatives would acquire warehousing and marketing facilities, purchase and hold farm commodities until the volume of production, price, and other conditions made their sale more economically attractive, and establish clearinghouses for the more orderly marketing of perishable commodities. The President wanted no fee or tax imposed on farmers or farm commodities, and insisted that no governmental agency should engage directly in buying, selling, and pricing farm products, "for such course can lead only to bureaucracy and domination." Lacking specificity, his suggestions included improvement of waterway transportation and increased tariffs on farm commodities to protect the domestic market and induce farmers to diversify production.

The draft message also suggested that higher tariffs on selected industrial goods were needed. Higher wages paid in the United States placed us in a bad competitive position. Hence, he proposed using the flexible provisions of the Tariff Act of 1922 in making adjustments and would, if conditions warranted, submit new tariff recommendations to the Congress. For the time being he intended to alter Tariff Commission procedures and standards so that decisions concerning changes in duties could be made in a month or two, rather than over a period of years as in the preceding seven years.

The key concept in his message was that over a span of time farm prices would fluctuate and that co-operatives would buy and store commodities when prices were low and sell them as market recoveries occurred. I came from a Bible-reading family and was struck by the similarity to the ever normal granary operation of Egypt in biblical times.

Secretary Hyde and I read the message silently. He made no effort to conceal his approval. I swallowed hard and said that in my judgment the statement was on shaky ground. It assumed that farm prices would rise sufficiently to permit the federally financed co-operatives to recoup their funds and remain in business. While the nation generally was enjoying what seemed to be an economic boom and many were glorying in the unprecedented advance of the stock market, a few economists were warning that a general depression was possible, perhaps imminent.

With a bit of wind behind me, I sailed on. I spoke strongly against the recommendations for increasing tariffs on industrial products. I did not object, however, to tariffs on agricultural imports which were exacerbating our own surplus situation.

Hyde was not impressed by my comments. At this point George Akerson, assistant to the President, came into the room and Hyde told him I was concerned about the message and outlined my comments. This was my first contact with Akerson, but it was the beginning of a close working relationship.†

I can only speculate that my critique of the President's farm message never reached him or failed to impress him. Without change, the message was delivered to Congress on April 6, 1929. The agricultural recommendations were quickly approved. Unfortunately the farm depression deepened, the stock market crashed in the fall, general economic stagnation developed, farm prices declined with toboggan speed, and in three years the Federal Farm Board lost $345 million, a fact, among others, that was used in 1932 to drive Herbert Hoover from the White House.

Ironically, the Farm Board's loss seemed minuscule in comparison to the millions of dollars that were spent annually under the Agricultural Adjustment Act of 1933 and its successor, the Agricultural Conservation Act of 1936. These later enactments employed some of the concepts of the Hoover program but added payments to farmers for reducing production and direct government buying, storing, and selling of surplus farm products, often at huge losses.

The Congress debated the Hoover tariff suggestions for more than

† Several months later he said that if I did not object he would suggest to the President that I be added to the White House staff. This tentative offer never materialized into reality mainly because, as Akerson later explained, legislative and appropriation restraints on the White House made an additional appointment impossible. Incredible as it may now seem, the President at that time had authority to appoint only two principal aides. Sometime later, President Hoover created a furor in Congress and the press when he asked for and won authority for two more major positions. The restrictions of that day now seem ludicrous in light of the current gargantuan size of the White House staff.

a year. On June 16, 1930, it passed the Hawley-Smoot Act, which raised duties on farm and industrial products to an all-time high. President Hoover told the Congress in advance that he would sign the bill despite its imperfections. "No tariff bill has ever been enacted under the present system that will be perfect," he said. He intended to use the flexible provisions to correct inequities, and if this procedure proved insufficient, he would ask the Congress to increase the authority of the Tariff Commission.

The high tariffs simply ignored the creditor status of the United States, a status we had enjoyed for a decade. The high tariffs of the Hawley-Smoot Act further reduced our imports and hence our exports, especially exports of our farm surpluses. The total effect was to make the situation worse.

In a frantic effort to check the depression, the President recommended the establishment of the Reconstruction Finance Corporation with authority to make loans to imperiled banks and other institutions. It was a good move. Hoover asked that the loans, especially to banks, not be made public—for obvious reasons. However, John Nance Garner of Texas, then Speaker of the House and later Roosevelt's Vice-President, insisted on an amendment which required public disclosure of bank loans. Any observant person could plainly see what would happen; and it did. When a loan was made to a bank and the loan was publicized, the depositors, being able to add two and two, made a run on the bank. This was, in my opinion, a major cause of the panic that swept throughout the nation and led later to the closing of the banks—the "bank holiday" in the early weeks of the Franklin Roosevelt administration. For reasons I don't understand, this has been largely ignored in the literature of the period.

Agricultural prices continued to decline. Nearly twenty-five per cent of the working force became unemployed. Farmers used shotguns to prevent mortgage holders from foreclosing on their farms. And a spirit of dismay and pessimism gripped the nation. The funny stories of the Coolidge days were lacking. The attitude in the legislative and executive branches of the government and in the capital generally was grim. The initiation of a modest program of public works, including flood control and navigation projects, the construction of the Hoover Dam, and increased emphasis on the establishment of national forests and parks were flyspecks on a depression map. While Coolidge was

President he held federal appropriations below $2.9 billion; Hoover increased them to $4.5 billion, but to no avail.

In many ways the Hoover administration, 1929–33, marks the transition between the nineteenth- and twentieth-century presidencies. The crisis of the great depression shaped the executive branch into new forms as the government attempted to respond to the tidal wave of economic disaster. Calvin Coolidge was the last of a passing breed of Presidents who could let events swirl around them as they napped in the afternoons. Franklin Roosevelt was the first of a new genus of Presidents, grasping all the power the presidency would yield and using it to shape the times to their own vision. In between these two stood Herbert Hoover, inclined by instinct to be a nineteenth-century President and impelled by necessity to be a twentieth-century President.

Hoover's experience in the White House was a personal tragedy. He was extremely well prepared for the office. His education and professional background were excellent training for the job. He was an engineer, a manager, an accomplished administrator who knew more about the functioning of government than had any of his predecessors; his strength was in solving problems, mustering resources—whether human or material—and concentrating them on the matters at hand. He was comfortably, though not extremely, wealthy, and his fortune was the product of his own labor. Widely traveled and familiar with international problems, as they affected both continents and human beings, he was perhaps the first—possibly the only—United States President with a deep understanding of economic theory. He was no stranger to large problems—whether the harnessing of the natural resources of China or feeding the millions of Europeans left starving in the wake of World War I. As Secretary of Commerce in the Harding and Coolidge administrations, he transformed that small and indolent agency into an efficient and effective force for the economic improvement of the American people. However, like most men of his generation, Hoover's beliefs were grounded in a conventional interpretation of the American myth. For him, the individual was supreme; the efforts of the individual on his own behalf would guarantee the national prosperity. Government's role was most properly a limited one. Yet he advocated a more active involvement on the part of government in the general welfare than most of his predecessors. Hoover was a great humanitarian, liberal—even radical—in his sympathy for his fellow men. But he was also confident that private efforts, organized, channeled by the most efficient means, and often through government example and leadership, could overcome all obstacles. In the early days of his term in office he told his associates that he wanted to make the presidency far more active than had Coolidge and Harding.

Hoover intended, as his memoirs show, to be vigorous in exercising all the powers conferred upon him as head of state, chief of the executive establishment, principal adviser to Congress, constitutional head of the armed forces and of foreign policy, and spokesman for the American people. He wanted, he said, "to give constant leadership by promoting social and economic reforms." He wished to be the conserver of natural resources and to "encourage all good causes." But no one— not a Hoover, Roosevelt, Eisenhower, or anyone else—could have prevented the great depression in 1929. It is possible, I think, that, if proper action had been taken in 1921 when farm income began falling below its historic parity with industry, the most severe consequences of the economic disaster could have been avoided. But by 1929 it was too late to do much. All the manifold actions of the Roosevelt administration from 1933 to 1942 did not bring about significant improvement. Depression was cured by war.

Unfortunately, Hoover was not a politician. Prior to his 1928 campaign, he had never held elective office of any kind. In this respect he was far behind other Presidents. Handicapped by his political immaturity, he could not understand and could not compete with men experienced in the arena of congressional politics. One observer—his biographer, Eugene Lyons[2]—said that he was "always the thinnest-skinned executive in Washington." He was faced with a strong Democratic Congress and he had neither the skill nor the will to dominate the Congress or to carry his cause past it to the public. As a result, most of his legislative programs never got passed or were taken over by the aggressive leaders on Capitol Hill.

Herbert Hoover was a captive of his own limitations, for with all of his ability and personal resources he did not recognize the battlefield on which the war had to be waged. His tireless exertions on his country's behalf did provide some significant remedies against economic collapse, so that by 1932 there was some reason to hope for an early end to the trouble. The near total demise of the international financial structure—carrying with it many of our own large banks— was a crisis of confidence as much as one of economics: a conflict that could not be waged through policies and memoranda. Hoover could not combat fear—his administrative principles and engineering techniques did not provide such answers. The American myth was being challenged. Hoover, the able Chief Executive, faced what was fundamentally a political crisis—one which affected what people believed about themselves, about their government, and about their economic system. He simply did not have the weapons to meet this challenge.

President Hoover was the object of much vilification, both during and after his administration. It was unjustified. He did not cause the depression. He may have even foreseen it—as early as 1927, he warned against the inflationary practices of business and the financial community. As Secretary of Commerce, he did everything which he, within his firm concept of limited government, could do to prevent what later occurred. As President, he exerted full authority to revive the faltering economic system. Much of his effort was directed at what he knew best: galvanizing private initiative to public duty. He tried to inspire renewed business investment, to revive employment, and he was confident that private mechanisms, such as the Red Cross and religious organizations, could handle the temporary dislocation and misery caused by the economic collapse. Further, where he saw the clear need, he brought the government into action: witness the moratorium on intergovernmental debts, the Reconstruction Finance Corporation, the National Credit Association, the World Monetary and Economic Conference, Federal Land Banks, Mortgage Discount and Home Loan Banks, and other acts. But nothing he did seemed to help much and he steadily lost the support of the American people.

President Hoover had one trusted friend and confidant: Lawrence Richey. While he called on many individuals for consultation and advice, including such Cabinet members as Henry L. Stimson and Ogden L. Mills, and such staff aides as George Akerson, Walter H. Newton, Theodore Joslin, and French Strother, there was only one genuine confidant. From the moment that Hoover became active in the Food Administration and later as Secretary of Commerce, Richey was by his side. Richey knew everything Hoover did and planned to do. He never betrayed a confidence, not even to his closest colleagues in the White House.

Richey shared the President's burdens and suffered with his "Chief." When an unjustified allegation was made that Hoover had been associated with a robbery in England, years before, it was Richey who went to England to make an investigation and return with proof that Hoover had been called only as a witness in the case.

Richey, seeing a growing physical exhaustion in the President, organized what came to be called the "Medicine Ball Cabinet," a daily group exercise that involved tossing a large heavy ball among the participants—a substitute for golf but not for fishing, which Hoover loved. Hoover turned to Richey for major appointments. It was Richey, a former member of the Federal Bureau of Investigation, who recommended the appointment of J. Edgar Hoover to head the Bureau, an appointment that lasted into seven administrations.

The Hoover staff was not immune to criticism. It was dubbed the "vestal virgins" by the press. But Richey escaped all criticism. During his four years in the White House and in subsequent years when he continued to serve the Chief, Richey retained the respect of all who knew him. Though Hoover was stern, sensitive, and mostly devoid of a smile in his public appearances, he was an intelligent and warm-hearted man, and his feeling for Richey was genuine.

Eugene Lyons has noted[2] that the President had a multitude of enemies but no ex-friends. Casual observers and the general public never saw this other side—this enormously likable side—of the unfortunate Hoover. All through his life he attracted men who served him devotedly and remained loyal in spite of every adversity. In return, Hoover went out of his way to show his appreciation, encouraging these friends during personal reverses—even to the extent of anonymously extending financial support or locating them in new careers. He wanted no recognition or thanks, but his gratitude toward his close friends was intense. During my brother's administration I came to know Hoover better. I spent several fishing vacations with him in the Rockies. I gained much from his wit and wisdom.

Election night 1932 was a humiliating experience for Herbert Hoover. Richey, perhaps the most faithful and dependable assistant a President ever had, was with his Chief that night. Hoover received 59 electoral votes to 472 for Franklin Delano Roosevelt.

For some years after he left the White House there were few kind words for the "depression President." But Hoover lived long enough to witness a remarkable change in the general public attitude. People came to realize that he had been a victim of circumstances. He continued to serve the government and the American people in numerous ways, most notably as chairman of two Hoover Commissions which recommended many constructive changes in the executive establishment. Before his death he had won respect as a great American and humanitarian, enthusiastically acclaimed in his rare public appearances.

I met Hoover as a result of a bizarre development. An employee of the press service under my direction sent voluminous documents to a Republican senator, charging that I had manipulated information in ways which had helped the Democrats. The senator complained about me to Secretary Hyde. Questioned, I declared very clearly and as firmly as I could that I was as objective as humanly possible in my position and my work was non-partisan and impartial. Unfortunately, the Secretary did not defend me on that basis but rather insisted that I was as loyal a Republican as the senator himself. This depressed me. It did not frighten me, however, as it once would have, for by now my youthful feeling of insecurity was completely gone; I then had several other tempting offers on my desk, one a tentative but lucrative chance to become editor of a national magazine.

I remonstrated with Hyde about his defending a career man on the basis of his politics. I was deeply conscious of the fact that a civil service officer had to be nonpartisan in all he did. Of course he had to help carry out the policies of the Administration in power, and if he found it impossible to do this faithfully, the only other course was resignation. Hyde, however, was so completely the partisan politician that he would not accept my view. Without my knowledge, he took the issue to the White House, for it involved not a single individual but a basic principle. George Akerson called me to the White House and in a few moments he accepted my view and said that President Hoover would uphold the policy of non-partisanship by career officers.

Scarcely had this problem been resolved than the issue again came to a head. Economy in government was one imperative of the Hoover administration. Most members of Congress were insistent upon the rigid control of expenditures. Suddenly I found myself embroiled in a dispute about economy that raised anew the issue of non-partisanship, and this time the dispute reached President Hoover.

Senator Pat Harrison of Mississippi made a sarcastic speech on the floor of the Senate, charging that the Department of Agriculture was wasting large sums of money, taxpayers' money, by publishing unnecessary and even ridiculous farm bulletins. He waved one above his head and said: "I have here a bulletin on the 'Love Life of the Bullfrog'!" This juicy bit of erroneous information earned front-page stories in the nation's press, in some papers receiving two- and three-column headlines. What occurred in the ensuing weeks reminded me of Aristotle's comment: "The least deviation from the truth is multiplied later a thousandfold."

In the first week following this amazing declaration, my office received about a thousand requests for the bulletin on bullfrogs. Secretary Hyde, in a fury, demanded that I make a counterattack on Senator Harrison and expose the fallacy of his charge.

I went to my office and thought about the matter for a full hour. To this point my governmental career had been free of controversy—certainly free of any public controversy. Now I was at the center of a small storm that could blow up into a full gale. I did not like it much. I especially did not like being on the wrong end of a mischievous and fallacious accusation. Still, I could not, in view of the objectivity that had to characterize my work, make an attack on a senator of the United States. If the Secretary persisted in his demand, I would have to resign. The prospect did not at all appeal to me. By then I had become completely absorbed in and fascinated by the functioning of the federal government. I had declined the several outside attractive offers and very much wanted to remain permanently in the federal service. So I did not defy Secretary Hyde and I did not comply with his demand. I simply ignored his directive and issued a factual press release in which I did not mention the senator's name or question his "good faith."

The release I issued that afternoon explained that the Bureau of Fisheries was not in the Department of Agriculture, that the Department of Agriculture had never published anything about fish, frogs, or other aquatic life, and that most assuredly we had never published a bulletin entitled "Love Life of the Bullfrog."

I then learned a classic lesson about communications. The press now gave front-page coverage to a repetition of Senator Harris' charge, and buried in the story was my statement. Few persons read it. The next week my office received nearly *two* thousand mail requests for the bulletin. Now critical editorials appeared in some papers.

Secretary Hyde was beside himself and very angry with me. His concern was not for the integrity of the department but for the protection of the Republican Party. He summoned me to his office and said we would go to the White House and have "a showdown."

When we were ushered into the oval office President Hoover asked me to give him the background, which I quickly did. The President was obviously concerned, but not unreasonably so. Before we went to the White House, I had hastily phoned George Akerson. He gave the President enough information to have a calming effect. President Hoover readily affirmed the policy of non-partisan activity by career service personnel and suggested that I speak on the NBC Red network and give facts about what had been alleged.

In this conference, I was struck by the sadness on the President's face. I knew that he had been working long hours each day, struggling to adjust from the optimism he had felt at his inauguration when he had said: "In no nation are the fruits of accomplishment so secure," to the terrible disappointments he suffered as his efforts to stem the depression failed. My view was that he did not truly understand the complex economic forces that had combined with the Harding-Coolidge farm depression to bring on the worst panic in American history. Day and night he had held conferences with business, labor, educational, and other leaders, urging them to help restore confidence among the American people and through that confidence to achieve economic stability. At the same time he had courageously established a moratorium on European war debts to the United States (my Scottish friends must have been pleased), worked assiduously to improve relations with Latin America, reversed some of President Wilson's imperialistic policies by taking our marines out of Nicaragua and promising to do the same for Haiti—and all the while driving himself and his few White House assistants and Cabinet members to work round the clock. It was at this conference that I began thinking seriously about the enormous responsibilities we had placed upon the President of the United States. I had read all I could find about the man-killing job President Wilson had undertaken for eight years, had witnessed the relative calm of the Harding, then the Coolidge administrations, and was now witnessing a return of conditions to the White House that had eventually consumed Wilson. In subsequent administrations I would see these burdens grow to unbelievable proportions.

I returned to my office in Agriculture a somewhat wiser and disconsolate young man, and uneasy about my relations with Secretary Hyde, who had been politely chastened by the President.

Before going on the air, as President Hoover had asked me to do, I learned that the Bureau of Fisheries of the Department of Commerce had issued, years before, a technical bulletin on the production of frog legs for commercial marketing. This must have been the bulletin that Senator Harris had shouted about in the Senate. It had been out of print for years. So I called the Superintendent of Documents and suggested that he reprint the bulletin (it would sell for ten cents). In my radio discussion I intended to refer all inquiries to the Department of Commerce or the Superintendent of Documents.

I spoke for fifteen minutes over 134 radio stations that reached every part of the United States. Carefully I explained that the Department of Agriculture knew nothing about frogs and had never published anything about frogs. The only bulletin ever published by the Department of Commerce was scientific in character and had nothing to do with the love life of frogs per se but was valuable to anyone who wished to raise frogs for market.

Once again newspaper reporters found the original charge to be so newsworthy that the leading paragraphs of most stories quoted Senator Harrison's original charges and only incidentally mentioned the facts. That week my office received *five thousand* letters asking for "Love Life of the Bullfrog." We referred the influx of letters to the Superintendent of Documents.

Now Secretary Hyde was really seething. He had a flexible orator's voice which he could manipulate with the skill of a concert pianist. He went on the radio network himself and made a direct attack on Senator Harrison. His voice fluctuated from pianissimo to fortissimo and ranged from low G to high C. In the midst of his diatribe he scornfully attacked all Democrats. He told, as I recall, about a family in Senator Harrison's state which had a genetic sport in it. It seemed that "Pa and Ma had eight children, all of whom were God-fearing Democrats except John, the youngest, who turned out to be a Republican. Neighbors, concerned that such a thing could occur in their community, called on Ma and Pa for an explanation. Pa pointed out that he had raised all his children to be faithful to the Democratic Party but John, the ornery cuss, took to readin'."

To Secretary Hyde's chagrin and my secret pleasure, my office that week received *ten thousand* requests for the bulletin on the "Love Life of the Bullfrog."

This incident impressed upon me a truth which I have lived by. Once a rumor is started, it spreads like leaves in a gale; truth cannot gather the leaves.‡ On the other hand, if the truth is first known, then rumors, even newsworthy ones, are generally ignored. I have therefore always, in government and education, tried to keep the public accurately informed on all the activities within the sphere of my responsibility, especially incidents in which my colleagues or I have made a mistake or done something which could be misunderstood, for that is the type of incident which, if ferreted out by the press, can be ballooned into an apparent scandal. It has not always been easy to abide by this policy.

The head of the John Birch Society, years later, charged in a book which he eventually withdrew that President Eisenhower was a Communist and that I was head of the party. Even though the book had limited circulation, the rumor spread with flash-flood speed across the country. Letters from all parts of the nation, especially from California, which seemed to have a disproportionate number of gullible individuals, poured into the White House and my office. Many asked me why I didn't publicly deny the charge if it were untrue. To call President Eisenhower a Communist was worse than ridiculous and I, if I differed with my brother at all, was more conservative than he on economic and fiscal policy. We never differed on matters of human values and human welfare.

The head of the John Birch Society, in another widely publicized document, which was not withdrawn, said that at the time of the Cuban revolution I had visited Castro and arranged to ship arms to him. I had never even been in Cuba, had never met Castro, took no action of any kind during the Cuban revolution, and thoroughly disliked all that Castro stood for.

‡ Mark Twain once said, "A lie travels around the earth while truth is putting on his shoes."

The important consideration in these two incidents—there were many more—is that if I had issued statements of denial I would have multiplied many times the public consciousness of the original charge, and my denial, if noticed, would be suspect. McCarthyism in many forms is as old as civilization and always consumes the innocent.

Normally, one has to let lies fall of their own weight. This does not mean that I enjoy having misinformation about my actions or philosophy publicized or spread by cocktail rumormongers. I have a normal amount of pride. Many experiences of the type I have mentioned sensitized me to the problems faced by candidates for public office and ingrained in me a determination to avoid offering myself in the elective process. On three occasions I had opportunities in this regard. In two states I was urged by substantial groups to seek the Republican nomination for governor; in Maryland I was offered the Republican senatorial nomination without opposition at a time when the Democratic nominee might have been relatively easy to beat. In the first two situations, I declined, partly because of no more than lukewarm interest, but also because, as a man who abhors personal attacks and countercharges, I did not wish to expose myself to campaign rhetoric and experiences. I might have set aside this dislike to run for the Senate, since that was the one political position that greatly appealed to me. But I was in midstream as president of The Johns Hopkins University and could not, in good conscience, leave until I had accomplished the goals I had set.

One other aspect of incidents like the bullfrogs and the Birchers has always perplexed me, namely the failure of so many people to read or listen to the facts. Granted that the media will often obscure or distort the facts in an effort to sensationalize a story, but that still doesn't explain how intelligent people, even when confronted with the facts, can simply not see or hear them. In other controversial situations where misconceptions abounded, I clearly set forth the facts, in a speech or in writing, only to have persons approach me afterward and spout the same misconceptions—as though I hadn't said anything. I finally concluded that when people are aroused over issues that touch their basic convictions or their favorite orthodoxies they have an uncanny ability to simply blank out what they don't want to hear—an automatic filtering device of sorts. And this, as much as anything, has made it possible for humans to do some very foolish things and to commit some horrible and heinous crimes against their fellow men.

Secretary Hyde and Alexander Legge, chairman of Hoover's Federal Farm Board, both had business, not agricultural, backgrounds. They were friends. Because their responsibilities in the farm depression were interdependent, they often were in conference. One day Legge asked the Secretary for a brief economic analysis of the farm situation and the prospects for price advances or declines in the coming year. The task was given to the Bureau of Agricultural Economics. The Bureau took weeks to prepare its analysis, during which time Legge telephoned nearly every day to demand early delivery. Finally a tome of several hundred pages was presented to Secretary Hyde, who sent it at once by messenger to Mr. Legge. I was in the Secretary's office late that afternoon when Legge telephoned him. He was furious and sarcastic. He said that a messenger had had to use a wheelbarrow to deliver a massive report instead of the brief analysis he had requested.

"It is so filled with qualifications," he yelled, "that it doesn't mean a damn thing! If those economists of yours wrote the Declaration of Independence, they would say: 'It is estimated that all men (see footnote on page six) are created equal, in one sense at least, and they seemingly, though this is subject to several interpretations, are endowed with certain unalienable rights!' "

His voice rose to a scream: "Is that the way you damn fools in Agriculture prepare material for the public? If so, you're issuing a lot of hogwash!" The Secretary, surprised and stung, decided he had better read the report. He found that it made no clear-cut predictions of any kind. Indeed, conditions then were such that predictions were impossible—as both he and Legge might have known.

The last two years under Secretary Hyde were difficult ones for me and many of my associates. He continued in a caustic way to be critical of my refusal to be a Republican first and a civil servant second. The national economy continued to sink, and nothing the Administration did seemed to help. Gloom was pervasive and laughter was rare in the nation's capital.

In the campaign of 1932, Franklin Delano Roosevelt, promising a "New Deal" and rigid economy in government, captured the imagination of the American people. His buoyant spirit and ebullient personality exuded a confidence that was contagious—a confidence that Mr. Hoover, for all his efforts, simply couldn't produce. Roosevelt had a wonderful voice and his rhetoric was moving. He rolled over Herbert Hoover and into the White House.

Then began my intimate relationship with Presidents of the United States. During President Roosevelt's time in the White House I carried out directly for him many complex assignments at home and abroad. Despite our political differences, which he often chided me about, we became fast friends. Indeed, it was said around Washington that only a handful of persons could have a "conversation" with the President— the rest just listened. For some reason which I can't explain, I was one of the fortunate handful.

CHAPTER 5

The first challenge for a leader is to induce
the people to believe in him; the second is
to induce them to believe in themselves.

ON THE DAY that Franklin Delano Roosevelt moved into
the White House—March 4, 1933—the nation's sagging banking system
collapsed.

The great depression had bottomed out. Twelve million Americans were out of work. Agricultural prices fell to new lows and farmers were desperate. In the cities, breadlines formed. Families, anxiously waiting for a stubborn winter to pass, prowled railroad lines, picking coal from between the ties. Wall Street toppled with the economy, and each day brought business failures, bankruptcies, ruined careers, and suicides. The stock market was in a shambles, far below the 1929 crash, and industrial operations were only half their 1929 volume. The nation was gripped with despair and to say that the "noble experiment" was on the brink of failure was not being melodramatic.

If Franklin Roosevelt had misgivings about assuming the presidency in the midst of the worst national disaster since the Civil War, he didn't show it. He exuded confidence in himself and in the nation. In his inaugural address he had told Americans that they had nothing to fear "but fear itself," and he displayed no fear. In a series of addresses, he was able by the sheer force of his personality and his persuasive rhetoric to dispel much of the anxiety and frustration of the Hoover years and to instill a feeling of hope in the people. He told us the banks would reopen, and they soon did. He said action would be taken, that the tragedy of unemployment, hunger, bankruptcies, and smokeless factory chimneys would soon be overcome. And people believed him. Roosevelt smiled readily when there was precious little to smile about, and laughter was heard again in the legislative and executive halls of the capital.

I have never forgotten the incredible transformation in the public attitude and will. In what has been called "the miracle of a hundred days," President Roosevelt declared a bank holiday, discarded the gold standard, and induced Congress in record time to provide relief for the unemployed and to pass the Emergency Banking Relief Act, the Agricultural Adjustment Act, the Civilian Conservation Corps Act, the National Industrial Recovery Act, the Federal Deposit Insurance Company Act, the Home Owners Refinancing Act, and the Tennessee Valley Authority Act.

Before the year 1933 ended, the Congress created the Commodity Credit Corporation and sent to the states a constitutional provision to repeal the Twenty-first Amendment—which was ratified in record time.

Even as he worked feverishly to turn the economic tide at home, President Roosevelt began initiatives in foreign policy. Most notably he sent Secretary of State Cordell Hull to Montevideo, where he promised the nations of Latin America that henceforth we would observe a policy of non-intervention in their internal affairs and would recognize the juridical equality of all nations, large and small. This change from our traditional big-brother attitude was being formulated in the Coolidge and Hoover administrations, but it remained for President Roosevelt to act. The Roosevelt Good Neighbor Policy was a bold and imaginative step that eliminated much of the enmity toward the United States that had been building up over a long period of years. I was to be reminded of the Roosevelt policy many years later when I served as President Eisenhower's special ambassador to Latin America.

The swift and dramatic actions of President Roosevelt's first year surely touched in some ways the life of every American.

My own situation in the Department of Agriculture was certainly affected. A new style and vigorous action became apparent the moment Henry A. Wallace was sworn in as Secretary of the Department. He summoned the top officers to his spacious office, complimented the department for its research and educational work, and asked for our cooperation in initiating a New Deal in agriculture. He made clear that it was essential to transform the department immediately into a vast action agency to restore parity of income to American farmers.

Secretary Wallace was no stranger to the Department of Agriculture. His father had been Secretary under Harding and Coolidge. As editor of *Wallace's Farmer* in Iowa, Henry had kept himself well informed on the department's work and on world economic currents that affected the American agricultural enterprise. He was, at the time, one of the most dedicated and intellectually honest men I have ever known. He was also an ideal administrator—one who, once policies and programs were formulated, delegated major administrative responsibilities and trusted those to whom delegations were made. I would never have believed it if someone had told me then that Henry Wallace would one day be denounced (inaccurately) as a Communist. And I watched with sadness years later when his mysticism, coupled with political ambitions aroused in him by associates equally mystical, drove him temporarily to the far left in political thought. He abandoned that position eventually and again became, in retirement, the knowledgeable scientific scholar and economist he had been when I first met him.

Henry Wallace was a Keynesian. It was ironic, therefore, that one of his first acts as Secretary was to reduce all salaries by ten per cent, as the President had ordered done throughout the executive branch. Our consternation at this was short-lived, for the Roosevelt promise of economy in government soon gave way to a Keynesian approach—a change which apparently resulted from the counsel of the President's "Brain Trust." Appropriations were increased, salary levels were restored, federal expenditures jumped to about $6.7 billion, and the government deficit increased to $3.6 billion.

I was appalled by the growing budget deficits of the federal government and expressed my misgivings to Secretary Wallace. He argued that a governmental budget need not be balanced in any particular year; the important consideration, he insisted, was that it be balanced over an economic cycle. Much later, when deficits grew during the war to more than $50 billion, Henry asserted that, in fact, a federal budget need never be balanced; the important consideration, he then insisted, was the relationship of the accumulated deficit to the nation's Gross National Product. If he were living today, I do not know what he would say about an annual federal deficit of more than $20 billion in a time of serious inflation, an unacceptable level of unemployment, and a total accumulated debt of $450 billion against a Gross National Product of some $1.3 trillion.

An intimate relationship between Secretary Wallace and me quickly developed. Otherwise, I probably would have left the department. When a host of new personnel came into the department to administer the Agricultural Adjustment Act and other action programs, the demand was made (especially by the administrator of AAA) that I be replaced by a Democrat. Secretary Wallace, respectful of the career service, rejected the demand but divided the informational activities into two parts: one to keep farmers and the general public informed on new economic programs, and the other to continue to handle information emanating from what we called the "old-line Department."

The Agricultural Adjustment program, financed by processing taxes on agricultural products named in the act, was not too different from the general concept of the McNary-Haugen bill: surpluses would be sold abroad at whatever prices they could command, farmers would be paid to reduce production (industries voluntarily reduce output when demand declines), and thus domestic farm prices should rise so that they had an acceptable parity relationship to the prices farmers had to pay for machinery, goods, services, and taxes.

Secretary Wallace wrote with eloquence and spoke with quiet conviction. His rhetoric was always precise. His addresses were numerous—invariably written by himself. Strangely, though, he had difficulty in discussing problems with President Roosevelt, and it was this idiosyncrasy in human chemistry that brought me to the attention of the President.

Harold L. Ickes, Secretary of the Interior, had lost no time after his appointment in insisting that all conservation agencies of the federal government should be in his department and that, therefore, the Forest Service should be transferred from Agriculture to Interior. This initiated a bitter interdepartmental struggle that persisted for years. Secretary Wallace was strongly opposed to the move and had been trying to win the support of the President.

One day Henry said: "Milton, I just can't seem to get the President to listen to what I say about Ickes' attempts to dismember the Department of Agriculture. When I go to his office he immediately begins telling me stories which fill the full period allotted to me. We never seem to get to the real issues."

Henry was clearly very agitated. "I'm very much afraid," he continued, "that I've offended President Roosevelt and made myself unwelcome. When I saw him this morning he began telling the same stories. Unfortunately I lost my temper and told the President I had heard his blessed stories several times and now I wanted to take up with him a very serious matter. Well, as you can imagine, Milton, the President was startled. He glared at me for a moment and I braced myself for the explosion; then he broke into that hearty laughter of his. Finally he said, 'Okay, Henry, what's on your mind?'"

Henry was still so uncomfortable at the memory that I repressed the grin I could feel tugging at my cheeks.

"At last I had the President's attention," the Secretary continued, "at least for a moment, and I was able to explain that if there were to be transfers between Interior and Agriculture, then what really ought to be done is to transfer public lands, the agricultural portion of the irrigation service, and other activities from Interior to Agriculture. I insisted that what we now have is virtually two Departments of Agriculture—a national department and a Western department. I told the President this made no sense at all. In the West, public and private landholdings are checkerboarded. The programs and policies of one department are in conflict with those of the other. The irrigation people are bringing new crops into production while we are paying farmers to reduce production. Grazing on public land is so intensive that it causes erosion, and on neighboring private lands we are promoting less intensive grazing and soil conservation."

I knew how strongly he felt.

"Well, what did the President say?" I asked.

Henry shook his head in despair: "He said he would think about it and launched into another story."

As I was to learn later, Henry Wallace may have been one of the first, but he was not the last victim of the highly effective Roosevelt maneuver of not letting the visitor get a word in when the President didn't want to hear what he knew the visitor had come to say. Senators, congressmen, colleagues, and a variety of favor-seekers were doomed to leave the President's office filled with interesting information, stuffed with anecdotes, charmed into a kind of numbness, but with their mission unaccomplished—indeed without having completed a single sentence.

In 1943, at an informal reception for new senators and congressmen, the President was apologizing for not being able to spend as much time with the legislators as he would like. Then, with characteristic ingenuousness, he remarked: "I think that part of it is my fault. . . . When somebody comes in on a ten-minute appointment, I start to do the talking. I get enthusiastic, and the result is that at the end of ten or fifteen minutes my visitor hasn't had a chance to get a word in edgewise. . . . So I say, please bear with me, and if you do come in, say to me quite frankly, 'Now listen, before you talk, Mr. President, let me have my say.' I think it would be a grand thing."

But that insight, or at least the public expression of it, came much later. Meanwhile Secretary Wallace took me with him when he next called on the President, and later sent me alone on his behalf, for I had no difficulty in conversing with Roosevelt. I don't recall that he ever prevented me from saying what I had to say. Indeed, I developed a genuine liking for him, and enjoyed my sessions with him. I rather think the feeling was reciprocated. In any case, the Secretary was getting his messages through to the White House much more effectively through a third person and I was delighted to be the intermediary.

On one occasion shortly after my first meeting with President Roosevelt I had a noon appointment to see him. When I entered the oval office, he said to me: "Milton, let's have lunch." He pressed a buzzer and a White House attendant pushed to one side of the President an aluminum container that looked like a very large filing cabinet. As he talked to me, the President opened one door of the container and extracted hot plates. From another he served fish and small potatoes. Hot rolls completed the luncheon. In the years of his administration this happy experience was often repeated.

The President was quick to laugh, as readily at his own quips and stories as at another's, and his laughter was contagious. Laughter is an Eisenhower characteristic and I inherited my share. So our conversations were invariably sprinkled with humor. Nevertheless, camaraderie did not prevent us from settling the problem that had brought me to his office.

In the next two years President Roosevelt got through the Congress much additional legislation, notably the Social Security Act. More proposals for agriculture, which originated with Secretary Wallace and Rexford G. Tugwell, a close friend of the President's, were also enacted. I helped with the preparation of bills and, at the Secretary's request, accompanied Tugwell to the White House for analytical discussions. Thus there came about the enactment of legislation creating the Resettlement Administration, the Rural Electrification Administration, and the Soil Conservation Service. Also enacted was legislation establishing the Export-Import Bank, an institution of considerable interest to farmers. For a young man in his early thirties from rural Kansas, it was a heady experience.

Late in 1935 the constitutionality of the Agricultural Adjustment Act was challenged. Secretary Wallace, in a major address, defended the act and, in doing so, made a statement I shall never forget, for it was prophetic: "The greatest feature of this act," he said, "is the processing tax. The funds obtained from this tax—and from compensatory taxes—are financing the farm program. Farmers themselves are paying for the help the government is giving in trying to restore prosperity to the people on the land. Farmers know this. They accept it. If this feature is declared to be unconstitutional and farmers dip into the Treasury of the United States to pay for their program, it will not only be immoral, but it will set loose in this country forces that no one can stop."

He was discouragingly right. When, in 1936, the Supreme Court, dominated by men of conservative philosophy, declared parts of the Agricultural Adjustment Act, especially its tax provisions, to be unconstitutional, the Congress did dip into the Treasury to finance farm programs. From the enactment of agricultural conservation legislation (which replaced the Agricultural Adjustment Act) to 1973, the Treasury has been called upon to provide as much as $7 billion a year to finance farm programs which, economically, have had only indifferent success. Indeed, the only time agricultural prices have achieved the goal of parity following our change from a debtor to a creditor nation in 1918 was during World War II when farm production was greatly reduced abroad and demand for our commodities exceeded the supply.

My interest in governmental affairs was consuming. If not an academic-type scholar of our political system, I became at least, a serious student of it. I had known there were flaws in the division of power our founding fathers had written into the Constitution and realized that the checks and balances system had built-in problems. But on the whole I had been convinced that for all its shortcomings our political system was the most ingenious and effective ever developed.

Now, for the first time in my life, I had some serious doubts. In my judgment, the action of the Supreme Court in declaring the Agricultural Adjustment Act unconstitutional was one of the worst mistakes it ever made. More important than whether it was right or wrong in its decision was the fact that the high court seemed to be assuming the position of what Mr. Justice Brandeis called "a superlegislature." The court had been very conservative throughout the twenties and appeared to be becoming more so. Despite the obvious need for bold reforms, despite the popular mandates of 1932 and 1934, and despite the very substantive support of the Congress, the Supreme Court was beginning to strike down almost systematically the key legislation of the New Deal.

I was torn. I sensed that over the longer cycles of history more good than harm resulted from one branch of government acting as a kind of brake on the other two. In such a situation, the Republic would be less likely to lurch too far in one direction or another. While I appreciated the need for change to meet new conditions and solve new problems, I also believed that lasting change had to be built carefully—even painstakingly—on a solid legal foundation and a substantial base of public acceptance. Moreover, like most Americans, I believed that the Constitution was a sacred covenant that embodied lasting principles of wisdom and justice, and I was loath to see it violated.

On the other hand, the need for action was urgent. Lesser nations had exploded into violent revolution in crises less crushing than the depression which stifled the United States in the early 1930s. The people had responded to President Roosevelt's confidence and action, and they had begun to emerge from the depths of their despair. But the fact was that the real substance of the problem had not yet been touched and the depression was still a virulent unsolved problem. The great majority of the citizens were solidly behind the President and the Congress in their efforts to bring a New Deal to America, and I was troubled that a handful of old men could and would thwart that will. Surely the Constitution was elastic enough to meet the needs of our modern society. I could not help but wonder whether the justices were interpreting the Constitution or expressing their own philosophical convictions.

It was a dilemma I did not resolve in 1934. It was a dilemma I would ponder on other occasions in the future. (It is a dilemma facing our society once again as I write this memoir, for the presidency, the Congress, the courts approach a constitutional crisis over the so-called "Watergate tapes.")

Even so I had no doubts about the consequences that would flow from the Supreme Court's rejection of the Agricultural Adjustment Act. As Henry Wallace had said, it set loose forces no one could stop.

Once the government undertakes a program it seemingly becomes eternal. A critical newspaper columnist wrote in 1936, referring to expanding federal bureaucracy, "Give it a shot of publicity and watch it grow!" Today, with federal, state, and local public programs consuming more than a third of the total national income, and deficits abundant, little thought is given to reordering our priorities. This is tragic in light of our neglect of many problems that threaten the quality of American life. If the crippling social problems of our society—from crime to racial discrimination—are to be attacked and gradually corrected, it is imperative that we re-examine existing programs, give up or reduce the less essential, and thus obtain the resources for new initiatives. This kind of reform is as imperative today as President Roosevelt's New Deal was in the 1930s.

In 1972 we were still spending many billions of dollars each year in an effort to achieve parity of income for American farmers. At the same time the government, worried about inflation, was doing what it could to hold down the prices of meats, wheat, and other agricultural commodities. Even these contradictory actions did not elicit from either executive or legislative leaders suggestions for possible changes in the policies or the cost of agricultural programs. That change came in July 1973.

On a sunny day in the spring of 1937, Henry Wallace called me and said he had something serious to discuss. He suggested that we walk over to the Washington monument and then to the dining room of the Agriculture Department. Henry, a vegetarian, exercised each day and was in good physical condition; he felt everyone should keep fit.

When we arrived at the base of the Washington monument he said: "Let's walk up!"

I had climbed those winding stairs only once before, with my wife, and she had fainted as we reached the halfway mark. The very memory of it left me weary. But now I had no choice. Trudging after Henry, the pace caused me to pant audibly. While he enjoyed the view, I sagged against the rail and gasped for breath. After a few moments

Henry led the way back down. That, of course, was easier. From there we walked to the South Building of the Department of Agriculture, where, to my amazement, the Secretary insisted upon walking up eight flights to the dining room. I remember nothing about what I had to eat that day. I couldn't have cared less, I was so exhausted. But I shall never forget our discussion.

Henry began with a question.

"Milton, are you aware of the conflicts in the action programs of the department?"

I was. The Agricultural Adjustment Administration was paying farmers to reduce the production of wheat, cotton, and other commodities, while the Soil Conservation Service was advising farmers, under certain circumstances, to plant them.

The Farm Security Administration was lending and giving money to farm families to enlarge their holdings and was inducing them to plant the same commodities that the AAA was trying to reduce. The Soil Conservation Service and the Federal-State Agricultural Extension system had agents on the same farms giving contradictory advice. And the conflict in programs was also interdepartmental, especially between Agriculture and Interior, as I have mentioned. The Tennessee Valley Authority administered a conservation program which conflicted with the efforts of both the Agricultural Adjustment Administration and the Soil Conservation Service.

The public was becoming aware of serious waste in the massive agricultural expenditures. Leading agriculturists in the states were outspoken in their criticism.

Henry now placed before me a breath-taking proposition.

"I want you to set up an agency with the mission of overcoming these conflicts," he said. "I've thought about this a great deal. I've discussed it with Paul Appleby and Rex Tugwell and they agree on what has to be done. You'll get our full support."

I knew enough about the complexity and the politics of American agriculture to be awed by the Secretary's proposition. He seemed to sense my concern.

"I don't expect you to perform miracles. This will be an extremely difficult task and you will surely make mistakes. But I hope you can make steady progress so that I can assure the President and the Congress that the problems and the conflicts are being resolved."

79

Frankly, I was thinking that even steady progress would be a small miracle. But I kept silent and let the Secretary go on.

"We will call the agency the Office of Land Use Planning," he said, "and make it a unit of my immediate office. You can draft the personnel you need; I'll call the agency heads and tell them to co-operate fully."

"What about my present job?" I asked.

Henry smiled. "If it doesn't tax your energies too much, you can continue as director of information while you carry out the duties of the co-ordinator of the Office of Land Use Planning."

Here was the most complex and difficult task I had faced. I was nervous about it and perhaps a bit intimidated.

Secretary Wallace knew that he was placing in my hands—I was thirty-seven—a responsibility which could cause me to stumble. He was also taking some risk in giving me this new task. He and I differed a good deal in matters of political philosophy. Only a year before I had gone to his office and offered my resignation, explaining that as a career officer I felt I had no choice but to resign when I was not in sympathy with his policies. He asked me to elaborate on what was bothering me and I did. I cannot recall the details, but I was concerned at the time about his position on certain international problems affecting agriculture. I do remember his smiling and saying that he liked to have persons associated with him who expressed their disagreement with his thinking. We respected one another and both of us clearly were dedicated to the general purposes of the Department of Agriculture. So, having remained with the department, I was now being placed in a position second in responsibility to the Secretary's.

Although it was a formidable assignment, I was not completely unprepared. For several years the Secretary and his able assistant Paul Appleby had called me frequently to serve as departmental trouble shooter, a role that caused me to become deeply involved in problems of administrative reorganization and "human engineering." I had come to realize that in any organization, particularly one involving large numbers of individuals, an organization chart in itself is not of first importance. The success of an enterprise depends primarily on the quality and the attitudes of the people in it. Then, I would say, it is very important that those who need constantly to consult with each other should be in as close proximity as possible. And a final consideration is to determine the proper staff and line responsibilities of personnel, grouped within a logical organization possessing closely related functions.

As the administrative trouble shooter in a department which had grown rapidly from a small research and educational agency into what was then probably the largest executive department, I learned another principle of human behavior: when one is attempting to change the thinking of people, or their functions or organizational relationships, one must be patient as well as persistent. It is well to use an evolutionary rather than a revolutionary approach. If large numbers of individuals are suddenly torn loose from their accustomed duties and shuffled quickly into a new organizational pattern with new duties, chaos may develop. It is best to determine the ideal pattern, then work toward it as rapidly as the people involved can understand and accept the new ideas and the new functions involved.

My work in the Department of Agriculture had taught me that it is not possible to develop a vast national undertaking in a short period of time without inefficiencies, conflicts, and a tremendous waste of resources. First, a relatively small organization should be established and only then, after personnel are thoroughly trained and are devoted to the philosophy and purpose of the undertaking, expansion can succeed. Then it is possible to transfer trained personnel to regional, state, and sometimes local offices where a new period of training must go forward.

What had obviously occurred in the Department of Agriculture was that three nationwide, generously financed, organizations had been built quickly. Each was filled with individuals who had a passionate interest in achieving a single objective, with no reference to what other agencies were doing; each, too, had many individuals who were inadequately trained and sometimes even lacking an understanding of the basic difference between serving in a public agency and serving in a private one.

So, with some insights into organizational problems generally and the Department of Agriculture particularly, I began.

First I called together the administrators of the Agricultural Conservation Administration (formerly the AAA), the Farm Security Administration, the Soil Conservation Service, the Forest Service, a few other agencies, and the chief of the Division of Soil Surveys. I explained the objectives of the newly created Office of Land Use Planning and how I might proceed, with their help, to eliminate the difficulties that were bothering the Secretary. The meeting was not a fruitful one. The head of the Agricultural Conservation Administration, who had at his command vastly more funds than all other agencies and bureaus combined and who felt he had a mandate to restore prosperity to American agriculture, made it clear that if the conflicts were to be resolved the other agencies would have to make the changes. He would not.

The head of each of the other agencies was similarly emphatic in stating that what was being done was absolutely essential to stopping soil erosion, or protecting the national forests, or giving aid to the low-income families in farming. It was evident to me that I would achieve nothing merely by banging heads together. I couldn't help thinking that it is no wonder that social groups or national governments develop such intractable attitudes and fail to understand and co-operate with one another. Here in a single department, responsible executives could not see past their own narrow interests.

Co-ordination would have to begin in the rural communities, counties, and regions rather than in Washington. Each of the agencies had local advisory groups, comprised of farmers, and some of these groups had considerable policy and administrative responsibilities. If we could persuade local groups to determine the maximum economic potential of their farm lands, consistent with a conservation objective, then there would be hope that nationally issued rules and regulations would be adapted at the local level to the point of eliminating conflicts. With this as a goal, I brought together a small staff of some twenty-five persons—economists, survey experts, lawyers, clerks, and secretaries—and instituted a nationwide program of land-use planning, the key elements being the local farmer committees.

This required each locality to understand the productive capacity of the land in the county or area, as well as its maximum use, consistent with conserving resources. Federal soil surveys and conservation surveys were available for many of the local communities, and these provided the scientific basis for local plans.

Since the land grant colleges and universities, with their agricultural extension services, were active in and highly respected by the local communities, it became necessary to bring about an agreement between these institutions and the Department of Agriculture. This proved to be a most difficult and time-consuming task. At one meeting of the directors of extension of the forty-eight states, one director shouted at me: "Co-operation with you federal folks is merely *operation* on your part! It's time you learned that we have something to say about all these programs too!"

The agreement I was trying to get approved consisted of twelve double-spaced typed pages. We read each sentence and paragraph aloud and then discussed suggestions for changes. Often we would argue about a single point for half an hour. The matter might be trivial but it was invariably cause for a full-scale debate. Finally a man from New Jersey raised his hand and I recognized him.

"Mr. Chairman," he drawled, "on page three, paragraph two, line four, after the word 'and,' I move we insert a comma."

Someone automatically seconded the motion.

Now a man from Texas objected, centending that the comma was unnecessary. "Why do you make such a motion?" he asked.

My friend from New Jersey—I knew him well and respected him —said innocently: "Well, my motion is just like lots of others being made here. It just occurred to me that there are millions of little commas in the world and they must be lonesome. I thought it would be nice to give one of them a home." For a few seconds there was silence; then the room filled with laughter. Thereafter we made better progress.

It took me two years to draw up and get unanimous agreement of the states on the methods of co-operation that were mutually beneficial. At least I had thought we had achieved complete agreement at the final drafting session, but when we met the following year to review progress I found that there were at least a dozen interpretations of the language in the document we had solemnly signed the year before. (After this experience, I had a new appreciation for the immense difficulties involved in international negotiations or treaty discussions and I marvel that any agreement ever survives.)

Nonetheless, my first effort at local co-ordination had at least modest success, avoided the worst of the program conflicts, and satisfied the President and the Congress that we were working diligently on the problem.

Each of the action agencies of the Department of Agriculture had divided the country into regions for administrative purposes and each had its own regional headquarters. The regions were not coterminous and rarely were there two regional headquarters in the same city. Certainly there were never two in the same building.

After a great deal of thought, I recommended to Secretary Wallace that all of our agencies be required to have identical regions (about twelve as I recall), common regional and state headquarters, and that all personnel at these headquarters be housed in the same buildings. This would reduce administrative costs and would be a vital part of a total co-ordination program. It also fulfilled my belief that persons with interdependent functions should be close to one another to enhance mutual understanding. I knew full well that my proposal to Henry was political dynamite.

Henry knew it too, but he approved with enthusiasm.

"Milton," he said, "I have two suggestions. First, you better get the approval of President Roosevelt, because that's where the political heat will be the hottest. Second, I think you ought to launch your program in the North Central States. That's my country. And if you make Milwaukee the headquarters for this region, you're going to have to move an office out of Des Moines, my home town. Maybe if we demonstrate the importance of putting selfish interest aside for a nobler cause it will set a good example."

Carefully I prepared two maps, one showing the crazy-quilt pattern of regions and offices then existing and a second indicating the outlines of coterminous regions for all federal agricultural agencies and their regional, state, and local headquarters. My meeting with the President was again at the noon hour. When I was admitted to the oval office I placed the two maps before the President and explained the urgency of going ahead with a program that would help alleviate many of the problems of the Department of Agriculture.

The President seemed relaxed as he served our simple lunch of tea and sandwiches. He had listened to my proposal without comment; now we discussed the merits of the plan and its political implications. Finally President Roosevelt leaned back in his chair and said:

"You know that the political criticism will be substantial. And you can bet that some of the loudest critics will be the very same senators and congressmen who have been condemning the program conflicts you are trying to correct." He paused for a moment, then continued. "I think what you want to do is right, Milton. So go ahead with your plan. I'll stand by you."

With the help of my able staff, I went to work in the North Central States. Things went more smoothly than I had dared hope. Then we turned our attention to the southeastern section of the country. We chose Atlanta as the city for the common regional headquarters. This required, among many other moves, the transfer of the regional office of the Soil Conservation Service from Spartanburg, South Carolina, to Atlanta.

Within two weeks after the public announcement of this change, Senator James Byrnes of South Carolina called on the President with a petition signed by many of his constituents, protesting the move.

Shortly afterward, President Roosevelt sent for me. As I walked into his office I noticed that the ever present cigarette, in a long black holder, was slanting jauntily toward the ceiling. But the President's eyes were focused on a document on his desk. He didn't look at me as he remarked:

"Milton, we're in trouble on that co-ordinating program of yours."

On his desk was the petition presented to him by Senator Byrnes. Thousands of the senator's constituents had signed the petition. My memory is that there were 120,000 signatures, but that doesn't seem possible.

Senator Byrnes had served for fourteen years in the House of Representatives and was now in his second term as a senator.

"I need Jimmy Byrnes," the President said, looking up at me. "I will be depending heavily on him to get some of my most important programs through the Congress." He went on to explain that he was certain that Senator Byrnes was a man on whom he would call in the future for higher responsibilities. In short, the President could not afford to alienate Senator Byrnes.

"I'm sorry, Milton, but I have to ask you not to go ahead with the move of the Soil Conservation office out of Spartanburg."

I understood what the President was saying and why. I was in no position to question a decision of the President, but I felt he needed to understand the full consequences of his decision.

"If it were just this one move, Mr. President, I could consider it a necessary compromise and move forward. But you know as well as I that this really means the end of the plan in all parts of the country. If we surrender to political pressure in a single city or region, the next move we try to make will bring even greater pressure to bear on this office."

"Yes. I understand that, and I still must ask you not to proceed with the move."

The President went on to explain that he favored efficiency in government and the wise administration of federal programs, but that the duties of the President were manifold and every decision had to be made in the much larger context of the over-all goals of his administration. He had to manage the executive establishment, maintain close relations with Congress, and keep the people informed and supportive, all to the end that the highest objectives of government could be realized. This sometimes required compromises and decisions that were not ideal.

Perhaps because my disappointment was so apparent, President Roosevelt talked candidly at some length about the problems he faced. While he had got through the Congress much of the legislation he felt was needed, more was in the planning stage, and his influence with the Congress had been diminished by his effort to reform the Supreme Court. At the moment, his goal was to get Congress to approve a fair labor standards act, which, among other things, would establish minimum wages throughout the nation for the first time. The expropriation of American and other foreign oil resources in Mexico was causing serious criticism by many members of the Congress. War clouds were gathering over Europe and in the Pacific, causing serious worry among his Cabinet and some of his best friends in the Congress. In all these and other matters, which he had to consider in balance, he needed the help of Jimmy Byrnes.

Personally dejected, but sympathetic with the enormous responsibilities of the President, I returned to the Department of Agriculture and informed Secretary Wallace that one major aspect of our coordination plan had to be abandoned. Henry took the news rather well, with an air of resignation. He suggested that we have lunch in the department dining room. As usual, we walked up the eight flights of stairs to improve our appetites—or, at least, his. As we walked, he said, "You know, Mordecai Ezekiel is one of the smartest men I know. He is a brilliant economist. But he's not very savvy politically." He went on to explain that it was Ezekiel who had induced him to issue a statement advocating the abandonment of the American merchant marine. The reason was that the cost of shipping by American carriers was much higher than shipping in foreign bottoms. Further, from the standpoint of agriculture, it would be advantageous for foreign countries to earn dollars which would aid them in purchasing our farm exports.

"No sooner was this statement in the press," Henry said, "than labor leaders began taking me apart. Zeke had forgotten about the Seamen's Act. That act causes wages of men on all American ships to be much higher than they are on foreign ships. So my statement has been interpreted as being anti-labor. I'll have to retract it." Henry, too, had to consider immediate actions in a larger long-term context. And it was well that he did, for otherwise he would not have been acceptable as the vice-presidential candidate later.

When Germany invaded Poland on September 1, 1939, foreign policy took precedence over domestic issues. Two months after the European war began, President Roosevelt issued two Neutrality Proclamations. One proclaimed that a state of war existed between Germany and France, Poland, the United Kingdom, India, Australia, Canada, New Zealand, and the Union of South Africa. The second placed restrictions on the use of ports or territorial waters of the United States by submarines of foreign belligerent states.

On September 3, 1940, he notified the Congress that the United States had been given at no cost the use of naval and air bases in Newfoundland and the island of Bermuda; the United States had obtained similar bases in Jamaica, St. Lucia, Trinidad, and Antigua by "the exchange of fifty over-age destroyers." (The destroyers actually were in good condition.)

"This is not inconsistent in any sense with our status of peace," the President said. "Still less is it a threat against any nation. It is an epochal and far-reaching act of preparation for continental defense, in the face of grave danger. Preparation for defense is the inalienable prerogative of a sovereign state."

All of us in Washington felt that we were being placed on a ready alert.

It was soon evident that we in the Department of Agriculture would undergo a reversal of many of the programs, for it was certain that the demand for American farm commodities would increase. This might for several years eliminate some but not all of the program conflicts I had been trying to solve. So I began concentrating on difficulties existing between the Soil Conservation Service and the Federal-State Extension Services, between the department and TVA and, again, between the Department of Agriculture and the Department of Interior.

At the Democratic National Convention in 1940, President Roosevelt defied tradition by accepting the nomination for a third term. He selected my boss, Henry A. Wallace, as his running mate. Though the Republican nominee, Wendell Willkie, reduced the large majorities that Roosevelt had previously received, the Democratic ticket was easily elected.

Claude R. Wickard, who had served for a time as Under Secretary of Agriculture, became Secretary on January 20, 1941. This was a ghastly mistake. Wickard, with a background in practical farming but only a modicum of administrative experience, had little talent to head the work of a massive federal agency. His most serious trouble, I thought, was that he did not trust anyone. Hence he could not delegate authority as Wallace had done. Problems accumulated on his desk, decisions were not made, and many of us in the department became restless and uneasy.

For the first time I began to lose interest in the department. For fifteen years I had been convinced that, with all our problems, the Department of Agriculture was the best-administered agency in the executive branch. I had been proud to be part of the department. In those years it surely had not occurred to me that I would ever leave Agriculture. I was deeply devoted to its purposes and I was fond of my colleagues. Despite prolonged arguments about policies and administrative matters, we were a close-knit team. Now this was threatened.

Having had some inkling of Wickard's bumbling methods before Secretary Wallace left to assume the vice-presidency, I resigned as director of information in order to devote all my time to the arduous and frustrating task of program co-ordination.

When Secretary Wallace decided to name as director of information one of my principal aides, Morse Salisbury, who had served brilliantly as head of the Radio Service, a major section of the Office of Information, I was delighted. He was keenly intelligent and dependable. He had always insisted, much to my pleasure, on having a high degree of independence in meeting his responsibilities, while invariably checking with me on policy matters.

Six weeks after he assumed the top informational post he came to my home on the verge of a nervous breakdown. The responsibility of directing a large-line undertaking, serving in a staff capacity for the Secretary in co-ordinating information activities of bureaus and agencies of the Department, and making numerous appearances before congressional committees had caused sleeplessness which exacerbated an underlying nervous condition.

I suggested that Morse take a month's vacation and leave his burden with me for that period with no legal or formal change in his status or mine. He did so, and when he returned he resumed the directorship. But he resigned a year later, went to New York to work with the Committee for Economic Development, and finally came back to Washington as director of information for the Atomic Energy Commission— a position he filled with distinction until his untimely death. He was a good man, a fellow alumnus of Kansas State, and one of my revered friends.

That experience, and similar ones later, impressed on me the vast difference between serving in the second post and serving in the top one in any human organization. Truman obviously had this in mind when he said: "The buck stops here." Subordinates in an organization can check their suggestions and convictions with the chief before undertaking an innovative action or making a crucial decision. It is the top man who has to say yes or no and bear the consequences of that decision. In government, when a Cabinet member resigns it is natural that consideration should be given to replacing him with an under secretary or one of the top deputies. Invariably there is some degree of gamble in this or in the appointment of an inexperienced person from the outside. Certainly President Roosevelt had gambled in promoting Claude Wickard to the post of Secretary of Agriculture. And he lost the gamble.

Shortly after Secretary Wickard assumed his new responsibilities, an assistant to the Secretary came to my office and asked: "What is the purpose of this co-ordinating agency of yours?"

I was astonished by his ignorance, but fortunately I kept my composure and explained the original problem of costly program conflicts, how we had tackled the problem, and what progress had been made. The record was by no means perfect. The human tendency for those in each program to work passionately for a single objective, oblivious or insensitive to the unhappy consequences for parallel programs in the same department, was still prevalent. Considerable progress was apparent at the county level where farmers themselves insisted that one agency should not jeopardize the gains being made by another.

Two weeks went by. Then another assistant to the Secretary, Sam Bledsoe, a man skilled in public relations but ill informed on agricultural and administrative problems, came to my office. He said that Secretary Wickard felt that I should take, on an additional responsibility of serving as associate director of the Agriculture Extension Service. This was demoralizing to my small but highly competent staff (a fact which later enabled me to move them from Agriculture to a war agency where I desperately needed them).

I now admitted to myself that I could not remain in the department working for a man who was inept, insensitive, and ignorant about the mission to which I was so dedicated. But I had no idea of what I would do if I left the department. President Roosevelt solved that problem.

During 1941, I was called to the President's office frequently to consult with him, not on agricultural problems usually, but on broader organizational and informational ones.

Germany was making devastating progress in Europe. The tension in the nation's capital was almost tangible.

On January 6, 1941, President Roosevelt in a message to Congress enunciated his famous Four Freedoms declaration, a statement now engraved in history: freedom from want, freedom of speech, freedom of worship, and freedom from fear. In March the President, while insisting that the United States would remain aloof from the conflict in Europe, nonetheless took a step toward our involvement by instituting the lend-lease program. This called for new administrative procedures at home and abroad, and for carefully planned informational programs on which I became a trouble shooter.

By this time, with nearly all of continental Europe under German control, President Roosevelt concentrated much of United States assistance on the United Kingdom. In August he met with Winston Churchill on a destroyer off the coast of Newfoundland and there the two leaders proclaimed the Atlantic Charter. It emphasized the freedom of the seas, the territorial integrity of nations, the right of nations to trade peacefully, and the right of all nations to choose freely the type of government they wanted.

At the request of the President I assisted the director of the Bureau of the Budget in establishing in October 1941 an Overseas Information Agency under Robert Sherwood. The agency had the responsibility of keeping the world informed of our attitudes and activities. At the same time we established an Office of Facts and Figures under the brilliant leadership of Archibald MacLeish. This office became a research and information organization highly useful to the President. The information division of the War Production Board was expanded and became in effect a bureau to keep the American people accurately informed of many war-related developments of the government.

I have often speculated on what the position of the United States would have been in the war had the Japanese not attacked Pearl Harbor—if Germany and Japan had proceeded with their powerful military attacks without taking an action guaranteed to bring the United States immediately into the war. President Roosevelt's attitude changed progressively and remarkably between October 1940 and December 1941. In Boston, on October 31, 1940, he said: "I have said this before, but I shall say it again and again—your sons are not going to be sent into any foreign wars." More than seven months later, in speaking about freedom, he emphasized: "We, and all others who believe as deeply as we do, would rather die on our feet than live on our knees." Three months later, on September 11, 1941, in one of his famous fireside chats, he seemed to be preparing the American people for war when he said, "When you see a rattlesnake poised to strike, you do not wait until he has struck before you crush him."

Then the strike at Pearl Harbor stunned the nation. On December 8, 1941, in his war message to Congress, he pronounced solemnly that December 7, was a day which "will live in infamy."

Now the many actions the President had previously taken, from the modification of the Neutrality Act and lend lease to obtaining military bases abroad in exchange for destroyers, had new significance. We were suddenly involved in the most massive war of history.

My personal problems with Claude Wickard seemed trivial, but my restlessness was suddenly magnified. As I was pondering the ways that I could best spend my time and energy and make some contribution to the war effort, President Roosevelt was acting to take that decision from me.

CHAPTER 6

The unique contribution of history is perspective; most great movements cannot be fully understood until their myriad elements have been assembled and illuminated by historians.

SEVERAL WEEKS AFTER Pearl Harbor, President Roosevelt asked me to make a study of all war-related informational activities of the federal government.

A variety of agencies and bureaus, scattered throughout the government, disseminated information about the war, and the President wanted these brought together and co-ordinated. He expected me to recommend a system that would (1) keep the American people completely and truthfully informed about our participation in the war; (2) direct adequate information to our allies so that they would not misunderstand our methods and purposes; (3) influence neutral countries to enter the war on our side or at least to remain neutral; and finally (4) counteract the vicious propaganda our enemies were using to strengthen the support of their own people.

John Bird, a colleague in my office in Agriculture, later associate editor of *Country Gentleman* and a writer for the *Saturday Evening Post*, helped me make the study. Because we knew a great deal about the various informational activities, the study required only a month or so.

My report to President Roosevelt recommended the creation of the Office of War Information (OWI) with both foreign and domestic branches. I proposed that OWI have full authority to co-ordinate related activities of other governmental agencies, including the War and Navy departments, the War Production Board, the Departments of State, Agriculture, Interior, and Treasury, as well as recently established agencies to deal with lend lease and other functions. I suggested that OWI have a large enough staff to develop and disseminate information relevant to all war activities. The head of the new agency should report directly to the President and should see to it that the policies of the President were observed in both domestic and foreign war information.

I did not use the word "propaganda." I did not even want to imply that falsehoods should be used when they might seem to serve our immediate interests. I stressed in the report that misleading information or outright lies might appear to be temporarily useful but would eventually destroy the credibility of our efforts at home and abroad. Since our cause was just, since we sought no advantage or territory for ourselves, since we fought only to retain our own freedom and restore the freedom of others, our real strength lay in telling the truth, sticking to the facts, and presenting a full and accurate explanation of our war purposes.

The President said he would study my recommendations and react to them as soon as possible; in the meantime he would ask Harold Smith, the Director of the Budget and a close presidential adviser, to review the report.

I had gotten behind in my other duties, and so plunged into my work. Several weeks later I left for a tour of Tennessee and other states involved in the Tennessee Valley Authority. I was trying to resolve the continuing conflicts in the conservation program of the TVA, the Agricultural Conservation Administration, the Soil Conservation Service, and the Federal-State Agricultural Extension Service.

I made the trip in a small plane through highly turbulent air. On occasions in the past I had been slightly seasick or airsick, but never to the point of thinking—indeed almost wishing—that I might give up the ghost. The trip was memorable. I stepped off the plane on wobbly legs, and I'm sure my face was green. One of the members of the TVA Board met me and said that the President's appointments secretary, Major General Edwin M. "Pa" Watson, had phoned and wanted me to call the White House as soon as possible. The way I felt, that could be a week. I was led to a nearby building where I took a large dose of Bromo Seltzer, lay down for an hour, and inhaled ammonia. Then I called the White House.

Pa Watson told me that I should leave for Washington "at the soonest" and come directly to the President's office. That was one of the few messages I could have received that would make me get into an airplane at that point.

By the following morning—March 10 or 11—I was at the White House. So was Harold Smith. He was obviously going to accompany me into the President's office, but he gave me no hint of what the problem was or what I might be asked to do. I secretly prayed that it would not involve flying. My illness of the day before was largely past, but I was still green around the gills—a fact which seemed to amuse the otherwise sober-minded staff in the President's outer office.

As we entered the oval office I was startled by the change in the President. In all my previous work with him I had never seen him without his jaunty air. No matter how difficult the problem, he was buoyant, smiling, and confident. Now, as he studied the paper before him, his face lacked color, his lips were a tight grim line, and, as he looked up at me, I saw his eyes were bloodshot.

Normally he would have exchanged a pleasantry or two, perhaps passed along an amusing anecdote, before turning to the problem or chore he had in mind for me. It was understood of course that the President's request was in fact a command, but Franklin Roosevelt was always so considerate and charming that I found myself wanting to do what he asked without needing a directive. I was about to experience the first exception to that.

He was blunt. His first words were:

"Milton, your war job, starting immediately, is to set up a War Relocation Authority to move the Japanese-Americans off the Pacific coast. I have signed an executive order which will give you full authority to do what is essential. The Attorney General will give you the necessary legal assistance and the Secretary of War will help you with the physical arrangements. Harold"—he nodded at the budget director—"will fill you in on the details of the problem."

He looked back at the paper he had been reading, and I realized the interview was over. My mind full of half-formed questions, I turned to leave. The President looked up at me again and said:

"And, Milton . . . the greatest possible speed is imperative."

I seized the opportunity to ask the first question that had come to my mind. "Mr. President, may I move my staff from the Co-ordinating Office in Agriculture to the Relocation Authority?"

"Just let me know who you want with you on this job," he replied, "and we will take care of it."

That was all.

Like most Americans at the time, I knew very little about the problem of the Japanese-Americans on the West Coast. As I walked with Harold Smith to his office, I tried to recollect what I had heard or read over the three months since Pearl Harbor.

I recalled that immediately after the Japanese attack newspapers and radio had reported a roundup of enemy aliens across the country by the Federal Bureau of Investigation. This included some Japanese aliens on the West Coast.

I also remembered reading that a General John DeWitt, who was in charge of the army on the Pacific coast, believed that an invasion of the United States was a real possibility and, in such an event, our armed forces and citizens would not be able to distinguish friend from foe. A few weeks earlier President Roosevelt had signed the executive order he'd referred to which, I mistakenly thought at the time, directed that all persons of Japanese descent, whether citizens or aliens, be removed from the West Coast. Finally, I was aware that a California congressman was holding hearings of some sort on the West Coast having to do with the evacuation of Japanese.

I knew no more than this.

In his office Harold Smith explained the situation. He told me that there were some 120,000 Japanese in California, Oregon, and Washington. Some were *Issei*, immigrants from Japan, many of whom had lived in the United States for a very long time but were not citizens; unlike German and Italian aliens who chose not to become citizens, the Issei had been prohibited by law from becoming naturalized United States citizens. A second and larger group of Japanese were *Nisei*, mostly the sons and daughters and grandchildren of the Issei, born in this country and therefore citizens by right of birth. A much smaller number were *Kibei*, persons born of Japanese parents in this country but educated in Japan and recently returned to the United States. Smith indicated that among the Kibei were people who probably posed the threats to our security.

According to Smith, Lieutenant General DeWitt, commander of the Western Defense Command, did not believe initially that one could tell the difference between a loyal and a disloyal Japanese-American, and the FBI and other intelligence units agreed. The army feared a "fifth column" on the West Coast that would be active in a Japanese attack on our mainland.

Smith said that there was great concern for the safety of the Japanese-Americans themselves. The mass media on the Coast were inflaming the people against the Japanese-Americans and several had been murdered in the fields where they worked. Greater turmoil and increasing vigilante action were threatened.

The budget director himself had not been much involved in the problem, having only read memos and correspondence and listened to some of the discussions in the White House. He offered helpful suggestions on space, organization, personnel, and other procedural questions. But on substantive matters he urged me to see Attorney General Francis Biddle and Assistant Secretary of War John McCloy. Biddle had been concerned with the Japanese-American situation even before the war and had studied all the legal aspects of the problem, including the President's war powers which later gave the War Relocation Authority its authority. McCloy had been in close touch with the military on the West Coast and was thoroughly familiar with all aspects of the situation. These men, Smith said, would give me whatever help I requested.

As he rose to end the meeting, Smith also stressed the need for speed and told me that the army was ready to move the Japanese-Americans into temporary camps on the West Coast and was anxiously waiting to see how the newly established War Relocation Authority would proceed. Smith told me the President would issue an executive order in about a week (it was signed on March 18) establishing WRA and naming me its director.

I asked about German and Italian aliens, and he replied that WRA would have the authority to deal with them also but that the German and Italian nationals were not expected to constitute a problem.

As I left the White House on that blustery March day it was clear to me that the question was not *whether* to evacuate the Japanese-Americans (since that process was already under way) but rather how to carry out their relocation to the interior.

Hurrying back to my office, I was deeply troubled. My instincts told me that the course we were embarked on was an extreme one. But I must confess that I spent little time pondering the moral implications of the President's decision. We were at war. Our nation had been viciously attacked without warning. We had been badly mauled by the Japanese forces and the enemy had been rampaging almost without resistance in the Southwest Pacific. The Philippines and Malaya had fallen; Hong Kong and Singapore were in enemy hands. There was no effective Allied armed force between Cairo and San Francisco. President Roosevelt was the Commander-in-Chief and he had given me my war assignment. I was determined to carry it out as effectively and humanely as possible.

When I assumed my new duties, I did not know what events had transpired between December 7, 1941, and mid-March 1942 which led President Roosevelt to make his evacuation decision. Indeed, it was not until years later, when historians reconstructed those events and wove them together into a coherent chronology, that I fully understood the situation I stepped into in March 1942.

I must rely upon these historians for background against which President Roosevelt's decision can be evaluated and my own role in the relocation of Japanese-Americans can be related. Stetson Conn, Yale-trained historian and general editor in the Office of the Chief of Military History, carefully documented the evacuation of Japanese-Americans in the U. S. Army's official history of World War II (*Guarding the United States and Its Outposts*).[3] Bill Hosokawa, in his book *Nisei: The Quiet Americans*,[4] records the history of the Japanese-Americans and the terrible tragedy of their evacuation in late 1941 and through the first half of 1942. Morton Grodzins' *Americans Betrayed*[5] details the events of that period. And others, such as Attorney General Biddle[6] and Secretary of War Stimson,[7] contributed to the mosaic through their published memoirs. From these men and others, I have pieced together the story that I did not know on March 18, 1942, when I began what turned out to be the most difficult and traumatic task of my career.

Although the Japanese attack on Pearl Harbor came without warning, our relations with Japan had steadily deteriorated in the preceding months, and war with Japan was increasingly likely. Some preparations, therefore, had been made, and on December 8, by 6:00 A.M., while broken ships still burned in Pearl Harbor, the FBI had taken some 733 Japanese nationals into custody. These were mostly aliens who had been under surveillance for many months. During the next four days, acting under presidential warrant, the FBI rounded up some 1,370 Japanese on the West Coast.

98

Most of the Issei arrested during those dark days after Pearl Harbor had done nothing wrong. But the Department of Justice had received reports of sabotage by Japanese residents in Honolulu (later proved false) and was taking no chances. There was real fear that Japanese air forces might strike the West Coast of the United States. There was also concern that local citizens, frightened and outraged by the sneak attack, might take action against the Japanese population on the Pacific coast.

Attorney General Biddle issued a statement to reassure both the American people and the Japanese-Americans. "So long as the aliens in this country conduct themselves in accordance with the law," he stated, "they need fear no interference by the Department of Justice or by any other agency of the Federal Government." He indicated that the government had disloyal aliens and citizens under control, and he assured the Japanese-Americans and loyal Japanese nationals that every effort would be made "to protect them from any discrimination or abuse."[6]

The fear of discrimination and abuse was well founded. Secretary of the Treasury Henry Morgenthau, Jr., wrote in his diary, *Years of War:*[8] ". . . deep-rooted hostility to the Japanese generated frequent rumors about espionage and subversion and frightened demands for repressive treatment not only of local Japanese residents but also of *Nisei*, American citizens of Japanese descent."

Secretary Morgenthau also reported that three days after Pearl Harbor he was urged by some of the staff in the Foreign Funds Control Office to take over thousands of small businesses owned by Issei and Nisei in the area between the Pacific Ocean and Utah. Morgenthau immediately asked FBI Director J. Edgar Hoover for his opinion, and Hoover insisted that the FBI had matters well in hand and that no additional steps against the Japanese were required. The next morning Morgenthau rejected the proposal as "hysterical" and "impractical."

The Department of the Treasury's general counsel, Edward Foley, objected to Morgenthau's decision, declaring that civil liberties must yield to the security of the country. Morgenthau records his response in his diary: "Listen, when it comes to suddenly mopping up 150,000 Japanese and putting them behind barbed wire, irrespective of their status, and consider doing the same with the Germans, I want at some time to have caught my breath. . . . Anybody that wants to hurt this country or injure us, put him where he can't do it, but . . . indiscriminately, no."

Also a few days after the attack on Pearl Harbor, a federal intelligence agent told West Coast military officials that some 20,000 Japanese in the San Francisco area were "ready for organized action." In fact, there were only 13,000 Japanese in greater San Francisco (men, women, and children of all ages). Nonetheless, the IX Corps Area staff hastily drew up a plan to evacuate the Japanese, and the plan was approved by their commander. Fortunately the plan was abandoned because the FBI learned of it and dismissed the rumor as the ravings of a discharged former FBI agent. This illustrates the way in which panic and rumor swept the Pacific coast after the Japanese attack.

Newspaper and radio stations were filled with stories of the roundup of Japanese and there were sensational reports of mysterious activities in the Japanese community. The public's fears were greatly heightened when Secretary of the Navy Frank Knox reported on his hasty inspection of Pearl Harbor and Honolulu. The report was issued on December 15 and it made no mention of sabotage or subversion by Japanese residents. But Secretary Knox held a press conference in connection with the release of his report, and the newspapers quoted him as saying: "I think the most effective fifth column work of the entire war was done in Hawaii with the possible exception of Norway."[4]

It is interesting to note that in those fearful days following Pearl Harbor, when rumor and panic were rampant, two senior members of the President's Cabinet stood firm and acted with reason and judgment. The notion of interning Japanese-Americans or depriving them of their constitutional rights was rejected. Even Mrs. Roosevelt spoke out—in a statement she said was approved by the Departments of State and Justice—saying: "I see absolutely no reason why anyone who has had a good record—that is, who has no criminal or anti-American record—should have any anxiety about his position. This is equally applicable to the Japanese who cannot become citizens but have lived here for 30 or 40 years and to those newcomers who have not yet had time to become citizens."[4]

Military officials, however, were taking a different view. On December 19, General DeWitt had asked in a memo to his superiors "that action be initiated at the earliest possible date to collect all alien subjects fourteen years of age and over, of enemy nations and remove them to the Zone of the Interior."[3] This may have been the first official call for evacuation, though General DeWitt was referring only to aliens, not citizens, and to all enemy aliens, not just Japanese.

General DeWitt was responsible for protecting the West Coast, and in those early days of the war, as the Japanese armed forces systematically crushed all opposition in the Southwest Pacific, the threat of an invasion of the United States mainland was viewed as very real. Half of the nation's military aircraft production was located on the West Coast; so were many naval facilities and oil fields. The military was understandably worried about the activities of enemy aliens should an invasion be launched.

General DeWitt rejected mass arrests and expressed the concern that such action would alienate loyal Japanese. He stated: "An American citizen, after all, is an American citizen. And while they all may not be loyal, I think we can weed the disloyal out of the loyal and lock them up if necessary."[4] This was a position—shared with Hoover, Biddle, and Morgenthau—that he held during the month after Pearl Harbor.

The military, nonetheless, continued to worry about enemy aliens and an invasion. In San Francisco early in January a two-day meeting of representatives of the Departments of War and Justice was held. Its purpose was to work out arrangements for controlling enemy aliens.

Official reports of that meeting indicate that General DeWitt continued to oppose mass arrest or evacuation of citizens but expressed distrust of both Issei and Nisei. The representatives at the meeting finally agreed that the army should designate strategic areas on the Pacific coast from which enemy aliens would be barred. In addition, there was agreement on a new program to register enemy aliens and concurrence that the FBI should increase spot raids to round up those who constituted a threat to security.

One of the participants in the San Francisco meeting was Major Karl R. Bendetsen, chief of the Aliens Division of the Provost Marshal General's office. Historian Stetson Conn attributes to Bendetsen the proposals for the designation of strategic areas and a new alien registration program. Major Bendetsen was to play a most influential role in the months ahead.

During December the mass media on the West Coast continued to carry sensational stories of the roundup of some Japanese. Early in January a newspaper columnist and a radio commentator fired the first salvos in an inflammatory campaign to discredit Japanese-Americans. On January 4, Damon Runyon, popular writer for the Hearst papers, wrote: "It would be extremely foolish to doubt the continued existence of enemy agents among the large alien Japanese population. Only recently, city health inspectors looking over a Japanese rooming house came upon a powerful transmitter, and it is reasonable to assume that menace of a similar character must be constantly guarded against throughout the war."[4] Official records show that no secret transmitter was ever found in Japanese-American hands.

The next day John B. Hughes ("News and Views by John B. Hughes") of the Mutual Broadcasting Company began a series of radio broadcasts declaring that the great majority of Japanese-Americans were loyal to Japan and berating the Justice Department for not moving against them.

These malicious attacks touched off inflammatory columns by other writers. Westbrook Pegler of Scripps-Howard wrote: "The Japanese in California should be under guard to the last man and woman right now and to hell with *habeas corpus* until the danger is over."[4]

Columnist Henry McLemore wanted all Japanese-Americans taken into custody and packed off to the "badlands." He wrote: "Let us have no patience with the enemy or anyone whose veins carry his blood. . . . Personally, I hate the Japanese. And that goes for all of them."[4]

The message reached the man in the street loudly and clearly and prompted a flood of letters to West Coast congressmen and senators. In response, Congressman Leland Ford of Los Angeles County wrote to Cabinet members and other federal officials demanding that all Japanese be placed in inland concentration camps. On January 20 he spoke in the House of Representatives and on a radio broadcast urging the mass internment of Japanese aliens and Nisei alike.

On January 21, General DeWitt forwarded a recommendation to the War Department, as agreed at the San Francisco meeting of Justice and War representatives earlier in the month. He proposed the exclusion of enemy aliens from eighty-six Category A zones and control of enemy aliens by a pass and permit system in eight Category B zones. Secretary of War Henry Stimson forwarded the memo to Attorney General Biddle for implementation with a covering letter:

"In recent conferences with General DeWitt, he has expressed great apprehension because of the presence on the Pacific Coast of many thousand alien enemies. As late as yesterday, 24 January, he stated over the telephone that shore-to-ship and ship-to-shore communications, undoubtedly coordinated by intelligent enemy control were continually operating. A few days ago it was reported by military observers on the Pacific Coast that not a single ship had sailed from our Pacific ports without being subsequently attacked. General DeWitt's apprehensions have been confirmed by recent visits of military observers from the War Department to the Pacific Coast. The alarming and dangerous situation just described, in my opinion, calls for immediate and stringent action."[3] Two interesting points about the Secretary's comments: first, Stetson Conn reports that there had been no Japanese submarine or surface vessels anywhere near the West Coast during the preceding months and that reports of hostile radio communications were completely without foundation; indeed, with the Japanese navy in complete control of the Pacific, it is not surprising that United States ships were consistently attacked. Second, the Secretary's letter was drafted in the Provost Marshal General's office.

General DeWitt had been in constant touch with Provost Marshal General Allen W. Gullion and Major Bendetsen. Late in January, General DeWitt, in a phone conversation with General Gullion, said: "The fact that nothing has happened so far is more or less . . . ominous in that I feel that in view of the fact that we have had no sporadic attempts at sabotage that there is a control being exercised and when we have it it will be on a mass basis."[3] In other words, the Japanese-Americans and Japanese aliens on the Pacific coast were now suspect because they had *not* committed acts of sabotage.

The publication on January 25 of a report of the Roberts Commission which had investigated the attack on Pearl Harbor heaped fuel on the fire. The report charged that Japanese consular agents and Japanese residents in Oahu had committed acts of sabotage before Pearl Harbor. (After the war this charge too was proved false.)

By late January the pressure generated by the newspapers and radio and by California politicians was beginning to have its impact on the military. General DeWitt met with the governor of California, Culbert L. Olson, to discuss the "alien problem." Afterward DeWitt reported to Major Bendetsen by telephone:

"There's a tremendous volume of public opinion now developing against the Japanese of all classes, that is aliens and non-aliens, to get

them off the land and . . . they are bringing pressure on the Government to move all the Japanese out. . . . It is being instigated . . . by
the best people in California. Since the publication of the Roberts
report they feel that they are living in the midst of a lot of enemies.
They don't trust the Japanese, none of them."[3]

Just who the "best" people were, in DeWitt's judgment, he did
not say. But the forces pressing for action against the Japanese population included the mayor of Los Angeles, the mayor of Seattle, the
Native Sons of the Golden West, the American Legion, the Military
Order of the Purple Heart, the California Joint Immigration Committee, and various agricultural associations. It is not too surprising that,
when Governor Olson suggested that the Japanese population should
be moved out of California, General DeWitt agreed and offered to accept responsibility for the enemy alien program if it were to be transferred to him.

At the end of January the California congressional delegation met
to formulate recommendations for action. The congressmen approved
a program calling for the evacuation of aliens and "dual" citizens from
critical areas. Major Bendetsen attended their meeting and reported the
next day to General Gullion that the congressmen were in fact demanding that all Japanese, including citizens, be removed from the West
Coast. He said that they wanted an executive order authorizing the War
Department to carry out the evacuation. The Justice Department had
approved General DeWitt's earlier memorandum and announced publicly the designation of eighty-six Category A zones, stating that all aliens
should be removed from these zones by February 24.

The growing public clamor, the hardening line of the War Department, and the recommendations of the California congressmen alarmed
Attorney General Biddle. On Saturday, February 1, he called a meeting
in his office and invited representatives from the War Department, including General Gullion, Colonel Bendetsen (he had just been promoted), and Assistant Secretary McCloy. Biddle distributed the draft
of a press release which he proposed be issued jointly by the Department
of Justice and the War Department. The release indicated that the two
departments concurred on the alien control steps taken so far. The release also included the following, significant sentence:

"The Department of War and the Department of Justice are in

agreement that the present military situation does not at this time require the removal of American citizens of Japanese race."[3]

It must have been clear to Biddle that the push for evacuation was gaining momentum, and this sentence was an obvious effort to head off a decision he felt would be wrong. He recalls the meeting in his diary and declares that he made very clear that his department would have nothing to do with interfering in the rights of citizens or with the suspension of the writ of habeas corpus.

Gullion, Bendetsen, and McCloy agreed with the wording of the draft release but took exception to the sentence quoted above. Biddle's release was withheld pending the approval of General DeWitt and the outcome of a meeting scheduled for the next day in Sacramento of DeWitt, Governor Olson, Tom Clark (who had been appointed coordinator of Alien Enemy Control Programs in the Western Defense Command a few days earlier), and various state and federal officials. After the meeting in Biddle's office, Colonel Bendetsen told the Chief of Staff's office that Biddle's release was being delayed because General DeWitt was ready to recommend the evacuation of the entire Japanese population from the West Coast. In fact, the Provost Marshal General's office had plans for mass evacuation well under way and had even located shelters to house most of the Japanese residents temporarily.

A few days later General DeWitt reported on the Sacramento meeting with Governor Olson and the others. The California officials had proposed a plan to move both Issei and Nisei from the coastal area to agricultural belts in eastern California where they could work on farms. He stressed that the movement of the Japanese would be voluntary, if possible with the collaboration of American-born Japanese leaders. He was confident that a plan could be worked out in about ten days.

Despite Colonel Bendetsen's remark about mass evacuation, John McCloy responded to DeWitt's report by warning him against advocating a position of mass evacuation. Assistant Secretary McCloy and Secretary Stimson were reported to be opposed to mass evacuation and any illegal interference with citizens.

By early February, then, the situation was confused, and it could have gone either way. Biddle was resisting mass evacuation; DeWitt was wavering and couldn't seem to make up his mind; McCloy and Stimson apparently were influenced by Biddle and were still opposed to relocating Nisei. Colonel Bendetsen appeared to favor mass evacuation. Under his direction, the registration of enemy aliens in California (worked out in early January) was under way. The Nisei and Issei affected by it were becoming increasingly apprehensive.

A navy report published in October 1942, several months after I had completed my work for WRA, gives some idea of what the Japanese on the West Coast were suffering, even as early as February 1942. The report found:

> . . . loss of employment and income due to anti-Japanese agitation by and among Caucasian-Americans, continued personal attacks by Filipinos and other racial groups, denial of relief funds to desperately needy cases; cancellation of licenses for markets, produce houses, stores, etc., by California State authorities; discharges from jobs by the wholesale; unnecessarily harsh restrictions on travel including discriminatory regulations against all *Nisei* preventing them from engaging in commercial fishing.[3]

Despite the hardships and apprehensions, many Japanese-Americans on the West Coast continued to believe that the government would recognize their loyalty; they simply could not believe that they would be evacuated from their homes.

The movement which had begun immediately after Pearl Harbor as an effort to control and detain potentially dangerous aliens evolved during January into a sentiment for controlling and evacuating all Issei from certain restricted areas. Then, in February thinking escalated into evacuation and control of all Japanese aliens and Japanese-Americans on the Pacific coast.

Early in February 1942, Colonel Bendetsen wrote to Provost Marshal General Gullion, pointing out that the evacuation of Issei would accomplish little, since most Issei were elderly and virtually harmless. Indeed, he stated, their removal would arouse the Nisei—their sons, daughters, and grandchildren. Bendetsen proposed a three-step program: first, an executive order authorizing the War Department to designate military areas; second, the actual designation of such areas by General DeWitt; and, third, the prompt evacuation of all persons except those licensed to remain. Such a plan in his judgment provided a legal way to remove the Japanese.

At this point the Provost Marshal General's office lent impetus to the eventual evacuation. Colonel Archer L. Lerch, Deputy Provost

Marshal General, supported Bendetsen's plan, while rejecting the voluntary movement of the Issei to eastern California farms, as suggested by Governor Olson. Lerch said the Olson scheme smacked "too much of the spirit of Rotary" and did not conform to the "necessary cold-bloodedness of war." His boss, General Gullion, took a similar stance and told John McCloy that the Olson voluntary relocation plan was "dangerous." He recommended to McCloy prompt action to eliminate the "great danger of Japanese-inspired sabotage on the West Coast." General Gullion wanted mandatory removal of all alien Japanese to areas east of the Sierras with as many Nisei members of their families as would voluntarily accompany them. The remaining Nisei would be excluded from restricted zones and resettled with the help of the federal government.

It is interesting to note that even as some military authorities were proposing evacuation to prevent widespread sabotage, General Mark Clark and Admiral Harold R. Stark, chief of naval operations, were dismissing the threat out of hand. They testified before a committee appointed by California's senior senator, Hiram Johnson, and chaired by California Senator Mon C. Wallgren to deal with the problems of aliens and sabotage in California. General Clark declared that the West Coast was unduly alarmed and that any chance of a sustained attack or invasion by the Japanese was "nil."

It is also well to remember that Colonel Bendetsen's military areas plan did not distinguish between Japanese aliens and German and Italian aliens. If the proposals for removing aliens from Category A zones had been carried out, some 90,000 aliens would have been removed—25,000 of whom would have been Japanese.

Attorney General Biddle did not want to evacuate Germans and Italians. Moreover, the scope of such an enterprise clearly exceeded the capacity of the Department of Justice. If it was to be done, he said, the military would have to do it. In fact, Biddle wanted nothing to do with the evacuation of citizens, as he had made clear all along.

Biddle's resistance resulted in the drafting of a memorandum by the War Department of the "questions to be determined *re* Japanese exclusion." Although it is reasonable to assume that some assessment had been provided to the President during the weeks following Pearl Harbor, it was this War Department memorandum drafted on February

11, 1942, that was probably the first official acknowledgment of presidential involvement. The following questions were drafted:

(1) Is the President willing to authorize us [the War Department] to move Japanese citizens* as well as aliens from restricted areas?

(2) Should we undertake withdrawal from the entire strip DeWitt originally recommended, which involves over 100,000 people, if we include both aliens and Japanese citizens?

(3) Should we undertake the immediate step involving, say, 70,000 which includes large communities such as Los Angeles, San Diego, and Seattle?

(4) Should we take any lesser step such as the establishment of restricted areas around airplane plants and critical installations even though General DeWitt states that in several, at least, of the largest communities this would be wasteful, involve difficult administrative problems, and might be a source of more continuous irritation and trouble than 100 per cent withdrawal from the area?[3]

Secretary Stimson describes in his diary what happened at that point. After meeting with McCloy and General Clark, the Secretary tried to see the President. Roosevelt, confronted with global problems, was too busy and could not schedule an appointment. Shortly after lunch, however, the Secretary and the President talked by phone and, according to Stimson, the President was "very vigorous" in response to the situation as described by Stimson and "told me to go ahead on the line that I myself thought the best." Stimson acknowledged in his diary that the best course of action in his view was the immediate evacuation of citizens and alien Japanese from the most vital places of army and navy production.

McCloy called Colonel Bendetsen and reported, "We have carte blanche to do what we want as far as the President's concerned." President Roosevelt had specifically authorized the removal of citizens. The President was aware of possible repercussions but that military necessity had to dictate the course of action. "Be as reasonable as you can," President Roosevelt had cautioned his Secretary of War.

The President's reaction put wind in the sails. General DeWitt hastily submitted a new plan which called for the enforced evacuation of Japanese-Americans from the Category A areas already designated.

* The War Department phrase "Japanese citizens" really meant American citizens of Japanese ancestry.

The same day the new plan was submitted, the Wallgren committee recommended the immediate evacuation of all persons of Japanese lineage first from the specific vital areas, but eventually from the entire Pacific coast. President Roosevelt forwarded the committee's recommendation to Secretary Stimson for a reply.

On February 17, Provost Marshal General Gullion telegraphed the corps area commanders on the West Coast:

PROBABLE THAT ORDERS FOR VERY LARGE EVACUATION OF ENEMY ALIENS OF ALL NATIONALITIES PREDOMINANTLY JAPANESE FROM PACIFIC COAST WILL ISSUE WITHIN 48 HOURS. INTERNMENT FACILITIES WILL BE TAXED TO UTMOST. REPORT AT ONCE MAXIMUM YOU CAN CARE FOR, INCLUDING HOUSING, FEEDING, MEDICAL CARE, AND SUPPLY. YOUR BREAKDOWN SHOULD INCLUDE NUMBER OF MEN, WOMEN, AND CHILDREN. VERY IMPORTANT TO KEEP THIS A CLOSELY GUARDED SECRET.[3]

In a subsequent letter General Gullion explained that 100,000 enemy aliens would be evacuated and interned east of the Western Defense Command; 60,000 would be women and children.

The plan for a mass evacuation came into focus in a meeting on February 17 of Secretary Stimson, Assistant Secretary McCloy, General Gullion, General Clark, and Colonel Bendetsen. General Clark objected to mass evacuation (on the grounds that it would require the use of too many troops) but Secretary Stimson decided to instruct General DeWitt to move immediately.

That evening Bendetsen, McCloy, and Gullion met with representatives of the Justice Department at the home of Attorney General Biddle. General Gullion read a draft of an executive order that would be presented to the President for his signature. Morton Grodzins, in his book *Americans Betrayed*,[5] describes that meeting. Edward Ennis, chief of the alien enemy control unit in the Department of Justice, was present as was James Rowe, Jr., Biddle's assistant. Both men were stunned by General Gullion's proposed draft. At first they thought it ludicrous, then they reacted with such biting criticism that General Gullion became angry. The two Justice Department representatives argued vigorously for the rights of citizens and pleaded for an examination and decision of loyalty in each individual case. The Attorney General remained silent, and draft of the executive order moved forward.

Ironically, Biddle had sent President Roosevelt a memorandum that very day as background for a presidential press conference. He indicated that the FBI had no evidence of an imminent attack on the West Coast and no evidence of any planned sabotage. He outlined the way in which he had co-operated with the War Department in designating critical areas and in planning for selective evacuations of aliens. He pointedly referred to the legal limits on the Justice Department which prevented him from evacuating citizens. Much of Biddle's memo was a rebuke of columnists who were inflaming the public on the West Coast. Specifically, he mentioned Walter Lippmann, who had advocated mass evacuation of the Japanese population in a column on February 12. (Eight days later, on February 20, Lippmann would write another column echoing the peculiar charge of General DeWitt a month earlier that the absence of sabotage by Japanese-Americans on the West Coast was an indication that they were lying low and awaiting orders from Tokyo to commit sabotage on a massive scale.)

By mid-February the congressional delegation from the West Coast had closed ranks, finally overcoming the reluctance of some members like Senator Sheridan Downey and Congressman Jerry Voorhis. In their demands for the evacuation of Issei and Nisei, the Westerners had attracted support from many Southern senators and congressmen. On February 18, Mississippi Congressman John Rankin addressed the House of Representatives on the question.

"This is a race war," he proclaimed. ". . . The white man's civilization has come into conflict with Japanese barbarism. . . . I say it is of vital importance that we get rid of every Japanese, whether in Hawaii or on the mainland. . . . Damn them! Let us get rid of them now!"[4]

Senator Tom Stewart of Tennessee told his fellow senators: "They [the Japanese] are cowardly and immoral. They are different from Americans in every conceivable way, and no Japanese should have the right to claim American citizenship. . . . A Jap is a Jap anywhere you find him, and his taking the oath of allegiance to this country would not help, even if he should be permitted to do so."[4]

Executive Order 9066 was signed by President Roosevelt on February 19, 1942. It did not direct that the Japanese should be evacuated, as I thought when the President referred to it during our discussion in March. Rather, it gave Secretary Stimson the power to evacuate both citizens of Japanese descent and aliens from the Pacific coast by authorizing him to designate certain military areas and exclude "any or all" persons from them.

Even after the signing of Executive Order 9066, the Nisei and Issei hoped that the evacuation would not be carried out. Hearings held by Congressman John H. Tolan of California offered some hope. The hearings were to look into the problems of evacuation. Japanese-Americans looked forward to demonstrating their loyalty to the United States.

The hearings, which moved like a traveling road show along the West Coast, were essentially superfluous. Before they were half completed, General DeWitt had designated the western half of California, Oregon, and Washington, as well as the southern part of Arizona, as restricted military areas from which all persons of Japanese descent would be evacuated. Simultaneously with the close of the hearings, the general established the Wartime Civil Control Administration, with Colonel Bendetsen as its director, to implement the evacuation program.

Still, the hearings are revealing. Various officials and leaders of civic organizations argued for evacuation on the grounds that (1) there was a danger of invasion and sabotage; (2) that loyal and disloyal Japanese were indistinguishable; (3) that the economy of the Pacific States would not be adversely affected by the removal of the Japanese; and (4) that evacuation was necessary for the safety of the Nisei and Issei themselves.

Japanese-Americans pleaded their case with fervor, but it was soon apparent that the Tolan committee was building a justification for mass evacuation rather than looking for objective information. Some distinguished citizens helped to build that case. California Attorney General Earl Warren, later to become Chief Justice of the United States Supreme Court, fell victim to the same curious reasoning that afflicted DeWitt and Walter Lippmann. He testified that the absence of sabotage was "the most ominous sign in our whole situation," because "we are just being lulled into a false sense of security."[4]

On February 14 the navy had designated Terminal Island (across from San Pedro) a restricted zone and ordered all Japanese out by March 14. On February 25 the navy changed the deadline to February 27. The heartbreak of evacuation became suddenly evident in this forty-eight-hour period as families with no place to go hurriedly gathered the belongings they could carry and fled Terminal Island. Many left behind possessions of a lifetime, either abandoning them or selling them for virtually nothing.

The mass evacuation of Nisei and Issei was beginning.

At a Cabinet meeting on February 27, 1942, President Roosevelt asked for a report. Apparently he had thought little about the problem of transporting and resettling the Japanese population.

Secretary Stimson summarized the situation, pointing out that General DeWitt's proclamation of restricted zones in early February had not, as he had anticipated, resulted in substantial voluntary migration. Some 15,000 persons, including many Nisei, had already voluntarily left the prohibited zones designated by the Justice Department in January but had moved into zones subsequently restricted by the War Department. Despite DeWitt's assurance that if they moved again voluntarily they would not be disturbed any more, only about 2,000 persons did so. Their unwillingness to move a second time was surely caused by the failure of federal agencies to help solve the inevitable problems of abrupt dislocation.

Stimson pointed out that the task was enormous and that General DeWitt was hampered by the lack of manpower. At that point, Stimson says in his diary, "There was general confusion around the table arising from the fact that nobody had realized how big it was, nobody wanted to take care of the evacuees, and the general weight and complication of the project. Biddle suggested that a single head should be chosen to handle the resettlement instead of the pulling and hauling of all the different agencies, and the President seemed to accept this; the single person to be, of course, a civilian and not the Army. . . ."[7]

And so, on or about March 10, President Roosevelt summoned me to his office and told me that I would be that "single head to handle the resettlement." Even as we talked, General DeWitt and Colonel Bendetsen on the West Coast were launching the Wartime Civil Control Administration to carry out a mass evacuation program.

Summarizing what happened during those three months after Pearl Harbor, I can hardly believe that at the time of the events I knew so little about them. But this, I feel sure, was equally true of most Americans. The newspapers and radio broadcasts of those opening months of the war were filled with news of bloody battles in Europe and Asia. The United States was rapidly mobilizing, and the war had already become a very personal matter for each of us. Like nearly everyone else in Washington, I was working day and night, and the task of conducting the information study for President Roosevelt during January was an added burden. The problem of the Japanese-Americans on the West Coast seemed remote and insignificant to the average American on the East Coast.

In any case, when I left Harold Smith on March 10, I knew only what he had told me during our brief conversation at the White House. Before seeing Assistant Secretary of War McCloy or Attorney General Biddle, as advised, I hurried to talk with my own staff. When I proposed that nearly all of them move directly to the new War Relocation Authority, the staff responded with enthusiasm. This was about the only heartening experience in those first few weeks of my new job. I knew their individual capacities; they were a well-knit team.

I met with Assistant Secretary of War John McCloy within the next two or three days. My recollection is that McCloy emphasized the need to relocate the Japanese population from the West Coast for their own safety, as well as to assure protection for vital industrial and military establishments. He also urged speed and said that the army was under orders to give me whatever assistance I required.

I took Philip Glick, attorney in the Co-ordinating Office of Agriculture, who had agreed to join me, with me to see Attorney General Biddle. We discussed the legal implications of moving Nisei into the interior. The Attorney General assured me that I could do almost anything I found necessary: I could transfer the evacuees into private employment if that proved feasible and, in doing so, I could specify the conditions which would have to be met in such employment. If private employment proved impossible, I could establish evacuation centers, set up schools, develop work programs, create courts and all the other facilities and procedures essential to making the relocation centers as nearly self-governing as possible.

Neither McCloy nor Biddle revealed in their conversations the interagency or individual conflicts and uncertainties that had preceded the President's decision. Their concern—and mine—was to carry out the evacuation as smoothly, quickly, and humanely as possible.

It was clear that I would have to maintain an office in Washington but I would also need an office, perhaps several, on the Pacific coast, where the actual movement of some 120,000 Issei and Nisei had to be carried out.

The next three months were a nightmare. In that period I seldom slept in my own home. I traveled from Washington to San Francisco and back on the average of once a week, always by night sleeper plane. The "night" description applied; the "sleeper" part did not—at least for me.

My first trip to the West Coast as the new director of the War Relocation Authority came a few days after the March 18 announcement by the White House. I wanted to meet with General DeWitt and Colonel Bendetsen and see for myself what the situation was. I also wanted to talk to some of the leaders of an organization of Japanese-Americans that I had heard about—the Japanese-American Citizens League. I had to assemble a West Coast staff and find office space for them.

In San Francisco, I met with Colonel Bendetsen. Our first session lasted for four hours. Bendetsen was all military—straight, serious, grim, and completely confident of his own judgments. From him I got the most thorough and detailed briefing of the current situation I had so far received.

The colonel explained that General DeWitt had divided the West Coast states into two military zones: Military Area No. 1 included the western halves of Washington, Oregon, and California and southern Arizona. In early March residents of Japanese ancestry in Military Area No. 1 had been advised that they would shortly be removed from this zone and they were urged to move voluntarily into the interior. Military Area No. 2, the zone into which it was expected that many Nisei and Issei would voluntarily migrate, included the eastern halves of Washington, Oregon, and California and the northern half of Arizona. As head of the Wartime Civil Control Administration created by General DeWitt on March 11, Bendetsen had the responsibility of supervising the move.

He told me that the voluntary evacuation plan unfortunately was a failure. He insisted that the voluntary relocation program be terminated and that compulsory evacuation of the entire Japanese population in Military Area No. 1 be undertaken at once.

I expressed dismay. I strongly resisted the idea of complete evacuation, hoping some less drastic solution could be found—though at that moment I knew too little of the situation to offer an alternative and workable proposal. I insisted that WRA, having been established only a few days earlier, was unprepared to cope with an immediate mass evacuation.

Colonel Bendetsen said that he shared my dismay but he was convinced that total evacuation was the only possible course. As to WRA's unpreparedness, he explained that the army in early March had selected two sites for relocating as many as 30,000 Japanese. One of these was in Arizona, along the Colorado River, and the other was in the Owens Valley of California. Within hours, the colonel said, he could have a group of Nisei volunteers recruited from the Los Angeles area on their way to one of these camps to make preparations.

Bendetsen went on to say that his agency had developed a plan for mass evacuation which would divide the coastal zone into 108 exclusion areas, each containing roughly 1,000 Japanese. The plan called for the systematic transfer of Japanese from these areas into temporary assembly centers, where they would be housed until WRA could relocate them. The army was building some fifteen such assembly areas, in addition to the two camps he had mentioned (Manzanar in Owens Valley and Poston in Arizona).

Deeply troubled, I replied that I wanted a few hours to consider the colonel's recommendation and to consult with others.

Before our meeting ended, Colonel Bendetsen suggested that Tom Clark was familiar with the problem, had been of some help to him and General DeWitt, and might be available to serve as my legal counsel on the Pacific coast. Later I spoke with Tom Clark and, to my everlasting thankfulness, he agreed to serve.

The next days were hectic. I became a one-man raiding party of government agencies in a search for staff for the West Coast offices of the WRA. Taking President Roosevelt's assurance as a mandate, I drafted experienced administrators from several offices, beginning with the Department of Agriculture, where I knew several well-qualified persons. Especially helpful were officials from the Department of Interior's Indian Service, Irrigation Service, and the Public Land Office.

Then I rented an entire floor in the Whitcomb Hotel and delegated the task of prying out of the federal bureaucracy telephones, typewriters, file cabinets.

It did not take me long to conclude that Colonel Bendetsen was correct about one thing: the voluntary evacuation program was a failure. Even if the Issei and Nisei had wanted to comply, they were virtually unable to. Families heading for Colorado, Idaho, Utah, and other Western states were met with hostility. Signs greeted them with the blunt message: "No Japs wanted here." They could not get hotel accommodations or service in restaurants. There was no work for people considered by their government to be potential saboteurs.

I first met with General DeWitt at the Presidio on March 25, and we agreed to terminate the voluntary evacuation program. He said he would issue a proclamation within a few days prohibiting movement in or out of Military Area No. 1. The general was an austere man, rather forbidding, and, like Colonel Bendetsen, supremely confident in his own judgment. He talked like a machine gun—fast, incisive, and seemingly without stopping to breathe. In our first conversation he covered much the same ground that McCloy and Bendetsen had, except he put greater emphasis on the military risks. He feared an invasion (though by late March that was an extremely remote possibility), and he was sure that there would be chaos in the coastal states should the enemy invade. He believed that a high percentage of both the Issei and the Nisei would support Japanese forces should they attack the West Coast, and he was adamant that one could not tell the difference between a loyal and a disloyal Japanese-American.

I sensed that General DeWitt had somehow blocked out the human implications of evacuation. He wanted the area cleared at once, so that he could make all feasible preparations for a possible invasion. I got the distinct impression that he intended to evacuate German and Italian aliens as well, though we did not discuss this. (Six weeks later General DeWitt formally recommended a limited collective evacuation of German and Italian aliens from Military Area No. 1. Secretary Stimson and Assistant Secretary McCloy rejected the recommendation, and General DeWitt insisted that he receive written instructions so that he would be exempt from all responsibility for the consequences of overruling his recommendation.)

Although I agreed that the voluntary relocation program should be terminated, I struggled against going ahead with a complete evacuation. I hoped that the people of California would accept a plan in which only men were evacuated, the women and children remaining in their homes and carrying on business enterprises as best they could, especially such businesses as florist shops, grocery stores, drugstores, and similar establishments where closing would involve serious economic losses. Colonel Bendetsen was certain that this would not be acceptable, and in a host of hurriedly called conferences I reluctantly became convinced that this was so.

I next wired the governors of the intermountain states and asked them to meet me within a week in Salt Lake City, Utah. My hope was that the governors would co-operate in a program to move the maximum number of evacuees directly into private employment. If mass evacuation were essential, at the very least it should be undertaken in a way that would permit families to stay together and the heads of these families to provide for their needs through gainful employment. The meeting was arranged for April 7.

I completed two other very important tasks during that first visit to San Francisco in late March.

I met with a group of Japanese-Americans and we established an advisory council to represent those who were affected by the President's executive order. This was the wisest thing I did in that whole traumatic experience.

The advisory council was headed by an attractive twenty-one-year-old Japanese-American, a Nisei, Mike Masaoka. He was secretary of the Japanese-American Citizens League, a graduate of the University of Utah, a man of great perception and heart. He was deeply respected by Japanese-Americans of all ages. After the establishment of the advisory council, I did not make a single major decision without first conferring with this young man and, when necessary, with the advisory council.

The other important action I took at that time was to meet with officers of the Federal Reserve Bank in California. I obtained their agreement that the bank would do all it could to protect the physical assets of the evacuees. It would protect property, try to rent properties and deposit the income to the credit of the right person or family, and give any other assistance in this area that it could. (Unfortunately, at this writing, some thirty years after those tragic events, two million dollars in claims by the Japanese-Americans have not been resolved.)

The governors (or their representatives in some cases) of the ten Western states met with me in Salt Lake City on April 7. I explained that the hysteria on the Pacific coast need not prevail in the intermountain states. None of the evacuees had been charged with disloyalty. In my judgment, there was no evidence to indicate that these people would indeed be disloyal in any event. I emphasized that they were being evacuated at the insistence of the military as a precautionary defense measure. Finally I suggested that the labor shortages in the intermountain states, especially in sugar beet production and other agricultural enterprises, was a problem that could be partially solved if the governors would co-operate in moving as many evacuees as possible into private employment. They would have to explain to their people that there would be no danger and they would also have to provide protective services in the event that misguided or uninformed persons attacked or harassed Japanese-Americans.

I was prepared to outline my idea for establishing small inland camps on the model of Civilian Conservation Corps camps which would serve as staging areas for the evacuees as they were moved into private jobs as soon as possible and could resume something like a normal life away from the Western Defense zone. I was prepared to discuss policies about prevailing wages, health care, and other factors. But I could get no further. The governors literally began shouting at me. They had been deaf to my opening assurances.

One governor shouted: "If these people are dangerous on the Pacific coast they will be dangerous here! We have important defense establishments, too, you know." Another governor walked close to me, shook his fist in my face, and growled through clenched teeth: "If you bring the Japanese into my state, I promise you they will be hanging from every tree!" Some governors demanded that the evacuees be kept under armed guard.

Only Ralph Carr of Colorado took a moderate and reasonable position. He said he had no objection to having loyal Japanese-Americans moving into his state and that co-operation with the relocation project was a citizen's responsibility. He was the single exception. The others were angry and hostile. That meeting was probably the most frustrating experience I ever had. During two weeks on the West Coast I had met many Japanese-Americans and had become convinced that the overwhelming majority were loyal and would remain so. I had hoped against hope that the governors would make it possible for us to resettle these people with the very least pain and to give them the maximum opportunity to live normally and contribute to their communities as they desperately longed to.

There was no doubt in my mind as I left Salt Lake City that the plan to move the evacuees into private employment had to be abandoned—at least temporarily.

Time was getting short. The longer WRA took to develop relocation centers, the longer the evacuees would be kept in the assembly centers along the coast. And the assembly centers were makeshift quarters of tar-paper shacks thrown up at racetracks and fairgrounds. There was virtually no privacy; conditions were primitive, with overcrowding and minimal facilities.

I hurried to Washington and held a meeting of the chiefs of the National Forest Service, Irrigation Service, Public Land Office, and National Park Service. I asked them to prepare for me at once a map which showed publicly owned lands that were destined for subsequent development, preferably as irrigation projects which would involve an enormous amount of work. I also asked for a list of the best people in these agencies who might be drafted for service in the War Relocation Authority.

I told Assistant Secretary of War McCloy of meeting with the governors and explained that there seemed no alternative to the unhappy one of creating evacuation camps where the people could live in modest comfort, do useful work, have schools for their small children, and thus retain as much self-respect as the horrible circumstances permitted. McCloy said that as soon as I gave him a map of the locations for the evacuation camps, and some direction regarding the facilities I wanted, the army would move in and construct barracklike buildings which could be subdivided into family apartments. Schools, churches, and other essential buildings would be erected.

I had decided that the fifty or seventy-five smaller CCC-type camps were not feasible and that larger, semipermanent centers were needed. I anticipated recruiting the evacuees as a kind of work corps, who could help in clearing and developing the land, who could plant crops and manufacture products for the war effort, such as tents, camouflage nets, and cartridge belts. These items could be sold to the government and the evacuees could share in the profits.

The search for the relocation centers proceeded during April and into May. It was not an easy task. The sites had to be on government property and had to be large enough to accommodate five thousand or more persons. They had to be located away from strategic installations. They had to provide useful work opportunities.

The various agencies compiled a list of three hundred sites. Two thirds of these were eliminated for various considerations and the remaining one hundred were visited and studied by teams of WRA and staff officials from other federal agencies.

In late April 1942, a very special problem arose. Some 3,500 Japanese-Americans were enrolled in colleges and universities in the three Pacific coast states. Evacuation made it necessary for them to either withdraw from college or transfer to another institution away from the West Coast. I felt deeply about the necessity of finding a way for these young men and women to complete their education. If they could be widely distributed throughout the nation's colleges and universities they would be accepted in a friendly spirit. So I set out to establish a committee of leading educators.

I must confess that I am still distressed by the excuses I received from the educators I approached. All declined. Then someone suggested that I telephone Clarence Pickett, the prominent Quaker leader. He accepted. All Americans should have undying gratitude for the work he did. He obtained complete information about the Japanese-American students on the Pacific coast, traveled to hundreds of colleges and universities seeking admission for a few of these in each place, finally induced a prestigious group of educators and industrialists and cultural leaders to form the National Student Relocation Council, and succeeded in moving the students to other institutions. I should emphasize that many of these Japanese-Americans were graduate and professional students in the arts and sciences, law, medicine, public health, dentistry, and engineering.

Shortly after I had recruited Clarence Pickett to help relocate the students, President Roosevelt received a letter from California's Governor Olson, expressing the concern of the Western College Association that the evacuation would interrupt the education of many loyal Japanese-American young people. The President spoke to me about the letter. I told him that we had already made progress on the problem, but I also related the trying experience I had had trying to find help in getting the students placed in other institutions. By then I had had many dealings with Japanese-Americans and was now personally and painfully aware of the tragedy of the relocation.

The President replied to Governor Olson, saying: "I am deeply concerned that the American-born Japanese college students shall be impressed with the ability of the American people to distinguish between enemy aliens and staunch supporters of the American system." I felt that the President had gained an insight into the human problem that, had it come in February rather than May, might have prompted him to decide against mass evacuation.

During the month of May, as the site selection was under way, we tried the "work corps" idea on an experimental basis at Colonel Bendetsen's Assembly Center in Portland, Oregon. The experiment was a failure. Only about fifteen men out of several hundred signed up. I suspect that the men feared their participation in the work program would somehow result in permanent confinement in the Assembly Center. Then, too, there was considerable and understandable bitterness among those in the centers—particularly among the men in the age group from which most of the volunteer workers could be expected to come.

But even as the experiment in Portland was failing, an even more hopeful development was taking place. Government officials, particularly agricultural officials, from the intermountain states began to request relocation centers in their states. Having rejected the Japanese-Americans so forcefully in early April, they were now petitioning WRA for workers. Why? To rescue farm lands that were going to ruin from lack of manpower.

We decided to try another experiment, this time allowing a small group of workers from the Portland Assembly Center to become agricultural workers in Malheur County in southeastern Oregon. The reports of the first participants encouraged many more to apply for such work, and WRA drew up "seasonal leave" procedures to allow the men to leave the camps for temporary work and return when the job was finished.

Now, however, we were calling the tune. We insisted that the local officials guarantee the safety of the Japanese workers, pay them the prevailing wage, and provide adequate housing and transportation. The program was a success. A few incidents of harassment of the Japanese workers were called to my attention, and I threatened to withdraw all workers. The local officials soon put an end to the bullying. By the time I left WRA in mid-June hundreds of evacuees were working in the intermountain states and the demand was growing. By autumn half of the males between twenty and fifty years of age—some ten thousand Japanese-Americans—were on seasonal leaves and officials were complaining because we could not meet the demand for more workers.

By June 5 we had selected ten sites for our relocation centers: Manzanar and Poston (both had begun as assembly centers and were transferred to WRA), Tule Lake in northeastern California, Heart Mountain in Wyoming, Minidoka in Idaho, Topas in Utah, Gila River in Arizona, and Granada, Rohwer, and Jerome in Arkansas.

Now I found myself signing orders which created schools, police forces, courts, stores, and recreation centers. Positions in the evacuation centers were filled by evacuees themselves where possible. The troublesome problem of pay came up. In a press conference I said we were considering prevailing wages for all positions. This brought a storm of protest from members of Congress, who demanded that pay not exceed that provided for privates in the army. Politically, we had to accept this. So the evacuees were provided free living quarters, food, and education, and army pay to cover incidentals from toothpaste to toilet paper.

We called the relocation camps "evacuation centers." Never did we think of them as concentration camps. Technically, the Japanese-Americans were not restricted to the camps, although in fact they could not return to the Pacific coast and movement without safeguards to any other location would probably have endangered their lives, at least in the beginning.

Although much of the building of the centers was completed after I left WRA, the construction had begun in June. The army was eager to get the evacuees out of the assembly centers and, despite our protests that the WRA centers were not ready, the movement of Japanese-Americans began in June.

On the ninetieth day of this grueling assignment I flew to Washington to handle ever pressing legal details. I never carried out those intentions. I was met at the airport by a White House employee who said a car would take me at once to see President Roosevelt.

The President had a new war task for me. He asked whether someone was prepared to take my place as director of the War Relocation Authority. I asked him for a few days to think this over and make a recommendation.

A day or so later I received an invitation to a party at the home of

Mr. and Mrs. Dillon S. Meyer. I had known Dillon in the Department of Agriculture and he had helped me select staff for WRA back in March. Although he had not been involved in any of the work of WRA, Dillon Meyer struck me as an excellent choice for the difficult job I was about to leave.

I enjoyed the party, for most of the guests were friends and acquaintances from the Department of Agriculture. The Meyers had a piano, and I was a self-taught key thumper, so I sat down and played for an hour or so late in the evening. When the other guests had gone, I spoke to Dillon about taking over WRA. I pulled no punches. The past three months had been the toughest of my career and I had lost a year's sleep in ninety days. I also stressed that we had turned the corner and a good strong leader could do a great deal to ensure that the Japanese-Americans could maintain some dignity, contribute to their own and the country's well-being, and eventually be brought back into society.

Meyer agreed to take the position if the President approved.

I spoke with President Roosevelt on Tuesday, June 16, and recommended that he appoint Meyer to head the War Relocation Authority. The next day the President made the appointment official.

In departing from WRA, I wrote a memorandum to President Roosevelt which summarized my feelings about the relocation program and suggested a future course of action. This was also my legacy to my successor. I wrote:

> The future of the program (WRA) will doubtless be governed largely by the temper of American public opinion. Already public attitudes have exerted a strong influence in shaping the program and charting its direction. In a democracy this is unquestionably sound and proper. Yet in leaving the War Relocation Authority after a few extremely crowded weeks, I cannot help expressing the hope that the American people will grow toward a broader appreciation of the essential Americanism of a great majority of the evacuees and of the difficult sacrifice they are making. Only when the prevailing attitudes of unreasoning bitterness have been replaced by tolerance and understanding will it be possible to carry forward a genuinely satisfactory relocation program and to plan intelligently for the reassimilation of the evacuees into American life when the war is over. I wish to give you my considered judgment that fully 80 to 85 per cent of the Nisei are loyal to the United

States, perhaps 50 per cent of the Issei are passively loyal; but a large portion of the Kibei (American citizens educated in Japan) feel a strong cultural attachment to Japan.

I then recommended four steps to the President:

1. Recommend to Congress a program of repatriation for those who preferred the Japanese way of life.

2. Issue a strong public statement in behalf of loyal American citizens who were now bewildered and wondered what was in store for them.

3. Call for a more liberal wage policy for evacuees.

4. Ask Congress to enact a special program of rehabilitation after the war to help the evacuees find their place in American life.

Dillon Meyer remained with WRA throughout the war. He performed even beyond my high expectations. He was often abused, but he never lost his composure.

Meyer and all our evacuees were greatly helped when citizens of Japanese descent formed the Nisei 442nd Regimental Combat Team. The Nisei soldiers fought on our behalf in some of the bloodiest battles of North Africa and Europe and took incredibly heavy casualties. The 442nd suffered some 9,500 casualties in seven major battles and won 18,000 individual decorations for heroism. It became one of the most decorated units in the war and opened the eyes of the American people to the loyalty and dedication of our Japanese-Americans.

The only pleasant memory I have of three agonizing months with the War Relocation Authority involves a gift from the Japanese-American Advisory Committee when I made a hasty trip to San Francisco before leaving for my next task. Mike Masaoka gave me a fifty-year-old bonsai, a beautifully sculptured dwarf pine tree, a form of art mastered only by the Japanese. In making the presentation, Mr. Masaoka said that the bonsai was to indicate the conviction of the Japanese-Americans that I had done all I could in their interest in view of the executive order for evacuation and the hostile attitudes then prevailing in the western half of the country.

I believe to this day that most of the evacuation could have been avoided had not false and flaming statements been dinned into the people of the West Coast by irresponsible commentators and politicians. There was surely some underlying and latent dislike for Japanese in that part of the country and that provided fuel for ignorance, intolerance, and bigotry to spread like fire.

The evacuation of Japanese-Americans from their homes on the coast to hastily constructed assembly centers and then to inland relocation centers was an inhuman mistake. Thousands of American citizens of Japanese ancestry were stripped of their rights and freedoms and treated almost like enemy prisoners of war. Many lost their homes, their businesses, their savings. For 120,000 Japanese the evacuation was a bad dream come to pass.

How could such a tragedy have occurred in a democratic society that prides itself on individual rights and freedoms? How could responsible leaders make such a fateful decision?

I have brooded about this whole episode on and off for the past three decades, for it is illustrative of how an entire society can somehow plunge off course.

It would be comforting to heap the blame for the evacuation on some individual or group of individuals. General DeWitt is a likely candidate, as is the unyielding Colonel Bendetsen. Perhaps General Gullion, the Provost Marshal General, or Assistant Secretary McCloy. Or even Secretary Stimson. President Roosevelt signed the fateful order and must be ultimately responsible; perhaps he should bear the blame. Certainly his approval of the evacuation was a glaring example of how a busy President often makes a decision on inadequate evidence, simply because he is preoccupied with seemingly more pressing matters.

All of these men—and many others—played key roles in the tragedy and all must share the responsibility. But I am convinced that *no one* fully understood at the time, or even knew about, all of the events that transpired between December 7, 1941, and March 1942 and which led ultimately to the evacuation.

Only after the events had taken place could historians work their magic and reconstruct chaos into neat, logical, linear chronology. But, at the time, many forces were at work—military, political, economic, emotional, and racial. The principal actors in the drama frequently acted independently of each other. Often they were unaware of what the others were doing or thinking or how their decisions or actions related to other decisions or actions. I doubt that anyone saw the over-all pattern that was emerging or how his actions contributed to that pattern.

Misunderstanding, rumor, fear, misinformation, prejudice, and ignorance were dark winds that blew across the land. An incident here, a rumor there, a political move, a military decision, an official memorandum—all fell like pieces into a mosaic that no single individual could perceive or had created. And as the days passed and the pressures mounted, the ultimate decision began to take shape.

Those who hold a conspiratorial view of history will find a plot behind the evacuation of the Japanese-Americans. Those who subscribe to a "good guys and bad guys" interpretation of history will find a scapegoat to blame for the tragic events. Such simplistic views are certainly more reassuring than the reality, for the reality is that in such major movements the decision is not *made*, it happens.

By the time the situation was presented to President Roosevelt in February of 1942 the decision was all but inevitable. The pattern was largely formed; the course was nearly set. The alternative courses of action at that point were limited and generally all undesirable. And so, as often happens, the President's action was less a decision than a validation. This might be said of President Truman's decision to drop the atomic bomb, or President Kennedy's Bay of Pigs decision, or President Johnson's decision to bomb North Vietnam.

In all of these instances the President's final decision was influenced by a variety of factors—by events over which he had little control, by inaccurate or incomplete information, by bad counsel, by strong political pressures, and by his own training, background, and personality.

The evacuation of the Japanese-Americans need not have happened. If public officials had provided strong and positive leadership at the outset they might have calmed the public. If the media had been responsible they could have cooled instead of incited passions. If the military had been more effective, it might have assessed the situation more objectively and, thus, not have pressed for evacuation. If the political leaders had resisted the pressures of the misguided public opinion perhaps they could have influenced it rather than succumbing to it. If those closest to the President had given him better advice, perhaps he would have decided differently. If the President had asked harder questions, demanded better information, been more skeptical, perhaps he would have overruled those who counseled mass evacuation.

Two decades afterward, Attorney General Biddle also played the "what if" game. He wrote:

"If Stimson had stood firm, had insisted, as apparently he suspected, that this wholesale evacuation was needless, the President would have followed his advice. And if, instead of dealing almost exclusively with McCloy and Bendetsen, I had urged the Secretary to resist the pressure of his subordinates, the result might have been different. But I was new to the cabinet, and disinclined to insist on my view to an elder statesman whose wisdom and integrity I greatly respected."[6]

Again, Attorney General Biddle contributes an insight in his memoirs. He said of President Roosevelt: "I do not think he was much concerned with the gravity or implications of this step. He was never theoretical about things. What must be done to defend the country must be done. The decision was for his Secretary of War, not for the Attorney General, not even for J. Edgar Hoover, whose judgment as to the appropriateness of defense measures he greatly respected. The military might be wrong. But they were fighting the war. Public opinion was on their side, so that there was no question of any substantial opposition, which might tend toward the disunity that at all costs he must avoid. Nor do I think that constitutional difficulty plagued him— the Constitution has never greatly bothered any wartime President. . . . Once he emphasized to me, when I was expressing my belief that the evacuation was unnecessary, that this must be a military decision."[6]

When the war was over a special court was established to cover a major portion of the economic losses of the Japanese-Americans and in time a test case was taken to the Supreme Court which ruled that the President had acted legally under the war-power provisions of the Constitution in doing what he did. Some cases, as I have said, are still pending. Monetary awards by the special court cannot, of course, cover more than a fraction of the true losses suffered by people needlessly uprooted and subjected to indignities of historic proportions.

CHAPTER 7

The greatest threat to tyranny and the greatest protector of freedom is truth.

O N J U N E 13, 1942, President Roosevelt signed an executive order which established the Office of War Information I had recommended to him in late 1941. He selected Elmer Davis, correspondent, columnist, and broadcaster, to head the new agency. Davis indicated that he would accept, provided the President would appoint an associate director who was "skilled in governmental organization and information matters." He explained to the President that he had never had anyone work for him, other than a part-time secretary. He confessed that he knew nothing about organizing or administering what obviously would be an agency with thousands of employees.

And so the President sent for me. Elmer Davis was with him when I was ushered into the oval office. My first impression of Davis was his eyes—they were piercing, almost accusing. They were made even more prominent by his ruddy complexion and plentiful white hair. Davis scowled when we were introduced and began abruptly to question me about my background, attitudes, and experience.

Apparently satisfied with my biographical data, Davis fastened his sharp eyes on me and asked bluntly: "Can you get control of the information being issued by all these government agencies, especially the War and Navy departments? That's the important thing," he said without waiting for my answer. "I just don't have much faith that very much of the information being handed out is reliable," he continued, "and that must change. This is a people's war and the people have a right to know what is going on. There must be no camouflaging of unfavorable information and no sitting on bad news until it can be offset by good news." He gestured sharply to emphasize how strongly he felt about these matters. "We must establish at once in the minds of our own people and the rest of the world that the United States Government will tell the truth day in and day out about all developments, policies, and objectives in the war."

I was delighted to accept this new assignment (fortunately, for I really had no choice), partly because it relieved me at once of the unhappy task in the War Relocation Authority, but also because I felt that Elmer Davis and I, coming from differing backgrounds and with varying views, would have interesting experiences together. I thought we could co-operate without difficulty. And we did.

The first task was to start the organization the President had approved. We created two major divisions of the Office of War Information: a domestic branch, headed by Mike Cowles of the Cowles Publications, and an overseas branch headed by Robert E. Sherwood, playwright and intimate friend of the President. To unify operations, the central office consisted of the director, the associate director, an assistant director for planning and policies, and an assistant director who was given responsibility for financial, personnel, and business management aspects of the agency. The top policy council was comprised of these four, plus the domestic and overseas directors.

OWI was directly responsible to the President and it was understood that we were to have access to him at all times.

At first Elmer himself kept in touch with the President, the Secretary of State, and the Secretaries of the War and Navy departments about policies and programs affecting the world-wide information effort. Soon he insisted that I accompany him on such visits. I had the task of forming and administering the work of the organization and seeing to it that the informational output of all federal agencies from Agriculture to Treasury was co-ordinated with the central program and adhered strictly to the facts. There was to be no slanting of the news, no "propaganda" in the normally accepted meaning of that term.

The first serious problem for OWI came as a result of two naval engagements in the South Pacific. American ships were attacked at night by a portion of the Japanese fleet, the result being disastrous for us. One cruiser was sunk, two others were seriously damaged, and two destroyers and one transport were crippled beyond repair.

Fortunately the Japanese fleet withdrew in darkness and did not realize the extent of the chaos it had caused. Replacement ships were speedily transferred from the Atlantic to close the gap in our naval forces. On the very eve of their arrival in the South Pacific, the Japanese fleet attacked again, but this time American ships were victorious. While the two engagements occurred a week or so apart, news of them came out on successive days—August 11 and 12, 1942. The first news release cautiously acknowledged the Japanese victory. The next one gave the facts about the American victory. Combined, the two stories indicated that gains by the United States naval, air, and land forces in the Tulagi area of the Solomon Islands "outweighed our losses."

Elmer Davis was uncontrollably angry. To him this was proof that the military establishment was managing the news, in direct violation of the policy approved by President Roosevelt. With fire in his eyes, he hauled me off for a confrontation with the United States Navy.

We met first with the navy information officer, but Davis was not satisfied with his explanation and demanded to see Admiral King at once.

Admiral King was a dignified man, impressive in his neat uniform. He never smiled, but he was not unfriendly. Patiently he explained that news had been withheld about the defeat of our ships for two reasons: first, if the Japanese had known about the extent of the damage they had done, our remaining military forces in the South Pacific would have been at their mercy; we needed desperately to get reinforcements into the area before the Japanese discovered how crippled we were. Second, it was the policy of the Navy Department to notify next of kin about casualties before the news was made public. These two purposes had been fulfilled on the day the news of the Japanese victory was issued— more than a week after the battle. Admiral King insisted that it was sheer coincidence that the next day, upon the arrival of our ships from the Atlantic, a significant victory had been scored against the Japanese.

Davis did not accept this explanation and bluntly said so. Admiral King's reaction was instantaneous. He rose from his chair, militarily erect, and said in a neutral tone, free of anger, "Mr. Davis, our conversation is finished. If you wish to see Secretary Knox, that is your privilege."

My own reaction to King's explanation was mixed. I was struck by an apparent contradiction. A news release delayed until next of kin could be notified? No such delay followed the second naval engagement in which the U. S. Navy was victorious. Perhaps there were no American casualties in that second battle, and so no need to delay while next of kin were contacted.

More important by far was the admiral's explanation that the first battle was kept secret until reinforcements could reach the South Pacific. As I pondered that situation I was struck as I have been so often in my life by the complexity of most situations. Here were two admirable principles in conflict. Elmer Davis insisted, and I agreed, that accurate and truthful information about the war should flow freely to the people. On the other hand, the immediate release of the Japanese victory could well have resulted in great American losses of life and matériel. Davis was apparently convinced that the navy had withheld news of the first battle primarily to avoid embarrassment and loss of face. That may well have been a consideration, but how could one ever really know?

From the time of our meeting with Admiral King, Davis assigned me the task of keeping in touch with the War and Navy departments. I believed in the integrity of the officers and the Secretaries of War and Navy with whom we dealt, and thus had no difficulty in carrying out the assignment.

In meeting the responsibility of co-ordinating the informational activities of the multitude of federal agencies that were not part of OWI, I created an informal council of the heads of the relevant information offices. At one of our weekly meetings I learned that the President had divided the Department of Agriculture into two separate agencies; one became the War Food Administration, headed by Chester Davis, a superb administrator, a sound policy man, and a thorough student of American agriculture. It comprised essentially all of the action agencies previously in the Cabinet department. Its task was to speed the production of food and fiber and to arrange shipments to Allied nations. For the first time in more than twenty years agricultural prices soared to heights that exceeded the parity objective of the federal farm program. Unlimited demand had achieved what crop reduction and payments to farmers could not do in times of surplus production and sluggish demand.

Remaining in the Department of Agriculture in this reorganization were the "old line" bureaus, namely research, regulatory, extension, and informational agencies. Claude Wickard remained as Secretary of the humiliated department. I was distressed by this totally unnecessary division of an important executive agency. It was clear to me that once again President Roosevelt was unwilling to fire an appointee in whom he had lost confidence. We had often seen the President kick a man upstairs or create a special project for him rather than take the difficult step of discharging him.

My work in OWI was not unrelated to the responsibilities that began to devolve on General Eisenhower.

Shortly after the Japanese attack on Pearl Harbor and before the Office of War Information was established, Brigadier General Dwight D. Eisenhower was summoned to Washington to become assistant head, then head, of the War Plans Division under General George Marshall. Mrs. Eisenhower remained in Texas for several months to close the house, arrange for the move to Washington, and settle other personal affairs. She once said to my wife, "From long experience I know that when I finally get new draperies hung in our quarters Ike will be transferred and I have to start the moving process all over again."

In their long and happy married life, Ike and Mamie were to own only one home of their own—the magnificent estate at Gettysburg. In the early thirties they had been stationed in Washington. There, the two Eisenhower families lived within a few blocks of one another. It was then that Ike and I found satisfaction and mutual helpfulness in working together. He was my best critic, and I was his. The two families were together a great deal, often several nights a week, having potluck suppers and playing acceptable games of bridge. It was a happy time. Later we would laugh about the fact that Ike, then a major, was referred to as "Milton's brother."

We would also recall that often when we worked together rather late I would call Mamie and he would call my wife Helen, and each of us would say: "Darling, I'll be home about eight o'clock." Our voices were identical on the telephone, and our wives never caught on.

When General Eisenhower was called to Washington after Pearl Harbor, he made his home with us while waiting for Mamie to move from Texas. He would leave our home in Falls Church, Virginia, early in the morning. Our cook and houseman would get up at six-thirty in order to serve his breakfast by seven. He was in his office by seven-thirty each day. When he came home, usually late at night, having had a skimpy lunch and dinner at his desk, he would go at once to our children's bedrooms, waken them, and have a relaxing chat. Our son, Milton—called Bud—was then eleven, and our daughter Ruth, three. They loved Uncle Ike and happily responded when he woke them. A moment after he said good night and left their rooms they were sound asleep again; it is an unhappy fact that I have never been able to achieve this kind of relaxation. Fortunately my children, now married with families of their own, did not inherit my difficulty.

While these nightly visits were under way my wife would go to the kitchen and prepare a light but nutritious meal, nearly always including a pot of cocoa, which helped Ike get to sleep.

It was during this period that Ike came home one evening, rather excited for him, and obviously with something he could hardly wait to tell me. He had received orders to go to England as commander of American forces there, and that afternoon he had been summoned to the White House for a conference with President Roosevelt.

The war was still going against us and the mood of the country was one of somber concern. Ike expected that President Roosevelt, with all that was obviously weighing on his mind, would be deadly serious and harried. The conference, Ike was sure, would be businesslike, full of military and strategic considerations.

As he entered the President's office Roosevelt looked up and said abruptly:

"Well, General, your baby brother is causing me an awful lot of trouble and I've just had to spend an hour on him."

Taken aback, Ike replied: "Do you mean my brother Milton?"

"I do," said the President. "Four different government departments want him, and I have to decide which one will be lucky enough to get him."

When Mamie arrived from Texas and established a new home in a spacious apartment on Connecticut Avenue beyond the Taft Bridge, our place lost a warm presence. We greatly missed Ike.

Shortly afterward, he was transferred to the United Kingdom as head of American forces in Europe. Mamie's life at this point was a trying one. Ike's specific activities and his whereabouts were necessarily secret. Although Mamie understood the need for secrecy, she could not help worrying about Ike's safety and the safety of the forces under his command. During this period she spent nearly every weekend at our Virginia home, which greatly pleased Helen and me, for Mamie, in addition to being a relative, was one of our closest friends. We thoroughly enjoyed her company.

In connection with my duties at OWI, I learned that General Eisenhower had been named Allied commander for the invasion of North

Africa. On the night of the invasion—November 8, 1942—Mamie, several friends, my wife, and I were playing cards in our recreation room. Knowing that the announcement of the invasion, with a message from General Eisenhower, would be broadcast at nine o'clock that evening, I kept a radio turned on so that we would not miss the initial part of the announcement. Mamie was puzzled at this and perhaps slightly annoyed.

"Milton, why do you keep that radio going?" she asked. "You're the one who always complains about the radio when we're playing cards!"

I said that the President was expected to make an announcement of interest to OWI, and that seemed to satisfy her.

When the invasion announcement was made, and a personal statement by General Eisenhower rang through the room, Mamie was silent. Tears came to her eyes, but for a long time she said nothing. When the program ended and the excitement had diminished, Mamie turned to me and said: "Milton, I am proud of you for not telling me."

The OWI task in the North African invasion was to place certain men on the invasion ships and have them use every method they could to persuade the French not to oppose the landing of Allied forces. They were to emphasize that the United States had no quarrel with the French; we only wished to move against the occupying Germans and Italians. After the landing, OWI people were to do what was essential to see to it that truthful information about all aspects of the Allied operations reached the local population and the outside world.

France at the time, it will be remembered, had surrendered to Germany at Compiègne. Half the nation was in the hands of Adolf Hitler; the rest was governed by an odd combination of idealists and defeatists at Vichy. Marshal Pétain, hero of World War I, had been designated as the leader of the Vichy government and had called on all French citizens to be loyal to it.

By signing an armistice with Nazi Germany and establishing the Vichy government, the French scored two significant gains: first, they retained their great naval fleet under Admiral Jean Darlan—Pétain's deputy—and thus kept it out of the hands of Germany; even more importantly, they kept their colonial empire intact, particularly North Africa, which was a stable and thriving economy untouched by Europe's wars. North Africa was the heart of France's overseas empire. There were 125,000 first-line troops in Morocco, Algeria, and Tunisia, and another

200,000 in reserve. The native populations were seemingly content with the benevolent colonial regimes.

But the armistice and the creation of the Vichy government also bitterly divided Frenchmen. There were not many Frenchmen who were sorry to see the fall of the Third Republic, for it was weak, unstable, and uninspiring. Nonetheless many of the French, epitomized by Charles de Gaulle, who headed an exile government in England, considered the Vichy government traitorous; calling themselves the "Free French," they were determined to fight Germany to the death.

In planning the invasion of North Africa, the United States was anxious to avoid combat with the French troops there. Since these troops were under the command of the Vichy government, which was technically neutral, they would be compelled to resist the Allied landing. Nearly all of the French officers were either supporters of the Vichy government or had sworn not to bear arms against Germany as a condition of their release after Germany had defeated France. Marshal Pétain was unwilling to co-operate with the Allies and maintained that his forces would have to resist an invasion, for otherwise he believed Germany would take over the whole of France and its colonial empire in retaliation. It is important to understand that the French forces in North Africa were professional soldiers. Their pay and subsequent pensions depended on their obeying the head of the French government, no matter what their opinion of the provisional government might be.

The United States, therefore, through its political representative, Robert Murphy, convinced General Henri Giraud to work with the French forces in North Africa to try to persuade them not to fight the Allies. Giraud was a war hero—one of the few to emerge untainted from the debacle of 1941. He had escaped from the Nazis and had a price on his head. He had not sworn to refrain from fighting Germany. It was agreed that Giraud would become the senior French military and political leader when the invasion had succeeded and order had been restored.

As soon as the Allied forces had landed at Rabat, Oran, and Algiers, Murphy contacted General Alphonse Juin, the Vichy commander-in-chief of ground forces for all North Africa, to arrange an immediate cease-fire. To his amazement, Murphy discovered that Admiral Darlan himself was in Algiers and, since the admiral outranked Juin, the latter was powerless. Moreover, General Giraud simply did not have the stature to overcome the great prestige which all loyal Frenchmen accorded to Darlan.

Admiral Darlan's unexpected presence there in Algeria was apparently accidental, since his son had contracted polio and was undergoing treatment in an Algerian clinic. But Darlan may have known in advance of invasion plans, since he had his own intelligence service. In any case, his presence upset Allied plans. As the number two man to Pétain, the highest-ranking French military officer on active duty, and the esteemed commander of the powerful French navy (which, for the most part, was resting quietly in harbors around the world), Darlan was able to dominate the situation.

After some heavy fighting, Darlan was captured by Allied forces. An agreement was quickly hammered out whereby he would proclaim a cease-fire throughout all of French North Africa and would enlist the loyalty of all Vichy officers in the common cause of liberating France from the Germans. In exchange, the Allies would confirm Darlan as the political and military head of all North African French on a temporary basis until a permanent settlement could be worked out.

I was in President Roosevelt's office when he approved what he termed a temporary co-operation with Admiral Darlan. He did this, he said, solely to save American and British lives, and to accelerate our primary mission, which was to defeat the German and Italian forces in North Africa. He insisted that co-operation with Darlan would end as soon as our major goals had been fulfilled.

The President stressed the "temporariness" of the Darlan deal because he knew very well that it would generate considerable criticism from the Free French and from liberal Americans. Admiral Darlan was considered a renegade and traitor by many Frenchmen and Americans. For more than two years he had worked closely with the Nazis and had been broadcasting anti-De Gaulle and anti-British propaganda. It is also true, however, that many French people viewed Darlan as something of a saint. He had helped to save unoccupied France from German domination; he had arranged for the repatriation of many French prisoners of war; he had, in effect, kept part of France alive during the two years since the German victory.

When the deal made with Darlan became public, it precipitated one of the sharpest controversies of the war. American columnists and commentators were highly critical. My friend Ed Murrow, whose daily reports were informative and lucid, issued a blast against the Darlan arrangement. "What the hell is all this about?" he wanted to know. "Are we fighting Nazis or sleeping with them?" Didn't we see, Murrow asked, that we could lose this war in winning it? Why this play with traitors?

Raymond Gram Swing took a temperate view. Frazier Hunt was critical. Walter Lippmann was cautious. Ernest Lindley felt the United States was saving American and British lives, avoiding trouble with the French, and focusing on the need to destroy the real enemy.

Archibald MacLeish, the poet, a dedicated public servant and an indispensable member of the OWI policy team, met with Secretary Stimson and Secretary Morgenthau. Morgenthau demanded a repudiation of the agreement, but Stimson said that he would consider anyone who opposed the Darlan arrangement at that stage a traitor. Word came in that Wendell Willkie was about to make a radio speech in which he would denounce Darlan. Stimson telephoned him and used blunt, even violent language to change his plans. Willkie made appropriate deletions.

The President, in a press conference, again emphasized the temporary nature of the arrangement with Darlan. No one should think that we had chosen to work with Vichy France as opposed to the Free French, he explained. When France was liberated, as it surely would be, the French people would establish their own government and certainly no one doubted that the choice would be for a form of representative government. This seemed to calm the situation for a time.

Then two other things happened. Reports began coming in from Britain that the British government had not been consulted about the agreement, that Eden was "standing up" for De Gaulle, that De Gaulle had to be censored to prevent him from completely upsetting the applecart, and that De Gaulle wanted to come to the United States to protest to President Roosevelt.

A second incident was, in some respects, even more serious. Secretary Stimson issued a public letter to Archduke Otto of Austria—son of the last Hapsburg emperor and pretender to the throne—authorizing him to recruit an Austrian legion in the United States to fight on the side of the Allies. This was seized upon by some of the same persons who had criticized the Darlan arrangement. What was this? A restoration of the Austrian dynasty? Had we more agreements up our sleeve that would affect Czechoslovakia, Hungary, Poland? Wasn't this proof that our recognition of Vichy France was an indication that we did not distinguish between true friend and foe?

I rushed to the office of the director of information in the War Department, General Surles. From him I learned that Stimson had issued the letter at the insistence of the State Department. So I asked Surles to have Secretary Stimson make the State Department letter public, and then rushed back to see Elmer Davis with the suggestion that he see Secretary of State Cordell Hull at once and develop the facts. Davis got the facts—from Under Secretary Sumner Welles. The *President* had given the order to the State Department, which had transmitted it to Secretary Stimson. The next day Secretary Stimson, in a press conference, said that the letter to Archduke Otto was the result of consultation between State and War, the authorization had no political implications whatsoever, and any other foreign national, Austrian or otherwise, who wished to recruit forces to fight on the side of the Allies would be welcomed by the United States Government.

This might have settled the matter but now we faced a continuing difficulty. We in the United States were receiving very few dispatches from Algeria. The press carried monitored reports from Radio Moroc at Rabat—a flood of material from London which was a rewrite of Radio Moroc broadcasts. All this material had an undertone of criticism of the Allies. It was obvious to us in OWI that distortions were the rule rather than the exception. We wanted to know why this was so.

I urged President Roosevelt to send Harry Hopkins to North Africa for a personal investigation and a report to the American people. Hopkins, a recognized liberal and close to the President, would on his return aid in quieting the fears of an important segment of our population. I also wanted Hopkins to make clear that political decisions were made by politicians and not by military commanders. I was of course concerned about the criticism being leveled at General Eisenhower, but I felt it highly important, as I looked to the larger issues that would come when an invasion of Europe was mounted, to have the American people understand that political decisions in war, as in peace, had to be made by the President. The Constitution surely made that clear.

Evidently I was persuasive up to a point in my presentation, for the President concurred as to the need for clarifying information. Instead of sending Harry Hopkins to North Africa he pointed his finger at me and said that I would have to go.

He gave me four specific assignments: (1) to study the work of OWI in psychological warfare and make changes if they were needed; (2) to find out why the Darlan agreement and our military actions were being misrepresented and make corrections if I could; (3) to develop at least the preliminary phases of a plan for psychological warfare in succeeding military operations (which turned out to be Sicily and Italy); and (4) to see what could be done with the French refugees who were fleeing from occupied France through Spain and Portugal to North Africa, where they threatened to impede our military operations.

Hastily I obtained a special passport, a high-priority transportation number, visas, and inoculations. Late that afternoon I returned to the White House and had an hour alone with the President. He expressed great confidence in General Eisenhower and in Robert Murphy, who was serving as American political adviser at command headquarters. He explained in detail why for the next several months it was essential for Admiral Darlan to co-operate with General Eisenhower. He felt that a straightforward statement by General Eisenhower on the current situation was needed, and perhaps a subsequent statement by Admiral Darlan would help. He discussed what the future might bring in a political way but expressed confidence, as he had in his press conference, that all would turn out well so far as France was concerned.

I left Washington on December 7 and flew from New York to Bermuda, then on to Gibraltar, and to Algiers. The flight from New York to North Africa was frightening. I was accompanying General Walter Bedell Smith, who was being sent out to serve as General Eisenhower's chief of staff. He was one of the ablest men I ever knew—a man whose exterior gruffness and abrupt speech hid a great inner warmth. The seaplane fought turbulent weather all the way to Bermuda. The next day, as we approached Gibraltar, General Smith became concerned about the absence of American planes that were supposed to provide us with air cover, for German planes were very active in that area, mainly in attacking Allied shipping. As we flew, finally, from Gibraltar to Algiers in an army bomber, we saw damaged planes on the ground beneath us.

Upon my arrival at General Eisenhower's quarters, I became ill from the series of inoculations I had received. As I lay in bed with a fever and an aching body, I could hear bombs exploding uncomfortably nearby. It was my first experience in an active war zone.

As soon as I was able to carry on I sought the facts about the misleading information pouring from North Africa into every area of the world, including the United States. Command headquarters had been much too busy with problems of supplies, transportation of forces, military organization, and preparation for an advance against the enemy to be concerned or even informed about misleading propaganda being disseminated.

I learned what was going on from several newspapermen. Invasion ships, in sinking, had cut the cable connection between Algiers and the United Kingdom. The limited military communications system was clogged with official messages. So American newsmen had no way of transmitting dispatches to their newspapers. The news reaching the world was obtained exclusively by the monitoring in London of the broadcasts of Radio Moroc, a powerful station which, amazingly, was in the hands of Free French sympathizers. Understandably the broadcasters were furious over the agreement with Darlan, whom they detested, so they lost no opportunity to broadcast unfriendly reports about all that was developing in North Africa.

I conferred immediately with General Eisenhower and General Smith and explained how the erroneous information was undermining morale at home—especially how it was causing dissension between liberals and conservatives. General Eisenhower telephoned Darlan and said he wished the admiral would see his brother, who was at headquarters as a personal representative of President Roosevelt. In five minutes a staff car took me to Darlan's headquarters. With the help of an interpreter, though Darlan understood a good deal of English, I explained the problem.

"What do you want me to do?" he asked.

I replied that I wanted the personnel of Radio Moroc relieved of their assignments. OWI men who had moved into the area with General Patton would be placed in charge.

Darlan smiled, but the smile was bitter. He picked up the telephone, called Rabat, and issued orders in French which were not interpreted for me.

"Very well, Mr. Eisenhower," he said, "your people can take charge of the radio station tonight at midnight."

I started to thank him, but he waved my remarks away and said:

"I know what you Americans think of me. Your President thinks that I am a lemon to be held until all the juice has been squeezed out. Then the rind will be discarded. That is all right with me. I am co-operating with you not for the benefit of the United States or Great Britain [he hated the British], but for the good of France."

My one visit with Darlan left me with the impression of an enigmatic and complex man. If his hatred of the British was readily evident, I did not sense in him any liking for the Nazis. Rather I felt he was a conservative patriot, prepared to do whatever he had to do for the benefit of France. His personality was purely a military one, austere, stern, confident of his ability to command, not unfriendly but making no effort to impress me.

As it turned out, Admiral Darlan's telephone call did not solve the problem. Setting out to replace the Free French sympathizers running Radio Moroc, I witnessed once again the difficulty of building a large organization quickly and having it function effectively and in harmony with government policy. Most of the men and women who had been recruited into the overseas division of OWI were former foreign correspondents, an independent group, usually more at ease criticizing public policy than in disseminating information concerning it. Many of them were indifferent to the distinction between their previous roles as private newsmen and their responsibilities as representatives of the United States Government.

The President of the United States had approved a temporary agreement with Darlan, exclusively to advance our own central war purpose. He expected, and had a right to expect, everyone connected with the government, in military or civilian status, to abide by his decision. This was not accepted by some of the persons I put in charge of Radio Moroc. They were sympathetic to the Free French and opposed to Pétain and everything connected with Vichy France. They openly opposed our dealing even temporarily with Darlan. While their broadcasts, still being monitored in London and flashed to the world by Reuters and the Associated Press, were somewhat more restrained than before, nonetheless their hostility to the general situation was evident in all they did. It soon became necessary to replace them as quickly as possible. The situation did not become satisfactory until C. D. Jackson, a leading journalist from *Time-Life,* flew to North Africa and took full charge of OWI operations.

When cable communication to London was restored, the complex situation in North Africa was clarified and I felt that thereafter the people of the free world obtained a factual picture of all that was going on. Most dispatches to the United States were now written by American correspondents and sent directly to their papers, not through a monitoring and rewrite office in London.

I completed the four assignments President Roosevelt had given me shortly before Christmas, and so went to Oran to arrange for a return flight to the United States. Six of us, all civilians, boarded a plane at three o'clock on the morning of the twenty-fourth of December for a flight to Accra, where we would change to a plane that would take us to Ascension Island, then to Belém in Brazil, and from there to Washington.

The plane out of Oran was unheated. The metal bucket seats were very cold and very hard. As we climbed over the Atlas Mountains and set a course across the Sahara Desert, the temperature inside the plane kept falling. Even with a heavy overcoat, two pairs of heavy trousers, and thick woolen socks, I nearly froze. The cockpit was moderately warm, so each passenger was permitted to go there in turn and stay for about ten minutes. We had no food or refreshments.

When we arrived at Accra, I was asked for my health certificate and was at once told that, since I had not had a yellow fever shot, I could not proceed. I could obtain an inoculation in Accra, of course, but would be delayed there for some weeks while the shot "cooked." At first I was desperate. Then I remembered that Accra was under General Eisenhower's command. My name and the urgency of my assignment enabled me to gain an exception and I was permitted to proceed—with the warning that if I came again without a yellow fever inoculation I would be held.

I spent Christmas on Ascension Island, a speck of land in the South Atlantic just large enough to accommodate a large airport, housing for a small contingent of troops, and a mess hall. Christmas dinner was an omelet made from dried eggs, canned Spam, and a glass of powdered milk, followed by a cup of coffee that had undoubtedly been made from laundry water and brewed a week before.

When we put down in Belém, an American officer gave us startling news: Admiral Darlan had been shot on Christmas Eve by a young French Algerian who was executed by a firing squad two days later, before much could be learned about his motives. No matter that Darlan was not the type of French leader I could admire; he had by one command stopped the French forces in North Africa from fighting us. He had thus enabled us to concentrate our efforts against the Germans and Italians. I was sorry that by assassination he was prevented from telling his own story when the war was over.

My arrival at the Washington airport was a tense end to a harrowing experience. The airport was fogged in, as were possible alternative landing strips. We circled, awaiting a change in the situation. Finally, after about an hour, we received instructions from the pilot to congregate in the rear of the plane. He explained that we were almost out of fuel and we were going to attempt a landing; if there was an accident there would be less danger of the plane's nosing over and causing great damage, possibly fire. Fortunately we broke out of the fog at about one hundred feet and made a bumpy but safe landing. Mamie and Helen were at the airport to meet me. They were as nervous and exhausted as I was, for they had heard the droning of the plane overhead, had been kept informed of our problem by a man in the control tower, and obviously feared that we might not make it.

Not infrequently when I relax in a comfortable seat in a modern jet with its temperature controls, and am served dry martinis and rare steak by a pretty stewardess while I listen to stereophonic music and zoom through the skies at six hundred miles an hour, I remember that endless and miserable flight from Algiers to Washington.

Early the next morning I went to the President's office. When I had completed my report and rose to go, the President motioned for me to sit down again. He was in a pensive mood.

"Did you notice the agricultural situation in Algeria and French Morocco?" he asked me.

"To some degree," I replied. "I drove into the rural areas of Algeria but did not get into Morocco." I added, however, that I knew in general that before the area had been ravaged by war the fertile lands lying between the sea and the Atlas Mountains had produced wheat, barley, fruits, vegetables, mutton, wool, olive oil, and wine—very good wine. Climatically and topographically, the coastal region was similar to the San Joaquin, Sacramento, and Salinas valleys of California. Prior to

143

the war, French North Africa had exported surpluses to the continent of Europe. Most farms were very small, but estates of the native nobility were large. If production could be brought back to normal, there would be enough food for North Africans and a good amount for the British and American forces in the area. And if we could supply machinery, fertilizers, seeds, and even clothing and food, the restoration of a productive agriculture could be speeded up.

Unfortunately, I went on, the Nazis, having taken all they could from continental France, had seized everything they could get their hands on in North Africa—food, clothing, pharmaceuticals, pipe, cement, and anything else that was movable. Even articles such as soap, shaving cream, brushes, and the like were now unobtainable. Many stores were closed. Goods were so scarce that money was useless. Barter was the rule. Men would work for wheat or meat or sugar or salt, but not for money, which couldn't buy anything.

President Roosevelt was deeply interested. I knew from previous discussions with him that he had an amazing knowledge of world food and fiber production. He seemed to know a great deal about every major river system and drainage basin in the world.

"You know, Milton, when the war is over," he said, "it would be wonderful to go to North Africa and trap the waters that now flow from the Atlas Mountains into the ocean. We could build dams and create one of the finest irrigation systems in the world."

The President knew very well that I was a conservative on matters of fiscal policy, though in agreement with him on questions of human values and programs. So I realized he was needling me when he added, "Of course, it would cost a lot of money; but who cares about cost?" He laughed heartily and waited for my retort.

"You might find, Mr. President, that when the war is over and our own surpluses again depress prices of farm products American farmers would not look kindly on using American dollars to expand agricultural production in North Africa."

We enjoyed a good laugh together.

Afterward I met with General Surles and the Secretary of War to report. General Surles, after our major business was complete, said to me: "Mr. Eisenhower, you must stop the press from calling General Eisenhower 'Ike.' It isn't dignified for the commander of Allied operations to be called by his nickname. No one calls General MacArthur 'Mac' or General Gerow 'Gee.' "

Obviously there was nothing I could do to change the practices of newsmen and editors. Had I been prescient I might have replied, "But, General, I like Ike." The fact was that the name "Eisenhower" was too long for easy headline writing, while "Ike" was a head writer's dream. (As the years passed, the name Ike became universal. In trips to Latin America with the President, I heard millions of people shout, "EE-kay!" Wherever Ike went, as general or President, the crowds shouted, with affection and joy, "Ike!"—or a curious mispronunciation of it.)

Before that long day ended, Elmer Davis and I had a serious conversation about what I deemed to be insubordination, almost treason, in the overseas branch of OWI. Not only had personnel not been adequately trained to carry out presidential policies, but our control offices for broadcasts to friendly, neutral, and enemy nations were in New York where the top personnel were not directly in touch with changing policies or with persons authorized to explain them. I insisted that these offices be moved to Washington and that the head of each major branch be given responsibility, under our direction, for keeping in touch with the State, War, and Navy departments, the War Production Board, and even, when necessary, the White House, so that their directives to writers and broadcasters in New York and throughout the world could give us assurance that our work was in harmony with official war policies and plans. Reluctantly, Davis agreed to do this. Although the problem was not completely solved by this move, there was noticeable improvement. Still, when Mussolini fled and was murdered, and Marshal Pietro Badoglio became provisional head of the Italian government and arranged for the surrender of Italian troops, OWI overseas personnel were openly critical of this political arrangement approved by the President. Before the war was over, Edward Barrett, an extremely intelligent man who understood government operations, became director of the overseas branch. He quickly got control of the world-wide operation and, so far as I know, there never again was a blatant disregard of the President's orders.

Late in the spring of 1943, President Roosevelt directed me to go to Quebec and make preparations for a conference which he, Winston Churchill, and their military advisers would attend in August. I was cautioned about one point: Prime Minister Mackenzie King would serve as host for the bilateral conference, but it was important that the conference not be considered to be a tripartite one, for this would be offensive to other Allies. The major purposes of the conference were to extend limited recognition to the French Committee of National Liberation, headed by General de Gaulle, and to agree on military plans for a landing in France in 1944.

An American military plane took me to Montreal, where I boarded a small, single-motor, unreliable, shaky plane that took me to Quebec. I had no difficulty in bringing about an understanding among the British, Canadian, and American personnel who were on hand, or in reviewing and approving the arrangements for the conference itself. The same small plane returned me to Montreal, where I faced a difficulty. No American military plane was available to take me to Washington, yet I was expected to report back to the President that night. A Captain Hall located an American-made, British-operated two-engine ship which was idle; the pilot and copilot said they would gladly fly me to Washington—indeed, they would enjoy a respite from routine duties in Montreal. As we sped down the runway for the take-off, the right motor seemed to explode, black smoke spilled out, and the motor died. We taxied back to the terminal building and the British pilot said, "I think we can get this ship in shape in about half an hour."

An hour later we were airborne, but we had not been more than twenty minutes in flight when black smoke began pouring into the cabin. The copilot rushed back, helped me put on a parachute, and said, "Move back to the door. If we are high enough, jump, count three, and then pull the cord. If we are not high enough, just jump and pull!" Then he added, "Wait just a moment. I have to help the captain. I'll be back to open the door."

I am not an especially brave person. In fact, I suspect I have more nerves exposed to worry than is normal. For some strange reason, though, I remained perfectly calm for the time being. I took off my glasses, carefully placed them in a shirt pocket where I hoped they would not be broken, and moved my suitcase as near the door as I could. I did not intend to leave my personal belongings, along with official papers, in a plane that might crash and be burned. I planned to push the suitcase out and then jump myself. There flashed into my mind an inane story a soldier had told me in Washington. He and others had been taken up for the first practice jump in a parachute division. When the plane was in proper position, eleven men jumped but one private remained in a bucket seat. The sergeant in charge yelled for him to make the practice jump but he replied, "I don't believe in practicing what you have to do right the first time anyway!"

The copilot who was going to shove me out of the plane returned in about three minutes and said that the automatic fire extinguisher had functioned. The fire was out. The pilot intended, if he could, to put back to the Montreal airport, where a rocky landing was in prospect. I could jump or stay with the plane. I looked out the window. We were losing altitude and were in the center of the vast expanse of the cold and forbidding waters of the St. Lawrence River. So I stayed where I was.

We made a fairly normal landing. Out the window as we taxied to a stop I saw a fire engine, an ambulance, and several sedans. As the door was opened and I stepped out, a British officer, grinning, remarked, "Well, sah, we had the meat wagon all a-waitin' for you!" All the pent-up nervousness now broke forth. I started to fall, shaking uncontrollably. Captain Hall supported me and suggested I come to his office where he had just the thing to fix me up. From his desk he took a bottle of bourbon and poured about five ounces of the stuff, neat, into a glass. I gulped it down like a gunman in a Western movie. It helped.

Now the task was to get to the White House. No other military plane was available and I had no intention of trying that British-operated ship again. I found that a commercial flight would take me to New York. In New York I took an overnight sleeper on the Pennsylvania Railroad to Washington, and thus arrived at the White House early in the morning, about fourteen hours late.

When my official report was made, I told the President of the experience. It cheered him a good deal. He laughed heartily and reported on several narrow escapes he had had during the past year.

Elmer Davis and I had many conversations about the possible life of the Office of War Information. We agreed, of course, that what we were doing was an essential part of the war effort. But we were convinced that the transmission of news, ideas, and explanations of national policies and programs should be a private undertaking when the war was over. Information internationally disseminated by governments in peacetime could be dangerous. That issued by unfriendly nations could keep leaders and peoples on edge, could mislead masses of peoples, and might even be a cause of a future war. At the right time we would need intellectual disarmament as much as we would need to reduce the warmaking powers of all nations. While the United Nations Educational, Scientific, and Cultural Organization concept had not yet been formulated, we found agreement between us that the development of genuine understanding among the peoples of the world was one of the indispensable ingredients of a total program for peace. Understanding would not guarantee peace, but there would be no peace until leaders and peoples had full knowledge of the histories, customs, problems, and purposes of at least the leading powers of the world. There might therefore be a place for an unbiased international organization which would have the responsibility for developing this type of genuine, peace-building understanding, but it should not be the task of individual governments. Our view proved to be in vain, for, as is well known, immediately after the close of hostilities the Soviet Union began broadcasting to all areas of the world in forty-two languages (today, eighty languages) gross misrepresentations of the actions and purposes of the United States and other free nations, and misrepresenting its own intentions and methods. In self-defense, the United States, Great Britain, France, and other countries had to maintain regular programs of information, a practice which still obtains. Mutual intellectual disarmament has not occurred and is not today seriously considered. It should be.

Either Davis or I, sometimes both, attended most of the President's press conferences. Normally, these were held in the President's oval office. He would remain seated at his desk while newspapermen stood, close together and filling every foot of the large office. Once, in early April as I recall, I was standing near the President's desk when the newspapermen filed out. I started to go with them but the President motioned for me to remain. He obviously wanted to say something in confidence, so I went to his side of the desk, as close to him as propriety permitted. As I leaned slightly toward him the President reached to my side and picked up his burning cigarette in the inevitable long black holder. With a gleam in his eye he said, "Milton, watch Joe Barnes. He's running Wendell Willkie for President!" Joseph Barnes, on leave from the New York *Herald Tribune*, was a valuable member of the OWI staff. I knew that Barnes was a close friend of Willkie's and had traveled extensively with him, but I had no hint that Willkie, defeated in the 1940 election, had any thought of running again. My only comment to the President was that it seemed to me that Dewey would be the Republican nominee for the presidency in 1944. President Roosevelt waved jauntily and dismissed me with a final "Just watch Joe Barnes!" This was the first and only intimation I had, before leaving the federal service, that President Roosevelt, by now a tired man, was thinking of running for a fourth term.

CHAPTER 8

A President may employ the knowledge and inspiration of many confidants, but they have no recourse if he outgrows and abandons them.

EARLY IN MAY 1943 a member of the Board of Regents of the Kansas State University (then called the Kansas State College, my alma mater) came to my office and told me that I was under serious consideration for the presidency of Kansas State to succeed Dr. F. D. Farrell.

Elmer Davis was agreeable to my looking into the matter, so I flew early one morning to Kansas City, spent several hours with the Board of Regents, and then returned to my work in Washington. By mail, I subsequently received a formal offer of the presidency of the college. For six weeks Helen and I discussed the alternatives of beginning a new career in educational administration or remaining in the federal service. While for the past eighteen months I had accepted presidential assignments outside the career service, I was entitled to resume my former status when the war ended.

On May 22, to keep a speaking engagement I had accepted months before, I flew to Topeka and met with the Kansas Bankers' Association. This gave me an opportunity to renew acquaintances in my home state, from which I had been absent for nearly two decades, and to talk further with one member of the Kansas Board of Regents who was publisher of the Topeka *State Journal*.

As soon as I returned to Washington I wrote to General Eisenhower, not as has been reported often to get his advice on my decision, but to ask whether he felt I could in good conscience leave a war task before the conflict was over. He said in his reply that we had to be as concerned about the strength of the nation in peace as we were about winning the current conflict. The United States would be a leading power in the world, and we would need young minds adequately trained in all fields, but above all minds that possessed true wisdom. I wish I had kept a copy of Ike's letter, for it was prophetic. The nation and the world, he wrote, would be far different from what we had known. Science and technology would dominate our lives. Military threats would keep peoples everywhere nervous, insecure, worried. We had to be prepared for constant change, and one of the heavy responsibilities of our colleges and universities was to prepare young people who could function effectively in a constantly changing and somewhat threatening environment.

In the six weeks of doubt, my wife and I made parallel lists: for and against going to Kansas State. Finally and ironically, the point that tipped the balance toward acceptance was my belief that at last I would have an opportunity to read, do some serious studying, and write several articles each year for leading magazines, something I had hoped to do earlier. This decision-making bit of misconception has always amused me. I thought I had worked faithfully and hard in government and I thought, as I am sure others leaving federal service for a private position have thought, that by comparison my new position would be a "cup of tea." I was to learn that serving as a university president was, in fact, far more difficult, time-consuming, and worrisome than anything I had ever experienced.

So on July 1, 1943, not quite forty-four years old, I became president of the institution where I had done my undergraduate work and from which my faithful friend, Dr. Jardine, had summarily "fired" me in the summer of 1924.

My feelings about this new venture were mixed with anticipation and regret. Naturally I looked forward to a new environment, a change of pace, meeting new people and new challenges. Frankly I was eager to be, for the first time in my life, the top man in an organization—a role I had studied with real interest in every position I had held. At the same time I was sorry to be leaving the exciting, frantic, and fulfilling life of Washington and the federal government; one easily develops the attitude that Washington is the center of the universe—a malady called Potomac fever.

I was also somewhat sorry to be leaving the immediate orbit of President Roosevelt, for the relationship that had grown between us and the sudden and unexpected assignments he gave me had added a special zest to my life.

I did not see the President in person again after I departed for Kansas. On April 12, 1945, as the second year of my presidency of the university drew to a close, President Roosevelt died. He had used his last ounce of energy in the service of this nation, and a saddened and deeply grateful people mourned him as a departed family member. One of the most devastating contrasts in photographs I have ever seen is of President Roosevelt: one taken at his first inauguration and the other snapped as he made a television talk when he was running for a fourth term. In the first his face is unlined. His appearance is youthful, with head tilted slightly upward, eyes sparkling, and a trace of a smile showing. The other photograph, showing him in a wheel chair before a microphone, is of an ill, exhausted, worried man. The deeply lined face is the color of whole wheat dough. Those photographs indicate vividly the toll the presidency had taken of the man.

Franklin D. Roosevelt was more a man of his time and had more influence over national and global events than any previous Chief Executive of the United States, with the possible exception of Lincoln. During his twelve-year presidency the United States faced two monumental crises—the great depression, then World War II. Both threatened the survival of our democracy; both called for a leader who was decisive and bold and who could bring forth the best of the American people. Nothing in Roosevelt's background prepared him to deal as a specialist with either crisis. He was neither economist nor military strategist. Although he had been governor of New York and Assistant Secretary of the Navy before that, neither position gave him the perspective or the special skills to cope with the awesome and hazardous complexities of depression and global war. For that, he had to rely on his own seemingly unlimited inner resources.

It is obviously a cliché to say that the man makes the presidency and the presidency makes the man, but that is surely true in the case of Franklin Roosevelt. He was a man of immense complexity, and he brought to this unique job a variety of indispensable personal characteristics.

He had a style all his own, comparable to no other President I have known, and he demonstrated, as John Kennedy would years later, that style can be a powerful force in a democracy. Despite his aristocratic origins, he cared deeply about the fate of ordinary men and he communicated this concern to them. Indeed, he had more in common with them than with the privileged and the powerful in his background. Nonetheless, his presence in the White House bore an air of grandeur. And he was without question a gentleman in the true sense of that word.

Roosevelt exuded confidence in himself and in the strategy he used to achieve his goals. He really believed that if a man were good and true and did his best, then everything would somehow work out in the end. With such supreme self-confidence, he could tolerate the incredible pressures of his office; he could make a critical decision, then put it from his mind and relax; he had an uncanny ability to sleep soundly at night while the storm of crisis raged about him. He was constantly outwitting his opponents. Even after he had an occasional defeat, such as in his effort to "pack" the Supreme Court or purge his party, he did not lose his confidence. Years later Merriman Smith would write: "To many he was a fabulous monarch, a dramatic king. He could be and usually was socially democratic, but always with a regal air that never let you doubt that he was in full command of the situation. . . . Roosevelt's press conferences showed his flamboyance, his wit, his lordly self-assurance."[9]

Roosevelt was a man of unusual courage. It may well be that in conquering the polio that threatened to leave him a helpless cripple he tapped some deep wellspring of courage and confidence. In any case, he seemed to have no fear, and in situations of despair or panic he was invariably calm and steady.

Fortunately for this nation, Franklin Roosevelt was an activist. He believed that every problem could be solved if only men were bright enough and daring enough to act. Very little fell outside his range of interest, and I marveled on numerous occasions at the scope of his concerns, the breadth of his vision, and his grasp of details. I'm sure that the greatest disappointment of his life was that there were problems to be solved that he would never get to simply because there was not enough time and energy for them. He wanted to do everything. Despite his killing pace, in peace and war, he had been able to do, as he once told me shortly before I left Washington, only a fraction of what he had hoped to accomplish. Most men assuming the presidency when Roosevelt did would have been highly ambitious if they had as their goal finding a solution to the economic disaster that paralyzed the nation. But that was a preliminary goal for President Roosevelt; he was determined to save the system so he could go on and reform it. And there is no doubt that, prior to World War II, he brought about the most far-reaching peaceful revolution in history. I was bothered—a feeling I have never lost—by his fiscal irresponsibility and by his seeming indifference at times to the maladministration of the programs he launched, but I never quarreled with his purposes. Perhaps he would have demonstrated more administrative concern later, had not the war intervened and commanded his full attention. But I doubt it. Roosevelt was many things, but he was not, in my judgment, a good administrator. Efficiency in execution was a question left to a subsequent administration and would not be dealt with for another eight years.

One of Roosevelt's most notable and most useful qualities was his finely honed sense of human relations. Many have referred to this as his "charm," and it is true that few people ever came within range without being captivated by him—including many of his proclaimed "enemies." It is also true that he developed to perfection a technique for bending people to his will—a technique which came to be known as "the Works" and which was the model for "the Treatment" developed by his young protégé from Texas who would occupy the White House two decades later.

But Roosevelt had more than charm. He genuinely liked people and was interested in them. He could draw people close to him and inspire them to stretch themselves beyond their limits to solve a problem or reach a goal—even when he himself was not sure what should be done. It has been said of him that he *used* men to suit his own ends, drained them, then often discarded them. I understand how this opinion could be held, but I think it is too harsh. Certainly my own experiences with him were always characterized by honesty and sincerity. My view is that many who became personal or professional confidants or who sidled into the shadow of his power were too assertive or too self-serving or too power-hungry. Some simply taxed his patience by disagreeing with him too often.

Although he created a complex and sprawling bureaucracy of unprecedented proportions, Roosevelt's administrations were highly personal. He kept real power very close to him and the handful of men he trusted most. Eventually the government became so large and so complex that he could not control or even know of everything important going on. Even then he seemed to protect his own influence by creating agencies that overlapped or conflicted with each other, by keeping others in partial confusion or only partly informed, by playing men, agencies, and forces off against one another.

Roosevelt's Cabinet, as a Cabinet, was not a very important part of government. One Secretary called it a "delightful social occasion" at which nothing was ever decided and no problems were solved. Roosevelt preferred to work through people rather than positions and he would rely on individuals for what they offered him rather than because they occupied particular posts. He was served by a variety of aides and confidants during his long tenure—all different. It is in these relationships that one can discern much about the President's personal qualities, his assets and shortcomings.

In his campaign for the presidency and during his first term he needed ideas and expertise, so he assembled, at the suggestion of Samuel Rosenman, a "Brain Trust" of Moley, Tugwell, Berle, O'Connor, and others. During his second term he needed the legislative and political skills of such a feisty person as Thomas Corcoran. During his third term Roosevelt's greatest need was for administrative trouble shooters, so he turned again to old friends, Harry Hopkins, Samuel Rosenman, and sometimes to me. It was a mark of the man that he had a remarkable ability to learn on the job and he used scores of people to help him, to serve as eyes and ears and sometimes just as sounding boards.

Because Roosevelt skillfully selected his aides to meet his most compelling needs at a given time, it is not possible to say that one or another had more influence on him, or was more loyal or more trusted, though certainly historians give first place to Harry Hopkins, a tough-minded, bold, incisive, but physically frail friend. But each confidant had his moment in the sun; some saw their influence rise and fall, then rise again, depending on the President's need for a special talent.

Roosevelt tolerated a certain amount of independence in those he worked with, so long as they did not distract too much from his own press and his own public image. Indeed, he sometimes seemed to amuse himself by baiting his aides and his Cabinet members and pitting them against one another. There was always a good deal of jealousy among those closest to him and among his staff—considerable jockeying for position. Louis Howe and Harry Hopkins were unequaled in their maneuverings, and both carried tales to the President about men who threatened to exceed them in the President's good graces. Roosevelt had a way of making everyone who talked with him feel important, even to the point of seeming to agree with each of them. Many a man left the President's office feeling he had just influenced the course of events only to learn later that not to disagree is not necessarily to agree. When an adviser or assistant became tarnished or a political liability, the President would exile him to a special foreign mission or to a remote spot in the growing federal bureaucracy. Hardheaded Dutchman Roosevelt could be, but he seemed unable ever simply to fire someone.

Louis McHenry Howe undoubtedly occupied a special and unique place. For twenty-one years he devoted himself to Roosevelt, beginning in 1911 when FDR was seeking re-election to the New York Senate. Howe became determined that his idol would be governor, then President, and he dedicated himself to those objectives.

Howe's biographer, Alfred B. Rollins, Jr.,[10] summed up the relationship between the two men this way:

"After 1912 it would be impossible to think of Roosevelt or Howe without the other. They operated as parts of one political personality. They complemented each other in strengths and weaknesses. With smiles and warmth enough for both of them, the genial Roosevelt specialized in the high level generalization, in persuasive speeches and personal charm in public contacts, and in the broad questions of public policy. Sardonic, cynical, shrewd, and chronically suspicious and worried, Louis Howe concentrated on the secret loyalties and patronage hunger. . . . Roosevelt could absorb the credit, Howe the blame. But between themselves they understood that they rose and fell together."

Howe's great service to Roosevelt prior to the presidency waned simply because Howe became increasingly ill and because President Roosevelt quickly "outgrew" him. The President now needed broader and more varied help; Howe's influence dwindled accordingly. Nonetheless, until his death in 1936 Howe was one of the few persons who could challenge Roosevelt, question, nag, goad, and shame him if necessary. He always forced Roosevelt to face his own fallibility.

James Farley's service to Roosevelt was focused in the run for the presidency. Roosevelt and Howe carefully selected Farley in 1929 to build and direct the political machine that would nominate and elect Roosevelt to the White House. Farley, an excellent choice, was a big, likable, easygoing fellow. He liked people and rarely forgot a face or a name.

Moreover, he was no threat to Howe or Roosevelt, for although he was ambitious he knew his limitations and had no desire to influence Roosevelt in matters of public policy or programs. Indeed, Farley's openness was a useful balance to Howe's mysterious, sometimes cynical maneuverings.

Farley's greatest usefulness to Roosevelt was between 1929 and 1932, but he remained part of the team until the end of the second term. I knew Farley and respected him highly. In placing loyal Democrats in influential positions in all federal departments, he insisted upon ability and integrity of the candidates and upon the willing acceptance of each man by the Cabinet member concerned. His objection to a third term for Roosevelt was, I am convinced, a matter of principle rather than a desire on his part to be the candidate.

If Howe and Farley were Roosevelt's political team, Raymond Moley and Rexford Tugwell were his "idea men." Moley came to Roosevelt's side early in 1932 when Samuel Rosenman suggested that Roosevelt call in some university professors to consult with him on major issues. Moley was then a forty-six-year-old professor at Columbia. Patrick Anderson[11] writes: "Moley burst across the political heaven like an errant sky rocket; few men have soared so high so fast or fallen so far so soon."

Moley headed the Brain Trust during the campaign for the nomination and the race for the presidency. He and his fellow intellectuals spent long hours with Roosevelt, tutoring him, discussing economic strategies, seeking bold new ideas to cope with a sick nation that had lost confidence in the national leadership. Moley drafted many of the major speeches during that period; he offered advice freely and the President accepted much of it.

Moley lasted only six months in the new Administration, but during that half year he wielded enormous influence. He met each day with the President, briefed him on critical issues, advised him on appointments, and suggested new programs. The President would set policy and leave the details to Moley—but the details could involve millions of dollars and millions of persons. Moley was also influential in bringing new faces into the inner circle, such as Felix Frankfurter, who in turn brought Thomas Corcoran and Benjamin Cohen. Then suddenly, following a dramatic conflict between Moley and Secretary of State Cordell Hull—the details of which I have forgotten—Moley was banished and subsequently wrote a syndicated newspaper column that often was critical of the New Deal.

Thomas Corcoran was in his early thirties when he joined the President. Educated at Brown University and the Harvard Law School, he served in a clerkship to Justice Holmes and later on Wall Street. He replaced Moley as confidant and speech writer and Farley as political consultant. He was brilliant, personable, witty, enormously talented, and at times unscrupulous. In the second term he served as a hatchet man who engineered the abortive purge of conservatives in the 1938 party primaries. He also played a key role in the President's effort to pack the Supreme Court, a chore he shared with Harry Hopkins; Hopkins proved more agile and managed to leave Corcoran "holding the bag" in the widely criticized maneuver.

Corcoran thrived on personal power and he exploited his relationship with Roosevelt to build a power base that made him one of the most influential men in the capital. He recruited scores of young lawyers into federal agencies and they formed an intelligence network that made "Tommy the Cork" Washington's best-informed power broker. Corcoran, however, shunned personal publicity and deliberately created an air of mystery about himself. He served as speech writer, legislative draftsman, political fixer, policy adviser, chief lobbyist, frequent companion, and court jester—replete with song and dance. Amazingly, he did all of these tasks extraordinarily well.

Corcoran, Cohen, and Rosenman were the basic speech-writing team for the President during the campaign of 1936, and Corcoran is credited with some of Roosevelt's most famous phrases, including "a rendezvous with destiny."

Corcoran's impact was great when his star was ascending. The Federal Securities Exchange legislation he and Cohen drafted for Roosevelt was about the only legislation that withstood judicial assault; he schemed, managed, and won against conservatives in the Administration a campaign to move the President on a trust-busting, "get tough with business" policy during the second term.

He understandably made hundreds of enemies during his heyday at the White House.* He was often denounced on the floor of Congress and in the oval office of the President. Most of Roosevelt's other staff

* Like so many others who worked directly for the President, Corcoran's office was not in the White House but in the Reconstruction Finance Corporation.

members disliked and distrusted him. Rexford Tugwell has said that Harry Hopkins ultimately ended Corcoran's White House career by systematically and successfully undermining him with the President. Rosenman has indicated that Corcoran ran roughshod over so many important political leaders that he became a millstone for the President and had to be banished.

Harry Lloyd Hopkins became a standard against which future presidential aides would be measured, even if mistakenly. He was probably the most versatile of Roosevelt's succession of confidants—a man for all seasons, politically astute, brilliant administrator, hard-nosed pragmatist, analyst, man of action, and ultimately consummate diplomat, despite his physical weakness and haggard appearance.

As governor of New York, Roosevelt in 1930 appointed Hopkins chairman of the state's Emergency Relief Administration. After his election to the White House he appointed Hopkins head of the Federal Emergency Relief Administration. Hopkins quickly caught the spirit of the New Deal, and during his first two hours on the job he spent five million dollars. Later that year he put four million men to work in the Civil Works Administration.

Roosevelt admired Hopkins' zeal and energy, his boldness and eagerness to take risks to get the job done. Moreover, Hopkins was a good companion—candid to the point of bluntness, sharp of mind and wit. In the early thirties his health began to fail, perhaps because he was given to the high life of Washington night life and gala parties. He and the President genuinely enjoyed each other and learned from each other, but Hopkins learned more from Roosevelt. As Hopkins grew closer to Roosevelt, it began to be rumored that the President was grooming a successor. The President encouraged the rumors, appearing with Hopkins publicly and praising him to party leaders. He may have been using Hopkins as a stalking horse, or he may actually have been laying the groundwork for a young liberal President to succeed him. Hopkins believed the latter and his appointment as Secretary of Commerce turned rumors into a boomlet in 1938.

A year earlier Hopkins had had half of his stomach removed to stem what was said to be cancer. In 1939 he became gravely ill and survived to live nearly seven more years only because Roosevelt personally directed doctors at the U. S. Naval Hospital to try every new experimental medicine, every possible treatment. Hopkins lived but his hopes for the presidency died.

In May 1940, Hopkins was dining with the President in the White House when he again fell ill and was immediately put to bed. Partly recovered, he remained in the White House for three and a half years and thus entered a new dimension in his relationship with the President.

Hopkins' first assignment in his new role was to get Roosevelt re-elected to a third term. Farley and Corcoran were no longer in the President's inner circle—and the decision to run for a third term was one of the issues that had led to the split. Hopkins engineered the Democratic Convention.

William Lawrence in his book, *Six Presidents, Too Many Wars*,[12] said that Hopkins had a direct line from his Blackstone Hotel suite to the White House. In calling the signals for the convention he paid "little heed to the sensibilities of Democratic Chairman James A. Farley." When Roosevelt was renominated Hopkins at once demanded that Henry Wallace be nominated for the vice-presidency, saying that otherwise Roosevelt would withdraw. Wallace was nominated. This has always puzzled me, for as I have previously explained the President did not like Wallace, nearly always avoided talking to him, and rarely consulted him on policy matters. It may be that Wallace's popularity in the farm states was the decisive point that led to his selection.

A few weeks afterward Hopkins resigned from the Cabinet, ostensibly because of poor health, but mainly because his role as arbitrary "fixer" and his absence from Commerce for many months had made him subject to serious political criticism. So he withdrew from the crucible of the White House—this time to private life in New York. But his withdrawal was short-lived.

Hitler was rampaging across Europe, and the newly re-elected President was preoccupied with the strategy of war. With the election safely behind him, he turned again to old friends like Hopkins. As 1940 drew to a close Roosevelt increasingly felt the need to do something to reassure Churchill and the British people. He did not yet want to travel to England and could not make up his mind whom to send in his place. Harry Hopkins volunteered and pressed the point when Roosevelt demurred. Finally the President relented and in January 1941 sent Hopkins as his personal emissary to improve personal relations between the President of the United States and British leaders, especially Churchill.

Hopkins succeeded beyond all expectations. His candor captured Churchill. Surrounded by his aides, many of lordly birth, Churchill referred to Hopkins as "Lord Root-of-the-Matter." Hopkins' outspoken support and admiration for the British people and his tangible sincerity won the hearts of the people. Now Hopkins was back in the White House. He made five trips to England during the ensuing years, and he joined Roosevelt and Churchill in several historic conferences. He also represented the President in dealings with Stalin, who also became an admirer. It is said that Hopkins was the only American, except for Roosevelt, whom Stalin would cross the room to greet and shake hands.

Hopkins became a liaison, a buffer between the great leaders (particularly between Roosevelt and Churchill), easing the way, heading off conflicts, preparing the groundwork for major agreements.

Meanwhile, pressure mounted for the President to appoint one man to head the war mobilization effort, but both he and Hopkins were wary of sharing their power, so they handled the task between them. Trusted friend Judge Samuel Rosenman was persuaded to leave the New York bench and become special counsel to the President (setting the precedent for Clark Clifford and Theodore Sorensen). Rosenman drafted a reorganization plan for wartime production and set up the War Manpower Commission and the Office of Economic Stabilization. Rosenman was no rival for Hopkins and the President, and the power stayed with them.

At the apex of his power, Hopkins moved men and material at all levels. He was the second most powerful man in America. He could open doors, break log jams, make or break bureaucrats and generals. He was the constant close companion and adviser of Roosevelt.

In such a role it was inevitable that Hopkins should become a lightning rod for criticism. As the 1944 election approached, the President once again followed his uncanny political instincts and grew noticeably cool toward Hopkins. Hopkins moved out of the White House and out of the action. Most officials in Washington were convinced that Hopkins was at last finished.

Early in 1945, however, Hopkins, on a visit to the White House, discovered that Roosevelt was about to send a cable to Stalin indicating that Churchill could speak for him at a conference on postwar matters to which Roosevelt did not intend to go. Hopkins felt that Stalin would interpret this to mean that the United States was not interested in how Europe would be dealt with after the war. With no authority, he intercepted the message at the White House communications center, confronted the President, and showed how serious a mistake it would be to convey such a notion to Stalin. Once again Harry Hopkins was back in the President's good graces and back on the job.

His last assignment was to accompany the President to Yalta. He played an important role, but by now his health was failing rapidly. Too ill to return by ship with the President, he was flown back to the States and immediately put in the Mayo Clinic. Roosevelt was displeased that Hopkins had not sailed home with him. The President went immediately to Warm Springs without seeing Hopkins, and shortly thereafter he died while Hopkins was still in the Mayo Clinic.

Harry Hopkins died on January 29, 1946. Before his death he had recovered sufficiently to serve Harry Truman in 1945 by making a special trip to meet with Stalin. Stalin agreed to compromise a Soviet proposal which could have wrecked the United Nations Charter conference in San Francisco, and Harry Hopkins may have been the only American who could have persuaded him to do so.

President Roosevelt depended upon others for the writing of speeches more than most chief executives. Raymond Moley for half a year and then Thomas Corcoran for a fairly long period were the mainstays of the President in this difficult field. Later Robert E. Sherwood, famous playwright and for a time head of the Overseas Division of the Office of War Information, where I came to know him, and Judge Samuel Rosenman took over almost the complete responsibility for preparing talks, State of the Union messages and other state documents. Many of Roosevelt's famous phrases are attributed to them. Normally, Roosevelt's editing of the copy that came to him was minimal, a fortunate thing for a President who was always tremendously overworked, often tense, and gradually losing his energy and his health in the most man-killing task on earth.

As one studies the role of Roosevelt's aides, some of whom I knew intimately—their relationship with him and with each other—one senses that the wiliest of our political leaders allowed each to feel indispensable but depended completely on none. When Moley felt that he had almost exclusive access to the President he was sometimes shocked to discover that the President had not only consulted with others to a great degree but had actually made up his mind to follow a course different from the one Moley advocated. When Howe and Hopkins were unable to perform because of ill health, the President quietly turned elsewhere and the ranks closed swiftly—to the despair of the two "irreplaceable" aides. When an assistant became a liability or an inconvenience, the President could exile him without a pang. As Patrick Anderson described the dismissal of Corcoran:

"Roosevelt in one of those computer-like calculations that master politicians make in the blink of an eye, realized the young Irishman had outlived his usefulness, so he sighed and waved his cigarette holder and sent him on his way."[11]

While I do not approve of the methods many of President Roosevelt's confidants employed—by-passing as they did the responsible members of the Cabinet—I recognize that they usually satisfied the President and to him that was the important consideration.

Early in the morning after President Roosevelt's death, the faculty and students at Kansas State filed silently into the auditorium for a memorial service. The choir sang two hymns in respectful tribute, and I spoke in a very personal vein, mindful of the close association I had enjoyed with him. What I said then was heartfelt: "History, weighing the evidence with objectivity and precision, will determine that Franklin Delano Roosevelt was the greatest world leader our nation had produced."

CHAPTER 9

It is less difficult to make changes than to make changes which endure. Even a revolutionary, if he wants a tree to grow, must plant a seed.

FOR NEARLY TWO years following my departure from Washington I devoted most of my time to education. Occasionally I undertook a short-term government assignment. One of these turned out to be hair-raising.

Because of my work in North Africa I knew a good deal about the military, economic, and human situation in the Allied war zone. Consequently the Secretary of War telephoned me in September 1943 and urged me to give the commencement address at the army bombardier school at Big Spring, Texas. The army would provide air transportation.

I drove to the Topeka, Kansas, airport where an army plane was to pick me up at four in the afternoon. The twin-engine plane, equipped for practice bombing and capable of accommodating six passengers, arrived at six o'clock, two hours late. The crew consisted of a single pilot—a young captain who looked sixteen years old but was probably all of twenty-one. An embarrassed flush making his healthy pink cheeks even pinker, he explained that he was late because he had made a little mistake and had landed at an airport in Missouri. That should have tipped me off and I should have become suddenly ill or something. But I didn't. We took off and headed south, I in the copilot seat. Shortly after we passed Wichita we ran into a dark and menacing front. The wall of clouds was as straight as the side of a huge building.

We had been bouncing around in the storm for what seemed hours when the captain informed me that the radio and electric gauges were out of order—perhaps because of the lightning. Only the magnetic compass was functioning.

"I think we must be over Oklahoma City," he said. "I'm going to put down and we'll get up early in the morning. You are due to make the commencement talk at nine-thirty tomorrow. Don't worry; I'll get you there." Despite his reassurance, I worried.

He nosed the plane downward and we broke out of the soup at about five hundred feet. We were not over Oklahoma or any city. In fact there wasn't a light to be seen, only unbroken blackness. So he took the plane back into the storm. After a few minutes he turned to me and said: "We have only enough fuel left for about thirty minutes of flying. What do you think we should do?"

What did I, who knew nothing about airplanes, think we should do?

With superficial calmness I suggested that with the use of the compass we turn north, hoping that we would break free from the storm. I also said we should climb higher, adjust our parachutes, and be prepared to jump in case the motors failed. In about thirty minutes, at an altitude of some nine thousand feet—with the fuel gauges showing empty—we saw a brilliant searchlight break through the clouds. It had to be an airport. The captain slowed the motors and glided toward the light. It was an army airport at Dodge City, Kansas. When we landed and stepped from the plane, a sergeant in a jeep began to swear at the captain for not having followed landing instructions. The captain explained that, with no radio, we could not receive messages.

I went to bed while the plane was being repaired. At six-thirty the next morning we took off again. Now we encountered a head wind so strong that by ground speed we were virtually crawling. The young captain said that to make as much time as possible we would continue at a high altitude and then circle to a landing when we got to Big Spring. I had the awful feeling we would end up at another airport in Missouri. But we landed at the right airport at 9:45 A.M., fifteen minutes late for the ceremony.

My ears were so stopped up that I could not hear a word said by the major general who met the plane. I was escorted formally into an auditorium where the graduates of the bombardier school were standing at attention. On the stage I had no idea what was being said. Only when the general turned to me and nodded did I know that the time for me to speak had arrived. I had no difficulty in making the talk, but I did not know whether I shouted or spoke in a normal tone. Not until lunchtime did my hearing begin to return. The facts about our flight were well known by that time, so a more experienced pilot returned me—without incident—to the Topeka airport.

To Kansas State, a major land grant institution, I as a neophyte president brought a consuming desire to institute educational changes, reforms designed to achieve goals not unlike those that Thomas Jefferson had in mind when he wrote the charter of the University of Virginia. Jefferson reasoned that democracy, entrusting as it does the basic social power to all the people, required a rising level of understanding among all the people and especially needed minds capable of "harmonizing" the divergent desires and intentions of specialized groups. He believed that this was a major purpose of higher education. But in most of the twentieth century, and especially in the period between wars, the Jeffersonian concept was largely ignored: the nation, in its frantic rush for physical and industrial development, had come to worship specialization. Training had become so intense that we had modern towers of Babel, with specialists in one field unable to understand the jargon of specialists in another.

In my inaugural address, several months after I arrived on the campus, I pleaded for more humanism, more breadth in education, a greater concern for the interdependence of specialized groups in our society which in turn required both a breadth of intellect and an open mind to new concepts and developments. We should not be so enamored of our ability to solve scientific and technological problems that we neglected the basic nature and needs of a free society. Modern complexity required that institutions of higher education help students achieve breadth of understanding and mature judgments.

Certainly minds capable of objective, critical, and creative thinking would be desperately needed when the war was over, as a nation inexperienced in international affairs sought to take leadership in a world that was by conflict earning the right to have permanent peace.

"We hold," I said, "that human beings are more important than the institutions they create." But our convictions about man, our convictions about human freedom and welfare, would not prevail, I went on, if we were complacent and indifferent to change. Victory in arms would do no more than offer a new generation a chance to work for a fuller life in an environment of individual liberty and social justice. Mere knowledge drilled into students was not enough. In the life we would soon

166

live we would need most of all citizen minds capable of making informed judgments in a multitude of critical fields.

"It will not be enough," I said, "for man to know how to build a Grand Coulee Dam or a Golden Gate Bridge . . . not enough to know how to till the soil and protect it . . . not enough to know how to heal the sick. For every man with a useful place in society will have several great responsibilities . . . using his specialized talent to make a living for himself and his family . . . applying his specialized talents to the solution of community, state, and national problems in his field of competence . . . and, as a citizen in a democracy, for making manifold decisions on problems outside his own discipline, decisions which, if made in ways compatible with our democratic ideals and methods, can spread the blessings of democracy, strengthen democracy, and guarantee its future."

In our scientific and technologically oriented colleges we faced the danger of encouraging a man to achieve genuine competence in one field but mere dogmatism on problems in other fields. A critical task of education, as of statesmanship, was to help people learn to *harmonize* seemingly opposed interests. This intellectual exercise called for creative compromise.

Inaugural addresses readily find comfortable places in dead files. I was determined that this should not be so at Kansas State. The university was a solid educational institution with a competent faculty and a wholesome, unsophisticated, eager, capable body of students. The curricula, however, were too specialized, containing only a modicum of courses in the humanities and social sciences—a fact my predecessor President Farrell had deplored.

With the help of the several faculties I set up a series of committees to plan educational reform. The chairman of each committee also served on a central co-ordinating group of which I acted as chairman. We made rapid, heart-warming progress. In a year and a half the faculties approved meaningful revisions in fifty-one curricula which combined general education with scientific and technical studies. We also established a new research and teaching institute devoted exclusively to experiments designed to find more effective ways of making general education exciting, acceptable, and valuable.

In my seven years at Kansas State co-operation was so dependable that we were able to expand the physical plant fifty per cent, increase faculty salaries seventy-five per cent, create a new foundation to obtain private gifts to pay for activities the state would not support, and involve hundreds of leaders of farm, industrial, social, and cultural organizations in the affairs of the institution. I believe, however, that the lasting contribution of that period, if any, was to change a college of quality and high ideals from fairly rigid specialization into a university which prided itself on offering undergraduate and graduate programs of genuine balance.

(In 1950, when I left Kansas State, one of the deans remarked that "Milton Eisenhower used democratic methods to achieve his dictatorial purposes." That may be. Perhaps I took to my first university presidency too much of the human engineering I had learned in the federal service.)

While educational changes were under way, another problem had to be dealt with. I had said in my inaugural talk that education must also work for social justice. This did not mean that a college should in any sense become a crusading political institution—far from it. An institution of higher learning stands publicly for research and education. It must remain aloof from the controversial streams of politics. The persons who comprise the institution—faculty members, administrators, students, trustees—are citizens, and as citizens they can be advocates or opponents in the social and political arenas. What an educational institution can do in the field of civil rights, for example, is to become a model of excellence, upholding mutuality in human relations, ridding itself of every vestige of discrimination.

To my astonishment, in the peaceful, self-centered state in which I had been raised, Kansas State stood as an institution with widespread discrimination against blacks. Most astonishing of all was the fact that the issue had never been raised. There was complete obliviousness to the problem. No one mentioned the ideal that ought to prevail. In a student body of about four thousand there were no more than one hundred and fifty black students. The blacks could not use the college swimming pool, could not have intramural teams, could not participate in intercollegiate athletics, could not belong to honor societies, and were not housed in college dormitories.

I was appalled and angered. I was also sorely perplexed. Tempted to issue a series of edicts which would quickly change the situation, I was aware that Kansas was half cavalier, half puritan. "Bleeding Kansas" had suffered, and effects of that historic period still lingered. A sudden and forceful change of the situation, however morally right, would provoke strong resistance, lead to discord, force people into fixed ideological positions from which they could not retreat, and possibly even lead to campus disruptions that might injure the educational enterprise.

On the other hand, if I moved slowly and cautiously, real change could be a long time in coming. It is easy to urge caution if you are not the one being intimidated or deprived of fundamental constitutional rights.

Pragmatism won out over emotion. I chose evolution over revolution because I reasoned that so long as one had a good objective, and adhered to it steadfastly, an evolutionary method of dealing with prejudice would succeed over a period of time far better than a revolutionary approach which might bring immediate changes that would not endure. Unless I acted prudently, I would defeat my own purpose.

The student council, fortunately, was comprised of open-minded young people, including an attractive black man, a true moderate. The council, especially the black student and its white president, helped me devise and carry into effect a series of changes over a period of six years. Discrimination in the swimming pool was eliminated almost at once. Soon blacks organized intramural teams and participated in intramural sports; later the intramural teams were integrated. The few cases of discrimination in the classroom were quietly handled with individual faculty members. Blacks were admitted to college housing. One edict was issued: any honor society or professional fraternity that discriminated on the basis of race, religion, or national origin would have its charter revoked. Finally came a knotty problem that went beyond the campus—permitting blacks to participate in intercollegiate athletics. Two members of the Big Eight Conference, Missouri and Oklahoma, said that if a Kansas State team came to their campuses with black members games would be canceled. We risked violating this ultimatum, and nothing happened. At the end of six years there was not a trace of institutionalized racial discrimination.

Of equal importance is the fact that *not a single story about this had appeared in the press, no protest meeting had been held, and I had not received one letter of criticism.* Timing was the key to success. Each change had been instituted after the previous one had been generally accepted.

A decade later, when the struggle for civil rights coalesced into a literally burning national issue, I recalled what we had done at Kansas State. I do not presume to say that I know all the answers to the complicated problem of civil rights, with white racism now countered by black racism. Only as a teen-ager did I know the answers to all difficult problems. Now I have more questions that need answering than I can personally resolve in my own mind. But I do believe that the nation would have achieved more, beginning with the Supreme Court decision of 1954 and the Eisenhower-sponsored civil rights legislation of 1957, if we had taken one critical step at a time, gained general acceptance for it, and then moved inexorably to the next logical change, than we have under the great outpouring of legislation and political promises of the sixties. In promising the unattainable, by adopting legislation the purposes of which could not be quickly realized, we raised the expectations of millions of underprivileged individuals; when realization fell far short of those expectations, we witnessed blood and riots, backlash, deeper intellectual divisions, and the proclamation of new extreme demands. We came close to becoming, in the words of the Kerner Commission, two societies, one white, one black. Now there is real doubt in my mind that the seeming progress resulting from the civil rights revolution will endure. Regretfully and sadly, I have a sense that, as the clamor has died down, the society is sliding back from the commitments made hastily in a period of turmoil.

Steady progress to overcome discrimination is vital to the stability and unification of our democratic society. Only when the task is completed can we achieve inner peace and be satisfied that we have reached the ideals set forth in the Constitution. A thousand "Kansas State" programs of quiet and evolutionary integration would have moved us closer to this important goal—and to each other.

At Christmas, in my first year at Kansas State, my faithful friend Dr. Jardine, then president of Wichita University, invited me to make the Yuletide address at his institution. Mindful of how very much he had done for me—what a vital part he had played in launching and guiding my career—I put aside pressing matters and journeyed to Wichita and there received from him my first honorary doctorate. Just before the ceremony he said to me, "Milton, I want to be the first to give you this honor. You will receive many, but you will never forget, I am sure, that in this ceremony today we celebrate what has been for me, and I hope for you, a most affectionate and rewarding relationship." That was my last formal meeting with him. He passed away some years later when he was in retirement in San Antonio. He did not live to see his prediction come true: in time there accumulated among my treasured possessions thirty-seven honorary doctorates, five from foreign universities, including the University of Bologna, the oldest university in the world. At each ceremony I remembered his words and struggled to keep tears from my eyes as I thought of how very much one kindly human being can mean to another.

In January 1944 a surprise family reunion took place in the official residence at Kansas State. General George C. Marshall telephoned to tell me that General Eisenhower was then in Washington. His movements were a secret. Following conferences with the President and the top staff of the defense establishment, he would see his son John at West Point and then make a quick trip to our home. I was to bring my mother, Mr. and Mrs. Doud (Mamie's parents), and my brothers to my home if possible, but this must be done without revealing the presence in this country of General Eisenhower. The Douds and my mother came. On the appointed night an army car took me to the airport at Fort Riley, a few miles away, and there I awaited the arrival of the plane from Washington. Rumors were rampant at the airport. Some thought General Marshall was coming. Several suggested that President Roosevelt might arrive. Since it was assumed that General Eisenhower was in Africa, the rumors did not involve him. At last the plane put down. The car in which I was riding drew up to the door of the plane and my brother, whom I had not seen since I was with him in Africa, hastily moved from the plane to the car. The trip to the campus home was without incident. Indeed, it was not until General Eisenhower was back in Europe and the world learned that he would become Supreme Commander of the European invasion forces that the people of the United States learned of the secret visit. The folks at Kansas State were thrilled and plied me with questions, but I could tell them nothing save that we had held a family reunion. By this time Mother's memory was failing, a defense against the grief she had suffered when my father died two years before, but she greeted us all with equal affection. She was never impressed by the worldly positions of her sons. There was no pretense in her statement two years later when, with five of her six sons beside her, a newsman asked, "Aren't you proud of your famous son?" and she instantly asked, "Which one?"

Of the brief visit to his wife, son, and the family gathering in my home General Eisenhower later wrote: "These family visits were a rejuvenating experience—until then I had not fully realized how far war tends to carry its participants away from the interests, objectives and concerns of normal life."

One of President Truman's early acts after taking office was to replace Secretary of Agriculture Wickard with Clinton P. Anderson of New Mexico. Anderson was appointed on June 2, 1945, and assumed office on the thirtieth of the month. At once he telephoned me from Washington and asked whether I would meet him in Topeka on a matter of highest importance. Three days later I did so.

Secretary Anderson was a man of probity, charming personality, and disarming forthrightness.

He came directly to the point. The War Food Administration and the Department of Agriculture had to be put back together. It was utter nonsense to have two interdependent agencies under different heads reporting directly to the President. President Truman insisted upon reunification as soon as possible and suggested that I knew more about government organization generally and specifically about the Department of Agriculture than anyone else. Would I come to Washington for whatever period was needed and recombine these two federal agencies? If I would consent he would take me to the White House where the President would make the request directly and give me whatever title I wanted.

To gain a few moments for thought I said I would first have to talk with the chairman of the Board of Regents, who was in Topeka, so I stepped into a side room and did so by telephone. I knew the answer would be affirmative. It is traditional in American higher education for presidents and other principal officers and faculty members to perform useful public services, provided only that extracurricular activities do not interfere with institutional responsibilities. The period of five minutes I had taken for this conversation gave me time to formulate my position.

I told Secretary Anderson that I would do what he requested under several conditions: I would do the work, not as a government employee or officer, but as president of the university. No pay would be involved. The government could meet my out-of-pocket costs. I would expect the Secretary to meet with me each day, preferably at luncheon, and I would complete the assignment in about six to eight weeks. He was agreeable but asked why I felt it necessary for us to meet every day.

"The reason is simple," I said. "I have seen many organizational studies made, some of them of great merit, only to have the agency head meet opposition from those most affected and, frustrated, to set the study aside and eventually adopt some other plan. I don't want to waste time in a useless exercise. Having spent sixteen years in the Department of Agriculture, I think I know what needs to be done but the important consideration is that you personally agree with each logical step as I present it to you. If you wish to confer with your associates, you should do so as the reorganization proceeds."

These conditions were met and a week later I took a train to Washington via Chicago. Because of enormous war traffic, I could not get a Pullman reservation from Chicago to Washington and so had to sit up all night.

My first meeting with President Truman was cordial but brief. I had heard a great deal about him from my oldest brother, Arthur, a banker in Kansas City. When President Truman was in the clothing business and Arthur was a lowly teller in a bank, the two of them, both then unmarried, had roomed together. My first impression of the President was that he was cocky but not arrogant; overwhelmed by the responsibilities of the presidency but poised and forthright; blunt but not offensive.

He was prepared to offer me an appointment as special assistant to the President, but when Secretary Anderson explained how I wished to function he nodded, smiled, and gave his approval. As we rose to leave, President Truman said to me, "I shall be calling on you for additional help, and I trust you will be willing to give it."

At least once a week for the next three months, often traveling at night in discomfort, I commuted between Manhattan, Kansas, and Washington, D.C. The mission was accomplished without difficulty. The President and the Secretary approved my plan. The department was again a unified executive agency under a single head. Secretary Anderson never ceased to be grateful and our friendship lasted through his Cabinet days and his many years in the Senate of the United States.

I had scarcely completed this work and caught up with my duties at Kansas State when I was summoned again. President Truman telephoned me and said he planned to establish a presidential fact-finding board to settle the General Motors strike which seriously threatened to disrupt the economy of the nation. He had already appointed Judge Walter P. Stacy, chief justice of the Supreme Court of North Carolina, and Lloyd Garrison of the Labor Relations Board. He wanted me to be a public representative on the board. He realized that I had no experience in labor matters, he said, but it was important that the interest of the public in this crippling strike be represented by one who would be completely objective.

The nation had been plagued with serious labor problems since the end of the war, largely as a result of the difficult problem of transforming our mighty industrial power back to peacetime needs. As war production ceased and millions of fighting men returned home, the task of finding them productive employment seemed overwhelming. Discharged soldiers expected to find their old jobs waiting for them and thousands of war workers faced unemployment. Take-home pay could not match wartime wages because of the end of overtime shifts and decline in the pressure to fill emergency military orders. While consumer goods once again returned to the market, the cost of living, which had been held down by wartime controls, rose sharply and the American people got their first taste of the inflation that would plague us intermittently over the next three decades.

Emergency legislation had sharply restricted the rights of both labor and management during the war years, but no sooner had the armistice been signed than labor trouble sprang up in every major sector of the economy and in every part of the country. There were strikes in the coal industry in the spring and autumn of 1945 and in April of 1946. A rail strike by twenty unions in May 1946 kept 300,000 workers off the job. Walkouts in other crucial industries affected oil, lumber, meat packing, telephone and telegraph, utilities, steel, and electrical manufacturing.

The most serious action was against General Motors, the industrial giant. Although many local plant issues were involved, the principal union demands summarized the grievances of labor across the land: they wanted a thirty per cent wage increase, seniority protection for displaced workers in reconverted plants, and the establishment of rules for in-plant transfers, filling vacancies, and newly created jobs. On September 22, 1945, the United Auto Workers-CIO filed notice of a labor dispute with the National Labor Relations Board. A strike vote was subsequently called and on November 21 more than 175,000 workers in nineteen states walked off the job. Although the union and the company proceeded directly into collective bargaining, there was no progress.

Earlier President Truman had summoned a White House conference of national business and labor leaders to recommend methods for the solution to the epidemic of labor disputes that threatened to paralyze an already crippled economy. A few small agreements were reached, but the conference adjourned without any significant results just as the General Motors strike was getting under way. Taking matters into his own hands, the President appeared before Congress on December 3 to propose enabling legislation for a way to mediate strikes —the Norton-Ellender bill, a labor fact-finding boards act. But the consequences of the strike were of such magnitude that Truman was forced to act on his own without waiting for the Congress to act. On December 14 he invoked the as yet unrepealed War Powers Act and appointed our Board. He requested that we investigate the case and be prepared to make recommendations within twenty days.

The first meeting of the Board was informal, held in the "Fishbowl Room" of the White House. After we arrived at a modus operandi we presented our plan to the President, who readily approved. As we rose to leave, the President motioned for me to stay. He smiled and told me a modified version of the story my brother had told me about President Roosevelt.

"President Roosevelt once told me he complained to General Eisenhower about you," Truman said. "Four different agencies were asking for your services. General Eisenhower remarked that he could use you too, but that would be nepotism!"

Shortly afterward Garrison and I met with GM President Charles E. Wilson ("Engine Charlie," who was later to serve as my brother's Secretary of Defense) and several of his associates to determine whether we could count on the company's co-operation. (Judge Stacy had become ill and had returned home.) Wilson looked at me skeptically and, I thought, with some disdain. "How did you get into this?"

he asked. I pointed out that the public had an interest in this strike and I was there to represent that interest—at the request of the President of the United States. The meeting was not successful. The General Motors officials felt that we would want to examine the company books and reveal the data to Walter Reuther, head of the union. Furthermore, Mr. Wilson declared, the company would refuse to present its case if we decided that prices and profits were pertinent issues to explore in considering union demands. It was clear that we would have to proceed thereafter without the co-operation of industry—a serious handicap in our study.

We called on President Truman to inform him of this development. He was quick to anger and uninhibited in the use of profane expletives. The strike had to be settled, he said, and we should move as fast as possible with or without the co-operation of the company or the union. The union, however, made public an immediate and favorable response to the creation of our Board.

The next day, December 20, President Truman blasted the company in a press conference. "Ability to pay," he said, was always relevant to the issue of an increase in wages and he insisted that fact-finding boards must have the authority to examine company records. He was speaking at the White House at the same time as our Board was holding its first day of public hearings in the Labor Department auditorium. Word of the President's announcement quickly reached us and we were encouraged by his support.

There was little that public hearings or private meetings could do to shed new light on the situation. The union held to its demand for an increase of thirty-four cents an hour (thirty per cent). With equal firmness, the company would offer only thirteen and a half cents an hour. Although they refused to disclose any figures, company officers contended that any greater increase would force a rise in car prices, which were then controlled by Chester Bowles's Office of Price Administration.

I called on Bowles to determine whether his research staff had data which would show the maximum wage increase possible without resulting in price increases. His agency had no facts to help us but Bowles said: "This strike is serious. Why don't you give Walter what he wants?"

I next went to the Department of Commerce to see Secretary

Henry Wallace. I had not seen him since early in his term as Vice-President. I was a bit self-conscious in his presence, remembering that only a last-minute decision by President Roosevelt had kept him from the ticket in 1944 and had led to the nomination and election of Harry Truman; otherwise Wallace would then have been President of the United States. One of the most revealing pictures I have ever seen is of Henry Wallace in the White House looking at Harry Truman as he took the oath of office as President. The facial expression was a blend of lost opportunity, peevishness, and envy.

Now, however, he was doing an acceptable job as Secretary of Commerce. I explained the problem being studied by the Fact-finding Board, insisting that we could not possibly recommend the increase demanded by the union, for that would certainly cause an increase in prices which OPA was not prepared to grant. Secretary Wallace suggested that we recommend a compromise amount, say, fifteen cents an hour increase, but insert an escalation clause which would provide for additional increases if productivity rose. When I suggested this to Walter Reuther he was violently opposed. He said that labor could not be held responsible for company mismanagement. The length of the work week was being reduced. The amount of take-home pay should not decline, and to prevent that the amount asked by the union was essential.

We began another round of hearings and had by this time gathered a small staff of experts borrowed from other government agencies. On December 28 minor company representatives angrily stalked out of our session, charging again that they could not co-operate with us so long as "ability to pay" was treated as an item for investigation. Nevertheless we pressed on with our work and concluded our scheduled public sessions the following day with a presentation from the union. Walter Reuther presented his case. I remember exchanging words with him during his testimony after I detected what I thought to be a flaw in the union case. He had introduced a government chart which demonstrated the steady increase in manufacturing industries over several decades. But the chart also showed a decline in production immediately after the two wars.

"You assume," I asked, "that in this industry the first postwar production year will be higher than before, contrary to the record for all manufacturing after the two wars?"

"Oh, but you cannot use the frying pan industry, the hairpin industry, the textile industry, and all the others to infer such conclusions," Reuther replied.

I smiled and said, "That was a rather catty remark. You introduced the chart."

He gave me a pained look, obviously annoyed with me for looking at the "wrong" part of his chart. "Yes," he said, "but the chart shows a general upward trend of industry over the years except after the two wars." He added that the auto industry also showed such an upward trend.

We worked for another week preparing our report. Judge Stacy's illness prevented his active participation.

Before the Fact-finding Board reported to the President we told Charles Wilson by telephone and Walter Reuther in our office that we would recommend an increase in the hourly wage rate of nineteen and a half cents; we had determined that a higher rate would result in higher prices. Wilson was noncommittal. Reuther angrily insisted that the union would not accept this and that the strike would continue. "If we accepted what you suggest," he said, "it would take us years to earn what we have lost during the strike." As it turned out, he would be right. Reuther was unyielding in his opposition to our proposal, which offered only six cents an hour more than the company had offered. "I don't even dare think in such terms as those," he declared.

On January 10, 1946—the fifty-second day of the strike—we presented our findings to President Truman, explaining our reasoning and conclusions. He was pleased because our recommendations were specifically non-inflationary and would not require a price increase, and he approved our report quickly and issued it with his endorsement.

Although Walter Reuther had denounced our findings privately, he now publicly announced that the finding was a great victory for the union—a statement which caused Garrison and me some amusement. The following day, GM President Wilson denounced the Fact-finding Board and rejected our conclusions without reservation. He accused us of reaching our conclusions on the basis of "unsound assumptions" and stated that the report was unacceptable "in whole or in part." He repeated his determination to stand on his original offer of thirteen and a half cents an hour.

The strike continued until March 13, 1946, ending on its one hundred and thirteenth day. In the final settlement, both sides agreed on eighteen and a half cents an hour, a penny less than our proposal. Although organized labor made some notable gains, the cost to the workers and the nation was immense. It was later estimated that the company lost more than $600 million in unfilled orders, the workers lost as much as $140 million in wages, and some $100 million was lost in retail commissions.

Before I returned home the President asked Garrison and me to join him for lunch at the White House. Although other fact-finding boards had been created by the Secretary of Labor to solve disputes, Truman said that this was the first presidential fact-finding board in history and he felt satisfied that our work had been of value. He said he intended to use a similar procedure whenever strikes threatened the economy of the nation. As it turned out, the GM strike was but a prelude to more major labor trouble in the next few years. The nation soon realized that a voluntary measure, such as ours, was not enough; something stronger than uncovering facts was needed to mediate between big business and big labor. So the Congress responded with the Taft-Hartley Act, which enabled the President to bring both sides to the bargaining table and gave him power to enjoin crippling strikes for ninety days.

Before we left the White House the President told me that he would soon establish a Famine Emergency Relief Committee to help alleviate suffering in the areas devastated by war and that he wanted me to be a member of the committee.

A few days after I returned to Kansas State, exhausted from the fourteen-hour-a-day work on the Fact-finding Board, a telephone call came through from Secretary of State James Byrnes. The leadership of the United Nations Organization was being selected. Secretary Byrnes kept me on the telephone for thirty minutes, saying that President Truman wanted me to become an Assistant Secretary General of the United Nations, and that he and his chief colleagues in the State Department felt it was imperative that an American occupy one of the high posts. The United States was satisfied to have the national of another country become Secretary General, but because we would have to provide more than forty per cent of the funds to support the UN and also because the United States and the Soviet Union had to be "on the inside" of all staff councils, he hoped I would accept. Our discussion developed the fact that the post he had in mind would be concerned mainly, indeed almost exclusively, with administrative, financial, and personnel matters. I declined. That was on March 7, 1946. I was not interested in a position which would not deal with major policy and program problems. Moreover, I had been at Kansas State for only two years, and I could not in good conscience leave at that time. A subsequent call from President Truman did not cause me to change my mind despite the fact that I was anxious to do what I could to support the new world organization; to the best of my recollection, this was the only time in a period of half a century of public service that I failed to respond to a request by a President of the United States.

The year 1946 was one of the busiest of my life. At Kansas State I faced the unending task of obtaining state appropriations for institutional operating costs and funds for plant expansion and renovation. I accepted the chairmanship of the Executive Committee of the Association of Land Grant Colleges which met regularly in Washington, D.C., a time-consuming task. I acceded to President Truman's requests that I be a member of his Committee on Emergency Famine Relief, headed by former President Hoover, serve as a delegate to the first international conference of the United Nations Educational, Scientific and Cultural Organization in Paris, become a member of the Executive Board of UNESCO in Paris, serve as the first permanent chairman of the United States National Commission for UNESCO, and accept membership on the President's Commission on Higher Education. Here were five rather formidable chores for the federal government, a fact which tires me even now as I look back.

I did little for the Committee on Emergency Famine Relief. Hoover was the master; he needed little help. The report of the President's Commission on Higher Education, on which we worked intermittently for months, did not have a significant impact on the President, the Congress, or the public.

The UNESCO task, however, became for a time a dominant interest in my life. Here, I thought, was a unique opportunity to work for intellectual disarmament and the development of better understanding among nations and peoples.

Wars are fought when appeals to reason and understanding fail. My work with OWI had convinced me that the struggle for men's minds is no less urgent, in terms of ultimate victory, than the struggle for men's blood. The battlefield is the physical expression of a conflict of convictions.

The most potent weapon in the war for men's minds is truth. The Nazis had demonstrated in World War II the immediate effectiveness of propaganda. They did not invent it; the armies of Genghis Khan had been preceded by secret agents who spread fear and defeatism among the people who were about to be attacked. But the modern science of propaganda warfare had been formulated in the laboratory of German militarism during the years that we and other democracies were too busy with the sciences and businesses of peace to worry about war. Just as they had adapted the highly mobile Panzer divisions to the tactical functions once performed by cavalry, so too had they adapted the use of radio, cable, radiophoto transmissions, the motion picture, and other current communication devices to an age-old tactic. The Nazis' use of propaganda had been skillful and successful. Hitler had launched his propaganda offensives well ahead of his armies with notable results. His advance propaganda had been partly responsible for his easy victories in Poland, Norway, and the Low Countries, and it had neutralized the opposition to the Nazis in their crushing march through France. Hitler's failure in Russia was due in considerable part to his inability to crack the Russian will to resist.

In the last analysis, however, propaganda could not prevail in the arena against truth. While the enemy resorted to manipulation, distortion, and outright lies, we told the truth, for what we needed to tell was in fact true. The striking power of truth was cumulative; in time the accumulated force of truth would explode like a bombshell in the faces of dictators and their false prophets.

Neither in war nor in peace did the people in totalitarian societies easily obtain the truth. Totalitarian methods of intellectual repression were awesomely effective. In a free country, propaganda based on lies was not effective, for all the means of mass communication kept the people adequately informed and the leaders of state ultimately honest. Lies cannot spread or be believed for long where the truth is allowed to compete.

When President Truman asked me to serve in UNESCO I accepted eagerly because I believed then, and I believe now, that since wars begin in the minds of men it is in the minds of men that the structure of peace must be built—and built solely on truth. And that conviction was to be a key proclamation in the constitution of UNESCO.

With my colleagues of the first United States delegation to UNESCO, I left in November for Paris with high expectations. My roommate in a suite on the U.S.S. *George Washington* was Chester Bowles, a leading New Dealer and Fair Dealer, who possessed an abundance of common sense. He said to me one day, "You know, the government is getting so large that it is becoming ineffective. Procedures are cumbersome. It is difficult to get a decision made." I replied, "Before I left Washington I followed the rule that if I could get a dozen initials on a document I considered it approved. Of course one disapproval always killed the proposal!" Chester Bowles—once governor of Connecticut, and twice United States ambassador to India—and I have kept in touch with one another by correspondence, but I have never asked him what he thinks of getting decisions made and action taken in the present gargantuan federal government.

The first responsibility in Paris was formally to make operative the constitution of the new international agency which had been written by a preparatory commission in London the year before. A major author of the constitution had been my intimate friend, the distinguished American poet, Archibald MacLeish, a man much admired by the delegates from all nations at that first conference.

Then two controversies kept us in session for about five weeks. One dealt with the program of the organization. The underdeveloped nations wanted UNESCO to become primarily a relief organization, channeling funds from the developed nations into their countries so as to equalize education opportunity. They contended that the "defenses of peace" could not be built in men's minds when illiteracy and lack of educational opportunity were rampant in many nations. One Bolivian delegate pointed out that, of the world's two hundred countries, dependencies, and territories, nearly half had illiteracy rates of more than fifty per cent, and twenty had illiteracy rates of ninety-five per cent. In these countries some 2,800 languages were spoken; communication within many countries was as deficient as communication between countries.

One nation wanted UNESCO to develop a treaty for the stand-
ardization of musical pitch, declaring that music was a universal language and we therefore had to depend upon it in developing that
mutual understanding which we all agreed was one of the ingredients of
international peace. Several nations, whose population lived at high
altitudes, asked that UNESCO finance high-altitude research. With the
United States delegation I worked day and night to try to get into
the program a major effort to tear down the barriers which obstructed
the flow of information across national boundaries—censorship of newspapers, magazines, and press dispatches, jamming of radio broadcasts,
quotas and tariffs on the importation of books, magazines, and other
informational documents. Even some of our best friends, such as the
British delegation, would not agree to the totality of my proposal, suggesting that a completely free flow of news and ideas between nations
was not necessarily desirable.

Eventually, to keep the conference from floundering, perhaps even
from disintegrating at its first meeting, the nations had to adopt one
hundred and thirty-eight separate projects. The total budget of the
organization was to be less than seven million dollars, a fraction of the
budget of a single American college.

The second controversy involved the election of the first Secretary
General. The United States felt that an American should occupy the
post in view of the fact that the nationals of other countries headed the
United Nations and several of the UN specialized agencies. Our
candidate was Archibald MacLeish. He would have been accepted
enthusiastically and unanimously by all the delegates at the conference.
But MacLeish balked. He did not wish to accept.

In an all-morning meeting in a huge salon of the Hotel Crillon,
our delegates and technical experts pleaded with MacLeish to accept,
even if he remained as Secretary General of the organization only for
its formative period. I wish I could remember his exact words when at
the end of two hours he stood at the table and explained in detail why
he had to adhere to his negative attitude. In conclusion he indicated
that he feared we did not understand. He remarked that, if he told us
that he was busy making a living in manufacturing refrigerators or in
selling insurance and that he could not afford to take on an international task, we would comprehend and accept his decision, but when
he truthfully said he could not accept because he had to devote his

thinking and energies to writing poetry we wouldn't understand. His final words were spoken with emotion.

He left the room. A full minute of silence ensued. Eyes literally filled with tears. Some of us, no matter how disappointed we were, did understand and inwardly applauded.

When word reached the conference that MacLeish was not available, a scramble for delegates to back particular candidates began. Finally Julian Huxley of Great Britain was elected. Huxley, of course, had an international reputation as a scholar and author. He had, in my judgment, no organizational or leadership qualities. He was a man of changing passionate interests. In the American delegation we commented that he could be as enthusiastic about surveying the butterfly species of Africa as he could about determining how the nations of the East and West could develop meaningful communication.

Despite my initial disappointment, UNESCO remained one of my deepest interests from 1946 to 1949, when I gave up the chairmanship of the United States National Commission for UNESCO. I finally dropped out of all UNESCO activities in 1951. In the meantime I served as vice-chairman of the United States delegations to UNESCO international conferences in Mexico City (1947), Beirut, Lebanon (1948), and Paris (1949). The chairman of our delegations at these conferences was William Benton, Assistant Secretary of State for Public Affairs, a dynamo of a man. He was brimming with ideas and always impatient, desiring prompt action. In business he had a Midas touch.

In Beirut one day he said to me, "Milton, if you will tell me how to get along in the city of Washington, I'll tell you how you can easily make a fortune." Unfortunately this mutual educational enterprise never got off the ground.

At a congressional appropriations hearing one day, Benton was supporting a request for funds which would constitute the United States contribution to UNESCO. About the room were fifty paintings that belonged to Encyclopaedia Britannica, which Benton headed when he was not in government. Some of these paintings were representational, others were of the French Impressionist period, a few were abstractions. They had been on a tour of many nations as one means of interesting other peoples in the American culture. A congressman sitting at the far end of the huge conference table in the hearing room suddenly shouted, "Secretary Benton, will you please tell me what this picture is all about?" pointing a shaking finger at one of the paintings. "You tell me," Benton said. "You are closer to it than I am." Since the painting was a total abstraction, artistically loud without seeming to say anything, I've always wondered whether Benton's response to the congressman had a double meaning.

CHAPTER 10

The essence of nostalgia is an awareness
that what has been will never be again.

THE FEVERISH EDUCATIONAL and governmental
activities of 1946 were interrupted by an event of consummate sadness.
My mother, Ida Stover Eisenhower, eighty-four years of age, died on
September 11. Only the day before she had been for a leisurely ride
with my father's sister and her husband. When she arrived home a
friend took a picture of her as she was about to enter her house. She
was laughing and apparently was in the best of health; the photo is a
precious keepsake. During the night she awoke, complained of a
stomach pain, asked her housekeeper for a drink of water, and went
back to sleep, not to waken again.

The five living brothers gathered at our home in Abilene, a home
filled with a thousand pleasant memories. Quietly and with gratitude
we spoke of the exemplary life our parents had led, and reminisced at
length about the methods Father and Mother had used in managing
six healthy, active boys.

Each of us had often been asked what influences existed in our
modest but comfortable home that resulted in six sons' achieving at
least modest success in their diverse life endeavors.

Arthur, the first-born, quiet and serious, had become a well-known
banker in Kansas City, executive vice-president of one bank and president of another; his specialty was the financing each year of the ava-
lanche of grain that flowed from the farms of the Midwest.

Edgar, a lovable, happy, and generous man, chose the law and made
a fortune, but used his legal talent for half a century to help others.

Dwight, possessing a slide-rule precision of logic, a student of history and a genuine humanist, achieved national and international leadership but never lost the modesty that characterized him as a youth.

186

Roy, a dedicated family man, became a pharmacist but died in his late forties, the same year that Father passed away.

Earl, just older than I, the redhead of the family and more exhilarated by argument than anyone else I have ever known, became a graduate engineer but later changed to newspaper, radio, and public relations work.

I, the youngest and perhaps a bit spoiled, cast my career in the field of public service.

Personal relationships in our family were ideal. Despite the rollicking activity of six sons, our home was dominated by serenity. I never heard a cross word spoken between Father and Mother, and corrections of their sons were always quietly spoken, never in anger. This serenity was a natural concomitant of our parents' utter devotion to their religious beliefs. They were fundamentalists. Mother, in her youth, had memorized 1,365 verses of the Bible in six months and received a medal for this achievement, something she always cherished. She was a living biblical concordance, with an apt quotation to meet every circumstance. Father was a member of the Brethren in Christ Church (nicknamed River Brethren), for his father had been a minister in the church. All of us boys were raised in the River Brethren Church, which was strictly fundamentalist in doctrine.

Father insisted that we read the Bible from cover to cover, not once but several times. He had a method of making this moderately exciting, but I'm not sure it enabled us to comprehend the Scriptures. One of us was permitted to read aloud until another discovered a mistake. The one who identified the error was then permitted to read. When Father read, I now realize, he deliberately made errors in order to pass the privilege of reading on to one of us. One of his Bibles was in German, a language in which he was fluent; he never spoke German in our presence, however, for in our early days in Abilene one was looked down upon if he spoke a foreign language and Father wanted none of that for his sons. He also read the New Testament in Greek and often pointed out to us that the Greek version did not have all the punctuation which appears in the King James version and sometimes commas would change significantly the meaning of a sentence.

The Ten Commandments were our constant guide. These were the imperatives of our youth. They became part of us. We had to observe them at home, at school, and in all other activities. Mother especially felt that a good person was one who lived by these concepts, a bad person did not. Indeed to her in a very real sense there was no glory to be assigned to anyone, including her sons, because of worldly achievement. The sole difference in human beings was between good and evil.

Another strong influence in our home was responsibility. The chores of running two acres of productive land in the town of Abilene were rotated each week by Mother, thus avoiding favoritism and complaints. One son was assigned to care for the orchard which, before it was destroyed by wind, had peaches, apples, persimmons, pears, and other fruits. Two worked in an enormous vegetable garden which produced more than the family could consume, surpluses being sold to others. The garden was kept so free of weeds that a neighbor once remarked, "You must use eyebrow tweezers in pulling the small ones." One took care of the chickens. One was assigned to milking the cow and caring for our wonderful horse, Silver, and one had to help in the house—the only responsibility that was seriously disliked. The house task required one of us to get up not later than five in the morning, build fires in two stoves (later, a furnace too), and make preliminary arrangements for breakfast. Helping with cooking, washing and drying dishes, and laundry were all part of this assignment.

When eight of us were at dinner, Mother had a unique way of preventing discord as dessert was served. A pie or cake was placed for cutting before one of us and the one who cut had last choice in the selection process. So we became expert in cutting pieces of uniform size; one had to use a micrometer to tell the differences between pieces.

The invariable rule was that, when chores were done, studies had to be mastered. After that, and only then, we were free to do as we pleased so long as our behavior met acceptable standards.

General Eisenhower, on his homecoming in 1945, had said, "The glory of our lives was that we were poor but didn't know it." Indeed we didn't. In fact I have never considered that we were poor. We had a tidy home, more home-produced food than we could consume, adequate clothing, and full opportunities for an excellent education. Though Father never made more than one hundred and fifty dollars a month, we never experienced deprivation. Our life style was such that each of us had to learn responsibility when we were very young. Responsibility was as natural as eating, sleeping, and going to school. We did not feel imposed upon by the tasks assigned to us or by the stricture that lessons had to be mastered.

Father, uninterested in politics but obviously a conservative, was a great admirer of Abraham Lincoln. He often quoted to us Lincoln's words: "You cannot bring about prosperity by discouraging thrift, strengthen the weak by weakening the strong, or lift the wage earner by pulling down the wage payer . . . or further the brotherhood of man by inciting class hatred, or help men permanently by doing for them what they could and should do for themselves." This last phrase became one of the guiding thoughts of President Eisenhower during his two terms in the White House. "Government," he often said, "should do for people only what they cannot do for themselves."

Learning responsibility at an early age is easier in a small town or rural community than it is in our great metropolitan centers. A youngster is quick to sense the difference between needful and contrived responsibility. If a family has a vegetable garden, and poultry and animals that must be cared for, responsible care is obviously necessary, and most youngsters thrive under responsibility and take pride in redeeming it. I often wonder how this valuable lesson can be learned in a family living in a city apartment, or in a ghetto with its street life, or even in a suburb where mowing the lawn is about the only work available to a youngster.

A fourth influence—or lack of it—was our parents' determination not to influence the career choices of their sons. My grandfather, minister and fairly well-to-do farmer, had wanted my father to become a farmer, but Father objected, choosing first merchandising and then "stationary" engineering, and eventually company management. I think it was this rebellion on his part that caused him and Mother to permit each son to choose for himself how he would make a living and contribute to the general welfare. After twenty-five years of working with young people as a university president, I am convinced that the worst mistake parents can make is to be insistent about the fields of study to be pursued by their sons and daughters. If the field so dictated is not in harmony with the young person's talents or preferences, he can and usually does become frustrated, academic achievement declines, academic failure often results, and his whole life may be injured. Parents should not even try to influence their children in the selection of a college or university. The consequences here, too, can be serious. Parents can make certain that their children consider the strengths and weaknesses of possible choices of colleges or universities, and they can help the children consider the requirements of each area of education and possible career potentials, but the ultimate choice should invariably be left up to the young people themselves.

Father died early in 1942 at the age of eighty. All the sons but Ike were at home for the funeral. Ike, burdened as head of the Operations Planning Division in Washington, could do no more than lock his office for an hour and sit in quiet contemplation at the time the funeral service was being conducted in Abilene.

Mother's gradual loss of memory became evident to me soon after Father's death. Elderly people often forget recent occurrences but continue to recall incidents of their youth. Mother's situation was different. She was throwing up a defense mechanism to ease the grief she felt in losing a lifetime companion, a life that I truly believe was ideal for both Father and Mother. Hence, as her memory failed, it applied to the entire sweep of her life. But serious loss of memory was not to come until the year of her death.

In October 1944 a lady whose name I never knew stopped in Abilene on her way from New York to San Francisco and came to our home to see Mother. The two sat on a swing on the front porch and for half an hour the stranger told Mother about what her son was doing in the army in Europe. Suddenly Mother, with a flash of memory, said, "I have a son in Europe too!" There was no cleverness, no pretense in this remark. She simply thought the visitor would like to know that the two had something in common.

Mother was indifferent to her inability to remember the past and became clever in avoiding direct answers. My wife and I had dinner with her one evening early in 1945, and as we stood up from the table I said, "Mother, can you tell me what you just had for dinner?"

She looked at me, her eyes sparkling with amusement, and replied, "It was good, wasn't it?"

On another occasion I tried to test her on a vital point: "Can you name your sons in the order of their births?"

"Certainly," she said, and then after a pause of a few seconds added, "You know them as well as I do!"

It was in 1945 that Mother was named Kansas Mother of the Year. She was also elected National Mother of the Year, but her health was such that she could not go to New York for the presentation ceremony, so the honor went to another, as of course it should. Many years later I would be named American Father of the Year, but I surely did not deserve such an honor in the sense that Mother did the designation offered to her. She was a thoroughly good, happy, talented person who devoted her life to her family, friends, and even strangers. She was never too busy to help the sick. She played the piano and sang beautifully, and took time to teach each of her sons to play the piano, a pastime which has remained with me, though now I prefer the organ.

It was that year that General Eisenhower came home from Europe in a triumphal tour through New York, Washington, Kansas City, and ultimately to our home town, Abilene.

Later, on July 17, 1947, the five Eisenhower brothers went to Wisconsin as guests of my father-in-law, L. R. Eakin, to spend a few weeks fishing together. On our first night in a cozy cabin we prepared fishing tackle for the next day, when we were going to try our luck at catching muskellunges, large, elusive fighting fish much sought after by anglers. As we worked in the cabin Earl sat down on a fishhook, jumped to his feet screaming, and reached behind for the invading hook. A photographer snapped a picture of the five of us at that moment. It won the Associated Press prize for the year, but I'm not sure we should have been proud of it, for shamefully all but Earl were laughing so heartily that one could almost see our tonsils.

With the help of several men from the Wisconsin Conservation Department, we fished a remote lake noted for muskellunges. General Eisenhower was the first to land a twenty-two-pounder, a respectable catch. Earl did the same. Arthur, who never before had fished, had his line taken by a twenty-pounder and succeeded in landing it. In the meantime Edgar, who had an inexperienced guide, hooked two muskellunges but lost them when the guide clumsily tried to gaff them. Luckily, he hooked a third. As he slowly reeled it toward the boat he said to the guide, "If you lose this one for me I swear I'm going to throw you right in the middle of this lake and I doubt if you can make it to shore." This time the guide struck the fish between the eyes with the gaff, stunned it, and pulled it into the boat. I had no luck with a bucktail with which I had been fishing, so tried a live bait and this time succeeded. The fish I finally landed after half an hour's struggle turned out to be a northern pike rather than a muskellunge, but since it weighed more than thirty pounds the gibes of my brothers, as we put in at the dock, were offset by my bragging about the biggest fish of the day. The picture taken then was published as a lure to summer vacationers.

Two years later we brothers were again together, this time in St. Louis where Ike, president of Columbia University, was to address the American Bar Association, an engagement insistently arranged by Edgar, who was active in the association. The speech Ike delivered at that convention was the nearest to a political talk he had ever given. I had worked with him on it in Wisconsin just before we went to St. Louis.

Fifty newspapermen and photographers gathered in our hotel suite and in the course of the interview a correspondent asked, "When were you brothers last together?"

Edgar quickly responded, "In June 1947 at Boulder Junction."

Ike interjected, "No, it was July."

"I'll bet you ten dollars it was June."

"I'll take that bet!"

"General, are you sure you are right?" a newspaperman asked.

"No," was the reply, "but I'm sure Ed is always wrong!"

Since his graduation from the University of Michigan Law School Edgar had lived in the Pacific Northwest, the most beautiful part of our country. He was immensely proud of the locality, as if the land were blessed by his presence upon it. We never ceased to josh him about his local pride. This time he lectured us on the superior merits of Olympic oysters, delicious but tiny tidbits from Puget Sound. He telephoned his secretary and had her ship by air express a large quantity of the oysters. When they arrived and were served at dinner, four of us pretended to gag on them and Edgar had to get the help of lawyer friends to consume the shipment.

We were not together again until 1952, this time in Chicago during the Republican National Convention. There hard work kept us from engaging in our usual banter. Following Ike's nomination, Arthur, Edgar, and Earl returned to their homes. My wife and I went to northern Wisconsin to join her parents for a couple of weeks of relaxation before I immersed myself in a mixture of campaign and university duties. Early one morning my father-in-law, then seventy-six years old, and I went out in a boat without a guide. We were not having much luck in our attempts to catch walleyes for dinner when, with no preamble of warning, he said to me, "You know, Milton, when you first married Helen, people referred to you as my son-in-law. As time has gone on they have referred to me as your father-in-law, and I don't like it!"

I was sympathetic, I said, for the cross I bore in that regard was worse and more persistent than his.

"Oh no, it isn't," he exclaimed, obviously irritated. "Now they refer to me as the father-in-law of Ike's brother!"

Several months later, when he was back in Washington, D.C., he attended a reception at the British Embassy. In a report of the reception in the social section of the Washington *Star* appeared this gem: "Many persons inquired about the tall, handsome, white-haired gentleman who was greeted in a friendly way by many of the guests. This was L. R. Eakin, father of Mrs. Milton S. Eisenhower, sister-in-law of the President." The next day I received a clipping from him, marked in red, "This is too much!"

While reunions of the brothers were a blend of gaiety and serious discussion, and relatively free of publicity, one departed from the norm. It was lacking in humor and received notorious publicity.

I was spending the weekend at the White House when a telephone call came from Edgar; he had just checked in at the Statler and would be so tied up that day and evening that he couldn't join us until the next day. On that first evening Edgar had what he thought was an off-the-record discussion with a newspaperwoman. He did not understand that anything involving the President of the United States vitiates all the normal ethics of the newspaper profession. So the press the next morning carried streamer headlines and a full-column story indicating that Edgar Eisenhower said that practically every law passed during the Roosevelt, Truman, and Eisenhower administrations was unconstitutional. This was a juicy story. Newspapermen were avid in their desire to get an answer from the President.

That evening Edgar was to join the President and me for dinner at the White House. Mamie was otherwise engaged. Before Edgar arrived the President indicated that he would not bring up the subject about Edgar's comments and if it did come up he would say very little.

The subject came up all right, almost as soon as Ed reached the oval room upstairs. Cocktails were being served when Ed said, "I suppose you're mad as hell about that story in the morning newspapers, but I've been letting this thing cook in my inside for a long time and I finally had to say something. I understood my comments were not for publication."

I suggested it was naïve to think a brother could make comments about the President, especially in Washington, and not have the remarks published.

"Well," Ed said, "I'm a citizen and have the same right as anyone else to speak my mind." He went on to explain what I knew was the fact: he was not basically opposed to most of the federal programs initiated in the period since 1933, but he felt that there was no constitutional authority for most of them. If constitutional amendments had been proposed for such things as welfare, Social Security, foreign aid, and so on, he would have voted for them.

"The trouble is, Ed," I commented, "that the newspapers and the public are not interested in your views as Edgar Eisenhower, or mine as Milton Eisenhower, but only as the comments of a brother of the President. If Harry Truman were still President and you made the comments you did, probably nothing would have appeared in the press. You have imposed upon a family relationship."

This was a new idea to Ed. After a long silence he remarked that he had not thought in such terms and we could be sure he would not do the same thing again.

He left the White House for his hotel at about ten-thirty. When he arrived at the Statler Hotel and reached his floor, he found some fifty newspapermen waiting for him. He succeeded in pushing his way through the throng, opened his door, and then impetuously turned and said in a loud voice, "Boy, did my brothers give me hell!"

That made top headlines too. It was days before the story died. When the President held his next press conference and the family question came up, the President grinned and remarked that he and Ed had differed on scores of subjects and what had recently happened was simply a continuation of a lifetime habit. This brought laughter and ended the subject.

The next reunion of the brothers was again in Wisconsin, shortly after President Eisenhower retired to his farm at Gettysburg. The five of us had a beautiful cottage on a private lake in Wisconsin and a separate dining room with quarters for my housekeeper and houseman, who were delighted to be with us and do the cooking and a few other chores; they, too, enjoyed fishing for walleyes, small-mouth bass, and trout.

Conversation was never lacking at these get-togethers. Arthur and Earl were moderate conservatives. Edgar insisted upon his role as constitutionalist. Ike and I maintained a middle-of-the-road philosophy. Discussions would begin early in the morning as we walked from our cabin to the dining room and would continue all day, save for the time we were in different boats on the Wisconsin lakes. We were together for two weeks. At our last dinner discussion we found ourselves essentially in agreement on domestic and foreign problems. That was the normal result at each of our reunions.

Our last reunion was on October 12, 1963, a birthday party given by President Eisenhower's closest friends, including members of the Cabinet in his two administrations, as well as members of the family. There were now only four of us brothers.

My task was to introduce President Eisenhower but the committee on arrangements asked me to depart from normal protocol and speak as long as I wished.

For once, I said, I was going to have the pleasure of presenting *my* brother. "This is really quite a switch," I said. "I was once asked to make a major speech in Wichita, Kansas, and in introducing me the presiding officer spent five minutes extolling the virtues of General Eisenhower, who was then Chief of Staff of the army. It suddenly occurred to him that he was being rude, so to redeem himself he exclaimed, 'But of course we should not refer to our distinguished guest tonight as the brother of General Eisenhower. We should refer to General Eisenhower as the brother of our eminent speaker!' "

This sort of corrective afterthought was unique, I commented. Usually folks weren't even aware of their mild discourtesy. "Some months before the Wichita incident," I went on, "I came into Paris from Berlin on a troop train so early in the morning that taxis were not available. A major commandeered a jeep for me. Just as we were ready to pull out of the station another civilian raced to the car and asked for a ride. He kept up a stream of conversation until we reached the Crillon Hotel. As I got out of the car he exclaimed, 'Boy, am I going to write home and tell my family I rode uptown with an Eisenhower!' "

Needless to say, I blushed, grabbed my bags, and started for the hotel entrance. He shouted after me, "Of course I won't tell them which one!"

This brought hearty laughter from the several hundred persons present at the birthday party. I think I heard Edgar roar most of all.

Jokingly, I said to President Eisenhower's friends, "One thing I have never understood: that is why anyone should ever have been in doubt, in 1948 or later, as to the political convictions and affiliation of Dwight David Eisenhower. Actually, the commitment began at birth and was solidified at a very tender age. In 1896, William McKinley came to Abilene and the political fathers decreed a torchlight parade. Because the town was one hundred per cent Republican, the elders could see no reason to make so much fuss when the outcome was already known. So the political managers frantically called upon the youth of Abilene. The first torch in the parade was carried by Dwight, six years old; then came Edgar, eight, then Arthur, ten. I have never been certain whether the real inducement here was William McKinley or a flaming torch!"

I suggested that many of the views of Dwight Eisenhower as President had developed in his early years. Indeed, two years before the McKinley parade, Dwight went to visit an uncle near Topeka. Uncle had a goose (I was mistaken, it was a gander) which, like the notorious one in *Friendly Persuasion*, would take after a youngster and chase him all over the farm. Young Dwight was terrified. So Uncle armed him with an old broom. The next time the goose (boo!) made an attack, Dwight gave the broom a great sweep and hit it in the exact center of its rear.

"That solved the problem," I commented. "And this was the origin of his conviction that a nation can negotiate only from a position of strength!"

I turned to the President's early life with his wife. The day after Dwight and Mamie were married, they had a wedding breakfast at our house and then came back a year later for their first anniversary. Dwight went uptown to meet old friends and got into a poker game. By dinnertime he was six hundred dollars down. He couldn't quit or call home to pacify the family, especially Mamie. It was two the next morning before he finally got even with the board and was able to rejoin the family. "I need not describe the homecoming," I said, "but I am sure it was at this moment that the future President determined that deficits are unsound, that fiscal integrity is a prime requisite of government!"

I suggested that since the presidential years were over, and members of the official families had resumed their own private personalities, even I, as a university president, could appropriately and without fear of a charge of plagiarism, resume my rightful title of *President* Eisenhower.

The President had been amused by these and a dozen other remarks I made, but this last one caused him to laugh uncontrollably.

In presenting my brother at that dinner—his own remarks were moving but brief—I pointed out that those of us who for eight years had enjoyed his hospitality at White House stag dinners had always been given a memento. It was now our turn to reciprocate. We presented to President Eisenhower a huge Steuben bowl, engraved in bold letters: UNITED STATES OF AMERICA.

"Not only we hosts but the people of the nation, of all political faiths, will say that this tribute is indeed appropriate," I concluded.

In our quiet visit in Abilene at the time of Mother's death, Edgar suggested that the home property was so meaningful to us that we could never permit anyone else to live there. This was an expression of love for all our parents had done for us. It would, Edgar thought, and we all agreed, be a desecration to their memory to pass the property on to others for what might be a less happy use. So my brothers commissioned me, with power of attorney, to handle the property in whatever way I deemed best. In a few weeks I offered the property as a gift to the Eisenhower Foundation which had been established to honor the war record of General Eisenhower. On that property today is our home, a magnificent museum, a beautiful library, a place of meditation where President Eisenhower is buried, and a set of entablatures which proclaim the simple and religiously inspired concepts that ruled the lives of our parents and their children. As I was preparing to sign the deed of gift to the Foundation, Mr. Charles M. Harger, my dearest friend in Abilene, said, "But, Milton, this is so much out of the way that no one will come down here." (We lived on the wrong side of the tracks, in the southern part of the town.) Since the Center, privately financed by thousands of gifts, was opened, more than five million persons have visited the property; they have come from every state and more than a hundred foreign countries.

Arthur passed away when the President was in his second term. Earl died at the time that David Eisenhower and Julie Nixon were being married in New York, so I missed the wedding, though my son and daughter were there. All know of President Eisenhower's death after a heroic battle with five heart attacks. Edgar died in 1971 when I was in Kiev, Russia, but I was able to get to the funeral in Tacoma, Washington.

It is strange, having had five brothers for most of my life, to be the only remaining member of my family. As I think back over the years and relive in memory our youth in Abilene, in an environment of splendid isolation, and consider with what affection we kept in touch with one another despite varying careers, opinions, and locations, I find myself satisfied that no family could have had a more rewarding relationship. For all American parents of all colors and creeds, I hope that we can reshape our national priorities, improve our style of living, and rededicate ourselves to the highest ideals of our country—that their children can enjoy the serenity and joy of home, learn the lesson of responsibility, and enjoy the full fruits of education that meant so much to the six sons of David and Ida Eisenhower.

CHAPTER 11

> Because we so often confuse idealism with
> naïveté, we frequently accept what *can* be
> instead of pursuing what *could* be; we will
> be more successful in building a better world
> if we stop thinking of idealism as an ado-
> lescent disease to which adults should be
> immune.

LESS THAN TWO months after Mother's death I was, as recounted, in Paris for the first international UNESCO conference.

Beginning then and for the next three years every moment I could take from my duties at Kansas State was devoted to the program of the United Nations Educational, Scientific and Cultural Organization and to the United States National Commission for UNESCO which carried out our national obligations in the international program. I was frequently in Washington, conferring usually with Assistant Secretary of State William Benton and occasionally with President Truman, who was enthusiastic about UNESCO's potential. I had to go to Paris several times as a member of the Executive Board of UNESCO which governed the organization between the annual general conferences in which all member nations participated. My travels throughout the United States to gain widespread co-operation with our National Commission were frequent and tiring.

The Preparatory Commission which wrote the UNESCO constitution had completed its work on November 16, 1945, in a London scarred by bombs. The members of the Commission signed the document and governments were invited to deposit instruments of acceptance with the government of the United Kingdom. At that time no one knew how many nations would co-operate in the fledgling organization.

Nearly eight months later President Truman signed Public Law 565, which authorized the creation of the United States National Commission for UNESCO with one hundred members—sixty representatives of national voluntary organizations interested in educational, scientific, and cultural matters, ten representatives of the federal government, fifteen representatives of the educational, scientific, and cultural interests of state and local governments, and fifteen persons chosen at large. I was selected by the President as one of the representatives at large and named as chairman.

The membership of the National Commission was excellent for the purpose. The voluntary national organizations—from the National Education Association and the American Federation of Labor to the League of Women Voters and the General Federation of Women's Clubs—had millions of members in their organizations who could be reached by their own national publications. The federal representatives were useful, for the commission was in fact a quasi-private institution with considerable governmental responsibility, especially in the field of foreign policy. State and local representatives gave reasonable assurance that schools of all levels, state boards of education, and related institutions would co-operate. The membership at large enabled the President to achieve balance and breadth of representation; it also permitted him to name individuals in whom he and the State Department officials had confidence and who could keep intimately in touch with official policies.

The legislation gave the commission several functions: to advise the government on matters affecting UNESCO, to help each year in selecting delegates to the annual UNESCO conference, to advise the delegates of the United States on activities the international organization should undertake and administer, and to promote the general objectives of UNESCO throughout the United States. This last function was the most important and would occupy a major part of the time of the commission members.

At the November 1946 inaugural meeting of the international organization in Paris, where the constitution became a living reality as thirty delegations officially participated—and a dozen national observers, still skeptical, attended—our time was spent, as I have said, mainly on troublesome program and leadership matters; we also argued endlessly about organizational and budgetary problems.

At the Mexico City General Conference, a year later, we dealt primarily with problems of program priorities and finances. (It was at this conference that I developed a deep interest in Latin America and began studies which in the two Eisenhower administrations would place upon me major responsibilities in the field of United States-Latin American relations.) When I returned home from Mexico I found myself to be ambivalent in my thinking about the UNESCO philosophy. I made half a dozen speeches which gave expression to my doubts, while still upholding UNESCO's central mission.

I believed that we could be initiating a crusade of historic importance, a crusade that had a chance over a period of years to change history. The central purpose of the organization, in the minds of many of us, was surely that of developing such significant understanding and common objectives among the peoples of the world that ultranationalism would decline and that transnational concepts and goals conducive to peace would develop, and that the cluster of international agencies being developed under the umbrella of the United Nations would succeed better in their specialized missions as a consequence of our work in the intellectual field.

On the other hand, I was poignantly aware of the fact that previous efforts throughout history to achieve a workable degree of universal cooperation had failed. Were we, as Franklin Parker later said, "touched by utopian idealism reminiscent of Plato's Republic"? Obvious to all was that social man had improved mightily his capacity to kill but had not found effective means of working peacefully for the settlement of serious international disputes.

The periods of uneasy peace which history had witnessed had been brought about not primarily through understanding or international compact but by one leader or nation achieving domination over most others. History was replete with attempts of this kind. Invariably they had been made through physical conquest—made by warriors whose prime motivation was the desire for personal power, glory, and wealth.

Alexander the Great, Attila the Hun, Genghis Khan, Tamerlane, Napoleon, Hitler—all of these attempted a unification of the world they knew on a basis of physical force. The wars each of them initiated were to lead to a universal order, an enforced world government, which would be an extension of the conqueror's private will and hence a multiplication of the conqueror's personal glory. There was no doubt that most of the conquerors regarded their egoistic will as a beneficent force in the world; they told themselves that its implementation through world control would be a great boon to mankind; but since the means they chose were flatly contradictory of the ends they professed, their attempts failed. In every case they failed.

But they failed in varying degrees. The vast empires of some of the conquerors vanished without a trace. The immense western conquests of Attila the Hun and Genghis Khan, for example, lasted a relatively few years as history is measured and, when they crumbled, did so with such completeness that there were no cultural or institutional remains. The conquests of Alexander and Napoleon, on the other hand, had cultural and institutional effects which are felt to this day. What was the inherent difference in the two? It seemed to me that the difference was in the fact that Attila and his ilk built their ephemeral empires out of pure action, so that when the force of action was withdrawn nothing was left—but in the conquests of Alexander and Napoleon, action was joined with ideas: many of the ideas remained and were embodied in social institutions long after the physical force had gone. While I did not regard either Alexander or Napoleon as great creative minds in themselves, each of them had ridden the crest of a wave of ideas—revolutionary ideas about the nature of man and of the universe. Behind Alexander was Aristotle and the magnificent climax of Greek culture. Behind Napoleon was Voltaire and the rational triumphs of the French Enlightenment. It was this force of mind behind the physical force which made an enduring impress upon the world.

The same was true of the Roman Empire. In many respects Rome was the most successful attempt in history to mold peoples of diverse languages, cultures, and allegiances into a single coherent social order with a central focus of authority. The Roman peace which covered the whole of the civilized world of the West was, of course, imposed initially by force, but not by force alone. Certainly it could never have been maintained over the many centuries of its existence solely by force. The Roman peace was more a creature of Roman ideas of justice and social organization than it was of the Roman legions. It was only when the Romans lost their commitments to these ideas that their empire fell. The ideas remained, however, articulate in the Latin language, to exert a persuasive influence through the medieval period and the Renaissance into our own time.

In short, the repeated attempts to conquer the world by force had been paralleled by or alternated with attempts to organize the world through ideas—and it was only when the two kinds of attempts had been linked that anything permanently valid had been achieved. Moreover, the permanence seemed to have resided in the ideas and not in the force with which they were initially imposed.

Was it possible, then, to unite the world through ideas alone—ideas divorced entirely from coercion? Could mental persuasion be counted upon, by itself, to extend and maintain social order?

Actually, this effort, too, had historic roots. I felt that the medieval period which succeeded the collapse of the Roman Empire was a classic example. During nearly all of that period Rome, the Eternal City, continued as the focus of whatever general social order prevailed throughout Europe. Rome was the seat of authority—but this authority was, in essence, spiritual rather than physical. The Pope in Rome was a weak person, if strength be measured in physical terms. He had direct command over no strong army. He ruled directly no great territory. There were then dozens of great lords in Europe whose feudal power exceeded his. Yet these lords paid him allegiance and, time and again, used their force as instruments of his will. This was the conquest of ideas. The great lords recognized the spiritual authority of the Pope as Christ's representative on earth.

The medieval synthesis was a religious one. The organizing principle of Europe, in so far as Europe was organized at all, was primarily a religious idea. And of the twin symbols of power, castle and cathedral, the latter, the symbol of faith, was clearly dominant. In those days the mental life of Europe was more unified than it has ever been since. Men of learning all over Europe had a common language—Latin. They had common intellectual traditions, inherited from the classic culture and sustained in modified form by the Church. They could be said to have understood one another to a greater degree than intellectuals in different countries understand each other in the modern period. Indeed, it was for this reason that Richard Johnson, who was American observer at the Conference of Allied Ministers of Education from 1943 to 1945, had said that the roots of UNESCO were to be found in that period of Western European history which was commonly referred to as the age of darkness. Certainly it seemed to me that it was this period of history which led to the creation of the International Institute of Intellectual

Cooperation in 1924 and the International Bureau of Education in 1925, the immediate predecessors of UNESCO.

But the medieval synthesis, the unification of Europe through a common faith embodied in a common church, was gradually undermined by the growing arrogance of unruly lords; as certain of the lords began to exercise the sovereign power of nation-states they paid less and less attention to the dictates of Rome. The idea of the nation-state proved stronger during the Renaissance than the idea of a universal church, and as the concept of unlimited national sovereignty was solidified in powerful states the ruling effectiveness of the Church was destroyed.

The dream, but not the reality, of a common world mind as a basis for world order still remained, however, and it inspired the internationalism of the great eighteenth- and nineteenth-century thinkers: Voltaire, Goethe, the Utilitarians in England, Kant and the utopian socialists.* The religious synthesis, derived from processes of faith, was to be replaced by a rational synthesis, derived from processes of logic and free inquiry. It began to be said by such men as Tennyson that international understanding, by itself, could bring world order, world peace. The very thought of physical coercion was repugnant to minds which inclined toward pacifism and philosophic anarchy, and there was wide acceptance among intellectuals of the belief that universal disarmament—the utter destruction of all coercive instruments everywhere in the world—would be an inevitable concomitant of universal peace. In summary, these men believed that a universal social order could derive solely from reasonable processes and rest solely upon commonly recognized truths.

During the one hundred years from the Congress of Vienna to 1914, these views gained an increasing number of adherents all over the world. Many statesmen came to believe that the precise balancing of power among the European states would make possible a simultaneous cutting of armaments and provide a basis for a permanently peaceful world order. Many socialist thinkers spoke of the state's "withering away" altogether as the necessities of government through force were removed. Even the catastrophe of World War I failed to destroy altogether what we came to label, eventually with some contempt, "nineteenth-century optimism." Vestiges of this optimism were institu-

* Earlier, Spinoza had written: "Peace is not an absence of war, it is a virtue, a state of mind, a disposition of benevolence, confidence, justice."

tionalized in the League of Nations and in the multitude of pacifist movements and international peace pacts which flourished in the 1920s. Enough of it remained so that many of us hoped that the Kellogg-Briand Pact of 1928 would do what it claimed it could do—outlaw war as an instrument of national policy. It died a slow death, this optimism, but it did die. Nazism and Fascism and World War II destroyed it utterly, at least for a time.

As I contemplated these facts and ideas following the UNESCO General Conference in Mexico City, and as I observed internal conflicts in China, Greece, Italy, and France, my thoughts returned to discussions I had often had with Elmer Davis in OWI. Since single nations, with common histories, ideas, cultures, institutions, and homogeneity of population often could not maintain internal peace, what could we expect in the larger world? Peace, wherever it existed—in Washington, New York, London, Paris, Tokyo, or the larger world of nations—was patently to a considerable degree the product of power. Man was (and is) an ambivalent being; he was both good and bad. Power must normally repress the evil in man. The good would prevail and we could live in peace only so long as events were compatible with group desires. Organized man, encountering forces which conflicted with his beliefs and major wishes, would again resort to the use of power. So any social system which ignored either the good or the evil in man was by that fact doomed to failure.

It seemed clear to me, therefore, that only a proper combination of force and ideas (involving genuine transnational understanding) had a reasonable chance of achieving the peace all the kindly peoples of the earth truly wanted. But who was to exercise the power? How was it to be constituted? Since the beginning of nation-states, the balance-of-power theory had always failed. It would fail again. It will always fail. There had to be a single power to enforce peace in the world. The United Nations Charter authorized the organization to establish a peace-keeping force, but that force was to be comprised of national units borrowed from co-operating countries, a fact which weakened, perhaps defeated, the entire concept. But at this time, 1947, my thinking did not go beyond the theoretical need. I was convinced, however, that if UNESCO was to help mankind, as quickly as possible, to develop the understanding which would lead to the transcendence of the good in both individual and organized man—to help men everywhere to accept as their highest priority a total program that would yield universal peace and security—we had to find a better answer to the problem of enforcement.

The United States National Commission for UNESCO proceeded with a series of large national conferences at home—in Philadelphia, Boston, Denver, Cleveland, Washington, D.C., and elsewhere. The purpose of each conference was to win acceptance for the UNESCO idea among the conference participants and through them to reach the minds of millions in the United States and stir them to form local study groups. Such groups did spring up in communities through the nation. It was a promising beginning.

Not at these conferences, where I presided, but in several personal addresses at universities late in 1947, I cautiously suggested that the Charter of the United Nations should be amended in such a way that, instead of borrowing national military forces for peace keeping, the UN should have authority to establish its own international police force. This really meant that we should have a narrowly limited world government. Not surprisingly, this brought biting criticism from the Daughters of the American Revolution and several other organizations; it also brought me an invitation to discuss my ideas with the House Committee on Foreign Affairs, which proved to be less quarrelsome than I had expected. Indeed, later the Senate of the United States would twice adopt resolutions favoring a directly recruited international peace-keeping force for the United Nations.

I have often speculated on what would have happened in our world if, when the United States had a monopoly on the atomic bomb and David Lilienthal and Dean Acheson offered to give it to the United Nations, the offer had been accepted, accompanied by an international agreement to prevent the development of atomic force by any nation. Could this central power have been used to enforce peace?

As vice-chairman of the United States delegation (the Assistant Secretary of State invariably served as chairman), I attended the UNESCO General Conferences in Beirut in 1948 and again in Paris in 1949. At these meetings it was apparent that the opposing ideas between East and West had become dominant influences. The moral and intellectual differences between democratic freedom and totalitarian Communism began to test men's souls and the vigor of their beliefs. We of the free world felt that we were face to face with the impassive countenance of a new and vicious tyranny.

This new tyranny wore a different label, yet it was as old and ugly as sin. The Communist tyranny, many felt, was even more frightening than Fascism or Nazism, for it was not so brittle and it had a passionate faith, no matter how tragically in error.

Most people seemed to look upon the diametrically opposed systems as something that had suddenly burst upon the world, but actually they had been developing throughout the whole sweep of human activity.

In the long history of mankind—before the dawn of freedom—two themes of human belief and organization threaded their way: the one that man and society are shaped by impersonal forces of destiny and circumstance; the other that the state is omnipotent and the source of all meaning. "Subjects were no more than shadows of shadows," said one historian in tracing these two themes through thousands of years.

As civilizations rose and fell the people remained in servitude to the state and the state and the people alike in bondage to destiny. All phases of human endeavor—behavior, ritual, even thought itself—were rigidly shaped and maintained. Men and women lived out their lives as pawns and prisoners of omnipotent government and omnipotent fate.

Then two peoples—the Jews and the Greeks—broke the fatalistic cycle and transformed the human scene with a new force of ideas. With the advent of the Jewish and Greek societies, the whole character of human development was altered and the "Western spirit" took hold. So dynamic were the ideas around which the Jews and Greeks built their civilizations that they seemingly obliterated the two previously dominant themes.

An understanding of the impact of Jewish and Greek ideas on the course of history is one important key to a comprehension of the fundamental issues which divided the world into two great parts after World War II. The Western civilization which evolved out of ancient Greece and Judea is truly revolutionary in its outlook, whereas Communist ideology, masking itself in revolutionary terms, is in fact completely reactionary.

Barbara Ward Jackson has spoken eloquently of the debt Western man owes to Greek and Jewish thoughts. She argued that men's thoughts became immersed in the idea that the totality of human affairs could by the human will be transformed and remade in the image of the Divine. Their desire to create, to seize on material circumstances and mold them as the artist transforms the material he works with, was the source of the energy injected into the Western world by the rational vision of the Greeks and the moral vision of the Jews. Thereafter, she contended, Western man could never again drive the fever of creation and progress out of his blood.

A second debt Western civilization owes to ancient Judea and Greece lies in the devastating attack that the Greek logician and the Jewish philosopher made upon the idea that the state was omnipotent. The Greek saw man as a creature endowed with reason and possessing inalienable rights, among them the right of self-government. The Jew believed that the divine image in man created in him moral responsibility for his fellows. From Cain's first question, "Am I my brother's keeper?" comes the Judeo-Christian doctrine of personal responsibility and moral accountability.

As inheritors of the legacy of ancient Greece and Judea, we are therefore the spiritual heirs to a revolutionary philosophy and a radical ideology. We believe that man, made in the image of a Supreme Being, is a creature of dignity and that social and political institutions must be designed to protect that dignity; Western man believes that ideas determine history and that man is capable of altering the course of history, of thinking and acting for himself—his eyes are on the stars and the limitless reservoirs of his mind are continually yielding more challenging ideas and greater standards of perfection, and hence he is committed to the ceaseless search for knowledge and truth. Western man also insists that the means to any end, even the most laudable, must be in comformity with certain moral standards; the end does not justify the means; in his letter to the Romans St. Paul said, "Do not be overcome by evil, but overcome evil with good." And of course a fourth element of Western man's philosophy, regardless of many divergences in areas of the world, is belief in a Supreme Being.

These Western ideas are in direct conflict with those of the Communist countries. Communism is not impressed by the worth of the individual; it holds that men are creatures of material forces; Karl Marx proclaimed bluntly, "The democratic concept of man is false . . . it holds that each man is a sovereign being . . . this is the illusion of Christianity." Certainly Communists do not believe that ideas determine history; history, they contend, is shaped by economic forces and man cannot change these forces; Marx argued that it is not the consciousness of men that determine their existence but, on the contrary, their social existence that determines their consciousness. Thirdly, Communists are scornful of the Western view about means and ends. Lenin, who today is deified in most Communist countries, argued that the dictatorship of the proletariat is a persistent struggle in which people should resort to schemes, stratagems, illegitimate methods, and lies so long as they served the ultimate Communist purpose; as Arthur Koestler, former Communist, said in one of his books, banned by the Communists, "A collective aim justified all means . . . and demands that the individual should in every way be sacrificed to the community." And, finally, a true Communist, a member of the Party, must be an atheist.

Thus it is clear that the legacy of the Western world from Judea and Greece is opposed in fundamental philosophic concepts to those of Communism. So I am correct, I think, in saying that democracy is a radical idea while Communism is in reality a profoundly reactionary philosophy which restores to men the old fetters of fatality and tyranny. Once again, in part of the world, we see the omnipotent state and omnipotent fate.

At this point in my reasoning about the task of UNESCO, I seemed to have worked myself into an impervious mental circle. If a peaceful social order depended upon both a judicious exercise of power, properly organized, and upon ideas—upon the development of genuine understanding and common conceptions among the peoples of the earth—how could UNESCO make a worth-while contribution in the face of the East-West philosophic divergence?

This was, it seemed, one of those times for creative compromise. The Cold War was burgeoning. We of UNESCO could have thrown up our hands and quit. But, after all, the intellectual divisions of the world were not solely between East and West. Indeed, there was precious little mutual understanding among non-Communist nations— Europe and the United States, the United States and Latin America, and the United States and the Middle East, for example. The few Communist nations in UNESCO could carry on attempts at disruption, as they began to do, but we of the non-Communist world should persist in our efforts.

By now, isolationism was disappearing from the American scene. People, especially members of the younger generation, were seeking new answers. These younger people were aware of the destruction and heartaches of World War II. War, they felt, was such a hideous evil that even the sacrifice of some small part of a nation's sovereignty—a sovereignty too often blindly worshiped—might be sacrificed to the nobler purposes of mankind's true aspirations. Older persons, especially most intellectuals, felt the same. So there was plenty of work to be done in the United States by the National Commission and by international UNESCO, at least among the nations dominated by Western thought.

So the United States Commission for UNESCO redoubled its efforts to develop local councils throughout the United States. Today, due to many circumstances, including the work of UNESCO, our schools, colleges, and universities, as well as the mass media, the American people, especially younger people, are better informed on international affairs and on American foreign policy than we have ever before been in our history.

Unfortunately, what happened in the United States was not matched in many other countries. Our National Commission found that eighty per cent of all the peoples of the world were obtaining information from other countries only after it had been filtered through some form of censorship. Tariffs, quotas, and other barriers seriously impeded the free interflow of books, magazines, motion pictures, and other materials. Winston Churchill spoke of the "iron curtain" but there were also lace curtains in essentially every area of the globe—in Latin America, Africa, the Middle East, the Far East. Because of these impediments to the flow of information and ideas, it was not surprising that we of the National Commission learned that the world thought of Americans as being superficial, all rich through no effort of their own, lawless and night-clubbish, imperialistic and incurably frivolous in our outlook upon the world. Other countries knew little of the real America: a spiritual people, an America that is generous and kind and serious in purpose and deeply devoted to ethical goals and purposes. They knew little, too, about our basic democratic concepts, our school system, life surrounding the rural church, the workings of our state and national governments, or the eighteen different nationalities working harmoniously in a single factory in Detroit.

Into the intellectual vacuum of many nations those hostile to the United States now intensified their broadcasting of lies. Aid to Greece and Turkey, the European Recovery Program, and the creation of NATO now came upon the world scene. Frantically, Russian, Polish, East German, and other broadcasts charged that the aim of the United States was to capture political and strategic positions in Europe; that the United States had initiated a race in armaments; that the Turkish army was being secretly run by the United States; that the United States had converted the Philippines to colonial status; that the income of the American people had declined by fifty per cent; that the United States was determined to conquer most of the countries of the Far East; and that the American policy in West Germany was to build an imperialistic peace based on the enslavement of nations.

Completely discarded now was the view I had held in OWI that governments should not engage in the dissemination of information when World War II was over. Lies, no matter how difficult the task, had to be countered. Better still, the truth had somehow to reach the peoples of the world so that lies, when broadcast, would not have receptive audiences. The work of the United States Information Agency became of vital importance.

With a larger budget at its disposal, UNESCO's efforts increased. It attacked illiteracy in many countries, initiated programs for the training of teachers, co-operated with private international organizations in the medical sciences, films, television, humanities, sciences, and architecture, each of which reached substantial audiences in many countries. It promulgated the Florence Agreement, in time adopted by sixty-two countries; this exempted from import duties books, publications, audiovisual material, scientific equipment, and even material for the blind. UNESCO negotiated the Universal Copyright Convention, to which sixty-two nations, including the U.S.S.R., are now signatory, to protect literary, scientific, and artistic works for a period of twenty-five years. An immense amount of travel by American citizens to most areas of the globe and lesser travel of foreigners in the United States helped. The Organization of American States carried forward its own UNESCO-type programs, with at least limited success in creating better understanding not only among governments but among peoples.

Two special stations in Europe—Radio Free Europe and Radio Liberty—financed partly by private funds but mainly by the CIA (later by direct congressional appropriations), developed skill in penetrating the iron curtain where an underground system of word-of-mouth information spread throughout the Communist countries. (I was to be deeply involved in this problem in the Nixon administration.)

But modest gains gave no reason for glowing optimism. A press survey indicated that nearly sixty-five per cent of the American people feared that another world war would occur within twenty-five years and that individual citizens could do nothing to prevent it. So I undertook a nationwide speaking tour, urging individual citizens to become intimately informed on all aspects of domestic and foreign affairs so that their actions, especially with their federal representatives, could be more effective in supporting efforts that might contribute to permanent peace and security.

I likened the building of peace to a three-legged stool. The stool would not stand with one or two legs, and would be wobbly unless all three legs were sturdy and of equal length. One leg of the stool was genuine human understanding, a deep, abiding understanding among peoples of diverse cultures and religions—an understanding out of which mutual agreements in social, economic, and political fields could be taken for peace building by all the nations of the world.

A second leg represented those economic, social, and political arrangements which are essential if peoples of all nations are to have the opportunity to earn for themselves a rising level of living conducive to a desire for peace. The world had become intricately interdependent. The United States drew raw materials from sixty other countries and shipped to them processed goods and farm products. Most advanced nations did the same and the developing nations, desperately in need of help, were also conscious of their interdependence with others, an interdependence which they felt was often to their disadvantage.

And the third leg was power, power which the peoples who wanted peace could use to enforce it against those who, out of ignorance or ruthless ambition, sought to foment war. I became a bit more outspoken on this third point; evidently the Daughters of the American Revolution felt it had argued enough, or possibly that I should be ignored.

At the end of three years of intensive work I gave up the chairmanship of the United States National Commission but remained a member for two more years.

In the ensuing years the most important single development in the world scene was the death of Stalin. Brutally, ruthlessly he had been the personification of the omnipotent state. In a conference with Churchill and Roosevelt he had admitted killing millions of individuals who opposed him, especially the kulaks, saying it was simply a surgical operation that had to be performed.

When Khrushchev, following temporary struggles for power, became head of the Politburo of the Communist Party and also chairman of the Council of Ministers, several important changes from the UNESCO point of view took place. He stated for all the world to hear that the two powers could annihilate one another; hence, war between them would be mutually destructive and must at all costs be avoided. He insisted that coexistence was not only possible but imperative. Limited cultural exchanges were instituted. In time, many visas were granted to American visitors, and some Soviet citizens, mostly scientists and other intellectuals, traveled throughout the United States. The Soviet Union and the United States exchanged exhibits. The fear of Communism in the United States, reaching its height in the Joseph McCarthy period, subsided considerably.

Even the deep-seated philosophic differences which separated East from West became modified somewhat. The Marx-Lenin-Stalin concept of using any means to achieve an end changed sufficiently that the West felt it could rely on international agreements with the Soviet Union, such as was done in the test ban treaty in the Kennedy administration and in the several agreements signed in Moscow and Washington in the Nixon administration. The Cold War was being replaced by a growing spirit of détente.

But we should not mistake the nature and scope of the evolving détente. We are greatly increasing cultural, scientific, and educational exchanges; we hope to establish a massive and mutually advantageous Soviet-United States trade; we look hopefully at the beginnings of a European security conference, and we are encouraged by the rapid growth of education in the Soviet Union, with the best-educated Soviet citizens becoming critical of the intellectual control within which they must work and live.

As I recount elsewhere, many developments in the Soviet Union are encouraging, but we should not assume that Communism, socialism, or state capitalism will disappear from that vast country, just as we must hope we shall be wise enough to keep the competitive enterprise system which is one indispensable element of the free system we cherish. Stated bluntly, détente, which we all want, does not imply a diminution of the ideological struggle. Indeed, Soviet theorists and political leaders, including Brezhnev, have made it clear that co-operation with the United States, needed for practical development purposes, *intensifies* the need to strengthen all their efforts, domestically and throughout the world, in the ideological field.

The need for UNESCO has not disappeared.

International UNESCO today has become a huge organization. The first appropriation of less than seven million dollars has grown to more than ninety million dollars, of which the United States pays about thirty per cent. But the funds available to the organization are ever so much greater than this. Today, the United Nations Development Program, the World Bank, participating nations being benefited, and other agencies entrust to UNESCO some 167 special projects involving an annual expenditure of nearly two thirds of a billion dollars; a major share of this amount comes from the participating nations.

Of the total projects, nearly sixty are in education, including teacher training, drives against illiteracy, and help in constructing educational facilities. More than one hundred projects are in the scientific and technical fields, including support of specific scientific studies and aid to engineering and other schools.

UNESCO has produced a library of special volumes, from statistical yearbooks to current evaluation of educational, scientific, and cultural programs in most nations of the world. It has even ventured into the field of national monuments, helping modestly to preserve some of the world's cultural treasures. The organization is co-operating with the International Bank for Reconstruction and Development, which has loaned as much as $365 million in the educational and scientific fields.

The international organization now has 125 nations as members, 60 of which did not exist when I attended the first general conference in Paris in 1946. The United States National Commission for UNESCO, still vigorously active, believes that today the high goals of mutual respect, equality, justice, and human dignity are a little closer to being attained by the member countries than they were when the international organization came into being. This may be true.

My disappointment is due to the conviction I held from the beginning about UNESCO's major duty. Of the three purposes of UNESCO —(1) to help in the advancement of education and spread of knowledge, (2) to give a vigorous impulse to the development and spread of science, and (3) to work for mutual understanding among nations and peoples—*greatest progress has been made in the first two, least in the third.* I still feel that greater efforts should be made toward this third goal. Despite limited progress, censorship still filters or denies information to a tremendous segment of the world's peoples from outside the borders of their own countries. I shall not be convinced that the enormous efforts made in intellectual international relations have succeeded until all iron and lace curtains have disappeared—until the free flow of facts, ideas, information, books, magazines, and travelers constantly crosses all national boundaries and refreshes all nations. Then perhaps UNESCO can, in terms of Article I of its constitution, be more effective in contributing to

> "peace and security by promoting collaboration among the nations through education, science and culture in order to further universal respect for justice, for the rule of law, and for human rights and human freedoms which are affirmed for the peoples of the world without distinction of race, sex, language, or religion, by the Charter of the United Nations."

If my deep commitment to these goals and my abiding hope that they will one day be realized characterizes me to some as a naïve idealist, then so be it. But the fact remains that we are one species living on one shrinking planet with the power of total self-destruction. The goal of universal brotherhood and permanent world peace is indeed a real long-shot—but, if you think about it, it is a long-shot in the only game in town.

CHAPTER 12

Every now and then someone comes along
and proves that any American boy can grow
up to be President. Truman performed well
above our expectations, but then our expectations were never very high.

ON APRIL 12, 1945, Vice-President Harry S. Truman adjourned the United States Senate at a few minutes before five. Unlike
many of his successors, Truman took his constitutional responsibility
seriously and regularly presided over the Senate. He had come from that
distinguished body, having been elected in 1934 and serving until he
became Franklin Roosevelt's running mate a decade later.

Following adjournment, the president of the Senate (as Vice-
Presidents are known on "the Hill") strolled over to the House side to
join old cronies who still welcomed him to the inner sanctum. Speaker
Sam Rayburn presided over a daily "salon" in his gilded chamber off the
floor of the House, known to intimates as the "Board of Education."
Here he and certain fellow representatives—including Lyndon Johnson—carried on a tradition begun by Cactus Jack Garner during prohibition: namely, to "strike a blow for liberty" with Bourbon and branch
water. Harry Truman was a special member of this elite club, never having been a representative.

When he arrived at the Board of Education, the Vice-President
found a message to call Press Secretary Steve Early at the White House
at once. He spoke briefly on the phone, then moved quickly and quietly
to the Executive Mansion to be sworn in to the office that had suddenly
become vacant with the death of President Roosevelt less than an hour
earlier.

Truman later recalled what happened this way:

Mrs. Roosevelt put her hand on his shoulder and said, "Harry, the President is dead."

He replied, "Is there anything I can do for you?"

She shook her head. "Is there anything we can do for you? For you are the one in trouble now."[13]

As I have said, I was at Kansas State when President Roosevelt died. Like most Americans, I suppose, I was too shocked and saddened about the man who was gone to think much about the man who had assumed his burdens. Indeed, Roosevelt had been President for so long that it was hard to remember what the government and the nation had been like before him, and it was virtually impossible to perceive what it would be like in the future without him.

Truman was not well known, even though he had chaired an important Senate committee investigating war production. In the contest for the number two spot on the Democratic ticket in 1944 he had backed his old friend Sam Rayburn, then shifted to the side of Jimmy Byrnes when Rayburn withdrew. But Roosevelt had other plans, as usual, and now Harry S. Truman was President.

The choice was not so strange as it might have appeared at the time. Determined that he must somehow solve the major problems that faced the United States, President Roosevelt in 1944 was already looking toward the postwar period. A victorious ending to the war was assured and virtually within sight. Roosevelt was planning for the aftermath, for the conversion to a peacetime economy, and for the organization of the United Nations. Although he had strong Democratic majorities in both houses of Congress, Roosevelt had not cultivated good relations with the Congress and he had bullied through the legislation he needed in recent years. That might be all right for fighting a war but it would not suffice for winning the peace that must follow. Roosevelt knew that he would need strong legislative support to make the United Nations an effective instrument for peace and he had no intention of making the mistakes that Woodrow Wilson had made. He needed for his running mate and his successor a man who could win the legislative branch to his side.

Truman was probably as well prepared a politician as any who ever entered the White House. He was a loyal Democrat, trained in the political school of Missouri politics when the Pendergast machine ran Kansas City. As a senator he was quickly welcomed into the inner circle of Democratic leadership. His close friendship with Justice Brandeis made him welcome in liberal circles. He knew the democratic process from the precinct up and he was a politician in the best sense of the word. Between McKinley and Truman, only Harding had had congressional experience, and his term in the Senate hardly qualified him for higher office. When President Roosevelt died none of his Cabinet had ever had legislative experience and none (except Henry Wallace) had ever run for national office. In his Vice-President, Roosevelt had a canny politician with close ties to the Congress and a man who was absolutely honest (and indeed remained so throughout his political career despite the corruption around him).

At the time of President Roosevelt's death Gerald Johnson, the Baltimore writer, wrote: "Great men go, but the average man is immortal." Truman was very much the average man. He was never what would be called "presidential timber." He was a small-town politician without much ambition except to serve his people and his party—and critics differ on his order of importance. Truman lacked a formal education and was one of the few non-military men to become President without having been a lawyer. But he was a hard worker who did his homework and paid attention to details, and in that sense he equipped himself well for each office he assumed.

The administration of President Truman was characterized by a blend of courage and greatness on the one hand with bad judgment, legislative failures, cronyism, and corruption on the other. He certainly presided over a troubled nation. The war had yet to be ended. Afterward, the country was plagued by unemployment, labor troubles, and rapidly deteriorating international relationships. Many of the crises he faced were new, not only for him but for the nation, and his administration was a process of trial and error. The record was a mixed one. Interestingly, it was the acts of statesmanship by Truman that played a crucial part in General Eisenhower's change of mind in 1952 and his determination to oppose Senator Taft for the Republican nomination.

My official relations with President Truman were excellent. I had seen him frequently and our conferences were pleasant and businesslike. There was no storytelling, as there had been with President Franklin Roosevelt. Truman was always quick to come to the heart of an issue and to make a decision.

My wife and I also saw the President and Mrs. Truman socially, including a memorable visit in the apartment of mutual friends, Mr. and Mrs. George E. Allen. Allen wrote *Presidents Who Have Known Me*, a book with a title which was not an expression of arrogance but typical Allen humor. That evening was fun—music, spirited conversation, a friendly game of cards, and a few scintillating stories by the President. I could detect no physical evidence of the torment he had experienced during the preceding six and a half years. They had been years which called for many quick and momentous decisions, often without sufficient time to consider alternatives and to arrive at judgments based on all the facts and the best available advice.

Less than a month after Harry Truman was sworn in as President Germany surrendered unconditionally: that was May 7, 1945. The United Nations Charter was signed on June 26. Then Truman went to Potsdam to meet with Soviet and British leaders. At that conference he made one fateful decision and confirmed another: to use the atomic bomb against the Japanese and to accept the help of the Soviet forces in the final stages of the war in the Far East. The consequences of these decisions will linger for generations.

When the scientists at the University of Chicago achieved the ultimate in physical power by releasing the energy of the atom—which Einstein had defined mathematically years before—they presented mankind with the possibility of entering a golden age or of making possible the annihilation of life. President Truman, whose relations with Roosevelt were not intimate, knew nothing about the atomic bomb before he became President. On the day Truman was sworn in as President, Secretary Stimson met with him privately to give him information about this new awesome warmaking instrument. On July 16, 1945, the first test bomb was successfully exploded in New Mexico.

President Truman, at the Potsdam Conference, decided to use the atomic bomb against Japan as a means of ending the war in the Far East. James F. Byrnes in his book, *Speaking Frankly*,[14] says that on July 16 at the close of the afternoon meeting of the Big Three—the United States, Great Britain, and the Soviet Union—President Truman walked around the large circular table to talk with Stalin. He told Stalin that after long experimentation we had developed a new bomb and that we planned "to use it very soon" unless Japan surrendered. Stalin's only reply was to say that he was glad to hear of the bomb and hoped that we would use it. Byrnes indicated that the President was surprised by Stalin's lack of interest; perhaps Stalin had not grasped the significance of the discovery, or, more likely, he already knew a great deal about it. Later Byrnes concluded that, since the Russians kept their new developments secret, Stalin probably thought it would be undiplomatic to ask President Truman for details.

The Potsdam Declaration was issued on July 26. It did not mention the atomic bomb but warned that unless Japan surrendered, her armed forces would be destroyed, her homeland devastated. On July 27 leaflets were dropped on Japan, warning that terribly destructive bombing was imminent. The next day the Japanese Premier rejected the warning.

"There was nothing left to do but use the bomb," said Secretary Byrnes. Secretary Stimson had already chosen targets deemed to be of military importance, and President Truman approved Stimson's recommendation.

On August 6 the first atomic bomb was dropped on Hiroshima. Three days later a second bomb was dropped on Nagasaki. The two cities were wiped out: civilians, military personnel and installations, business buildings, homes—became ashes.

It is indisputable that we would have won the war against Japan without the bomb. Victory was in sight. The justification for its use was the shortening of the war and the saving of many Allied lives.

Our employment of this new force at Hiroshima and Nagasaki was a supreme provocation to other nations, especially the Soviet Union, which decided to overcome as quickly as possible the superior coercive influence this power placed in our hands. Moreover, its use violated the normal standards of warfare by wiping out entire populations, mostly civilians, in the target cities. It seemed to me then, and does today, that had we kept the knowledge of the atom bomb secret until peace was restored, and then declared our intention to use this new power solely for peaceful development, we might have avoided the subsequent costly race in atomic armaments and might even have induced the Soviet Union to accept our proposal for the United Nations to become the sole custodian of the bomb. Certainly what happened at Hiroshima and Nagasaki will forever be on the conscience of the American people. Today, at least five nations possess these instruments of destruction. Other nations have the knowledge needed to produce atomic and hydrogen bombs and they can do so if they are willing to invest enormous resources in the complex engineering required for production. Proliferation of nuclear weapons would multiply geometrically the possibility of world catastrophe, so we must hope that the non-proliferation treaty will be universally observed.

One must recognize of course the historic milieu in which Truman made his hasty decision. The infamy at Pearl Harbor had created an intense hatred toward the Japanese. Furthermore, during the war Germany, with conventional, buzz, and V-2 bombs, had blasted many cities of the United Kingdom, some of which had no military value, and in retaliation the Allies had leveled German cities. One could argue that there was no difference in using a single bomb to accomplish what previously had required hundreds of flights and the dropping of thousands of bombs, many with proximity fuses. The peoples of the belligerent nations had certainly become conditioned to a new style of warfare that obscured normal concepts of morality. But this short-term consideration should not have induced Truman and his close advisers to ignore the ultimate consequences of a world dominated by the fear and the actual potential of the total extinction of life. Today, atomic stockpiles are massive. Much of the sweat and toil of workers, the intelligence of scientists and engineers, and the resources of the country reside in them. Their power can be released in seconds.

The decision to bring Soviet forces into the war against Japan was also confirmed at Potsdam. The possibility of Soviet military help in the Far East had been discussed at Teheran and an agreement on this had been reached at Yalta. When the Potsdam Conference was held, and it was evident that the end of the conflict in the Far East was near —especially with the use of atomic bombs—Truman's foreign policy and military advisers hoped that this aspect of the Yalta agreement would not be implemented, for they foresaw postwar complications if the Soviet Union participated in the defeat of Japan. Herbert Druks, in his book, *Harry S. Truman and the Russians*,[15] asserts that Truman went to Potsdam with the belief that it would be "easier to do business with 'Old Joe' directly." Truman's major concern was to "settle various differences so that American troops might be withdrawn from Europe as quickly as possible."

"Old Joe" was obviously prepared to send his forces to the East. No effort was made to dissuade him. He ordered Soviet forces into the Far East conflict on August 8 and thus gained a legitimate interest in the ultimate settlement, a fact which he obviously welcomed. At the conclusion of the war the Soviet Union demanded its pound of flesh in the form of northern Japanese islands which she still holds. Her presence in the Far East led in a demonstrably direct way to Stalin's decision to supply war matériel to North Korea and to induce that fragmented country to attack South Korea, a fact acknowledged by Khrushchev in the book alleged to be his memoirs, *Khrushchev Remembers*.[16] Our participation in the Korean War, in turn, enhanced our commitment to the maintenance of forces in the Far East and Southeast Asia and thus had some bearing on our entrance into the Vietnam conflict, a monumental error.

The Potsdam Conference was held when Truman was a neophyte in the presidency. As Vice-President he had attended Cabinet meetings, but serious problems had rarely been discussed. He once commented that as Vice-President he had seen Roosevelt only twice outside Cabinet meetings. Several advisers of President Truman have expressed the belief that Roosevelt's coolness toward Truman was due to Truman's having signed a ghosted article which was critical of the President. In any event, it is clear that Truman was not a working confidant of Roosevelt as Nixon was to be under Eisenhower. So it was that he came into the White House with little knowledge of the manifold military, political, and economic problems which had been on the agenda of meetings of Stalin, Churchill, and Roosevelt during the war years.

The moment Truman was sworn in as President, however, he began studying long hours each day. He had much to learn. His nervousness and uncertainty were hidden by hastily formed judgments, decisive actions, and fighting rhetoric. His early actions seemed to me to have been impulsively determined, rather than judgments based upon mature consideration of all facts and possible consequences. My charitable view is that had the Potsdam Conference been held a good deal later, when Truman had developed greater poise, knowledge, and confidence, he might not have committed the errors in judgment that made the conference the blot on American history that I deem it to be. Truman's memoirs, however, give no such impression. That is not surprising.

Presidents find justification in retrospect for most of the actions they took when they possessed that awesome responsibility.

The peace that Franklin Roosevelt had worked for was not to be. The Soviet Union, ignoring objections of the free world, seized control of Eastern Europe. This violated our traditional and most cherished foreign policy of freedom of choice and ignored agreements made by the Allies during the war. It raised fears of united military forces in Eastern Europe that would threaten the freedom of the Continent and possibly other areas of the world.

When the Soviet Union moved to support the Communist rebels in Greece after Great Britain pulled out, the United States Government envisioned a Soviet expansionism that would spread to Turkey, then to the Middle East. Our response was the Truman Doctrine. Economic and military aid costing four hundred million dollars was rushed to the assistance of Greece and Turkey. Representative John McCormack of Massachusetts, then Democratic whip, declared: "The issue is joined between the forces of democracy and Communism." The Marshall Plan for the reconstruction of Europe soon followed. Here were examples of President Truman's ability to rise to heights of statesmanship. It is for these courageous decisions that he will have a permanent place in history.

Then came the policy of containment which was to persist until altered slightly by President Nixon in 1970.

Secretary of State Byrnes, in an address before the Overseas Press Club on February 28, 1946, warned the Soviet leaders that the United States would not "allow aggression to be accomplished by coercion or pressure or by subterfuges, such as political infiltration." He declared that the United States would live up to the cardinal concepts of the United Nations Charter. "There must be," he said, "a stop to this maneuvering for strategic advantage all over the world and to the use of one adjustment as an entering wedge for further and undisclosed penetrations of power." Byrnes indicated that the United States would not "gang up" against any one state and would not do anything to break the world into exclusive blocs of influence. "We have openly, gladly and wholeheartedly welcomed our Soviet ally as a great power, second to none in the family of nations," he said, adding, "Only an inexcusable tragedy of errors could cause serious conflict between us in the future

. . . but in the interest of world peace and in the interest of our common and traditional friendship we must make plain that the United States intends to defend the [United Nations] charter."

Seven months later, in an address in the Stuttgart Opera House, Secretary Byrnes gave a detailed explanation of United States policy toward Germany. He referred to the wartime agreements which called for a disarmed and demilitarized Germany and for four-power control (France, the United Kingdom, the Soviet Union, and the United States) of Germany for as long as would be necessary to give positive assurance that Germany would not again become a threat to other nations. This warning to the Soviet Union that Germany should not be divided into blocs went unheeded.

Various writers ascribe the beginning of the Cold War to varying specific incidents or moments. My view is that the East-West hostility which dominated the world for many years—and still does to a considerable extent—was the consequence of many events, policies, circumstances, and years. By no means were relations between Western leaders and Stalin friendly during the war; co-operation was solely the child of necessity. After the war Communist threats which led to our aid to Greece and Turkey and the Marshall Plan to help rebuild Europe, Secretary Byrnes's forthright address at the Overseas Press Club (formally announcing the containment policy against Soviet expansionism as exemplified by her seizure of the nations of Eastern Europe), and finally the creation of NATO—all these cumulatively created what the mass media and then the peoples of the world came to call the Cold War.

The most potent aspect of the Cold War was and is the *policy of containment*. An ideological outgrowth of the Truman Doctrine, containment provided that the United States would oppose the coercive spread of Communism, unilaterally and with force if necessary, wherever it threatened to occur. In the minds of most Americans, Communism was a menace more frightening than Nazism had ever been, and Americans applauded the Truman Doctrine.

My own view is that containment as a policy was too sweeping. Built more on fear and emotion than on reasoned analysis, the policy would not permit any other interpretation of Soviet actions than the one which revealed a carefully conceived plan for global conquest. We seemed incapable of considering the possibility that Soviet moves in Eastern Europe, Greece, and the Middle East were defensive rather than offensive—that the Kremlin was acting out of fear for the security of a country badly mauled in World War II and terribly vulnerable to neighboring nations which had looked upon the Bolshevik Revolution with intense hostility.

Moreover, the policy of containment cast the United States in the role of Atlas of the world—global policeman charged with the responsibility for the entire non-Communist world. No one nation can enforce universal peace. No single nation can take upon itself the right to intervene in the affairs of other sovereign states, even when it is obviously "good for them." The policy of containment is too encompassing. It might have been a workable policy in certain circumstances where the direct interests of the United States were involved or where the delicate balance of world power was really at stake. But we did not contain our policy of containment, and it was used to claim legitimacy for President Kennedy to send many American troops to Vietnam in the early sixties and for President Johnson's massive escalation of our involvement in 1965–68.

Even as I write this, I am mindful that hindsight is usually twenty-twenty vision. I can recall vividly the bewilderment, then the shock, then the anger, and finally the fear that gripped us when the Soviet Union made its aggressive moves following World War II. The war was over. America had done its job and had begun disassembling the mightiest military machine ever built. Had we wished, at the end of the war, we could have conquered the world. We had the power and there was nothing that could have stopped us. But it was not an idea that would even have occurred to Americans who never wanted to fight anyway and could not wait to get back to their homes, families, education, and jobs. Hence, when the Soviet Union continued to develop its military capacity and to violate the sovereignty of other nations and the letter and spirit of agreements, Americans felt betrayed.

It will be a while yet before we can assess the rights and wrongs of our postwar foreign policy. Meanwhile, in the past two years a revisionist movement has been growing in this country, nourished largely by the tragic folly of the Vietnam War. And that, on the whole, is good. The time for clear rethinking of our role in the world is long overdue.

Perhaps, if our thinking is clear enough, we can avoid more Vietnams and really begin to wage the peace. In saying this, I do not endorse any specific set of revisionist policies now being advocated.

The profound international developments could have more than fully occupied the attentions of President Truman. As it was, America was confronted with enormous domestic problems. The transition from war to peace was painful. Our society had changed in significant ways during the war. Science had become a major force, producing a technology which was directly affecting the way Americans lived. Women had left the home to work in factories. The movement to the cities was under way. Mobility was increasing. Social structures and institutions were creaking in the winds of change. With all of our efforts directed to winning the war, the nation's agenda of problems and unfinished business had grown long.

President Truman initiated his Fair Deal domestic program on September 6, 1945. His message to Congress contained some twenty-one points of domestic legislation and was the longest message (16,000 words) since Theodore Roosevelt's legislative message (20,000 words). He urged the Congress to increase the federally established minimum wage, create a permanent Fair Employment Practices Commission, expand the Social Security program, grant federal aid for research, undertake federal power developments on the Missouri, Arkansas, and Columbia rivers, and initiate these and many other measures when the projected deficit of the government for the fiscal year 1945–46 was running above eighteen billion dollars.

The elections of 1946 produced the first Republican-controlled Congress in sixteen years (a fact which prompted Senator Fulbright of Arkansas to suggest to President Truman that perhaps he should resign). Back in power on "the Hill" for the first time in so many years, the Republicans were not disposed to co-operate with President Truman except in the field of international relations, and his domestic program, for the most part, was blocked. It was the "conservative" Senator Taft who was mainly responsible for the enactment of liberal housing legislation as well as the later passage of the Taft-Hartley Labor Act, which the President vetoed only to have the Congress pass it over his veto. The President did induce the Congress to approve the first step toward the unification of the army, navy, and air force into a

Department of Defense—a move that really did not unify the military services but nonetheless made possible subsequent reorganizations that came closer to achieving that goal.

The campaign of 1948 was one of the most frantic and surprising our nation ever experienced. Truman was seriously behind in the pre-election period according to the polls. Henry Wallace opposed him from the left and Thomas Dewey and Strom Thurmond were against him from the right. Everybody recognized that he didn't have a chance—except Truman. So the President traveled the country in a fighting mood, hitting the "do-nothing Congress," ridiculing the Henry Wallace forces, ignoring the Dixiecrats, and in crude language sneering at the "highroad" campaign of Governor Dewey, the sure winner. Truman's upset victory disproved a theory I had long held, namely, that campaigning by presidential candidates had at best only a modicum of influence on the outcome of an election. I believed that an electoral decision was formulated over a considerable period of time, with the voters taking into account economic conditions, the general trend of domestic programs, the management of international affairs, and the personalities and philosophies of the candidates. On the basis of these considerations, Truman couldn't win and his "hell-bent for election" campaign would surely be futile. But, amazingly, he won.

President Truman, displaying a cockiness that remained with him throughout his full term, placed an expansion of the Fair Deal before the Congress, but his success with a Democratically controlled House and Senate was not much better than it had been when the Republicans were in charge of the Congress. In international affairs he fared better. He established a technical assistance program to aid underdeveloped nations and obtained approval for the creation of the North Atlantic Treaty Organization, a development patently needed at that time and one that, late in 1950, moved General Eisenhower from the presidency of Columbia University to Paris as first commander of NATO forces.

The American people had given restrained support to Truman's programs in Greece and Turkey, enthusiastic approval of the Marshall Plan and his advocacy of NATO, accepted with reservations his program of general foreign aid, and offered no objection when, under the aegis of the United Nations, he sent American forces under General

MacArthur to oppose the invasion of South Korea by North Korea and, in time, China. With respect to the Korean War, however, public opinion wavered, especially when General MacArthur was removed from command (quite properly, I think). By the time of the election of 1952 opinion was hostile. His rating in the polls had dropped spectacularly.

With most political attention focused on foreign affairs, Senator Joseph McCarthy of Wisconsin startled the nation by launching his disgraceful and indiscriminate attacks on Americans whom he charged with being Communists or fellow travelers, attacks which wrecked the lives of many loyal individuals and families and humiliated the United States in the eyes of the world. Simultaneously charges of corruption in high places filled the halls of Congress and columns in the press. To all these charges, President Truman returned flippant denials of any wrongdoing on the part of his cronies who came under suspicion. (I became one of Senator McCarthy's targets, but that was later, during President Eisenhower's administration.)

While I had been mildly critical of several of Truman's decisions, especially the use of the atomic bomb and the containment policy, we remained friendly, but I never asked him why, on March 29, 1952, he announced that he would not be a candidate to succeed himself. He was then sixty-eight years old. Perhaps that was reason enough for, as I shall argue later, no man can redeem the responsibilities, even if he works eighteen hours a day, now placed upon the President. The responsibility of the President is not only enough to age a man prematurely, but omissions are an inevitable consequence of the limitations of time.

In all of his work, foreign and domestic, Truman's most intimate adviser for five years was the formidable Clark Clifford.

At the age of thirty-eight Clifford became an assistant to the President's naval aide, having left his law practice in St. Louis for service as a naval officer. Soon he replaced his friend Jake Vardaman as the principal naval aide. This would normally have been a dead end in the White House, for military men on assignment to the President (before Clifford and until General Al Haig) perform mainly ceremonial duties, with little opportunity to persuade government officials to elevate them to positions of power. But Clifford was to be unique. In 1946, Truman appointed him special counsel to the President and in that position, with constant and easy access to the President, he was able to have enormous influence until 1950.

From the beginning of his service as counsel, the press became intrigued with Clifford's style. Newspapers saw him, accurately, I think, as chief of the White House staff (as Sherman Adams was later for a time under Eisenhower and Haldeman was under Nixon), as principal speech writer (as Rosenman and Sherwood had been under Roosevelt), adviser on foreign affairs (as House had been under Wilson), and coordinator of domestic affairs (as Ehrlichman became for four years in the Nixon administration). In all these activities Clifford maintained an air of secretiveness. Trying to uncover his Achilles' heel or his hidden flaws, if any, became a favorite game at cocktail parties in the capital. *Life* magazine, in apparent despair, found nothing to comment on other than to emphasize his good looks.

One observer has characterized Clifford as one of the most successful advisers to a President of the United States. While he and the President were intimate friends, Clifford was never guilty of sophistry or flattery. He was never away from decision making and action at any juncture. He shouldered broad political and policy responsibilities, freely sharing every aspect of the presidency. He even engaged in legislative liaison work, a task normally assigned to a special adviser and several assistants.

His role was so unusual that writers have never ceased to write about him. Some have likened him to Ted Sorensen under President Kennedy. Others have compared him to Robert Kennedy, though qualifying this by saying that he did not have the "telepathic communication" (Arthur Schlesinger's description)[17] which prevailed between the brothers John and Robert Kennedy. A few have seen Clifford as the forerunner of Bill Moyers under Johnson: both were young, attractive, energetic, and able to get things done; both won the plaudits of their peers in government and the applause of the press; both were intimate advisers on key policy matters, handled managerial tasks with ease, dominated the entire communications processes for the Chief Executive, and developed numerous legislative proposals.

Perhaps his rise to prominence was due partly to the fact that he was an enormously talented person in a presidential staff which David Lilienthal described as a group of "third-raters." There was, however, another cogent reason. He was from Missouri. To Truman this was important. He was also a protégé of Jake Vardaman, a long-time crony of the President's. Personal friendship was something Truman was not likely to break.

The only other able man in the White House was a carry-over from the Roosevelt administration, Judge Rosenman. Rosenman was impressed by the young Missourian and soon they were working together on legal matters, legislative proposals, presidential speeches, and key appointments. Clifford, especially, took advantage of vacuums that developed in the Cabinet advisory system as men left and new men came in to fill their places. Twenty-four Cabinet members served under Truman in his seven and a half years, in contrast to the sixteen who served under Eisenhower in eight years.

In domestic affairs, Clifford persuaded the President to veto the Office of Price Administration and Taft-Hartley bills. He supported the President in the demand that the railroad unions call off their nationwide strike in 1946 and wrote the President's violent speech in which he asked Congress for enlarged strikebreaking authority.

One of Clifford's notable contributions was his famous forty-three-page memorandum on plans for the 1948 campaign. Prepared and delivered to Truman in 1947, the paper laid down a blueprint for what was to be the successful campaign against Governor Dewey. Following the Clifford plan, Truman concentrated on the industrial centers of the country and their large liberal constituencies. It was a blueprint for victory that astounded the political professionals, especially Governor Dewey and his sophisticated political staff.

Clifford was also influential in foreign affairs. He helped develop and, as legislative liaison, persuaded the Congress to establish the National Security Council and the Central Intelligence Agency. While supporting Truman's containment policy, he also urged, in a long memorandum, that the approach to the Soviet Union be a balanced one, including taking the initiative in working for the exchange of visitors, scientists, and others. It was he who was responsible for Truman's notable 1947 address that called for substantial aid to Greece and Turkey.

Some speech aides, such as Emmet Hughes and Arthur Larson in the Eisenhower administration and Raymond Price and William Safire in the Nixon administration, were ghost writers. Clifford was different, perhaps similar to Sorensen and Moyers, all of whom in helping with speeches also contributed greatly to ideas and helped the Presidents sharpen their own views.

Clifford has said, "If I rendered any service to President Truman in five years it was as the representative of the liberal forces." Clifford thought that the success of the liberals in that period was due, at least partly, to his role as principal presidential confidant. The conservative forces, mostly members of the Cabinet and key congressmen, were not so fortunate.

Acutely depressed by the corrupt, self-seeking, cronyist atmosphere in Washington following Truman's inauguration in 1949, Clifford's influence began to wane, mainly by his own choice. He resigned in January 1950. George E. Reedy, for a considerable time a member of Lyndon Johnson's staff, on the Hill and in the White House, has said that Truman's handling of the Communist spy scare opened the door for the McCarthy era, and other writers have contended that Truman's airy dismissal of charges of Communist infiltration in government as "red herrings" fanned fires McCarthy was lighting.

The Clifford liberal influence in the White House was now lacking. He had returned to the practice of law, but such was his talent that he was to serve two more Presidents, an unusual occurrence. He was pressed into service by President Kennedy to smooth the transition from Eisenhower to Kennedy, a transition remarkably free of clumsiness and discord. Clifford also helped Kennedy in reorganizing the Central Intelligence Agency following the Bay of Pigs fiasco. Still later President Johnson called on Clifford, his long-time friend, to serve as one of his confidants and as Secretary of Defense from 1968 to 1969. Here he faced a dilemma. He had to carry out the orders of the Commander-in-Chief but he soon strongly advocated a reversal of Johnson's Vietnam policy. His retrospective account of decision making on the Vietnam question was angrily denounced by Johnson. A final cause of the break in the relationship, prior to Johnson's death, was the favorable treatment given to Clifford by the press, usually by the same newspapermen and editorial writers who severely criticized Johnson's war policy. Mutual friends have said that the disillusioned President held his old friend accountable for stories which seemed to make Clifford look good at Johnson's expense.

Harry S. Truman may well turn out to be one of the most difficult Presidents to assess. Developments since his presidency may have proved, or may yet prove, that many of his decisions were poor ones. Surely, many were right. A disproportionately high share of the decisions he had to make, however, were fateful. Truman presided over a nation that had moved into a new era—an era in which there were totally new forces to contend with, in which the "tried and true" could no longer be relied on, in which the rules of the game were being rewritten.

Truman was a tough and active President. He was totally his own man. He worked at being President and he was determined to be effective in the job from the moment he assumed it to the moment he relinquished it. He understood the presidency and its problems and sought to make it more efficient and more effective. It was he who summoned the first Hoover Commission to give serious study to the organization of the executive branch. Speaking of the President's responsibility to co-ordinate the various executive agencies, President Truman aptly described the job as making a "mesh" of things. He brought the National Security Council into being and viewed it as "the place in the government where military, diplomatic, and resources problems could be continually appraised . . . to give the president a running balance and a perpetual inventory of where we stood and where we were going on all strategic questions affecting the national security." He had suffered from his lack of information and involvement when he assumed the presidency and determined that his successor should move easily and smoothly into the breach; so he instructed Clark Clifford to work out the transfer of power after the election of President Eisenhower.

"The presidency of the United States of America," Truman once declared, "has become the greatest and most important office in the history of the world." And when he remarked that if one couldn't take the heat, get out of the kitchen, he meant as well that while he was there, he *liked* the kitchen.

CHAPTER 13

To a politician there is no greater temptation than the intimation of electoral immortality.

A CONSTITUTIONAL AMENDMENT of historic importance was adopted during the Truman administration. The Twenty-second Amendment, limiting a President to two four-year terms, was submitted to the states in July 1947 and ratified three and a half years later, in February 1951. A principal motivation for this was the conviction of the Congress and a substantial number of the American people that the nation should not again have a President elected for three or four terms.

Edward S. Corwin, in analyzing the congressional debate on the amendment, pointed out in his book *The President: Office and Powers*[18] that the really critical issue in the minds of the Congress was "whether a President should be permitted to succeed himself at all."

My answer to that question is "No!" I was convinced then, as I am now, that the President should be elected for a single six-year term. When I have discussed this with friends, the normal reaction has been that my notion is radical, too great a departure from a tradition that has existed from President Washington to the beginning of the Roosevelt third term. In fact the idea is older than the Republic. A preliminary draft of the Constitution said: "The executive power of the United States shall be vested in a single person . . . [who] shall hold office during a term of seven years, but shall not be elected a second time." I have always thought that this provision was not adopted because of the unprecedented respect all had for General Washington and the assumption that he would be the first constitutional President. He was so revered that some spoke of his becoming only head of state, a surrogate king, with a chief executive under his general guidance.

The platform of the Democratic Party in 1912 called for a constitutional amendment which would limit the President to a single term, a political promise which President Wilson ignored.

My reason for favoring a single term for the President is based on my conviction that we should expect the President to foster only those programs and policies which he is convinced are in the interest of the nation as a whole—that he should have no incentive to propose and fight for measures conceived mainly to enhance his chances of re-election, or merely to confound the political opposition. I have seen too often the enormous power of the federal government employed by Presidents in seeking approval of ill-conceived or wasteful programs that seemingly would add temporarily to their prestige but in the long run would be detrimental to the country. This was surely true of some of the programs fostered by President Roosevelt, for they were so hastily initiated nationwide that ghastly inefficiency and serious program conflicts were inevitable. This view was confirmed later by actions taken by Presidents Johnson and Nixon.

In a previous chapter I have discussed the initiation of nationwide programs that failed or achieved only a modicum of success for the reason that persons trained to carry out the programs were not available. It did not appeal politically to the President to begin on a manageable scale, wait until personnel were trained and policy and procedural matters worked out before gradually expanding the programs as rapidly as training and efficiency permitted.

Too frequently the President and the opposition party in the Congress seek to outbid one another in welfare, educational, research, health, military, public works, and other programs in the hope of obtaining political advantage. And when the much-touted program turns out to be more promise than performance, citizens become disheartened, even cynical.

The task of statesmanship for all leaders, and especially for the President, is to stand for what is right and then seek to convince the people of the national advantage of the position taken. Theodore Sorensen has said in *Decision Making in the White House*,[19] "Public and political needs are often incompatible. . . . A President must remember that public opinion and public interest do not always agree," and President Truman in his memoirs acknowledged that "A President cannot always be popular." The incentive for statesmanship in the presidency would be enhanced if re-election were not possible and thus not an influence on the President's reasoning and judgment. But even apart from that, the drain on the energy and health of the President is always so inescapable that a period of six years is enough even for the most robust individual.

When President Eisenhower was deciding whether he would run for re-election, one of the negative points in his mind was his belief that he would have less influence in a second term because of the constitutional limitation on his running still another time. In effect, he thought he would be a "lame duck" in his second term. The power of the president, however, is not dependent on the possibility of another term or on patronage. His real power is in the respect and broad support of the people. If they believe in his credibility, character, basic purposes and policies, they will support him, even if they disagree with some of his specific proposals and actions. The voters' attitudes are well known to members of the Congress. If the people support the President, this to a considerable extent influences congressional attitudes and improves relationships between the Congress and White House, provided, of course, that the President regularly and in earnest meets with the congressional leaders in seeking common views. In my judgment President Eisenhower was more successful in his second term than he was in the first, though I realize some historians feel otherwise.

Corwin, in his book I have just cited,[18] calls the presidency a "killing job"; hence "An untried president may be better than a tired one." He goes on: "The chief objection to presidential reeligibility is just as valid against a second successive term as it would be against a third term. It consists of the fact that a president who is looking forward to reelection *will be apt to evaluate all programs primarily for their probable effect on his political fortunes and will, in fact, be expected by his party to do just that.*"

Edwin L. Dale, Jr., in an article in the July 16, 1972, issue of the Sunday New York *Times*, stated his belief that a major issue in the campaign would be the "runaway" nature of federal spending. He indicated that one of President Nixon's confidants had said to him that "in a second term Mr. Nixon *would be freer to act upon his convictions about spending. There would be no political necessity to allow various types of popular spending, inasmuch as the President is limited to two terms.*"

The incentive to spend or take any other action for sheer political advantage should not exist. It would not if the President were limited to one six-year term.

The reasoning for a single term for the President of the United States leads logically and even with increased force to the conviction that representatives should be limited to three terms of four years each and senators to two terms of six years each. The temptation to those who represent limited constituencies to neglect the national interest and stand for what they believe will contribute to their re-election is patently more pronounced than it is with the President. Much legislation is introduced and sometimes passed solely for the benefit of a single locality or for several local constituencies and often it is detrimental to the nation. This is a direct consequence of the belief of representatives and senators that to be re-elected they must satisfy the wishes, even the prejudices, of their constituents. The story is told of a senator, a sponsor of the prohibition amendment to the Constitution, who each year made an impassioned speech in the Senate memorializing the adoption of prohibition, although he himself liked to drink; senators had heard the speech many times, so normally they left the chamber when this annual address was made. At several points in the speech the senator would ask the presiding officer to call for order; this read well when his constituents received the *Congressional Record*. A friend asked him how he could reconcile this situation with his conscience—drinking himself but praising prohibition. His reply: "If I did otherwise, I would lose my place in the Senate and someone would be elected who is not half as capable as I in representing my state!"

Of course each representative and senator should be mindful of problems and conditions in his own geographic area, but they should be viewed in the national context. Citizens of his area should expect him to favor measures in the interest of the nation; it is his responsibility to bring about this type of enlightenment. Edmund Burke, in a talk with the Electors of Bristol in 1774, suggested: "Your representative owes you, not his industry only, but his judgment, and he betrays instead of serving you if he sacrifices it to your opinion."

The conflict of local political advantage versus national interest became evident in the Congress once again with the passage of the Rail Passenger Service Act of 1970 which created, effective May 1, 1971, a quasi-public Railroad Passenger Corporation to take over and operate a nationwide system of intercity passenger service. Since the private railroads had been losing seven hundred million dollars a year operating passenger trains, it was obvious that the new service, popularly called Amtrak, could make a profit—as it was legally supposed to do—only if it discontinued all trains which carried too few passengers and incurred annual deficits. The Amtrak plan of limited service was published in March 1971; it was pointed out that the organic act under which Amtrak would operate provided for the addition of services where the states were willing to assume two thirds of the operating losses. Only two states came forward, Illinois and Massachusetts.

A good many members of Congress, however, sought to expand services in their areas without state subsidies. Several of these succeeded at federal expense.

Senator Mike Mansfield, normally statesmanlike in his positions on most questions, demanded that the approved northern route across Montana be supplemented by a second one across the southern part of the state. Mansfield threatened the loss of Amtrak initial financing if his suggestion was not approved. As majority leader of the Senate he probably could have made good on his threat. The second route was established. The "Mansfield Special" is costing the taxpayers of all fifty states $2.6 million a year.

In the House, Congressman Harley O. Staggers, chairman of the Interstate and Foreign Commerce Committee which handled the Amtrak legislation, let it be known that there would have to be train service through his home district in the northeast panhandle of West Virginia. He won. The "Staggers Express" has been a financial flop. Often the trains run without any passengers, save for limited Washington commuter use in the first seventy-five miles of the 351-mile journey. So taxpayers are indirectly contributing a million dollars to the Staggers campaign fund by subsidizing an unprofitable train which the congressman feels helps him politically.

On July 28, 1973, Senator Vance Hartke of Indiana proposed that Amtrak add high-speed rail service between Chicago and South Bend, Indiana. Since the senator is chairman of the Senate Surface Transportation Sub-Committee, it does not require a Nostradamus to predict what the outcome of the proposal will be or that the operating deficit, financed by taxpayers, will be huge.

The process of logrolling is a dramatic example of how the desire for re-election supersedes a member's knowledge of what is right. Thus importation of shoes from Italy may temporarily disadvantage several states; the importation of textiles from Japan may hurt others; bringing in lead and zinc from Mexico may cause temporary trouble in two or three states. Representatives and senators who feel their areas disadvantaged by unrelated situations form a legislative coalition; they can then pass a bill which, if approved by the President, would be harmful to the country, for economic interdependence among nations is now such that archaic protectionism is no longer acceptable. Sometimes logrolling in the Congress impels the President, as a means of preventing passage of a tariff bill, to adopt a quota system on imports, for quotas are neither so rigid nor so difficult to remedy as are tariff laws.

It is true that for the time being the United States is at a disadvantage in world trade. But this is a problem of comparative wages, prices, and currency relationships, not of efficiency of production in the developed nations of the world. The fundamental problems should be tackled. Patchwork legislation is almost always harmful, as was the Hawley-Smoot tariff in the Hoover administration.

One may even question the assumption that voting merely to please local constituencies is actually good politics. Senator George Norris, a liberal in his time, came from a conservative state—Nebraska. He was the author of the TVA Act and many other measures which today are taken for granted but in the thirties were considered to be liberal. He was an honest and courageous man. *He was also skillful in explaining to the people of Nebraska his reasons for the positions he took in the Senate.* He was re-elected without difficulty, once without opposition. Senator Borah of Idaho, an arrogant conservative, and Senator LaFollette of Wisconsin, who cannot be categorized, also voted their convictions, arrived at after Senate hearings and through consideration of the needs of the nation. These men educated their own constituents. The people of their states were proud of them. I think Senator Mike Mansfield, Senator Charles Percy, and Senator Charles Mathias are such senators today.

More important than the foregoing is this: membership in the House and Senate of the United States Congress *should not be a career*. It is to maintain a career that members support bills on the basis of local prejudices and interests. Why do members of congressional committees sit for months holding hearings on a vital problem and having a research staff provide them with all possible facts about that problem, only to ignore the information they have obtained (knowledge obviously superior to that of their constituents) and vote in a way they believe will meet local approval? Again, statesmanship calls for more than this.

Tom Wicker in his book, *JFK-LBJ*,[20] writes: "The . . . most fundamental task of American politics ought to be that of public education —the enlightenment of the electorate the [President or congressman] represents, a constituency that in the nature of the case and in the press of its own business will not have the time, opportunity, or inclination that he has to inform himself about the realities of an ever more complex and shrinking world."

Service in the national Congress, instead of being a career, should be a contribution an individual makes to his country. Re-election should not be paramount and defeat at the polls should not be cause for personal frustration. Service in Congress should be an interruption to one's normal career, whether he or she be a lawyer, educator, manufacturer, finance expert, housewife, or social or cultural leader. One who temporarily takes leave from his normal career should end his political experience with the satisfaction that he has worked diligently for the total welfare of the nation.

The change I suggest—a change in somewhat different form and for different reasons from that made by President Eisenhower in *Waging Peace*[21]—*would break up the seniority system* in the House and Senate, an improvement now favored by Common Cause and many other agencies and individuals. Seniority is a legislative anachronism. Chairmen of committees have too much power. They tend to be satraps. Why should a single man decide for the entire population whether there will be congressional hearings on gun control? Why should another determine whether consideration will be given to tax reform?

The initial inauguration of limited service for representatives and senators could be on a staggered basis. Thereafter, since some would be re-elected and others would not, the membership in both chambers would, so far as tenure is concerned, be mixed. Possibly present members who have already served in the Congress for twelve years should be permitted to run for one additional term.

A single term for the President and limited terms for members of the Congress would result in better executive-legislative relations and co-operation. It would not and should not eliminate all differences between the two branches of government, and most assuredly not between Democrats and Republicans in the Congress. But with re-election made less important and with the transcendent problems of keeping the nation at peace, prosperous, and constantly altering social programs and policies to meet changing economic, social, and cultural conditions, it seems inevitable that a more co-operative spirit would be evident in Washington.

Probably, too, we would more often than in the past have the White House and the Congress under control of the same party. This would be meritorious for two reasons: it would make convention platform pledges more meaningful to the people and would enhance the opportunity of implementing the pledges made by a successful party.

Opposition to limited terms for representatives and senators would come mainly from the senators. The most likely opponents of incumbent senators are retiring governors and representatives who have achieved favorable publicity and standing in their states. Today, a representative is often reluctant to run against an incumbent senator because he must give up his House seat to do so—he cannot run for both elective offices at the same time. But if representatives had four-year terms, rather than two as now, many senators would be up for re-election when several congressmen in their states had served only two years of their four-year terms. Hence, representatives could seek the Senate seat and, if they failed, they would still be members of the House.

The Constitution provides for two methods of amendment. Throughout our history we have used only one: passage of a proposed amendment by the House and Senate followed by its submission to the states for ratification. We have never used the national convention method of amending the Constitution. It is clear to me that if there is merit in my suggestion we would have to employ this dormant constitutional provision, for otherwise the proposed amendment would never pass the Senate.

CHAPTER 14

There are times when the harness of duty
chafes the very soul.

GENERAL EISENHOWER'S WARTIME role had
made him a well-known figure in the nation and the world and inevitably led to public consideration of him as a strong contender for the
presidency. For a variety of reasons, however, he was not interested in
running for political office. He had an aversion, as I did, to the intense
public exposure, name-calling, and other shenanigans that too often
characterize political campaigning. Beyond that, however, he earnestly
believed that it would be wrong for him to take advantage of the wave
of popularity and affection that resulted from military victory, won by
the toil and blood of men under his command. In 1948, when he was
being proposed as a candidate, he wrote to New Hampshire publisher
Leonard Finder, stating:

"It is my conviction that the necessary and wise subordination of
the military to civil power will be best sustained, and our people will
have greater confidence that it is so sustained, when lifelong professional soldiers, in the absence of some obvious and overriding reason,
abstain from seeking high political office."

Standing on that conviction, he effectively squelched efforts to make
him a candidate for the presidency.

Two years later, in the fall of 1950, when General Eisenhower was
serving as president of Columbia University, Tom Dewey decided that
he would not try for the third time to win the White House. In announcing this decision, he stated that he would support General Eisenhower. The next day the general again told the press that he had
no intention of running for political office.

In December 1950, President Truman asked General Eisenhower
to assume command of the newly formed North Atlantic Treaty Organization in Paris. Although he despaired of being an absentee president

of Columbia and urged the trustees to act in the best interest of the university, Ike could not decline Truman's request. Nothing was more important to Western civilization, he believed, than an alliance of the United States, Great Britain, and Western Europe.

Despite his move to Europe, the public talk of him as a presidential candidate in 1952 continued. Many of his friends had been urging him to run, arguing that the nation needed a change in party leadership. I certainly agreed that a Republican victory would benefit the nation, but my position on this in discussions with my brother was an impersonal one. *I took it for granted that nothing would change his mind with respect to becoming a candidate.* I expressed in a detached way my feeling that in our pluralistic society it was dangerous to have one-party control for too long, considering the power vested in the presidency. Had the Republicans been in control of the White House for twenty years, as the Democrats would be by the next inauguration, I would favor a change just as fervently. Intellectual divisions within our society tended to deepen and grow bitter as one party remained in power. Opposition to an administration's program moved from a modest and rational posture to carping and irrational criticism, and eventually to bitterness and even hatred. A change of top leadership miraculously changed this almost immediately. The new administration rarely abrogated any of the programs of its predecessor and thus, de facto, tacitly approved them. Republicans might bitterly oppose Franklin Roosevelt's Social Security program for a decade or more, but once a Republican became President and did not press for its repeal, the Social Security program became a bipartisan one. Members of the opposition party now accepted, sometimes reluctantly, what was already in being. By 1952, after two decades in power, the Democrats would have enacted much legislation and created many programs that had not yet become sanctioned by the Republicans.

I recognized, of course, that the cycle would repeat itself—that the party newly in power would experience a so-called "honeymoon," then disagreements would again begin to build. But the disagreement would be on new issues, not the old ones. This had been true throughout our history. When the Federal Reserve System was created, for example, Republicans asserted, as did my elders in Abilene, that it would bring disaster to the nation. But when Harding, Coolidge, and Hoover followed Wilson in the White House they did not discard the system but rather strengthened it. The Federal Reserve System was no longer an issue in the adversary system of American politics. When the Republicans occupied the White House, after twenty years of Democratic rule, I was sure that most of the elements of the New Deal and the Fair Deal would remain and become largely removed from the arena of controversy.

This practice of dogmatic opposition, leading to serious divisions in our society, is not very complimentary to our democratic system and is repugnant to idealists and intellectuals who yearn for the time when problems, issues, and politics will be analyzed with objectivity and when judgments will be formed on the basis of rational evaluation. But the ideal was not reality in 1950 and is not now. I felt strongly that a change in national leadership was essential.

General Eisenhower fully agreed with me on the desirability of a Republican victory. But he had no intention of being the Republican President.

Some of his friends were much more personal and partisan on this matter than I. General Lucius Clay, former Senator Henry Cabot Lodge, William Robinson of the New York Herald Tribune, Senator James Duff of Pennsylvania, Senator Frank Carlson of Kansas, Governor Dewey, Herbert Brownell, and Clifford Roberts of New York, and others—all wanted a Republican victory in 1952 and were convinced that only General Eisenhower could guarantee that victory. They argued that he owed it to the country to respond to the call that was growing from coast to coast.

Although Ike remained adamant, even under pressure from close friends, he was not insensitive to the problems. Developments in the Truman administration were carefully noted at NATO headquarters in Paris, and General Eisenhower was very conscious of them personally and in his negotiations with the heads of governments of NATO countries, especially NATO itself, the European Recovery Program, aid to Greece and Turkey, and, in general, the concept of mutual security.

He became deeply concerned about one serious matter early in 1951. Senator Robert Taft was the leading Republican candidate. He seemed to have a good chance of winning, even running against President Truman. My brother's principal concern resulted from rumors that Taft was not friendly to the concept of mutual security.

In February 1951, General Eisenhower returned to the United

States on a brief visit. He arranged to meet secretly with Senator Taft. I did not attend the meeting. The two men were alone. To the best of my knowledge there is no written record of what was discussed, but my brother told me about it in detail, and I am sure that my memory of our conversation is substantially accurate so far as the critical point in the discussion is concerned.

Senator Taft and General Eisenhower met for several hours. On domestic questions no significant differences of opinion were apparent. Senator Taft, dubbed by the press a conservative, was in fact moderate in his views; several liberal enactments were results of his leadership, and he was open-minded on other domestic issues brought up in the meeting with my brother.

Their discussion on foreign affairs was not so harmonious. General Eisenhower was determined that the Republican Party should stand firmly behind the Truman-inspired policy of mutual security. His experience in World War II and as head of NATO and his awareness of the menacing situation in Eastern Europe convinced him that NATO was essential for the protection not only of Europe but also of the United States. He was deeply committed to a policy of mutual security even though the United States would have to bear a disproportionate share of the military and financial burden until our European allies could overcome the destruction and economic losses of the war. He insisted that the United States could negotiate successfully with the Eastern powers only from a position of economic and military strength. The Soviet Union and nations within its hegemony were scornful of weakness. Ike believed it would be sheer folly to underestimate the threat. The Soviet Union had seized the nations on her western and southern borders, had become belligerent toward Western nations, particularly Germany, and had become increasingly hostile toward the United States since the end of the war. In response, the United States and Western European nations must make clear that an attack on one of them would be considered an attack on all. General Eisenhower also foresaw the probable need for other alliances in the Middle East and Southeast Asia.

Senator Taft would not commit himself to such a policy. He did not know, he said, whether he would favor two or more United States divisions in Europe.

General Eisenhower's feelings about mutual security were so strong that he had taken into the meeting with him the draft of a statement. He would make it public if Senator Taft would commit himself to the policy of mutual security. The statement would say clearly that he would not authorize use of his name in the 1952 presidential contest and that he would repudiate any effort to make him a candidate. When Taft refused to commit himself, Ike tore up the statement and later said: "In the absence of the assurance I had been seeking, it would be silly for me to throw away whatever political influence I might possess to help keep us on the right track."

General Eisenhower returned to Paris and his duties as head of NATO. As the months passed, his concern about collective security increased and he worried about the consequences of a President who was not committed to NATO.

The first I knew that my brother was weakening in his resolve to keep free of elective politics occurred on April 4, 1952. Bill Robinson, publisher of the New York *Herald Tribune*, just back from Paris, joined me for breakfast in Washington and gave me a message that my brother had asked him to deliver. Robinson said that General Eisenhower had been deeply moved by Truman's announcement on March 29 that he would not again be a presidential candidate. This enhanced the chances of a Republican victory and, now that Senator Taft was a formal candidate running hard, it held the possibility of weakening NATO and the leadership of the United States in world affairs. Hence, said Robinson, "your brother now feels he would be unhappier in remaining out of the forthcoming Republican preconvention fight than he would be in abandoning the position on this question he has so long maintained."

I knew that Ike had been under tremendous pressure during the past year to run for the presidency, or at the very least not to oppose those who were making strenuous efforts in his behalf. I did not at the time, however, know just how persistently people were pursuing him. Senator Lodge and General Clay were two of the most persistent, but many of my brother's friends and admirers were involved. Ike had many visitors while he was in Paris and, whatever the reason they may have given for going abroad, they always seemed to wind up in Ike's office trying to persuade him that it was his duty to resign from NATO and come home and run for the presidency.

To all of these overtures his response was essentially the same. He declared that it was inappropriate for him in his present position to become involved in politics in any way and refused to take any action, positive or negative, in regard to matters of a political nature. There was absolutely no doubt in my mind that he meant exactly what he said, for he stuck by this position even when it hampered the efforts of admirers who were promoting his candidacy in various state contests. Later he would even refuse to declare his party affiliation when Henry Cabot Lodge needed such a declaration to enter his name in the New Hampshire primary.

In November 1951, General Eisenhower returned to discuss NATO matters with President Truman. His visit was an occasion for rampant speculation in the press about his political future. The trip was a nightmare for him. He was constantly harassed by members of the press, who followed him everywhere and camped outside his door, hoping he would say or do something to reveal that he was in fact considering the presidency. When Ike refused to say definitely that he would not run in 1952 (in keeping with his position that he would say nothing either negative or positive regarding political matters), the press and Eisenhower supporters interpreted this as a sign of his interest in the office.

Ike returned to Paris, glad to be away from Washington, and I remained convinced that he did not want to be President of the United States. I also realized, however, that my brother was a tormented man. He wanted desperately to stay out of politics, but his growing concern over foreign affairs and his high sense of duty made him somewhat vulnerable to the appeals and pressures of men and women he respected who truly believed that the welfare of the nation depended on him.

Shortly after his return to Paris, General Eisenhower, working through Cliff Roberts and Bill Robinson, established a personal advisory group of close friends to counsel him on this increasingly complex and confusing matter of presidential politics. He insisted that the group be completely independent of any political efforts to put him in the presidential race, and he wanted it to be hardheaded and objective in looking at the "propriety, decency, and desirability" of any proposition affecting him. He wanted his friends to keep themselves and him well informed of developments in the United States. General Eisenhower listed the following as members of that group: *Lewis Maytag,* retired president of Maytag Washing Machine Company; *Bobby Jones,* Atlanta lawyer and former golf champion; *W. Alton Jones,* president of Cities Service Company; *Ellis Slater,* president of Frankfort Distillers; *L. F. McCollum,* president of a Houston oil company; *Albert Bradley,* executive vice-president of General Motors; *Burton Peek,* board chairman of Deere and Company; *Philip Reed,* board chairman of General Electric; *Douglas Black,* president of Doubleday and Company, publishers; *Robert McConnell,* a retired oil executive of Denver; *Philip Young,* the dean of Columbia Business School; *Aksel Nielsen,* president of the Title Guaranty Company of Denver; *Lucius Clay,* who was then president of Continental Can; *Cliff Roberts* and *Bill Robinson,* and *Milton S. Eisenhower.*

I did not know, until some time later, just how frenetic the period of December 1951 to April 1952 was for my brother. Of course I was aware of several significant developments that were increasing the pressure on him, such as the massive Eisenhower rally in Madison Square Garden in early February 1952 (the films of which later moved Ike deeply as he witnessed the great outpouring of support for him) and the New Hampshire primary in early March which produced a significant plurality for Ike and a sweep of all delegates. These were public events; behind the scenes the intensity of letters, telegrams, and visits from those who were pushing his candidacy was growing week by week.

Thus, when Bill Robinson reported to me on April 4 that my brother was beginning to yield to the pressure, I was not terribly surprised. I had mixed feelings—immense pride and genuine sympathy for him.

One week later, on April 11, the White House announced that General Eisenhower was being relieved of his NATO duties at his own request and would be coming home on June 1. In effect, the announcement removed all doubt that Ike would be a candidate if the Republican Party wanted him. Even so, during his remaining months in Paris he refused to become involved in political matters or to assist those who were promoting his candidacy in the United States.

I was then president of the Pennsylvania State University. Penn State was only four hours by car from Washington, so it was easy for me to join a steering group in Washington when General Eisenhower came home on June 1, 1952. He agreed to participate in a limited campaign for the Republican nomination, but he also said that he was acting out of a sense of duty and not out of personal motivation. He would not tailor his opinions or his principles to win votes. He would say what he believed and stand on his own convictions, and if the Republican Party wanted him on this basis, he would accept.

It was decided that General Eisenhower's first address should be in our home town. That proved to be a near disaster. Fifty thousand persons gathered in Abilene, a town of only five thousand population. Obviously no hall or even stadium was available to seat so many people. So the address was to be held outdoors in Eisenhower Park, where all had to stand, and, as it developed, get wet. A cloudburst drenched the audience. The governor of Colorado stood right behind General Eisenhower during the televised address, wearing a typical Western hat and constantly moving back and forth. The multiple distractions of the heavy rainfall, shifting umbrellas, and the constantly moving Stetson made it difficult for the television audience to see or follow the candidate.

Campaign headquarters were established first in Denver, then in New York. Throughout the campaign, both preconvention and postconvention, I divided my time between my university duties and traveling by train for whistle stops and major addresses in key cities. I had offered to resign or take leave of absence from Penn State, but the trustees insisted that so long as I kept up with my university duties I was as free as any other citizen to participate in the campaign; indeed, they said, it would not be understood if a brother who for years had been extremely close to General Eisenhower did not participate actively.

My initial duty was to help prepare addresses on agriculture and notes on that topic for informal whistle-stop talks. But soon a small group of six individuals found ourselves working together to do research and prepare first drafts of addresses for my brother's consideration. We quickly learned, however, that nobody could "ghost" a talk for Ike. He would tear a draft to pieces and then revise his own copy time and time again. Years later, when I prepared for him drafts of thirty-two talks he would make on a good-will trip to Brazil, Uruguay, Argentina, and Chile, Ann Whitman and others on the White House staff said I "got off easier" than anyone else had during the Eisenhower presidential years.

During the convention in Chicago our offices and conference

rooms were in the Blackstone Hotel. We had a full floor at our disposal. Nearly every hour of each day delegations came to the suite or General Eisenhower joined them at their hotels. On one occasion my brother was confined to his room with a stomach disorder and I was assigned to meet with the delegations that came to the suite that day, doing my best to place before them the positions on domestic and international issues which I knew my brother would have done. I also met with a large group of young Republicans at a nearby hotel for the same purpose.

In the convention, the mistakes in political tactics were not made by the amateur Eisenhower forces but by the professionals in the Taft camp. The critical fight on the convention floor involved the seating of portions of certain state delegations, a dispute the Credentials Committee, dominated by Taft, had decided in the senator's favor—much to the irritation of the Eisenhower forces. Since there were several other candidates for the nomination, including Governor Warren of California and Governor McKeldin of Maryland, there was a different outcome when the Credentials Committee decisions came to the convention for a vote. Since the senator was believed to be the leading candidate, the delegates for the other candidates voted to seat delegations which opposed Taft. That practically determined the outcome of the convention, for delegates were seated who subsequently shifted to Eisenhower.

Dwight David Eisenhower was nominated on the first ballot.

Indelibly pictured in my mind are the actions which immediately followed the convention victory. Half a dozen of us had remained in the hotel suite with my brother during the voting. When the outcome was announced, the General rushed to Mamie's room. As we awaited his return, we became aware of shouting outside the hotel. From the windows we saw General Eisenhower attempting to push his way through a happy, noisy crowd, on his way to Senator Taft's headquarters at a hotel directly across from ours. On television we watched a meeting of the two men who had been opposing candidates only moments before.

My brother returned to his suite. Then we silently witnessed a scene that brought tears to our eyes. He wrote a telegram resigning his post as a five-star General of the Armies of the United States. He had been in the military service for forty years, believed deeply in the need for an efficient American military force, and was personally devoted to the service. Although he might soon become Commander-in-Chief, he resigned with utmost reluctance.

In the suite with us was Sergeant Moaney, General Eisenhower's personal and devoted valet. General Eisenhower called the sergeant, showed him his resignation, and said: "Moaney, I am no longer entitled to have you as my personal valet, though we will always be friends. You cannot afford to resign your army commission. I may not win this election. You cannot give up your army income and the retirement privileges you will get someday."

Without hesitation Moaney replied: "General, you and I can always make a living!"

As I heard this, I thought back to the time when Moaney and his charming wife were married. General and Mrs. Eisenhower were then living in the official residence of Columbia University at 60 Morningside Drive. Following the inaugural ceremony, my brother said to Moaney that, while there would always be a place for him in his personal entourage, he doubted that there would be a post for his bride, Dolores, in view of the fact that the residence was fully staffed by the university. Under these circumstances Moaney and Dolores might prefer to have a position where they could work together. In his charming Southern drawl Sergeant Moaney had responded: "General, I knowed you before I knowed her." The relationship of Sergeant Moaney and his wife with the Eisenhower household became permanent and continues to this day with Mrs. Eisenhower.

At the insistence of President Truman, the Democratic Convention nominated Governor Adlai Stevenson of Illinois, a moderate liberal and a man of exceptional verbal talents. The President, who had offered General Eisenhower the Democratic nomination in 1948 and had been his friend and admirer until 1952, now turned viciously against him. I have always thought the animosity began as a result of a casual statement made by Stevenson in Seattle, early in the campaign. He undiplomatically referred to "the mess in Washington." This was widely quoted in the press. It became a constant phrase of the Eisenhower forces: "We'll clean up the mess in Washington."

Significant factors in the outcome of the election were several. There can be no doubt that the popularity of General Eisenhower was important. His name was a household word, most admired him, and few had anything against him. The fact that he was not a politician helped him, for it became evident during the campaign that the people of the country had become satiated with politics during the preceding twenty years, and especially during the preceding seven years. Time and again people at Eisenhower rallies would come up to me—persons of all ages —and say, "I'm going to vote for your brother because he isn't a politician. He is an honest man and I believe in him." My brother's strong support of the concept of mutual security also appealed to the American people; that this popular concept could prevail without the help of a slogan-issue like "the mess in Washington" was a real plus.

During most of the campaign we of the Eisenhower staff felt that the tide was running strongly in our favor. The only doubt developed (and it was temporary) when charges were made that vice-presidential candidate Richard M. Nixon had benefited from a "political slush fund" allegedly given him by a "millionaires' club" in California.

The press asserted that General Eisenhower was shaken by this revelation. The press was wrong. I was with my brother throughout that period and he was one of the few prominent Republicans who was not panicked by the story. General Eisenhower had learned long ago not to judge a situation on partial evidence; his decisions too frequently involved the lives and fortunes of young American fighting men for him to act precipitously. He wanted all the facts he could get, not rumors, before he arrived at a judgment.

Over the next few days, as the story gained in significance and as political opponents expressed righteous indignation, telegrams and telephone calls flooded in urging either that General Eisenhower dump Nixon at once or immediately denounce the story as a vicious attempt to smear Mr. Nixon. General Eisenhower would do neither. He ordered a team of lawyers and accountants to make a thorough investigation and report back. Until they did, he simply said that the facts would all come out and he was certain that they would exonerate Mr. Nixon. When the study was completed, in very short order, it was clear that the charge was without foundation. The fund was no different from those of many politicians; it was controlled by a trustee; Mr. Nixon had no direct access to it; contributions to it were limited to five hundred dollars; and all expenditures had been for legitimate political expenses.

It was agreed that Senator Nixon would go before the American people and lay the facts before them. And so he did, making his famous

"Checkers" speech. Many people called that speech "corny" and an "emotional stunt." Certainly it was an emotional performance, but no more so than the situation called for. Senator Nixon had a right to be emotional and indignant, for he was fighting for his political career against a completely false allegation. General Eisenhower heard the speech in Cleveland where he was about to make a speech. He sent a telegram to Senator Nixon expressing complete confidence in and admiration for him and urging him to fly the next night to Wheeling, West Virginia, and join the presidential campaign. Then Ike tore up his speech on inflation and came out with a rousing, crowd-pleasing tribute to his vice-presidential candidate.

The Nixon incident taught me a sobering lesson. Some days before it occurred, James Hagerty, in charge of press relations for the Eisenhower campaign, had arranged for me to have an off-the-record visit with a distinguished newspaperman whom I considered to be the best in the profession. The newsman wanted me to summarize for him what I considered to be the significant points General Eisenhower was making in the campaign. Unfortunately the meeting in my stateroom on the train took place on the morning the news broke about the Nixon fund. Our discussion dealt solely with this one issue. I emphasized that General Eisenhower believed in Senator Nixon's honesty but that he would not make any judgments in the case until all the facts were before him. In an offhand way, when I was pressed for a suggestion, I said the problem could be referred to the Senate Committee on Ethics; surely everyone would accept the judgment of such a committee. Within five minutes after our conversation ended, rumors were rampant among newsmen on the train: Eisenhower forces were divided; some wished to "sit tight" while others wanted to "dump" Nixon, and some wished to refer the Nixon problem to the Senate Committee on Ethics. I complained to Jim Hagerty that the confidential nature of my discussion had been violated and an off-the-record comment was being made public.

"Milton," Hagerty said, "when an issue involves the President of the United States or a major presidential candidate, all the normal rules of newspaper ethics are suspended." I never forgot that lesson.

The Eisenhower forces received the election returns at the Commodore Hotel in New York. When victory was assured, my wife and I, exhausted but happy, skipped the celebration and retired for the first solid and peaceful sleep in many weeks.

A few days after the election I inadvertently walked into the library of the university residence at a time when General Eisenhower was in conference. Hastily I turned to leave, but he called, "Milton, you're the one we need!" A delegation sponsoring the national Heart Fund drive had called to ask my brother to make a speech at the Waldorf Astoria Hotel, initiating the national and New York State campaigns for funds. He had explained that he was too tired to consider it. When he saw me, however, he suggested that if I could be persuaded to make the address he would accompany me and perhaps follow my talk with a few words of greeting. The delegation was delighted, not because of my participation, but because this assured the presence of the President-elect and hence a large audience.

I worked hard on that fifteen-minute speech, a talk touched with humor but with the serious theme of what voluntary giving meant, not only to indispensable activities, but also to the spirit of the people who gave. At the conclusion of the talk Ike, touched by what I had said, rose to his feet and chatted informally for nearly twenty minutes, much to the delight of the audience, and especially of those who had asked him to be present. At the opening of his remarks he said that if his brother made more speeches of the type just delivered many would feel that not only had the wrong Eisenhower been chosen as president of Columbia University but such thinking might extend to the office to which he had just been elected. Light as it was, Ike's comment was his way of giving public expression to the way he felt about the intellectual and affectionate relationship that had developed between us.

The week preceding the inauguration and the inaugural itself were hectic. Eisenhower family chores had been my responsibility ever since Father died in 1942. I suppose it is natural for a family to impose upon the youngest member. For the arrangements in Washington, it was inevitable that relatives should look to me, for I lived closer to the national capital than did the others, and I was an old-time Washingtonian. For several weeks prior to the inauguration, my wife and I stayed in the spacious quarters of her parents in the Mayflower Hotel in Washington. I had to make hotel reservations for brothers, their families, and other relatives. I had to obtain tickets for all events for everyone, and that proved to be time-consuming, which surprised me, for I had assumed a brother of the President would have everything done for him. I also had to arrange for cars and drivers, and for seeing to it that all relatives arrived at the right place at the right time for each event.

While this was driving me close to collapse, the telephone at my father-in-law's apartment was ringing constantly; people from all over the United States, claiming to be old friends, wanted tickets for the inaugural parade and the inaugural ball. One man, whom I did not know, telephoned from California and said he would like a parade ticket in or near the President's personal box! When I said that all the tickets were taken and I could do nothing for him, he shrieked on the telephone: "You haven't heard the last of this! I have a cousin, a schoolteacher, who knows Senator Knowland!" I always regretted that I did not reply: "Friend, it wouldn't help if you knew the President's brother!"

That was a mild introduction to what I would encounter for the next eight years. I became rather adept at either avoiding special pleaders completely or using skillful methods of having them gently escorted from my office or home without serious offense and invariably without agreeing to be a conduit to the White House or any individual in it.

CHAPTER 15

Learning to cope with incredible complexity
has become an imperative. Orderly change
is the best assurance of stability.

For TWO MONTHS following his election General Eisenhower conferred constantly with Herbert Brownell, Sherman Adams, and other close advisers in deciding whom he would ask to serve in his Cabinet and in other important federal posts. Surely he did not need to be told that the quality of the personnel he would bring into government with him would determine to a great extent the success of his administration; throughout his adult life he had been uniquely successful in selecting the right person for the right job.

Nelson Rockefeller, Arthur Flemming, and I were consulted occasionally about potential Cabinet appointees, but our main assignment was that of studying the entire federal organizational structure in order to identify the type of individual needed for leadership in each of many specific posts, and to consider organizational and procedural changes that would increase federal efficiency and promote economy. The President-elect felt that for twenty years the nation had experienced a social revolution, that many of the national programs were wasteful and inefficient, and that for a few years the task would be to consolidate gains, improve the federal structure, and obtain full value for the billions of dollars spent on fairly new social programs.

Late in November General Eisenhower asked us formally to become a Permanent Advisory Committee on Government Organization, an arrangement that was made official on January 24, 1953, by an executive order which defined the functions of our group, popularly known as PACGO. This was to be one of four responsibilities I would have for the next eight years, the others being personal representative of the President in United States-Latin American relations, consultant in speech writing, and personal confidant of the President. In addition, I occasionally was given emergency assignments for which no one else seemed to be available.

The President-elect had firm views about the functions of a member of the Cabinet. We occasionally discussed this matter late at night after others had left. He felt, as I did, that each member of the Cabinet had responsibilities that transcended the task of administering a single department. A Cabinet member should certainly not be thought of as a spokesman for a specialized economic group in our society; thus the Secretary of Agriculture was not to be merely a conduit for the views of farmers, or the Secretary of Labor exclusively a representative of labor, or the Secretary of Commerce a spokesman for business. Rather, each member of the Cabinet, competent in his field of primary responsibility, should bring that competence to bear in the formation of total government policies and functions. In other words, each Cabinet member was to be a broad-gauged adviser of the President, taking into account the total national welfare, not merely the concerns and needs of one segment of society. To the extent that this higher function preempted much of the time of the Cabinet member, there should be an able Under Secretary to devote full time to internal administration of the department, under the general guidance of the Secretary.

It is axiomatic that the interest of any one major economic group may not be in harmony with the total national interest. For example, during World War II we brought into production marginal, high-cost lead and zinc mines, for these metals were needed for military purposes and could not be obtained in sufficient quantity elsewhere. When the war was over, however, and less expensive ores from foreign countries, especially Mexico, became available, the marginal mines of our intermountain states continued to produce, and regional interests brought pressure in the Congress to provide protection (either tariffs or a quota system) against the competition of lower-cost production from abroad. This raised the price of lead and zinc domestically, but simultaneously reduced United States exports to Mexico, which depended on our purchases of her ores to earn the dollars needed for the purchase of a great variety of our manufactured products. Both nations suffered. It would have paid dividends for the United States Government to let marginal mines close while helping the producers to become relocated in more profitable enterprises.

A second example of the conflict of groups and national interests was evident from 1968 to August 1972. With the cost of labor increasing four times as fast as productivity, the entire nation suffered enormous losses through an inflation which caused us to lose much of our normal world market and thus intensified our problem of imbalances in international payments.

These two examples could be expanded into dozens. So the task in selecting Cabinet members was, hopefully, to find men who had the confidence of specialized groups but who understood that the needs of those groups had to be viewed within the context of the total requirements of the nation.

Further, General Eisenhower was determined to have the Cabinet become a major policy and program force in his administration. It was common knowledge that the Cabinet had been of little consequence in the administration of President Franklin Roosevelt. President Roosevelt preferred to discuss and resolve problems with individual members of the Cabinet, or with his staff, or with other small groups drawn from the larger organization. In the Roosevelt years the Cabinet, as discussed, was often referred to as a discussion and social group, not a policy-advisory one. The situation was little different in the Truman years. Each national leader has his own style of working. Many feel that one may not be better than another, but I shall argue otherwise later. General Eisenhower felt it imperative that the men and women who headed the major executive establishments should be consulted constantly in policy formation, for then they would more intelligently and enthusiastically carry out the agreed-upon policies and programs. Further, he did not want Cabinet meetings to become merely a compromise of the preconceptions of its members. He wanted policies and programs of consequence to be analyzed and discussed thoroughly and candidly, with evidence and views based on careful research, reserving to himself, of course, the making of final decisions.

As experience indicated to him the ways in which the Cabinet could be most effective, he made a number of organizational and personnel adjustments which he believed would enhance the value of the Cabinet as the primary advisory group to the President. He appointed a special assistant to the President who became secretary of the Cabinet; this officer, working directly with the President, the White House staff, and individual Cabinet members, developed an agenda for each meeting; often a bibliography of authoritative documents relevant to agenda items was attached. Similar arrangements were instituted with respect to the National Security Council, a body smaller than the Cabinet but comprised mainly of Cabinet members, to deal with foreign policy and security problems. Here, too, an officer of outstanding ability was made secretary of the National Security Council and was given a small professional staff to help with agenda preparation and the conduct of studies for Security Council consideration.

The formation of policies and programs is one important function in government, but effective and dependable execution is equally important; in a massive and far-flung organization one cannot take for granted that policies, even those approved by the President of the United States, will be carried out by the myriad of executive agencies. So President Eisenhower established the Operations Coordinating Board and provided it with a small staff, its function being to follow through on policy determinations and to assure him that they were faithfully being carried out. Indeed, the Cabinet, the National Security Council, and the Operations Coordinating Board became interdependent; often agenda items for the policy groups arose in the co-ordinating mechanism. In general, the two policy groups were comprised of Cabinet members, the co-ordinating agency of under or assistant secretaries of executive departments.

A prominent adviser of President Roosevelt once remarked that the appointment of a co-ordinating officer (as I had been in the Department of Agriculture) or the creation of a co-ordinating body (such as the Operations Coordinating Board) was an indication that the government was not properly organized. This is nonsense. There is no way to organize a large human undertaking that does not require transorganizational consultation and co-ordination.

Thus, within a single executive agency are many bureaus, but these bureaus must all operate within the larger policies and toward the central objectives of the department of which they are a part. Similarly, there is no way to bring about clusters of bureaus within a single department that makes transdepartmental co-ordination unnecessary. A well-known example has to do with the development of the nation's water resources. The Department of Agriculture has considerable responsibility in this area in the administration of the national forests, the soil conservation program, the water facilities program, and the land phase of flood control; it should be noted that these activities belong in the Department of Agriculture, for each involves wise utilization of lands, which is the major function of that department. These activities obviously require constant co-ordination at the level of the Secretary or Under Secretary of Agriculture. But the Department of the Interior also has important functions in water development. The Bureau of Reclamation and to some extent the administration of public lands are involved. These two activities could be transferred to the Department of Agriculture, but they have always been in the Department of the Interior and powerful Western pressure groups insist that they remain there; it is logical for the two programs to be in the same department, for irrigation in the West involves, among other things, more intensive use of what has been part of the public domain. Important water development functions are also lodged in the Department of Defense, the Army Corps of Engineers being the administering agency. For years, consideration has been given to transferring this activity out of Defense, but the planning never reaches implementation, mainly because the Corps of Engineers is essential to the military establishment in times of war and helps with strategic and tactical planning in peacetime. The Corps has the competence and needs the experience in peacetime of building such large engineering structures as dams on the Columbia and Colorado rivers and of managing such undertakings as the construction of the Panama Canal as was done between 1904 and 1914. Finally, the Federal Power Commission has broad statutory responsibility for river basin planning. It is clear that these functions in four federal agencies could readily conflict with one another; so it is the task of the Cabinet to avoid policy conflicts, the job of the Office of Management and Budget to help the President determine budgetary priorities in water development, and the function of a White House staff member (though unfortunately sometimes of the President himself) to achieve co-ordination in program execution.

A more important example is in national security. Each of the departments concerned with this crucial objective has numerous bureaus and divisions, as well as special committees which handle matters that bear upon the central objective; synthesis within each agency is the task of the Secretary. Co-ordination at the presidential level must involve the President personally, the National Security Council, and others. National security involves essentially *every* department of the federal executive establishment, especially such major agencies as the Defense

Department, State Department, Agency for International Development, United States Information Agency, the Treasury Department, and the Central Intelligence Agency, and to a lesser degree the Departments of Agriculture, Labor, and Justice.

These thoughts were uppermost in the mind of the President-elect as he selected each member of his Cabinet. He made one serious mistake in this process. Just as he chose a man skilled in agriculture to head the Department of Agriculture but with the understanding that he would function at a level broader than this single-interest field, so, too, did he choose Martin P. Durkin, a practical labor leader, to head the Department of Labor. I watched Secretary Durkin try to live up to the responsibility the President placed upon him, but he could not; having spent his adult life fighting for the welfare of the workingman, and especially the trade unionist, he could not suddenly view labor as only one major element in the total economic complex of the United States and arrive at judgments which, while fair to labor, were also compatible with the national interest. Unable to meet the requirements of the office, he properly resigned.

When the President's Advisory Committee on Government Organization was formally established, we appointed a small but able staff, headed by Arthur A. Kimball, a career officer of broad experience in public organizational, personnel, and administrative matters. We obtained the constant help of Jarold A. Kieffer of Arthur Flemming's staff, and of William Finan of the Bureau of the Budget.

The work of PACGO was tedious, time-consuming, and exacting. It called for precise analysis of each problem and many hours of conferences with the leaders of the agencies to be affected by proposed reorganizations. Our intention was, if possible, to take to the President in final form orders under the Reorganization Act, or, when necessary, proposed legislation, which had the approval of affected agencies. This would save the President a good deal of time and would give reasonable assurance of willing acceptance by the personnel of the reorganized agency, if the President approved our proposals. We achieved this objective most of the time, but not always. Occasionally we had to recommend approval of a plan by the President that was opposed by one or more members of the Cabinet.

For three months following President Eisenhower's inauguration, Nelson Rockefeller, Arthur Flemming, and I met almost daily. Gradu-

260

ally we were able to rely on the staff for fundamental studies, so thereafter we met less frequently. In the eight years of the Eisenhower administration, our committee met about one hundred and twenty times. Informal and formal conferences with the President were numerous—in all probability ninety meetings, sometimes for as much as an hour for the consideration of a single proposal. We also attended Cabinet meetings when our proposals were on the agenda for Cabinet consideration. The score card of our endeavors was this: Fourteen plans became effective under the Reorganization Act (which authorizes the President to effectuate changes if the Congress does not disapprove within a specified time). Seven reorganization measures were put into effect by executive order, congressional review in these instances not being required. Two became law through congressional enactments. In addition, many helpful changes in working procedures were brought about by presidential letters addressed to appropriate agency heads.

For two years of PACGO's work, from 1953 to 1955, the Second Hoover Commission, concerned with all aspects of federal procedures, was also functioning. When it had completed its work, the President appointed Meyer Kestenbaum to work with all agencies in achieving an acceptance of some of the four hundred recommendations of the commission. More than two hundred of these were in fact adopted wholly or with only minor modifications, while about one hundred and seventy-five were accepted partially. PACGO and the Hoover Commission avoided conflict or duplication by having Arthur Flemming serve on both bodies. In no way did the Hoover Commission studies and recommendations—on budgetary procedures, accounting methods, depot utilization, paper-work management and control, civil service reform, extension of the merit system, creation of a senior civil service for top career personnel, business management in defense, elimination of federal activities that compete needlessly with private enterprise, discontinuance of the postal savings system, authority for the federal government to send selected personnel to universities for further training, and a host of other activities and studies—impinge upon our responsibility.

The massive records of PACGO and the Hoover Commission—volumes that fill many file cabinets—are available in the Federal Archives. The most important of them pertain to the creation of the Department of Health, Education and Welfare, the United States

Information Agency (the successor to OWI), the International Co-operation Administration (now called Agency for International Development), the Federal Aviation Agency, the National Aeronautics and Space Agency, and the Federal Council on Science and Technology.

We helped with the studies that resulted in two congressional enactments that operationally unified the Department of Defense, placing highest policy authority and control in the Secretary of Defense and under him in the Secretaries of the three constituent military departments, thus assuring civilian control of the largest agency in the executive branch of the government. In presenting these two plans to the Congress and in subsequent executive directives, the President made clear that, in addition to having unchallenged civilian responsibility in the defense establishment, it was essential to achieve: (a) effectiveness with economy; (b) efficient and constantly ready military plans that were sound strategically, scientifically, industrially, and economically; (c) maximum decentralization consistent with control, thus leading to the abolition of the Munitions Board, the Research and Development Board, the Defense Supply Management Agency, and the Office of Director of Installations, responsibilities of these cumbersome and ineffective agencies being transferred to Assistant Secretaries of the Army, Navy and Air Force; (d) centralizing considerable authority in the chairman of the Joint Chiefs of Staff, principal military adviser to the President; and, most important of all, (e) providing for unified field commands, as exemplified in the Allied forces in World War II, each unified command being under the direction of one of the military Secretaries, acting as executive agent for the Joint Chiefs of Staff. So what President Truman had started, though then of only symbolic value, finally resulted in effective unification. It may be that someday the United States will have a single military service, rather than three, with only one uniform, and all men subject to control by the head of a single agency; but at best that is for consideration in the future, at a time when possible temporary loss of morale is not a problem.

Some of our recommendations, approved and put into effect, were less dramatic but important to efficient management, such as transferring certain congressionally mandated authorities for administration from subordinate officers in a department to the Secretary of that department. Thus, in the Department of Agriculture the Congress had placed specific executive responsibilities in the administrator of the

Rural Electrification Administration; this hindered the policy control of the Secretary (who nonetheless was held responsible for results by the President) and made for inflexibility in organization and management; hence, this mandated authority was transferred to the Secretary.

This same kind of change was made in numerous departments and agencies. One of special interest in this regard was in the Department of Justice. A law of 1870 had specified that the Solicitor General would become the Acting Attorney General in the absence of the Attorney General; but the Solicitor General's sole responsibility was and is to represent the United States in cases before the Supreme Court; he has nothing to do with the many other activities of the department. The Deputy Attorney General, on the other hand, is familiar with all phases of the department's work. So by reorganization order the authority to be Acting Attorney General in the absence of the head of the department was transferred to the Deputy Attorney General.

In a slightly different category, legislation had placed management authority for the affairs of the Export-Import Bank in the hands of a five-man board, some members of which had other heavy responsibilities; it is axiomatic that a board or committee cannot handle daily administration, so full authority was placed in the hands of a managing director, one of the five members of the board.

One of our more pleasant experiences, since rarely is a federal function discontinued, was to liquidate the affairs of the Reconstruction Finance Corporation. The few remaining functions of the RFC were divided among the Export-Import Bank, the Small Business Administration, the National Mortgage Association, and the Secretary of the Treasury.

We made the studies that resulted in the reorganization of the Office of Defense Mobilization, primarily a consolidation of the National Security Resources Board and the previous Office of Defense Mobilization. This change brought about a unification of planning for military, industrial, civilian, and economic mobilization, and involved transfers to the new agency of functions lodged in five other federal departments, including responsibility for strategic stockpiling which previously had been assigned to the General Services Administration.

We did a great deal of work in the field of foreign affairs, but with only limited success. Secretary Dulles was firm in his belief that the Department of State had too many administrative functions that took his time and that of principal associates from the major function of policy formation under the close direction of the President. Secretary Dulles said to me one day, "Far too much of my time is taken up with internal administrative matters, and a fourth is involved in appearances before congressional committees." To reduce his testimony before Congress, the Secretary one year made an opening statement about his department's request for funds to a subcommittee of the Appropriations Committee of the House and then left, trusting to the Under Secretary to handle details. On the day of his first absence a clerk of the committee called him and said, "The chairman has asked me to tell you that the subcommittee has just reduced substantially the appropriation of your own office. If you wish to have this restored, the chairman suggests that you remain throughout the hearings on the State Department appropriation bill as you have in the past."

PACGO proposed to Secretary Dulles a plan, considered radical at the time, that would have relieved him of details and would have enabled him always to be available to the President in the formation of foreign policy which, constitutionally, is vested exclusively in the President. Secretary Dulles objected at that time, although before his untimely death he decided we were right; but it was too late to implement the plan. I shall deal with this in some detail later.

We did succeed in taking out of the Department of State some of the agencies which annoyed Secretary Dulles, but by having these report directly to the President, a new problem arose. The President now needed help in co-ordinating such activities, an assignment for the Operations Coordinating Board. In the Kennedy, Johnson, and Nixon administrations the need for co-ordination by the White House itself led to a major expansion in White House personnel. Today the foreign policy assistant to the President has a large staff,* half of whom are professionals; similar expansion in other White House activities has caused the staff of the Executive Office of the President to increase to 2,236, in my judgment an intolerable situation. Correction will call for radical change and legal enactments, possibly constitutional amendments.

Always in our minds was the realization that far too many individuals reported directly to the President. He could not possibly see them all, much less confer at length with them. Ideally, the executive

---

* In September 1973, this assistant, Henry Kissinger, also became Secretary of State.

establishment should be organized in a pyramidal pattern with certainly no more than about twenty persons reporting to the President.

By the first week of August 1960 we were satisfied that we had arrived at logical answers to some, but by no means all, of the problems inherent in this concept. We discussed our conclusions for several hours with President Eisenhower. He considered submitting a series of proposals to the Congress at that time but refrained for two reasons: first, the Reorganization Act had been permitted by the Congress to expire, and in the President's judgment sound results in executive reorganization could be obtained mainly through the procedures established in that act—procedures we had employed in most of the reorganizations that had been accomplished; second, he felt that lacking authority of the act and thus being required to submit proposals for legislative action could lead to their being injected into the political campaign which was then under way. Problems of executive management are patently complicated and technical, remote from general public understanding, and should be considered on a non-partisan basis. They should not be subjected to campaign debate, as are policy and program proposals.

So the President decided to incorporate the gist of some of our proposals, though in greatly abbreviated form, in his budget message to the Congress just four days before the end of his second term, hoping that the recommendations would meet the approval of his successor and would be acted on favorably by the Congress or, preferably, by reorganization orders after a renewal of the relevant legislation.

Nelson Rockefeller had by this time left PACGO and had become governor of New York. The task of drafting our final recommendations to the President fell primarily to me and Arthur Flemming, ably assisted by Arthur Kimball and Jerry Kieffer. The abridgment of our lengthy set of recommendations for inclusion in the President's budget message to the Congress became my responsibility.

The President placed emphasis on the need for authority to reorganize the President's office. The duties placed upon the President by the Constitution, a myriad of laws, and tradition had become so burdensome that no President could discharge them adequately. The Congress should enact legislation authorizing the President to reorganize the Executive Office as he personally found to be necessary, including the authority to redistribute statutory functions among units of the office; to change the names of units and titles of officers within the office; to make changes in the membership of statutory bodies in the office; and, within the limits of existing laws and appropriations, to establish new units in the Executive Office and fix the compensations of the officers. This flexibility would enable the President to shape the units within the Executive Office in ways he found best to get the help he needed in carrying out his responsibilities.

As suggested to him by our Advisory Committee, the President also recommended to the Congress that his successor should have authority to establish an Office of Executive Management, headed by a director, responsible to the President and discharging many of the President's managerial responsibilities. In an enterprise as large and diversified as the executive branch of the government there was and is an imperative need for effective and innovative central management to strengthen program planning and evaluation, promote efficiency, identify and eliminate waste and duplication, and co-ordinate numerous agency operations within approved policies and statutory objectives.

The President did not spell out the details of this broad proposal, although our committee had done so in our report to him. We felt that the organization of the Executive Office suffered from the rigidities created by statutory prescriptions of individual units and offices. Often, temporary staff arrangements, special assistants to the President, temporary study groups, and even presidential advisory committees, including ours, had been resorted to unsystematically to meet emergency situations.

While the Bureau of the Budget had carried a wide range of management activities and could be used as the organizational structure within which an Office of Executive Management could be constructed, functions other than budget preparation and control *should not be the responsibility of the director of the budget.* This we considered to be of first importance. Rather, we insisted, the budget office should be *only one co-ordinate unit within the larger organization handling a multitude of management functions.*

A second co-ordinate office under the director of the Office of Executive Management should deal with problems of government organization. If an advisory committee such as ours were felt to be essential as an aid to the full-time staff, it should be advisory not directly to the President but to the director of Executive Management, or to the head of the specialized unit devoting full time to this area. Property management, data processing, and research and systems analysis might constitute another division of the office. Legislative clearance surely should not be the responsibility of the Bureau of the Budget but of the director of Executive Management, who would need a small expert staff for the purpose. (Most bills passed by the Congress and sent to the President for approval or disapproval are normally circulated by the Bureau of the Budget among all relevant departments for comment; these are synthesized into a single document and presented to the President for his information. Clearly, considerations other than budgetary ones are normally involved, and often these other considerations transcend sheer budgetary evaluations.)

A small unit for public works planning and co-ordination then handled by an officer responsible to the President should be placed in the new Office of Executive Management.

A statistical division, then subordinate to the budget director, should become a co-ordinate unit.

Personnel management, one of the most important tools available to the President in supervising the vast federal establishment, and handled by a special assistant to the President, should be another unit of the office.

When President Nixon appointed George Schulz, formerly Secretary of Labor, as head of the Office of Management and Budget, he achieved part of what President Eisenhower had recommended to the Congress in 1961, but only part. It sometimes takes a long time to get results in Washington, especially if the problems involved are technical and non-partisan in nature. Why this should be so I do not know. It may be partly because there is no pressure group in this area. There is no political advantage to be gained by anyone who gives time and provides leadership at the congressional level in getting results. Or it may be that, as in economic affairs, everyone assumes he is an expert, persists in his preconceptions, and thus a committee or the Congress as a whole is slow in reaching agreement.

In our final report to President Eisenhower, we also devoted much argument to the need for the President to have higher-ranking help in the field of foreign affairs. He did not accept the details of a plan I personally proposed, and shall discuss later, but did accept the central idea and so suggested to the Congress that, to aid the President in correlating all aspects of foreign political, economic, social, and military affairs, there should be authorized the appointment of an official who would rank higher than Cabinet members, possibly with the title First Secretary of the Government. This officer should assist the President by consulting constantly with the departments in the formation of national security objectives, by co-ordinating international programs, and by representing the President at meetings of foreign officials above the rank of foreign minister and below the rank of head of state. If this last phrase seems incomprehensible, it must be recognized that the President of the United States is one of the few leaders in the world who is both head of state and chief of government. Hence he personally must be the host for kings, queens, presidents, and prime ministers who come on official missions to Washington in droves, a task which continues to increase now that our national capital has literally become the crossroads of the world.

In 1957, President Eisenhower spent the better part of thirty-five days in fulfilling his duties as host to foreign dignitaries, including Queen Elizabeth and Prince Philip, the King of Saudi Arabia, Chancellor Adenauer, the King of Morocco, and the Premiers or Prime Ministers of France, Great Britain, Japan, Vietnam, and Pakistan. Nineteen fifty-eight was a lean year in this regard—foreign dignitaries were the President's guests for only twenty days. In 1959 the President was tied up for twenty-nine days in serving as host to visiting heads of state and chiefs of government, and in the same year spent twenty-four days with the heads of state in various countries of the world, especially in Europe, the Near East, and the Indian subcontinent.†

In the meantime, of course, he had to carry on the normal duties of the presidency. In the midst of this intense activity, horrendous for one who had suffered a major heart attack, an ileitis operation, and a mild brain spasm, he suddenly felt the need for relaxation. So on a moment's notice he flew one Saturday morning to Augusta for a round of golf, an outing which is presumed by the public to be an escape from duty. But accompanying the President on the quick trip were (as al-

† Official White House guests in 1959 included the Presidents of Argentina, El Salvador, Ireland, Mexico, and Guinea; the Kings of Jordan and Belgium; and the Prime Ministers of Great Britain, Italy, the U.S.S.R., and Iran. President Eisenhower's visits with heads of state and prime ministers abroad included Mexico, Germany, Great Britain, France, Italy, Turkey, Pakistan, Afghanistan, India, Iran, Greece, Tunisia, France (again), Spain, and Morocco. He also spent two days at NATO headquarters.

ways) several assistants and the inescapable and able members of the Secret Service who, even on the golf course, carry communication equipment which the President may use if any authorized person feels the need to reach him. I went with the President on the trip to Augusta but did not play golf, for I was suffering from a slipped disc. At the conclusion of the game one of the President's assistants told me of an incident that I believe to be accurate. To me it is hilarious. I told the story a number of times in my brother's presence and he neither verified nor denied its authenticity.

His visit that Saturday was so unexpected that his regular caddy was not available. So the club officials hastily searched for a substitute and brought back a man in his seventies who had not caddied for several years. When the foursome had driven off the first tee, the elderly caddy went close to the President and said, "Keep your head down, Baldy!" The President smiled and nodded.

One of the other caddies was horrified and said to the elderly man, "Don't you know who that is?"

"Nope." (Indifferently.)

"That's the President of the United States!"

"Oh?"

After the foursome had driven off the second tee the elderly caddy walked to the President and said: "I *told* you: keep your head down, Mr. Lincoln!"

If the tale is true, I'm sure no one was more amused than President Eisenhower. It probably contributed to the relaxation he was seeking.

Amidst the flood of foreign visitors, I was usually involved officially only when the Presidents of Latin American countries were guests of the United States. It was my good fortune, however, to attend formal dinners for others. One impressed me deeply. When Queen Elizabeth and Prince Philip were White House guests, it happened that in the Blue Room after dinner I found myself next to Prince Philip. He began asking me questions about conditions in Latin America generally and about important problems that were then high on the agenda in United States-Latin American relations. His detailed knowledge of these numerous and complex problems astounded me. He spoke not from the point of view of the United Kingdom in its relations with the nations of Latin America but knowledgeably about the problems the United

States was having with specific countries. In that half-hour discussion I became a great admirer of Prince Philip, an admiration that has not diminished as the years have passed.

The President in his final budget message to Congress also included several other recommendations we of PACGO had given him in our August memorandum.

He recommended the creation of a Department of Transportation with all but the regulatory functions in this field transferred to the department. This cryptic recommendation was based upon a detailed analysis I had worked on, with occasional help from my colleagues, for several years. We pointed out that not only were public transportation responsibilities split among federal, state, and local units of government, but within the federal establishment air transportation was promoted and regulated by the Federal Aviation Agency and the Civil Aeronautics Board; rail, truck, bus, coastal steamers, and certain inland waterway and some pipeline forms of transportation were regulated by the Interstate Commerce Commission; the Federal Power Commission regulated other pipelines; highway construction and financing were the responsibility of the Department of Commerce; the transportation functions of the coast guard were under the Secretary of the Treasury; the operation and regulation of the merchant marine were divided between the Department of Commerce and the Federal Maritime Board; and international maritime traffic through the Panama Canal was under the jurisdiction of the Secretary of the Army. Clearly, there was no federal transportation program or policy. No one was in a position to give the President a balanced view of the over-all transportation requirements of the nation, including the transportation requirements of the military forces.

The only form of transportation then enjoying economic health was handled by pipelines. Although PACGO did not so state to the President I had become convinced not only that we were plagued by fractionated organizations and authorities but that the laws governing the many forms of transportation were obsolete. The basic concept in transportation regulation was developed when the railroads essentially had a monopoly. It is a credo of American economic thought that all productive enterprise should be privately owned and operated, so long as the self-regulative element of competition is present; if, on the other hand, an enterprise is more efficient as a monopoly, then it should be publicly owned or regulated. With this credo uppermost in public thinking, most of the regulatory legislation has been passed to control a monopolistic enterprise. But there was no longer any semblance of monopoly in transportation. Airplanes, trucks, buses, ships, and privately owned cars were competitive with the railroads and with one another; 138 different railroads were often highly competitive with one another. Eminent scholars in the transportation field had convinced me that we could reduce the annual cost of transportation to users by two billion dollars a year, and yet each form of transportation could make a profit, provided each in the competitive market could perform those functions for which it was best suited. To me it was ridiculous for the Interstate Commerce Commission to require a railroad to maintain an unprofitable branch line to a remote spot when buses and trucks were handling most of the traffic; it was wrong to require railroads to maintain passenger services at losses amounting to seven hundred million dollars a year when airplanes, buses, and private cars were carrying most travelers. I therefore thought we needed to unify all federal activities relating to transportation, have the new department develop a consistent set of policies and programs, and that the laws governing federal regulation should be drastically amended.

But PACGO limited its recommendation to the President by suggesting that the coast guard, the Federal Aviation Agency, certain services and administrative functions of the Interstate Commerce Commission, transportation activities of the Department of Commerce including the Bureau of Public Roads, the Coast and Geodetic Survey, the Federal Maritime Administration, and the Canal Zone Government and Company—and possibly even the Post Office Department— should be placed under a Secretary of Transportation. Much of this was eventually brought about in the Johnson administration. Later, the Post Office Department was dissolved and a special federal corporation to handle the duties of the former department was created during the Nixon administration.

These fairly recent administrative changes are correct, but most forms of transportation in the United States are still in economic difficulty. The bankruptcy of the largest rail system in the United States, the Penn Central, was a blow to the entire economy and a signal that something more needs to be done. In my judgment, we should rely primarily on competition among all types of transportation, with a bare minimum of public regulation, to enable each form of transportation to develop efficiency and make at least enough profit to keep its equipment up to date and its service adequate to the needs of our modern industrialized economy.

Conditions constantly change, and so must government, all levels of government. But changes in government become more difficult as it grows larger and larger. The federal government today is almost unmanageable. It is filled with inefficiency. Obsolete activities, or ones of diminished importance, are carried on in sheer inertia. An entrenched civil service has become a burden. Bureaucracy in foreign affairs, as Galbraith has said, has made for terrible rigidities in foreign policies, but the same thing may be said about most functions of government. Studies and recommendations for elimination of less essential activities, for reorganizations, for increased efficiencies—essential as they were in 1953 when PACGO began working—are an imperative need today. But innovative and appropriate actions will be taken only if stimulation and broad guidance are provided at a very high level. Herbert Hoover, twice head of commissions to study the federal establishment, and drawing on his own experience as President of the United States, suggested to a Senate committee that serious consideration be given to the appointment of an Administrative Vice-President with high responsibilities placed upon him by the President. With this, too, I shall deal in the final chapter.

The most persistent misunderstanding about the Eisenhower administration, still extant, has to do with his method of administration. Certainly he had his own style. Erroneously, it is assumed that he delegated policy, program formulation, and administration so extensively to Cabinet members and other high officers of the government that he served in effect as "Chairman of the Board." Especially it is assumed that Secretary Dulles, one of the ablest men I have ever known, was responsible for the development of most strategic and tactical phases of our foreign operations and policies. "Eisenhower," it is said, "turned his constitutional duties over to the Secretary."

The simple truth is that President Eisenhower reserved to himself—and was insistent upon this—leadership in all discussions and studies leading to policy and program formulation, and in giving final approval to all important policies and programs. Secretary Dulles was scrupulously careful in this regard. When he was in Washington he normally came to the White House at about five-thirty or six o'clock, often to the President's personal quarters on the second floor of the mansion; in these meetings every current situation was analyzed and often decisions were made; though always these detailed decisions were made within the broad policies determined by the President in Cabinet and National Security Council meetings; potential developments were also considered and possible responses were discussed. When Secretary Dulles was abroad, as he had to be much of the time, he telephoned to the President *every day* for guidance, ordinarily in the evenings; if a telephone conversation was not possible, the Secretary sent the President a cable in code.

There are probably three reasons why President Eisenhower's executive functioning has been misunderstood. One of these involves his style of administration, another has a psychological and philosophic base, and the third has to do with the affection in which he was held by the people, even those who disagreed with him.

President Eisenhower, during his presidency, as he had done as Supreme Commander in war, almost instinctively wished to "build up" those who worked with him. I do not recall his saying, "I have *directed* the Secretary of Defense (or the Secretary of State) to take" a certain action. Rather he indicated his approval of a given policy or action, often saying, "I have approved the Secretary's proposal." Further, in administering the executive branch of the government and in dealing with a Democratically controlled Congress, he relied upon a collaborative process, believing in his power of persuasion. The stature which the Cabinet as an institution achieved and the institutionalization of the National Security Council are proof of this. In his dealings with the Congress he was careful to bring both majority and minority leaders to the White House for consultation. There is a vast difference between the collaborative style of administration and the assertive style—one that relies upon constant presidential directives which give the impression of vigorous executive leadership. It is a fiction, however, to say that one man, even the President, possesses all the wisdom needed in arriving at judgments on all the complex problems of administration and policy formation that arise in the mammoth federal structure.

The psychological and philosophic aspects of the Eisenhower administration recognized that in the previous twenty years the United

States had undergone a social revolution as well as the most devastating and costly war in history. Vast national programs had been launched hurriedly without adequate training of personnel; inefficiency was rampant, as was waste of resources. It was a time for consolidation, for promoting efficiency, for permitting officials, federal employees, and the general public to adjust to new conditions brought about by the immense changes in public programs and public authority. This does not mean that President Eisenhower in any way failed to insist upon amendments to existing programs or the launching of new initiatives. It does mean that the aggressiveness and turmoil of the previous twenty years were subordinated and a period of calm, consolidation, better understanding, and efficiency came to the fore.

The other factor contributing to the misconception about the Eisenhower method of administration may be due to the regard in which he was held by most of the people. Thus, those who disagreed with the foreign policy of "brinkmanship," or the decision to withhold financial assistance from Egypt for the construction of the Aswan Dam, or the refusal of the United States to identify itself with the British-French-Israeli attack on Egypt tended to place the blame on Secretary Dulles, rather than on President Eisenhower. If *blame* were to be so misplaced, then the myth had to be maintained that the Secretary was the real policy maker. But in all these situations the decisions were made by the President.

In the more assertive type of presidential leadership this misconception does not arise. Yet undoubtedly Secretary of State Dean Rusk gave Presidents Kennedy and Johnson the same kind of help Dulles gave Eisenhower, and McGeorge Bundy and Walt Rostow certainly provided staff assistance, as Robert Cutler, Sherman Adams, and General Wilton B. Persons had done in the Eisenhower years.

Of my several continuing responsibilities in the Eisenhower years in the White House, this task of improving the federal structure and procedures was the least interesting, the most time-consuming, and possibly the most important.

CHAPTER 16

It is ironic that Congress has yielded so much of its power to the Chief Executive, but has denied him authority that is rightfully his.

M Y WORK FOR the President on organizational problems convinced me that several legislative enactments, possibly constitutional amendments, would enhance the President's authority to improve the management of the executive branch of the government, would reduce somewhat the trivial but time-consuming things he is now legally required to do, and would clarify the President's veto privilege as was clearly contemplated by the framers of the Constitution.

Reorganization is an unending task. As conditions in the country change and new laws are passed to meet changing social and economic conditions, it becomes imperative to realign departments and move activities from one agency to another. New national priorities may require the elimination of some government agencies and the creation of others.

The Congress has always limited the President's authority to deal with organizational and procedural problems, even though the Constitution makes the President responsible for the faithful execution of the laws enacted by the Congress. One might reason that, since the executive, legislative, and judicial branches of the government were very deliberately created to be separate and equal, the President should have complete authority to shape the executive structure in ways that make it possible for him to execute the laws most effectively and most efficiently. Not so! Although the President cannot tell the Congress what its committee structure and procedures should be, the Congress can and does dictate, to a considerable extent, at least, how the executive branch is to be organized. Then, having done so, it holds the President responsible for the effective management of the executive branch as the Constitution requires.

From the beginning of our history to 1932, the President had little power in this area. The Congress by law shaped the executive structure and specified the duties of the department heads and subordinate officers, sometimes with ludicrous results. When Congress created the Treasury Department, it specified that it should have five offices—Secretary, Comptroller, Auditor, Treasurer, and Registrar. It defined the duties of each office, then blatantly required the Secretary of the Treasury to report, not to the President, but directly to the Congress; then, despite this meddling, the Congress held the President responsible for the policies and actions of the Treasury Department.

In 1838 the Supreme Court upheld the right of the Congress to determine by legislation the structure of the executive branch. Whether the congressional enactments in this area were wise or ill conceived did not concern the court; it merely confirmed that Congress could by legislation establish, change, or eliminate agencies just as by legislation it could fix tax rates, authorize new programs, declare war, and change federal priorities.

The impeachment of President Andrew Johnson in 1868 was built on this very issue of Congress' authority over executive organization and procedures. The Tenure of Office Act of 1867 forbade the President to remove civil officials, including Cabinet members, without Senate approval. President Johnson rightfully rebelled, considering the act an unconstitutional assault on the separation of powers. In defiance, he fired Secretary of War Edwin Stanton and replaced him with General Lorenzo Thomas. Stanton also became defiant and barricaded himself in his office when his successor showed up to replace him. Of the eleven impeachment articles subsequently drawn up against the President, ten dealt with Stanton's removal and one was a ridiculous catch-all article covering everything from the President's bad manners to his profanity. The Supreme Court in this instance refused to act on the matter.

President Taft was the first to take an important initiative in this field. In a message to Congress on efficiency in government, on January 17, 1912, he said: "In the past, services have been created one by one as exigencies have seemed to demand, with little or no reference to any scheme of organization in the government as a whole." This observation led to no constructive action by the Congress. In 1913, Taft, therefore, took the matter into his own hands. He discarded the previous practice of each department's taking its annual budget through the Treasury Department and by that department directly to the Congress as it had always done under its original legislative mandate. By executive direction to all departments, Taft formed a consolidated executive budget and sent it to the Congress which, with grumbling and ill grace, acknowledged, at least negatively, his right to do so.

On December 8, 1914, President Wilson in his second annual message to the Congress said: "Governments grow piecemeal, both in their tasks and in the means by which those tasks are to be performed, and very few governments are organized, I venture to say, as wise and experienced businessmen would organize them if they had a clean sheet of paper to write on." This message in time evidently impressed members of Congress but no action was taken for nearly seven years; then the Congress passed legislation which created a Bureau of the Budget under presidential supervision; this central agency, in considering annual appropriation requests, could have some influence in reorganizing federal agencies, though its findings and judgments, if approved by the President, would still have to be submitted to the Congress for legislative enactment.

It was in the closing year of the Hoover administration that Congress was persuaded to grant the President limited but useful authority to effectuate organizational changes by reorganization orders rather than by legislation. This modest beginning led to broader authority by enactments in 1939 and 1945, substituting the broad presidential authority of the reorganization plan for the executive order authorized in 1932. In granting this authority, the Congress insisted upon two reservations: each plan promulgated by the President was subject for a period of sixty days to veto by either the House or Senate, and the legislation carried a termination date. Since then the Reorganization Act has lapsed and then been renewed from time to time under Presidents Truman, Eisenhower, and Johnson, but in each instance the act has carried a date on which the act was to expire. Hence there have been periods since the act was first approved when the President had no authority. This is the situation today. In such times the President had to submit recommendations for legislative action to the Congress, relatively few of which have been approved. When the act has been in effect, good results have been achieved. President Truman promulgated thirty-five reorganization plans, of which twenty-seven were not vetoed by either the Senate or House. I have previously indicated what President Eisenhower did in this field, and none of his plans was disapproved. President Johnson issued seventeen plans, and all but one became effective. Since 1949 five Presidents have submitted ninety-one plans to the Congress and Congress allowed seventy-one to become effective.

President Nixon sent a series of recommendations to the Congress. His recommendation to change the postal service from a Cabinet department to a government corporation had to be implemented through legislation, for this type of change was never delegated to the President by the Reorganization Act. Similarly, his sweeping recommendation for the consolidation of seven Cabinet departments into four—Natural Resources, Human Resources, Community Development, and Economic Development—had to be submitted to the Congress, for this type of major change too was not authorized by the Reorganization Act. This last recommendation by the President has been ignored by the Congress, though desultory committee hearings have been held in the House. It seems obvious that even if the Reorganization Act had given the President authority to bring about this type of major alteration in status, his reorganization plan would have been disapproved by the Congress.

Four changes in the Reorganization Act are in my judgment needed:

First, a presidential reorganization order, to be disapproved by the Congress, should require, as did the original act, a constitutional majority vote (one requiring a majority of all members of the House or Senate) rather than, as provided in all renewals of the act, a simple majority vote of those members actually voting.

Second, congressional disapproval should require a constitutional majority vote in both the Senate and House.

Third, the amended act should carry no termination date. The President and all who advise him on reorganization problems should carry on their work carefully, often with outside specialized consultation, with assurance that presidential authority is intact when the proposal is finally in shape for presidential action. This is especially important, for some problems in reorganization may require several

278

years to develop with precision and with the requisite understanding among all officials who will be affected by the contemplated changes.

Fourth, since the Congress and the people hold the President responsible for effective management of the executive branch, there should be no limitation on the types of actions he is authorized to take. If he wishes to consolidate the Departments of Agriculture and Interior, which many have long advocated, he should certainly have authority to promulgate a reorganization plan to this effect; if the Congress wishes to disapprove, it can do so and that disapproval would be final, for a vote in Congress on this matter is not subject to presidential veto.

Another congressional enactment would remove considerable trivia from the President's desk and would to some degree improve the functioning of the Congress.

On a single day, late in the 1950s, I saw President Eisenhower veto ten private relief and private immigration bills and sign scores of others. He studied each bill with care, knowing that justice to some individual was involved. In the first two years of his administration he approved 1,002 such bills and vetoed a host of others. The number of private immigration bills has declined since the revision of the Immigration and Nationality Act several years ago, but for the President to spend time on such matters is still annoying at best and time-consuming and distracting at worst. President Kennedy signed 684 such bills in 1961–62; the number dropped to 409 in the next two years and the flow of these bills to Presidents Johnson and Nixon continued at about that level. There is no assurance, however, that the number will not increase; this is more true of private relief than of immigration bills. Each bill must be introduced by a member of Congress, undergo committee and floor scrutiny (utterly routinely, of course), and then be sent to the White House where a conscientious President must consider each on its merits.

The Congress should pass organic legislation which sets the general standards for special immigration cases and for claims against the United States Government. It should assign to the United States Court of Claims authority to hear evidence and make decisions on private relief claims. It should authorize a purely administrative court in the Division of Immigration with power to deal with special immigration problems. Congress has not hesitated to delegate quasi-legislative, executive, and judicial powers to numerous regulatory agencies; why it continues the anachronistic practice of passing hundreds of individual relief and immigration bills is a puzzle to me.

Of greater import to the President are hundreds of laws passed over a period of a hundred years which require him to make decisions on problems that never should come to his attention. President Truman recommended and Congress passed an act which permits the President to delegate by executive orders legislatively mandated decision making to Cabinet officers or agency heads unless a specific act prohibits this practice. Thus a foolish legal mandate for the President to approve rules affecting operations in the Panama Canal Zone was delegated to the Secretary of the Army, to whom the governor of the Canal Zone reports (but preferably should be the task of the Secretary of Transportation, to whom responsibility for canal operations should now be transferred). Amazingly, one law requires the President to determine whether a new drug is an opiate; he may delegate this responsibility to the Secretary of Health, Education and Welfare. And certainly he may delegate the legal requirement that he decide whether the Marine Band may leave the District of Columbia to the Secretary of Defense or Secretary of the Navy. Fortunately the requirement that the President personally appoint postmasters of the first, second, and third class has been abrogated.

Some of the responsibilities placed upon the President by 350 laws cannot be so delegated, however, because numerous departments and agencies are involved in the problems dealt with in certain acts. He obviously cannot delegate his responsibility in such circumstances to a single Cabinet member who has a vested interest in the decisions to be made. To remove from the President the need for dealing with the less important of these interagency problems will require a constitutional amendment and this I shall deal with when I suggest the creation of two supra-Cabinet positions, with limited constitutional authority.

A minor needed improvement involves those laws in which decision-making authority is legally vested in a subordinate officer of a department or agency. I have previously explained that by reorganization orders President Eisenhower cleared up many of these ill-conceived and bad administrative situations, and none was disapproved by the Congress. The simplest solution, however, would be for the Congress to enact legislation that would automatically transfer to the Secretaries of Cabinet departments and heads of independent agencies authorities previously vested in subordinate officers. This would assure that Cabinet members and agency heads can be held responsible by the President for all activities within the organizations they supervise.

A procedural practice in the Congress that impinges upon the constitutional authority of the President and causes him much anguish should be corrected by either legislation or constitutional amendment.

The framers of the Constitution evidently assumed that each bill introduced, considered, and passed by the Congress would deal with a single subject, from a simple bill authorizing the creation of a Board for Public Broadcasting to a complex bill on many aspects of civil rights. With this as standard practice, the President may sign or veto the bill on its merits or on the basis of its harmony or conflict with his total program. Thereafter, the Congress by two-thirds majority vote may override the veto.

Many years ago the Congress found a way to prevent the President from vetoing a measure which it knew he vigorously opposed. It began placing unrelated legislative riders on bills it believed the President could not veto because of the need for an appropriation or the importance of a substantive problem dealt with in the legislation. This has become standard practice today. No bill coming before the President occupies so much of his time, including hours of consultation with members of the Cabinet and White House aides, as does an enactment of this kind.

When the Congress, without consultation with the President, Secretary of State, or Secretary of Agriculture, attached a rider to an important agricultural bill that compelled the payment of a subsidy ranging from five to eight cents a pound on the export of American cotton, the subsidy to remain in effect until the United States had regained its historic share of the world market for cotton, the President considered for days what he should do. The bill bearing the rider was one he had worked for several years to obtain. The Congress had reluctantly agreed with his proposals. In desperation, the President signed the bill, including the rider, though he knew that this would cause serious international problems with Mexico, Peru, Egypt, and other countries. They would be especially critical of our failure to consult with them in advance before any such drastic action was taken. Under the Agricultural

Adjustment Act and its successor, the Agricultural Conservation Act, the United States had substantially reduced land devoted to cotton production. In that period Mexico, Egypt, Peru, and other countries expanded their production of cotton by a similar amount. Cotton became Mexico's principal earner of foreign exchange, which she used in full to buy processed goods from the United States. When the President signed the bill with its harmful rider, Mexico did not blame the United States for trying to regain its share of the world market. It bitterly criticized us for not giving a friendly nation warning so that it could begin to make adjustments to the radically changed situation. Mexico's purchases from us declined as her exports of cotton suffered.

In mid-1972 the Congress passed a bill increasing the debt ceiling to $450 billion. Attached to it was a rider increasing Social Security payments twenty per cent. An increase in the debt ceiling was imperative, for deficit financing was such that the government would be paralyzed had the Congress not taken the appropriate action. Cleverly, the timing in the Congress was perfect from its point of view. It sent the bill, with the rider, to the President the day before the previous debt ceiling would become the limiting factor. So the President had to sign the bill. He did so with utmost reluctance because of the inflationary influence of the increase in Social Security payments at a time when inflation was a serious danger to the nation. The President had been agreeable to a five per cent increase in Social Security payments, no more; hence the Congress knew he would veto an independent bill which required the twenty per cent increase. By its action, the Congress denied to the President his constitutional right to veto the undue increase; a Machiavellian aspect of this was that members of the House and Senate were reasonably certain that a veto by the President on this issue could not be overridden by a two-thirds vote in the two houses.

A related problem is the congressional practice of appropriating far more funds for a given activity than the President feels is wise or than can be prudently expended. This is most common when defense appropriations are under consideration. If the Congress appropriates more for a given defense activity than the President, National Security Council, Secretary of Defense, and Joint Chiefs of Staff believe to be wise, the President is often unable to veto the entire bill, for most of the appropriated funds are needed at once for essential defense activity.

The first of these two problems—riders on unrelated bills—can be corrected by several methods. The Congress could pass an act which forbids the practice; if, subsequently, the Congress sought to repeal this restriction upon itself, the President could veto the bill authorizing repeal. Another method would be to adopt a constitutional amendment, harmonious with the intentions of the writers of the Constitution, that each bill in the Congress should deal only with one substantive issue.

The best method, I think, would be to adopt a constitutional amendment which would give the President line-veto authority. This would permit the President to veto, for example, an increase in Social Security payments while approving that portion of the bill which increased the debt ceiling to $450 billion. The line-veto authority would also permit the President to disapprove a single fund item in a major appropriation bill.

In some of the states governors have line-veto authority. If the bill is an appropriation, the governor may eliminate or reduce items but he cannot increase the amounts appropriated. The same line-veto privilege permits the governor to veto an unrelated legislative rider.

Legislative riders are wrong in principle and few practices of the Congress take so much of the President's time as does this improper procedure.

What I advocate is quite different from President Nixon's refusal in 1972–73 to spend many of the funds appropriated by the Congress— an action that caused acrimonious congressional and press criticism. This was deemed to be unconstitutional power exercised by the Chief Executive. Had the Congress in making appropriations included a provision requiring the President to spend all the funds appropriated, and had he then impounded many of them, I think the President would have been subject to censure, perhaps even to impeachment and subsequent trial by the Senate. The facts were otherwise. An irresponsible Congress had appropriated far more funds than was prudent in the light of the dangerous inflationary situation, an inflation that would be exacerbated by the increased deficit financing. Someone had to act responsibly and only the President could do so. The appropriation acts which provided the funds did not carry a congressional mandate that they be spent.

The President's action can be made unnecessary and unconstitutional in the future. As is now proposed by a number of bills in the

Senate and House, the Congress can establish a ceiling on total appropriations for a given fiscal year. If the passage of individual appropriation acts exceeds this ceiling, a joint committee of the Senate and House can make essential reductions so as not to exceed the predetermined ceiling. The joint committee action would then have to obtain Senate and House approval. This final act, a responsible procedure in my judgment, would require that all funds be expended as stipulated. A presidential impoundment of funds under these circumstances would surely be unconstitutional. We would therefore not have another situation in the funding field in which it was charged that the President was impinging upon the prerogatives of the Congress.

But neither should the Congress impinge upon the constitutional authority of the President. Line-veto power for the President would restore his authority to disapprove unrelated substantive riders which he deems to be unwise, without at the same time jeopardizing the fate of important measures to which they may be attached.

CHAPTER 17

The wine is *still* bitter.

ONE OF THE most exciting and absorbing responsibilities I had during the Eisenhower years was serving as the President's personal representative and special ambassador to the nations of Latin America. My assignment was to make continental studies of conditions in Latin America and suggest changes in policies and programs which would strengthen the bonds of friendship between the United States and its neighbors to the south.

This new assignment began on April 12, 1953, when President Eisenhower told the Organization of American States:

"I am anxious that the government of the United States be fully informed of the economic and social conditions now prevailing throughout our continent and of all the efforts being pressed to bring a better life to our peoples. . . . Because my present duties make impossible my making personal visits . . . to the countries of Latin America, as I wish I could do, I have asked my brother, Dr. Milton Eisenhower, to visit shortly . . . these great republics. He will report to me on ways to strengthen the bonds of friendship between us and all our neighbors in the Pan American Union."

In 1963, I published a full account of my work in this field.[22] My thesis, as I reviewed eight years of hard but rewarding labor, was that in the period 1953–61 the United States had done more for the nations of Latin America, and had changed more fundamental policies affecting our relationships with Latin America, than in any other period in history. But despite commendable progress, the nations of Latin America were literally on the verge of revolution. The question was whether revolution would be bloody, as in Cuba, or peaceful and characterized by rapid social changes which would eliminate historic oligarchical systems inherited from Spain and Portugal—systems that kept most of the people in poverty and ignorance, while a few privileged families in each country lived in luxury, owned a high percentage of all productive resources, and exercised the powers of government.

The national and international legislation and agreements which initiated programs that could help to change this anachronistic situation were adopted in September 1960 and were later verified at the ministerial level in the 1961 Charter of Punta del Este. This agreement for social reform became known as the Alliance for Progress. The reforms, agreed to by all nations save Cuba, involved land reform ("land for the landless"), better education and health facilities, more equitable systems of taxation honestly administered, and economic advances within political systems that assured personal freedom for all the people.

I felt then that the domestic legislation and international agreements of Bogotá and Punta del Este marked a turning point in history. Gone was the "big brother" period of the Monroe Doctrine, amplified by the Theodore Roosevelt corollary to that doctrine, and the indefensible Platt Amendment to our treaty with Cuba. Gone, too, was the imperialism of the Woodrow Wilson regime. Building on the good will of the Good Neighbor Policy of Franklin Roosevelt, we would now give meaning to non-intervention proclaimed by that policy, and achieve the kind of partnership that would bring justice to the masses. Certainly in 1963, I was cautiously optimistic that in time the rigid control of the oligarchies would diminish, education would gradually become the privilege of all, illiteracy would be overcome in time, forms of democracy suitable to each country would begin to flourish and, with our help, amounting to some two billion dollars a year, per capita economic advances would be about two and a half per cent a year, with the benefits reaching most, not just a few, of the people.

When, in *The Wine Is Bitter*,[22] I wrote about my eight years of work in Latin America and about the major changes the United States Government had made in our policies toward our southern neighbors, I was somewhat provoked by the fact that the mass media as well as university scholars and others seemed to take it for granted that the Alliance for Progress was originated by President Kennedy early in his administration. Essentially what President Kennedy had done was to give a catchy new name to a substantive program that was already provided for in 1960 domestic and inter-American enactments. I was therefore pleased when Dean Rusk, Secretary of State under Presidents Kennedy and Johnson, wrote later in the March 23, 1971, issue of the

New York *Times*: "Foreign policy doesn't change a great deal simply with the election of new presidents. . . . Let me confess one thing. The *Alliance for Progress*, for example, was started by Milton Eisenhower in the closing days of the Eisenhower Administration.* . . . President Kennedy took up the idea, gave it a new name, and articulated it brilliantly to the nations of the hemisphere. But the essential idea for the *Alliance for Progress* was not a new invention. So there are elements of continuity that cut across administrations."

Since my brother left the White House, my responsibilities in the field of United States-Latin American affairs have been limited, though I have tried to keep up with developments. At the request of President Johnson, I again became special ambassador to Latin America and headed in January 1968 a United States delegation to an inter-American conference at Maracay, Venezuela, where delegates diligently sought to agree upon improved programs in education and science. Also in the Johnson administration I became one of the five members of a presidential advisory commission charged with trying to solve the perplexing problem of bringing stability to the operation of the Panama Canal and determining how the transit capacity of the present canal or a new sea-level canal might best handle the constantly increasing maritime traffic across the Isthmus of Panama, the prospect being that a traffic jam would develop as early as 1990. These efforts with Panama will be discussed briefly in a later chapter.

A quasi-official mission took me to Mexico in 1966 where one official of our government and three of us from private life met with four Mexican leaders and for several days publicly discussed in televised meetings how Mexico might improve the production, distribution, and sale of agricultural commodities.

The farm problem in Mexico was acute, an inheritance of neglect. For many years Mexico had concentrated on industrialization, improved marketing, mining, and a vast increase in public utilities. For quite some time she enjoyed the most rapid increase in gross national product of any of the Latin American countries, approaching ten per cent in some years. This was largely a consequence of producing domestically manufactured products which she previously had imported. But this substitution of domestically produced goods for former imports

---

* The basic legislation of the Alliance was passed five months before the end of Eisenhower's second term.

was approaching an end by 1966, so Mexican officials became concerned about the fact that her farmers, constituting nearly fifty per cent of her population, were so poor as not to be a significant element in the money economy of the nation. With a relatively few exceptions—isolated and efficiently operated irrigation projects—most of the farms of Mexico are of handkerchief size, scarcely producing enough for home consumption, almost none for sale that would provide funds for farmers to purchase processed goods.

The difficulty went back to the Mexican Revolution of 1910. During the long dictatorship of Porfirio Diaz ninety-five per cent of the ownership of Mexican resources fell into a few hands, some American, some Mexican, but always to the enrichment of Diaz. So "land for the landless" became a battle cry during the revolution and in time became almost sanctified in Mexican tradition. To provide land for the maximum number of persons, vast areas were carved up into small plots, averaging about twelve acres each. This doomed farmers to impoverishment. To have agriculture become a profitable enterprise, with farmers receiving roughly a parity income and therefore becoming buyers of industrial products, paying taxes, and sending children to school, farms would have to be enlarged greatly.

Two forces operate against such a change. Even with its growing prosperity, Mexico has incredibly bad slums on the periphery of her major cities, especially Mexico City. There was and still is consuming fear of additional migrations from the farms to the cities. The other force is political. Most farmers do not own the land but occupy the small tracts at the sufferance of the party in power. This assures that the ruling party in each election will receive a favorable vote from the farmers, for otherwise, they fear, they might be ejected from the land. One cannot talk publicly about this second point in Mexico. In our discussions, therefore, we concentrated on the first.

I spoke time and again about the need for industrial decentralization, thus permitting farms to be increased in size but keeping displaced farmers in the same general areas, only now as industrial workers. To Mexican leaders, decentralization means that all industry is not in Mexico City; some is in Monterey, Guadalajara, and a few other cities. The concept of having a plant of some kind in nearly every village had not entered their thinking and I doubt that my arguments convinced many persons. I pointed out, for example, that in my home state of Kansas the farm population has constantly decreased while total farm production has increased spectacularly, but the population of the state has not declined. On the contrary, it has increased, for every city, town, and village in Kansas has a tire plant, or a meat-packing plant, or a cannery, or a salt mine, or grain elevators, or flour mills. Landing boats for the United States Navy were built during World War II in Kansas City, Kansas, about as far from the two oceans as one can get. Wichita has become a major airplane manufacturing center. Even the United States, good as is its record of industrial decentralization, must do more in this regard, for accelerating urbanization is threatening the quality of life in our country. If our problem is worthy of serious attention—as it surely is—it is painfully acute in Mexico. And it remains true that if Mexico is to advance economically it must so shape its future that fifty per cent of its population, now destitute, can become part of the private competitive buying-and-selling economy of the country. I see no way of achieving this save by enlarging farms into viable economic units and keeping the displaced population employed in hundreds, even thousands, of towns and villages in all parts of the nation.

The Mexican experience is relevant to revolutionary movements in other Latin American countries. A firm pledge in the Act of Bogotá and the Charter of Punta del Este is to provide "land for the landless." It will be an almost irreversible error if the Mexican pattern is copied. Farming, like any other enterprise, should be a viable part of the interdependent economy. Each farm, therefore, must be an economic unit capable of bringing to the farm family an income sufficient for it to pay production costs and achieve sufficient profit to enable it to buy essential goods and services from other producing elements in that economy.

What is the record in this regard in the Alliance for Progress? Have the other reforms promised in the Alliance made headway? Or have they been as glacial in their movements as seems evident from reading the American press?

The most impressive single change in Latin America is a new attitude in both public and private enterprises. When I was making studies in our neighboring countries during the fifties, a major roadblock to progress was the inability of most Latin American governments to formulate effective policies and to manage programs efficiently. In the pre-Alliance period, a pervasive scarcity of technical and managerial competence, coupled with archaic and unserviceable procedures and organizational structures, was characteristic of most governments of the hemisphere. Recently the Agency for International Development, in a report to the House Committee on Government Operations, pointed out that this has been greatly changed during the past decade. There is now reasonable competence and a genuine commitment to progress in nearly all governments of the hemisphere. Thousands of public servants have for the first time received relevant training. Government posts are no longer sinecures for the incompetent. Governmental policy making is more realistic and better balanced. Executive agencies have been strengthened. AID believes, and I agree, that the Alliance has led to a genuine commitment for sustained development, and the means for attainment have become more realistic. This is a momentous achievement. Hence, though the data I shall cite indicate that what has been accomplished is not impressive, I believe that the cautious optimism I expressed in 1963 is still justified.

Perhaps the most crucial test of social change—of the success of the Alliance—is in the area of land reform, partly because such a high percentage of the people live on the land and partly because a substantial change for the better must involve considerable loss of economic privilege and political influence on the part of the oligarchists who have historically owned most of the land which is in private ownership and controlled the destiny of their countries.

Sixteen countries have passed agrarian reform laws, providing either for breaking up the internal empires of land, the *latifundias*, or for granting ownership or other permanent tenure arrangements on what previously had been land in the public domain. The passage of such legislation is mildly encouraging, but action to implement these legislative enactments has been minimal, save in Chile, Peru, Brazil, and Bolivia where progress has been noticeable, though I fear not notable. At present there are vague promises of favorable land-reform movements in other countries. Late in 1971 representatives of twenty-two nations of the hemisphere met in Peru to foster accelerated land reform and colonization. At the conference Argentina and Brazil indicated that they would proceed with land settlement schemes; certainly they possess enormous areas of undistributed public land to provide for many of the landless. Bolivia and Mexico at the conference contended that they have already achieved land reform, though as I have pointed out the Mexican program has doomed the rural population to poverty and the Bolivian experience still leaves the country with a serious food deficit.

Fifteen of the Latin American representatives indicated that their governments had granted nearly ninety-six thousand titles to new owners and had settled sixty-four thousand families on more than ten million acres, including natural pasture land. Thus, Bolivia granted more than forty-three thousand land titles, Colombia twenty-two thousand, and Guatemala, Peru, Chile, the Dominican Republic, and Nicaragua each more than four thousand.

In addition to granting titles to new lands several Latin American countries have authorized individual ownership to families who previously operated land as sharecroppers or employees of large landowners. The Organization of American States reports that the number of rural families benefited by this type of action has been twice as great as those who gained by receiving titles to new lands; this program has been notable in Colombia, Peru, Honduras, and Bolivia.

Unfortunately the Mexican error in agriculture is not being avoided in most other countries. Too many farmers are being provided enough land only for a bare subsistence type of farming, sixteen acres to the family on the average. These sub-family farms make up forty-three per cent of all farms in Argentina, thirty-seven per cent in Chile, and ninety per cent in Ecuador. Despite what has been done, sixty per cent of all farm workers in Brazil are landless, as are forty-eight per cent in Chile and thirty-five per cent in Ecuador. These data are indicative of the entire hemispheric situation.

So it must be said that on a continental basis land reform has progressed at a snail's pace. Progress has not been sufficient to reduce appreciably the danger of revolution, peaceful or bloody, in most of the nations of Latin America.

Only recently has a new program been initiated that promises the type of land reform that may give farmers the same opportunity for reasonable incomes as are obtained by industrial owners and workers. A gigantic homesteading program is in its initial stages in Brazil. The Brazilian government plans to resettle more than half a million people in the Amazon basin, which comprises nearly sixty per cent of the national territory and is larger than the entire land area of Mexico.

The first effort is to build some nine thousand miles of roads which will crisscross the vast emptiness of the Amazon basin. Each farm is to have slightly less than 250 acres and each will have frontage on one of the new highways. To avoid crop failures, the first crops will be those suitable to the area, including rice, beans, corn, manioc, soybeans, and other short-cycle crops. As research finds appropriate answers, crop production will be expanded to include pepper, cocoa, coffee, guaraná, palm trees, cashews, rubber, and sugar cane. Started only a few years ago, more than ten thousand settlers have already been located in the area. As development proceeds, there will be three types of population center in Amazonia: farm villages with fifty family houses, an elementary school, a health center, and a few shops; larger towns with as many as a thousand families along with essential services; and intermediate towns. The gamble in this is the danger of vastly changing the ecology as trees are removed and the thin topsoil is exposed to the burning sun. The topsoil could be severely damaged or even washed away by torrential rainfall. A judicious retention of trees, planting of new trees as windbreaks, and the adoption of sound soil and water conservation practices may avoid much of the trouble. Certainly this effort to open and tame a frontier is commendable and deserves whatever assistance Brazil may need from the United States.

Chile has expropriated three thousand large farms, totaling nearly ten million acres, and on this vast area is settling previous farm workers. Under the law, the government will hold title to the land for from three to five years. In that period the government will organize farm workers into co-operatives and pay many of them wages. This implies the possible development of a mixture of collective farms and state farms as in the Soviet Union, where agriculture remains the most inefficient enterprise in that country. There are two other difficulties: first, there are three times as many people who want land as the government can provide and, second, large sums of money are needed to purchase fertilizers, tractors, and other farm equipment and supplies, and still more cash to build farm-to-market roads. In a State of the Nation report, the late President Allende said nearly fifty per cent of the farm land of the nation had come under the land-reform plan, that many of the holdings would be "kept as economic units," and that decentralized industries would be developed to keep rural workers from rushing to the cities.

The effect on Chile's progress in this area of the recent coup and Allende's death is yet to be determined.

Another major reform promised in the Alliance is to increase greatly the number of students in formal education and to reduce the number of illiterates. Specifically, the objective was to offer at least six years of elementary education for the entire school-age population; in a single decade the ambitious goal was to increase primary school registrations from twenty-six million children to forty-five million. In 1971 there were forty-two and a half million students in primary schools —not a bad record. Unfortunately, though, over a period of years only eleven per cent remained in school long enough to complete elementary education. Hence only a small percentage of the population, fifteen to twenty-four years of age, was eligible to enter secondary schools, with this situation being far worse in rural areas than in the urban centers. Even so, in 1971 there were nearly nine and a half million students in the secondary schools, with the dropout rate being extraordinarily high. Finally, in that year there were 1.6 million in higher schools—colleges, universities, technical institutes, vocational training schools. As compared to 1960, these enrollments represented an increase of better than 165 per cent at the elementary level, nearly 350 per cent at the secondary level, and about 260 per cent at the higher level. In this period the percentage of illiterates in Latin America dropped from 40 to 24 per cent, but due to the immense increase in population the decrease in the actual number of illiterates was only from 41 to 39 million. These 39 million illiterates (all over fifteen years of age) are a terrible drag on the economy, political creativity, and over-all progress, especially in some countries where the illiteracy rate is still as high as 70 per cent of the total population, a sharp contrast to one country where illiteracy is now only 10 per cent.

In education, our neighbors to the south must be given A for effort. They are now devoting more than 20 per cent of their gross public expenditure to education. Further, even in the face of the highest population growth in the world, school enrollment in the sixties rose twice as much as the increase in the school-age groups—no mean achievement.

The dark side of the picture, however, is the fact that there are still more school-age youngsters outside the educational system than are inside. Further, the efficiency of the educational system is still low; the large number of "late starters," the almost unbelievable number of "repeaters," the number of over-age children who block entry of younger students, and the huge number of dropouts at all levels of education (as high as seventy-five per cent in some countries) are stern and discouraging evidence of this. Other factors of inefficiency are unqualified teachers, poor physical facilities, lack of textbooks, and a lack of relevant relationship between education and the need of the individual students; on this last point less than a quarter of all Latin American students are pursuing a type of education which will prepare them for productive roles in a society that must become increasingly dependent on science and technology.

A third reform promised in the Alliance is improved health facilities, personnel, and programs. In the pre-Alliance period the death rate per 1,000 live births ranged from 43.4 in Honduras to 94.1 in the Dominican Republic and 105 in Bolivia, an incredible infant mortality rate. The hope set forth in the Alliance was that these rates would be reduced fifty per cent in ten years. Unfortunately infant mortality rates have increased in Guatemala, Nicaragua, Paraguay, and Uruguay; there were satisfactory reductions in eight countries and modest reductions in others.

The nations declared their intentions to eradicate malaria and smallpox. I had worked hard for this goal in the meetings with the presidential representatives in the 1956–57 period and had offered, with President Eisenhower's approval, to have the United States pay a substantial portion of the cost of the eradication programs. So the Alliance goal to eliminate these two prevalent and controllable diseases had enthusiastic United States approval. But only Bolivia has thus far achieved satisfactory results. Argentina, Brazil, Chile, Peru, and three of the Caribbean island countries have made reasonable progress. In the other Latin American countries progress has been slight.

In fifteen countries comprehensive health plans have been developed. Nearly fifty new medical schools have been established and the number of physicians being graduated each year has increased about seventy-five per cent. Again, however, population growth minimizes the importance of the figures showing gains. Only five countries in Latin America have 6 or more physicians per 10,000 population, as compared to three countries ten years ago. In nineteen countries the ratio of graduate and practical nurses per unit of population has increased slightly, but such gains as have been made in health personnel are largely limited to the cities. In general, rural areas are without health aids. In several countries, programs which require physicians, upon graduation from universities, to devote several years to practice in rural areas have been initiated.

The most serious health menace in Latin America continues to be lack of sanitation. I had been appalled by what I saw in this regard in my eight years of travel throughout Latin America. So with great interest I read data prepared in this field by Dr. Abel Wolman, the greatest environmental engineer in this country, possibly in the world. I commented to him one day that his figures made me shudder as much as had the physical evidence. He commented that he was just back from India where he had made a study for the Indian government and that his latest experience had impressed upon him how superior the situation was in Latin America!

Under the Alliance program progress has been made in the sanitation field. In nineteen countries potable water is now provided for seventy per cent of the urban population. Again, the rural situation is much worse. In most countries potable water has been provided for less than twenty per cent of the rural population.

Only in El Salvador and Colombia are sewage disposal systems provided to as many as seventy per cent of the urban population, though Panama and Peru are close to this goal. Once again, the rural people are left to suffer; in all countries save Colombia (where the record is somewhat better) only ten per cent of the rural population has adequate sewage disposal.

Finally, in the Alliance years the number of hospital beds increased from only 685,000 to 843,000; hence, with the population explosion proceeding unabated, the number of hospital beds per unit of population remained unchanged and, needless to say, all hospitals are concentrated in urban centers.

Still another reform promised in the Alliance is improved tax laws, honestly enforced. Here commendable progress has been made. When I was serving as special ambassador to Latin America in the fifties, persons of low and moderate incomes paid a disproportionate share of all taxes, while the wealthy were usually successful in paying only negligible amounts. At that time most taxes were regressive—such as import duties and sales taxes. Today, most countries are moving toward tax systems that make them adequate tools for development and for better income distribution. In the hemisphere as a whole, tax collections have increased more than thirty per cent, in some countries the increase is sixty per cent, and in one it is eighty per cent. It has long been clear to me that if the nations of Latin America will tax their citizens on the basis of ability to pay and at rates comparable to what we have in the United States they will have available for education, health, housing, and other desirable developments a great deal more local capital than they now possess. Adequate local capital, in turn, will increase their credit-worthiness and thus will enable them to obtain a greater volume of private and public capital from abroad.

Since the Alliance was initiated, all Latin American countries have established or strengthened existing national housing agencies charged with the responsibility for providing low-cost housing. The agencies are in existence, but the record of accomplishment is a dismal one. The need for low-cost housing in Latin America is about twenty-three million units and this deficit, instead of being reduced, is increasing each year at a rate of about one million units—still another consequence of the population explosion.

The foregoing statistical indicators of progress in the field of social reform, while not impressive, do hold out the hope that a momentum is developing and that the second decade of the Alliance will show greater gains for individual citizens, even those in rural areas who now are obviously the neglected people of the hemisphere.

One other and inseparable part of the Alliance is economic development, with the benefits of increased national income going not exclusively to a few wealthy families but to an ever increasing percentage of the entire population. Data in the economic area are elusive. Those published by several congressional committees, by the Agency for Economic Development, by the State Department, and by the Organization of American States vary considerably. The data, however, are such that one may draw reasonable generalizations from them.

The economic goal of the Alliance is a per capita increase of 2.5 per cent in production each year. For the hemisphere as a whole, the gross national product from 1960 to 1971 may have increased annually more than 4 per cent. Population growth partially offset this gain. On the average the goal was not met, but variations by countries have been great. Thus in Bolivia the per capita growth in production was about .5 per cent; in Brazil, perhaps 1.5 per cent; Panama 3.8 per cent; Venezuela, better than 2 per cent. Fortunately, economic improvement in the second half of the decade was better than it was in the first half, so that in the past five years the Alliance goal has been met in some countries, exceeded in a few. This late improvement was due to increases of about 50 per cent in public expenditures to enhance production, both industrial and agricultural.

The most remarkable, almost unbelievable, development has recently occurred in Brazil. As I have just indicated, the per capita growth in Brazil during the decade of the sixties was only about 1.5 per cent. But toward the end of the decade a miracle happened. Its growth rate accelerated and today is the highest in Latin America; the gross national product last year increased nearly 10 per cent—one of the fastest rates in the world. Per capita income increased to about $550, not comparable to personal incomes in industrialized countries, but high for Latin American nations. That this remarkable achievement occurred under a dictatorship is discouraging, but it dramatically indicates the need for political stability in all nations of Latin America if they are to have economic growth and reach the other goals of the Alliance for Progress.

Industrial production increased appreciably in most countries during the past ten years. Manufacturing now contributes more than twenty-five per cent of the gross domestic product in the hemisphere, exceeding somewhat the contributions made by agriculture, forestry, and fishing. Countries with the largest industrial production are Argentina, Brazil, Mexico, and Chile, though lately there have been significant increases in Panama, El Salvador, and Peru.

In meeting the economic goal of the Alliance, the agricultural situation in Latin America remains discouraging. This is an area in which the United States Government and several large American foundations as well as numerous American universities have tried to be most helpful for a period of thirty years. This foreign assistance has established and maintained agricultural experiment stations, built access roads to open productive virgin lands, and helped set up extension systems to carry the results of research to people on the land. But the sad fact is that the increase of twenty-four per cent in gross farm production during the past decade has been offset by population gains, so that per capita farm production was slightly less at the end of the decade than it was at the beginning. Food production has a slightly better record than total production, including fibers. Per capita food production was better in 1971 than it was a decade earlier. Variations, however, were large. Thus, there were declines in Argentina, Bolivia, Colombia, Ecuador, Panama, Peru, and Uruguay, and increases in Brazil, Chile, Costa Rica, El Salvador, Guatemala, Honduras, Mexico, Paraguay, and Venezuela.

As per capita income increases, the Alliance commitment is to achieve more widespread distribution of the fruits of production. Here progress is negligible. It is still true that in most Latin American countries a relatively few persons are very wealthy; there is a small though growing middle class and oceans of desperately poor individuals. While solid data are lacking, the Agency for International Development has estimated that in Latin America as a whole the upper ten per cent of the population receives forty per cent of the national income, while the lower forty per cent receives only ten per cent. If these figures are reasonably accurate, they represent, bad as they are, considerable progress over what existed when I first began my work in Latin America in 1953.

Galo Plaza Lasso, Secretary General of the Organization of American States, former President of Ecuador, and one of the distinguished scholars of Latin America, recently said, "Latin America must achieve an economic growth rate of 7.2 per cent annually merely to prevent additional unemployment and provide jobs for new workers entering the labor force which is growing faster than that of any other part of the world—three times as fast as in the industrialized countries."

In 1900 there were 60 million Latin Americans. Today there are 290 million. Population increases range from 2 per cent per year in Chile to 3.4 per cent in Ecuador, El Salvador, Honduras, and Mexico. Hence, the population will double every twenty-four years. The population of Latin America by the end of the twentieth century will not be less than 580 million, perhaps a little more than 600 million. (World population, now 3.7 billion, will be 8 billion by the year 2000 if the current rate of growth—180,000 a day—continues.)

Under any set of foreseeable circumstances, this volatile rate of population growth would prove disastrous in Latin America, but it poses a special threat since most of it will be in the cities with slums that defy description. Some Latin American cities are experiencing a doubling of their population every ten years and the growth is greatest in the slums. City unemployment continues to increase. Schools, hospitals, and housing remain inadequate.

How can anyone doubt that both social reform and increased economic justice for the masses in Latin America demand a new population policy? The most unchristian thing a family can do is to bring into the world children who are doomed to privation, perhaps illiteracy, ill health, and early death. With population stablilized, increased productivity in agriculture and industry, and increased tax income to finance better education, health, and low-cost housing, Latin America could begin to realize the grand goals of the Alliance. Otherwise, I fear, it cannot.

The future of Latin America is of grave concern to the United States. While world events cause us to be preoccupied with Southeast Asia, the Middle East, Europe, and the Soviet bloc, nonetheless we realize that no area of the world is of greater importance to our own future than is Latin America. Our investment there is about thirteen billion dollars. Our trade with the area, five billion in exports and about the same in imports each year, exceeds that with most parts of the world, save Canada. We are dependent on Latin America for the importation of critical primary commodities and for the export to the area of large quantities of manufactured goods.

In the Alliance for Progress we promised to see to it that net foreign capital going into the Latin American countries would amount to two billion dollars a year, or twenty billion dollars in ten years, provided that they would devote eighty billion dollars of their local savings to social reform and development. Latin America has exceeded its quota. More than ninety per cent of the development capital in Latin America under the Alliance has been domestically generated. We have fallen slightly short of our promise. The net flow of foreign capital into the area has averaged $1.7 billion a year. This is a fairly good record considering the discouragements that have occurred—vast expropriations of American assets without compensation in Peru and Chile and, earlier, in Cuba, with threats of expropriation in other countries. It cannot be overemphasized that private capital cannot be forced to go to any part of the world. *It must be attracted* and that can be done only if the climate for investment in specific countries is favorable. It was foreign capital, mainly from Europe, that contributed to the rapid development of the productive capacity of the United States. We did not expropriate any of the foreign-owned resources. We gradually paid the debt, becoming a creditor country only in 1918. Latin America, still in a fairly primitive state, can hasten its development through the use of foreign funds, and it can repay them over a period of years, to her own benefit. She will make a terrible mistake if in the apparent temporary gain of expropriation she discourages further foreign investment in the hemisphere.

A final goal of the Alliance is that the social reforms and increased production I have discussed should take place within democratic frameworks, with increasing personal freedom for the people. Indeed, the declaration of Latin American ministers, made on the day of the signing of the Charter of Punta del Este, is as moving and explicit a plea for personal freedom and representative government as has been set forth in any state document, including our own Declaration of Independence and our Constitution. It therefore is not encouraging that the number of dictatorships in Latin America has increased from three at the time the Alliance was formed to eight today. But the modern dictatorships in Latin America are different from the typical ones of the past. Historically, most Latin American dictators—Perez Jiménez, Trujillo, Porfirio Diaz, and others—were extreme rightists, men on white horses who protected the privileged and did nothing for the masses of miserably poor, illiterate peoples. Today, some of the dictators tend to be more liberal than are the members of the constitutionally elected national assemblies. One hopes that the dictators and the legislators will find common ground to carry forward the enlightened goals of the Alliance, and that as soon as possible dictatorships will again be reduced, as they were during the 1950s.

Today my view of Latin America is not too different from what it was when I published *The Wine Is Bitter*[22] in 1963. The people are angry. They want a better life for themselves and their children. Though they still suffer from a low level of education and a pervasive illiteracy, they now know that the life they have led for generations and still lead is neither universal nor inevitable. So they demand change. The question still is, as it was a decade ago, whether change will be peaceful by democratic methods, as envisaged in the Act of Bogotá and Charter of Punta del Este, or violent and bloody as it was in Cuba. The modest advances I have outlined are commendable but not nearly enough. Social reform, greater economic development, increased foreign assistance, and the benefits of economic growth benefiting all the people—these are modern *imperatives*.

In September 1970, Chile became the first nation in the world to elect freely and democratically a Marxist President: Salvador Allende Gossens. Three years later, to the month, as the result of a sudden and bloody military coup, Allende was dead, his social revolution in a shambles, and his nation in chaos—perhaps for years to come.

The military coup was a compound tragedy, not just because of the toll it took in human life, but because it violated the free choice of the people of Chile. When Allende was elected I strongly believed that the United States would err most seriously if it changed its policies because he was a Marxist. This would make a mockery of a policy that we have proclaimed since Thomas Jefferson, that people have an inherent right to choose their own form of government. The overthrow of the Allende government will be viewed by many as proof that those who preach democracy do not have enough faith in it to abide by it.

I do not believe that Allende would have been re-elected in the next free election. He had gained office in a three-way election by winning a plurality of only slightly more than one third of the vote. Despite his promise that he would bring to Chile a government "authentically democratic, popular, national and truly revolutionary," he defied the Chilean Congress, flaunted international law by expropriating vast foreign-owned properties without providing compensation, forcibly put down dissent by those who disagreed with his policies and methods, and generally led his country into turmoil.

I think Salvador Allende truly believed that he could bring to Chile long-overdue reforms. Early in his term as President he won widespread support among the working classes by embarking on social reforms and raising wages while holding down prices. But, perhaps because he was pressured by his Marxist supporters, he pushed his people too far too fast and earned the wrath and distrust of Chile's large middle-class population. His agrarian reform programs caused sharp drops in farm production. His expropriation of United States copper companies lost him American aid and shattered Chile's foreign exchange position. Inflation soared more than three hundred per cent and shortages in food and other products swept the country. Finally, when Allende proposed to replace the Congress with a unicameral parliament and to nationalize such industries as Chile's all-important trucking industry, he aroused widespread anger and massive strikes. In response, President Allende began arresting people and, it is said, to develop a secret police force.

There are many lessons to be learned from Chile. One of them is that the rooted and horribly tangled problems of our Latin American neighbors simply do not yield to ideology. The social reform and economic development so desperately needed in Latin America will be brought about only when those in control can unite their people in an effort that will require great energy, enormous intelligence, and unprecedented political skill and sensitivity. The people of Latin America will not tolerate much longer the anachronistic social system inherited from Spain and Portugal. Those in power, whether rightists or leftists, will either lead a peaceful revolution or be consumed in a violent one.

I remain proud of what we did in the Eisenhower period: we doubled the flow of private and public capital to the nations of Latin America; increased the capital of the Export-Import Bank to the point that it could meet all legitimate demands for financial help from our country; strengthened the role of the Organization of American States in economic and social affairs; instituted the Development Loan Fund to provide "soft" loans to Latin America, a sharp departure from traditional policy; discarded a hundred-year-old policy which opposed common markets and did all we could to increase efficiency and credit-worthiness by promoting common markets in three great regions of Latin America; created for the first time commodity study groups with a view to minimize the fluctuations in the prices of primary commodities which Latin America sells to the world; established the Inter-American Bank as an instrument that could make loans with conditions requiring social reform, something that could not be done by our national lending institutions without violating the all but sanctified policy of nonintervention in the internal affairs of other states; tripled cultural exchanges; tripled the shipment of food to needy countries, especially Bolivia, and in Public Law 86-735 of September 1960 and the Act of Bogotá one week later laid the legal basis, domestically and intergovernmentally, for the social reform and economic development program we came to call the Alliance for Progress.

While my work in Latin America as personal representative of the President was the most time-consuming of my assignments in the international field, there were a good many others. I lived, for two years, in Great Britain. My first official trip to the Soviet Union was in 1959, followed later by a long personal study there in 1970 and a semi-official trip in 1971. My assignments for UNESCO took me for six-week periods each to Paris, Mexico City, Beirut, and again Paris. Trips to Africa, Europe, and Canada were undertaken for President Franklin Roosevelt. Indeed, foreign assignments have taken me many times to some continents and to every area in the world except the Far East and Southeast Asia. I therefore have had an opportunity over a long period of years to observe the functioning of American foreign policy and the officials we have in foreign countries to carry out policies constitutionally determined by the President of the United States.

I concluded many years ago that our foreign service—including especially the representatives of many federal agencies—has grown much too large—so large, in fact, that we often create more problems for ourselves in country after country than we solve. Theoretically, all United States personnel in a foreign country are under the co-ordinating guidance of the United States ambassador, regardless of whether they serve as political or economic counselors, first, second, or third secretaries, representatives of the United States Army, Navy, and Air Force, agents of the Departments of Agriculture, Labor, and Treasury, CIA personnel, United States Information Agency workers, Agency for International Development personnel, or representatives of the Export-Import Bank, Peace Corps, or other agencies.

In Mexico, 1,200 officials of the United States Government are permanently stationed in various parts of that country and, as I have said, the ambassador is supposed to be sufficiently aware of their activities that he can provide policy guidance, prevent duplication of effort, see to it they do not violate any domestic or foreign United States policy, and carry out their assignments efficiently. In Brazil we have 1,000 employees. These are representative situations.

I agree with Dr. John Kenneth Galbraith, who contended, in an address at The Johns Hopkins University, that the foreign service of the United States is no longer the personalized activity it once was when such eminent persons as Thomas Jefferson, Benjamin Franklin, and, much later, Dwight Morrow represented us abroad. These men were truly, not just theoretically, the personal representatives of the President of the United States. They spoke with the authority of the President. They were respected abroad in that capacity.

Today, our officials abroad constitute a massive bureaucracy. An unmanageable bureaucracy has several built-in faults. It develops a rigidity in policy and personal views at a time when conditions are rapidly changing; new policy directives from Washington are slow to reach and be accepted by field personnel. Often attitudes do not change in harmony with the new directives. In other words, the activities of many of our representatives abroad are out of date, ineffective at best, harmful at worst. Second, with personnel located in far reaches of each of the countries, often not in touch with the embassy for weeks or months at a time, officials often create problems that would never have developed had they not been in the field. Third, the cost is unnecessarily high. I am convinced on the basis of my personal observations that we would be much more effective in carrying out the President's foreign policies if we reduced our personnel abroad by at least fifty per cent; raised salaries and station allowances appreciably; kept in each country well-educated, distinguished persons who commanded the respect of that country's public officials and private leaders; and changed approaches and personal negotiations promptly as changing conditions require the President to make essential shifts in policy.

While I have great respect for many persons in our embassies, I must in candor say that there are others of mediocre quality who seem to be permanently entrenched.

I may be quite blunt in giving a relevant example about this. When the first global Mercury flight was being planned, it became apparent that we had a critical need for a control system at Guaymas, Mexico. Our able ambassador and his entire staff insisted that President Lopez Mateos would never consent to our stationing a control operation on Mexican soil, primarily because the entire operation was presumed to have a military flavor and it was notoriously true that we could not reach agreement with Mexico on anything of a military nature, even on a radar belt that would be as valuable to Mexico as to us. The bureaucracy of the massive United States staff was convinced that it would be a mistake to approach the Mexican government on any such matter. When it was suggested that I, then serving as a special liaison agent between President Lopez Mateos and President Eisenhower, might take the problem to the Mexican President, there was no objection by any of our embassy personnel; indeed I suspect that they secretly smirked and awaited my failure.

Even though Manuel Tello, then the Foreign Minister, was a personal friend of mine of long standing, I decided that I would take the problem directly to the Mexican President. I explained to President Lopez Mateos why a control station at Guaymas was imperative; this would be our first flight girdling the globe and if anything malfunctioned it would be at Guaymas that the signal would have to be given to the orbiting astronauts, headed by John Glenn, that would bring them down into the Atlantic near the Bahama islands. I carefully explained that the only military participation was the actual launching of the Mercury satellite. Everything else was under the civilian control of the National Aeronautics and Space Agency. Indeed, we would be happy to have Mexican scientists stationed with our personnel at Guaymas and Cape Canaveral—and, if the President of Mexico preferred, we would make our installation a portable one so that if, after one or more flights, discontent with the arrangement developed in Mexico we might by that time find another way to handle our problems. Finally, I said that if for any reason Mexico could not accede to our request, we would have to station a flattop just three miles off the coast of Mexico near Guaymas; this would be unfortunate notice to all the world that the two neighboring countries, which really were good friends, could not cooperate even in a scientific experiment of first importance. President Lopez Mateos listened to me with care. When I finished my presentation he asked whether it would be possible to have Australian, British, and perhaps African scientists at the Guaymas station, and Mexican scientists not only there but at other control stations in Antigua, Africa, Australia, and perhaps elsewhere; this would enable the Presidents of the United States and Mexico to announce the spectacular space flight as truly an international scientific experiment. At once I agreed to his proposal. I did not even call President Eisenhower or Dr. Keith Glennan, head of the Aeronautics and Space Administration, to obtain their approval, for the proposal was obviously a good one and I knew our people would approve.

President Lopez Mateos asked me to brief Manuel Tello and Dr. Nabor Carillo Flores, rector of the University of Mexico and head of the Mexican Atomic Energy Commission. The President then indicated that he would give me an answer soon. His approval came a little later when he was making an official visit to the United States and I was with President Eisenhower, who was taking President Lopez Mateos on a delightful trip down the Potomac to Mount Vernon. When the Mexican President called me to his side and gave approval for what I had asked, I rushed to tell my friend Antonio Carillo Flores, then Mexican ambassador to the United States. Toni smiled and said I surely did not expect the President to turn me, a brother of President Eisenhower and known to have his confidence, down on such a vital matter.

Diplomacy should be a highly personal affair, conducted by persons who command the respect of their counterparts in the countries where they are serving. I would not venture a guess as to the precise numbers of personnel we should have in Mexico or Brazil or Chile or the United Kingdom or France or the Soviet Union. Obviously there must be a wise political attaché who himself has such prestige and standing that he may, in behalf of the ambassador, deal directly with relevant officials of the foreign office of the country in which he is serving. The same is true of economic and commercial affairs, agricultural and labor matters, military affairs. In countries where we carry on aid programs there should be talented personnel to see to it that the aid program is efficiently conducted. But I have no hesitancy in advocating an immediate reduction of fifty per cent in all of our personnel stationed abroad; the largest percentage of the reduction should involve representatives of federal agencies other than the State Department.

My conviction regarding this problem is shared by many career officers in our foreign service. Ambassador Ellis Briggs, a career diplomat who served as head of United States missions in five countries and in lesser capacities in twelve others, points out in his book, *Farewell to Foggy Bottom*[23]: "Practically every diplomatic mission in the world is so stuffed with unnecessary personnel that the handful of State Department officials trying to perform substantive diplomatic functions can scarcely find a chair. . . . Of over one hundred American Embassies in the world today [1954] a majority could perform twice as effectively with half the persons now cluttering up the premises. . . . Practically every department in Washington is represented abroad." He specifies Commerce, Agriculture, Coast Guard, Treasury financial attachés, Customs, Internal Revenue Service, Immigration Service, FBI, Interior, Tariff Commission, Public Health Service, Federal Communications Commission, Civil Aeronautics Board, Bureau of Public Roads, and a miscellany of others, and I add the Peace Corps, AID, CIA, science attachés, military attachés (in great abundance), and labor attachés.

"The average size of a mission a decade ago [1944]," Briggs goes on, "was about a dozen Americans, including clerks, stenographers, and attachés. . . . Today everybody wants to play diplomacy . . . [this] is playing havoc with our international relations. . . . The only American official who can resolve the expensive confusion caused by unneeded personnel abroad is the President himself."

In mid-1973 a distinguished United States ambassador wrote me: "In Rome in the early 1960s there were twenty-five governmental agencies represented. It took a very large room—an auditorium—to hold the weekly staff meeting. In London at that time more than forty agencies were represented in our Embassy."

Most career diplomats blame our present problem of overstaffing on the proliferation of federal agencies assigned to our foreign missions. State Department personnel constitute only twenty per cent or less of the total abroad. Most ambassadors do not know what all these federal people do, though they are held responsible. They also feel that the State Department in Washington is burdened with peripheral activities while those handling the vital problems of intergovernmental relations are seriously overworked.

When Ellis Briggs, then ambassador to Greece, discovered that the Coast Guard had a representative attached to his embassy, he asked one of his top attachés what the man did. The attaché said he could only guess. He might be counting icebergs in the Mediterranean!

CHAPTER 18

Expected to be all things to all men, a
President sorely needs someone with whom
he can simply be himself.

SINCE MY BROTHER and I had worked together intermittently but intimately for twenty years prior to his election to the presidency, it was natural for me to become one of his closest confidants.

We were philosophically compatible. We shared a passionate belief in the American system of representative government. Distilled from long and vigorous discussions over the years were a number of views on which we agreed wholeheartedly: the supremacy of the people who delegate limited power to the federal government; the necessity of maintaining a responsible federal posture in all domestic and foreign financial affairs; the need to advance human values in our rapidly changing society; the essential need to strengthen the competitive enterprise system as one of the bulwarks of retaining personal, political, and economic freedom.

As Ike often said: "All freedoms are a single bundle; lose one, and we lose them all."

Our relationship did not change merely because he now occupied the highest office in the land. It may seem incredible, but I did not view him primarily as a leader with great power. I saw him as I always had: a brother with whom I enjoyed an unusually strong affection which, fortunately, was mutual. Our work together had always been, and would be for the eight presidential years, characterized by trust, unqualified openness, and good will.

Ike sometimes lost his temper, but he never did with me. Often he said to friends, and once in a press conference, that if I were not his brother I would be in a top Cabinet post. We had mutually decided, following his election, that it would be a mistake for him to appoint me to the Cabinet. It would smack of nepotism. My public pronouncements would not be accepted as my own but as an echo of the President's views. I was insistent upon being recognized not as a brother but as an individual in my own right, and with this he heartily agreed.

With this understanding, the White House was my weekend home for eight years, although I ceased staying there when I learned that the President always paid a guest charge for me. Even though I was there on official business, he felt that a brother should be considered a guest. So I spent the nights at my father-in-law's apartment in the Mayflower Hotel after that. But every Friday, Saturday, and often Sunday I was in the oval office or the family rooms of the White House, save when assignments took me abroad.

My constant trips from Penn State to Washington, from 1953 to 1956, required four hours by car, about forty minutes by small plane. These trips became tedious, for I soon learned that I became nauseated if I tried to do serious work in the car or plane. After 1956, when I became president of The Johns Hopkins University, I wasted little time in travel, for a car could get me from my home to the White House in less than an hour; by helicopter, used only in emergencies, the travel time was fifteen minutes.

I felt ambivalent about my role. I knew President Eisenhower found it helpful to reveal his innermost thoughts and plans to one who was not subservient to him, was not an advocate of special interests, had no selfish purpose to serve, and would raise questions and facts solely to help the President think through his problems without pressing for a particular decision.

On the other hand, I found the role difficult for two reasons. I feared it would be misunderstood and possibly resented by principal officers of the executive establishment, and I confess that at times, as any human would be, I was tempted to urge a policy decision. It was difficult to discipline myself and put the temptation aside. Yet, as I think back on those eight years, I am satisfied that my policy was correct in making specific suggestions solely in my three official areas— and even then only after I had first obtained the agreement of the appropriate Cabinet officers and White House counselors. I was determined not to create a schism between the President and leading members of his administration with whom he worked daily and on whom he depended for the execution of policies and programs. Further, I was not so arrogant as to think my judgment was better than that of the President and his official family.

I had seen disastrous effects of confidant-presidential decisions in previous administrations. Harry Hopkins, for example, had often persuaded President Roosevelt to act without consulting relevant Cabinet members. The decisions, whether right or wrong, often caused resentment and confusion among those who had to carry them out. Certainly it was ridiculous for Roosevelt, on Hopkins' advice, to split the well-run Department of Agriculture into two agencies, with Secretary Wickard in charge of the "old line" research bureaus and Chester Davis in charge of the agricultural action agencies, called the War Food Administration. The obvious solution was to replace Wickard with Chester Davis as head of a consolidated department. Hopkins, knowing that Roosevelt hated to fire anyone, had urged a solution that fitted the President's temperament but which caused needless inefficiency and higher cost.

Any policy, any set of rules, however, should not be so rigid as to preclude exceptions. In 1958–59, I made a mistake in not going around a Cabinet officer directly to President Eisenhower on a matter of genuine urgency. From my studies in Panama in 1958, I was convinced that serious difficulty was inevitable. We had violated an amendment to the original treaty of 1903 between Panama and the United States. We were not, as we had agreed, buying all supplies from either of the two countries; we were not as persistent as we might have been in training Panamanians for promotion from unskilled and lower-paying jobs to the professional higher-paying posts. For many years we had been delinquent in developing among the people of Panama an understanding of the fact that the United States did not make a cent from the Canal —that, on the contrary, we subsidized its operation. Worst of all, Panamanians were enraged by assertions on the part of some congressmen that the United States was the sovereign power in the Canal Zone, when in fact Panama retained titular sovereignty and the United States only exercised administrative control "as if it were sovereign." In response to these "provocations," Panamanians were becoming increasingly critical, even belligerent.

On the basis of my studies, I developed a nine-point program which I felt would ease the difficulty, at least for some years. I have explained this in detail in *The Wine Is Bitter*.[22] Secretary Dulles and his associates in the Latin American Bureau of the State Department approved my recommendations. I then discussed them with Secretary of the Army Brucker, to whom the governor of the Canal Zone reported. He objected. I therefore did not go to the President and that was my mistake. Trouble did develop. The American flag was torn down, a U. S. Information Office was stoned, and anti-American hostility gained ground in Panama, to burst forth again in the Johnson administration.

A year after I had met with Secretary Brucker, just before the trouble erupted in Panama, the Secretary decided that I had been right, but it was too late for the President to take action. To do so in the face of a confrontation would have created the belief that the way to get the United States to take action was to cause turmoil and become insulting. So months had to pass before remedial action could be taken, and even the changes made then merely postponed the difficulty for a few years.

I can think of no other time when I would have been justified in going directly to the President. President Eisenhower understood and accepted my position on this, for he knew very well that confidants of Presidents, by interposing themselves between the President and department heads, had often disrupted good relations and injured the confidence and trust that should prevail between the President and the principal members of the executive branch of the government.

My brother and I agreed that on certain assignments, such as my work as special ambassador to Latin America, I would be in the public eye and would at times have to hold press conferences, especially when I was making studies in specific countries. In all other ways, however, I would maintain what Franklin Roosevelt once called "a passion for anonymity."

To avoid any possible criticism of my special relationship and also to maintain the inner feeling that I did not work for the President and was therefore not subservient to him, I accepted no compensation from the government for my work in Latin America, on the President's Commission on Organization, for speech writing or for special assignments. Normally, part-time consultants are paid ($117 per day now, plus their actual expenses). I accepted only travel by government planes and cars.

Even this once exposed me to criticism by a senator. My daughter and I had driven to Wisconsin to relax and fish prior to what was obviously going to be a tiring trip to the five republics of Central America, Panama, and Puerto Rico. It was to be a strenuous tour, one filled with personal tension, because Vice-President Nixon had been humiliated and threatened in Venezuela only a month or so before, and intelligence reports from Guatemala and Panama were not favorable for my trip. Suddenly, for reasons I have never understood, the date for my departure was set forward, the first stop being Panama. There was no time to drive back to Washington to begin the trip. So a small government plane, an Aerocommander, picked me up in Wisconsin and took me to Washington; I hired a driver to return my car. Senator Proxmire criticized the President for having a government plane transport his brother. Keeping in mind the lesson on issuing corrective statements I had learned in the Hoover administration, I said nothing, but David Lawrence and other columnists came to my defense; Senator Proxmire did not apologize but did insert the David Lawrence column in the Congressional Record!

Most Presidents of the United States have had one or more confidants. Franklin Roosevelt holds the record for the number and diversity of men on whom he relied for counsel. The press has always shown great interest in confidants and I was no exception. Newspaper columnists and television commentators, mindful of the roles of Colonel House, Harry Hopkins, Clark Clifford, and others, found it difficult to accept my role for what it actually was. In a cover story in the September 8, 1958, issue of *Time* magazine, the editors wrote:

> The guest followed the servant across the hall to the spacious south bedroom occupied by the President of the United States. He entered and found Dwight Eisenhower in his shirt sleeves, already wading through the morning papers and his usual breakfast steak (rare). At the sight of the visitor, Ike's face broke into a grin of particular welcome . . . within seconds the two were deep in informal, give-and-take discussion covering the breadth of U.S. policy. . . . The special guest was Milton Stover Eisenhower, president of Johns Hopkins University, top flight educator, a government pro of thirty years' experience, youngest of the brothers Eisenhower and the man nearest to Ike in all the world. Dwight Eisenhower's inner circle includes many top aides. Yet none of these friends approaches Milton Eisenhower in the heart and mind

of his brother Dwight. The relationship between Dwight and Milton can be traced in part—but only in part—to specific examples of his influence on Ike's political career and presidential administration.

Time editors asserted, "Having contributed to Dwight Eisenhower's basic middle-road political philosophy, Milton helped persuade Ike to run for President in 1952." Anyone who understood our intimate relationship of more than two decades would know that I would not presume to do such a thing; at most I would discuss alternatives for my brother to consider.

"Milton advised and encouraged Dwight Eisenhower to go before the United Nations in 1953 with his historic atoms-for-peace proposal," the *Time* article said. This statement was based on the erroneous assumption that I was behaving as another Harry Hopkins. The decision for the atoms-for-peace speech was the President's and his alone. My only part was to work with C. D. Jackson, who helped the President draft the talk.

The editors were kind enough to say that, "By any standard, Milton Eisenhower is well qualified for his role," and then, departing from its view of me as another Harry Hopkins, conceded, "It is in striving . . . for objectivity that Milton Eisenhower is most valuable to his brother." *Time* correctly quoted me as saying, "In this lonely job it is good for him to have someone who is a good listener and a sympathetic friend who can serve as a sounding board." And *Time* was also right in saying, "[Their] conversations run the whole range of policy problems and mutual personal interests. . . . In their policy talks neither Eisenhower is yes man to the other. . . . The President thoroughly respects Milton's experience and skill, but far from blindly. Once when Milton was uninhibitedly polishing a presidential speech, Ike took one look and said gently but firmly, 'That's fine. But that's not what I want to say.'" (I don't know how *Time* got this quote, but I heard it many times as Emmet Hughes, or Malcolm Moos, or C. D. Jackson, or Arthur Larson, or I prepared an initial draft for the President only to have him revise our copy a dozen times. He had an irrepressible urge to revise any copy placed before him, including his own. Even when he gave a copy of a speech to Jim Hagerty for release to the press, he kept making alterations, so reporters had to follow each speech and insert changes in their mimeographed copies.)

Demaree Bess, in a long article in the *Saturday Evening Post*, September 17, 1955, came a bit closer to my White House role:

> In Washington today there is one person-to-person relationship which seems to have no exact parallel in the history of American politics. That is the relationship between President Eisenhower and his youngest brother, Milton. . . . Dr. Milton Eisenhower has publicly stated that he will not accept any paid office under his brother's administration. . . . And yet Milton Eisenhower has served the present administration in so many ways and is known to be so close to the President that his influence has been compared to that of two previous famous presidential confidants: Woodrow Wilson's Colonel Edward M. House and Franklin D. Roosevelt's Harry Hopkins. . . . Most American Chief Executives have felt the need for congenial unofficial counselors to whom they could turn for consultation, and President Eisenhower has found such an intimate in his own brother. The President [has] an exceptional respect for his youngest brother's judgment and for his knowledge of government. . . . Once General Eisenhower introduced him as "the brightest member of our family. That is no idle compliment. It is the plain truth." . . . What makes this brotherly relationship unique is that Milton Eisenhower possesses none of the driving political ambitions of such former presidential confidants . . . as Harry Hopkins, either for a place in the show window or for power behind the scenes. . . . He has a pronounced aversion to . . . those who take delight in bypassing Cabinet officers. . . . Among the scores of chores which Milton Eisenhower has undertaken for the President since January, 1953, I have not been able to find one instance in which he failed to work through channels with the officials formally concerned.

Robert Donovan in his book, *The Inside Story*,[24] understood my role as a listener and questioner, rather than as an advocate, when he wrote: "When Milton is in Washington the two will sit together in the President's bedroom for hours while the President grinds out his ideas on different subjects. This is the process the President uses habitually to clarify his thinking and plot the line where he is and where he wants to go."

Perhaps the most precise interpretation was expressed by Frederick W. Collins in an article, "How to Be a President's Brother," in the August 23, 1959, issue of the New York *Times Magazine*:

> A unique role is played in this government by Dr. Milton S. Eisenhower, the President's brother. Day in and day out, whether visit-

ing at the White House . . . or traveling to Latin America . . . or flying to the Soviet Union, he conducts a subtle and delicate operation. . . . The best judgment is that, through a complicated array of circumstances, Milton has become perhaps the most helpful member of the multitude, official and personal, around his brother. . . . A President must have at least one friend, and this friend must know what he is talking about when he discusses public affairs. . . . The only person who really qualifies is Milton. He has no vested interest. He is not subservient. He owes nothing to any one element of the national society, and thus can talk without partisanship or localities—without, to use one of the President's words, parochialism. . . . His discussions with the President have one quality the President considers priceless—inviolate privacy. . . . When Dwight Eisenhower became President of the United States, he had a brother who had a sense of the world, a detailed knowledge of the Federal bureaucracy, and special competence in the fields of agriculture and education. . . . Theirs is a relationship in which neither has had to finish a sentence. . . . Those who have watched them work together report that Milton considers his older brother to have one of the most logical minds in the world. . . . The Twenty-second amendment means that his career as a brother of the President cannot continue after January, 1961. But he has served other administrations than the Eisenhower one. Unique as his relationship to this Presidency may be, he could well go on rendering distinguished service to another President not his brother.

Late in 1955 and early in 1956, before President Eisenhower, still concerned about his heart attack, announced his decision about running for a second term, nearly every columnist, every radio and television commentator, speculated on possible Republican candidates in 1956. Normally four or five were mentioned, and my name was among them. A special friend of mine, Roscoe Drummond, talented columnist for the *Christian Science Monitor*, thinking that too many Republicans considered me a left-wing liberal, wrote, on January 20, 1956, a column, widely copied, to show that I, like the President, was a philosophic centrist on questions of human values but a conservative on matters of fiscal policy; indeed I had often expressed the fear that most extremists in the liberal area, impervious to the realities of revenues and expenditures, did not realize that the most humane, the most liberal programs can be demolished by reckless fiscal management. I suppose this view is why both President Eisenhower and I usually have been referred to as middle-roaders.

Drummond wrote: "There are three reasons why we are going to be hearing more, rather than less, about Dr. Milton Eisenhower . . . during the coming months. Milton Eisenhower is the closest, most trusted, most influential adviser to the President. He is spending more time working with his brother than ever. If the President decides not to run, Milton, regardless of his own wishes, will be in the political picture."

During this spate of speculation about possible Republican candidates, the question came up in one of the President's press conferences. He said he was glad the question had been asked, for he wanted the public to know that he and I were in complete agreement that under no circumstances would I become a candidate if his decision when given was a negative one. The Eisenhowers, he said, did not seek a dynasty. On a later occasion, to a friend, he remarked that if all other considerations did not keep me from entering the political arena a final and compelling one would: Milton, he said, refused to ride on anyone else's coattails, including his. "He's sensitive," he added. "As a candidate, he would feel that he would be identified not as a personality in his own right but as a brother, and that would crucify him."

Though many years have passed since I worked closely with President Eisenhower, I do not consider it appropriate to reveal the substance of our confidential discussions as some others have done in their diaries or memoirs. The exceptions to this pertain to personal situations and to those of an official nature on which even today there continue to be serious misunderstandings. I hope I can clarify some of these.

During the campaign of 1952 and the early years of his presidency, nothing troubled President Eisenhower so much as the issue of McCarthyism. He loathed McCarthy as an individual and as an elected official who, using the immunity of the Senate, blighted the lives of hundreds of good American citizens. "Guilt by association" became rampant. Because President Eisenhower did not publicly denounce McCarthy, some critics mistakenly felt that he either supported him or was intimidated by him.

Even such a respected newspaperman as William Lawrence, in

his book, *Six Presidents, Too Many Wars*,[12] says that President Eisenhower never spoke in support of General George Marshall after McCarthy had attacked him. This statement by an honest newspaperman surprises me. As military leader, candidate, and President of the United States, my brother time after time expressed his unbounded admiration for General Marshall. In war and peace the relationship between these two men, though not characterized by the intimate emotional attachment normally associated with true friendship, was one of mutual and complete admiration.

I was long deeply bothered by McCarthyism, not only because of the senator's despicable methods and his patent hypocrisy but also because he was seriously injuring the reputation of the United States throughout the world. In my fury I discussed with the President my belief that the time had come for him directly to attack McCarthy. Calmly he pointed out two basic convictions of his: first, as President he should never deal critically with a single personality, only with principles; second, if he attacked a member of the Senate, that body might rally behind its member with the result that the President would make a martyr of McCarthy. He would vastly increase McCarthy's own publicity appeal. Instead, he wrote and spoke time and again of the fundamental American concept that all men were innocent until proved guilty, that charges of guilt by association should be universally condemned. In a two-column boxed article on the front page of the *Herald Tribune* he set forth his statement of principles in such clear language that he hoped the nation and the world would understand his attitude on the McCarthy problem. Once he said to me: "Only the Senate can censure and destroy McCarthy."

On one occasion, when McCarthy had demanded the withdrawal from American libraries abroad of books which he said contained Communist propaganda, the President went to Dartmouth College and delivered his "Don't join the book-burners" address.

There is no doubt that McCarthy wanted the President to engage in a personal feud with him, believing that this would enhance his own influence. When all else failed to achieve this result he turned on me. Evidently he thought if he attacked the President's brother, who was known to have the President's affection, he would blast open the President's ability to become enraged and thus cause him to depart from his firm policy.

One night when I was having a large reception at Penn State, Senator McCarthy by radio spent thirty minutes attacking me, stopping short of calling me a Communist but certainly leaving no doubt that he considered me to be an evil influence in government and favoring policies that helped the Soviet Union in the Cold War. When the reception was over friends repeated to me nearly word for word all he had said.

The next morning I flew with my daughter and her friend Ann Brownell (daughter of Attorney General Herbert Brownell) to Land-O-Lakes, Wisconsin, where my father-in-law was vacationing. That evening he gave a dinner party for thirty persons in the main dining room of the hotel. McCarthy and his wife were in the dining room, far removed from our table. When he saw me he came over and tapped me on the shoulder. I stood up and deliberately turned my back to the folks at the table. McCarthy threw his arms around me and hugged me, then vigorously shook hands and said how happy he was to see me in Wisconsin. I refused to introduce him to anyone, turned back to my place, and sat down. He then proceeded to go round the table and speak to every one of the thirty guests, though he had not previously met any of them. When he came to Ann Brownell he leaned over and kissed her on the cheek. This made her so ill that she left the table for a time to recover. This single incident is to me irrefutable proof of the man's hypocrisy and of my belief that his attack on me was designed to provoke my brother into an attack on him. There is an old saying about a contest between an individual and a skunk which, though true, is too crude to state here.

In the end, I conceded to President Eisenhower that his method had been the correct one and I had been wrong. The Senate eventually censured Senator McCarthy, his influence waned rapidly, then collapsed.

Another situation in which there had been much misunderstanding involved Emmet Hughes, who for a time helped President Eisenhower with speeches and later became critical of the Administration. Hughes was a beautiful writer, capable of purple prose or memorable phrases. His difficulty was that he could not write what the President wanted to say, only what his own views dictated. Normally the President would outline to Hughes (or anyone else helping with a speech or federal document) what he wished to say and then the drafting would begin.

If the Hughes draft departed from what the President wanted, the two would meet again and the President would ask for revisions. But Hughes could not revise. He might insert a subjective clause containing the point the President wished to make, but it would be obscured in the total impact of the manuscript.

This was not always true, for on one important matter Hughes agreed completely with the President, namely, that because of the President's personal and friendly relations with other world leaders he was in an especially favorable position to work with them in building the structure of permanent peace. As Supreme Commander of Allied Forces in World War II and as first Supreme Commander of NATO forces, he had become universally known and had developed intimate friendships with the leaders of many nations. His innate honesty, an enviable quality in a leader, was never doubted. It was known that he hated war. Who knew better the horrors of war? So as he began moving with passionate interest and devotion to help lead the world into an era of peace, his integrity and selflessness were never doubted. Hughes saw this as a great plus; he, too, felt President Eisenhower was in the key position to work systematically and patiently for peace. So there was no difficulty when he and I worked with the President on his address before the Council of the Organization of American States on April 12, 1953, the address that propelled me into eight years of labor in the Latin American area. Nor was there any trouble in Hughes's helping the President with the address, "The Chance for Peace," delivered before the American Society of Newspaper Editors on April 16, 1963. Much of the poetic phrasing in that talk was suggested by Hughes:

"Every gun that is made, every warship launched, every rocket fired, signifies, in the final sense, a theft from those who hunger and are not fed, those who are cold and are not clothed.

"This world in arms is not spending money alone.

"It is spending the sweat of its laborers, the genius of its scientists, the hopes of its children.

"The cost of one modern bomber is this: a modern brick school in more than thirty cities. It is two electric power plants, each serving a town of 60,000 population. It is two fine, fully equipped hospitals. It is some fifty miles of concrete highway. We pay for a single fighter plane with half a million bushels of wheat. We pay for a single destroyer with new homes that could have housed more than 8,000 people.

"This, I repeat, is the best way of life to be found on the road the world has been taking.

"This is not a way of life at all, in any true sense. Under the cloud of threatening war, it is humanity hanging from a cross of iron."

It was C. D. Jackson, not Hughes as some have said, who went with the President to a conference with Churchill on the island of Bermuda and worked with the President in the preparation of the famous "atoms for peace" address delivered before the General Assembly of the United Nations on December 8, 1953. The President revised the address, to my certain knowledge, six times, but there was no conflict between him and Jackson.

I have always thought that my brother's most eloquent address was that made in the Guildhall of London following the victory over Hitler, an address that contained no word from any aide: "Humility must always be the portion of any man who receives acclaim earned in the blood of his followers and the sacrifices of his friends." But the United Nations address was significant, beautifully stated, and persuasive. After picturing accurately the atomic power of the United States and the growing knowledge of the atomic art in other nations, including the Soviet Union, and describing the horrible consequences of atomic war, the President proposed that the nations of the world begin to transfer fissionable material to a world Atomic Energy Commission, under the aegis of the United Nations, with the understanding that the scientists of the world would co-operate in making this ultimate source of energy serve the true human needs of all countries.

Trouble between the President and Hughes soon developed. Hughes considered himself to be an expert in international affairs. He differed constantly with Secretary Dulles, yet yearned for a top post in the Department of State. The President became irritated as time and again Hughes found it impossible to prepare even in draft form what had been requested. He began referring to Hughes as a "word carpenter." So inquiries were begun looking to the transfer of Hughes to the State Department, but the most that Secretary Dulles was prepared to offer was a minor spot in the vast and beautiful woodwork of State. Hughes left in a huff. Later he wrote books, bitterly critical of the Eisenhower administration, and especially of Secretary Dulles, an attitude that was completely opposite from the glowing things he had said as he roamed through the White House offices during his short tenure there.

Presidential press conferences, useful in keeping the American people informed, have been a painful chore to some Chief Executives, a joyful experience to others. President Coolidge, dour and normally aloof, seemingly enjoyed press conferences and maintained cordial relations with members of the press corps. He would summon to his office only the correspondents who were stationed in the press room, make an announcement, sometimes lightened with a curious New England wit, and then dismiss them. Hoover was somewhat wary of the press, especially as the depression worsened. Roosevelt, a master in dealing with the press, was invariably in command of the situation. He was gay, humorous, informative. Bill Lawrence has said that in his twelve years in the White House Roosevelt held an average of more than eighty news conferences annually—a figure that is even more astounding if one notes that President Nixon held only four news conferences in and out of Washington during 1970.

President Eisenhower normally held a news conference each week. He was the first to open the press conference to television. Attendance by reporters and commentators had become so large that most meetings were held in a large room in the Executive Office Building or occasionally in the East Room of the White House.

It is understandable, I think, that historians and others should have decided that President Eisenhower often had difficulty in expressing himself, charging that his syntax was unfathomable. This view was based on his responses to press conference questions. The President, always honest, seeking never to mislead anyone, would think out loud as he considered and replied to specific questions. He would start a sentence, stop, begin again, and sometimes ramble on until he felt he had correctly stated his view and had properly added all essential qualifying statements. He was very conscious that his remarks could have a profound impact on foreign affairs, the economy, and other sensitive issues.

A reading of the verbatim accounts* of Eisenhower's press con-

---

* The stenographic records were never edited to correct syntax, rhetoric, or even punctuation. This was a departure from previous and subsequent practice in the White House.

ferences would surely cause an Archibald MacLeish to raise his brows. Actually, however, President Eisenhower wrote with logic and clarity, with good choice of words, and often with eloquence. His formal speeches and state documents were invariably his own. Even when he spoke extemporaneously after having had time to get his mind in order his presentations rang with sincerity, there was no problem about syntax, and his thoughts came across precisely as he intended.

I saw him write parts of his first book, *Crusade in Europe*, in longhand. He wrote on yellow legal-size paper, sometimes at my home, sometimes riding in a car, often at his desk. That book is a classic.

I gave little help in his writing *Mandate for Change* and *Waging Peace*—I merely reviewed the final manuscripts. I saw him follow his regular practice in preparing these books, namely, revising each page many times. Only when he wrote *At Ease* did I see him dictate first drafts, each of which, as usual, went through numerous revisions.

My principal contribution to speech writing was an unusual and amusing one. After the President had told a writer—Hughes, Jackson, Larson, Moos, Lodge, or others—what he wanted to say and a first draft was placed before him, he might find it disorganized. Busy with other pressing affairs of state, he might have a feeling of helplessness in starting his own revision, so often he would call me on the White House telephone in my study at home and say he wished to send a draft over to me for suggestions. I knew what this meant. He wanted me to rearrange the material so that it started at an appropriate point and moved logically to a conclusion. He would send the draft to me by messenger. Often I would work from eight in the evening to one or two in the morning to produce a new triple-spaced draft. Seldom did I add new material, for I did not possess it at my residence. I nearly always rewrote the speech completely, giving it a normal progression in fact and thought and easily using the President's own phrases which were not different from my own. Early the next morning this draft would go to the President by messenger. He would then begin his revision and when he had finished one would have thought that a dozen chickens with dirty feet had found delight in scratching on every page. Mrs. Ann Whitman—obviously a skilled cryptographer—would then retype this draft, which would go back to the original office with suggestions for insertions.

I think Dr. Malcolm Moos, former professor of political science at

The Johns Hopkins University and until recently president of the University of Minnesota, gave the President especially effective help. He is a highly educated man and is politically wise. His knowledge of history, literature, and government is unusual. His ability to quote authorities without reference to original sources always amazed me. His major problem was that he did not uniformly satisfy the President's passion for absolute logic in whatever he said in an address, a letter, a State of the Union message, or other state documents. Any help I gave on the Moos drafts was fairly easy, for the subject matter and ideas were usually complete and pertinent. Rearranging that kind of material was an easy task.

Anyone who helps with a speech is to some extent also helping make policy and program suggestions. That is inevitable. However, when President Eisenhower had revised each document numerous times, the final product was his and his alone.

It has been said ad nauseam that President Eisenhower completely neglected his responsibility as head of his political party. It is true, I think, that he was one of the most non-partisan Chief Executives in history, ranking in this regard with Washington. It is also true that he was discouraged by the attitude and behavior of the Republicans in Congress during his first two years in the White House when the Congress was in control of his own party. The Republicans in Congress had for twenty years opposed the President of the United States and they found it difficult to break the habit. Even though he conferred with them regularly, the legislators failed to realize that a time for constructive co-operation had come. Also pertinent is the fact that President Eisenhower never, as I recall, made an official decision or proposal that was formed merely to aid a vested-interest group. Idealistically, perhaps, but in my view quite correctly, he formed each judgment on the basis of what he felt would be the best for the United States as a whole and for all its people.

But it is not true that he was indifferent to his responsibilities to the Republican Party. He believed in the two-party system. His preference was for a Republican-controlled Congress, but with not too great a majority, his conviction being that sounder legislation would result from adversary considerations in congressional committees and debates in the House and Senate. And though he was surely not a flaming left-winger, neither was he as conservative as were many of the Republicans in the House and Senate. So he set out to try to rebuild the party, a task with many aspects. He asked me to help him in one of these, for he wished to encourage younger, intelligent men and women in all the states—persons who had already established reputations in business, law, education, and social affairs—to begin rebuilding the party at the precinct level, to attain state office in the electoral processes, and in time to enter the Congress and the Senate. So with the help of Postmaster General Arthur Summerfield, Governor Sherman Adams, Thomas Stephens—the able, dependable, and politically astute appointments secretary to the President—we set up a continuing series of black-tie dinners at the White House. To each of these we brought from a single state some fifteen to eighteen persons who met the standards the President had set. I attended most of these. They were a delight and highly educational. They followed a pattern. We met in the President's oval study on the family floor for a cocktail, then proceeded to the state dining room for dinner, and finally to the Blue Room for coffee and round-table discussions. My guess is that over a period of years about five hundred individuals were involved in these happy and useful meetings. The results were not all the President hoped for, but they did make a contribution. Able young leaders became active in party affairs throughout the nation, much to the disgust of some old-timers such as Senator Duff of Pennsylvania, who feared my friends in Pennsylvania were preparing me to run against him in the next election. Nothing was further from the President's mind and mine. As time went on and the President had to deal with a Democratic Congress for six of his eight years in the White House, more Republican governors were elected, such as William Scranton of Pennsylvania. For some years Republican governors were in a majority in the states. To the House and Senate came new faces, mostly of moderate persuasion, including a man of great intellect, charm, and judgment, Charles Percy of Illinois—one my brother and I helped directly.

While the President's efforts at reform of the Republican Party were not an unqualified success, I think the misunderstanding about his attitude stems from the fact that for six years he had to co-operate with leading Democrats in the Congress to get bills adopted and to have presidential vetoes sustained. Indeed, I suspect President Eisenhower

holds a historic record: only two of his vetoes in eight years were overridden and both of these were the inevitable and undefeatable pork-
barrel bills, an atrocious congressional practice that should be stopped.

In his role as party leader President Eisenhower never said much
publicly, but in *Mandate for Change*[25] he wrote: "I have never enjoyed the luxury of being head of a majority party. Perhaps the leader
of such a party can be uniformly partisan. But the leader of a minority
party has a different set of references." Indeed he does. In the United
States the Democratic Party has by far the largest membership, independent voters represent a significant influence, and the Republican
Party is a minority. For a Republican to be elected, he must be more
than a political partisan. To serve successfully as President, he must
avoid what George Reedy refers to as the monarchic complex and the
constant use of assertive demands; he must win by persuasion and co-
operation.

A misunderstanding that has persisted to this day has to do with
the relationship of Eisenhower and Nixon. In choosing his running mate,
Ike relied on political advisers, but from the moment that Dwight Eisenhower was sworn in as President and Richard Nixon as Vice-President,
a friendly relationship developed. The President at once began placing
a variety of responsibilities on the Vice-President. In Cabinet meetings,
at the conclusion of a major discussion when all points of view had been
expressed, the President expected the Vice-President to present a balanced summary of the various points of view and alternative suggestions, which he did with consummate skill. He never recommended
what decision should be made, respectfully leaving this to the President.
He was made head of several important study commissions. Indeed,
President Eisenhower, possibly telling no one but me, began grooming
Nixon for the presidency, even at a time when the President was in the
best of health and a second term seemed certain. The President sent
Nixon on foreign good-will and study trips which caused the Vice-
President to travel some 160,000 miles to fifty-four nations. His con-
fidence in Nixon was unquestioned.

The President honestly felt, perhaps naïvely, that the vice-presidency was not a politically potent steppingstone to the presidency itself, save through the death of the President. So he discussed with
Nixon, prior to the 1956 campaign, the possibility of Nixon's giving up

the vice-presidency and accepting a high Cabinet post. He emphasized that the choice was Nixon's. I can understand Nixon's concern about this. He was more politically minded than the President, realized that his position was wholly dependent on the President's personal wishes, and therefore tortured himself, as he has written, in deciding what his answer should be.

I write with absolute confidence about this, for my brother and I discussed it at length. He explained to me, word for word, what he had said to the Vice-President, and he was deeply concerned that Nixon had not fully understood his reasoning or his motive. I was not as confident as my brother that Nixon would make a good President or even that he could be elected, if nominated. I felt that Nixon was so steeped in partisan politics that he lacked a deep and abiding philosophy that would guide him carefully through the shoals of the hourly and sometimes treacherous situations a President must handle. I have never had sympathy for the politician who takes polls of constituent opinion and then acts accordingly, for, I repeat, the true task of statesmanship is to do what one deeply believes is right and then try to persuade the people of the correctness of that decision.

My brother was aggrieved that I did not share his high opinion of the Vice-President. This remained in his mind long after the Eisenhower-Nixon ticket was swept back into office. Early in 1958 he arranged for the Vice-President and me to meet often to discuss United States-Latin American problems. We found ourselves reasoning together with no difficulty. Within weeks after the Vice-President's trip to many South American nations which nearly ended in disaster in Venezuela, where Communists sought to embarrass and harm him because of a triumph he had had over their fellow travelers earlier in Brazil, Uruguay, and Argentina, the President had me resume my Latin American work, this time in Central America, Panama, and the American Commonwealth of Puerto Rico. On my return, Nixon and I again found ourselves in agreement on all vital issues between the United States and Latin America. He joined in Cabinet approval of my formal reports on this question in 1953 and 1958, reports which became accepted United States policy.

But my brother, though happy about this camaraderie that was developing between Nixon and me, was not satisfied that I respected the Vice-President to the degree he felt I should. So he asked me to accompany the Vice-President, Mrs. Nixon, and others to the Soviet Union in July 1959, where our principal official task was to open the United States exposition in Moscow, but actually we were official guests of the Soviet government, which involved long discussions in the Kremlin and trips to Leningrad, Sverdlovsk, and Novosibirsk, then home by way of Warsaw.

The Vice-President made me unofficial vice-chairman of the group, so that he, Mrs. Nixon, and I were the guests of the Soviet leaders in their famous dachas and in all critical meetings. Our work together impressed upon me the intellectual flexibility of the Vice-President, and I developed an affectionate regard for him and Mrs. Nixon. I also had some of the most interesting and dramatic experiences of my life, experiences which have caused me for years to study the Soviet Union and make two more trips to that vast country.

One day, when the Nixons and I were guests at Khrushchev's dacha on the Moscow River, he took us for a ride in his speed boat, stopping half a dozen times to introduce us to some of the fifty thousand persons who were spending the Sunday holiday swimming and picnicking along the river. That incident and others later convinced me that Khrushchev, unlike his predecessor, craved above all else the applause of his own people. I felt this was a hopeful sign, for to gain acceptance he had to reduce some of the severe restraints imposed upon the people, stop the wholesale killing that characterized the regime of Stalin, replace fear with hope, and begin to satisfy the desires of the people for more consumer goods, better education, and a better life. At the conclusion of the hour on the river we had luncheon under an outdoor canopy on the grounds of the dacha. We sat down—Chairman and Mrs. Khrushchev, Vice-President and Mrs. Nixon, Ambassador and Mrs. Llewellyn Thompson, Assistant Secretary of State Foy Kohler, and two interpreters, one ours, one Khrushchev's. That luncheon, with never an interruption in conversation, lasted six and a half hours, until nine-thirty at night. The conversation was spirited and candid. Nixon was skillful in dealing with many knotty problems.

The most publicized event in our visit to the Soviet Union was the famous kitchen debate between Khrushchev and Nixon.

The drama began when we called on Khrushchev at his office in the Kremlin. We were scarcely seated when, with some heat, Khrushchev told the Vice-President that the Soviet Union regarded the Captive Nations Resolution passed by the United States Congress as a serious "provocation." Nixon replied that "provocation" was the wrong word. The Captive Nations Resolution was an expression of indignation, emanating from the American people as a whole. Millions of American citizens, many of them emigrants from Eastern Europe who still had relatives in those countries, were resentful of the fact that their relatives and millions of others had by force been absorbed into a system they did not select or want. They, like all Americans, believed that human beings everywhere should have the right of free choice. But the Captive Nations Resolution did not imply that the United States would intervene or that we would support revolutions in the occupied nations if they broke out; it only expressed our moral support for those whose freedom had been violated.

The second act in this play took place at the United States exposition in a small television studio which was demonstrating color television, a recent American development. Khrushchev, something of a ham actor, though shrewd, knowledgeable, and never lacking for words, especially when he faced a radio microphone or television camera, launched into a boastful speech. Within seven years, he said, the Soviet Union would be on an economic level with the United States. Then the Soviet Union would pass the United States, waving to us as it did so. "Then, if you wish," he said, "we can stop and say: 'Please follow up.'" Again he castigated the Captive Nations Resolution of the United States Congress. He ended his televised "greeting" by wrapping his arms around a Soviet workman and asking, "Does this man look like a slave laborer? With men with such spirit, how can we lose?"

The Vice-President, conscious of being a guest in a foreign country, was restrained. "Your remarks," he said, "are in the tradition of what we have come to expect—sweeping and extemporaneous. Later on we will both have an opportunity to speak and consequently I will not comment on the various points that you have raised, except to say this —this color television is one of the most advanced developments in communication we have." He added with a smile, "After all, you do not know everything." Khrushchev retorted, "If I don't know everything, you don't know anything about Communism except to fear it."

This ended the second act of the play and created great expectations for the third.

From the television studio we walked a short distance to a typical

American worker's house. In this brief interval Nixon decided that he would not again permit serious charges to be made without adequate response. Being a guest must not deter him.

The house we entered was a masterpiece of showmanship. It was a six-room structure, sliced down the middle and separated with a corridor of about ten feet between the two parts. On one side were two bedrooms and a bath, on the other, a living room, a kitchen, and a dining room. A worker for General Motors might have been living in it; he would have a car and probably two children in school. The kitchen was modern, with electric dishwasher, electric stove, and of course a refrigerator. The kitchen was custom-designed to fit the architectural arrangement of that single dwelling.

At once Khrushchev attacked the United States for its wasteful methods, for the inefficiency of having custom-made kitchens when mass production would be cheaper. He said it was the competitive spirit of families in America, each trying to outdo the other, that would enable the Soviet Union soon to surpass the United States.

(On November 17, 1956, in a Kremlin reception for Western ambassadors, Khrushchev had said, "We will bury you!" This remark had been persistently interpreted as a threat to the free world, but Khrushchev repeatedly explained that he meant only that Communism had more vitality than capitalism and thus would outproduce Western nations, especially the United States. His comment in the kitchen debate was a repetition of what he had said a dozen times.)

Nixon was prepared for Khrushchev this time. As I recall, his main theme was that the private competitive enterprise system would always outproduce socialized production, since it decentralized decisions, increased the capacity and responsibility of workers, and gave them greater pride in what they were doing. If every family wanted a house of different architectural style and internal arrangement from all others, that was its privilege. That was an inseparable part of freedom. This contrasted, he said, with the monotonous sameness of Soviet apartments, the style and arrangement dictated by central authority.

But the debate did not remain on a high level.

Khrushchev, waving his arms at the house (it cost fourteen thousand dollars), exclaimed, "You think the Russian people will be dumfounded to see these things . . . all you have to do to get a house is to be born in the Soviet Union . . . in America if you didn't have a dollar you have the right to choose between sleeping in a house or on the pavement!" His tirade was extensive.

"If you were in our Senate," interposed Nixon, "we would call you a filibusterer. You do all the talking and don't let anyone else talk!" Then in an effort to be conciliatory he added, "You can learn from us and we can learn from you. There must be a free exchange. Let the people choose the kind of house . . . the kind of ideas they want."

Nixon turned the debate from housing to more fundamental matters. He suggested it would be better to compete in the relative merits of houses and washing machines than in the strength of rockets.

"Your generals say, 'Let's compete in rockets,'" Khrushchev shouted. "In this respect we can show you something!"

Nixon with some heat said that one side could not put an ultimatum to another. "I shall ask you about this later," he said in an effort to conclude a discussion before hundreds of witnesses.

"Who is raising an ultimatum?"

"We will discuss that later."

Khrushchev, pressing against Nixon, exclaimed, "Why not go on with it now while people are listening? Let your correspondents compare watches and see who is filibustering." He was still referring to the talk about ultimatums, which he ostensibly considered a threat. "We, too, are giants," he shouted, stabbing a finger into Nixon's chest. "You want to threaten. We will answer threats with threats . . . we have means at our disposal. Ours are better than yours."

Nixon suggested that who was best was not material. "My point was that in today's world it is immaterial which of the two great countries at any particular moment has the advantage. In war, these advantages are illusory. . . . The government of the United States is for peace. . . . To have peace . . . there must be a sitting down around a table. There must be discussion. Each side must find areas where it looks at the other point of view."

These few excerpts from a heated discussion that lasted for half an hour do not convey the intensity, the emotion, or the sheer drama that existed in that workman's house on July 24, 1959, in Sokolniki Park in Moscow. Later Nixon, in his book *Six Crises*,[26] wrote: "As we walked away from the model to view the rest of the [American] exhibition, I began to feel the effect of the tremendous tension of the past two hours. Holding back when you have something you want to say is far more wearing on the system than letting yourself go. I felt like a fighter wearing sixteen-ounce gloves and bound by the Marquis of Queensberry rules, up against a bare-knuckled slugger who had gouged, kneed, and kicked. I was not sure I had held my own. But two widely different sources of opinion buoyed me up on this score . . . a correspondent for the United Press . . . whispered in my ear, 'good going, Mr. Vice President,' and . . . later . . . Mikoyan [said] . . . 'you were very skillful in debate.' "

To the best of my knowledge, the debates in the television studio and in the workman's house were the only times modern political leaders conducted what may loosely be called official discussions in front of a large audience, including newspapermen.

I felt that Nixon had, on the whole, come off fairly well.

As we traveled about the country we soon learned that everywhere we went goons (young Communist agents) were strategically located to ask questions. Nearly always a goon would pose two questions. The first pertained to an incident which happened on our first day in Moscow. The Vice-President, an early riser, had left the United States Embassy early on our first morning to take a stroll toward the central part of the city. With him was only one Secret Service agent. The two came to a farmers' market. At once he was recognized and many persons gathered around him. They complained about their inability to obtain tickets to the United States exposition which we were there formally to open. Against our wishes, the Soviet government had decided to charge admission to the exhibit but had distributed tickets to faithful members of the Party so that for a week or more no one else could obtain a ticket. But the Vice-President, not understanding Russian, thought they were saying they could not afford to buy tickets, so he started to hand money to the head of the farmers' market with instructions to distribute tickets among the people. Just then an interpreter from the embassy caught up with the Vice-President, gave him a correct interpretation, and the incident seemed closed. But suddenly, by radio, television, and questions by goons at every stop, it was charged that the Vice-President had tried to "bribe Soviet workers!"

The second point invariably brought up by the goons had to do with the Captive Nations Resolution our Congress had passed just before our trip to Moscow. The goons were adroit in making their charges in loud voices that all could hear and then in preventing the people from hearing Nixon's response. An interpreter would turn to the Vice-President and explain in English the goon's charge about the bribe, Nixon would answer, but as the interpreter started to explain in Russian what Nixon had said, the goon would in a loud voice begin a tirade about the Captive Nations Resolution. It soon became evident that Nixon's replies were not being heard by the people. So I suggested to him that wherever we went, sometimes among as many as ten thousand workers at one time, he give one standard answer, namely, that before he left the Soviet Union he would speak on national television and would explain the truth about the charges. This he did.

The Nixon speech to the people of the Soviet Union before our departure for Warsaw was calm and well balanced. He, Ambassador Thompson, Assistant Secretary Kohler, and I stayed up all night as Nixon prepared that speech and we occasionally made suggestions. The address was a blend of the basic American philosophy and achievements, on the one hand, and our desire to reach an accommodation with the Soviet Union so as to enhance the chances of peace, on the other. During the address he told the truth about the bribe charge. The next day I took a taxi, driven by a Russian, to the center of the city to buy some mementos. The interpreter with me asked the driver whether he had heard Vice-President Nixon's speech. "Oh yes," the driver said, "I have a television set and ten of my friends listened with me. We were glad to learn the truth about the bribe charge, for we knew it wasn't true!" The underground communications network in the Soviet Union is more efficient than many Soviet leaders realize.

Mrs. Nixon and I had two experiences which caused me to develop genuine affection for her and to realize that she would make a great First Lady of the United States.

In Sverdlovsk, a city of a million persons in the heart of the Urals, we had been given a large community luncheon. Immediately after the luncheon Mrs. Nixon was to visit a Russian family in an apartment and I was scheduled to go with the Vice-President and descend into the depths of a copper mine. I was tired of visiting steel plants, subways, mines, and industries, so I asked Khrushchev's protocol officer whether I might accompany Mrs. Nixon. To my surprise he agreed.

At that time nearly all apartments in the Soviet Union were communal—that is, one kitchen and one bathroom served several families, while only bedrooms were private, a situation which has now been changed. The apartment we entered, however, was for a single family, testimony to the standing of the occupant, the head cutter of the copper mine. There was a small kitchen, bathroom, tidy and well-furnished living room, and one bedroom. These quarters were occupied by the husband, his pregnant wife, and a two-year-old child. On the table of the living room were cake and wine, identical to those we had had at the official luncheon. The wife was charming; the husband was huge, strongly and beautifully built, and as expressionless as a stone statue. When I was introduced to him he formally held me at arm's length, did not smile, and merely nodded his head.

Conversation was strained until I noticed an accordion in the corner of the room. Inquiry indicated that the husband loved to play it, so Mrs. Nixon and I asked that he play some Russian folk songs. He did so with considerable skill. Fortunately we had learned one song ourselves—our Russian no doubt was terrible—so we asked that he play it. He did and we began to sing. We were joined by the interpreters who were with us. This changed the atmosphere. As we prepared to leave after half an hour and I held out my hand to say good-by, the head cutter of the mine looked at me for a moment, pulled me to him and gave me a tremendous hug, and tears flowed from his eyes.

As I thought of this later I recalled the touching scene in *War and Peace* in which a Russian soldier, under orders to shoot any Frenchman who did not keep up with the retreating forces, lifted his gun and then looked into the eyes of the doomed Frenchman; at that moment the Russian suddenly realized that there is a commonalty to mankind which transcends geography, nationality, and even war. The head cutter of the mine had never before seen an American. He was overcome when he realized that Mrs. Nixon and I were mere humans, friendly, and not too different from himself and his wife.

The other incident with Mrs. Nixon occurred at the United States exposition in Moscow. As part of our massive exhibit, we had arranged a style show, as the Soviet Union had done in New York previously. The show was given on a raised U-shaped platform outdoors, under a plastic roof. The platform was about four feet above the ground and at the center of the U was a small building where the participants could quickly change clothes. The young men and women in the show were attractive American university students; two were married and had two children, a boy about five and a girl about three. The announcer, an

American girl, spoke excellent Russian. She would explain that the young people would show how Americans dressed for work, sports, vacations, informal dinner parties, formal parties, and so on. After each such announcement the young people would come out appropriately dressed and do a brief dance, then disappear to prepare for the next scene. Always there would be about five thousand persons surrounding the platform. The climax of the exhibit came when the announcer said, "Here is what Americans wear at a formal wedding." Out would come the ushers, best man, bridesmaids, ring bearer and flower girl, all in formal dress. Finally, to the tune of Mendelssohn's Wedding March, would come the lovely bride and handsome groom. At once all the older folk in the audience would begin weeping, loudly and uncontrollably. They could remember when ceremonial events were important in their country. Mrs. Nixon also got tears in her eyes, as did I, and we turned away quickly. I saw this exhibit four times, always with the same result.

This visit was, I think, the beginning of Mr. Nixon's true understanding of the Soviet Union, climaxed by his trip to Moscow in 1972 and Brezhnev's return visit in 1973. Certainly it was the beginning of my own education on Soviet affairs which I continued on a more informal basis in the Nixon administration.

If further evidence is needed of President Eisenhower's respect for Nixon, one should recall three other facts.

First, in the 1960 campaign the Vice-President asked my brother to make only a few selected speeches, understandably not wishing to be thought of as one who was dependent on the President's great popularity; in the last weeks of the campaign, with polls being unfavorable to Nixon, President Eisenhower, especially at the urging of the citizens' organization which had been formed by Mrs. Mary Lord and Walter Williams and had served him magnificently in two campaigns, made a series of fighting speeches for the Vice-President that nearly turned the tide.

Second, he later said that his greatest disappointment in politics was the defeat of Richard Nixon in 1960.

Third, in 1968, breaking his policy of never interfering in a primary or convention fight prior to a nomination, he rose from his sickbed in the Walter Reed Hospital and, in a brief press conference, urged the Republican Party to select Richard Nixon.

As a consequence of my work at home and abroad with Vice-President Nixon, and from dinner sessions with him in my home and his, I came to feel that he was a man of broad knowledge, amazing memory, a fighter, and politically astute. I did not, however, to the disappointment of President Eisenhower, reach the conclusion that he would be a good President. Of course I did not anticipate the difficulties that would engulf the White House in 1972 and 1973, but I was concerned about the fact that the private Nixon and the public Nixon seemed to be two different persons. In private, Nixon was gracious, warmhearted, friendly, humorous, and devoid of pretense. In public, he appeared to be austere, remote, often devoid of personality, given to self-praise, and for reasons I have never understood a pictorial affirmation of the "Tricky Dicky" syndrome. Privately, he exuded integrity. Publicly, he lacked credibility.

So much has been written about the U-2 incident and Khrushchev's rude destruction of the 1960 Paris summit conference that I can add only one historic fact which even President Eisenhower in his writings did not reveal. Since the Russian spy system in the United States was such that the U.S.S.R. knew all it needed to know about our major military developments, while we had little information about theirs, the U-2 flights were begun in 1955 to provide us with essential information on Soviet military developments. About six months before the Powers plane came down in the Soviet Union, *the President at a meeting of the National Security Council suggested tentatively that the United States had obtained all the useful information it could and that the flights should be discontinued.* The heads of the State and Defense departments and of CIA felt strongly the other way, so a decision for change was postponed. When the Powers plane came down a "cover" story was issued automatically. *The President did not see it or know about it in advance.* When the facts became known the President took full responsibility, something I thought he should not do. His response to me was that if he blamed the situation on a subordinate he would have no choice but to discipline, probably discharge him, and he would not be guilty of such hypocrisy.

Khrushchev and his associates in the Kremlin had been aware of the U-2 flights almost from the beginning. They told their people nothing about them. Why, then, when one plane was brought down, was the incident highly publicized? Khrushchev could have kept it quiet. I think the answer is obvious. He wanted to prevent President Eisenhower from coming to the Soviet Union on a visit reciprocating the one he had made to the United States. Khrushchev's star was already sinking in the Soviet Union owing to the failure of his agricultural program, and also because of his combative control of both the Communist Party and the government. He had seen the warmth of the welcome Nixon received the year before in his country, had witnessed an incident in which some thousands of workers had acclaimed me when they learned that I was a brother of President Eisenhower, and was aware of the millions who had emotionally welcomed President Eisenhower in other countries. He clearly did not wish to have the people of the Soviet Socialist Republics acclaim an American President. He wrecked the Paris conference to keep Eisenhower out of the Soviet Union.

Since I had spent more than fifteen hours with Chairman Khrushchev when Vice-President Nixon and I were in the Soviet Union, it was natural for me to be a member of the party that entertained the Soviet leader when he was President Eisenhower's guest at Camp David. My brother had had a difficult time getting agreement on what Khrushchev would be willing to do on his official visit to this country. The Soviet advance agents, for example, had vetoed the suggestion that President Eisenhower take Chairman Khrushchev on several helicopter trips, especially over Washington at the height of the evening traffic problem. Since Khrushchev stubbornly insisted that our data about automobiles in the United States were mere propaganda we wanted a method to impress him and change his mind.

President Eisenhower outfoxed the advance planners. At the end of the first discussion between the two leaders in the White House, the President said that he usually took a short helicopter ride over Washington just for relaxation and he would be glad to have the Chairman accompany him. So Khrushchev had his first helicopter ride. He not only was amazed by the traffic congestion, but he also became intrigued with the machine, two of which he bought before his return home. Most of us had gone to Camp David by helicopter. At Camp David I mainly listened, but one afternoon Khrushchev wished to take a stroll on the large lawn in front of the President's cottage, so I accompanied him. Through an interpreter we had a vigorous and friendly discussion. I said to Khru-

shchev that I had been somewhat amused by his tirade on television
after he had been denied a trip to Disneyland (a trip his own secret police had vetoed). I said that when I was in Novosibirsk I had asked his
chief protocol officer to permit me to visit a collective farm rather than
another industrial plant. The protocol officer had declined. Khrushchev,
with genuine astonishment, said he did not know why such a decision
had been made. I thought I knew: everywhere we had been taken there
were obvious signs of recent renovation, painting, or cleaning. We were
being shown only the best. A collective farm had not been prepared, so
I could not be permitted to visit one.

From the moment he entered the White House President Eisenhower was determined to achieve fiscal responsibility in the federal
government and to check inflation, which had been so serious as to
cause a rise in prices of more than forty per cent during the years of
the Truman administration, partly due, of course, to the costs of the
Korean War. Despite two mild recessions in the Eisenhower eight years,
the trend in production, in the gross national product, was upward, and
inflation was only ten per cent in those eight years, one and a quarter
per cent per year. During the first mild recession the President completed and recommended to the Congress a budget which was not in
balance. Though this was agreed to by all members of the Cabinet, the
Secretary of the Treasury, George Humphrey, spoke critically of the
budget in an open press conference. President Eisenhower has been
criticized for trying to smooth over publicly the difference between himself and the director of the budget, on the one hand, and the Secretary
of the Treasury, on the other. His action and his attitude have been
interpreted as weakness in the exercise of presidential power. At the
time I was uneasy. I knew of the great confidence my brother had in
George Humphrey. I also knew that he preferred to find a way of minimizing the situation without "breaking up any part of the team."

Most political scientists who analyze the presidency write constantly of the "power of the President." Of course the President of the
United States has more power than any other leader on earth, save the
heads of the Communist parties in the Soviet Union and in the People's
Republic of China. When necessary, President Eisenhower used this
power. He was not a stranger to power. He had used both personal and
military power in commanding the Allied forces in World War II. But

politically, he always thought in long-time terms, not just in terms of the momentary situation. He wanted to keep Humphrey. So he made the most of a bad situation, which may be analyzed for years in political science classes as having been a great error.

Again, my admiration for George Humphrey was not as great as my brother's but, unlike the Nixon situation, I did not this time change my mind in the slightest. I thought Humphrey was arbitrary, stubborn, and much too sure of his own infallibility. It was he more than anyone else who induced the President to favor our co-operation with Canada in the construction of the St. Lawrence Seaway. It is true, of course, that in his military career my brother had long thought that the seaway would be of military importance and as President he became convinced that it would also be to our economic advantage. Further, he once said to me, if we refused to participate in the project, Canada would alone go forward with it, and we would then have no control over the long-time situation. Here, perhaps more clearly than in the other examples I have cited, I can make clear my own role as a confidant. On this problem the President had a volume of written evidence, drawn from all relevant departments. It was a problem which he had thought about for many years. As we discussed the project one night I asked that he take into consideration a factor not mentioned in the documents before him: the St. Lawrence Seaway would take from the financially shaky railroads a good deal of traffic, perhaps even most of it, for seven months or more a year, but in the severe winter only the railroads could carry the traffic. The Interstate Commerce Commission would require the railroads to operate year round, even at a loss. He agreed that the railroads were in a difficult situation. Indeed he said that the whole transportation enterprise of the United States had to be restudied and new laws passed, for our laws and our attitudes were anachronistic. Each form of transportation should be permitted to perform that function for which it was best fitted, and under the right circumstances all forms of transportation should have sufficient income to keep up their plants and to make a modest profit. But we could not stop new and promising developments in the transportation field, any more than we could stop a growing technology merely because each technological improvement was disadvantageous to some group. To exaggerate the problem, what would happen to America if we closed our research laboratories and declined to accept each improved method or system discovered by scientists and engineers because of temporary unemployment caused by technological change? I did not contest his conclusion. It was not, I emphasize, my function to do so. Further, I had not discussed the problem with the Secretaries of State, Defense, Treasury, and Commerce, who had much to do with the decision about the St. Lawrence Seaway. But on one matter I was right, my brother wrong: he thought the seaway would be self-supporting financially; I was sure it would have to be subsidized—and this has been the situation.

On occasions I had the happy privilege of representing the President at formal and sometimes quite important meetings; others were trivial. Thus when our grandfather's home at Elizabethville, Pennsylvania, was memorialized with a large permanent marker, I was sent to represent the President and the family. In March 1956, I helped entertain President Ruiz Cortines of Mexico and Prime Minister Louis St. Laurent of Canada at the Greenbrier Hotel, my principal task being to serve as host to the President of Mexico when the other two principals were in conference. I represented President Eisenhower at the installations of several Latin American Presidents.

One of the most interesting of these special assignments occurred when President Gronchi of Italy was President Eisenhower's official guest late in February 1956. Before President Gronchi left for home, he was to be entertained by the large Italian-American colony in New York and nearby states at the Waldorf Astoria Hotel. Some 1,500 persons were there. I was sent to New York to represent the President and with suggestions from the State Department I had prepared a twelve-minute official address, the time allotted to me for the purpose. We were all informed that precisely at nine o'clock that night television would carry President Gronchi's address. Unfortunately the garrulous and insensitive toastmaster of the dinner had arranged for addresses by four or five persons before Ambassador Ellsworth Bunker, an old friend of President Gronchi, and I were to speak. Each exceeded the time allotted to him. So Ambassador Bunker and I, sitting side by side, took out pens and began cutting paragraphs from our talks. As the ambassador's time and mine came to speak, we tried to put the program back on the right time track. He spoke three minutes, I about six. Then the toastmaster, instead of giving the formal introduction that international protocol demands, namely, "Ladies and gentlemen, with pride and pleasure I present the President of Italy," made about a ten-minute talk, as if he were introducing the superintendent of schools to the Abilene Kiwanis Club. Then, to our astonishment and despair, he repeated his entire introduction in Italian. The unfortunate consequence was that the obscure master of ceremonies was on television nearly as long as President Gronchi, and if the President's facial expression was an indication of his inner feelings, he was not pleased.

Some of the most intimate and analytical discussions my brother and I had about federal affairs were not in his office or official residence. Often he would enjoy a half day of fishing, or an hour's relaxation in my library, or chatting as we rode in a golf cart. His mind was never free of his responsibilities and never was he more than a few seconds removed from a communications system with the White House. On all such occasions we would chat about the major problems confronting him, but these were often interrupted by amusing incidents.

President and Mrs. Eisenhower came to the Pennsylvania State University for its hundredth anniversary. Most of the Eisenhowers were there. The President was to make the commencement speech. Shortly before eight o'clock on the morning of commencement the President and I were in the breakfast room chatting about Dulles' famous word "brinkmanship," when the meteorologist of the university joined us to discuss weather possibilities. He carefully reviewed them for the President, saying that the chances of rain at eleven o'clock were fifty-fifty. This posed a baffling problem. We would have twenty-five to thirty thousand guests for commencement, so the ceremony was to be in the stadium. If we had to go indoors we could seat at most six thousand. Naturally I waited for the President to suggest what we should do. He grinned, waved his hand at me, and said, "You decide. I haven't worried about the weather since June 6, 1944!"

As we marched into the stadium at eleven a drizzle, which had been continuous for two hours, was still falling. A mass of humanity with umbrellas, plastic covers, and even newspapers for protection was a ridiculously funny sight. But as we stepped onto the speaker's platform the rain stopped, the sun soon emerged. D-Day at Penn State was a success!

On another visit to my Pennsylvania residence we went trout fishing, and catching trout was essential, for we had guests, plus eight Secret Service agents, and fish were needed for the planned outdoor luncheon. Like President Hoover, my brother was a purist in fishing. He used only dry flies. When we were getting no results I, not a fanatic in the sport, used a wet fly and began pulling in rainbow, brown, and brook trout—real beauties. With some disgust the President used a wet fly, at once caught a three-and-a-half-pound brown trout, and then calmly went back to his own non-productive style, upstream. We had more than enough fish for lunch.

I had stopped playing golf—a terrible thing for an Eisenhower to do—having been in a body cast for eight weeks with a slipped disc. I was not willing to risk the twisting of the body involved in the use of woods, so often I would drive the electric cart as the President played. Sometimes, if he made a bad shot, he would show anger and swear. One day at Palm Desert I said, "Ike, you're getting profane in playing this game," and he quickly replied, "I am not profane. I just use cuss words as adjectives!"

Entertaining a President of the United States in one's home, even if he is a brother, is not as simple as some may suppose. Twice the President and Mrs. Eisenhower came to my official residence at The Johns Hopkins University for informal dinners. The day preceding each dinner, the Secret Service would inspect the residence, the surrounding gardens and buildings, and examine the guest list. All guests were notified by me to be on hand on the evening of the dinner before the President and Mrs. Eisenhower arrived. The arrival itself was like a parade: a Maryland escort car in the lead, the President's car, two Secret Service cars filled with eight or ten agents, then finally the local university constabulary, not to be left out, ending the procession. Since my amazing housekeeper of long standing, and her permanent and temporary help, could not take care of the dinner for the presidential party and the small army of Secret Service agents simultaneously, there would be prepared in advance boxed dinners for the Secret Service, served in my housekeeper's dining room. Much as I loved my brother and his lovely and charming wife Mamie, I always heaved a sigh of relief when the occasion was completed without mishap.

Even at an informal dinner of this type the conversation closely resembled that of the White House stag dinners I have already described. The guests were knowledgeable persons. The President was happy to hear their views and answer their questions, no doubt a disappointment to the ladies, who wanted to question Mrs. Eisenhower about the duties and pleasures of the First Lady.

The desire of the public personally to encounter the President was dramatically demonstrated on one of the visits the President and Mrs. Eisenhower made to my home at Penn State. The residence had a large lawn and beautiful gardens and a huge lily pond; the grounds were completely surrounded by a high hedge so that one could not see the residence without entering by the formal walk or through the hedges. The President and I had been chatting for an hour in my library when about nine o'clock in the evening he suggested that we walk about the grounds and see the flowers; a little fresh air would be good for us. We went out the front door and got about halfway to the lily pond when— this is no exaggeration—two or three hundred persons began pushing through the high hedge. We would have been mobbed. We raced for the house and just made it. I've often pictured the scene of several hundred persons chasing the President of the United States across the lawn!

It is much easier to be with the President when on rare occasions he can be isolated from the world, save for the inevitable communications system that links him to the White House. I shall never forget a weekend when President Eisenhower asked former President Hoover and me to accompany him to Aksel Nielsen's delightful ranch high in the Rocky Mountains, at the Great Divide. On the ranch is a clear stream filled with rainbow trout.

When we arrived the President had a headache, so he sent President Hoover and me to the trout stream to get fish for dinner while he "worked off" the headache in the kitchen. When we came in for lunch the President's headache was gone. He was in gay spirits. I assumed he would join us in fishing that afternoon, for we had had no luck in the morning. But he had with him several hundred bills which had been enacted by the Congress and it was necessary for him to begin to approve or veto them. So President Hoover and I returned to the stream while the President worked on an improvised table outdoors.

Dry flies were ignored by the beautiful rainbows in the clear mountain stream, but President Hoover, like my brother, was a purist and would do no more than change dry flies every few moments. I was practical; we needed food for dinner. So I tried a wet fly and soon had landed half a dozen rainbows, each weighing three pounds or more. That evening, when the fish had been cleaned, the President said, "They are too big to fry. I'll try something else." He was an imaginative cook. So he rubbed salt, pepper, and other condiments into the fish, wrapped them in several thicknesses of aluminum foil, and then tossed them directly into a white-hot charcoal fire. When they were served, they were brown and crisp on the outside, soft and juicy on the inside—the most flavorable trout I have ever eaten. President Hoover actually consumed two three-pound trout for dinner!

Two days later, when we drove from Frazier to the Brown Palace Hotel in Denver, Mamie and my daughter Ruth were waiting for us at the hotel entrance. The photographers at once lined us up, Ruth on the extreme left, I next to the President, and then Mrs. Eisenhower and President Hoover. The caption, in identifying us, said, "Miss Ruth Eisenhower, *her father,* Milton S. Eisenhower," etc. That pleased Ruth. Now married to a Johns Hopkins doctor and with three sons, and active in social and charitable affairs in Baltimore, she keeps the picture and the caption for her friends to see.

My brother and I went to Key West, Florida, on January 5, 1956, primarily to provide the President with complete relaxation and mild exercise—no more than hitting a few golf balls which I shagged for him. For hours in the evening we discussed the decision he would have to make in the near future: would he run for a second term? These talks were in a relaxed atmosphere and were devoid of emotion. I was opposed to a second term as were the President's son John and a good friend, George Allen. However, even on this point I asked more questions than I tried to answer.

We were staying in the home of the commander of the naval base. There were only two interruptions to our isolation. Jim Hagerty kept all newsmen and photographers off the property and no official visitors, to the best of my recollection, came from Washington. There were, of course, constant telephone calls between Key West and the White House.

The first formal interruption occurred when we learned that Mr. Kubitschek, who had been elected President of Brazil, was coming to the United States, prior to his inauguration, on an unofficial visit, and it seemed to the President that courtesy required him to invite the President-elect to stop in Key West for an informal chat. The President-elect arrived, of all times, for breakfast. Kubitschek and I had a spirited conversation, for now we were dealing in one of my areas of expertise, and because I took the lead, my brother, still recovering from his heart attack of September 24, 1955, could relax, listen, and interject a comment when he wished. It was a delightful occasion. I liked the President-elect. I had no idea then that his presidential policies would trigger an uncontrollable inflation in his country, caused partly by financing the construction of Brasília with printed money, a project which, nonetheless, may many years hence prove to have been a critical move in opening the interior of the vast unsettled spaces of Brazil. It is unfortunate that he could not have done this through traditional methods that would not have robbed the people through inflation.

Two days later the President prepared to put in his regular half hour in hitting golf balls with irons—no woods. It was a sunny day, so I wore a pair of shorts and a Trumanesque sport shirt, the loudest I owned. Since the public was excluded from the area, I was not concerned about my appearance. At the conclusion of the golf exercise my brother suggested we walk to the wharf and look at several submarines that were tied up there. He knew and did not tell me that on this one occasion Jim Hagerty would permit newspapermen and photographers to interrupt our isolation. Whether he forgot to tell me about this or took whimsical delight in what he knew would later be my embarrassment, I do not know. As we stood looking at a submarine I suddenly saw fifty—perhaps seventy-five—newsmen and photographers rushing toward us. I attempted to step out of the pictures but the President laughingly held me by the arm. The pictures were flashed that very day to every part of the country. At ten o'clock that night the unlisted telephone in my bedroom rang, and when I answered my son in New York shouted, "Hi, there, shorty pants!" The New York *Times* carried a double-column cut of this ghastly picture on its front page, so when I got back to the Pennsylvania State University, where I still served as president, students were ready for me with posters and many signs.

For some strange and unjustified reason I had been listed a couple of years before as one of the ten best-dressed men in the United States, so I'll always remember one mammoth poster which read: "What the best-dressed men in America must now wear!"

The Key West discussions were the forerunners of the more formal talks that began in Washington about the possibility of my brother's running for a second term. Mrs. Eisenhower made it clear to the President that she was ready to accept and support his decision, no matter what its nature. Cabinet members asked for special appointments in order to express their views. Then, on an evening in January 1956—about the thirteenth as I recall—a key group met in the President's oval study on the second floor of the White House for an analytical discussion of the problem. From previous conversations with many of those who were to participate, I feared, with justification, that all would urge the President to run again, ignoring the negative factors. So I went to two of them in advance and extracted promises that they would state both the pros and the cons. I did this because my brother had told me he did not want me to express a personal judgment, only to summarize the discussion just prior to adjournment. The participants were Herbert Brownell, Leonard Hall, Foster Dulles, Cabot Lodge, Sherman Adams, Jerry Persons, George Humphrey, Arthur Summerfield, James Hagerty, Howard Pyle, Thomas Stephens, and I.

Starting with Secretary Dulles, the President asked each member of the group to speak. To my dismay, not a single person, even the two who had promised me to be objective, recognized a single negative factor. All urged the President to run. So when the President called upon me to perform my chore of summarizing the conversation I said that I would have to go beyond my assignment and state both sides of the question. When I had done so one participant, my good friend Jim Hagerty, joined me in recognizing that all points to be considered were not in favor of a second term.

Several days later I wrote my brother a memorandum, summarizing what had been said at the meeting and adding a few comments I had made to him after the others had left. Since this memorandum is of some historic value and has never before been published in full, I quote it here:

Dear Ike: January 16, 1956

It occurs to me you might like to keep a record of the main points made by the group at your private dinner last Friday evening.

All felt that, because you command the respect of the peoples of the world, you are in a better position than anyone else to prevent global war and to work steadily toward permanent peace. It seemed doubtful to some that you could do much in this regard as a private citizen, particularly if a Democrat succeeded you as President.

The Republican Party is being rebuilt (thirty-nine new state chairmen have been elected during your administration) and this reform will be more meaningful and dependable four years hence. Since it is believed that only you of all Republicans can be elected in 1956, the continuation of present policies and programs for peace, rising levels of well-being, fiscal stability, and promotion of the general welfare is dependent on your being a candidate for re-election.

However, all present fully understood that only you can decide whether you would feel able to complete your present term, and also serve another four years, and all would respect your decision whether it be negative or affirmative.

It was said emphatically that you have earned the right to do as you please, free of criticism if you decide to lay down the burden. No man is indispensable (at least two contended) and a party should recognize this fact now as well as four years hence. You will be sixty-six when the next presidential term starts. You've had a heart attack. You could not make a vigorous campaign. It would be calamitous if you had a setback during the campaign, and difficult for the nation if such occurred any time during your second term. Are we sure that another Republican, who believes in your policies, could not be elected? Will the situation within the party and in domestic and world affairs really be materially different four years hence? Is it possible that the very people who like and respect you most would vote against you in 1956, feeling that the party and the nation are now asking too much of you?

The foregoing is based on the notes I took. I would add what I said upstairs after the others had gone.

If I were in your place, I would do all my reasoning within a framework of conviction that, everything considered, I had the full right, beyond all possibility of reproach, to decide negatively, if I wished. It is within that framework that I would consider (a) purely personal desire, (b) the probabilities of the future, (c) the alternative opportunities for service, (d) what duty might require.

Finally, may I point out the obvious, more personal, perhaps more selfish view: if you decline to run, you will clearly go down in history as one of our greatest military and political leaders, with no major domestic or international difficulty to mar your record. If you go on, you might enhance your standing, contribute mightily to peace and to sound principles at home; or you might face serious economic setbacks at home and upheavals abroad. You might jeopardize your health and your ability to carry the burdens of office.

That seems to be it. I know what loneliness you must experience in working toward a decision which only you can make. I wish I could help.

Devotedly,

Milton

The President, after reading my memorandum, drew a long line beside the next-to-last paragraph and scribbled beside it in ink:

Of no great moment; even though history might condemn a failure it cannot weigh the demand of conscience.

It was on February 29, 1956, that the President announced he would be a candidate for a second term, explaining with care to the American people the limitations he would place upon himself in the campaign and in the next four years in the White House if re-elected.

Of course he was swept back into office.

CHAPTER 19

Considering that President Eisenhower
faced, among other things, the Korean War,
McCarthyism, Hungary, the Suez crisis, the
U-2, and Little Rock, I am sorry he did not
live long enough to enjoy hearing his time
in office referred to as "the good old days."

THE FINAL MONTHS of President Eisenhower's first term
and the beginning of his second term permitted no relaxation in
the White House. Sharp differences between Western Allies, the na-
tionalization of the Suez Canal, military action against Egypt, the danger of a major war, hurried travels by the Secretary of State and his top
associates to Britain, France, and Egypt, and constant telephone calls
from the White House to 10 Downing Street—all were part of a fast-
moving, tense drama.

Developments in Egypt, the United Kingdom, France, and Israel
from April to December 1956 were on the presidential agenda every
day, sometimes every hour late into the night. Six weeks traveling in
the Middle East did not equip me to contribute much to the complex,
dangerous, and rapidly changing situation, so my role was one of sympathetic listener with whom the President could think out loud and
share his doubts, his deep concerns, and his tentative judgments. The
Western Alliance to which he was deeply committed was now in jeop-
ardy and I know how greatly he suffered when he felt compelled to oppose actions contemplated and eventually taken by our friends, Britain,
France, and Israel.

The problem was rooted in the creation of the independent state
of Israel in 1948 following British withdrawal from the area. President
Truman was the first to recognize the new nation. His action brought
the fury of the Arab states upon us and reversed the close relations

we had enjoyed with them for a century. The United States became a principal supporter of Israel, and the Soviet Union gradually moved into the vacuum as the ally of the Arab nations. Whether a delay in the timing of our recognition of Israel would have made a significant difference has stimulated much speculation. I think it might have.

The specific difficulties of 1956 began when President Nasser tentatively rejected an offer of the United States to provide monetary assistance directly and through the World Bank for the construction of the Aswan High Dam. The project was estimated to cost more than a billion dollars and to take two decades for construction. President Eisenhower explained to me that if our offer was accepted it would be at best a mixed blessing. Our help over a period of years would finance the cost of imports needed for the construction of the dam and the technical requirements of irrigation. The Egyptian people would pay local costs, which were a high percentage of the total. "Whatever government provides the outside assistance may in time be thoroughly disliked by the Egyptian people, who will feel the oppressive weight of taxation," he said.

After a series of negotiating sessions the United States felt it would probably have to withdraw its offer of support. Nasser announced a tentative arms agreement with the Soviet Union and began to negotiate with the U.S.S.R. for financial help for his pet project. The President shared with me his concern about Nasser's "playing one nation against the other, and blackmailing both."

In June, Nasser agreed to purchase $200 million in arms from the Soviet Union and indicated that the Soviets would provide more funds and technical help for the Aswan Dam than were offered by the United States. This angered President Eisenhower and many members of the United States Senate. In July the Senate Appropriations Committee added language to the Mutual Security Act which forbade use of any funds to help finance the dam in Egypt.

I shall never forget the discussion the President and I had late the night of the Senate Committee's action. He understood its attitude. He realized that the United States' offer to Egypt had to be withdrawn, partly because of Nasser's blatant tactics in trying to sell to the highest bidder, but also because our help would not be approved here at home. Nonetheless, he foresaw that Soviet assistance to Egypt would widen the East-West division that was developing in the Middle East. The struggle between Israel and the Arab states had created a tinderbox in the Middle East in which the possibility of a big-power confrontation would exist for years to come. A hot enough spark, which Arab leaders were in a position to strike, could ignite a major war.

Nasser was ready to provide the spark. His next move was to nationalize the Suez Canal. Legally, he was entitled to do this, for Egypt was the sovereign power in physical control of the canal area. The United States had often faced expropriation by foreign powers of the assets of United States citizens and had been able to do nothing provided that just compensation was paid as required by international law.

The canal had been built in 1869 by the French. French citizens still held more than fifty per cent of the stock of the canal company, but the British government was the largest single owner, holding forty-four per cent of the outstanding stock. In 1888 at Constantinople nine nations, including Britain, France, and Turkey (which then occupied Egypt), had entered into a convention which provided for a canal company to operate the waterway and carry on normal housekeeping functions. But the convention did not internationalize the area or provide for international political control of the canal. Even though Egypt had a legal right to nationalize the canal, as I said, tempers flared in Britain and France. A parade of diplomats crisscrossed the Atlantic for hastily called conferences. The President's daily, sometimes hourly, communiqués were by coded cable, telephone, and letter, and also by the dispatch of Under Secretary Herbert Hoover, Jr., and later Secretary Dulles (who was in Latin America when the difficulty began), to Britain and France in an effort to prevent precipitate action. Tension mounted rapidly.

Always in the minds of British and French leaders was the belief that force would be needed to restore the canal to its previous position. Otherwise Nasser would become a hero in the Arab world. With increased prestige and power, he could control the oil supplies on which Western Europe and the United States were dependent. As Prime Minister Anthony Eden put it: Europe would be at the mercy of an ambitious and unpredictable man.

The President received a flood of messages from Eden but, as he told me, this was a time for patience. He decided to try to arrange a meeting in London of the major maritime nations, including those signatory to the Constantinople Convention. If they could agree on a position they could select a group to negotiate directly with Nasser. This was preferable to direct British-French-Egyptian talks, for there was too much bitterness among these three. In any case, the move would buy time, which the President felt was justification enough for trying it.

The conference reached agreement, though not unanimously, and a small delegation headed by the Prime Minister of Australia went to Cairo to meet with Nasser. The negotiations failed.

A second effort proposed by President Eisenhower, somewhat different from the first, involved the creation of a "users' association." Britain and France felt that Egyptians could not operate the canal. Most of the pilots and other personnel were British and some were French; only a few were Egyptian. The users' association, as I recall my brother's explanation, could, with the combined power of the pilots and other technical personnel and the maritime nations using the Suez Canal, open direct bargaining sessions with the Egyptians. This would be something like labor-management bargaining in a large industry. Nasser also rejected this proposal.

In September the Western pilots left their jobs, believing that their action would close the canal and put pressure on Nasser to become more conciliatory. They were mistaken. Egyptian pilots took command and in the first week took more than 250 ships through the canal without a single accident or serious delay in the transits.

At this point President Eisenhower and I had a long discussion about the implications of Nasser's move for the United States' problem in Panama. The two situations were similar only in that they were both potential crises. The Panama Canal is a lock canal. The maintenance of a water supply for lock action, the transit of large ships through the locks with only inches to spare, the management of slides, and other complex technical problems made the operation of the Panama Canal distinctly different from that of the sea-level Suez Canal. Nonetheless, critics of the United States in Panama, infiltrated by aliens who were presumed to be Communists, became active in proposing that Panama seize the canal and all property in the zone which bisected the Panamanian Republic. This was a potential problem that had to be put on the back burner (a major amendment to the treaty of 1903 was completed a year later and for a time greatly eased the tensions in Panama).

Without consulting President Eisenhower, the British and French took the issue of Suez to the United Nations. The President told me of his concern over this move. It was possible, he thought, that the British and French sincerely wanted the help of the Security Council or possibly the General Assembly in finding a peaceful solution to the problem. But if this were so, why had they not informed him of their plans and asked for our support? It was also possible that this was a preliminary move toward the use of military force, an action that might be acceptable to a nervous world if the United Nations failed to find a solution.

Chagrined by the failure of close friends to confide in us, the United States nevertheless supported the British-French proposal. It was vetoed by the Soviet Union in the Security Council. Secretary General Dag Hammarskjold now took personal charge of the problem, developed a set of principles he wanted accepted as a basis for settling the dispute, and personally opened discussions with the countries most involved.

The Secretary General's initiative proved to be too late. Israel, having secretly obtained additional war planes from France, began maneuvers seemingly directed against Jordan, which was then in a weakened condition. But this was only a tactical diversion, for on October 26 Israeli forces suddenly turned on Egypt and touched off a war in the Middle East.

The United States rushed to the United Nations with a resolution calling for the cessation of hostilities. This was done in haste to have a resolution on the agenda ahead of one that assuredly would be presented by the Soviet Union. Not unexpectedly, it was now France and Britain that cast vetoes in the Security Council!

At this point President Eisenhower faced one of his most difficult problems. The United States, Britain, and France were signatories to a tripartite agreement which obligated us to oppose an aggressor nation that violated the Egyptian-Israeli frontiers and armistice lines. Anthony Eden said the agreement was obsolete and inoperative. The President emphatically said that an agreement could not be abrogated by one or even two of the parties concerned. For half an hour he thought out loud with me in his upstairs study about the sincerity of the United States, as a member of the United Nations, in seeking to settle international disputes by negotiation, and living up to its commitment to help prevent aggression in the explosive Middle East. Thoughtlessly, with no intention of diverting his mind from the central issue, I commented that it would not be popular politically at home for the United States to help protect Egypt against the armed might of Israel.

To this day I marvel at the fact that the well-known Eisenhower temper did not blast forth and consume me at that moment. My brother glanced at me. His eyes and facial expression were the epitome of grief. After a long silence, during which he overcame his first impulsive response, he commented quietly that the 1956 election was farthest from his mind. Great decisions involving not only the United States but many countries of the world had to be based on rules of law and justice, not on their effect in domestic politics—and I of all people ought to know this and fully understand his strong feeling in this regard. If need be, and despite the opposition of the other signatories to the tripartite agreement, the President said he would stand on our solemn commitment. This might require him to call a special session of the Congress, for only it could authorize the use of military force. Of course he prayed this could be avoided. He would do all he could to find a peaceful solution.

When British and French forces moved into the canal area the President was not surprised. The timing of the attack by Israel and the quick military response by Britain and France showed conclusively that plans had been carefully co-ordinated in advance. On this, too, the United States had not been consulted.

On November 2 a cease-fire resolution before the General Assembly, introduced by the United States, was adopted by an impressive vote, only Britain, France, Australia, New Zealand, and Israel dissenting. This resolution was supplemented by a motion, introduced by Canada, to provide a United Nations emergency force to occupy the canal area until through negotiations a permanent and peaceful solution to the entire problem could be found. Britain and France rejected the cease-fire order of the General Assembly but accepted the proposal for United Nations forces to control the canal until Egypt and Israel reached a peaceful agreement and satisfactory arrangements had been made for the management of the Suez Canal. Fighting in the area ground to a halt on November 7, but it was not until the latter part of December that Israel pulled her forces back from the canal, Britain and France withdrew their forces, and Egypt began clearing the canal of ships she had sunk during the fighting to make transits through the canal impossible—a task that would require a long time.

The Middle East crisis was enough to frustrate any free-world leader who was committed to the peaceful solution of international problems, but before it was concluded other worrisome problems commanded top headlines in the press.

On October 20, Khrushchev, rebuffed by Polish Communist leaders who had brought Gomulka back into power and ousted Khrushchev's hand-picked man, Rokossovsky, from the Politburo, sent Soviet troops into Poland. Sporadic fighting began. Students and workers joined with Polish military forces in opposing the invaders who, fortunately, did not press the fighting to a crucial point. In the nervous peace that followed, agreement was reached under which Poland obtained greater control over its internal affairs, Gomulka would remain in power, but Poland would faithfully recognize the lead of the Soviet Union in all matters of international concern.

That evening my brother and I discussed the Polish problem, which was not too different from that of the other Eastern European countries within the Soviet hegemony. Poland's cultural orientation was to the West. Her people had known freedom from time to time and under the right conditions wanted to regain it. Her rural people had rejected farm collectivization, religion was deeply ingrained in the people, and most Poles wanted good relations with the United States and other Western powers. But she was in a seemingly impervious circle. Part of her territory to the east had been taken from her in the World War II settlement dictated by the Soviet Union, and in return she had been given rich agricultural lands to the west, previously part of Germany. The new border of Poland had not been recognized by West Germany or by the United States and Britain. The nation could not exist economically without the annexed lands. Her only protection was the military strength of the Soviet Union. No matter what her secret desires might be, she could not escape into freedom. We speculated, not too seriously, on whether, had the Western nations not then been in such disarray, military aid might have been given to Poland. That was patently out of the question. The Poles were not seeking to overthrow a Communist regime; indeed they would have rejected any such effort to help them. Intervention would have been the beginning of a major conflict of ominous proportions and certainly a war-weary Europe and preoccupied Britain and France would have rejected intervention, even if the Poles had requested it.

The Polish situation led directly to the historic uprising in Hungary. Hungary had a long list of grievances against the U.S.S.R., which controlled every important action taken by Hungarian Communist leaders. This was widely resented, even by loyal Communists. By October 24 fighting was raging in Budapest. Mobs tore down Soviet flags and monuments. Within three days the revolt had spread to all parts of the country. A week later Hungary renounced the Warsaw Pact and appealed to the United Nations for help in protecting its proclaimed neutrality. The Soviet response was to move massive forces of tanks, planes, and ground troops into Hungary. Thousands of civilians and Hungarian soldiers were indiscriminately murdered. The revolt was crushed. The Soviet Union was again in complete control of all aspects of life in her satellite.

Many persons in the United States expressed the view that we should have gone to the aid of Hungary. Emotionally, I think, President Eisenhower agreed. He was aggrieved by the slaughter that had taken place. But he could not yield to his emotions. He said to me: "Look at a map. Hungary is inaccessible to any Western force. Austria is a neutral country, thanks to our efforts in her behalf. If Western forces had sought to cross Austria to reach Hungary, the main fighting would have taken place on Austrian soil and most of the killing would have occurred there. A non-Communist force could not have reached Hungary through Yugoslavia. Despite Tito's insistence upon independence from the U.S.S.R., his country is still Communist and we have no desire to fight the forces of Yugoslavia. The difficulty would have been as great or greater in trying to get through Czechoslovakia. Air-borne assistance would have been futile. And it goes without saying that, had armed assistance been geographically possible, it could not have succeeded without the full co-operation of all NATO countries and you know as well as I do that action by NATO, with Britain and France dissenting, would not have been possible."

He considered the Hungarian revolt and its murderous suppression by the Soviet Union to be one of the modern tragedies. Unlike the Poles, most of the people of Hungary had no reason not to want freedom at once. The cries of the revolters and the Hungarian appeal to the United Nations proved that Hungary wanted to be released from Soviet domination. "It is a crime against all humanity for the forces of an alien government to occupy another nation against the wishes of its people," President Eisenhower said. "Every country should have the right of free choice."

All the United States could do was to rush supplies of food and pharmaceuticals to Hungary, express our indignation to the world, and press for action in the General Assembly of the United Nations.

In the midst of these problems—reviewed here so briefly as to fail to indicate their complexity and the anguish they caused the President and his associates—national problems, from civil rights to economic maladjustments, and a national election were demanding attention at home. President Eisenhower made a minimum number of trips to carry his campaign to the people. He was too busy to do otherwise. It was gratifying to all of us when the returns came in and the margin of victory was larger than it had been four years before. This did not cause elation among those who were close to the President. If we needed experiences to impress upon us the awful responsibility we expected a single man to carry for all of us, we were surely seeing it demonstrated in 1956.

Near the close of the 1956 campaign Adlai Stevenson, apparently becoming desperate and seeking, as candidates often do, for something to "smear" the opposition, charged that the Eisenhower administration, on my recommendation, had given Juan Peron, the dictator of Argentina, $100 million. My brother hit the ceiling, almost literally. I have seldom seen him so furious. The Truman administration had approved loans of $130 million to Argentina, the Eisenhower administration none. But, since I had been in Argentina in 1953, Stevenson attributed the charge of a United States loan to my influence. The President's instinct was to reply directly. I'm sure he would have been angry if the Stevenson statement had been aimed at any federal official. That would have been bad enough. But that the misrepresentation was directed toward me affected him especially. Fortunately I was able to calm him, and the next day official documents were issued to show the facts.

One problem my brother and I discussed dozens of times was civil rights. We agreed completely that the American philosophy and our Constitution demanded mutuality in human relations and equal opportunities in education, employment, promotion, housing, and other areas of life. He was convinced, as I had always been, that in dealing with masses of people of varying backgrounds, prejudices, and levels of education it is better to employ an evolutionary approach in seeking change rather than a revolutionary one. I have already discussed my own experience at Kansas State in this area. So when he asked the Congress to pass the Civil Rights Act of 1957, the first since the Civil War, he looked upon it as only the first in a series of laws that would have to be enacted over a period of years. The House passed the bill. The Senate weakened it at the insistence of the majority leader of the Senate, Lyndon Johnson, who later became the exponent of revolutionary change in this field. My brother discussed this subject early in 1961 with President Kennedy at the latter's request, and explained why he felt it would be better to take one major step at a time, have it accepted without major discord, and then take the next logical step. This reasoning did not appeal to President Kennedy, who introduced an omnibus bill which was passed under President Johnson. It has always seemed to me that President Eisenhower's sponsorship of the Civil Rights Act of 1957, his vigorous action in the Little Rock incident, his elimination of discrimination in programs and agencies under his direct control, and his repeated statements that additional legislation should be enacted at propitious times, should leave no doubt about his position on civil rights.

Anyone close to the President—certainly a brother of the President—is assumed by the public to be a direct channel to the White House. If the President is inaccessible, a brother in private life is not— or so it is assumed. My able assistants and secretaries became gratifyingly competent in convincing callers at my office that they would waste their time if they appealed to me to carry information, ideas, or recommendations to the President. Letters declining to serve as a go-between took a great deal of my time. Occasionally, though, a group would break through my defenses. One day about ten well-dressed men appeared at my Johns Hopkins office and told my assistant that they had made a special flight from Memphis, Tennessee, by private plane to see me on a matter of highest importance. They would not explain what they wished to say and I, in a moment of weakness, permitted them to come into my office. They wanted me to intercede with the President on a tax matter which was being discussed in Congress. The argument in Congress was that, since railroads, trucks, and airlines paid many types of taxes, water transportation was enjoying favoritism by using channels and docks, financed by the federal government, at no cost. The threat was that use charges might be imposed. The delegation said that this would wreck their businesses and would be especially harmful to all cities and rural areas bordering on the navigable portion of the Mississippi River. With as much courtesy as I could muster under the circumstances I said that the talk in Congress made sense to me and that in any case, even if I agreed with them, I would under no circumstances carry their views to the President. They should go, I said, either to the appropriate congressional committees or to the Assistant Secretary of Commerce, who at that time was the major policy adviser on transportation matters.

This incident was one of hundreds, though few were admitted to my private office. The most annoying aspect of the problem was when I was approached at a dinner party, pushed into a room where private conversation was possible, and compelled to keep my temper as a courtesy to our common host and hostess. So far as I know, privileged appeals to the President through confidants or relatives are far fewer than most Americans believe, but I do know that none occurred through me in the eight Eisenhower years.

President Eisenhower and I had often discussed in detail the work I had done in UNESCO during the Truman administration. He was as convinced as I was that one of the ingredients of a total program for peace was genuine understanding among the governments and peoples of the world. On one occasion he had said to the staff of the United States Information Agency that he had been frustrated many times as he learned how little the peoples of many countries, including well-educated persons in friendly countries, knew about the United States. He found that this had grave consequences from time to time. He expressed his belief that the government could not conduct foreign relations satisfactorily unless it took positive steps to let the world know what was deep in the American heart, the psychological reactions of Americans to given sets of problems and circumstances, and the motives of the United States in its major international efforts.

One evening we had an interesting conversation about the need to improve understanding among the peoples of the Soviet Union and the United States. We were in the President's study upstairs, the President with a weak scotch and soda, I with one of Sergeant Moaney's incomparable old-fashioneds. The President was especially concerned about the fact that the Soviet officials could learn anything they wished about our open society but permitted their own people to know only what the Communist leaders wanted them to know. United States short-wave radio broadcasts and the broadcasts of Radio Free Europe and Radio Liberty penetrated the iron curtain, but anyone who has visited the Soviet Union, as I have done on three occasions, knows that a high percentage of the people of the U.S.S.R. are ill informed, with ghastly misconceptions about America's philosophy, institutions, and purposes.

The President began speculating about the fact that the "old-timers" in the Soviet Union probably were beyond redemption on this problem, but the younger people, who one day would be in control, ought to be reached with the truth, the whole truth.

"Do you think the Congress would approve a proposal for our sending ten thousand typical American university students to the Soviet Union, and the Soviet Union sending a similar number to us?" he asked. He was half serious about this, though I know he realized that the possibilities of doing such a dramatic thing were negligible. Of course I was enthusiastic, though I, too, presumed that it would be years before such a massive exchange could take place.

The President called the Secretary of State and asked for a judgment. At that time the United States and the Soviet governments were renegotiating an exchange agreement. The Secretary said, "We are having a devil of a time to get the Soviets to agree to the exchange each year of a few scientists and teachers, a few students, and theatrical, musical, and ballet groups. If we suggest such a huge undertaking as you ask about, all negotiations will cease!"

Even as late as April 6, 1972, the United States and the Soviet Union could agree only on the annual exchange of eight professors, six performing arts groups, twenty individual performers, and indeterminate numbers of technicians and cultural exhibitions.

Late in 1960 my brother and I had many discussions about American forces in Europe. He was concerned about two major problems: first, an increasingly large balance-of-payments deficit was beginning to be troublesome and, second, European nations were failing to live up to their commitments to assume a greater share of the burden of maintaining a protective shield against possible Communist military action.

Imbalances in international payments were new for this country. From 1868 to 1918 our exports of goods and services had exceeded our imports sufficiently that at the end of World War I we changed from a debtor to a creditor country. Nonetheless, from 1918 to 1957 we continued to have a favorable balance, despite growing military expenditures, foreign aid, and the movement of private capital overseas for investment. Even in 1957 and for nearly fourteen years thereafter our exports of goods and services exceeded our imports. But escalating military expenditures around the world, foreign aid (not of great importance, for most aid was in goods, not money), large expenditures abroad by United States tourists, and the continued movement abroad of American capital for investment caused the United States for the first time to experience an imbalance in international monetary affairs. A major cause of this was the fact that we maintained some 310,000 military personnel in Europe, plus about 235,000 wives and children, and some 14,000 civilian employees, at a cost of more than $14 billion. (By 1973 the cost had risen to $17 billion.)

Since our NATO cost is today being constantly discussed in the United States Senate, it merits explanation. If one assigns to each contingent of United States armed forces, no matter where located, its pro rata share of the total defense cost, then the dollar outlay for our military personnel and their families in Europe is now $17 billion. On the other hand, if we brought these troops home, and they remained in the service, the savings would be only about $1.5 to $2 billion. To achieve the full savings implied by the total cost, we would have to discharge our NATO personnel from the service, an action which few propose. At the same time the significance for our imbalances of international payments in maintaining troops and their families in Europe is much greater than the $1.5 to $2 billion that could be saved by bringing them home, for the dollars paid to them in Europe are largely spent there.

The other consideration—the failure of Europe to meet its NATO commitments—was equally worrisome. When NATO was established Europe was by no means recovered from devastation caused by war, but the Marshall Plan was making commendable progress, so it was understood that the United States would carry a disproportionate share of the mutual-defense burden only until the nations of Europe were economically healthy. We would then reduce our troops and costs, and European countries would take up the slack. Unfortunately only West Germany in 1960 was fulfilling its obligation. Some members of Congress were urging the President to withdraw some troops from the European continent, perhaps fifty thousand, as a warning that we expected Europe to pay its full share for its own protection. President Eisenhower, however, was convinced that at that time the psychological effect in Great Britain, France, Italy, West Germany, and other countries would be extremely bad; they would feel, European leaders told him, that the United States was beginning to "welch" on its own commitments.

President Eisenhower, after conferring with the National Security Council and some of his own staff, including General Goodpaster, decided not to reduce our troops—that should come later—but to bring home many dependents. This would reduce our annual cost in Europe and thus would have a beneficial effect on the problem of imbalances in international payments. (By 1973 our imbalances were annually fluctuating from a few to as much as $12 billion a year.)

It is important to keep in mind that at many locations American military personnel overseas cannot take their wives and children with them. This is true in Korea and all of Southeast Asia, for example. Certainly in wartime military men must leave their dependents at home. Even a Supreme Commander must do this.

So President Eisenhower issued an executive order providing that thereafter the number of dependents of military and civilian personnel abroad should be reduced, the total being subject to review annually by the President. The reduction was to be accomplished at the rate of not less than fifteen thousand a month, commencing on January 1, 1961.

The same executive order called for a reduction in foreign military purchases and foreign military aid; required the coast guard to reduce foreign expenditures; instructed the International Cooperation Administration, in managing foreign aid, to emphasize the shipment of American-produced goods, rather than their purchase abroad, and called upon all departments and agencies with personnel stationed abroad to reduce such personnel when this could be accomplished without impairing United States policies and objectives.

At once many military leaders, including the American who then headed NATO forces, said that this action by the President would injure the efficiency of our troops in Europe. I thought this was nonsense. I had been in Europe a number of times and had seen military personnel of every rank having a fairly good time, trips with families on weekends being a standard practice. My son had been with the NATO forces; he was stationed in Berlin, but on every weekend he made pleasure trips by military planes to many other countries. I was convinced that if our troops were there without their wives and children they would pay more attention to the plans and exercises for the defense of Europe than I witnessed on my trips to the Continent.

President Eisenhower was unmoved by the protests. His executive order stood. One of the first acts of President Kennedy, however, was to rescind it. Military personnel had convinced Secretary McNamara that the move was wrong and he in turn had persuaded the President to this point of view.

Today, in the Congress, a demand is growing for massive reduction in our military personnel and dependents in all areas of the world. Senator Mansfield wants a reduction of five hundred thousand men in three years.* The pressure is so persistent that it cannot much longer be avoided. The major conflict between the executive and legislative branches of the government now is whether the United States should unilaterally reduce our forces in Europe, as many senators advocate, or whether we should await the outcome of mutual force negotiations contemplated in discussions now under way, as President Nixon wishes to do. Because of the intransigence of France—ejecting NATO from France and essentially removing French forces from the NATO command—NATO is weaker than it was. My belief is that in the foreseeable future our troop strength in NATO will be reduced by as much as a hundred thousand men, and I strongly suspect that something comparable to the Eisenhower executive order will be revived; dependent personnel will remain at home and the tour of duty in Europe will be limited for each member of our armed forces.

My final work during the Eisenhower administration began early in January 1961. My brother was seriously concerned about the ulti-

* In mid-November 1973, the military procurement bill, signed by the President, required that troops be withdrawn from Europe in relation to the failure of NATO countries to offset the balance-of-payments deficit incurred by the United States in stationing its forces there.

mate consequences of the growing partnership between the military establishment and many American industries. He evidently foresaw what I encountered nearly three years later when I was serving as chairman of the Republican Critical Issues Council in 1963–64. I sought the co-operation of the vice-president of one of America's largest corporations, but despite his desire to work on the space program with me, his board of directors disapproved on the grounds that his co-operation with a Republican group might imperil the continuation of large war contracts, which constituted an appreciable part of the company's business. Similarly, when I asked a distinguished professor of a leading American university to help on another study, the president of the university suggested that he assist me quietly with no publicity for fear it would lead to the cancellation of research grants and contracts that yielded the institution a third of its annual income.

President Eisenhower and I discussed at length the situation as it existed in January 1961 and what future developments might be. Without being alarmist, we both felt strongly that a situation was developing in this nation which could ultimately seriously injure it. My brother felt that his long military career and his eight years in the White House put him in a better position than anyone else to issue a warning to the American people. So he prepared his farewell address, weighing every word. It was delivered on January 17, 1961, just three days before he turned over the burdens of the presidency to his successor.

One phrase of that address has become a part of everyday language: "the military-industrial complex." President Eisenhower said:

"In the councils of government, we must guard against the acquisition of unwarranted influence, whether sought or unsought, by the military-industrial complex. The potential for the disastrous rise of misplaced power exists and will persist."

The words were prophetic, and in the years since they were uttered the situation which prompted them has worsened in my opinion and now justifies alarm. Events during the past few years have convinced me that the industrial-military complex has already attained a pervasive power which reaches and influences the highest levels of government.

Lest I leave the impression, by citing the foregoing examples of my service as confidant to the President, that I was the only one in this capacity, I emphasize that President Eisenhower had many official advisers whom he trusted, and a few personal friends who often conferred with him. Certainly among his official family he had unbounded admiration for Foster Dulles, Robert Anderson, Gabriel Hauge, Andrew Goodpaster, Herbert Brownell, and Thomas Stephens, among others. He had great confidence in James Hagerty, dubbed by William Lawrence the finest presidential press secretary in his experience. Persons who had no official federal post and who were of help to him included General Alfred Gruenther, William Robinson, and General Lucius Clay. Good friends who seldom discussed policy or program matters but helped the President relax at bridge, light conversation, or golf included "Slats" Slater, Pete Jones, George Allen, Clifford Roberts, and many others.

As I think back to those eight busy years I am convinced that as time goes on students of government will agree with what is already becoming a general judgment: the period 1953–61 will be looked upon as the best period of this century for the United States. Though our country has engaged in four wars in this century, there was none in the Eisenhower years; the President's policies, a strong gamble at times, worked in Iran, Lebanon, Austria, Berlin, Europe generally, and the Far East. We did not go into Vietnam and get bogged down in an unjustified and unwinnable war. The Communists made no advance with their military forces or through subversion save in Cuba where Castro, having driven the despicable Batista from power, changed a year later from democratic preachments to rigid Communist control. A feeling of security was again restored to the people of the United States. The urban crime wave that began in the sixties was not yet launched. The people trusted the President, with complete faith in his integrity and credibility. Despite two mild recessions, the economy moved upward. Inflation was at an all-time low.

The President's major purposes, seldom articulated comprehensively but often discussed in our evening sessions, were based on an unshakable middle-of-the-road philosophy. In international affairs he wanted above all else to help build a solid base for a total structure of peace that would have to be constructed over a period of decades; in his time in office he would depend a good deal on his close personal relationships with many of the leaders of the world. By many actions, at home and abroad, he greatly reduced the inflammatory aspects of the Cold War, a trend which was reversed in the Kennedy and Johnson administrations but renewed in the right direction by President Nixon, who, despite unprecedented difficulties in domestic affairs, made commendable progress in muting the Cold War and in working toward détente.

Domestically, President Eisenhower felt that it was not a time for inaction—far from it—but for consolidation, for achieving stability. The nation in the previous twenty years had been through two wars and had experienced a social revolution in the Roosevelt and Truman administrations. There were more fundamental social changes and in government activity than we had ever before witnessed in our history, and they were not without intellectual bitterness that needed to be healed. New Deal and Fair Deal programs were filled with inefficiency when he assumed office in 1953. *None of these social programs was abrogated.* Every effort was made to stabilize them and to eliminate inefficiencies and glaring conflicts.

The spirit in which he worked on domestic matters was shown when he said: "My job . . . is not to create friction, not to accentuate differences, but to bring people together so we can actually achieve progress—not to be dramatic or do something to get another headline, but to get progress for the United States." But new undertakings were also on the agenda: massive increases for research, especially in our universities; an unprecedented thirteen-year road-building program; increased Social Security, both in greater coverage and in size of payments; a new and much-needed farm program which substituted flexibility in price supports for the rigid and high supports initiated during World War II; the National Education Act with its many facets, including spectacular aid for graduate students; unprecedented changes in our relations with Latin America, including the legal basis for the Alliance for Progress (enacted 1960); a sound beginning in civil rights, the first such effort in eighty years; fiscal responsibility; a major change in defense, including especially the creation of unified commands and a shift from overdependence on conventional weapons to increased reliance on the deterrent effect of atomic weapons, and sustaining the treaty-making power of the President by the defeat of the Bricker Amendment to the Constitution. This was not all. Statehood was granted to Hawaii and Alaska. The St. Lawrence Seaway was built in co-operation with Canada. The largest tax decrease in our history up to that time was enacted. A massive space program was initiated, with successful orbital flights in three years after starting from scratch. Polaris and ballistic missile programs were successfully launched. Medical care for the aged (Kerr-Mills Act) was begun. Good-will journeys to more than a score of nations in Europe, Asia, Latin America, and the Pacific paid dividends in increased understanding and friendship.

It indeed was not a period of inaction, either in improving programs inherited from his predecessors or initiating new ones, with initiations being carefully planned and spaced so as not to deter the efforts toward consolidation and stability which the President considered to be of prime importance. And his relations with the Congress in the last six years of his administration were excellent, even though he had to work with Democratic leaders who controlled both houses; one test of this was the fact that of his 169 vetoes only two were overridden, and both of these were pork-barrel bills.

This chapter and the previous one have dealt with selected examples of my work with the President as his intimate confidant, the emphasis being on matters which have been misunderstood by a great many persons. Each of these has been related from memory and from my point of view. It is not inappropriate, I trust, to conclude with two statements, one written, one oral, which indicate President Eisenhower's view of the help I tried to give him. In his book, *Mandate for Change*,[25] he wrote: "My brother, Milton S. Eisenhower, President of The Johns Hopkins University, undertook the onerous work of reading the entire text . . . and offering notes on its contents. He is the only individual who could have done this to my satisfaction, not only because of the close association between us . . . [but also] because during the period of my two administrations he was a constant adviser, confidant, and, at times, personal representative."

In the Walter Reed Hospital, two days before President Eisenhower died, he sent for me, even though his doctor had asked him not to tax himself by speaking. I left Mamie Eisenhower for a moment and entered my brother's suite. He motioned for me to lean close to him, and he whispered, "I want you to know how much you have always meant to me, how much I have valued your counsel." I choked up, pressed his hand, and left the room. I then tried to repeat his words to Mamie, but I confess unashamedly that I could not do so. I cried.

CHAPTER 20

Few things are sadder than a promise un-
fulfilled.

M Y ACQUAINTANCE WITH the Kennedy family be-
gan in the late 1950s with Sargent Shriver, a brother-in-law of the future
President. At my request he joined a distinguished advisory council I
established, under a grant from the Ford Foundation, to study the
problem of political intrusion into higher education. Shriver was then
chairman of the Board of Education of Chicago. I liked him. He was
gracious, co-operative, and helpful.

Not long thereafter I had luncheon with Mrs. John F. Kennedy in
a spacious home in Palm Beach, Florida, at a time when Senator Kennedy was in the hospital with serious back trouble. Later Sargent Shriver
and his wife, representing the Kennedy Foundation, came to my office
at The Johns Hopkins University to discuss the possibility of the Foundation's making a substantial grant toward the construction of a huge
children's medical center, the problem of handicapped children being
of prime interest to the Foundation.

When the contribution was made it was presented to me by Ted
Kennedy. His brother was then fighting vigorously to win the Democratic primary in West Virginia. After a cordial conversation and the
usual picture taking as the check was presented to me, Ted Kennedy
pinned on my lapel a "Kennedy for President" button. I laughed and
said that in the unlikely event that John Kennedy became President of
the United States he as a brother would find that life would become
complicated. Little did I know then that the Kennedys would have no
hesitation in using the prestige of a presidential brother to achieve political prominence for themselves. I say this with no intention of being
critical. President Kennedy was the first in American history to appoint
a brother to the Cabinet. This was a step which President Eisenhower
and I had rejected out of hand, but what the Kennedys did may in the

future be recurrent rather than abnormal. And the nation may be better served, depending, of course, on the ability of the persons involved. Americans are suspicious of nepotism, so if it is practiced the abilities of the appointee or the candidate for election must actually be superior if criticism is to be avoided.

The nomination of John F. Kennedy as the Democratic candidate for the presidency was a surprise to most of us in the White House circle. We saw him as an engaging young man whose positions on public issues were obscure. Soon we were angry about his assertions that the United States was falling behind the Soviet Union in certain military areas (a misrepresentation corrected by Secretary of Defense McNamara a few months after Kennedy's inauguration). To our further irritation, Kennedy charged that the world reputation of the United States was at an all-time low (it has been going down ever since, especially after our commitment in the Vietnam War) and that the economy was in a mess (inflation had been stopped and production was steadily upward).

We were confident that Nixon would win, partly because he was better known and also because it seemed doubtful that a Catholic could be elected.

When word reached the White House that Kennedy had challenged Nixon to several television debates, President Eisenhower quickly called Nixon and advised him against accepting. He argued that the debates would automatically give Kennedy a wider public audience than he could achieve on his own, and would not make Nixon any better known than eight years in the vice-presidency had already done. He also pointed out that Nixon, as a responsible member of the Eisenhower administration, would as best he could have to adhere to the well-known facts in all policy and program matters, whereas Kennedy could indulge in charges and distortions which would be difficult to correct. Finally, my brother thought that debates did not constitute the appeal to reason and careful statement of facts and views that would best serve Nixon's purposes. He much preferred forthright exposition.

Nixon, however, felt that he would be branded a coward if he declined. The debates, in my judgment, were a major cause of Nixon's loss in 1960. Kennedy took the initiative in making charges and stating views and never lost it. His youth, vigor, and inimitable style made a great impression. Nixon, on the other hand, seemed tired, even ill, especially in the first debate.

There continues to be, even to this day, a difference of opinion as to whether Henry Cabot Lodge as vice-presidential candidate on the Republican ticket did or did not contribute to the Republican defeat. William Lawrence insisted that Lodge was selected as vice-presidential candidate long before the Republican convention began. He was wrong about this. Immediately following his own nomination Nixon called a conference in his hotel suite with about twenty-five of us attending. Each of us was asked to speak candidly about possible vice-presidential nominees. Four or five leading Republicans were seriously considered. Many of us supported Lodge. I did so because of the superb job he had done as ambassador to the United Nations, a position in which he had often spoken to the American people by radio and television. Further, the name Lodge, like Nixon, was a household word. In the campaign Senator Lodge was much less effective than I expected. I agreed with those who felt that he added no votes to the ticket and may have caused some to shift to Kennedy.

My relations with Senator Ted Kennedy and Sargent Shriver continued on a friendly basis after John Kennedy became President. Twice the senator came to Johns Hopkins at my request to speak to the students and faculty and, later, in the Johnson administration when I appeared before a Senate committee of which he was chairman, he was elaborate in his comments on my public service.

My last meetings with Shriver were amusing. He was seriously considering running for the Democratic gubernatorial nomination in Maryland against the incumbent Marvin Mandel. Twice he came to my house to suggest that the liberals of the state, Republicans and Democrats, should form a coalition and for that purpose I would make an ideal chairman of the campaign committee. I declined, suggesting to Shriver that a Republican as head of a campaign effort in a primary—in a state with four times as many registered Democrats as Republicans—would guarantee that most Democrats would support the regular ticket. He wisely decided not to make his initial effort in elective politics a losing one.

(As things turned out, in 1972 when he was the vice-presidential nominee, his defeat in elective politics was a humiliating one.)

I must confess at the outset that John F. Kennedy is the most difficult President for me to characterize or categorize. This is partly because I begin with a natural bias against him; he campaigned against the Eisenhower administration in his contest with Richard Nixon and he said and did things which could only hurt and alienate those of us who were part of that administration—especially his blatant misrepresentations. I don't need to be reminded that politics is like that, or that Eisenhower campaigned against the Truman administration in 1952 and Nixon against the Johnson administration in 1968. That doesn't change the bias; it only explains it. Moreover, I never got to know President Kennedy very well. I carried out one major assignment for him, and that was not a pleasant experience.

But even if this were not the case I would find it difficult to evaluate Kennedy the man and Kennedy the President. Like most Presidents, he was complex. He was an odd blend of liberalism and conservatism, of impulsiveness and wisdom, of pragmatism and idealism. In his first year in office he made monumental errors. But he showed wisdom and courage in the Cuban missile crisis of 1962. Since he learned rapidly and never made the same mistake twice, it is possible that, had his life been spared, he might have become a great President. And that, of course, is another reason why it is hard to assess President Kennedy: he was not permitted to finish what he began.

The Bay of Pigs fiasco hurt the American pride, injured the reputation of the United States abroad and especially in Latin America, gave Khrushchev erroneous views about American leadership, and was subsequently responsible for Kennedy's taking unwise actions to prove that the presidency of the United States was not in weak hands.

Shortly after President Kennedy took office the Cuban exiles in the United States for the first time put aside their internecine quarrels and agreed upon their own leadership, essentially a government in exile. That leadership approved of the insistent desire of the exiles to invade their homeland and convinced the CIA and the Joint Chiefs of Staff that a successful invasion would cause an uprising in Cuba against Fidel Castro. The United States was to provide ships, air cover, and weapons. The exiles would do the fighting.

During the presidential campaign John Kennedy said his policy would be to give United States support to democratic forces opposed to both Batista and Castro, and he advocated an invasion by the exiles. So with the United States' approval and help the exiles set forth in mid-April on their ill-fated mission of liberation. Whether they would have succeeded even if the United States had kept its promises for air cover is questionable. The only certain fact is that the Castro regime crushed the invasion. President Kennedy took full responsibility for our part in the action, and he said:

"I intend to profit from this lesson. . . . There is an old saying that victory has a hundred fathers and defeat is an orphan."

It was in the aftermath of his first serious mistake that President Kennedy called upon me to perform a most difficult assignment.

When the Bay of Pigs effort failed, more than 1,200 Cuban invaders were imprisoned in Cuba. President Kennedy feared for their lives and wished to free them. Their possible fate was obviously on his conscience. He knew that Castro had practiced genocide ruthlessly following his defeat of the Batista forces. The likelihood was that he would continue the practice.

An opportunity to free the men came when Castro, speaking expansively and boastfully to Cuban farmers, offered to trade the prisoners for tractors. President Kennedy went into action at once. As had happened so often in the past, I answered my home telephone to hear that familiar female voice say: "Dr. Eisenhower, one moment, please; the President is calling."

My first reaction was one of curiosity and some puzzlement. Why would John Kennedy call me? I had no time to speculate, for the young President was on the line at once, and his first words were: "Dr. Eisenhower, I want to ask you for some help."

After three decades, my reaction was almost a conditioned response. Without knowing any more, I replied: "I'll do whatever I can." But I was genuinely surprised. Although I had run errands for every President since Hoover, I had opposed John Kennedy's election and I expected no presidential assignments during his term.

The President explained that Castro was sending ten prisoners to the United States to negotiate for the release of the Bay of Pigs prisoners. Our government felt an obligation to these men but could not deal with Castro directly, for we had severed official relations with Cuba.

The President, therefore, asked me to serve on a committee with Mrs. Eleanor Roosevelt, Walter Reuther, and George Romney to raise private funds to buy the tractors and free the prisoners. (Romney declined, but Joseph Dodge accepted.)

I accepted on the condition that the President or the Secretary of State announce at once that the policy underlying the committee's work was a presidential one. The promise was given, and the President said he would explain the matter to the American people the next day.

Later that evening Walter Reuther called to discuss with me how the committee should proceed with its task. During the conversation he said something that kept me awake most of that night: "As I understand it this is to be a wholly private effort and we aren't to mention that the President has asked us to undertake this."

I quickly demurred, pointing out that private citizens cannot meddle in foreign affairs and that to do so would put us in violation of the Logan Act. Reuther pooh-poohed this, saying that everything had been cleared with the State Department.

I have recorded subsequent incidents in all their tiresome detail in *The Wine Is Bitter*[22]—how a storm of protest developed when President Kennedy failed to notify the Congress and the American people that the policy decision in this grave matter was in fact his. The President's failure to carry out his commitment to me brought upon the ad hoc committee charges that it was flagrantly violating the Logan Act, was setting the dangerous precedent of giving in to ransom demands, was trading in human lives, and was dangerously playing a game with a Communist power.

Not only did President Kennedy not keep his promise to inform the American people that he had asked our committee to serve, but before a week had passed he issued a statement urging Americans to support our committee. At the same time he declared that the United States Government had not been and could not be a party to the negotiations with Castro and that the government was neither hindering nor helping the wholly private effort.

After ten days of personal abuse and bitterness, led by leaders of the President's own party, I wrote a brutally frank letter to the President, charging bad faith on his part. The letter was referred, possibly by a staff member, to Secretary of State Dean Rusk, who telephoned me to say that it was the first time he had been consulted on the matter and that he would at once make an appropriate explanation. For the remaining three weeks of our abortive effort our committee was under Rusk's guidance, but now I was persona non grata at the White House and the White House was in no better standing with me.

Dean Rusk had for many years been a friend of mine, so it is probable, despite my opposition to the President's election, that I would have been called upon to carry out non-partisan missions abroad during the Kennedy administration. Unfortunately, the Tractors for Freedom episode removed any such possibility.

The Bay of Pigs crisis was only one of many. President Kennedy faced Soviet-East German threats against Berlin, a vexing problem of what to do about Vietnam, the serious prospect of abrogating the Skybolt missile agreement with the British and substituting the submarine-launched Polaris missiles, rumblings from President de Gaulle about France's desire to have its own nuclear capability, and to be militarily independent, and his own mistaken belief, repeatedly stated during his campaign, that the military posture of the United States was not what it should be. During the campaign he had been critical of the deliberate and composed methods of the Eisenhower years and therefore tackled these and other problems with "vigor."

As early as mid-May, President Kennedy pondered the possibility of a meeting with Khrushchev, believing that he might obviate any danger of a miscalculation by Khrushchev of United States firmness with respect to Berlin and other critical areas as a result of setbacks in Cuba and Laos. In a meeting with the Soviet leader he would demonstrate that the American President was a man of strength and action.

He called for an expansion of America's military might and directed the Defense Department to begin training guerrilla troops—the Green Berets—who might enter South Vietnam to halt Communist expansion and prevent a "domino-loss of nations in Southeast Asia." He sent Vice-President Johnson—later Walt Rostow and General Maxwell Taylor—to the threatened area for a personal appraisal and on Johnson's return asked the Congress for an additional hundred million dollars in aid for South Vietnam, Thailand, and Pakistan. He was giving tangible proof of his inaugural statement: "Let every nation know that we shall pay any price . . . in order to assure the survival and success of liberty. This much we pledge."

373

Before the year was out he sent about 1,500 United States troops, especially guerrilla forces, to Vietnam. In 1962, 10,000 more were sent. By 1963 we had 16,000 men in South Vietnam. For the first time in that political-military jungle our forces participated in the fighting. Whether Kennedy would have further escalated our part in the war, as President Johnson did, or withdrawn our troops is a question hotly disputed by those who were closest to him. His only revealing statements on the subject were two. In a press conference he said, "In my opinion, for us to withdraw from that effort would mean a collapse not only of South Vietnam but of Southeast Asia. *So we are going to stay there!*" On television shortly before his shattering assassination he commented, "If Vietnam went it would have given the impression that the wave of the future in Southeast Asia was China and the Communists." Interestingly, between these two presidential statements Secretary McNamara said, *"We are winning the war."*

Walt W. Rostow, close adviser of the President on many matters, including the development of counterinsurgency forces, has said that if Kennedy had lived he would have followed the same plan that Johnson did, only he would have done it sooner. Kennedy would not, he insisted, have countenanced another Cuba. On the other hand, Kenneth P. O'Donnell, top aide to Kennedy, and Theodore Sorensen, counselor to the President, have said that Kennedy, influenced by General MacArthur and Senator Mike Mansfield, would have withdrawn United States forces sometime after the 1964 election and no later than mid-1965. The only irrefutable facts are: actual participation in the Vietnam War by United States forces began under Kennedy; the same advisers who worked with Kennedy remained for some time with Johnson; what action the United States should take in the future became a prime issue in the Johnson-Goldwater campaign; following his election and contrary to his statements during the campaign, Johnson began a major escalation, leading to a total force of about 550,000 United States troops, numerous ships, and massive air forces, which began the bombing of military targets in North Vietnam.

Our participation in the war was, in my judgment, the second crucial error made in the first year of the Kennedy administration.

The anguish and turmoil of the early Kennedy period was not without humor. President Kennedy for five years had enjoyed a high-backed rocker which he moved into the oval office, much to the pleasure of his physician, who felt that rocking was an aid to health. Newsmen and television commentators gave this homey bit of news wide coverage; the chair became the most photographed piece of furniture in the United States. The North Carolina company that made the rocker was swamped with orders. Stores carried full-page advertisements about other rockers that furniture stores carried in stock. Then the United Furniture Workers of America spread the news that the President's chair was made by non-union labor—that the non-unionists were paid a dollar an hour less than union workers. A New York commentator quipped that the rocking chair had become a hot seat. The head of the national union said he was displeased with the President and that in any event a union-made rocker was more comfortable than the one the President used. The White House press secretary diplomatically made no comment.

The President began a feverish activity involving many conferences with Prime Minister Harold Macmillan of Great Britain, Chancellor Adenauer of Germany, Prime Minister Diefenbaker of Canada, and President de Gaulle of France, not only to discuss bilateral and broad international problems but also to obtain a common view for guidance in a meeting with Chairman Khrushchev in Vienna. Conferences with Macmillan began late in March 1961 in Key West, where the two leaders agreed on a policy of preserving the neutrality of Laos against Communist threats; the two were together again in Washington in the second week in April when, among other things, they emphasized publicly the critical problems of Laos and South Vietnam. At this conference the first word of a possible development of a unified nuclear force for NATO reached the press; the communiqué at the conclusion of the conference explained: "One purpose of the effort to develop a unified nuclear force is to prevent the proliferation of nuclear weapons to many other countries."

In mid-April Adenauer was in Washington. The Chancellor and the President were of one mind that military defenses of the West had to be strengthened, that Germany should be reunited, and that the West should defend the freedom of the people of West Berlin.

Next the President went to Canada to confer with Diefenbaker. Here, once more, the problems that would come up in Vienna were discussed: the situation in Southeast Asia, the need for a test ban treaty, the need to stem Communist advance in Latin America, the defense of

West Berlin, and the need to strengthen conventional forces in the NATO complex.

On June 1, Kennedy flew to Paris to see De Gaulle before proceeding to Vienna. The two Presidents achieved an identity of views on Western actions to counter any threat to Berlin by the Soviet Union but differed on many NATO matters.

Before leaving Paris, President Kennedy, at a reception in his honor, engaged in a charming bit of humor for which he was famous: "This city is no stranger to me," he said. "A Parisian designed the city of Washington . . . who laid out our broad boulevards. . . . When he finished he presented a bill to the Congress for $90,000, and the Congress of the United States, in one of those bursts of economic fervor for which they are justifiably famous, awarded him the munificent sum of $3,000. Some people have been so unkind as to suggest that your clothes designers have been collecting the bill ever since."

From June 3 to 5, 1961, Kennedy and Khrushchev discussed world problems in Vienna. Reports of the meeting are confusing and contradictory. It is known that Khrushchev ruled out atomic and hydrogen wars and those limited wars that could lead to holocausts but was adamant in saying that "wars of liberation" were not only permissible but necessary and would have the support of the Soviet Union. The President retorted that this was a fallacious and highly dangerous policy.

The two leaders apparently reached a limited accord on Laos (which proved to be meaningless) but divided sharply on the Berlin issue. Khrushchev rattled sabers on this problem. Kennedy made it clear that NATO would defend the city and keep access to it open. The two also disagreed on key issues of armaments; Kennedy wanted the two nations to maintain the status quo in armaments, but Khrushchev objected because the United States was then superior in military strength.

Some newsmen on the scene said that the two leaders got along well and that Khrushchev developed respect for the young and vigorous President. A military historian, Stephen E. Ambrose, said that Kennedy got "nowhere with Khrushchev." Ambassador George F. Kennan, who read the verbatim account of the meeting, was reported by the press as saying that Kennedy was a "tongue-tied young man, not forceful, with no ideas of his own," and that the impression Kennedy conveyed may have encouraged the Soviet Union to risk sending offensive missiles to Cuba. Subsequently James Reston in an interview on the National

Educational Network said that Kennedy "got off the track" with Khrushchev. He believed that the "bullying" of Kennedy by Khrushchev was the result of United States indecision in the Bay of Pigs fiasco and that President Kennedy afterward decided to send troops to Vietnam in order to make United States power "credible" to the Soviet Union.

Upon his return from Vienna, Kennedy moved to increase the military budget. He activated Army Reserves and National Guards, adding 300,000 men to the troops available. Forty thousand were sent to Germany to add to our retaliatory capability.

The Soviets responded to these moves by increasing their military budget. This caused the United States to make further increases in its conventional and nuclear power. A new and costly arms race was under way; it was, indeed, the largest peacetime arms race in history. Later Secretary of Defense McNamara, with the advantage of hindsight, said that "the whole thing was wrong."

Military historian Ambrose, in his book, *Rise to Globalism,*[27] states that under President Eisenhower the Soviets believed that an accommodation with the United States in military matters was becoming possible but that as they witnessed the new Kennedy effort they changed their minds.

On August 13, 1961, two months after the Vienna conference, the Soviet Union and East Germany began building the Berlin Wall, which still stands as grim evidence of the sharp division between West and East. Khrushchev broke the moratorium on atomic testing and built an atomic bomb several thousand times as powerful as the one the United States had dropped on Hiroshima. In August 1962, Khrushchev began putting offensive missiles in Cuba and we now unleashed a spate of boastful publicity about our military superiority. It was not a favorable or quiet period.

In 1962 two crucially important developments took place, one of which was harmful to the Western powers, though President Kennedy probably did the right thing despite the unhappy and perhaps inevitable consequences. The other showed the new wisdom and mettle of the President.

The first of these involved a complex web of Britain's desire to enter the European Common Market, Britain's uneasiness over the prospect of the scrapping of Skybolt, the development of multilateral atomic capability in Europe, and De Gaulle's sudden actions which weakened NATO. This complex of problems began on January 28, 1961, when MacMillan met with De Gaulle to discuss Britain's desire to become a member of the European Economic Community. The two met again in June. In these conferences De Gaulle was friendly, even encouraging, but he made no commitment.

In Great Britain a debate extending over months involved an agreement between the United States and Great Britain, under which the United States would produce Skybolt missiles for British and American planes which, when launched, would have a range of about one thousand miles. Britain would produce her own planes and atomic warheads for the missiles. The United States had spent nearly one billion dollars on the project, Great Britain about $200 million. Rumors of adverse United States views about Skybolt had reached British leaders and this was the cause of the continuing debate.

Kennedy and Macmillan met in the Bahamas shortly after mid-December 1962. Hard bargaining continued for days. On December 22 the two issued a joint communiqué which provided that the Skybolt project would be discontinued (tests in the United States had met with failure), the United States would instead provide Great Britain with submarine-borne Polaris missiles which Britain would provide with warheads in her own submarines, Britain's submarines would become part of the NATO nuclear force and would have their targets designated by NATO, the United States would match the British contribution to NATO's nuclear capability, and the two nations would immediately contribute to NATO a portion of their existing nuclear forces in Europe (though the United States would keep the greater part of its nuclear forces outside the NATO command).

Kennedy and Macmillan jointly signed an urgent invitation to De Gaulle to enter into the same agreement.

In January 1963, De Gaulle, who had not been consulted on these matters, made his position clear. He did not approve of a multilateral NATO nuclear force. Further, since by law the United States reserved to itself the final decision about the use of its atomic power, its assignment of nuclear capability to NATO was meaningless; hence, France also would develop and control its own.

He then for the first time expressed open opposition to Great Britain's entry into the European Economic Community; commentators said that De Gaulle felt the Nassau agreement made Great Britain a satellite of the United States and he had no intention of co-operating in or having France follow such a course.

His intransigence over a period of time became increasingly embarrassing to the Western Alliance. He withdrew French naval forces from under the NATO command, demanded that American air bases in France be turned over to the French government, later recognized Communist China, then ejected NATO from France (which cost the United States immense sums of money), and recognized North Vietnam.

After studying the voluminous records of that period, my view is that De Gaulle seized upon the Bahama communiqué as an excuse to hasten actions which he had long wanted to take; he was not a party to the Nassau agreement and he could therefore use it as a pretext for declaring France's independence. Only six months after the NATO alliance was created, De Gaulle had said that France "must first count upon itself, independent of foreign aid," and "NATO takes away from the initiative to build our own defense." In mid-1957 and again early in 1958 he indicated that when the NATO agreement was open for renegotiation in 1969 he would insist upon many modifications, though he would not repudiate NATO. A month later, on February 28, 1958, he was reported as having said privately that "NATO is against our interest." NATO had been established, he felt, to counter any possible Soviet threat but he thought there was no longer such threat. "After France has regained her own independence," he had said, "perhaps she will be linked with the Western countries . . . but we cannot accept a superior like the United States to be responsible for us."

These attitudes were well known during the Eisenhower administration, but Presidents Eisenhower and De Gaulle had worked successfully together during World War II, General Eisenhower had escorted De Gaulle triumphantly into Paris to the acclaim of the French people on their day of liberation, and as personal friends they subordinated their differences for the general good of the West. It is possible, as I have said, that De Gaulle merely bided his time and seized upon the Nassau declaration as an excuse to begin a series of actions, detrimental to the Western nations, that he had been planning for years.

Kennedy's moment of greatness came in the Cuban missile crisis late in 1962, shortly before the congressional elections, in which the danger of offensive missiles to the United States and many nations of Central and South America was debated. The situation was fraught with peril, one that might lead to World War III. For two weeks the President's advisers studied every possible alternative, from bombing the missile sites to invasion of the island. Finally, of all the options open to him, Kennedy courageously adopted the only one that had a chance of success short of war. He imposed a blockade of Cuba with United States war vessels; the ships would be supported, if necessary, by air power; the purpose was to bar the shipment of Soviet materials needed to complete the installation of the offensive missiles. At the same time he let it be known that a missile attack on the United States or any Western Hemisphere nation would lead to a nuclear attack on the Soviet Union itself. For days the nation lived in dread, glued to television sets, watching the approaching confrontation that could have destroyed much of the civilized world. Then Khrushchev backed down. He called back the Soviet ships that were on the way to Cuba. The crisis was over and the young President had won. The only concession by the United States was to assure Khrushchev that we would respect the independence of Cuba and that we would implement an earlier decision to remove our missiles from Turkey.

Kennedy's other significant success in foreign affairs was in having his representatives negotiate a test ban treaty with the Soviet Union, a treaty with some shortcomings, such as the clause which bans underground testing if such testing causes contaminated material, no matter how little, to cross a national boundary. This has seriously retarded research in the peaceful uses of atomic power, including its use in canal building. Over all, however, the treaty was a plus.

His performance on the domestic front was a great disappointment to President Kennedy. His bold New Frontier programs were in large measure stalled in committees of Congress at the time of his assassination, and it remained for President Johnson to make them legislation under the Great Society. One observer of congressional affairs has said that, of Kennedy's recommendations to the Congress, only thirty-seven resulted in legislation during his lifetime. Another observer presented a more charitable interpretation. He pointed out that Kennedy induced the Congress to pass the poll tax amendment, the nuclear test-ban treaty, the Peace Corps legislation, the Communications Satellite Act, and the Reciprocal Trade Act. In sheer routine affairs, the Congress approved 108 of Kennedy's 195 recommendations. The difference in these two views is no doubt due to congressional action on truly important measures; thus none of Kennedy's civil rights recommendations was approved.

Despite his mediocre record with Congress, President Kennedy had gained stature in the world, especially among young people. His style was indeed impressive—his natural appeal and good looks, his vigorous and colorful presentation of ideas tuned to the modern age, his flair for phrase making, his easy, often self-deprecating sense of humor. For many Americans the past was past, the mistakes he had made had been offset by his triumphs, he would thereafter lead the country to new heights. One can only speculate about what President Kennedy might have done, for the tragedy in Dallas brought a sudden end to the New Frontier. I believe that President Kennedy could and probably would have become a great President. His enthusiasm for the office never waned. In foreign affairs he had been through the crucible of difficult experience and had quickly become a veteran with a confidence in his own judgment and negotiating ability. There is no reason to doubt that he would have been re-elected, probably with a greater mandate than he received in 1960, and would have learned to work more effectively with the Congress. He had certainly created a new and positive spirit among large segments of the population, a growing sense that we could solve our problems and move beyond the obstacles that confronted us toward some new frontier.

Pierre Salinger, who served as press secretary in the Kennedy administration, has said that between the President and Robert Kennedy there "was a complete and mutual bond."[28] Salinger felt that the relationship between the two rested mainly on Robert's love and admiration for his older brother, who considered Robert to be his closest friend and chief confidant. The relationship endured throughout the period of John Kennedy's presidency. Indeed Robert Kennedy was the central figure who was consulted by the President on all critical issues.

Arthur Schlesinger in his book, A Thousand Days,[17] expressed the view that Robert Kennedy was his brother's "total partner," a relationship which Schlesinger felt had never been duplicated between a President and his confidant. Decisions were made jointly. Robert often used the plural "we" in describing the President's wishes and no one had the audacity to challenge his right to speak for his brother.

Robert Kennedy eagerly accepted the role of confidant when his brother set his mind on becoming President of the United States. Following Senator Kennedy's losing bid for the vice-presidential nomination at the 1956 Democratic National Convention, the brothers began to plan together for the presidential race in 1960. Senator Kennedy felt that only Robert could be trusted to perform the arduous work of collecting delegates and other supporters, and history shows that the trust was not misplaced.

There has been no exact parallel to this relationship. Certainly my relationship with President Eisenhower was completely different. I am not a political animal; I did not induce my brother to become a candidate either in 1952 or 1956; I did not supervise his campaigns; and I did not serve as a "total partner" of my brother.

It is a mistake, too, to compare the Kennedy situation to the Wilson-House or the Truman-Clifford relationships. House and Clifford were immersed in the partisan political campaigns and in the White House they were constantly consulted on a vast array of central issues, but neither had the complete and irrevocable trust displayed by President Kennedy for his brother.

It is not an exaggeration to say that President Kennedy viewed his brother as a fixed star in an ever changing constellation of government officials—as an alter ego. Patterned after the Roosevelt staff organization, the Kennedy staff was open, flexible, and highly competitive. Talented staff aides with boundless ambition clashed with one another as they competed for the President's attention. Whatever staff unity existed seemed to stem from a common distrust of bureaucracy—a view shared by the President himself—and the widely shared admiration of the President.

In this competitive milieu the President felt he needed someone on whom he could rely unreservedly, and this was his younger brother, whose judgment the President had tested for many years.

It was unique in American experience when the President appointed his brother Attorney General of the United States. Attorneys General had usually been drawn from among political advisers—Thomas Clark, Herbert Brownell, John Mitchell—for example. The fact that the Kennedys were brothers brought charges of nepotism; a great volume of letters to the Democratic National Committee ran a hundred to one against the appointment. Robert Kennedy, sensitive to criticism, was reluctant to accept the post but capitulated under pressure from his brother and father. In time the criticism vanished and the dual role of Attorney General and presidential confidant proved to be appealing to the combative and activist-oriented Robert Kennedy. He became the second most influential man in Washington and did all he could to advance the President's domestic and foreign programs. Sorensen tells how a phone call from the Attorney General interrupted the President in conference, and John Kennedy turned to his visitors with a smile and said, "Will you excuse me a moment; this is the second most powerful man calling."[29]

Ralph de Toledano[30] has described Robert Kennedy as the most political Attorney General since Harry Daugherty under President Harding. He shouldered, Nick Thimmesch and William Johnson have said, White House decisions "almost as often as the President."[31]

In domestic affairs the Attorney General's influence was pervasive. In collaboration with his brother he developed and steered seven anti-racket bills through Congress, carried on anti-crime efforts as chairman of the President's Committee on Juvenile Delinquency and Youth Crime, launched a relentless vendetta against Jimmy Hoffa and worked assiduously, though not successfully, to obtain passage of the Civil Rights Bill of 1963, with its strong section on public accommodations, a bill which was finally put through Congress by President Johnson in June of 1964. In May 1961, when the Freedom Fighters were attacked in Alabama and state and local police did nothing, the brothers agreed to employ whatever force was necessary to restore order, an action which led to the dispatching of federal officers. On September 29, 1962, they faced another crisis together—the registration of James Meredith at the University of Mississippi. The President and his brother conferred by telephone with Nicholas Katzenbach, the Deputy Attorney General, who was on the scene in Oxford, Mississippi; following adamant refusal of Governor Barnett to let Meredith register, a mob began to move toward the dormitory in which Meredith was staying; the Kennedys ordered military police and federalized National Guardsmen into action. Sixteen thousand troops descended on the campus. Meredith was registered. The cost was two dead and more than two hundred wounded.

Robert Kennedy, a partner also in political affairs, played a decisive role in dispensing patronage appointments at high and low levels; he helped the President identify people for judicial and Cabinet-level appointments and singled out individuals for jobs as postmasters throughout the country.

The President soon began to rely on his brother in foreign affairs. As the President's suspicion of the regular federal establishment grew— a direct consequence of the Bay of Pigs fiasco—he had his brother participate in meetings of the National Security Council and help with a reorganization of the National Security policy system.

Robert Kennedy joined the President at the command post during the Dominican Republic crisis in 1961, following the assassination of dictator Rafael Trujillo; the same occurred in August 1961 when the East Germans began to build the Berlin Wall, at which time it was Robert Kennedy, not the Secretary of State, who met with the Soviet ambassador to the United States to convey the views of the President. In the Cuban missile crisis of October 1962 the President placed his brother in the middle of the debate over appropriate American response to the installation of Russian offensive missiles in Cuba. After days of intensive discussion Robert Kennedy's suggestions formed the core of the key letter sent to Chairman Khrushchev. Robert Kennedy had persuaded his brother and the other members of the National Security Council to ignore a more belligerent note from Khrushchev and respond instead to a positive inquiry sent earlier from the Soviet Union. After the Soviet ships turned back on the high seas and did not challenge the quarantine imposed by the United States, John Kennedy thanked his brother and Ted Sorensen for being the most useful advisers during that historic period.

Interestingly, the Kennedy brothers transacted their governmental business almost exclusively during working hours. They socialized only rarely together, thus limiting the time for extended and relaxed conversations. Perhaps lengthy discussions were not necessary. Having interacted with one another since they were children, they could communicate almost by osmosis. Their minds were as one.

Though Robert Kennedy was without doubt *primus inter pares*, Ted Sorensen was of invaluable assistance as an adviser to the President. Sorensen's intimate relationship began before Kennedy revealed his aspirations to become a presidential candidate. A graduate of the University of Nebraska Law School, where he performed brilliantly, Sorensen joined the Kennedy senatorial staff, and demonstrated his unstinting devotion to the senator's political career. It was not long before Kennedy trusted Sorensen implicitly with virtually every aspect of his senatorial job.

There were no lifted eyebrows when President Kennedy's first White House appointment was Ted Sorensen. He was named special counsel to the President. The relationship grew and solidified. Sorensen demonstrated around-the-clock devotion. In contrast to Robert Kennedy, who maintained his distinct personality, Sorensen became virtually indistinguishable from the President. He possessed the "passion for anonymity" which Roosevelt had advocated; indeed, his place in history might have remained obscure had it not been for his subsequently writing a book on his many years with Kennedy.

After the Bay of Pigs fiasco Sorensen became a general adviser to the President. He helped develop legislative proposals and established a liaison with many government departments. But the greatest acclaim came to him for his ability as a speech writer for the President. He could match Kennedy's passion for colorful rhetoric, and in doing so he often placed new ideas before the President. Especially did he constantly express his liberal and internationalist views, which often were different from those of the somewhat centralist President.

President Kennedy's inaugural address will remain as a symbol of the effective and close interaction between the two men. The writing of that talk was a joint enterprise. Much later it was Sorensen's participation with Robert Kennedy in studying alternatives and finally arriving at a possible solution to the Cuban missile crisis that won for him Kennedy's unbounded respect.

In September 1963, at the urging of my brother and under the sponsorship of the Republican Citizens Committee of the United States, I became chairman of the Republican Critical Issues Council. Associated with me on the council were twenty-four nationally known economists, financial experts, former military personnel, publishers, welfare experts, bankers, internationalists, agricultural specialists, educators, lawyers, and a former Secretary of Labor. Our purpose was to conduct serious research on the major problems facing the nation and to propose solutions different from those advocated by the Administration.

A party in power has at its disposal in the federal agencies research help on every conceivable question. Normally its proposals are an outgrowth of manifold studies. What it advocates can be supported with abundant evidence. But the party out of power has essentially no research assistance. Hence opposition statements, usually newsworthy only if expressed by important members of Congress, are often lacking in substance and so in persuasiveness. Further, many of the nation's problems, from imbalances in international payments and troublesome agricultural problems to international alliances and civil rights, are so complex as to be beyond the comprehension of most private citizens. We felt, therefore, that alternatives to the Administration's proposals, each based upon careful research, should be widely distributed among the people so that they could better decide what they deemed to be the correct courses of action. We said in each publication we issued: "Seldom before have the needs of the nation so called for principled, clearly reasoned analyses of national problems and fresh programs to meet them. The Critical Issues Council seeks to provide American citizens with an honest evaluation of matters of vital concern to the Republic, to offer evidence instead of emotion, purpose in place of polemic, and to follow criticism with positive proposals."

We set up twelve task forces, each comprised of nationally known individuals who had special competence in the problem assigned to it. For example, the task force on Imbalances in International Payments was chaired by Dr. Henry C. Wallach, economist of Yale University, with Elliott V. Bell, William Fellner, Neil H. Jacoby, Clarence R. Randall, and Frazer B. Wilde as members, and Dr. Raymond Saulnier and Dr. Arthur Burns, both former chairmen of the President's Council of Economic Advisers, as consultants. Each task force was similarly constituted.

We prepared studies entitled: *Panama; A Free and Prosperous Agriculture; The Atlantic Community and United States Security; Republicans and Civil Rights* (prepared with the help of the scholarly Ripon Society of Boston); *Cuba; America's Space Program; Balance of Payments; The Future of Foreign Aid; Fiscal Policy for National Strength and Prosperity; The U.S. Position in the Far East* (the only one about which I had serious reservations); *Resources and the Future;* and *Population.*

Just as we were ready to issue the first of these studies the President was assassinated. So of course we delayed publication, recognizing that the stability of the nation was for a time at stake, and also determined to await the attitude of the Administration when the new President had an opportunity to make his views known.

Early in April we began releasing our studies, usually one each week. Most studies were given front-page space in the nation's press, as much as two columns in the New York *Times* and other leading papers. I felt we were making an unprecedented contribution to the information and political reasoning of citizens.

Senator Goldwater had from the very beginning of the Critical Issues Council's work been flatly opposed to it. Through the Republican National Committee he tried to bring about the council's dissolution. Since the council was sponsored not by the Republican National Committee but by the Republican Citizens Committee, Goldwater's efforts did not succeed. So he appealed to my brother Edgar, who was chairman of Goldwater forces in the state of Washington, and Edgar in turn insisted that I have a conference with the senator. That conference, a breakfast meeting in the Capitol building, was held two days prior to the California primary in which Governor Rockefeller and Senator Goldwater were the opposing candidates.

When I entered the senator's private room in the Capitol at eight in the morning he came forward, shook hands with great cordiality, and said, "I have read every one of the documents published by the Critical Issues Council and I agree with all your positions with the exception of your recommendations on civil rights. In that booklet you have gone beyond what I could accept."

We had a pleasant chat at breakfast, and then as he accompanied me into the hall outside his office a dozen photographers began taking pictures of the two of us. They were carried in the press nationally, but especially in California on the day before the primary, thus creating the impression that the Critical Issues Council, the Republican Citizens Committee, and a brother close to President Eisenhower were not, to say the least, unfriendly to Goldwater's candidacy.

In the press the same day, news of the birth of a child to Governor and Mrs. Nelson Rockefeller was on the front pages of most California newspapers. This renewed, especially among women voters, criticisms that previously had been rampant of Rockefeller's divorce and remarriage.

The California vote was close, only about a one per cent advantage going to Goldwater. It was said at the time that the two stories made the difference. Certainly it is true that if Rockefeller had won the Republican primary in California his strength added to Governor Scranton's might have brought about in the 1964 Republican Convention a result different from what developed.

Concurrently with these activities, which commanded much of my time, preparations were under way in Maryland to select delegates to the Republican National Convention. I was chosen as a delegate at large, subject to ratification by the state convention. Before the convention met, Governor William Scranton of Pennsylvania announced that he would not be a candidate for the presidential nomination. This was a shattering disappointment to me. Several months earlier I had spent a day with Scranton, urging him to announce his candidacy, but he demurred. So, believing that the nomination of Senator Goldwater would make a Republican defeat certain—though I say this with reluctance, for I like him as a gracious and sincere person—I withdrew my name as a candidate for delegate at large.

Then one of the most amazing things in my long public career occurred. I received a call from Governor Scranton. After a moment of amenities he said:

"Milton, I want to ask a great favor of you."

"What can I do for you, Bill?" I asked.

"Tomorrow, at the Maryland State Convention," he said, "I intend to announce my candidacy for the Republican nomination for the presidency. I am hoping you will agree to come to San Francisco and nominate me."

I was completely taken aback. "I am not a delegate," I said, "I withdrew my name some time ago."

"We'll take care of that," he said.

I was delighted at his decision, but I had not anticipated a role for myself at the national convention after I had withdrawn my name as a candidate. Yet I replied: "If you are sure this is what you want and if you can work out a seat in the delegation for me, I will certainly do what you ask."

Before Governor Scranton hung up he said something very interesting: "By the way, Milton, you know that Dick Nixon is in London. Well, he called Mac Mathias and asked him to set up a breakfast meeting with a number of key people in Washington for next Tuesday. Apparently he is going to announce his candidacy for the nomination."

After I hung up I sat at my desk recalling a long talk I had had with Nixon at my home earlier that spring. He had come to Johns Hopkins at my request to address our students and faculty. Prior to his address we had sat in my living room talking mainly about the political situation. Nixon had an amazing grasp of organizational and grass-roots politics. He seemed to know every county chairman and half the committeemen by name. He indicated that the Goldwater forces had been working diligently and successfully to build a wave of support that would sweep the senator to the nomination.

"Barry is a good man," Nixon said, "but he would not be a good President. He has to be stopped. I am not sure it's possible to stop him, but someone has got to try; whoever tries it may himself be committing political suicide."

Now, apparently, if Scranton was right, Nixon had decided to make the effort. He did not know that Bill Scranton had just made the decision to enter the race. The following Monday Nixon arrived at Kennedy Airport and was greeted by a battery of reporters and television commentators, all eager for his reaction to the announcement that Scranton was in the race. I remember clearly the television clips of that interview. Nixon was clearly piqued. He said something to the effect that a man who could not make up his mind whether or not to run for the presidency would not make a very decisive President—evidently referring to Scranton's on-again, off-again posture during the preceding weeks regarding the nomination. I remember being surprised that Nixon would be so critical, in light of his comment that someone had to stop Goldwater even at the risk of political suicide. Apparently he was upset at Scranton's entry into the race just a few days before his own announcement as a candidate.

The day after Governor Scranton called me he came to Maryland, attended the state Republican Convention, and announced that he would be a candidate for the party's presidential nomination.

True to his word, Governor Scranton arranged for me to become a delegate, and he did so in a unique but legal way. The delegate from my district resigned and his alternate automatically attained delegate status. I was selected as the alternate of my district. Next, the new top delegate resigned, and I automatically moved up to the delegate post. I then nominated the original delegate to be my alternate and this was approved.

At the meeting where this unusual procedure was planned, Senator Goldwater's Maryland leader, Fife Symington, himself a delegate, was prepared to make a fight against me. I hoped this would occur, for, as happened in the 1952 convention when my brother was nominated, the fight (if we lost it in the Maryland caucus) would be carried through the Credentials Committee (controlled by the Goldwater forces) to the convention floor. This might, I thought, possibly change what promised to be a kangaroo type of convention. Unfortunately, at the very moment the fight in the Maryland Central Committee was about to begin, a telegram from Senator Goldwater came to me and to Symington, approving my selection.

A few days later I was at the University Club in New York City. At midnight the telephone in my room wakened me from a deep sleep. For a few seconds I failed to recognize Richard Nixon's voice. Soon, however, we were in a serious discussion. He indicated that the drive for Goldwater, if successful, would result in a terrible defeat for the Republican Party. Hence he was going the next morning to Gettysburg to discuss the problem with President Eisenhower. He felt that President Eisenhower was the only person who could make a public statement that might change the course of events. Nixon speculated that if Governor Romney would declare himself to be a candidate three men— Scranton, Rockefeller, and Romney—might gain enough voters to deadlock the convention. He did not say so, but I felt he had in mind the probability that in the event of a deadlock the convention might again turn to him.

At the Gettysburg meeting President Eisenhower reiterated his stand that it would be improper for him to interfere in the nominating procedure; he should save his influence for the vigorous support of the Republican nominee, whoever he might be. I thought Nixon felt so strongly about the matter that he might make a public statement, but he did not.

A great deal of misleading information was being carried by the press at this time. It was reported repeatedly that President Eisenhower had induced Governor Scranton to run on the promise that he would support the governor's candidacy. When this failed to occur the press said that President Eisenhower had changed his mind and that this guaranteed the nomination for Goldwater. I can say without qualification that there never was any such promise—that my brother at no time had any intention of interfering either in the preconvention or convention procedures, a practice based upon a firmly held policy which he was eventually to break in 1968.

Then, in the midst of what seemed to me to be a dismal political picture, an amusing development occurred. Nixon was scheduled to come from a meeting of governors in Cleveland to Maryland to make a major political address and I was to introduce him. Prior to the dinner Mr. and Mrs. Fife Symington gave a cocktail party at their home for Nixon and a hundred of the persons who would attend the dinner where Nixon was to speak. Nixon appeared late. He did not know that Symington was leader of the Goldwater forces in Maryland. Most members of the party were on the lawn. Without speaking to Symington of his intention, Nixon stepped up on the porch, faced the group, clapped his hands for silence, and then with much earnestness suggested that the party urge Governor Romney to become a candidate and thus create a genuine competitive situation in the convention.

His remarks were greeted with vast silence, for most of the guests were Goldwater supporters. Mrs. Symington grabbed my arm in anger and said: "You put him up to this!" I protested, saying that I had had no advance warning of Nixon's intention. She did not believe me and said so in unrepeatable language. The incident merited full coverage by the Baltimore *Sun* the next day.

The 1964 Republican National Convention in the Cow Palace in San Francisco was generally a rather morbid affair. The anti-Goldwater forces skirmished and plotted for several days prior to the balloting, but deep down I think we all knew that the Goldwater juggernaut, which had stubbornly beat back all efforts to modify the conservative platform, would roll on to a first-ballot victory.

Whatever the outcome, I was determined to nominate with great pride my friend Bill Scranton—a man of keen intelligence, sound and moderate philosophy, political and administrative experience, and a vote-winning charisma. The only salve to my wounded feelings was a comment by Huntley and Brinkley that my address was the highlight of the uninspiring events and speeches in the Cow Palace. As I recall, it ranked in the ratings only slightly behind Goldwater's acceptance speech.

I shall never forget the experience of writing that nominating speech. I had scrawled some rather complete notes on a pad on the trip to San Francisco but they were far from satisfactory. My assistant at Johns Hopkins, Ron Wolk, an able writer who had helped me with the Critical Issues papers (despite his being a Democrat), arrived in San Francisco a few days after I did, and I asked him to expand my notes into a draft. Malcolm Moos, who had served as an assistant to President Eisenhower, volunteered to help him. I was in meetings day and night, trying to round up delegates and planning strategy with the Scranton forces, and had not a minute to spare.

The speech went through several drafts, getting closer to what I wanted each time. But Governor Scranton's aides were not happy with the general tone of it. Finally, on Wednesday morning, the day before the nominations, the Scranton lieutenants insisted that Ron Wolk and Mac Moos join them in a suite in the Scranton headquarters to produce a draft acceptable to them. I was not aware of this and learned later from Ron what happened. Four of them, each at a typewriter, began to compose a speech as a committee. One of them would try a few lines, another would modify it slightly, then they would agree and commit it to paper. Ron had worked for me long enough to know at the outset that the very political and highly rhetorical speech emerging from that ad hoc committee would be totally unacceptable. After the first fifteen minutes he left his typewriter and sat quietly on the window sill while the new draft was hammered out.

The new speech was finished just about noon. I was picking Ron up at noon to drive to the Cow Palace. The Scranton men asked him to give me the speech, and he replied that he wanted no part of it. But everyone else had other commitments, so Ron climbed into my car with the speech in hand. As we pulled into traffic he leaned over the front seat and said: "Here is a new draft of the speech, written by a committee, of which I was not a part."

The first sentence I read named the candidate, which I realized would touch off a demonstration immediately and prevent me from going any further for fifteen or twenty minutes. A few paragraphs later the drafters had me shouting questions at the convention to elicit a loud and unifying response. It was a speech I would never make, and in my irritation I hurled it against the dashboard and gave vent to some strong feelings.

Later that night, after President Eisenhower had addressed the convention, I hurried back to my hotel room, somewhat desperate to get my nominating speech written. Ron and I went back to the previous draft, which was pretty nearly what I wanted to say. I rolled up my sleeves and manned the typewriter. Ron spread the previous three or four drafts out on the floor. Then we went at it sentence by sentence, and I picked it out on the ancient typewriter in my two-finger style. I believe it was two or three in the morning when we finished and I woke President Eisenhower's trusted secretary, Lillian Brown, to retype my heavily edited draft on the large-type-face speech typewriter.

Bill Scranton listened to my speech on television in his hotel room. Shortly after I had completed the talk and hours before balloting began, I received a telegram from him saying: "Regardless of the outcome, your nominating speech was the best I ever heard. You made me very proud."

A week or so later a Washington columnist, speculating about whom President Johnson would select as a vice-presidential candidate, said something like this: "One possible candidate is Milton S. Eisenhower, a prominent Republican. This is not as farfetched as it might sound. Dr. Eisenhower nominated liberal Governor Scranton at the Cow Palace last month with a ringing speech that could easily have been made at a Democratic Convention."

I suppose he meant that as a compliment.

No speech, probably no candidate, could have prevented Goldwater from winning the nomination. Richard Nixon, heaping fulsome praise on Goldwater, presented the nominee to the convention for the acceptance speech, thus gaining favor with the conservatives whose support he would need in 1968.

Had Scranton been nominated by some miracle, the documents issued by the Critical Issues Council probably would have constituted a substantial part of the party platform. As things turned out, our work was wasted so far as party declarations were concerned. But I still think that the idea of an opposition party's conducting research and issuing thoughtful alternatives to the Administration's proposals is superior to the type of polemics we normally have in the American political scene.

CHAPTER 21

A society which insists on running its quadrennial conventions like circuses should not be surprised to get tightrope walkers as presidential candidates.

THE SELECTION OF presidential and vice-presidential candidates should be a profound exercise of representative government—an exercise that would command the pride and enthusiastic support of the American people. As it is, this important task is carried out under conditions that are comparable to those of a carnival, circus, or prize fight.

If each of the two major political parties is to nominate the individual best prepared to meet the awesome responsibilities of the President of the United States, we must take prompt steps to reform substantially the national conventions. I am convinced that changes must be made in the selection of delegates and in the rules of the conventions themselves, especially the rules and traditions involving the nomination of the presidential and vice-presidential candidates.

I have been a delegate to two conventions and a spectator at many. In 1964, when I sought support for and nominated Governor William Scranton, the noise level in the Cow Palace in San Francisco was so high that I could not hear what the speakers on the platform were saying. The babble of voices was incessant, ranging from mid-volume to fortissimo. At times the brass bands and organ were deafening. It was impossible to move about the convention floor to confer with other delegates. At one point in the convention I wished to talk to the chairman of another state delegation, for I had been told that he might be leaning to Governor Scranton. I could not even get out of my chair. The aisles were jammed with television reporters who carried portable cameras, radio men with microphones which were constantly being shoved in the faces of delegates who had to shout to be heard, newspaper reporters, and hundreds of pages who were unable to carry messages because of the congestion.

President Eisenhower, in an article in the July 1966 issue of *Reader's Digest*, called the quadrennial conventions "thoroughly disrespectful" and "exercises in chaos and tumult—unmannerly, undignified, ridiculous." The 1964 Republican Convention provided a blatant example of this by booing Governor Rockefeller so loudly and so long that he could not speak. The incident was disgraceful but not unique.

William S. White, in the October 1960 issue of *Harper's*, characterized conventions as being "irresponsible . . . a solemn farce which even a cynic in politics wants to reform. . . . We put the worst possible foot forward . . . in a grimy spectacle which is the beginning of the grand and solemn task of choosing a new President of the United States." When the party platform is taken before the convention, he says, "not one-twentieth of the delegates will hear it or read it, then or later, or ever give it the slightest heed."

Clinton Rossiter,[32] distinguished political scientist, has written of the vocal opposition throughout our history and in all parts of the country to the sloppy methods we use in choosing a President.

Aaron Wildavsky, in the July 12, 1964, issue of the New York *Times* magazine, wrote: "The convention brings [the delegates] together to participate in making an important decision in a terribly short time, under hectic conditions, in a strange place where most of them never find out precisely what is going on and many are full of misinformation." He goes on to say that "confusion is the hallmark of conventions," with the typical delegate floundering around, unsure of where he is to be, what he is to do, or whom he should believe. Wildavsky categorizes the delegates in three groups, some leading, some following: "The party boss or state leader who controls many votes . . . the delegate of independent standing . . . who because of his high personal prestige . . . plays a significant role . . . and the rank and file members whose votes are determined by party leaders, especially in the large delegations." The rank and file delegate follows his governor and does what he is told. However, if a front runner does not succeed in getting the nomination on an early ballot and bargaining and trading begin, as in the 1912 convention when Wilson was nominated, the rank and file delegates assume more importance, for they are the ones most wooed by the several contenders.

Televising this noisy chaos can only serve to disillusion the people of the United States and degrade our reputation abroad. Worse, in the cacophony of noise, quarrels, shouting, and emotional indifference to the solemn business of the convention, there is no possibility of thoughtful and helpful discussions which ought to precede the adoption of a party platform and the nomination of candidates for the highest offices in the land.

Reform must begin many months before the conventions are held.

The selection of delegates to the quadrennial conventions varies by states, the two principal methods being by convention vote and by direct primary. Experience has not indicated that one method is better than another, but both parties should do all they can to improve the quality and balance of their delegations. In both the primary and convention selection systems, some preference goes to those who have at least modest financial resources, for delegates must pay their own travel and living expenses, running from a few hundred dollars for one from a nearby state to as much as fifteen hundred dollars for one from a remote location.

The state convention or state committee method tends to give priority to the selection of those who have been faithful party workers—about eighty-five per cent of the total—regardless of whether these faithful ones have the intelligence, integrity, and judgment essential to the important task they are performing. Often the governor and a small clique select the at-large delegate slate, and the state committee or convention merely rubber-stamps its approval. Nelson W. Polsby of the Brookings Institution, writing in the September 1960 issue of the *Western Political Quarterly*, asserted: "The elected chief executive . . . generally has the most political power. [He] comes closer than any other individual to possessing unilateral control over the party organization . . . hierarchical controls . . . will assert themselves in the national convention. . . . A substantial number of delegates will be controlled hierarchically."

Local conventions and caucuses are different. "Local conventions can sometimes directly select delegates to the national convention, ignoring the wishes of voters, state leaders and national leaders alike," wrote Richard G. Niemi and M. Kent Jennings in the March 1969 issue

397

of the *Western Political Quarterly*. "The path to the Goldwater convention was paved with painstaking, successful efforts in both local and state conventions." County conventions and caucuses are often routinely, almost negligently, handled. Niemi and Jennings indicated that in county conventions in Michigan in 1964, a fourth of the county delegates were absent from a majority of all the meetings. The governor and other state party leaders tend to ignore the smaller desultory county meetings but bring great pressure on the meetings in the large counties, hoping to obtain delegates who will support their position.

Since World War II the national party conventions have become more show and hoopla than actual decision-making bodies. State convention, state committee, local convention, local caucus, and primary methods of selecting delegates have more and more sought to commit the delegates well in advance of the national convention. The real business of the national conventions is done well before they convene and the delegates are lined up and counted to the extent that they often simply go through the motions at the national convention. Although the possibility always exists that there will be substantial shifts in power or sentiment at a national convention, it has become for the most part in recent years an occasion for the public ratification of decisions already made.

The state primary system of selecting delegates places emphasis on popular judgments at a particular moment, with preference often going to a candidate who has spent the most time in the state or has the best-financed campaign. So many states now have primaries, from early March to mid-July, that a candidate cannot campaign strenuously in all of them. Even if he had the time to do so he might well lack the funds. So the candidate must pick his targets carefully, weighing the return he will get for his investment of time and effort and being mindful of the damage to his campaign should he lose in a state where he has made an all-out effort to win. Further, as I have said elsewhere, most personal campaigning by the aspirants, including that involved in primaries, is largely an effort to win support through emotional appeals and does not provide information about a candidate's philosophy, purposes, and views on major issues.

Under federal and state constitutions and laws, as well as national, state, and local party rules, delegate selections are a hodgepodge.

Eleven states, including California, Florida, Ohio, and Wisconsin, select delegates at large and congressional-district delegates exclusively by primaries.

Seventeen states use state and district conventions to choose all delegates. In this group are Connecticut, Idaho, Minnesota, and Missouri, for example.

Twelve states and territories, including Delaware, Montana, and Wyoming, give power exclusively to the central convention to select both delegates at large and district delegates.

Five states, including Michigan and Indiana, modify this slightly by using state conventions to choose delegates at large and district caucuses to select the others.

Five states—Massachusetts, Pennsylvania, Illinois, Maryland, and New York—permit the state committee, rather than a convention, to name delegates at large but resort to primaries in choosing district delegates.

Arkansas and Texas entrust final selection of all delegates to the state convention, but district delegates, nominated by local committees, must be recommended to the state convention. The District of Columbia has a single primary. Oregon resorts to a variety of methods: some delegates at large are chosen by primary, others by state convention, and district delegates are selected by primaries.

As though this weren't complicated enough, the primaries differ in significant ways. Most are presidential preference primaries in which voters cast their ballots directly for a presidential candidate, save for five in which votes are cast for delegates who have announced a preference for a particular candidate.

Under current state laws less than one third of the delegates to the 1976 Republican Convention will be *legally* bound to a candidate on the first ballot, less than one fourth on the second ballot, and less than one seventh on subsequent ballots.

At present, then, a minority of delegates to a convention is *legally* committed to a candidate. Many others, selected by conventions, caucuses, committees, and non-preferential primaries, are committed to candidates by personal pledges, state party convention resolutions, or simply by moral commitments. But these delegates are not *legally* bound to adhere to these stated preferences. They are at least legally free to exercise individual judgments at Republican Conventions in the event that what they hear and learn there induces them to change their minds. Democratic rules differ, but not appreciably.

Unfortunately the trend today is in the wrong direction. More states are considering legislation to initiate preferential primaries as their method of selecting delegates. Delegates selected by preferential primaries can exercise independent judgments in a national convention only if the candidate to whom they are pledged releases them or, differing by states, after the first, second, or subsequent ballots.

Beginning with 1968, but more importantly in the 1972 national conventions, emphasis was placed on balanced delegations—on an acceptable mix of minorities, younger people, older persons, trade unionists, men, women, and so on. The effort to strike a better balance in representation at national conventions is commendable, but I would suggest that educational background should receive equal emphasis, along with experience, philosophy, attitude, judgment, and character. A delegate has a historic mission. His decision should not be routinely or carelessly reached and should not be based on emotion. For reasons which will become clear in my suggestions for convention reforms, it would be advantageous if delegates were not irrevocably committed in advance to a particular candidate. This may be expecting too much in the near future, but it seems to me reasonable that those who seek delegate status in support of particular candidates should not be bound to adhere to such commitments regardless of what develops or what compelling new evidence is presented in the convention. To achieve this, laws governing primaries would have to be changed in a number of states. And unfortunately, as I have said, the current trend is not too promising in this regard. Immediate change in the right direction can be made, however, in party rules governing state and local conventions and caucuses.

Indeed, late in 1973 the Republican National Committee was engaged in discussions that could vitally affect the make-up of delegations chosen by convention and committee methods by reducing the undue influence which a relatively few leaders in each state have heretofore had on the votes of their state delegation. Thus, if a rule of the convention is interpreted as requiring that half of each delegation be women, that minority groups and youth be adequately represented, and that more open procedures be used in delegate selection processes, it is obvious that the governor, state party chairman, and their cronies will lose much of the influence that they have had in the past. Further, if a suit filed by the Ripon Society of Boston, challenging the method of determining the number of delegates permitted for each state, is successful in the courts, the delegate strength of the Northeastern and Midwestern states will be increased by as much as ten per cent at the expense of other regions of the country; the new delegates would reflect different values from those they would replace and would, I think, exercise a greater degree of independent thinking.

Another complication in the present situation is the "winner-take-all" rule in some states. In California, Massachusetts, Oregon, Rhode Island, and the District of Columbia the candidate who wins the primary, however slim the margin, gets all of the delegates. In 1964, for example, Goldwater defeated Rockefeller in the California primary by winning only about fifty-one per cent of the popular vote, but the entire California delegation was bound to Goldwater. Some states have rules which permit mixed delegations, split roughly proportionately to the votes received by presidential candidates or delegates.

We do not have in the United States, nor should we have, a pure democracy (what students in the late sixties called a "participatory democracy")—that is a system in which all the people participate directly in the settlement of all issues, enactment of laws, or, in many situations, the selection of personnel for important positions. Instead, we have a representative form of government at every level—city, county, state, and federal. When we elect a senator, for example, we understand that as a candidate he cannot commit himself on votes he will cast on every issue he will face in his six-year term. If he did, he would make a mockery of the long Senate hearings to gather data on proposed legislation, of the serious research done by his own staff and committee experts, and of all the other methods he uses to achieve a full understanding of the facts and alternatives before he decides how to vote.

In this light, my suggestion that delegates be selected as representatives of their constituencies, with considerable freedom to exercise their best judgment on the basis of evidence obtained at the convention, does not seem to me to be unreasonable or a departure from representational procedures.

Many thoughtful individuals have suggested the elimination of the quadrennial national conventions and the substitution of a direct primary system of choosing presidential and vice-presidential candidates. I think that would be a mistake. Normally, each major party would have from three to as many as six candidates for the presidential nomination. The likelihood of one of these obtaining a majority vote would be minimal. Hence a second primary would be needed, most likely between the two receiving the highest number of votes. This would be expensive and time-consuming.

Moreover, in a nationwide primary the preference would almost automatically go to a well-to-do candidate or to the one best able to obtain substantial financial backing. Once a candidate is chosen, the entire party machinery is used in obtaining funds to finance the campaign, but the party structure and personnel cannot be used for the support of numerous candidates in a primary contest. Even if we eventually provide some public funds to finance presidential campaigns, it seems unlikely that such funds would be provided for primary candidates who, in abundance, would wish to test their strength in a national primary.

Finally, I would oppose a national primary because I have doubts about placing this type of serious problem before the voters directly, rather than before a convention of carefully chosen delegates who will represent the voters in making the fateful decision. A system of representation is essential in most human activities. A large university cannot place final educational decisions in an entire faculty; if decisions are ever to be made, they must be made in a representative university senate or academic council. A city council speaks for the people of a city, as a state legislature does for the residents of a state. In industrial and financial institutions, relatively small boards of directors, working with top management (whom they have chosen), make the major policy decisions. And in all of these instances those being represented have the ultimate power to approve or disapprove and to replace their representatives if they choose. Only in a very small community, such as the old New England town meeting, can difficult decisions be left to the entire body of citizens.

The convention method with all its faults is better than direct primaries in selecting presidential candidates, but only on the condition that far-reaching reforms of conventions be instituted.

The national nominating conventions should be occasions for education, analysis, debate, and the serious consideration of the important domestic and international issues confronting the United States. Addresses and debates should be conducted under rules similar to those now enforced in the Congress. To make this possible, only delegates and a few pages should be permitted free access to the floor. Alternates should sit in the gallery save when an alternate takes the place of an absent delegate. One television camera, representing all networks and stations, should be focused on the platform. Roving television, radio, and newspaper reporters and commentators should not be permitted on the floor where they can, as now, constantly buttonhole delegates for comment and thus divert attention from the main proceedings. Instead, they should have facilities off the floor in which they may interview delegates who are willing to speak. I realize that much of what emanates from the platform is dull or routine or inane political rhetoric—much of it of poor quality. But if the main business of the convention was transacted at the convention and not somewhere else in advance, and if the objective was to provide real substance, the quality of presentations would merit full media attention. I venture to say that a majority of the voters who watched the 1972 conventions were at times annoyed by the constant "cutting away" from the platform to the media sideshows and the endless punditry.

I would further recommend that the number of pages be severely limited. Spectators should be required to maintain proper decorum as is the rule in the Congress. Bands and other artificial methods of stimulating enthusiasm or showing support for a candidate should not be permitted. Sometimes these demonstrations are conducted by persons who have no official standing in the convention; on more than one occasion I have seen doors opened following a nominating speech and hired bands and loud-voiced persons rush in to carry on a senseless, ear-splitting parade for half an hour, much to the disgust of the delegates.

The first reform in this regard occurred at the 1972 Democratic Convention; bands and parades were not permitted following nominating speeches. But the congestion, noise level, and other impediments to judicious consideration of issues were as malodorous and disgraceful as ever. Unfortunately matters of principal interest—platform debates, platform adoption, voting for the presidential and vice-presidential candidates, and acceptance speeches—took place when most persons in the East and Midwest had gone to bed.

To facilitate discussion among delegates of different states, and especially between chairmen of delegations, there should be, as President Eisenhower once suggested, a closed-circuit telephone system, unconnected with an external switchboard. For outside calls, delegates should leave the floor. The internal communications system should flash call signals by lights rather than by bells.

Traditionally candidates have not appeared in the convention, though there have been exceptions. Normally they have made their headquarters in hotels and maintained telephonic communications with their floor leaders. A major change is desirable. Each candidate for his party's nomination should be required to appear before the delegates and to explain in detail his support of or differences from the party platform which was hammered out prior to the nominating procedure. This would be a candidate's last opportunity before final evaluation and voting to make his position clear on major problems, policies, and issues. The awful truth is that many delegates *do not know what position candidates have on the critical issues*. Preconvention addresses by candidates before crowds throughout the country, I repeat, are not intended to enlighten so much as to obtain favorable audience responses. Clichés, popular at the moment, take precedence over thoughtful exposition.

James Harvey Robinson, in *The Human Comedy*,[33] wrote: "Political campaigns are designedly made into emotional orgies which endeavor to distract attention from the real issues involved and they actually paralyze what slight powers of cerebration men can normally muster." Debates, which achieved some popularity, are not as helpful as one might think, for they are more a test of reaction time than of elucidating a candidate's honest views, and each exchange between the debaters is too short to permit either participant to explain his position on complex problems, such as imbalances in international payments, tax reforms, crime control, military posture, and a host of other problems of prime importance. Moreover, in the heat of debate a candidate may take a position more extreme than his philosophy dictates in order dramatically to make a point or confound his opponent. He then is committed to the extreme view expressed. As Plato said: "The partisan, when he is engaged in dispute, cares nothing about the rights of the question, but is anxious only to convince his hearers of his own assertions."

In a convention, following presentation by candidates, analytical discussions by delegates should proceed under House rules, including limitations on the number of speakers and time allotted to each speaker. This process might—in my opinion should—take two days. It would be an enlightening experience to the delegates and highly educational to the people of the United States. The people could be legitimately proud of this important democratic process.

The same procedure should be employed in nominating a vice-presidential candidate. Certainly we must do better than nominate a "party hack" who presides over the Senate for four years and then "passes into oblivion," an outcome which Clinton Rossiter has said often occurred in our country's history. Presumably the tradition of permitting the presidential nominee to suggest his running mate will continue on the assumption that he can best "balance the ticket" and select someone whose philosophy is compatible with his own. But here a contradiction exists. To balance a ticket implies not a similarity but a difference in political philosophy and voter appeal. The overriding consideration in nominating a vice-presidential candidate should be that delegates are selecting a person who may become President. So all vice-presidential nominees, including the one suggested by the presidential candidate, should appear before the convention and expose their basic views. Thereafter there should again be a thoughtful debate by delegates, with all possible facts and views being expressed. Had this procedure been followed in the 1972 Democratic Convention, the embarrassment that ensued in removing the vice-presidential nominee from the ticket might have been avoided.

I have been distressed, particularly in recent national conventions, by the fairly obvious fact that the presidential nominee had not given much serious thought in advance to possible vice-presidential candidates. Spiro Agnew in 1968 and Thomas Eagleton in 1972 appeared to be last-minute decisions in a very real sense. Their names were surely on somebody's list, but they had not received the scrutiny they should have from either the presidential nominee or the convention. When one considers the screening process that most high-level presidential appointments go through en route to Senate confirmation, it is ironic that the man next in line for the presidency is identified, selected, and nominated all in the matter of a few hours.

William S. White, patently seeking the same result as I am, though by a somewhat different method, wrote in an article in the October 1960 issue of *Harper's*: "I suggest the following: Let the convention itself appoint a subcommittee of fifty voting delegates, one representing—and truly representative of—each state delegation. Let this subcommittee meet, *always in public* (presumably sitting with the convention), in serious and businesslike session to hear *before the nomination* each serious presidential candidate. Let each candidate come forward with a plain statement of where he stands on every important issue of the day. . . . Then let the convention itself proceed to the business of nominating, with no further chit-chat—and no horseplay whatever. Let us be done with the so-called seconding seconding speeches. Let there be an end to the witless 'floor demonstrations' which are as spontaneous as the idiot's card held before a TV performer. . . . Finally, let the successful candidate *at once* address the convention and the country, without the aid of ghost writers, without time to think out clever explanations and elaborations of what he had said before."

I realize that the convention reforms I have advocated may cause some old-line politicians to label me (William White, too) a spoilsport, seemingly trying to transform what has long been a political circus of sparkling colors and emotional orgies into a solemn wake. Is a session of the United States Senate when it is considering a presidential nomination of a Cabinet member (or even of a Vice-President under the Twenty-fifth Amendment to the Constitution) to be considered a wake? Not at all. However, for those who prefer drama to judgment, hoopla to wisdom, I am willing to offer a mild compromise. After the issues and candidates have been presented and thoughtfully discussed, after the substantive business preceding the balloting has been attended to, I would not object to a brief recess with some good rousing music, perhaps a bit of sign waving, and even the release of colorful balloons filled with helium. The balloting about to begin does involve a certain amount of tension and drama. So a bit of hell raising at just the right time might be irrepressible and might actually relieve tensions and thus prepare delegates better for the final act of balloting for the presidential and vice-presidential candidates.

The campaigns by the nominees should be limited to about two months, with increased emphasis on a series of half-hour television talks by the candidates. The national election should be held not later than the last week in September or the first week in October. The successful candidate should be inaugurated by mid-November. This, too, was once suggested by President Eisenhower. The reason for this change is important: the incoming President by late January must determine the position he will take on the federal budget for the ensuing year; in his State of the Union message he must set forth his legislative priorities and soon thereafter present a comprehensive economic report to the Congress. He surely needs at least two months to prepare for these vital messages.

The financing of presidential campaigns has become a major concern to the people of this nation. And rightly so, for a very important reason. The sums now required to mount a successful campaign for the presidency are so astronomical that candidates either must be wealthy or must cater to wealthy backers. It may sound cynical, but I simply do not believe that many persons make six-figure donations to a candidate's campaign just because they believe he is the best candidate. Many of the largest donors are buying influence or favors and some of the most generous surreptitiously have supported both candidates just to hedge their bets.

Most Americans believe that throughout our history many campaign committees and treasurers have concealed the source and amount of some of the campaign funds. In recent years, and especially in the 1972 campaign, this became a major issue and insistent demands arose for reforms that could be policed. Tom Wicker, the New York *Times* columnist, wrote of "rivers of money flowing into and out of the Committee for the Re-election of the President." Testimony of the principal fund raiser of the campaign indicated that huge campaign contributions were received in cash and often disbursed in cash, for purposes apparently unknown to him or the treasurer. Apparently as much as fifty million dollars was raised for the campaign, twenty million of this before changes in the law, effective April 7, 1972, made non-accountability a criminal offense.

Senator Charles McC. Mathias, Jr., of Maryland and Senator Charles H. Percy of Illinois, men of intelligence and integrity, have proposed in the Senate bills that would limit campaign costs for each major candidate in a presidential election to fifteen or twenty cents per person of voting age. Of this total, one third would be provided by a federal appropriation. The other two thirds would be provided privately, not more than five thousand dollars from an individual or single group.

Other bills in the Senate have suggested increasing the federal appropriation and decreasing the private donations, but all seemed to be satisfied that an average of fifteen to twenty cents per eligible voter would be sufficient. Such a formula would apparently reduce campaign costs to about one half the amount spent by Republican committees in 1972.

Senator Mathias would limit *cash* contributions by an individual or group to twenty-five dollars. Contributions above this amount would have to be by check.

Equally important to limiting campaign costs is how the money is spent. A presidential campaign, I have long contended, should be a vast educational experience for the American people. Certainly *public* campaign funds should not be used to buy votes, or wasted on extravagant travel, car stickers that do not enlighten, short Madison Avenue television commercials that confuse, or false charges and countercharges that alienate voters rather than inform them.

While it is traditional for candidates to roam the country by train and plane, with whistle stops at crossroads and in cities, actually a small fraction of the people is so reached. Television presents to candidates their best and safest method of reaching the electorate with an exposition of their positions on major issues and on what they would hope to accomplish if elected. The candidates of the two major parties should have equal television time on all three networks either free or at reduced rates; this suggestion is in harmony with federal law, which requires radio and television stations and networks to serve the "public interest, convenience, and necessity." At least six, preferably more, half-hour programs in prime time in each time zone of the United States should be available to the two major candidates.

A troublesome problem is what to do about candidates of minor parties. Senator Mathias has dealt with this problem in his bill, which would make federal funds available to minor candidates on the basis of their parties' showing in the previous election or, if a party entered an election for the first time, through a petitions procedure. Time on television for minor party candidates should be proportional to the federal subsidies evolved from the computations provided in Senator Mathias' proposal. This would require an amendment to the Federal Communications Act.

The most important consideration, however, and the one most difficult to deal with in legislation, is that funds be so used as to enlighten the American people on the complex issues facing the nation and each candidate's proposals for dealing with those issues. This presentation of views on issues should, of course, include a clear exposure of the candidate's basic philosophy that would guide him in making decisions on hundreds of problems that cannot possibly be anticipated during a campaign, for, as I have suggested, a President should be elected for a single six-year term, and in our fast-moving world no one can possibly foresee all the critical domestic and foreign issues that will arise during that span of time.

The effort to keep the American people informed on basic problems and possible solutions should not cease with inauguration of a President. In his eight years in the White House, President Eisenhower held 193 press conferences, spoke to the nation by television and radio, and before groups—ranging from the United Nations and the National Association of Newspaper Editors to labor conventions, agricultural meetings, and conferences of governors—more than nine hundred times. In addition, State of the Union, economic, budgetary, and special messages to the Congress were voluminous and frequent. This was not a record. President Franklin Roosevelt in his first eight years exceeded this, most notably in the famous "fireside chats" by radio.

Dr. Malcolm Moos, formerly a special assistant to President Eisenhower, until recently president of the University of Minnesota, and a distinguished political scientist, in an address early in June 1973 said: "It is proper for the President to speak to the American people and use them as a megaphone to react upon the Congress, but *I believe the time has come in the confluence of events when the chief executive should speak to the Congress openly and regularly.* The time has come to institutionalize a means of restoring the tide-marks of trust between the executive and Congress. In essence, I suggest the functional equivalent of a vote of confidence for having the President continuously accountable to the legislative branch." Senator Mike Mansfield on July 11, 1973, in a press conference, suggested that the President hold weekly bipartisan meetings with congressional leaders at the White House, try to establish friendly and personal relations with individual members, report to the people more often through television talks and press conferences, consult with key congressional committee chairmen, and strive to develop a true executive-legislative partnership.

With Senator Mansfield's recipe for co-operation I am in complete agreement. I also applaud Dr. Moos' suggestion that the President appear formally, openly, and regularly before the Congress, not only as a means of promoting better executive-legislative relations but also to enlighten the American people. I do not agree, however, as Moos indicates, that the purpose of this should be to make the President accountable to the Congress as a substitute for the parliamentary system of requiring a vote of confidence in the nation's leader. Such a concept or practice would vitiate the constitutional separation of powers—the co-equal status of the executive and legislative branches of government. The President's major responsibility is not to the legislative branch but to the people, and it is from them that he needs the constant equivalent of a vote of confidence.

This question of presidential responsibility—to the Congress or to the people—was given serious consideration in the Constitutional Convention in 1787. Many felt that the President should be elected by the Congress. This would have some appeal today if the quadrennial conventions are not quickly changed. But the reason given in the Constitutional Convention does not appeal to me. The thought was that the President ought to be accountable exclusively to the Congress, which was considered to be "the depository of the supreme will of society." Indeed, this provision was in several drafts of the Constitution as tentatively approved by the convention. Finally, however, the reasoning prevailed that the President was responsible to *all the people* and hence should be elected by the people through electors chosen by voters in each state.

This makes it highly essential that the President and his principal spokesmen (Cabinet members, for example) restore and maintain absolute and unchallenged credibility, and speak frequently not only to the Congress as Moos suggested but also directly to the people by television and radio and through press conferences. I shall deal with the problem of credibility later in analyzing aspects of the Johnson and Nixon administrations.

Since no human being, including the President, is infallible, the party in opposition to him should be in a position to place alternative proposals before the people. This is an effective educational method which enables citizens better to arrive at judgments. Hence, the opposition party should maintain ongoing research and publicize its conclusions as did the Republican Critical Issues Council in 1963 and 1964; this would change opposition from polemics and emotional tirades into suggested alternatives worthy of citizen consideration.

When the President is given free television or radio time to present his views to the nation, and if those views deal with controversial issues or otherwise have political implications, equal time should be provided free of charge to an opposition spokesman. This should be a legal requirement, not subject to decisions by network and station executives. This practice on a regular basis would contribute to better citizen understanding and would give substance, not merely lip service, to the fact that the ultimate social power in our society resides in the people.

CHAPTER 22

Leadership involves the ability to make difficult choices; unable to choose between his Great Society and the Vietnam War, Lyndon Johnson lost both.

I FIRST MET Lyndon Baines Johnson in 1937, just after he had been elected, at the age of twenty-nine, a New Deal congressman from Texas. In 1942, in my capacity as associate director of the Office of War Information, I invited him to participate in a national radio program. It was his first exposure to a national audience, something he never forgot during our association over the next three decades.

When Johnson became the Democratic whip in the Senate I began seeing him frequently, for he was often at the White House to confer with President Eisenhower. From 1955 on, co-operation between Johnson and Eisenhower became imperative, for Johnson's control as majority leader of the Senate was so complete that the President could get legislation through the upper chamber only with Johnson's help. At that time the senator from Texas was a moderate on most questions and a conservative on some; he was an effective compromiser and a "fixer."

Like his hero Franklin Roosevelt, Johnson wanted very much to be President and, like Roosevelt, he had his own great vision of America and an obsession to make that vision a reality. When his maneuvering for the Democratic nomination in 1960 earned him only the consolation prize of the vice-presidential nomination, he could not have been too surprised. In 1958 he had expressed the belief that a Southerner could not be nominated for the presidency and, if somehow nominated, could not win. With his landslide election in 1964, he became the first President since Zachary Taylor to be elected President from a Southern state.

The difference between a politician's responsibility to a limited constituency and to a national one was vividly demonstrated by Johnson's change of attitude when he left the Senate to become Vice-President, then President. In my work as special ambassador to Latin America I had suggested a solution to the age-old Chamizol dispute with Mexico—a dispute that arose when the Rio Grande changed course and a question of national ownership of land became a hotly contested international issue. Senator Johnson, behaving as a loyal Texan, objected to my solution, which would have given about two thirds of the contested land to Mexico, one third to the United States. As Vice-President, he concurred in the solution proposed by President Kennedy —a proposal which was little different from mine.

Again, as a Texan, he was far from being liberal on the question of civil rights. President Eisenhower introduced a proposal in 1957 which would have guaranteed voting rights to all citizens, authorized the federal government to seek preventive relief in civil rights cases, created a Civil Rights Division in the Justice Department, and established a Civil Rights National Commission. The bill passed the House in its original form. *Majority Leader* Johnson forced the Senate to weaken the bill. But *President* Johnson became a militant civil rights leader. Campaigning in 1964, he made one of the most daring political speeches in American history. He went to New Orleans, then known as Goldwater country and bitter about the passage of Johnson's strong Civil Rights Act earlier that year. There, in blunt language, he attacked the racial prejudice which had divided this country throughout its history.

"Whatever your views are," he told a hushed and stunned audience, "we have a Constitution, and we have got a Bill of Rights, and we've got the law of the land. And two thirds of the Democrats in the Senate voted for it [the 1964 Civil Rights Act] and three fourths of the Republicans. And I signed it, and I am going to enforce it! And I am going to observe it!"

Johnson had been President only several months when he sent a helicopter for me and brought me to the White House for a general discussion. Interestingly, instead of our sitting in the large oval office, he took me to an adjacent small room, once a bathroom, later converted to a room for President Eisenhower to rest, and there we talked for fully ninety minutes. Our discussion covered the whole sweep of domestic and international affairs, with considerable concentration on his arduous and unfamiliar task of administering the federal establishment.

Johnson was addicted to hyperbole; he declared in a speech in Nashville: "We've passed more bills, spent more money, reached more people, provided more comprehensive efforts in three years than in the rest of history." Nonetheless, his legislative accomplishments were herculean. His record on domestic legislation equaled that of Franklin Roosevelt. In his first administration he induced the Congress to pass an omnibus Civil Rights Act, the Economic Opportunity Act (War on Poverty), a major act to help education, and a whole series of appropriations bills that had been tied up in committee. But it was in his second administration that the Great Society (Madison Avenue again) blossomed: water and air pollution measures, more civil rights legislation (especially in housing), more aid to education, medical care for the aged, a housing program, immigration reform, and a nationwide attack on heart disease, cancer, and stroke. His fertile mind was constantly finding new ideas which, regardless of what was happening to the American economy, he put before the Congress with demands for quick action.

He called me early in 1964, following riots in the Canal Zone which resulted in twenty-five deaths, hundreds of injuries, and continuing furious protests by Panamanian citizens. I had already prepared the document which the Critical Issues Council would issue on this question, so I briefed the President on the history of United States-Panamanian relations, a history which went back to 1846 when the United States entered into a treaty with New Granada (Colombia) which guaranteed the neutrality of the Isthmus of Panama and New Granadan sovereignty over it in return for permission for the United States to develop transit across the isthmus. With that beginning, there had been nineteen treaties, studies, commercial developments, and presidential orders dealing with the problem of the right of the United States to provide for Atlantic-Pacific transits. The most important of these was the Hay-Bunau-Varilla Treaty of 1903 which was quickly negotiated immediately after Panama declared its independence from Colombia, believed to have been done with the help of the United States Navy as ordered by President Theodore Roosevelt. That treaty gave the United States exclusive authority "as if it were sovereign" over a strip ten miles wide through the central portion of Panama and the right to build and operate a canal, free of all interference, in this strip. Construction was completed in 1914. Half a century of successful operation was behind us at the time the President sent for me.

But, while operations had been successful, our relations with Panama had always been difficult. Panama was interested in the canal merely as an economic resource and with understandable pride insisted upon its titular sovereignty over the Zone, a fact which three Presidents of the United States had acknowledged. The United States, on the other hand, though not indifferent to Panama's aspirations, was interested primarily in maintaining an efficient world transportation facility. Unfortunately the problem was filled with misunderstanding. American politicians, especially in the House of Representatives, kept insisting that the Zone was part of the United States, that we were the sovereign power, when patently we were not, though having a right in perpetuity to administer all affairs within the Zone. Misunderstandings in Panama were rife, fomented by politicians who found it possible to turn discontent about domestic poverty and maldistribution of income against the colossus of the north which, it was claimed, was making a fortune out of the canal. The truth was that the United States had never made a cent of profit from the canal; indeed, by low interest rates on the debt, by modest annual payments to Panama, and by other means we subsidized canal operations and improvements to the extent of about six million dollars a year.

In the Critical Issues Council paper I wrote and published on this question, I advocated a thirty per cent increase in canal tolls (they had not been changed since 1914), an annual payment of fifteen million dollars to Panama, amortization of the debt the Canal Company owed the United States Treasury, improvements in the canal which would enable it to handle most traffic for another twenty-five years, higher wages for Panamanian employees in the Zone, and the ultimate construction by new agreement with Panama of a sea-level canal.

My recommendations could not be adopted for two reasons: first, President Johnson had made a commitment to the President of Panama that he would renegotiate the treaty of 1903, something I thought should be postponed until much later; and, second, he knew that attitudes in Congress were such that he would have to recommend enactment of a law which would provide for a detailed and time-consuming study of the canal problem.

On September 22, 1964, the Congress, at the President's request, passed Public Law 88-609, authorizing "a full and complete investigation . . . for the purpose of determining the feasibility of, and the most suitable site for, and the construction of a sea-level canal connecting the Atlantic and Pacific oceans; the best means of constructing such a canal, whether by conventional or nuclear excavation and the cost thereof." The President's recommendation for this legislation had been made after one of our extended discussions.

As specified in the act, President Johnson set up a five-man commission to make the study. I became one of the five members. Raymond A. Hill, a well-known consulting engineer of California; General Kenneth E. Fields, former head of the Army Corps of Engineers; Dean Robert G. Storey, Texas lawyer and frequent federal adviser; and Robert B. Anderson, former Deputy Secretary of Defense and Secretary of the Treasury, were the other members, with Mr. Anderson serving as chairman with great distinction. Mr. Anderson was also appointed by the President to be the United States chief negotiator, with the rank of ambassador, to develop a new treaty with Panama, a function related to but outside the responsibility of our study commission.

We worked for five and a half years on this problem, meeting as frequently as studies in engineering, atomic explosives, shipping trends, ecological factors, costs and revenues, and other matters were ready for us.

When we began, we were optimistic that a sea-level canal could be constructed with the use of atomic explosives at a cost of only one sixth to as low as one tenth the cost of conventional construction. Eventually, for several cogent reasons, the possibility of using atomic construction had to be discarded: for political and legal reasons, research on the use of massive underground explosives did not go forward as rapidly as we had anticipated; the use of atomic explosives would violate the test-ban treaty; geological studies showed that atomic explosives would create a degree of bank incline which in much of the shale involved would result in frequent slippages that would tend to fill the canal, thus requiring constant dredging; the seismic shock from the use of large explosives might do damage as far away as Panama City, one hundred and twenty-five miles distant; and finally, even if in the distant future atomic excavation became feasible, the cost advantage would not be as great as we had thought.

On December 1, 1970, we reported to President Nixon that only conventional construction of a sea-level canal was feasible for as far in the future as we could foresee. The most suitable site, we said, was on a route only ten miles from the present lock canal. Construction would cost about three billion dollars, which, if traffic projections proved to be reasonably accurate, could be amortized over a long period of years, assuming higher toll charges and an appropriate agreement with Panama. We felt that any possible shortfall in amortization payments would be offset by national defense and foreign policy benefits to the United States.

Since it would require about fifteen years to construct a sea-level canal by conventional methods, we recommended to the President that he give serious consideration to the problem fifteen years before a traffic jam developed in the present lock canal—something that could occur as early as 1990 or as late as 2000. We urged that treaty negotiations with Panama keep both the lock canal and a new sea-level canal under United States jurisdiction at least until all costs were amortized. I doubt that Panama will agree to a treaty acceptable to the United States, but if she does I would not object if, when all costs have been amortized, operation by a joint United States-Panamanian corporation, or Panama, or some form of international organization were negotiated.

The United States will probably have to reach a decision on this problem in the latter half of the 1970s. If an acceptable treaty with Panama cannot be negotiated I see only two alternatives: first, we could continue to operate the present canal and, when a traffic jam developed, the maritime nations of the world, including the United States, would have to build larger ships which without too great an additional cost could handle world oceanic transportation by the far longer route around the tip of South America; second, we could raise tolls, repay the canal debt to the United States Treasury, and then open negotiations with Panama under these changed circumstances.

During the campaign of 1964, I invited the two presidential candidates to speak at The Johns Hopkins University. Both accepted. Senator Goldwater later canceled, but President Johnson came. Because the crowd was huge we erected a special platform in a beautiful quadrangle on the campus and only the President and I were on the temporary stage. Considering our membership in different political parties, I introduced the President not as a candidate for re-election, but mainly as a friend. He at once said, "Milton, that's the second best introduction I ever had. The only better one occurred in Kentucky when the governor was supposed to present me. He failed to appear, so I introduced myself!"

Johnson's speech was recorded on a new teleprompter which carried in bold black type material that even a nearsighted man could read, but to the audience nothing was seen save two large pieces of glass. The copy on the teleprompter would have taken him about fifteen minutes to deliver. With skill, he extemporized time and again, but always coming back with logic to the prepared text. This was a dexterous and professional performance. In extemporizing, Johnson kept turning toward me and bringing roars of laughter from the crowd by comparing his record in supporting President Eisenhower with that of Senator Goldwater. At one point he said: "Read the record. As majority leader of the Senate I supported President Eisenhower ninety-two per cent of the time. My opponent in this campaign voted with the President only twelve per cent of the time!"

Throughout the campaign Johnson was moderate in expressing his views and by most voters was deemed to be the "peace candidate." Goldwater, favoring a large increase in United States forces in Vietnam and the bombing of North Vietnam, thus seeking peace through military victory, was dubbed the "war candidate." Johnson's popular vote was the largest ever received by a presidential candidate. Voters also swept into office a huge majority of Democratic representatives and senators.

Shortly after his election, Johnson greatly expanded United States participation in the Vietnam War. This decision was to haunt him throughout his remaining time in the White House and eventually to cause him not to be a candidate in 1968.

It was late in March 1965, when opposition to the escalation of the war began to be increasingly evident on campuses of colleges and universities, that I thought it would be wise for the Johns Hopkins faculty and students to hear authoritatively what was happening and what the potentials might be. I therefore asked a friend of mine, McGeorge Bundy, assistant to the President on foreign policy and security matters, to speak at the university. He accepted. He was due on a Monday. On the Friday before the scheduled talk he telephoned me to ask whether I would mind his sending a substitute. Anyone who has handled public addresses anywhere, certainly at a university, knows that the idea of accepting a substitute speaker is anathema. As I hesitated, Bundy chuckled and said, "The President is my substitute."

Preparing for the appearance of a President is a mammoth job. Secret Service agents must swarm over the campus, give instructions, clear out all offices facing the quadrangle where the speech is to be delivered, and determine the flow of traffic. Arrangements with television and newspaper people must be precise and approved by the White House. I wondered how we could make necessary arrangements on a weekend. On Saturday morning Bundy called again and said that the President had changed his mind and he, Bundy, would keep his original engagement. He arrived at my residence about forty-five minutes prior to his lecture, so we had an opportunity for a leisurely chat in the library of the university's official residence, a talk that was enlightening to me. Bundy gave me details about the invasion of South Vietnam by North Vietnamese forces that had been much in dispute, the question being whether we had interceded in a civil war in South Vietnam or had actually gone in to help repel an invasion from the north. As we rose to go to the auditorium the telephone rang in my library. It was the White House calling for Bundy. The President told Bundy that he had again changed his mind and would make a speech on Vietnam at Johns Hopkins on April 8. Bundy's mental dexterity was put to a test that day. He had planned to speak on Vietnam. Now he found it inappropriate to do so. As we rode to the auditorium, which took only a few moments, he got his mind in order, stepped on the stage, and made an interesting and informative speech on the decision-making process at the presidential level. He was adroit in the question and answer period, frankly handling all inquiries with poise and precision, but saying that for confidential reasons he could not reply to questions about Vietnam.

Now I faced a dilemma. I was scheduled to be in Seattle, San Francisco, Los Angeles, and Denver from April 8 to 14 for alumni meetings which were of importance to the university, for alumni assistance was contributing to an upward momentum at the university that enabled us to do many necessary things. I explained my problem to Bundy at the conclusion of his address. He felt that my relations with the President

were such that the President would understand my absence and that
Charles S. Garland, chairman of the Board of Trustees, could preside
and present the President. The President arrived on schedule and, following Mr. Garland's proper formal presentation, said, "Thank you,
Mr. Garland. Dr. Eisenhower, distinguished guests, ladies and gentlemen!" and then proceeded with an address that was televised nationally
and proved to be of historic importance. It was his first offer to Hanoi
of "unconditional negotiations."

One of the few chores I ever performed for a President that was
sheer pleasure, free of strain and worry, was serving as first chairman
of a Presidential Commission to select Presidential Scholars. The idea
had originated with Dr. Eric Goldman, a professor at Princeton but on
leave as a special assistant to the President. I was aided by a distinguished
group that included noted musicians, educators, scientists, authors,
and secondary school administrators. With evidence of scholarship and
extracurricular and civic activities, we selected two individuals from
each state, American territories, the Commonwealth of Puerto Rico,
and the Canal Zone. I continued this activity for three years and then
turned the task over to a successor. The program is still under way and
merits support. The scholarships carry no stipends, but the recipients
are brought to Washington, are received by the President, and are
shown a good deal about federal operations. The recognition given these
young people each year is prized in their home communities and in the
colleges and universities where they enroll.

During the Dominican crisis President Johnson called and said he
was sending his helicopter for me. When I walked into his office he rose
and asked, "Milton, would you mind walking around on the south
grounds? I want to chat with you about the situation in the Dominican
Republic." Needless to say, such a suggestion by the President of the
United States is always observed. For half an hour we walked slowly
on the circular drive of the south grounds; I think we made about eight
laps. In that period I did not make a comment or ask a question. The
President began with the first word of trouble that had reached him
and then told of cables and telephone calls that came to him each day,
and what response he had made to each new bit of information. It was
one of the most amazing demonstrations of memory for detail and tim-

ing I have ever experienced. Not a fact was omitted. Much later in the day he asked me to look over his file and I could find no deviation from what he had told me from memory. One of my prized photographs among the thousands I possess is one taken of the two of us walking on the driveway of the south grounds; it shows us from the rear, but no one could mistake who the figures are, the President tall and I of medium height. The picture came to me several days after the chat, autographed "To Milton, with affection, Lyndon B. Johnson."

Briefly, what the President had told me was this: Rafael Trujillo, dictator for thirty years, had been assassinated in 1961. In the turmoil that followed, President Kennedy had threatened to intervene when Trujillo's heirs tried to seize control, but fortunately they failed. Late in 1962 Juan Bosch was elected President but, presumably owing to inept administration and an alleged move toward Communism, a military coup occurred a year later. The revolt against the military junta was ostensibly to restore Bosch to power, but the President was convinced that the forces were really under the control of Cuban-trained Communists. When he ordered 21,000 marines into the country, his sole purpose was to save American and foreign lives. Even the American Embassy was under attack and one telephone call from the United States ambassador was said to have been made from under his desk while bullets blazed through the room, though this was later denied by Ambassador Tapley Bennett. As rescue operations proceeded it appeared that the Communist-led forces would overcome the government. It was at this point that the President sent in more United States forces and intervened in the war.

As he completed his recital the President suggested that we return to his office. There he asked me to comment on all he had done. Did I approve of his actions? If not, what should he have done? What changes might now be made?

As we sat down he asked an aide to bring each of us a glass of root beer!

For the next twenty minutes I commented on the Dominican crisis as I saw it. As I spoke, the President kept glancing about the room, giving me the impression that he was not listening to a thing I said. But I carried out the assignment. In my opinion, I said, he was justified in sending in the first contingent of American marines to save American lives and the lives of other foreigners who wished to flee from the country. This was accepted international practice, and no one had any justification for criticizing such action. But I felt he had made a serious mistake in sending in more troops and participating in what was surely a civil war, even if he feared, as he had stated, that "this was another Communist take-over, as in Cuba." He should have called an emergency meeting of the Council of the Organization of American States, and the military action to protect the group in power in the Dominican Republic should have been under, not our auspices, but those of the OAS. Indeed, a few days after our intervention the OAS had condemned the war and had given authenticity to the military action, some Latin American nations even sending troops and ships as authorized in the Mutual Defense Treaty of 1947. However, an American was still in charge of the military forces and essentially all statements emanating from the country and being disseminated world-wide were from American officials, including our ambassador and several special assistants the President had sent there. At once, a military leader from a Latin American country should be placed in charge of all troops, I said, and all statements coming from the island should be issued by an official of the Organization of American States. As soon as the civil strife was under control we should withdraw United States forces at the earliest possible moment. If it was necessary for a protective force to remain it should be made up exclusively of troops from Latin American countries.

When I had completed my recital the President asked me to have lunch with him in the family dining room on the second floor of the mansion, a facility which had not been there in the Eisenhower years. He asked, "Do you mind if I ask some of my staff to join us for lunch?"

For the first time that day I grinned, and said, "You're the President!"

Upstairs, he introduced me to Mrs. Johnson, who obviously was a keen observer and an influential adviser of the President. During our visit a dining table miraculously appeared in a room across the hall with settings for ten. When we sat down and started to eat, the President said, "I want to tell you what Milton Eisenhower has just said to me." He then repeated almost word for word all I had said, another amazing demonstration of memory. Actually, most of my suggestions were already planned. The major difficulty was one of timing. Had our intervention been delayed a few days, the military operation in the Dominican Republic, following the initial effort to save American lives, would have been under the aegis of the Organization of American States as our intervention in Korea had been an action of the United Nations.

I was consulted by President Johnson only once about the war in Vietnam. This was when the fighting was at its height, including the bombing of North Vietnam, and massive protest movements against the war were under way in this country. The meeting was exceptionally difficult for me. I had been bitterly opposed to our intervention in the war from the beginning for several reasons: I did not believe the area was essential to our own security; I did not subscribe to the Truman Doctrine that we should play Atlas and alone oppose the coercive spread of Communism wherever it occurred. I felt we were intervening in what was primarily a civil war, though I accepted McGeorge Bundy's word that an invasion from the north was also involved; and, most important of all, I thought our costly involvement was futile—that no matter when the fighting stopped South Vietnam would be so demoralized that organized Communist forces ultimately would take over. Our sacrifice would have been in vain.

But I felt it would serve no good purpose for me to explain my views on what I deemed to be the mistakes that led up to the situation then existing. So as diplomatically as I could I discussed Johnson's several statements on television to the effect that he was carrying out policies and programs which had originated with Presidents Truman and Eisenhower. I said the statement was incorrect. President Truman had extended economic aid during the French war in Indochina and President Eisenhower had continued this. There was no commitment for United States military action, only assistance in training local troops. The record on this was clear.

Early in his administration President Eisenhower kept urging the French, as he had done when he was Supreme Commander of NATO forces, to declare to the world that the war was not to retain a colonial empire but only to prevent the spread of Communism by force. As French forces in Indochina became more imperiled, some military leaders had suggested to President Eisenhower that we aid them by air assaults. The President disapproved, pointing out that the French and Vietnamese forces were widely deployed and hidden in the jungle. Hence air strikes would be ineffective. In any event, he said, he would not have the United States engage in a conflict that had as its major purpose the re-establishment of a colonial empire.

In February 1954, President Eisenhower had publicly expressed his abhorrence of getting involved in the war, saying, "No one could be more bitterly opposed to ever getting the United States in a war in that region than I am." (He had said to me many times that if developments which he did not then foresee caused him to change his mind about intervening he would certainly not do so without the formal approval of Congress.)

Several days after his public announcement he had sent Secretary Dulles to the Senate Committee on Foreign Relations to explain our policy of non-involvement.

On July 21, 1954, the French agreed to a cease-fire and the partition of Vietnam. The United States did not participate in the Geneva Conference where these arrangements were made but did tacitly agree to what had been done. Later in the year Secretary Dulles, Senator Alexander Smith, and Senator Mike Mansfield signed for the United States the Manila Pact, the other national signatories being Great Britain, France, Australia, New Zealand, the Philippines, Pakistan, and Thailand. A protocol to the pact extended its protective provisions to Laos, Cambodia, and Vietnam.

What were our commitments to Vietnam through SEATO? The SEATO nations had agreed that if a member faced armed aggression each of the member states would meet the danger *in accord with its constitutional processes.* Second, it was agreed that if the political independence of a state were threatened by any other means that could violate the peace of the area the signatory nations would *consult in order to agree on measures to be taken for the common defense.* It should be noted, I emphasized, that these SEATO provisions were never employed.

Apart from SEATO, the United States had made it clear that to help protect the independence of Laos, Cambodia, and South Vietnam it would provide economic and technical assistance, military advisers, and training—nothing more.

I recalled the gist of an article by Fletcher Knebel in a February 1955 issue of *Look* magazine in which he indicated his belief that history would credit a number of men with helping keep the United States out of war for "the last ten months." He named Eisenhower, Dulles, Ridg-

THE PRESIDENT IS CALLING

way, Anthony Eden, and Nehru, adding, "The strongest voice for peace was that of President Eisenhower."

Non-involvement militarily remained the policy throughout the Eisenhower administration. In a press conference on January 14, 1960, President Eisenhower had said with respect to Indochina that "there was never any plan developed to be put into execution." When he left office only 600 United States troops had been stationed there, their sole mission being to help train South Vietnamese forces. It was President Kennedy who had sent our guerrilla troops into the area and it was under his orders that our forces, increased by then to about 16,000 men, engaged in ground fighting. I did not know, I said, whether President Kennedy would have dispatched additional United States forces.

At this point in my recital President Johnson, seemingly genuinely puzzled, said to me that President Eisenhower in public statements had given him every support. Why had he done this if throughout his own administration he had been opposed to our intervening?

One reason was clear to me, I said. Following the passage of the Tonkin resolution which gave the President authority for what he was doing, *the war was a fact*. We were in it. Whether we should have been involved was quite a different question. President Eisenhower had often said to me that force was the ultimate authority available to a nation; once used, the full resources of the nation should be marshaled to bring the conflict to a conclusion as quickly as possible. To use the authority of force and then withdraw suddenly would greatly injure the credibility of the United States, the Soviet Union would become the dominant power in the world, and possibly all of the Far East would come under Communist domination, a situation that would indeed involve the security interests of the United States, even if Vietnam as an isolated situation did not.

His second reason for publicly supporting President Johnson's war actions, I indicated, was purely Eisenhoweresque. I did not know that any other former President would hold the conviction that he did. He felt that a former President should feel free to criticize the domestic activities of the incumbent but that in foreign affairs the United States should be, or at least appear to be, united. Further, the incumbent President had at his command immense amounts of information available to no one else. My brother would not assume that his information in retirement was equal to that of a President in office.

His third reason for not publicly opposing Johnson's Vietnam policy, I indicated, was his conviction that a critical statement by him would give comfort to the enemy, might contribute to the failure of any possible peace negotiations, and thus might prolong the conflict. He had never said so to me but I was sure he felt that, if American leaders in positions of power had abided by the position he had taken, leaders opposed to the war could readily make their views known directly and forcefully to the President and thus avoid creating the feeling in North Vietnam and among the Vietcong that in time the United States, in the face of growing criticism, would withdraw its forces and thus permit them to take control of all of Vietnam.

After I came home from that discussion I reread President Eisenhower's relevant public and private papers of eight years and proved to my satisfaction that he scrupulously avoided direct military involvement in Vietnam during his two terms in office and so stated publicly; second, there was no official, personal, or any other kind of commitment, by Truman or Eisenhower, that would have made our participation in the war a legal or moral necessity, and, third, he would not have permitted United States troops to enter the fighting had he still been President in the heartbreaking years that followed his retirement. His support of President Johnson's actions in the mid-sixties did not, as I have explained, conflict with these conclusions.

President Johnson did not have a confidant who had the intimate relationship of a House with Wilson, or a Hopkins with Roosevelt, or a Robert Kennedy with his brother. He turned to a number of individuals who had served him well in the past—to younger men for ideas and action, to older men for advice and philosophic discussions.

Prominent among the younger men was Bill Moyers, who helped on a multitude of problems and followed through on policies determined by the President. Johnson worked with Moyers on the whole sweep of presidential responsibilities: national and international problems on which Moyers advised; activities in the vast federal bureaucracy which he often supervised in the President's name; the campaign of 1964 in which he was a key operator; public relations, especially as the President's efficient press secretary; legislative programs which he helped prepare; and speech writing in which he excelled. It was Moyers who worked constantly with Johnson in preparing the program after the 1964 election which was euphemistically called the Great Society.

The relationship between Johnson and Moyers has been described as a father-and-son one. Moyers, a former Baptist minister, challenged the President's ideas with regularity. In one sense the two were polar. One was a technician in power politics, the other a youthful and messianic idealist. Both, however, were preoccupied with results and manipulated people and agencies to get the results they wanted. Moyers exhibited a high degree of independence in this curious relationship. This led in time to trouble. Moyers received favorable press coverage at the time the President's image worsened, even after Moyers became press secretary. In 1966, after twelve years together, the two came to a parting of the ways beyond the possibility of reconciliation. Moyers left to become publisher of *Newsday*. Thereafter Johnson criticized him for a multitude of alleged faults.

Joe Califano became the principal young aide after Moyers' departure. I saw a great deal of him. He was a human dynamo. He was constantly on the telephone or in conference, dealing principally with the Great Society program. In the lengthy struggle for a Department of Transportation, the President told his Cabinet: "When Joe speaks, that's my voice you hear!" Once when I sat in Califano's office for a full hour, trying to get a decision that could have been reached in ten minutes, he was called into the President's office four times.

The central figures in the older group of presidential advisers were Abe Fortas and Clark Clifford. They were long-time cronies of Johnson's. While Clifford was influential, it was Fortas who became the close confidant.

Michael Gartner of the *Wall Street Journal* called Fortas the President's closest adviser. Johnson had never forgotten Fortas' legal prowess, which had helped put him in the Senate after a disputed election in Texas—which Johnson won by 87 votes. But Fortas' influence was not based on gratitude. A man of vast knowledge, precision in reasoning, and a sound political prophet, he suited Johnson's need for intimate consultation.

His intellectual capacity was unquestioned. Justice Harlan said that Fortas was the most brilliant advocate ever to appear before the Supreme Court in modern times. Certainly the President admired Fortas' intellect, his liberal views, his political acumen, and his judgments, which were always reasonably and quietly expressed. He was self-effacing about his role; he acknowledged that he met frequently with the President and the White House staff but contended that his role was limited to summarizing discussions and clarifying issues; aides in the White House, however, attributed a far more extensive and influential role to him.

Fortas left the government with a cloud over his head but, unlike the Moyers situation, the President was not directly involved in the Fortas fall. When the Senate considered the President's nomination of Fortas for Chief Justice of the United States (he had readily been confirmed earlier as one of the associate justices), the propriety of certain of Fortas' financial dealings made top headlines, as did questions about his continuing relationship with the President after he became an associate justice of the Supreme Court. Rather than prolong the embarrassing situation, Fortas resigned and returned to the private practice of law.

Clark Clifford, as I have indicated, was for a time a confidant of Johnson's. Later he became Secretary of Defense. The differences between the two men over the Vietnam War led to an estrangement which was beyond healing.

Johnson was an extremely difficult man to work for. He expected those who worked for him to keep up with him, and he set a wicked and exhausting pace. In fact he invented a "two shift" working day to get everything done. He would begin work at six-thirty or seven in the morning, break for a lunch and long nap, and begin his second shift at about 4:00 P.M. Usually he worked until midnight. When he wanted Moyers or Califano, they were expected to be at hand, regardless of the time of day or the day of the week. He demanded total dedication and total loyalty. He persuaded key members of President Kennedy's staff to remain in the Administration after the assassination, because he needed them. But as his reliance on them lessened and their greater loyalty to "their President" increasingly rankled Johnson, he turned to others.

Johnson was quick to lose his temper, and stories of his towering rages, falling indiscriminately on hapless aides, are well known. He could be cruel with those closest to him, baiting them, needling them unmercifully. After his Vietnam speech at Johns Hopkins the President hurried to a nearby lounge where three television sets had been installed for him so he could watch each major network. He had invited a dozen or so leading Maryland Democrats to join him there. When Richard Goodwin, a speech writer for Johnson, entered the room the President pointed to him and said sarcastically: "This is Goodwin, the great speech writer. Say something eloquent for us, Dick." He continued to jibe at Goodwin, to the embarrassment not only of Goodwin but most of the guests as well. Eric Goldman, who also felt Johnson's wrath, tells of an old Johnson friend who said, "He will probably do more for the United States, destroying everybody around him, than any other President."

Since I knew most of the men who worked with President Johnson I have often reflected on the fact that men came and left with great frequency. Ted Sorensen remained with Johnson for a time and was his major speech writer, but he left in 1964. McGeorge Bundy was a keenly intelligent national security adviser, but he resigned to become president of The Ford Foundation. Dick Goodwin, a young and troublesome man, and no doubt still smarting from his humiliation at Johns Hopkins, departed in 1966 and thereafter was unrestrained in his attacks on Johnson's policies. Harry C. McPherson, Jr., undertook serious responsibilities only after 1966. For a time Horace Busby was a confidant; it was he who worked with the President on the address in which Johnson declared he would not be a candidate in 1968. Willard Wirtz had an interesting experience; he wrote most of the President's 1964 campaign speeches and then, early in 1968, spent four hours with Johnson outlining a program of addresses for the 1968 campaign—this only two days before Busby and the President completed the television address in which the President announced he would not be a candidate for re-election.

My judgment is that, while Moyers, Califano, Fortas, Bundy, Clifford, Rusk, McNamara, and many others were of help to President Johnson, he suffered from the fact that he did not have someone he could trust completely and who would remain with him through his years in the White House.

On March 13, 1968, President Johnson appointed me a member of the Board of Directors of the Corporation for Public Broadcasting. This for me was a happy climax to a public campaign I had been prominently engaged in for eighteen years.

It was early in 1950 that I accepted membership in a national citizens' group which insisted that the miraculous development of television provided a new and unmatched opportunity to contribute to the education of the American people in social, cultural, political, and even foreign affairs. My associates and I did not believe that commercial television could or would fill this role. We did not criticize or seek to weaken the commercial networks or stations. Rather, we wished to parallel the commercial system with a publicly supported educational set of stations and, in time, an educational network. We campaigned for the reservation by the Federal Communications Commission of both normal and ultra high frequencies for educational purposes. Gratifyingly, the campaign succeeded. More than 140 reservations were made, mainly in the ultra high frequency bands, a few in the normal bands. Shortly thereafter The Ford Foundation set up an independent Foundation for Adult Education, of which I was a director, and under the driving force of its president, C. Scott Fletcher, major attention was given to financing the construction of non-commercial television stations and the creation of a central agency which would receive and distribute nationally tape recordings of many of the best programs originated by individual stations. Many millions of dollars went into this enterprise.

It was not until 1968 that the Congress was induced to establish a non-profit Corporation for Public Broadcasting and to provide some of the funds for the operation of individual stations and regional interconnections. The act called upon the Board of Directors to "facilitate the full development of educational broadcasting in which high quality programs will be made available to non-commercial educational television and radio stations; assist in the establishment of interconnections to be used for the distribution of educational television and radio programs . . . ; effectively assure maximum freedom of non-commercial educational television and radio systems; obtain grants from individuals, institutions, organizations, etc. and make contracts for educational television and radio programming."

The Board of Directors began meeting frequently, our first task being to devise a system of public financing which would not endanger the independence of the non-commercial stations. Discussions centered on the possibility of creating a special fund built up by a designated tax, either on the sale of new television and radio sets or possibly, as in the United Kingdom, on all existing sets.

My tenure on the Board was short, for only three months after its establishment President Johnson called upon me for a new task which was so arduous and time-consuming that I was compelled to sever my connections with the educational effort, which meant a great deal to me.

Lyndon Johnson had ascended to the presidency in the midst of the national crisis caused by the assassination of John Kennedy. His dignity, firmness, and skill during the transfer of power—always a somewhat precarious procedure—calmed and reassured a stunned and uncertain nation.

Swept into office a year later by the greatest landslide vote in history, Johnson had the mandate to accomplish the goal he so ardently sought: to unite Americans in the cause of the Great Society. He saw himself as a "healer," and he pleaded for national unity as though it were some kind of religion. "Come, let us reason together," he said. As the unequaled master of consensus politics, Lyndon Johnson seemed the ideal man to lead the nation through the sixties.

How ironic and tragic, then, that he should finally decide that he could only hope to accomplish his great goal of national unity not by holding the presidency but by yielding it. On March 31, 1968, Lyndon Baines Johnson, a tired and disillusioned but still proud man, partially halted the bombing of North Vietnam and announced that he would not accept renomination for the presidency.

His legacy to his successor was to be a highly unpopular war that could not be won on the battlefield; serious inflation, caused by his insistence that we could proceed with costly social programs while fighting a war that caused defense costs to soar to eighty-two billion dollars a year, while wages rose at a rate about four times the increase in productivity; and a loss of faith by millions of Americans in their government and many of their social institutions. The term "credibility gap" was invented to characterize the Johnson administration. It began mildly with our involvement in the Dominican crisis and then became a major issue with the escalation of the Vietnam War. The people had not forgotten that he had worn the mantle of healer and peacemaker during the 1964 presidential campaign. It intensified as official reports from the White House and the Defense Department differed significantly, sometimes completely, from the facts developed by dependable correspondents in the war zone. Cynicism swept across the nation. So turbulent were the popular protests, and especially by the young, that President Johnson became a virtual captive in the White House.

Walter Cronkite, in an address at The Johns Hopkins University on February 9, 1967, said: "Honesty has become old-fashioned and the very use of the word subjects its user to that guttural 'yech' that is the younger generation's bronx cheer. . . . We . . . stand at Thermopylae, which is not that Grecian pass where the Spartans stood but the gap at which our credibility rests. Today truth and honesty are surrounded by untruth and dishonesty, by dissembling and distortion, by cynicism and disbelief. Through apathy and unnecessary helplessness, we can lose to these black forces the great bastion of mutual confidence that is the guardian of our democracy. . . . Misleading the public has become general armed forces policy. . . . U Thant's revelation of Hanoi peace feelers was denied by Washington and confirmed only after Eric Severeid reported them. . . . Just this week the Pentagon finally admitted that American air losses in Vietnam were almost double that of previous statements. . . . As the power of our individual officeholders grows with the inevitable growth of government, that which William Fulbright has called the arrogance of power grows too, and not alone in his context of foreign policy, but as well in the treatment of the truth and of those who speak it."

President Johnson, while crushed by the criticisms that engulfed him, and despite his decision to remove himself from the next presidential election, continued vigorously to carry on the great responsibilities of the presidency. It was in the midst of the most anguished period of his years in the White House that he telephoned me and insisted that I serve as chairman of a presidential Commission on the Causes and Prevention of Violence.

CHAPTER 23

I am convinced that the danger to America from within is far greater than from any external force.

My LAST CHORE for President Johnson began on June 10, 1968, when I, with foreboding, was sworn in as chairman of the National Commission on the Causes and Prevention of Violence.

Ten of us who became members of this new presidential commission that day gathered to await the appearance of President Johnson. We were reading a draft of the executive order. An assistant to the President entered the room and asked us to wait for a moment longer; the President, he said, wished to make a last-minute change in the order.

The draft before us directed that we investigate and make recommendations with respect to:

(a) the causes and prevention of lawless acts of violence in our society, including assassination, murder, and assault;

(b) the causes and prevention of disrespect for the law and violent disruption of the public order by individuals and groups;

(c) such other matters as the President might place before the commission.

The President's last-minute change in the order was the inclusion in paragraph (b) of the additional phrase "disrespect for public officials." Surely this reflected his concern that the President, as well as other government leaders, could rarely appear in public without provoking vigorous, often disruptive, public demonstrations.

When the amended order had been retyped we were summoned to the Cabinet room where television cameras, reporters, and a host of White House staff members were waiting. The gloom and despair of Senator Robert Kennedy's assassination hung heavily over the nation, and there was an air of tension and solemnity about the occasion. The commission members sat in assigned chairs on one side of the table, facing the cameras. Then President Johnson strode in, greeted each of us quietly, took his usual chair in the center of the huge table, signed the executive order, and began speaking.

He held the executive order in his hand and glanced at it occasionally. He appeared to be speaking extemporaneously, but actually he was reading from a teleprompter below the lens of one of the television cameras. Suddenly he waved his hand and stopped the proceedings. With some asperity he directed that the final amendment to the executive order be inserted in the teleprompter copy. After this was done he began again. This time all went smoothly.

I was amazed by the great change in the President. I had always known him as a man of immense energy, with an almost passionate interest in each person he dealt with, a stern self-control, and a conventional rhetoric expressed in a disarming Texas drawl. Now he seemed distraught, tired, aloof. His speech was clipped and he seemed on the verge of anger. As I had observed with other Presidents, the vast responsibilities and worries of the office were taking their toll. And as I sat there I realized that this brief time with our commission was only one of dozens of responsibilities devolving on him that day.

It was clearly a trying time for Lyndon Johnson. His announcement some two months earlier that he would not be a candidate in 1968 had not brought him peace of mind. Nor had his decision finally to reduce the bombing of North Vietnam. American casualties in Southeast Asia had reached an all-time high, some 1,111 dead in the two weeks ending May 26. Some military leaders were criticizing his limitation of the bombing. Student riots at Columbia University threatened the existence of the university, the leader of the uprising declaring: "We will either politicize the university or destroy it!" On scores of other campuses student protest movements were gaining momentum and demonstrations against the war were closing classes and leading to violence which destroyed property, made hostages of university officials, and eventually claimed lives. The Reverend Ralph Abernathy had brought three thousand elderly poor people to Washington, set up Resurrection City, and declared that they would remain to "plague the Pharaohs on Capitol Hill." He demanded new housing and jobs for the poor and did not intervene when some of his people threw stones through the windows of the Supreme Court.

Peace delegates in Paris, after quarreling for days about the shape of the negotiating table, were waging a propaganda war. In the Democratic primaries Robert Kennedy, until his assassination, and Senator Eugene McCarthy had been making scathing comments about the Administration. Ominously, Soviet troops were crossing the borders of Czechoslovakia and tensions there were mounting. A nationwide strike of students in France was causing widespread violence and was imperiling the French government. A truculent and frustrated Congress was insisting that the President accept a six-billion-dollar cut in federal expenditures and was roundly condemning United States imbalances in international payments. To top it all off, a United States submarine, the *Scorpion*, had disappeared in the Atlantic.

The patience and energies of any President would have been sapped by such troubles. Staff members told me that the President had risen before seven, had conferred at breakfast with congressional leaders, reached his office at nine, put in half a dozen phone calls to the Defense and State departments, and then began seeing a string of visitors, one every thirty minutes, each with a different problem. The Commission on the Causes and Prevention of Violence, being sworn in, was a mere interruption, for the frantic pace would continue long after our departure.

Following our swearing-in ceremony, we returned to the fishbowl room of the White House (principal reception room for presidential visitors) to plan our first official meeting. We decided on an early date when the three absent members (yet to be appointed) could be present.

That meeting was held in a spacious conference room in the Senate wing of the Capitol. As I glanced about the table I was consumed with misgivings. Four of the thirteen members were political liberals, five were conservative (two extremely so), and four were moderates. Nine were lawyers, two of whom were judges; one was a labor leader and philosopher, another was an archbishop soon to be a cardinal; two were black; four were Republican; seven were Democrats; and two were political independents. Two of the members were congressmen and two were senators.

It was clear to me that if we merely sought to find common ground in our preconceptions our report to the President would be of no con-

435

sequence. I suspected that such a diverse group would have difficulty in agreeing on any matter of substantive importance.

Evidently other members shared my fear, for we quickly determined that we would set up a nationwide network of research scholars to dig deeply into the subject of violence. We would begin by assembling a smaller group of leading sociologists, psychiatrists, historians, political scientists, criminologists, lawyers, and others to help us define the parameters of the subject and to determine what each scholarly discipline could contribute to a well-rounded study.

The wisdom of the President in suggesting Lloyd Cutler as executive director became apparent from the outset. He was able to give only part time to our work, as was the case with the commissioners themselves; but he suggested the appointment of James Campbell, a young lawyer in the Justice Department, as the full-time general counsel, and Mr. Campbell, under the direction of Mr. Cutler, proved to be a tower of strength. Whenever some aspect of our work seemed to falter he had a genius for intervening and putting everything back on a solid track.

After meeting with our group of specialists we decided to divide the subject of violence into seven major areas:

Individual Acts of Violence

Group Violence

Assassination and Political Violence

The Effects of Violence in the Mass Media

Firearms and Violence

The Criminal Justice System

The History of Violence (with comparative cross national studies)

At this point we arrived at an ingenious organizational approach to our study. We decided to create a task force to investigate each of the seven areas. Each task force would have as co-chairmen a lawyer and a scholar. A lawyer, by training, is devoted to getting the facts and making the best possible case. He must be able to become reasonably expert on a given subject in a relatively short time and then be able to present logical and compelling arguments; his objective is to make the best possible case on the basis of the facts available to him. The scholar, on the other hand, dedicated to searching for the truth is inclined to reserve judgment until he has gone as far as research can take him. Having a lawyer and a scholar sharing responsibility for the study in each of the seven major areas would create a healthy tension and would hopefully produce substantive data for the commission's consideration. Each of the task forces would enlist the aid of research scholars throughout the country to study and analyze the complicated aspects of the causes of violence.

Lloyd Cutler had an amazing nationwide acquaintance and with his help we soon induced two leading scholars to become co-directors of our research effort and to work with all of the seven task forces. Marvin E. Wolfgang of the University of Pennsylvania and James F. Short, Jr., of Washington State University, both sociologists with specialization in criminology, joined the staff and began the search for some two hundred scholars who were needed to carry out the research in the seven areas we had agreed upon. Cutler then contacted leading law firms around the country and recruited bright young lawyers to serve as co-chairmen of the task forces.

At this early stage we made another sound decision. We knew that most of the leading authorities we needed were engaged in teaching and research, that their commitments were firm, and that they would not lightly give up their ongoing research just to help our commission. Only by guaranteeing them the same kind of academic freedom they had on their campuses to follow their research where it led them and publish their findings without editing or censorship by the commission could we hope to attract the scholars we needed. Our problem was made doubly difficult by the fact that in the summer (it was then late in July) we would have trouble reaching all of the scholars we selected and they would be hard pressed to rearrange their previous commitments. Frantically, by telephone, cablegram, and letter we located the researchers we wanted. We made this basic agreement in approaching each one: providing only that they would develop for us the facts, interpretations, and recommendations in each of the seven areas we had outlined, we would assure them that they would have the normal academic freedom to do their work independently; we would not edit their manuscripts; we would guarantee that their final report to us would be published by the government or that they would be free to publish it themselves. The commission would neither approve nor disapprove what they reported to us. Their findings would be reports *to* the commission and not reports *by* the commission.

I still marvel at the fact that within a month all seven research groups were hard at work.

We decided that while research was under way the commission itself would hold public hearings in the Senate Office Building, hearing witnesses such as the Attorney General, the director of the FBI, youth leaders (including extremists), police chiefs, leaders of the mass media, religious, educational, and social leaders, and many public officials, including those dealing with the pervasive problems of drugs. Over a six-month period we would take testimony from some 150 persons.

In planning the commission hearings we had our first disagreement. The congressional members insisted that our hearings be open to the public and the mass media, as nearly all congressional hearings are. Some of us objected in the belief that witnesses (to say nothing of commissioners) would be overly conscious of the television cameras and would make speeches; worse, they would be sensitive to the public reaction to their statements and would tend to be less candid in giving us honest opinions on such controversial matters as civil disobedience, gun control, and correlations (if any) between race and crime.

The congressional view prevailed, which was inevitable, I suppose. Consequently the hearings were not as helpful as they might have been. One network, at least, kept a television camera trained on us throughout the hearings, but most of the time it was not operating. Only when a note of controversy was struck or a very prominent witness appeared would the TV cameraman lay his paperback novel aside and photograph the proceedings. Eric Hoffer was certainly the most flamboyant of the commissioners in his interrogation of witnesses. His blunt, passionate eloquence made interesting viewing, even though it often took the form of statements rather than questions. So it was not surprising, as the questioning moved around the dais, that the TV cameraman would focus his lens and turn on his camera when it was Hoffer's turn to examine a witness.

Although the television networks had been adamant about their desire and right to cover the commission's hearings, they did not present much of the commission's activity to the American people. When something significant or controversial occurred in a hearing, the evening news would include a brief film report. These brief vignettes were no more representative of the day's hearings than the paperback novel. I recall one such distortion when a young nihilist made a passionate statement about the many evils he saw in the American society and demanded that the "establishment" be destroyed. I tried in vain to have him state what form of human organization he would advocate. He would only say that he favored "participatory democracy." We all believe in citizen participation, I replied, could he be more specific? When I failed to get an answer I asked him whether he would submit to the commission a memorandum spelling out his alternatives to the American system of representative government. He said he would but never did.

As we were getting the commission's activities properly organized and launching our research effort, massive violence erupted at the Democratic National Convention in Chicago. The commission staff and the White House staff quickly agreed in mid-September that we should create a special task force to investigate the convention violence. To head that task force we chose Daniel Walker, then an executive with Montgomery Ward and now governor of Illinois. We were all agreed that speed was essential, that our investigation should begin while the incidents were still fresh and should be completed as soon as possible.

Mr. Walker took his mandate very seriously. In a matter of days he had assembled a staff of investigators, developed a plan of attack, and by September 27 had begun gathering data. Fifty-three days later Mr. Walker had a draft of his report. His task force had taken more than 1,400 eyewitness accounts of the Chicago violence, had collected and studied more than 180 hours of motion picture film and television tapes, and had examined more than 12,000 still photographs.

The Walker Report, of course, made headlines and created controversy—some of it in the commission itself. The report was blunt and shocking. It castigated the Chicago Police Department and civic authorities, and charged that a "police riot" had triggered much of the violence in Chicago in August 1968. Some of the commissioners were upset by the report—by its blunt attack on the Chicago police and by its inclusion of the obscene language that characterized the Chicago demonstrations.

The report was ready by November 18. At that point the commission had not yet had to reach any decisions on substantive issues and certainly had not had to take any public positions. Now, suddenly, we were faced with a bombshell of a report, prepared under the commission's auspices, but with no real participation by the commissioners.

I am sure that some of the commissioners would have voted to withhold the report, at least for a while, and to edit it substantially.

439

(This and other investigatory reports were in a different category from research studies on which we had promised freedom of publication.) Dan Walker obviously anticipated such a reaction, for when he delivered his report it was not a typed but a multilithed copy, stapled between printed covers. It was immediately clear that there would be little if any editing and that the release of the report was a moot question, for by that time, I am convinced, copies were already in the hands of certain persons outside the commission. Dan Walker was polite but firm in response to pressures for changes in the report. He agreed to one significant change: he had given his report the title, in strong stencil type face, *DEMCON 1968*; it was published as *Rights in Conflict*. And it was published as a report *to* the commission.

As our study proceeded, we created other special investigatory groups, like the Walker team, to investigate the shoot-out in Cleveland between police and Black Muslims, the violence at San Francisco State College, and the inauguration of President Nixon, which had been threatened with violence. All were published, but none had the impact of the Walker Report.

When the public hearings were completed the commission began to meet frequently to develop its own views. At most meetings the chairmen of the task forces would join us and inform us of their progress, as well as of any preliminary findings or tentative conclusions. Thus we did not have to await the final written reports of seven task forces and five investigatory groups before we could fulfill our own serious responsibility.

President Johnson had hoped that we would complete our studies and report to him before the end of December 1968. It was clear to us early in the fall, however, that we simply could not meet the President's charge to us in such a short time. Any consideration of the causes and prevention of violence would require at least a year if a creditable job was to be done. President Johnson, of course, would be leaving the White House in January, and I could understand his impatience to have our report before then.

Beginning in late summer and continuing through the fall, the commission staff reported to me that the White House was exerting pressure to get the report completed before the first of the year and to hasten that part of our study dealing with violence and the media. There was some sense on the part of the commission staff that the

THE PRESIDENT IS CALLING

White House was harassing us in subtle ways. One not so subtle problem was a recurring one in the early months of the commission's life:
we simply couldn't get the funds we needed. Congress had not appropriated money for the commission; the President's aides assured us that
funds would be transferred to us from other executive agencies. Colonel
William G. MacDonald, our chief administrator and one of those highly
competent career officers who has mastered the bureaucratic maze,
spent hours every week for many weeks trying to track down funds.
On one payday the Treasury remained open after closing time for an
extra few minutes while a messenger hand-carried a form authorizing a
transfer of funds from the National Institute of Mental Health budget
to ours. With the form in hand, the Treasury official handed Colonel
MacDonald the pay checks and he hurried over to our building where
commission employees were waiting at the front door for him.

The problem became so serious that the commissioners, in executive session, considered calling a press conference and resigning for lack
of support from the White House. I could not understand why the
President or his assistants would want to harass the commission, and
so assumed that in its lame-duck situation the present Administration
was having trouble getting funds from career bureaucrats. In any case,
at an executive meeting of the commission we delegated to commissioner Leon Jaworski the task of raising our problem with the President.
Mr. Jaworski had been invited to the White House that evening for a
black-tie dinner.

The next morning, prior to our public hearings, the commission
gathered in the staff offices of the hearing room to receive Jaworski's
report. He explained that he had indeed had an opportunity to speak
alone with Mr. Johnson and that he had told the President of our financial problems and the sentiment that perhaps the commissioners
should publicly resign. As Jaworski told it: the President, towering
above him, grasped his left shoulder, crushing the shoulder pad of his
tuxedo in his fist. Then the President sternly lectured his old friend
about the impropriety of threats of resignation, all the while emphasiz-
ing each point by jerking up on Jaworski's tuxedo jacket shoulder pad.
Jaworski demonstrated as he reported, and all of us had a good laugh.
But the financial problem continued until, much later, we obtained a
special appropriation from the Congress.

It was just about that time that an item in Drew Pearson's column infuriated me. The article said that Lloyd Cutler, executive director of the commission, was also attorney for the Columbia Broadcasting System and that the commission would take a soft line on the question of media violence because of this. We learned from reliable sources that the Pearson item had come as a "tip" from the White House. I was quite upset. When he was asked by the President to serve the Violence Commission, Lloyd Cutler pointed out that his firm represented a major television network and that this could create a conflict-of-interest situation. The President waved this aside, saying that Lloyd could simply remove himself from considerations of media violence. Mr. Cutler accepted the assignment but he put on the record a statement acknowledging his connection with CBS, and he scrupulously avoided an involvement in that part of our work that touched on television violence.

A day or so after these incidents I was riding home to Baltimore with my special assistant, Ron Wolk. Ron had worked for me at Johns Hopkins for eight years and had left a position in California in August to join me on the Violence Commission. I knew I could speak candidly with him, so I gave vent to my concerns about the White House's role in our problems. The more we discussed the problem the more apparent it became to me that I would have to speak with President Johnson directly. When we arrived at my house we went right to my study and I placed a call to Joseph Califano and told him I wanted to see the President as soon as possible. It was then Wednesday or Thursday. Califano said the President could see me late Saturday morning. I told him I would bring with me two other commissioners, Senator Phil Hart and Senator Roman Hruska.

The Saturday meeting was an unusual one. President Johnson appeared weary and subdued. I got right to the point, explaining to him that the commission and its staff were working at a backbreaking pace on an extraordinarily difficult assignment; we simply could not do our job without his full support and I was there to determine whether or not he wished us to continue. I was as blunt as I could be without being disrespectful.

The President turned in his chair and gazed out of the window for a full minute without speaking. Then he turned to me and said:

"Milton, you know how much I admire and respect your brother and how I feel about you. I want you to finish this job and you will have my support. But I must tell you that I am very worried about the effect that the mass media are having on this country." He then went on, almost in monologue fashion, to speak of the erosion of traditional values in our society and the role played by television and motion pictures in shaping the attitudes of the nation's young people. He spoke for nearly half an hour, quietly and with great sincerity and concern.

When he finished I told him that we would make as thorough a study as possible of the mass media influence but that the commission would not conduct a witch hunt. I also said that while it was impossible for us to finish our work by the end of December we would give him a progress report which would include preliminary findings. I know he was disappointed that our final report would not be submitted while he was still President, but he understood the problem we faced and accepted the reality gracefully.

From that moment on we had no further evidence of harassment, subtle or otherwise.

We wanted to give the President as thorough a progress report as possible, so the commission and major staff members spent a long weekend at a rural retreat and hammered out, in spite of serious disagreements, a statement which indicated in general terms what would be set forth in detail and with precise data in the final report.

In the progress report we were mainly assertive and philosophical. We said that the people of America were deeply concerned about violence. They had seen a President, a senator, and a great civil rights leader assassinated in a few short years. They had seen flames rising from the skylines of their cities as civil disorders spread across the land —"holocausts of rioting, looting, firebombing and death." They had seen students disrupt classes, destroy educational buildings and scientific equipment, physically attack public figures, shout obscenities and the "strident rhetoric of revolution," and then ask for clemency. Further, we said, the American people had seen the violence of overseas war, of police dogs, and of fire hoses and police clubs. And they had seen slaughter on highways and violence all but glorified in motion pictures and television programs.

At this stage of our work we were still seeking for a perspective that would guide us in our deliberations. So, in the progress report to President Johnson, we reflected on the fact that Aristotle,* viewing

---

* Even the peace-loving Aristotle thought that violence could be justified under some circumstances. He said: "We make war that we may live in peace."

man as a social animal, with ambivalent instincts, had nonetheless marveled at man's ability to create a social order which enabled him to embrace for social purposes the challenges and opportunities of the environment. Social order came to be known as the state, and the rules of its maintenance as the law. But from Genesis and the *Iliad* to the morning's newspaper, civilization had witnessed man's violence toward other men.

And man did not consider that all violence should be avoided. We of the United States did not do so. Our nation has always accepted some violence as legitimate and some as unacceptable. The task for every society was to draw moral and legal distinctions between legitimate and illegitimate violence. Thus we felt our own Revolutionary War, killing in self-defense, appropriate discipline of children, war against an enemy, and use of violence by the police in certain circumstances were acceptable. At periods in our history we had not been greatly shocked by the violence of vigilantism, shoot-outs in the opening of the West, Indian wars, the hanging of rustlers, and even lynchings by the Ku Klux Klan. Today we were more discriminating, more civilized. In volumes of federal and state statutes we had drawn sharp distinction between legitimate and illegitimate actions, even down to distinctions in the rearing of children; a parent might spank a child but he could not break the child's arm. Certainly lynchings, vigilantism, and indeed all violence that impinged upon the rights of others or employed violence without the sanction obtainable in legal processes were unacceptable. So were the obvious crimes of homicide, rape, robbery, assault, and larceny.

We felt that the elimination of all violence in a free society was impossible, for the coercive use of power to achieve such an end would be so tremendous as to give us essentially a police state in violation of our basic concepts of freedom, mutuality in human relations, and democratic decision making.

Our conclusion was—and this the President had said to us in the television broadcast in his office on July 10—that the commission's study of violence in contemporary America must, if it were to reach meaningful conclusions, include a study of American society itself, past and present, and the traditions and institutions which accept or condemn the various forms that violence takes in our society. We expressed our regret that we could not give him the definitive report he had asked

444

of us. Disappointed, but gracious and understanding, he accepted our statement.

I have often speculated since then on what President Johnson would have done had we been able to report to him the objective, logical, and well-documented material we gave President Nixon on December 10, 1969. Would he have used it in framing his own recommendations to the Congress? I shall indicate what I think should be done in this regard in the next chapter.

As July 10, 1969, approached—the legal termination of the commission under the original executive order—it became clear that we could not complete our work by then. At this stage some research had been completed, hearings had been studied, staff members had prepared many preliminary chapters of a report, and the commission was meeting weekly. I was spending more than half my time in Washington, commuting comfortably in a White House car between my home in Baltimore and our Washington office.

On May 23, 1969, President Nixon signed an executive order which continued our legal life to December 10, 1969. Many of us worked long hours each day to meet the new deadline. By doing so we met the deadline and we were on the whole satisfied with our work.

I confess, however, that we failed to deal with at least one relevant and highly sensitive subject. The research study on the influence of the mass media was the last presented to us. With the help of the research staff we did reach the conclusion, and so reported, that programs of violence on television had a deleterious effect on the attitudes and behavior of the young, especially in the ghettos where the fiction on television was not dissimilar to the life of the street; young persons therefore did not distinguish between fact and fiction. But we did not reach agreement on the possible consequences of the way the mass media dealt with violence in the news columns and on the television screen. We considered two drafts prepared by distinguished American journalists and one by our research group. We discarded all three.

In the final months of our deliberations every word of the report was read aloud in the presence of the entire commission. Often we would spend an hour discussing a point in a single paragraph. Occasionally a member of the commission would make a speech, seemingly differing with a statement in a given paragraph. Then I would ask, "What specific change would make this satisfactory to you and to the commission?" On more than one occasion the member, after a pause, would say, "Let it go, it's all right as it is."

I dislike mentioning the contributions made by various members of the commission, for an omission could be offensive to all and would be a shame to me. But I must, in spite of this, say that I have never worked with a more knowledgeable and creative person than Ambassador Patricia Harris. Further, whenever she differed with a viewpoint in the tentative text, she would not make a speech in the hope that someone else could produce a satisfactory draft; she would present an alternative draft herself and nearly always she was right. Senator Hart of Michigan and Congressman McCulloch of Ohio were faithful in attendance and keenly intelligent in their suggestions. Cardinal Cooke displayed an amazing knowledge of human behavior and ill behavior and a true liberalism in suggesting actions which he felt should be taken to achieve improvement. Judge Higginbotham, Leon Jaworski, Albert Jenner, and Walter Menninger were invariably constructive. But no commissioner deserves more credit for the quality of our work, including the writing of the final report, than do the top staff members, Lloyd Cutler and James Campbell.

On the final day of our legal life I held my tenth news and television conference (each major section of the report had been released separately) and then Mr. Cutler, Mr. Campbell, and I went to the White House to report to President Nixon.

The President permitted me to speak for about forty-five minutes without interruption. In that period I tried to give him in capsule form our major findings and recommendations.

We had found that each year some ten million serious crimes are committed in the United States. Of these as many as a million are violent crimes: homicides, aggravated assaults, forcible rapes, and armed robberies. Of all crimes, each year only twelve per cent result in an arrest, six per cent in a conviction or plea of guilt, and only one and a half per cent in incarceration. As Mr. Cutler had remarked in one of our commission meetings: "It would be hard to argue that crime does not pay. The sad fact is that our criminal justice system, as presently operated, does not deter, does not detect, does not convict, and does not correct."

The United States has the unenviable distinction of being the most criminogenic of the modern, stable nations of the world. The United

States, with two hundred million population, averages fifty times as many gun murders a year as do England, Germany, and Japan combined, with their total population of little more than two hundred million.

Our rate of violent crime per unit of population is five times that of Canada, thirty times that of Great Britain, and ninety times that of the Netherlands.

In the great urban areas, where more than two thirds of the American people live—and this trend toward urbanization is increasing—violent crime is rising and fear is rising in its wake. The rate of violent crimes in the cities is eight times that of the rural countryside, six times that of the smaller town rate. But fear is nationwide, manifest in locked doors, empty streets at night, an alarming increase in the number of handguns bought for an assumed self-protection, the refusal of bus drivers to carry cash, and a rush of those who can afford to do so to escape from the cities and seek refuge in suburbs which are themselves becoming armed camps.

Violent crime has increased about one hundred per cent in the past ten years. It is significant that the rate of crime in the United States had declined from the turn of the century to the early forties, increased somewhat from then to the late fifties, and suddenly doubled in the sixties. Before I mentioned causes to the President I amplified on the statistics.

First was the problem of urbanization. If one lives in a poor section of Chicago his chance of suffering a violent crime is one in twenty-seven each year. If he lives in the best section of the city his chance would be one in two thousand, and in a rich suburb one in ten thousand. In my home city, Baltimore, the mathematical chance of being a victim of a serious crime is one in about fifty, so the odds are in favor of one's becoming a victim sometime during his lifetime.†

Second, violent crime is concentrated mostly in the ghetto slums where most black people live. But one race is no more criminogenic than another. Prolonged research by many scholars has established this fact. The correlation is not between crime and race but between crime

† In December 1969, when I reported to the President, the rate of crime in Baltimore was the highest of all cities in the United States. In the ensuing four years Baltimore has made substantial progress in reducing many types of crime so that in October 1973 the city ranked sixth, not first, in crimes per unit of population.

447

and the human and environmental conditions in which people live.

Third, violent crime in cities is overwhelmingly committed by males.

Fourth, in the cities, by far the most crimes are committed by young males between the ages of fifteen and twenty-four; the rate of crime for this age group is three times that of any other. Alarmingly, however, there has been a startling increase in crime among the ten-to-fourteen age group—nearly a three hundred per cent increase in the past decade.

Fifth, while the public believes that violent crime is a kind of inter-racial warfare, the facts are that most crimes are intraracial. Victims have the same characteristics as the offenders: they tend to be males, youths, poor persons, and blacks. Nine out of ten urban homicides, aggravated assaults, and rapes involve victims and offenders of the same race. We found that only robbery is largely interracial, young blacks robbing somewhat older white males.

Sixth, many violent crimes, especially those of rape, homicide, and assault, are acts of passion among intimates and acquaintances. Indeed, half of all homicides are committed within the family, eighty per cent within the family or among acquaintances. But robbery, a calculated crime, is committed by a stranger eight times out of ten.

Finally, an amazingly high percentage of violent crimes is committed by recidivists. In one study we found that in a given age group six per cent of the members of the group committed fifty-three per cent of the homicides, rapes, and assaults and seventy-one per cent of the robberies. It is a well-known fact that persons out on bail commit more crimes while they await trial, and those on parole have a wide incidence of recidivism.

In sum, then, violent crimes in the cities involve males rather than females, youths rather than older people, the poor and unskilled rather than the more successful, and ghetto blacks rather than persons living in the more affluent city sections.

Violent crime, however, is not exclusively the province of ghetto youth. All strata of society have alcoholics and drug addicts. Alcoholics are mainly a danger in traffic. Drug addicts are not made prone to crime physiologically or psychologically by drugs; rather they enter a life of robbery to obtain the funds needed to support their addiction. It is unfortunately true that the thin shell of civility that houses our aggressive instincts often breaks open and spills violence in some of the so-called finest families of America. This should not detract us from the fact, however, that the social pathology in the ghettos breeds the most crime, or that even in the ghettos a majority of the poor, young Negro males rise above their environment and lead useful law-abiding lives.

On several occasions Attorney General John Mitchell had asserted that poverty is not a cause of crime. I had been irritated by this, for his repetition of his belief seemed to be a criticism of thinking that was developing in our commission. But we were not correlating crime and poverty as Mitchell could easily determine. Certainly one could cite areas of poverty where the rate of crime is low. The commission did not ascribe the problem to poverty alone. It is important to understand that socially destructive forces—environmental and human—are at work in the ghettos. There is in the ghettos an acrid awareness of the fact that throughout our history the realities of American life have made a mockery of the American dream so far as most blacks are concerned. In the ghetto there are few, if any, examples of educated, successful men. The youth notes that his father, if he has one, and the men up and down the block sweat at menial and intermittent jobs. If one man has a fancy convertible, he isn't working for a welfare agency or in an industrial plant; he is probably pushing drugs or robbing grocery stores.

There is no place for quiet study or contemplation in crowded ghetto apartments. There are few books or serious magazines, and little or no conversation to stimulate the intellect. But there is the constant lure of the omnipresent television set. The young ghetto resident by the time he is eighteen has spent more time watching television, *mostly programs of violence*, than he has spent in school. The lure of television is matched by the lure of the street. There youngsters band together, often late into the night; to be accepted into the peer group one has to engage in crime or use drugs. This is the situation which our director of research, Professor Marvin Wolfgang, has called the subculture of violence. His book on this subject should be required reading in every school in the country.

In the ghetto schools are ill equipped, accommodated to defeat. Teachers expect no more than a modicum of discipline. They have little time to give special help to exceptional students; everything is pitched to the average. Promotions to the next higher grades must be made so that younger entrants can be accepted. It is not surprising that the dropout rate is high. Then, in the American value system, the dropout is a failure and the affluence promised by advertising cannot be his, at least by legitimate means.

The young, between the ages of ten and twenty-four, turn in increasing numbers to violence. Guns are easily obtainable. A gun makes each young man, regardless of size, the equal of the biggest man he might meet.

In our report to the President I then turned to what most uninformed citizens consider to be a paradox, namely, that since conditions in the ghetto are gradually improving, why should crime be increasing?

The percentage of blacks completing high school has been rising appreciably, as have the numbers of blacks in colleges and universities. Unemployment in the ghettos has decreased appreciably.

The explanation for this seeming paradox is not to be found in a single circumstance. Many forces have combined to give this amazing result.

Urbanization is increasing at an accelerated rate, with whites fleeing to the suburbs and blacks swelling the ghettos. One would therefore expect crime to increase proportionately.

The age group most involved in violent crime has soared not only in numbers but in proportion to the total population, from eleven per cent to fifteen per cent, from a total of twenty million to nearly thirty million.

The instability of American families is a factor. Divorces and separations are on the rise in every segment of the population, especially among the poor blacks of the cities, partly a consequence of our archaic welfare system.

The increasing number of firearms in private hands is a major cause. In a four-year period, late in the sixties, the sale of long guns doubled; in the same period the sale of cheap handguns, having no sporting value but efficient for killing people, quadrupled.

The speed of technological, occupational, social, and cultural change, we found, is an important consideration. Times of great change alter how we work, think, and live; great change loosens people from old moorings and creates tensions and uncertainties. It is a reasonable assumption that the speed of change has contributed to parental permissiveness, for parents have become somewhat unsure about what values to encourage in their children and what standards to impose.

And in the ghettos, since old-fashioned standards have yielded little for their parents, there is not much incentive to inculcate them in their children.

During the sixties we witnessed a general diminution of the respect accorded the institutions of government. When governors defied federal laws and Supreme Court decisions, when with impunity mobs looted stores with few arrests, when college students destroyed property and then were granted amnesty, when public officials were exposed in corruption—all these and more served to encourage a cynical disrespect for law throughout the nation and certainly in the ghetto slums. (As I made this report I of course did not know that the Nixon administration itself would become involved in alleged illegal acts which would be further encouragement to all persons with criminogenic tendencies.)

Possibly the greatest single cause of the tremendous increase in violent crime is a direct consequence of what academic scholars call the "J curve." Our research people gave us a long thesis on this. Briefly, it is axiomatic that in a period of rising expectations on the part of masses of people, followed by a period in which there is little realization, violence is certain to follow. Could anyone deny that for more than ten years we had been passing legislation and politically making vast promises about a better day in which all citizens would have equal opportunity? Had not most political leaders asserted that discrimination would be eliminated and that good housing, better education, and employment opportunities would be available to all? While some progress had been made, it was glacial in its movement. Politicians and movement leaders had made expectations appear almost utopian. Even if everyone had co-operated and been willing to achieve what was promised, it would have taken and still would take years to bring about the essential changes. So disappointment, then frustration, then anger, and finally militant enmity had resulted. The white racism proclaimed by the Kerner Commission is now matched by black racism, especially where blacks are congregated in ghetto slums.

Finally, the failure of the criminal justice system is a crucial fact. While one should not by any means be critical of most police, certainly some are undereducated, undertrained, and possessed of wrong attitudes. Charges of police brutality, true or not, are accepted as a fact in the black community. The low rate of arrests is partly due to lack of community co-operation. The court system is hardly beyond criticism.

Justice is not always equally dispensed. Court congestion, the long waiting period for trial, and the disappearance of witnesses during this waiting period, make it impossible for justice to be fairly and equally administered. And when a small percentage of those who commit crimes are placed in prison, they often find themselves in a school for crime, not an institution of rehabilitation.

These were only a few of the facts, I said to President Nixon, that had led us to make ninety-one recommendations for federal, state, and community actions which we felt would have a major beneficial effect in reducing the incidence of violent crime in the United States. Our conclusion was that the attack on the problem had to be twofold: simultaneously, we had to improve the criminal justice system and overcome the social causes of crime.

I did not elaborate on what we must do regarding the criminal justice system (the Katzenbach Commission had reported on this), other than to point out that in the judgment of our commission we would have to double the annual investment of federal, state, and local governments in this area. The total annual cost is five billion dollars, less than we have often spent in a single year on agriculture, not much more than we spend on space research and exploration. We must increase this to about ten billion as soon as financial resources are available and adequate plans for such expansion can be formulated.

With regard to overcoming the social causes of crime at an annual cost, we felt, of about twenty billion dollars, I emphasized that most of the things we have to do in this area are already well known to the American people and most of the essential legislation has been enacted; but finances are inadequate. Better schools, better teachers, full employment at fair wages, work opportunities for youth, especially those of the criminally prone ages, a rebuilding and restoration of the tax bases of our cities, better housing, reduction of dope addiction, and the ultimate elimination of the ghettos, by both dispersion of blacks and a countermigration of whites—all these are essential.

We recognized, and so said in our covering letter to the President, that this massive undertaking cannot begin full-blown until the federal government is in a position to reorder its program of expenditures. With the ending of the war in Vietnam, we should be able to reduce military expenditures by as much as twenty billion dollars a year. If the economy, in a peaceful climate, resumes its upward momentum, the federal government should annually have a large increase in revenues, even at prevailing tax rates. Convinced that the threat of crime and other problems within the United States is a greater threat to freedom than any foreign situation, we believe it imperative to take the many actions our commission recommended.

I purposely saved to the last an issue on which I felt deeply, so much so that my colleagues on the commission humorously dubbed me a radical. The issue was gun control.

I was perplexed by the blind, emotional resistance that greeted any reasonable proposal to bring the senseless excess of handguns under control. Every civilized nation of the world, other than our own, has comprehensive national policies of gun control. Yet in the United States we read almost daily of a junior high school student shooting a playmate during a quarrel, of a robber shooting a filling station employee, wives shooting husbands and husbands shooting wives. There are some thirty million handguns known as "Saturday Night Specials" in the United States. These are not sporting weapons. They have no other purpose than to intimidate and kill. So the commission, after most careful deliberation, came to the conclusion that we need a policy of restrictive licensing of handguns and a simple identification system for long guns. There should be a federal statute which provides that only those who can prove a need for handguns can purchase or possess them. Standards for determining need should be set forth in the law. The federal statute should not go into effect in any of the states for a period of three years, and then only if a state fails to enact its own law that harmonizes with the federal standards. It is almost useless for a few states to pass good legislation, as New York did long ago, for people can simply cross state lines and purchase guns with no difficulty.

Objectors say that law-abiding people will observe the law but criminals will not. In a very real sense, that will make for the success of the law. The police know who most of the criminals and potential criminals are, but they cannot now arrest anyone until a crime has been committed, and the record of proving guilt in court is not impressive. Knowing who most likely possess guns, however, police could, with a new law under rulings of the Supreme Court, frisk the suspects and if handguns were found the violators could be convicted on the physical evidence. In time, with the voluntary surrender of guns by law-abiding, right-thinking people, the police could greatly reduce the number of handguns in the hands of criminals. Since the handgun is the favorite weapon used in violent crimes, a reduction of the handgun inventory *would* have a beneficial effect.

I had spoken on television and to the press about this matter several months before. Vitriolic mail at once poured into my office, nearly all of it instigated by form letters and cards distributed nationally by the rich and politically powerful National Rifle Association. I was called everything from Facist to Communist (quite a wide spectrum) and charged with "besmirching the family name." So I told the President that if he accepted this particular recommendation he would not be praised by many, though every poll taken on the subject over a ten-year period showed that about seventy-five per cent of the American people wanted some such action as we had proposed. I quoted Edmund Burke's famous sentence: "The only thing necessary for the triumph of evil is for good men to do nothing."

During my forty-five-minute recital President Nixon had listened attentively. I appreciated his permitting me to make a fairly complete statement.

He indicated that he would read the commission's report with care. He asked me to go through the fourteen supporting documents and mark the most important sections I felt he should study.

He then commented that in determining priorities in federal expenditures in the future there would be great competition for funds. Existing legislation had built-in requirements for appropriation increases. Groups interested in education, pollution, civil rights, welfare, and a host of other problems and activities would wish to have the Congress appropriate vast sums if, as we hoped, defense expenditures declined and federal revenues increased.

In a twenty-minute question and answer period that ensued President Nixon showed that he was well informed on the problem of crime in the American society, and expressed his appreciation of what my associates and I had produced after eighteen months of difficult and time-consuming work. I left the White House with the hope, but no promise, that in due time the President would send to the Congress a well-rounded and soundly conceived program to attack the problem of violent crime in our country.

CHAPTER 24

*America has the wisdom and wealth to solve
its most pressing problems; it is only sufficient will that is lacking.*

For EIGHTEEN MONTHS after I reported to President
Nixon the White House was absolutely silent regarding our commission's study and recommendations. Evidently our report, like many
others, had been filed and forgotten. It is easier to talk about attacking
crime and violence than it is to do something about it.

Somewhat discouraged, I accepted an invitation of the Senate Subcommittee on Administrative Practice and Procedure (of the Committee on the Judiciary), chaired by Senator Edward Kennedy, to testify
on what federal, state, and local actions had been taken as a consequence of the findings and recommendations of the Commission on
the Causes and Prevention of Violence. I was also asked to suggest how
the work of presidential commissions might be made more effective.

With me were Lloyd Cutler and James Campbell. Our testimony
filled sixty-five pages in the printed report of the Kennedy subcommittee.

I acknowledged that very little legislation had resulted from our
work but I contended that the value of a presidential commission should
not be judged solely on that basis. A commission, if properly constituted
and comprised of able and conscientious persons, can make three important contributions to the solution of difficult social problems:

First, free of political pressures and partisanship, it can arrive at
objective, well-documented analysis of the problem.

Second, it can help inform the American people on the facts and
their significance.

Third, it can offer its reasoned judgment on the kinds of actions
required to help solve the problem.

I still marvel at the fact that thirteen individuals of all political persuasions, from various cultural backgrounds, representing different walks of life, and with views about violent crime that varied widely, in time agreed unanimously on the salient facts about the pervasive problem of violence in our society. We agreed, too, on a highly controversial major concept that in my judgment was impeding progress in a general understanding of the basic problem. A great many well-informed persons believed and passionately argued that it would be futile, even dangerous, to attack the problem of crime and violence by strengthening the law-enforcement agencies of society. One of our task force co-chairmen, Jerome Skolnick of the University of Chicago, pressed this point strongly. He and others believed that the only solution lay in a vigorous attack on the social causes of crime and any move to strengthen law enforcement would exacerbate the problem. Others, especially Attorney General John Mitchell, felt that law and order could be restored primarily through stronger and more coercive efforts on the part of the criminal justice system. President Nixon apparently shared this view.

These two opposing points of view, with numerous variations, were held by members of the commission. But after eighteen months of work we unanimously and without qualification determined that the only sensible approach was to move simultaneously in both areas—to launch a massive attack on the causes of violence, while at the same time strengthening our faltering system of criminal justice.

We also agreed unanimously on seventy-nine of the eighty-one recommendations we made to the President, federal, state, and local legislative bodies and many private groups.

Only on two issues did we fail to achieve unanimity. While nine of our members agreed on a system of firearms control that would involve both federal and state legislation, four felt that the problem should be left exclusively to the states. On another grave issue—one that has generated controversy from the time of Aristotle—the commission divided seven to six. This issue was civil disobedience.

Never before in our history has such a concentrated, comprehensive, and penetrative study been made of the historic roots of violence in America and the current magnitude and complex nature of the problem. I doubt that any other method could have produced the same results. Indeed, if the entire population of the United States could go through the long exercise of study and debate that we did, I am confident that there would be a national consensus for the prompt adoption of our recommendations.

The second value of the commission's work is still being attained. The American people today know much more about every aspect of the problem than before. When we began, there was not even a listing for "Violence" in the Encyclopedia of the Social Sciences. As the commission completed each aspect of its study, as, for example, student confrontations, or individual acts of violence, or assassination, it was released in a large newspaper-television press conference. The New York *Times* and the Washington *Post* usually carried each of our topical reports in full, and the press of the nation devoted many column inches to our findings. Television coverage was generally good. More than two million copies of the commission report and its research documents were sold and, of these, most were commercially published. Three nationwide organizations—the Urban Coalition, the American Jewish Committee, and the National Council on Crime and Delinquency—used the commission report for educational work throughout the nation. Later a distinguished symposium of fourteen separate programs at The Johns Hopkins University was carried nationwide by public television stations. Educational work is still under way.

I remember once, midway through our work, when many of us were a bit tired and skeptical, that some felt our efforts would have little if any real impact on the problem. One of our task force leaders admonished us. "Listen," he said, "the work we are doing will advance the state of knowledge about this problem by a decade or more. We should not be too disappointed if today's politicians do not respond to our study; we are writing for the students who are in college who will be influenced by our findings and will carry them further and will, in ten or twenty years, make them matters of policy." I hope that enough of our citizens will become fully informed and will decide on the imperative need for action. When they do, when they demand action, then we will begin to get solutions.

Our failure as a society to make significant inroads on the problem of crime and violence is to a large extent due to the fact that the President, the governors, and the mayors have been unwilling to formulate and fight for comprehensive programs. Our report is buried in some obscure file in the White House. President Nixon has not made a single

457

public comment about the commission's findings, nor have his Attorneys General.

So in testifying on May 26, 1971, before the Kennedy subcommittee, I made two recommendations which I believed would be helpful in the future in avoiding the fate of the Katzenbach, Kerner, Eisenhower, Scranton, and other commissions.

I suggested, first, that the President, upon deciding that a presidential study commission was needed, should be required to send an emergency recommendation to the Congress, seeking specific authorization as to purpose, asking for an appropriation sufficient to cover the total cost of the study regardless of the time needed for it, and asking for subpoena power the commission might need in obtaining evidence.

Normally a President establishes a commission by executive order and then tries to finance its work by transferring funds from existing appropriations in the executive establishment which have some relevance to the study authorized by the order. Thus, funds for our commission came from the Department of Justice, the Budget Bureau, the National Institutes of Health, and, later, a special appropriation by the Congress. As I have said, we were constantly running out of funds, and our administrative officer was always scrounging for the money to meet our costs, which totaled about $1.6 million over the eighteen-month period. So the sheer difficulty of keeping a study under way, without interruption, is a serious matter under present procedures. More important, however, is the fact that the Congress has not joined in the decision that a study is needed and thus may not be receptive, at least initially, to the findings and recommendations that result.

Secondly, I suggested that, by separate organic legislation, the President of the United States within a year at most, preferably within six months, be required to transmit each commission report to the Congress, along with his own suggestions, positive or negative.

I said to the Kennedy subcommittee: "While we have got into the British habit of appointing the equivalent of a royal commission to provide the government with experienced and non-partisan advice on major controversial issues, we have ignored the salutary British procedure by which the government responds to the advice provided by the commission. The British have a formal method of response—the Cabinet white paper. The publication of each royal commission report is usually followed within six months to a year by the publication of a

Cabinet white paper setting forth the government's views on the commission's recommendations and the government's proposals, if any, for action."

I cited a typical example, namely, the Redcliffe-Maud Commission on Local Government, appointed by Mr. Harold Wilson's Cabinet several years ago. It filed its report in 1969, recommending that the London model of a single urban area council with a lower tier of neighborhood or borough units be adopted in the fifty largest urban complexes in the United Kingdom. Six months later the government issued a white paper and accepted most of the commission's proposals, but modifying a few. Before the government's bill made much progress through the Parliament, the Labor Government was defeated and Mr. Heath's Conservative Government took over. The following spring, however, Mr. Peter Walker issued the Heath Cabinet white paper on the Redcliffe-Maud proposals, modifying them somewhat further, but adopting their essential principles.

Despite an intervening change in government, the Redcliffe-Maud proposals, dealing with one of the most controversial political issues in Britain—or for that matter in the United States—would, I feel, soon achieve concrete results. To me this illustration had particular significance because the Violence Commission made substantially similar proposals for change in local government structure—to my mind one of the most critical problems we face in managing our crowded urban society and thus reducing the incidence of crime.

I suggested that the Congress should consider institutionalizing the British system of administration in response to commission reports in the form of a presidential white paper. While Presidents usually take the initiative in forming commissions, and while these commissions report to the President rather than to the Congress, the Congress is also asked (indirectly and directly) to finance their work and in some cases to arm them with subpoena and other powers. It would make sense to me for the Congress to assure that the taxpayer gets his money's worth by having a requirement that the President issue a detailed response to the commission's recommendations—within six months or perhaps a year after the commission's report is filed.

It is now more than three years since the Violence Commission reported to the President. President Nixon has not made a substantial recommendation on this threatening problem other than to try to strengthen law enforcement in the District of Columbia and to appropriate additional funds under the so-called Safe Streets Act. The problems get worse year after year in most urban centers. Politicians always quote scare statistics when they are running for office but, once elected, they limit their attack on crime to finding ways of interpreting statistics to show that the situation is improving.

The commission's statement that the internal threat to our society may now transcend any possible external threat becomes more and more an inescapable fact. There is an echo from history in this. The commission said to the President and the American people:

> When, in man's long history, other great civilizations fell, it was less often from external assault than from internal decay. Our own civilization has shown a remarkable capacity for responding to crises and for emerging to higher pinnacles of power and achievement. But our most serious challenges to date have been external —the kind that a strong and resourceful country could unite against. While serious external dangers remain, the graver threats today are internal—haphazard urbanization, racial discrimination, disfiguring of the environment, unprecedented interdependence, and the dislocation of human identity and motivation created by an affluent society—all resulting in a rising tide of individual and group violence. The greatness and durability of most civilizations has been finally determined by how they have responded to these challenges from within. Ours will be no exception.

CHAPTER 25

It is often a paradox of leadership that the higher one rises the less one sees and hears. A President, isolated and aloof, may seek help, but characteristically he will not deign to be impressed by what is offered or to show appreciation for the effort made.

BEFORE HE FINALLY decided to be a candidate for the Republican nomination for President in 1968, Richard Nixon asked me to join him for luncheon in his spacious apartment in New York City. He had been meeting with leaders from many parts of the country in a quiet effort to evaluate public attitudes and his current political strength. I had no doubt that he would make an affirmative decision, but in our visit he gave no such indication. As we talked, I kept thinking of who might be an ideal running mate.

The name which stood out for me was Charles Percy—senator from Illinois, a newcomer to the Washington scene, and a keenly intelligent, hard-working, successful businessman with a Kennedy-like political charisma. I had known Chuck Percy for a good many years. When he was a candidate for the Senate I had joined three of my brothers, including President Eisenhower, at a fund-raising dinner in Chicago in support of Percy. Previously I had worked with him as a member of the Foundation for Adult Education, a subsidiary of The Ford Foundation, and had participated with him in an important colloquium he financed at the University of Chicago when he was a trustee.

I greatly admired Senator Percy. Before he arrived at a judgment on any state or national problem he conferred with the best minds in the field, weighed possible alternatives, and then announced his position. His public speeches were models of logic; his stature grew with each position he took and with each platform experience. He was a man

461

of such wisdom and integrity that I would have been willing to see him in the presidential chair in the unhappy circumstance that the President could not complete his term.

Dick Nixon at that time had only a casual acquaintance with Percy. I asked him whether he would be willing to come to my residence in Baltimore for a confidential visit with the senator. He accepted.

Upon my return home I called Chuck, who also accepted, and the two joined me at my home not long afterward for dinner and a four-and-a-half-hour discussion. We analyzed the problems of inflation, war, imbalances in international payments, crime, and fiscal irresponsibility —all problems the next President would inherit from the Johnson administration. We talked about the appeals the Republican nominees might best make to the electorate. The three of us had no difficulty in arriving at common judgments.

Nothing was said about the vice-presidential nomination. I felt, however, that Chuck Percy, reasonably well known nationally because of his phenomenal success as head of an American industry with domestic and world markets, and as a young and courageous senator, would greatly strengthen the ticket. He had received wide publicity during the Eisenhower administration as chairman of a Republican policy committee and also as a leading advocate for a national policy of freer trade, a fact that would appeal to urban voters, stronghold of the Democratic Party.

This was my only attempt to play the part of kingmaker. It failed, and that distressed me. Indeed, in the years since then Senator Percy has publicly disagreed with President Nixon on several occasions, and it is no secret that Nixon does not consider Percy one of his favorite people.

During the Republican primaries newspaper columnists and politicians speculated about the Republican vice-presidential candidate in the event that Nixon was nominated for the top spot. Senator Percy was usually mentioned.

Spiro Agnew was then governor of Maryland. I had known him when he was county executive of Baltimore County and I had supported him when he ran for governor against George Mahoney—an extreme and ill-informed reactionary. Agnew was considered to be a moderate— even a bit liberal. This view continued in the early period of his administration in the State House in Annapolis. The riots following the murder of Martin Luther King altered this view in the minds of many. Baltimore was hard hit. There was vast property damage and much human suffering. Governor Agnew summoned the black leaders of the city and proceeded to chastise them harshly for not controlling "their people" and for not having taken steps to ameliorate the difficulty. Stunned and resentful, the black leaders rose and left the assembly one by one, until only a few remained to bear the brunt of Agnew's rage. The press began to call him a conservative, and this image grew when the governor later sent the state police to put down protests at Bowie State College, a black institution.

Agnew had not yet really changed his political posture, however. Earlier, he had mounted a national campaign to obtain the Republican nomination for Governor Nelson Rockefeller. He asked me to become a delegate at large to the Miami convention, and I assented. Agnew was badly shaken when Rockefeller, without prior notice to him, announced that he would not be a candidate. Despite this rebuff, Agnew publicly persisted in his efforts to change Rockefeller's decision. Later, when Rockefeller announced his candidacy, he again did not notify Agnew in advance. This was a double insult—more than Agnew could tolerate. He abandoned Rockefeller and threw his support to Nixon. Then Governor Agnew asked me to withdraw as a delegate, saying: "The Central Committee fears you would not accept the majority decision of the delegation."

Agnew's change in midstream resulted in his becoming the vice-presidential nominee at Miami. I did not attend the 1968 convention, so I can only assume that the media people were correct in interpreting his selection as part of Nixon's decision to follow a so-called Southern strategy. A striking similarity was seen in the 1960 and 1968 strategies. Senator Kennedy, a New England liberal, had selected Senator Johnson, a moderate Southern conservative, as his running mate, even though the two had bitterly attacked one another in the preconvention period.

There is no doubt that Johnson, popular in some sections of the South, contributed to Kennedy's narrow victory in 1960. Similarly Agnew, admired in the South, perhaps for the wrong reason, added to the strength of the Republican ticket, which succeeded by a narrow margin.

Whether Agnew's change from a moderate, supporting Rockefeller, to a conservative who added Southern strength in the 1968 campaign was blatantly opportunistic, or whether he suddenly changed his political philosophy, I do not know, for I have not met with him since his nomination in Miami.

For three years after President Nixon's inauguration my official relations with the White House were minimal. The reports I made to President Nixon on the findings of the Violence Commission and, with Chairman Robert Anderson, on the Canal Commission were culminations of assignments from President Johnson. In these three years the friendship I had developed with the President and Mrs. Nixon in the Eisenhower years, the marriage of my great-nephew David to Julie Nixon, and Mrs. Mamie Doud Eisenhower's fondness for the Nixons led to several happy social invitations.

Fairly early in 1969, President and Mrs. Nixon were kind enough to have me as a White House guest for three days. They placed me in the Lincoln suite, the first time I had occupied those historic rooms. Later I spent a weekend with the family at Camp David, a happy experience. A memento of that visit, which I prize, is a red sports coat bearing the presidential insigne which the President had tailor-made for me.

As I watched the President at work and talked to him on these two social occasions about his routine I realized that he was a prodigious worker. An early riser, he began work before breakfast. Often he did not return to the family room for lunch, satisfying himself with a tray at his desk. Occasionally dinner was also sent to his office. Even when he joined the family for a quick dinner he often returned either to the oval office in the West Wing or to a special office in the Executive Office Building; occasionally he worked in the small living room of the Lincoln suite, a dictating machine beside him. When he went to his California or Florida homes for relaxation work went with him. The frequent temporary transfer of presidential headquarters to the two coasts was a public extravagance, for each trip required many members of the Cabinet and White House staff to be available—all traveling by special jets.

I was always amused, but also annoyed, when in the Eisenhower administration the press kept a running score card of the number of times my brother was away from the White House and especially the number of times he was on the golf course. The score card was not maintained in subsequent administrations, though the Kennedy, Johnson, and Nixon absences from the White House were more numerous than Eisenhower's. It must be remembered, of course, that wherever the President goes the responsibilities and work of the office go with him. A corporation executive on vacation can turn his duties over to an executive vice-president; a university president can delegate his duties to a provost or vice-president; and even a minister of the gospel can have an associate take charge in his absence. But, as Robert Gray said so succinctly in his book *Eighteen Acres Under Glass*,[34] the President of the United States can never stop being President. When he is on a golf course Secret Service men carry with them a golf bag containing a communication system. His airplane is equipped for instant communication. Even when the President is ill in a hospital he must still exercise the responsibilities of the presidency, and when he is on a plane headed for China or the Soviet Union he may have to approve or veto bills.

On the weekend with the Nixon family at Camp David the President and I reminisced about the trip we made to the Soviet Union in 1959. Subsequently Mr. Nixon, as a private citizen, had made several other trips to the U.S.S.R. and the information he gained from those trips intrigued me so much that I determined to go again and make some serious studies. So early in September 1970, with the blessing of, and briefings by, the State Department, but not as a federal official, I discussed with the minister of the Soviet Embassy in Washington persons I hoped to see on a trip of about a month. I wanted to go not only to Moscow but to Leningrad, Novosibirsk, Tashkent, and Kiev, and I wished to have long talks with several members of the Council of Ministers, the mayors of the five cities to be visited, rectors of universities, students, leaders of collective farms, workers, the head of the branch of the Academy of Science which studies the United States and advises the foreign office of the U.S.S.R., a representative of *Izvestia*, and others. The Russian Embassy made the appointments I requested and every one was meticulously kept. Indeed, for the entire trip (Dean Francis O. Wilcox of The Johns Hopkins School of Advanced International Studies and Mrs. Wilcox accompanied me), we were given "red carpet" treatment everywhere. A head of state could not have been more courteously received. Still later, in July 1971, I returned to Moscow and Kiev again, this time as a member of the Dartmouth Conference, in which some fifteen Americans and their Soviet counterparts discussed pending problems with candor; unfortunately I had to come home before the conference concluded because of the death of my brother Edgar, a hasty return trip I could not have arranged in time, save for the help of Soviet leaders and personnel in our embassies in Moscow and London. Upon my return from these trips, especially that of 1970, I reported in full to the State Department, and later had luncheon with Ambassador Dobrynin and gave him my impressions.

Changes in the Soviet Union in the eleven years since my first visit were notable. Education had burgeoned at every level. There were now 45 million students in preparatory schools and 4.6 million in universities and technical institutes. Illiteracy had essentially been wiped out in the fifteen republics. All preparatory curricula in the U.S.S.R. are standardized; students, whether in Tashkent or Leningrad, study precisely the same subjects from the same textbooks. Similarly, specialized curricula in universities and institutes are also standardized—in physics, chemistry, history, law, and all the fields of advanced study. Marxism-Leninism is taught at every level, from the first grade to the highest university class. The number of institutions of higher education, called "high schools," is now eight hundred. The quota of students permitted in each discipline, the subject matter, and even methods of teaching are centrally determined. I asked the Minister of Education in Moscow what would happen if he had told the University of Leningrad that it could have one hundred students in law but more were enrolled. He smiled and said that he might reduce the personal money allowances which are provided for seventy-five per cent of the students (education is free, plus money allowances to students, only the children of well-to-do citizens being ineligible and allowances being largest for the best students, gradually reducing to zero for poor students). He added that if this method didn't work he would simply pick up the telephone and tell the rector of the university to drop the surplus students from the law curriculum.

The rapid expansion in the number of educated persons in the Soviet Union will gradually have a significant effect on the future of the country. Obviously development in all areas of human endeavor will be accelerated. Attitudes will change. Leading scientists, noted and indispensable in their fields, have in polite language criticized Soviet practices, especially in the field of intellectual control, and most of them have not suffered severe reprisals. What the ultimate effect will be would be a hazardous guess.

I was especially intrigued by the language problem. In the fifteen republics 170 languages and distinct dialects are spoken. Often basic instruction is in the native language, such as Ukrainian or Uzbek. Students are required to study Russian and one foreign language; English is the first choice in the foreign-language option, with German and French being second and third. The translator who accompanied us on the trip could not understand many of the native languages, so local officials had to speak in Russian. Later I asked the Minister of Education whether an attempt was being made to unify the language of the fifteen republics. He said no. Local pride was involved, so much so that even the dictatorial control of the Communist Party did not care to deal with this delicate problem.

We spent half a day with Chairman Kosygin's son-in-law, Dr. J. Gvishiani, Deputy Chairman of the State Committee for Science and Technology, a supra-Cabinet committee which has charge of scientific and technological research and development in the Soviet Union, including that in the branches of the Academy of Science, universities, technical institutes, industries, and other agencies. There is no doubt that massive research and development programs are under way in all the republics, the emphasis being on applied research. Thus in Novosibirsk, in central Siberia, more than 10,000 scientists of high caliber are devoting full time to doing all they can to develop that vast region: agriculture, industries, mining, and social and cultural institutions. In the conversation with Dr. Gvishiani in 1970 and in visits with Dr. Georgi A. Arbatov at the Dartmouth Conference in Kiev in 1971, I learned how anxious the Soviet government is to normalize trade relations with the United States. I think the time is here when we will find it to our advantage to buy more ores, gas, and other products from the U.S.S.R. and sell them agricultural commodities and many manufactured products. I assume, of course, that we would not sell anything to the U.S.S.R. that would increase directly its military strength.

When the Nixons and I were in the Soviet Union in 1959 there were almost no cars in Moscow or other cities. The few we saw were those of Communist officials. In 1970 the mayor of Moscow told us with pride that in the city were 200,000 cars (I believe this; all appeared to be driven at reckless speeds) and that in another five years there would be a million. I suggested he would have the same pollution problem we face in the United States. He waved his hand and said that in the meantime they would develop a simple addition to the exhaust pipe, like a cigarette filter, that would solve the problem! Other industrial developments match what is happening in car and truck production. Unfortunately for Soviet citizens, first priority is given to capital projects and military matériel, so that shortages of consumer goods continue to be acute. Indeed, though wages are low, personal savings since my first visit have built up to more than fifty billion rubles; when cars, clothes, good meat, and other consumer products are available the people will buy.

Many Americans have the mistaken impression that the pay of workers in the Soviet Union is uniform—that the incentives we have for production in the private enterprise system do not exist in the U.S.S.R. This is not true. An apprentice in a steel plant may receive forty rubles a month, the average worker about 120 rubles, the skilled operators of large lathes about 250 rubles, and the manager of the plant 500 rubles; the manager also receives free a car and a chauffeur, the most spacious apartment in the city, and a substantial bonus if he meets his production quota each year. The bonus arrangement leads to a system of graft which Communist leaders have not been able to stop. Thus, if electrical equipment breaks down in a steel plant and the manager of that plant is threatened with a temporary interruption in production—for electrical equipment may be in short supply—he may go directly to the manager of an electric manufacturing plant and offer a portion of his bonus to get immediate delivery of the equipment he needs.

Pay differentials continue upward—from 800 to 1,000 rubles a month for a university rector, 1,800 rubles for an eminent member of the Academy of Science, and no one knows how much for top leaders of the Communist Party.

The shortage and poor distribution of consumer goods causes a behavior which is a puzzle to American visitors. Late each day long lines of people wait for as much as an hour to make small purchases—perhaps just enough meat for dinner. The cause is twofold: refrigeration is almost non-existent in apartments and the amount of consumer goods for sale each day may be so limited that rationing is needed.

Despite a frantic effort of some fifteen years to provide housing for the people, there is still an acute shortage of apartments, the only approved method of housing in the Soviet Union, save for dachas for the Communist leaders and a relatively few individual houses left over from czarist days. In Moscow the mayor told us that workers were building one hundred and twenty thousand apartment units each year and demolishing about twenty thousand old ones, and we learned that on a proportionate basis the same was true in other cities we visited. The waiting lists for housing are long.

An ingenious new apartment plan has been developed. Citizens are permitted to purchase co-operative apartments. This intrusion of a private enterprise concept seemingly does not bother anyone. The purchaser of a co-operative apartment must pay forty per cent of the total cost down and the remainder in fifteen years. When payments are completed there continues to be a charge for maintenance. Since the maintenance charge is about equal to the very low rental—five to seven rubles a month—I wondered why anyone would use his savings to make a purchase. I inquired of one family why it had done so. The answer was candid; the family could get immediate possession, thus not having to wait for three or four years for their turn for admission to a publicly owned apartment, and they could make their purchase in a section of the city close to their employment, thus avoiding hours of travel each day. Both husband and wife involved in this purchase were university graduates. Their combined income was three hundred rubles a month ($330). At the time of the purchase they lacked fifty rubles of the down payment. So they appealed to friends for a short-term loan. Some exclaimed, "Why do you come to us? You are rich! You own two rings. Why don't you sell them?" In time the fifty rubles were borrowed and the purchase was made.

Agriculture in the Soviet Union is unbelievably inefficient. More than a third of the population of the fifteen republics is engaged in farming. Farmers do not grow enough to satisfy demand. Fresh fruits and vegetables, good-quality meats, eggs, and other perishable commodities are in short supply and costly. The standard diet of cabbage, potatoes, fatty, low-quality meats, and bread is unappetizing and fattening. Only the rich can afford to buy the more expensive foods. The current Soviet plan for agriculture is to spend eighty-six billion rubles in five years for drainage, fertilizers, irrigation, farm machinery, new types of seed, research, importation of beef animals for breeding, and massive improvement in farm-to-market roads.

We visited two collective farms, one near Tashkent, the other twenty miles from Kiev. On the Tashkent farm, in the irrigated area of the country, cotton was the primary commodity, but much acreage was also devoted to diversified crops. In answer to my question, the farm manager, a man of Korean background, proudly told me that the average earnings of each worker were 200 rubles a month. I knew that the wage on nearby state farms was 160 rubles. So I said, "The state farms must want to become collectives." I was curious what his response would be, for one never hears a statement in the Soviet Union that differs from official policy. He smiled and said, "Both systems are excellent."

At a fairly efficient collective farm outside Kiev, where we were royally entertained with abundant food and vodka, the inescapable Communist agent was wearing the medal of a Hero of the Soviet Union. I inquired what he had done to earn it. He had been a major in the Soviet army that defended Kiev up to the moment of Germany's destruction of the city and the murder of two hundred thousand citizens. His recital of the facts about the Kiev defense was passionately spoken. I said to him, "If I had experienced what you did, I would hate the Germans as you obviously do. How, then, do you feel about the tentative agreement just made by your government with West Germany?" His answer was classic: "Dr. Eisenhower, I am a faithful Communist. The Party says this is right. So it is right!"

We discussed with many leaders problems in foreign affairs—the SALT talks, Vietnam, the Middle East, Berlin, West Germany, and trade possibilities. All expressed hopes for the success of the SALT talks, for peace in the Middle East, accommodation with Germany and the remainder of Western Europe, and quick improvement in trade relations with the United States. One scholar, editor of a magazine, was somewhat quarrelsome. I suggested to him that if the Soviet and the United States leaders agreed on a formula we could bring the war in Vietnam to a conclusion quickly and then other possibilities would open up. He said to me, "Why should we help you in the Vietnam situation? It is causing your people to fight one another and is sapping your resources. It isn't hurting us."

He insisted that the United States was the imperialistic power in Vietnam. We had, he contended, intervened in a civil war. Despite my opposition to the war, I pointed out that after World War II three nations were divided—Korea, Vietnam, and Germany. The U.S.S.R. had obviously been responsible for the attack by North Korean forces on those of South Korea. Khrushchev's memoirs concede this. I then asked him: "If West Germany should attack East Germany, would the Soviet Union intervene, and if you did would that constitute Soviet participation in a civil war and therefore imperialism?" He argued that the German situation was different—that it involved the Warsaw powers. I said there might be a legal difference but not a moral one. I then asked him about the Soviet armed intervention in Czechoslovakia, which brought an abrupt end to our discussion.

I had better luck with another Soviet leader, a most intelligent man. (I dare not identify him.) In his office in Moscow we found ourselves visiting in a friendly spirit. We both knew that, as always, our conversation was being recorded, so we were guarded in our comments. Later I saw him in the United States. Free of recording instruments, he was now much more candid, so I said to him: "The Soviet Union is always charging the United States with imperialism, but you seized all the nations of Eastern Europe, initiated the Korean War, brutally attacked Hungary and Czechoslovakia, and supported Castro in the hope that he would be the focal point to spread Communism in Latin America. How do you justify this?"

He indicated that each of these situations was different. He would comment on the Czechoslovakian problem. It was, he said, comparable to our action against Cuba. We did not like to have a Communist power ninety miles from our shores. So we had helped Cuban refugees mount an unsuccessful invasion. Then when the Soviet Union began placing missiles in Cuba, as we had done on the periphery of the Soviet Union in Europe, we risked World War III in finding a solution. "You did this for your own security," he said. The Soviet Union, fearful of Western Europe, especially Germany, insisted upon maintaining a band of "fraternal, friendly nations" between itself and Western Europe. When the members of the Politburo of the Communist Party saw Czechoslovakia moving toward Western practices and ideas, including a free press, the development was debated for eight months and when the decision was made to send in Soviet troops to rectify the situation it was by no means unanimous.

Because of our experience with goons in 1959, I was especially interested on my 1970 and 1971 visits to learn more about the Communist Party and its methods of control. There are only fourteen million members of the Party. It is not easy to become a Communist. An applicant undergoes numerous tests, must be recommended by party members who know him well, and, if accepted, must undergo severe training and accept serious responsibilities. Members are so strategically located throughout the nation that the Party knows essentially everything that is going on. The Party is alert to any deviation from approved policy, and punishment follows any deviation. Every major industry, university, school, sports complex, and cultural institution is headed by a member of the Party. The Party controls the Soviet of each republic. All are answerable to the Central Committee headed by Brezhnev from which every important decision emanates, including decisions administered by governmental agencies, headed by Kosygin, chairman, and the Council of Ministers. Billboards are mercifully absent from the Soviet Union, save those of the party; on most highways are immense signs, normally about fifty feet long and with large gilt letters, proclaiming, "The Party and the people are one."

Everywhere one goes the same official "line" is faithfully expressed —by students, workers, rectors, and others. I tried many times to obtain even a hint of criticism of official policy. At one university, where a dozen students and I became friendly, I asked, "Have any of you ever been outside the Soviet Union?" One whispered, "I wish we were permitted to go." In another city, as I walked alone with a university student, I heard a comment similar to one Ferdinand Kuhn reported following his visit to the U.S.S.R., only my young friend was not quite so outspoken. A student said to Kuhn, "They [meaning the controlling people in Moscow] know we are socialists. Why don't they let us alone?"

Museums, theaters, ballet, opera, motion pictures, and indoor circuses are plentiful and usually crowded. In Moscow I saw a beautiful production of *Swan Lake* when six thousand persons were in the audience. Competitive sports and superb sports facilities are abundant. I also attended a superb puppet show. The comment that drew prolonged applause occurred when a puppet remarked: "All the West is decaying very successfully."

Crime is not serious—nothing approaching what we have in the United States, and it is not reported by the press. Drunkenness is prevalent and hooliganism is said to be a consequence of this. Small use of narcotics is conceded. The party members know what is occurring and if a problem becomes serious the police move in quickly. Punishment varies from ostracism and exile (as for literary figures), to banishment to northern Siberia, to imprisonment and, worst of all, to confinement in an insane asylum.

Without doubt the Soviet Union has made enormous progress in the past dozen years. And I admire much of what has been done. I might even applaud if it were not for the relentless intellectual control which is so complete and intellectually stifling that as I left the U.S.S.R. after each of three visits I felt as if I were emerging from a dark dungeon into the bright sunlight of day.

I am convinced that Soviet leaders, though still suspicious of the United States—this seems to be an innate characteristic—want to find an accommodation with us. The modest success of the SALT talks, the settlement of the Berlin question, the keen Soviet desire for a European security conference (perhaps in time resulting in a reduction in NATO and Warsaw forces), their recognition of the need of the great powers to avoid war in the Middle East, and their constantly repeated desire to develop mutually advantageous trade with the United States convince me that now is the time to do what we prudently can, through treaties, executive agreements, and informal arrangements to make real progress in Soviet-United States relations. I therefore approve with enthusiasm what Nixon and Brezhnev were able to do in 1972 on Nixon's trip to Moscow, and in 1973 when Brezhnev came to the United States. The agreements announced were a small beginning, but a beginning. Just as Truman's containment policy marked the opening of the Cold War, so do I believe that Nixon's modest agreements with the U.S.S.R. may mark its close, though co-existence and improved cooperation do not imply a relaxation of the ideological struggle.

One of the most interesting discussions I had in the Soviet Union was with the Metropolitan of Leningrad, later to become Patriarch of the Orthodox Church. He was a charming, bright-eyed, intelligent man who had the longest beard I have ever seen; he kept stroking the beard as we talked, sipped wine, and munched on chocolates. In the course of our conversation I recounted to him what I had witnessed at the United States exposition in Moscow in 1959 which led me to believe that many people clung to their religious beliefs and their love of religious rites. As I have previously explained, older people openly wept when the participants in a style show appeared dressed for a formal wedding, for they recalled days when religious rites of dignity were observed in the Soviet Union.

The Metropolitan explained that under Stalin all churches had been closed and religious rites, including those involving weddings, abolished. Under Khrushchev and Brezhnev much liberalization had occurred. Churches had reopened. The Church and the Party had agreed to mutual toleration. Religious publications were permitted for all denominations save the Jewish. There were, he was sure, about "fifty million Orthodox believers" in the Soviet Union. There were also many Moslems in the south, Baptists, and, of course, many Jews. Discrimination against the Jews did not permit religious education (the Metropolitan had 165 seminary students in training), no religious publications, and severe restrictions on the emigration of educated Jews to Israel.

Four developments in the Soviet Union will, in my judgment, make internal changes inevitable and these may contribute to détente. One is a constant increase in the number of educated men and women in the Soviet Union who know, as I shall indicate later, much more about external and internal affairs than their rigidly controlled mass media and their leaders want them to know; a second is the prospect for trade, a problem which the leaders of the two countries have promised to pursue with vigor; a third is the increasing mobility of the Soviet people due to the coming of motorcars and some improvement in their miserable highways; and the fourth is a modest increase in human welfare, including more consumer goods. When the standard of living in the U.S.S.R. reaches a point that the nervous leaders in the Kremlin no longer fear comparison with life in the West, I think helpful developments that we do not now envisage may begin to occur. This does not mean that the U.S.S.R. will not maintain a socialized economy; I am sure it will for as long as one can foresee, just as I trust we will be wise enough to retain the more productive and more freedom-protecting competitive private enterprise system. Co-existence is possible between the two nations and for the sake of humanity we must seize every opportunity to strive for better relations.

My first official assignment from the Nixon administration came early in 1972 when a staff member of the White House said the President wanted me to join a citizens' group to counteract the efforts of

Senator William Fulbright, chairman of the Senate Foreign Relations Committee, who was trying to bring about the discontinuance of Radio Free Europe and Radio Liberty. These radio networks broadcast hundreds of program hours each week to the Soviet Union and the Eastern European countries within the Soviet hegemony. Senator Fulbright contended that they were relics of the Cold War and therefore not harmonious with the spirit of détente that was becoming evident.

I was only in a general way familiar with the programs of the two radio networks, but I felt that a precipitate discontinuance of efforts to penetrate the iron curtain—efforts that had been under way since the fifties—would be a mistake. I did know that the radios were bitterly criticized by leaders of the Communist bloc, but felt sure this was because they wished to have an absolute monopoly on what their people learned about domestic and foreign developments. I therefore joined a citizens' group under the chairmanship of former Under Secretary of State George Ball. Opposition efforts caused the Congress to appropriate funds to the State Department to make grants to RFE and RL for one more year on the condition that the President appoint a special commission to study every aspect of the problem and report to him and to the Congress. (The two radio networks had been financed from the beginning—1950 for Radio Free Europe, 1951 for Radio Liberty—by the CIA. For the fiscal year 1972–73 the CIA had been completely separated from both enterprises, and thus the State Department had become the funding agency.)

On August 9, 1972, the President asked me to become chairman of a Presidential Study Commission on International Radio Broadcasting, the other members being Edward Barrett, former Assistant Secretary of State when the Voice of America had been under his supervision; John Gronouski, former ambassador to Poland where he had become thoroughly familiar with Radio Free Europe broadcasts; Edmund Gullion, former foreign service officer, ambassador to the Congo, and deputy director of the U. S. Disarmament Commission; and John Roche, former special consultant to Presidents Kennedy and Johnson. The President indicated to us that we should consider the relationship of the radio networks to the nation's foreign policy objectives and, if we felt they should be continued, how they should be organized and funded. He asked that our report reach him not later than February 28, 1973. This date seemed late to me, for funds to support the radios would expire on June 30 and time would be needed to get essential organic legislation and appropriations through the Congress before that date.

We worked feverishly, determined to report to the President prior to the deadline he had given us. We reviewed the voluminous 1972 Senate and House hearings on this subject, the report on the two radio networks made by the research branch of the Library of Congress, and a study by the General Accounting Office on financial management of the networks. We conferred with top leaders of Radio Free Europe and Radio Liberty, held conferences with State Department and other federal officials, met with interested private individuals, and spent many hours with more than thirty senators and representatives who had been most interested in the problem.

We studied the hour-by-hour operations of the two radio networks. For this purpose we went to Munich, Germany, site of the studios, where we went as deeply as we could into the research, news-gathering, monitoring, broadcasting, and related operations. We interviewed recent émigrés from the Soviet Union and Eastern Europe in an effort to satisfy ourselves of the validity of testimony previously presented to Congress on the effectiveness of the broadcasts.

In Munich we spent much time with those who write and voice the broadcasts in order to satisfy ourselves of their attitudes, notably their restraint from harmful polemics and from temptations to attack individuals or governmental actions in the receiving countries. In our discussions we emphasized the absolute necessity of truth and objectivity.

The visits with senators and representatives at the outset of our study had raised repeatedly four pertinent questions:

Are the radio networks a positive encouragement or deterrent to détente?

If they are continued, what federal agency should receive appropriations and then make allocations to the two private corporations that operate them?

How can all concerned be assured that these private stations—operating essentially as a free press, which is necessary to their maintaining credibility in the listening areas—operate in a manner not inconsistent with United States foreign policy?

Should not European countries pay a substantial part of the costs involved in operating the stations?

Our studies convinced us that the dissemination of factual information and research-backed interpretations to the peoples of the six countries concerned (all of whom lived behind walls of severe information control) actually enhanced opportunities for détente. Stated differently, we feared a situation in which the peoples of the Soviet Union and Eastern Europe knew only what their leaders and their rigidly controlled mass media wanted them to know. We became convinced that a misinformed or partially informed people would be pawns in the hands of party and governmental leaders. Persons in possession of the facts about world and internal conditions, actions, and aims, on the other hand, do have an influence on leaders, even in dictatorial regimes.

I personally became convinced, and so reported in writing to the President and later said in testifying personally before the Senate Foreign Relations Committee and the House Committee on Foreign Affairs that a major motivation of the Soviet Union in developing better relations with the United States and other Western nations was a response to the expressed desire of her people for higher standards of living, a consuming desire that had gradually developed from their knowledge that human welfare was better served and advanced in Western countries, and that their own current condition need not be inevitable and should not be ignored. Their knowledge leading to this influence had come partly from Western governmental broadcasts, such as the Voice of America and the British Broadcasting Company, but mostly from the broadcasts of Radio Free Europe and Radio Liberty. Hence the Soviet Union was seeking better trade relations and agreements in the political and military areas which would permit her to emphasize more than before production to improve personal well-being.

In our report to the President and Congress we cited fourteen specific examples out of hundreds we had studied to indicate the effectiveness of the broadcasts in reaching listeners with the type of information that had a cumulative inducement to détente.

Alexander Solzhenitsyn, famous Russian novelist and Nobel laureate, had said in April 1972, "If we hear anything about events in this country, it's through them [Radio Liberty broadcasts]."

Two examples of effectiveness will suffice for my present purpose. The Soviet mass media have constantly reported all economic and military aid given by the United States to Israel but have not informed their people of the massive help given by the U.S.S.R. to the Arab countries, especially Egypt. Hence, when the Soviet government repeatedly accused the United States of being "Zionist" and the "imperialistic power in the Middle East," many believed the propaganda. Radio Liberty therefore gave all the facts. Its analyses, based on painstaking research, showed the vastness of the Soviet commitment of resources to the Arab states at a time when these resources were badly needed at home and showed that this aid did not contribute to a peaceful solution of the Arab-Israel conflict.

In the wake of an official announcement of substantial price increases on food and other consumer goods on December 12, 1970, workers in the Polish Baltic seacoast cities exploded into a series of angry demonstrations. The regime used severe police measures to suppress the demonstrations and imposed strict censorship on the information media outside the local area with a view to achieving a blackout of knowledge about these events. Radio Free Europe, however, had monitored the radio broadcasts in the disturbed areas. So it was able to inform the Polish population generally about the protests, the substance of the workers' demands, and the measures taken to crush them. Soon nationwide dissatisfaction of workers forced the government to stop its repressive actions and eventually to replace Chairman Wladyslaw Gomulka with Edward Gierek, who adopted new policies, negotiated with the workers, and accepted most of their demands. The Radio Free Europe broadcasts were cautious and scrupulously accurate. The facts contributed to the cessation of repression and the improvement of living conditions in Poland. Like the peoples of the other Eastern European countries and of the Soviet Union, the Polish people want still greater improvement in living conditions. Hence they favor better relations with the Western nations generally, and especially with the United States.

Radio Free Europe and Radio Liberty devote nearly half their broadcasts to reporting developments within the listening areas, the information about these being obtained by monitoring Eastern European and Soviet radio broadcasts, reading some 175 internal newspapers, obtaining typescript materials called *samizdat* (materials prepared by East European and Soviet citizens, but completely censored for use in local media), special materials given to the radio networks by reliable foreign correspondents, and by keeping current the research studies by expert staffs. The other half of the broadcasts are devoted to world news and interpretations.

Some feel that this penetration of the iron curtain—disseminating materials which the governments do not wish their peoples to have—is in fact intervention in the internal affairs of other nations. But the Declaration of Human Rights adopted by the General Assembly of the United Nations says: "Everyone has the right of freedom of opinion and expression; this right includes freedom to hold opinions without interference, to seek, receive, and impart information and ideas through any media *and regardless of frontiers.*" The Preamble to the Constitution of the United Nations Educational, Scientific, and Cultural Organization, to which the Soviet Union and most other Communist nations belong, says: "Since wars begin in the minds of men, it is in the minds of men that the defenses of peace must be constructed. . . . The States Parties to this Constitution . . . believing in . . . the free exchange of ideas and knowledge, are agreed and determined . . . *to increase the means of communication among their peoples* and to employ these means for the purpose of mutual understanding and a truer and more perfect knowledge of each others lives. . . ." And the Montreux International Telecommunications Convention, to which the Soviet Union is signatory, prohibits interference with international radio broadcasts. (The Soviet Union and three of her satellites spend at least four times as much trying to jam the programs of Radio Free Europe and Radio Liberty as we spend in maintaining the stations.)

The second and third questions raised by members of the Congress, namely, what organizational arrangements should be made to channel federal funds to the private corporations that operate Radio Free Europe and Radio Liberty, and how all could be assured that they operate in ways not inconsistent with United States foreign policy, caused our commission to confer with many public officials, especially those of the State Department, Government Accounting Office, Office of Management and Budget, and the United States Information Agency. The Congress never appropriates directly to a private corporation or organization. Appropriations are made to an appropriate agency of the executive establishment which in turn makes grants, under safeguards, to private universities, companies, and others. Thus the National Institutes of Health, the National Science Foundation, the

National Aeronautics and Space Administration, and the Defense Department make grants for research to private universities. The Army, Navy and Air Force departments make contracts with private industrial concerns.

We recommended the creation of a Board for International Broadcasting, comprised of five persons, skilled in foreign affairs or mass communication, nominated by the President and confirmed by the Senate, and two ex officio, non-voting members, namely, the executive heads of Radio Free Europe and Radio Liberty. This Board would obtain federal appropriations, make grants to the private corporations, and see to it that the funds were prudently spent and that programs were never inconsistent with United States foreign policy. We had in mind the need for economy and felt that by having the new Board and the executive offices of the two private corporations contiguously located in the same building, preferably in the Washington, D.C., area, the Board would need to employ no more than half a dozen individuals in carrying out its assigned tasks.

The final knotty question was the feeling that the constructive work of the radio networks, of value to all the free world, should be financed in substantial part by our European allies, perhaps fifty per cent of the total cost. The cost had been running at a level of nearly forty million dollars a year, but owing to devaluation of the dollar and inflation, it had increased to fifty million dollars a year; further, the transmitting equipment was becoming obsolete and overpowered by many new transmitters of other countries, the cost of equipment improvement being estimated at thirty million dollars over a period of three to four years.

Our commission felt that we should, through the official channels of our government, urge European nations to provide either public or private funds, possibly both, in support of some aspects of the operations. We indicated that efforts in this regard should begin as soon as it was known that the Congress would continue the broadcasts until there was a free flow of information across national boundaries—until information reaching the peoples of one power center of the world was not filtered through systems of control that harmfully distorted or withheld the facts. Efforts to obtain financial help should be, first, in support of the indispensable and accurate research of the two stations, this research costing three and a half million dollars a year. Further, we said, we should seek both foreign and domestic private and public funds to rebuild the transmitting facilities of the stations.

We were emphatic in opposing foreign financial help in support of *daily broadcasting*. United States experiences in many international organizations had demonstrated how time-consuming it is to get agreement in a multinational effort. In the editorial field, such as in preparing UNESCO publications, texts were often edited and re-edited until they met the objections of all, and the final result was often bland and meaningless. In the rapid-fire task of daily broadcasting, multinational control with inevitable delays and compromises would be fatal. We emphasized that a great strength of Radio Free Europe and Radio Liberty was that they often reached their audiences with both world and internal news and interpretations before the centralized censoring bureaucracy had released the governmentally sanitized versions. This caused increased listenership and enhanced credibility for the two radio networks. Furthermore, we argued, despite all the criticism of the United States heard abroad, the United States was more highly respected by the listeners than was any other nation. Hosts of them were grateful to us for helping them learn about the actual conditions that affect personal well-being and international relationships.

On June 12, in testifying before the Senate Foreign Relations Committee, I went beyond what was in our official report. I said that in my personal visits with many senators I had gained the impression that the problem of financing the two stations was caught in a much larger issue. Many senators and many of us in private life were chagrined, even angry, by the failure of the European nations to meet fully their obligations in support of Western security. Our costs were $16 billion in 1972 and would be higher in the future because of the devaluation of the dollar. Only one nation in Europe had lived up to its commitments. The United States, which purposely paid a disproportionate share of the cost when Europe was economically prostrate, continued to do so to this day, at a time when Europe could afford to do more. Hence came the strong feeling that we should make a unilateral reduction in our European expenditures. I indicated I would feel the same were it not for my earnest hope that in the military-force-reduction talks then under way we could achieve agreement for arms reductions in all Western and Eastern powers. If this were achieved, reductions by the United States should be greater percentagewise than those made by European nations, thus resulting in a more equitable situation.

It was, I contended, an unhappy circumstance to have the problem of the radio networks involved in this larger issue. The Soviet Union and nations within her hegemony, while working for détente, had made clear their intention to intensify the ideological struggle. They now spoke to the world in more than four thousand program hours a week —in 84 languages from Soviet Moscow alone. Of the total, 250 program hours a week were beamed to North America in English and a variety of foreign languages used by ethnic groups in the United States, a situation which seemed wasteful in view of the fact that our free press carried nearly everything the Soviet Union and her satellites said or did. All of the Western powers combined spoke to the world in 4,200 program hours a week, including limited programs to the Eastern European countries and the Soviet Union. Only Radio Free Europe and Radio Liberty were beamed exclusively to the Communist bloc. Essential as were the Voice of America, the British Broadcasting Company, and other public radio stations, their programs were different. They presented the official views of governments. This was useful, but many listeners assumed that they were characterized by propaganda, as they knew their own governmental news and analyses to be. Radio Free Europe and Radio Liberty, on the other hand, operated as does a free press in this country. They therefore had high credibility and an amazing listening audience, about fifty per cent of all persons over fourteen years of age in the Eastern European countries, and about ten per cent of the people in the Soviet Union; but in the Soviet Union students, teachers, and others often taped the broadcasts, put them into typescript, and circulated the typescripts clandestinely. Hence, I said, these two radio networks were unique, the most effective in reaching the power center with which the United States must find accommodation. An informed people would work for that accommodation. Since the cost of the stations was about one third of one per cent of other United States costs in Europe, and if an informed people succeeded in inducing their governments to enter into mutual force reductions and other cost-reducing agreements, the stations each year eventually would pay for themselves a hundredfold.

We succeeded in getting a typewritten copy of our report to President Nixon on February 5, 1973, and the final printed copies two weeks later. Then an amazing thing happened. Silence greeted our repeated attempts to learn whether the President agreed with the report and, if he did, when he would send a message to Congress. It was three months after the President got the report that he endorsed it, recommended it without change, submitted our draft legislation to the Senate and House, and wrote routine letters of thanks to the five of us on the commission. It was the first time, in chairing or serving as a member of numerous presidential commissions, that I had not frequently discussed facts and ideas with the Chief Executive as work progressed, and then personally participated in the presentation of the final report to him. The difference was, of course, that the palace guard system in the White House had broken down, issues that should have been placed before the President were held in desk drawers, and the challenges of the Watergate "cover-up," an uneasy cease-fire in Southeast Asia, and the most serious inflation in a quarter of a century occupied the full time of a frightened, nervous, frustrated, and dissembling presidential staff.

The bill in support of Radio Free Europe and Radio Liberty was reported favorably by the Senate Foreign Relations Committee by a 13–3 vote, despite the opposition of the chairman, Senator William Fulbright. It passed the Senate by a comfortable majority. Then the House Committee on Foreign Affairs brought out a favorable report, passage by the House was almost without opposition, and the President signed the new legislation into law. Two weeks later a member of the executive staff telephoned to inquire whether I would accept the chairmanship of the new Board for International Broadcasting. I declined. I did not wish to accept a post which I had had a significant part in creating. And I felt that at the age of seventy-four I could with a clear conscience say no. This, I'm positive, brought an end to my chores for Presidents—indeed, an end to my federal service which fell short by less than a year of spanning half a century.

CHAPTER 26

A President derives his power to govern not
only from the Constitution but even more
significantly from the trust of the people.

THE MILD AMBIVALENCE I felt as brother and confidant
of President Eisenhower was nothing compared to the emotional
schizothymia I have lived with during the administration of President
Nixon.

I have had a long and genuine friendship with the Nixon family.
As I have already reported, I was never able to share my brother's interest in Nixon as presidential material, but I liked him very much as
a person. It has always puzzled me, as I know it has others who have
known Richard Nixon intimately, that as a private man he could be so
different from his image as a public official. Over the years, in our personal dealings, I have always found him to be sincere, sensitive, warm,
intelligent. And I never ceased to be surprised, as I watched the public Nixon, that he so often appeared insincere, devious, insensitive, cold,
and self-serving.

Because of my friendship with Richard Nixon and my fondness
for David and Julie Eisenhower, I hoped from the moment he was inaugurated as President on January 20, 1969, that my earlier doubts would
prove groundless—that he would be an effective leader, demonstrating
the wisdom, integrity, credibility, and moral leadership needed to
unify a distressed and divided nation.

Indeed, with some misgiving, I supported Richard Nixon for President in the 1968 campaign, and, despite my disappointment with some
of his actions and policies during his first four years in the White
House, I had no difficulty in favoring him over McGovern in 1972.
I, like millions of others who had contributed to Nixon's mandate for
a second term, had no inkling of what was soon to come.

Of course I did not expect perfection in either the first or second term. Only when I was young, and especially during my blind admiration for President Wilson, did I believe in the infallibility of the President. My first disillusionment came early in the Coolidge administration when the Teapot Dome scandal of the Harding administration became public. I experienced a continuing dismay during the Truman years as the President's military aide, Major General Harry Vaughan, was repeatedly identified with "influence peddlers" in Congress and the executive agencies, as members of the Internal Revenue Service were allegedly involved in bribery and tax scandals, as high officials of the Reconstruction Finance Corporation and of the White House itself were charged with being involved in "pay-off" operations, and as Truman scornfully refused to do anything about obvious disloyalties of some of his cronies—disloyalties which opened the door to Senator McCarthy's spectacular rise to notoriety. And with great sadness I saw Governor Sherman Adams leave the White House in the Eisenhower years because he had accepted a coat and other favors from a business friend, and I lived with a growing despair during the Johnson administration as increasing numbers of intelligent citizens lost faith in the credibility of the President and many of his principal Cabinet members and staff aides.

But none of these prepared me adequately for the astonishment and deep anguish I now feel as I write these pages in the waning autumn of 1973. The Nixon administration has become embroiled in scandals, perjury, favoritism for sheer political gain, and possible misuse of federal appropriations that eclipse any wrongdoing we previously experienced in our nation's history. And no other administration has so alienated the American people.

Who would have believed that early in the second Nixon administration the Vice-President, whom President Nixon had twice chosen and lavishly praised, would be involved in plea bargaining with the Justice Department and would be forced to resign to avoid criminal prosecution? That two Cabinet members, including the highest law-enforcement officer in the land, would be formally charged with criminal offenses? That many of the men close to the President in the White House would resign or be fired and would face criminal prosecution? That, only a year after winning an electoral mandate exceeding even President Johnson's, President Nixon would have the support of only a quarter of the American public? That a second independent prosecutor would be needed to investigate White House activities? That the House of Representatives would be seriously considering impeachment proceedings and that millions of Americans would favor either the resignation or the impeachment of the President?

The promise of Lyndon Johnson's presidency was destroyed by numerous forces, but mainly by the Vietnam War. Richard Nixon inherited that war. It was a quagmire. It had divided the nation and sapped its financial strength, its pride, and its moral vitality. Nixon, in his campaign for the presidency, pledged to bring war in Vietnam to a successful and honorable conclusion. He did not provide a formula for "winding down" the war, but his promise was forthright, and a weary electorate accepted it as a commitment.

Although Nixon was politically wise enough to learn from his predecessor's example and although he realized full well that continuation of that futile struggle would erode his effectiveness, he decided to keep troops in Vietnam until a cease-fire was agreed to about four years after his first inauguration. Seven more months were to pass before the Congress would compel the President to stop all bombing and other United States military activity in Southeast Asia on August 15, 1973.

For many years historians, political scientists, and politicians will ponder the effects of the Vietnam War on our society and on President Nixon. Should he have precipitately withdrawn our troops from Southeast Asia, as many demanded he do, regardless of the consequences? Would that have avoided at least part of the tragedy of his presidency? Or was he right in following a policy of Vietnamization, remaining involved in the war on a gradually reduced basis, until South Vietnam seemed to be capable of defending itself and maintaining its independence?

I'm sure many Americans have asked themselves, as I did, what course they would have followed had they been President. No one despised this war more than I did, yet I worried about the consequences of unilateral withdrawal of our military forces. I worried about the credibility and world position of the United States in the event of a withdrawal. Would the Soviet Union have become the dominant world power? Would a massacre of South Vietnamese have ensued, which would have been a cancer on the American conscience as it was for a time on a much smaller scale when the lives of 1,200 Cuban exiles were threatened by Castro after the Bay of Pigs fiasco? Would a clear-cut North Vietnamese victory have led to the domino-type loss of other nations in Southeast Asia, as President Kennedy predicted? I am glad I did not have to make the awful decision facing President Nixon on this complex issue. To persist in the struggle meant the waste of more lives and more resources, deepening the dangerous intellectual divisions in our own country, and delaying positive efforts to reach a détente with Russia and China. To withdraw meant the abandoning of an ally, a loss of America's credibility and standing in the world community, and an unknown peril to the international balance of power.

During the war Nixon surely added a seventh to his Six Crises when he ordered an attack on the North Vietnamese and Viet Cong sanctuaries in Cambodia. At once millions of citizens, especially university students, deemed this to be an unwise and illegal widening of the war. Riots broke out. A bank was bombed and burned in California. Property damage by homemade bombs, axes, and clubs became rampant against universities and businesses that had no control over federal policy. What President Nixon failed to explain to the American people was this: his order to the military to attack the sanctuaries in Cambodia did not in fact widen the war in a *legal* sense. *It did not violate Cambodia's sovereignty.* It is a well-established rule in international law that if a neutral nation cannot expel one of the belligerents from its soil the other belligerent may attack the enemy forces in the occupied area without raising questions of sovereignty. The North Vietnamese and Viet Cong had used a portion of Cambodia throughout the war as a sanctuary, each post within the zone being the focal point of murderous attacks on the United States and South Vietnamese forces and civilians, and a haven for the enemy forces as they withdrew after each foray into South Vietnam. So long as we were in the war the President's order for the attack on the sanctuaries was justified. But by that time this was only a technicality to many Americans; the war itself was the issue and only an immediate end to it was acceptable to them.

The mystery, however, is why this single military action which lasted only six weeks was publicly announced, when for several years United States planes had been secretly bombing enemy forces in Cambodia and our officials had been lying about this to the Congress, the families of killed soldiers, and the American people. In 1973, when a military officer told a Senate committee that forces killed in Cambodia and Laos had been reported as having lost their lives in South Vietnam, a new wave of criticism swept the country. Military leaders explained that Prince Norodom Sihanouk and later Marshal Lon Nol had condoned our bombing in Cambodia on the condition that the air attacks not be made public. Silence might have been flimsily defensible; lying was unforgivable. As Elmer Davis often said in our OWI days: "This is a people's war and the people are entitled to know the truth, nothing but the truth." In war or peace a government which lies to its people, in order to sustain a policy at a given time, is undermining the very basis of democracy. If the people, through their elected representatives, will not support a policy in light of all the facts, then the policy should be changed. Leaders who are so convinced that they know what is best for the people—but do not trust the people to reach the right decision—are not entitled to lead. Official misrepresentation about important developments in Southeast Asia will not soon be forgotten, for this is now viewed as another example of immorality in government —simply an extension into international affairs of dishonesty in domestic affairs. The consequent loss of faith in government—in its credibility and its moral standards—has become a moral crisis unmatched in our history. Not only is this fuel for the flames ignited and fanned by the small group of nihilists who would destroy the government but, more importantly, it calls into question in the minds of good Americans everywhere the integrity of our political system.

The war and an attendant inflation (also inherited from the Johnson administration) dominated Nixon's first term and largely obscured his other efforts. The war and the economy dominated his press and television conferences, which were held, early in his administration, rather frequently. At first the President was informative and candid in his dealings with the press, skillfully responding to questions without notes to jog his memory. But his war and economic policies intensified public and media criticism, so he began to withdraw from public and congressional contacts, especially from leading Republicans who expressed disagreement with some of his policies. His press conferences became rare, separated by many months.

Nixon's isolation and its consequences were described by George E. Reedy, former assistant to President Johnson, in a speech at the Brookhaven National Laboratory—a speech incorporated in his latest

488

book, *The Presidency in Flux*[35]: "[The President] is isolated . . . because everyone around him is his subordinate. There are two ways to isolate a man. One is to lock him up in a padded cell and deprive him of human companionship. The other is simply to be certain that everybody in his vicinity is his servant. The two methods are equally effective. There is a chain of circumstance and it is vicious. Power breeds isolation. Isolation leads to the capricious use of power. In turn, the capricious use of power breaks down the normal channels of communication between the leader and the people whom he leads. This ultimately means the deterioration of power and with it the capacity to sustain unity in our society. This is the problem we face today."

An older devastating comment about the self-aggrandizement that grows in isolation is in Stefan Zweig's *Erasmus of Rotterdam*.[36] Erasmus was an observer of the human condition in the latter part of the fifteenth and early sixteenth centuries. Zweig offers this gem: "Eras about to be renovated project their ideal into a figure which shall manifest the soul of the age; for the Zeitgeist, if it is to grasp its own essence concretely, invariably chooses the type of man most suited to its purpose; and when this unique and chance-found individual outsoars his inborn capacities, it grows, in a sense, enthusiastic over its own enthusiasm."

The relevance of these generalizations is found in Nixon's high degree of isolation (greater than that of any other President) and to his rare public addresses and press conferences in which he became his own most enthusiastic advocate.

The outrage over Watergate and the incredible events which followed it in 1972 and 1973 have obscured the positive accomplishments of the Nixon administration. These must not be overlooked in any objective evaluation of his performance. Certainly his posture in foreign relations, in which on balance he has excelled, bears little resemblance to his distressing record in the management of domestic affairs.

President Nixon has all but ended the Cold War, begun in the Truman administration. He proceeded logically and courageously in carrying forward what President Eisenhower had started in minimizing Cold War psychology and working earnestly with the leaders of the world for universal peace and improved relationships between the two great power centers of the world. That effort, in my opinion, stalled and even to some extent was reversed under Presidents Kennedy and Johnson. But President Nixon picked up where President Eisenhower had left off. He demonstrated skill, bold diplomacy, and creativeness in improving our relations with the Soviet Union and the People's Republic of China and did so in such a way as to raise no suspicion of trading on the ideological conflict between the two most powerful Communist nations.

It is doubtful that Hubert Humphrey or George McGovern, had either been President, could have done what Nixon did. A Democratic President would have encountered polemical objections from many political leaders and a substantial proportion of citizens of our country. President Nixon, with a long background of anti-Communism, muted the opposition that otherwise would have come from conservative and moderate elements in our society, and he held the support of liberals of both parties who would have favored such actions no matter who was President.

The President's reliance on Dr. Henry Kissinger as an advance agent and intelligent alter ego in paving the way for specific accomplishments in his own summit meetings was as meritorious as his confidence in domestic advisers was ill conceived. Further, his timing in meetings with Chinese leaders in Peking and Soviet leaders in Moscow, later with Brezhnev in Washington, showed sensitive perception. The people of the United States, the peoples of the world, can breathe easier and quench to some extent their feeling of fear and insecurity as a result of his vigorous leadership. Much credit must go to Dr. Henry Kissinger, a wise and tireless worker, in whom the President properly has reposed complete confidence. But this does not detract from Nixon's own achievement. If the President is to be blamed for the ghastly errors made by his aides in the domestic and military realms, he must be applauded for what Kissinger has helped him accomplish.

The Moscow and Washington agreements included the first step toward mutual disarmament as painstakingly worked out in the SALT talks. Accords were also signed in the fields of transportation, oceanography, agriculture, and culture. Each of these accords provided for the exchange of scientists, publications, students, teachers, and researchers, each to be implemented by special U.S.S.R.-U.S.A. joint committees which are to meet at least annually to develop details of co-operation. Specific types of co-operation range from bridge building and traffic control to joint projects in biological oceanography. The most interesting accord includes co-operation in environmental protection, medical science, outer space, and exchanges in the performing arts, films, books, magazines, athletic teams, and members of legislative bodies. Finally, moving from the general to the specific, the two nations agreed that in 1974 and 1975 exchanges would include from each side forty graduate students, thirty language instructors, ten research professors, ten performing arts groups, and a series of seminars with twelve participants from each country.

Unresolved was the desire of Nixon and Brezhnev to develop substantial two-way trade, carrying forward the beginning made in the 1972 grain sale by the United States to the Soviet Union, a sale seriously misunderstood by the press and many citizens. Mutually beneficial trade, which can become significant over a period of years—our farm and industrial surpluses for Soviet minerals and gas—is dependent on the willingness of the Congress to grant favored-nation status in trade relations to the Soviet Union, a step not yet approved because of the insistence of many senators that the Soviet government first agree to the unrestricted emigration of its Jewish citizens. This is an unfortunate, though hopefully only a temporary, deterrent. Everyone is anxious for the Soviet Union to change its emigration policy. But international agreements, desired by and in the interest of both parties, cannot be consummated if one of the nations tries to intervene in the internal affairs of the other. We would resent the Soviet Union's demanding, as a condition of entering into an agreement on arms reduction, that we at once eliminate discrimination against minority groups in our society. While the two situations are not wholly comparable, the principle involved is the same. Our hope for freedom of emigration for Soviet Jews should be vigorously pursued through normal diplomatic channels, not used as a bargaining point in a trade negotiation that is in our interest.

The agreements reached in the past two years may seem to be a small beginning and, as compared to the free exchanges and co-operation the United States enjoys with other countries, they are. But the crucial fact is that a *beginning has been made.* Constant contacts of students, teachers, scientists, businessmen, manufacturers, financial experts, legislators, performing arts groups, and others may open a new era in Soviet-United States relations. The spirit of good will and accommodation shown by the leaders of the two nations seems to me to be as important as the agreements thus far reached. If this spirit prevails, it augurs well for arms-reduction talks, the possibility of a meaningful European Security Conference, an ultimate solution to the trade problem, and in time to *much greater exchanges* of personnel than are provided for in the 1972–73 accords.

The President's negotiation with the leaders of the People's Republic of China is also a notable achievement. By one visit, well planned in advance, Nixon reversed a policy of hostility and warlike threats that had persisted for more than a quarter of a century. The establishment of diplomatic offices, below the ambassadorial level— each nation represented by distinguished and seasoned diplomats— promises future co-operation in many of the areas dealt with in the U.S.A.-U.S.S.R. accords, and the sale of agricultural commodities to the People's Republic of China opened new doors of accommodation.

The parade of heads of state and chief executives of many foreign powers to the White House indicated that universal condemnation of the Vietnam War and alleged scandals in high circles of our government did not seriously weaken Nixon's leadership in world affairs. In fact, at the height of his domestic difficulties in October 1973, President Nixon exerted strong leadership in arranging a precarious cease-fire in the Middle East after all-out war had erupted between Israel and the Arab states. Dr. Kissinger, now Secretary of State, again played a crucial role, meeting with all parties involved, and especially with Soviet leaders. The most recent Mideast crisis tested the new détente with the Kremlin, and the world was reassured to see that the United States and the Soviet Union worked together to halt the fighting. If the cease-fire holds, and if Nixon and Brezhnev continue to work together, there is at least hope that a more lasting peace can be forged in that troubled area of the world.

The "Nixon Doctrine" has some significance. It modified the rigid containment policy established by President Truman. In a press conference on Guam, July 25, 1969, Nixon called for our allies to understand that in the future they must be responsible for the major burden of their own defense. We would no longer try to be the Atlas of the modern world. In explaining the new policy Nixon said, "Its central thesis is that the United States will participate in the defense and development of allies and friends, but that America cannot—and will not—conceive all plans, design all the programs, execute all the decisions and undertake all the defense of the free nations of the world. We will help where it makes a real difference and *is considered in our interest . . .* [we will] *insist that other nations play a role . . . a necessary sharing of responsibility.*"

A new agreement on Berlin apparently yielded stability to the legal status and peace of that city enclave. The nuclear non-proliferation treaty, finally approved by the Senate, was a distinct plus.

This commendable and historically important foreign relations record was unfortunately sullied somewhat by the President's public support of Pakistan in its genocidal conflict with East Pakistan, now Bangladesh. Why the President felt it desirable to speak vigorously in behalf of Pakistan may be a mystery until his personal memoirs are written. With destitute millions fleeing from East Pakistan into India, hundreds of thousands being slain in East Pakistan, and large numbers dying of disease and starvation—facts which shocked humanity—Nixon appeared heartless and impervious to criticism as he cast his prestige in support of aggressive Pakistan. It was a golden opportunity for the President to remain silent. Persons close to the President have suggested that he was overly conscious of Pakistan's membership in CENTO and our long reliance on that country as an ally, but this partnership had been perverted by Pakistan's support of the People's Republic of China in its difficulties with India. Nixon's attitude on this issue must have aggrieved even Henry Kissinger; he remarked at the height of the difficulty that the President had given him the devil for not being more outspoken in support of Pakistan. The lingering effect of Nixon's position is an India unfriendly to the United States and forced closer to the Soviet Union, a Bangladesh that is contemptuous of United States attitudes, and a weakened position for the United States in the Indian subcontinent.

This error in international leadership might have loomed larger in our international relations had it not been for the transcendent importance of developments with the Soviet Union and the People's Republic of China.

President Nixon's domestic program has had modest successes and, unfortunately, large failures. The successes have not earned wide coverage by the mass media or provoked citizen discussions.

Military forces were reduced in four years from 3.5 million to 2.4 million, though total military costs increased. The draft was ended on July 1, 1973, an action that gave young men an opportunity to plan their futures with greater certainty. An all-voluntary army was then instituted. The Twenty-sixth Amendment to the Constitution enabled eighteen-year-olds to vote in national elections. The annual rate of increased federal spending—amounting to seventeen per cent a year under Johnson—was reduced for a time to nine per cent by Nixon, a commendable change, but not enough as economic developments, especially inflation, indicated.

An effort to check the growth of the federal government was initiated in 1969 and came to modest fruition with the passage on October 20, 1972, of the General Revenue Sharing Act which provided that more than $30 billion in federal revenues would be allocated to state and local governments in the ensuing five years. Minimal success was achieved in one aspect of welfare reform—to place some welfare recipients in regular jobs—but the President's proposal for major reform of the anachronistic welfare system continued to be debated in committees of the Congress. Social Security was broadened in coverage and the total payments increased more than fifty per cent. Assistance to small businesses was increased from $820 million in 1969 to $3 billion in 1973. The National Railroad Passenger Service (Amtrak) was instituted as a means of saving this phase of rail service.

Modest gains against crime were recorded. In the second half of the sixties drug use in the United States reached alarming proportions; by increasing elevenfold the funds for domestic drug control and by inducing Turkey, chief source of opium and therefore heroin, to place a ban on opium production, progress was made in reducing the supply of hard drugs.

Under the Urban Mass Transportation Assistance Act of 1970, federal aid for mass transportation systems reached a billion dollars a year by 1973, and an amendment to existing law permitted some funds in the Highway Trust Fund to be used for mass transportation. The Postal Reform Act changed the Post Office Department from a Cabinet agency to a government corporation with broad powers.

New agencies to deal with pollution and other environmental problems were established and funds for these programs reached nearly $2.5 billion in 1973, four times the amount provided in 1968. Federal officials took legal action against municipal and industrial water polluters, prosecutions quadrupling in a two-year period.

Major gains were made in some phases of health care, especially in the training of doctors, nurses, and dentists, but reverses were experienced in medical research, training grants, and fellowships available to medical and public health students. Funds for hospital construction declined drastically.

New consumer agencies were established to eliminate dangerous products and to induce industry to improve consumer products. Surveillance in this field exercised by the Food and Drug Administration and the Federal Trade Commission was increased substantially.

Aid to elementary and secondary education was increased but serious damage was done to collegiate and university education by the elimination of graduate fellowships, research grants, and aid for essential construction.

Equal rights for women were stressed in federal appointments and in a constitutional amendment submitted to the states.

Sporadic successes were overshadowed by Nixon's dismal record in coping with serious inflation, by what I deem to be errors of judgment in establishing spending priorities, by downgrading the Cabinet and magnifying the power of the palace guard, and by the most serious crisis in presidential authority in our history, due to amazing developments which destroyed the faith of the American people in executive leadership and even, to some extent, in American democratic institutions.

The failure to bring inflation under control caused deep concern among businessmen, consumers, and investors.

Public enterprises in the United States now require for their support each year more than a third of the total national income. In 1929 spending by all levels of government amounted to about ten per cent of the dollar value of the national output; it rose to twenty per cent in 1940, thirty per cent in 1965, and thirty-five per cent in 1972. "It is time to call a halt," said Dr. Arthur F. Burns, chairman of the Board of Governors, of the Federal Reserve Board in testifying before the Joint Economic Committee of the Congress. Since the federal budget alone accounts for $270 billion of the total annual socialized cost, it follows that the federal government has a major responsibility for national economic management, the goal being to have low unemployment, increasing production, stable prices, and a satisfactory situation as regards the flow of international payments.

In the eight Eisenhower years the economy moved gratifyingly upward with inflation held to a surprisingly low level following the inflationary spiral during the Korean War. However, two mild recessions were experienced. The first began in 1957. President Eisenhower was prudent in managing fiscal affairs: essentially, he speeded up federal construction expenditures, and the Federal Reserve Board refrained from adopting a too easy monetary policy which would have laid the basis for later and troublesome price increases. In this he had the expert help of Raymond J. Saulnier, chairman of the Council of Economic Advisers, and William McChesney Martin, chairman of the Federal Reserve Board of Governors. The economy responded fairly well in 1958, but a second mini-recession was experienced in 1960–61. Careful management paid dividends, however, for the nation came out of the 1960–61 difficulty with wage increases almost in line with productivity gains, foreign trade accounts back to surplus, prices stabilized, and the inflationary psychology totally eliminated. Furthermore, this was accomplished without re-establishing wage and price controls, which had been removed in 1953 following the Korean War. And a basis had been laid for a series of good years in the first half of the 1960s.

Inflation broke out in the second half of the sixties. Presidents Kennedy and Johnson increased annual federal expenditures by nearly $87 billion and piled up $60 billion in budgetary deficits. President Johnson insisted that the nation could have both "guns and butter," a homely way of saying that soaring war costs need not deter us from instituting costly social programs. A sizable tax increase at this time might have had a salutary effect, and the President did in fact favor a ten per cent income tax surcharge for a temporary period. But President Johnson's unwillingness to assure Congress that spending would be held in check delayed enactment of the tax; this was a major factor in allowing inflation, which got an explosive start in 1965, to build up momentum. The money supply increased rapidly and wage hikes began exceeding increases in productivity by a wide margin. President Johnson instituted voluntary guidelines, accompanied by "jawboning"; this plan worked for a time and then failed, so prices moved upward.

When President Nixon assumed office the inflation rate was about five per cent a year and increasing.

When a new President takes office, especially when a change of party is involved, he likes to begin with protests over the state of affairs he has inherited. Certainly Nixon inherited an unpopular and costly war and he did, in fact, begin with a badly deteriorated economic situation. For a year or two he insisted upon significant reduction in the rate of increase of federal spending. A major change was in the area of monetary management. Whereas under Johnson the money supply had been increasing about ten per cent a year, the Federal Reserve Board, with Nixon's enthusiastic approval, instituted monetary austerity to the point that there was virtually no change in the money supply in 1969.

Unfortunately, in his second month in office, Nixon announced a policy of non-restraints on wage and price increases. In a press conference he said, "I do not go along with the suggestion that inflation can be effectively controlled by exhorting labor and management to follow certain guide lines. . . . [They] have to be guided by the interests of the organizations they represent."

He assured the country that inflation would be controlled by classical methods and without increasing unemployment. All the same, labor costs rose 7.1 per cent in 1969 and consumer prices rose 5.4 per cent, the highest since the Korean War.

Within a year the wage-price spiral intensified. Industries, threatened with crippling strikes, granted the largest wage hikes in history. In the construction industry wages increased 22.1 per cent; railroad wages rose 15 per cent a year for several years, and in the automobile and other major industries wage increases of 42 per cent over a three-year period were contractually approved. Naturally these costs had to be covered in prices charged to consumers.

Though not requested by the Administration, tax decreases were put into effect in 1969 and again in 1971. Unemployment increased to 6 per cent, and a recession developed.

The President became so concerned that he publicly declared he was departing from classical economic theories and was becoming a Keynesian. For the fiscal year 1971–72 he would submit a "full-employment" budget to the Congress, a budget with a proposed increase in expenditures of $16.4 billion and a deficit of $11.6 billion. (This increase, added to those of the preceding seven years, would result in federal expenditures being *precisely double what they were eight years earlier.*) The hope was that the enlarged budget would stimulate the economy to the extent that in time the projected deficit would be covered by revenues when full employment was in fact achieved. Unfortunately the President grossly underestimated expenditures and the size of the deficit. Congress, as usual, appropriated more than the President asked for. The deficit zoomed to more than $23 billion. These facts, along with some credit and monetary expansion, exacerbated the problem of inflation. The peak of consumer price increases at that time was six per cent annually, with unemployment as high as six per cent.

In the meantime Congress on its own initiative passed legislation authorizing direct control of wages, salaries, prices, and rents, but not raw farm commodities. The President announced that he would not use this authority.

In an interview with a staff member of *Challenge* magazine in its May–June 1973 issue, Walter Heller, chairman of the Council of Economic Advisers in the Johnson administration, explained that the nation had been contending with two types of inflation. One developed when total demand exceeded the reasonable limits that the economy could supply at full employment, that is, "excess-demand or demand-pull inflation." To curb this type "we have to use the instruments of monetary restriction and tough fiscal policy. Unless total consumer, business, and government spending is held in check, it will overheat the economy and pull prices up." Concurrently we had "cost-push inflation." We had persistent "cost-push where both labor and business units with excessive market power can set wages and prices within a considerable range of discretion. The role of government is to induce purveyors of market power to behave according to the rules of competitive society." In this event, Heller said, "we need a kind of permanent wage-price guide posts that work—guidelines for noninflationary wage and price behavior backed by the power to roll back wages and prices in cases of flagrant violation."

As early as December 1970, Arthur Burns, chairman of the Board of Governors of the Federal Reserve Board, had said, "In a society which rightly values full employment, monetary and fiscal tools are inadequate for dealing with the sources of price inflation such as are plaguing us now." He indicated his conviction that an incomes policy was needed.

Early in 1971 the President, with demand-pull and cost-push influences to contend with, hesitated, seemingly confused. In the first quarter of the year he was encouraged by a temporary drop in the rate of increase in prices, but soon the upward surge resumed, and unemployment hovered around six per cent.

Finally the President was pressed by congressmen and consumers to take new action. On August 4, 1971, he said in a press conference that while he continued to be generally opposed to wage and price controls he had an "open mind" with respect to what action should be taken. Eleven days later controls were imposed. This was labeled Phase I.

Phase I was in effect for ninety days. It froze prices for that short period. Simultaneously the President suspended the convertibility of dollars to gold for foreign treasuries and central banks, and imposed a temporary surcharge of ten per cent on imports. By and large the temporary program worked moderately well, in part because consumers were doubtful about their income prospects and increased their rate of savings.

Three months later Phase II was announced. The guidelines in this plan permitted flexible wage increases averaging 5.5 per cent a year, plus certain additional allowances, and placed fairly strict restraints on the prices of many industrial products and consumer goods, but not on raw agricultural commodities. Since there was ample excess plant and labor capacity, competition kept most prices at reasonable levels. The annualized rate of inflation, 5.9 per cent before Phase II, gradually declined to 3.4 per cent for consumer prices. Citizens felt that something useful was being done. In the fourteen months of Phase II the index of wholesale prices of farm products rose 28.5 per cent, all commodities 8.7 per cent, and industrial commodities 4.4 per cent. Most observers felt that Phase II changed expectations of employees and employers, slowed prices and costs, was fair to most elements of the economy, and fostered a minimum of price and production distortions.

For reasons few persons understood, Phase II was replaced by Phase III in January 1973. Some students of the problem charged that neither the President nor those who administered the control program really favored controls and wished to remove them as soon as possible.

Phase III was considered to be a step in that direction. Walter Heller said the change was a mistake. Later Herbert Stein, chairman of the Nixon Council of Economic Advisers, said the same but for a different reason; he felt it gave decontrol a "bad name." Dr. Arthur Burns told a congressional committee that Phase III made it easier to pass rising costs to product prices and to widen profit margins. Arthur M. Okun of the Brookings Institution bluntly told a House committee that Phase III was widely perceived as an abandonment of government price restraints; he called this a major error of economic policy making.

Inflationary pressures now became ominous. Only wages behaved moderately well, increasing at an annual rate of about six per cent. Consumer prices in the first three months of Phase III rose at an annual rate of 8.5 per cent and wholesale prices by a whopping 19 per cent. The index of wholesale prices of all farm commodities soared to 182 in June from 144 in January, of processed foods to 152 from 132, and industrial commodities to 127 from 120. Home-building costs skyrocketed. Retail food prices increased each week. Housewives complained bitterly, some trying to organize a nationwide boycott on meats, especially beef. On June 23, 1973, the President, alarmed by the political disadvantage of this, slapped a sixty-day freeze on most but not all prices. This was humorously labeled Phase III½.

The price freeze caused shortages of some foods. Farmers killed little chicks and pregnant animals. Beef producers withheld supplies from the market. Food prices increased more. The Secretary of Agriculture warned that a normal food basket might increase in price by as much as an additional twenty per cent.

On August 13, 1973, Phase IV was launched. It sought to restrain but not prevent the upward movement of wages and prices, as had Phase II, but now on a voluntary basis. Controls were removed from smaller industries and businesses, and large enterprises could increase prices commensurate with higher costs. The financial community indicated confusion, and many investors became panicky, not only because they did not know what price increases would develop and to what extent profits would be squeezed, but also because they were fearful that the new controls would do little to overcome inflation and might cause another recession. In August 1973 the rate of inflation reached a new high, with food items leading the way, up from a modest increase in 1972 to an annual rate of thirty-six per cent in 1973. Interest rates zoomed to historic highs. Federal expenditures hovered around the $270 billion level.

Controls are a palliative, not a cure. They may be likened to the construction of a large dam in a river with a history of periodic flooding. The dam will prevent flooding until the waters reach the top of the dam, after which the flow downstream will be as great as ever. Even more ominous, in this analogy, is the disaster that could occur if the dam breaks. The most that controls can do is to buy time while fundamental corrective action is taken.

One need not be an economic expert, with the knowledge of Raymond J. Saulnier, Arthur Burns, Walter Heller, Milton Friedman, Herbert Stein, and others to realize that in an inflationary period government expenditures must be rigorously controlled, reduced if possible; taxes must be increased; all limitations on production must be removed; money supply must be prudently managed; import quotas on some commodities must be liberalized; economic expansion must be slowed, for example by interest adjustments; a variable investment-tax credit and a tax-inducing savings plan should be instituted; dollar devaluation with floating relations with other currencies may have to be instituted, and until these actions take effect, wage, price, dividend, and corporate profit guidelines must be enforced.

Inflation in the United States is not unrelated to the persistent imbalances in international payments the United States has experienced. Until 1957 we were not concerned with this problem. Even our expenditures abroad after World War II for military forces and foreign aid did not for a time cause an imbalance in the total world transactions of the United States. While we continued for some time after 1957 to have a sizable favorable balance of trade, foreign military and foreign aid costs, as well as the export of American capital for investment, gave the United States a net deficit situation. Large trade deficits after 1970 exacerbated the problem. In 1971 we faced an imbalance in all international transactions of more than $20 billion annually. With inflation accelerating at home, the world lost confidence in the dollar, gold prices skyrocketed, and the value of the dollar declined sharply in terms of foreign currencies.

Some helpful actions were taken. Two planned devaluations of the dollar in time increased our exports sufficiently that in the second quarter of 1973 we had, for the first time in several years, a favorable balance in the exchange of goods and services. But imbalances in over-all payments continued because of high foreign military costs. The export of American capital for investment declined as domestic inter-est rates soared. A new farm bill, approved by the President, removed production controls, thus promising greater production of many com-modities in one year and of meat in about two or three years. These two actions in time will help reduce food prices at home, increase exports, and reduce the cost of the farm program substantially. If we also adopted Senator Mike Mansfield's suggestion for a phased reduction of troops abroad, and did what we prudently could to stem for a tem-porary period the flow of American capital abroad, hoping that repa-triation of capital through dividends, amounting to $9.2 billion in 1972, would thus yield a greater net inflow of dollars, the situation would indeed look better.

Inflation is one of the most insidious forms of taxation. Most per-sons suffer, especially disadvantaged men and women in retirement plans and others on fixed income. Millions who were barely able to be self-sustaining before have to be added to the relief rolls. But inflation, Dr. Arthur Burns has pointed out, hurts more than the disadvantaged. It injures the entire national economy. "Confidence of businessmen and consumers in the economic future is shaken, productive efficiency fal-ters, export trades languish, interest rates soar, financial markets be-come unruly, and social and political frictions multiply," he said to a congressional committee, adding, "Our nation is experiencing great prosperity, but it is a marred and joyless prosperity, and so it will re-main until we bring inflation under control. We cannot do so until we put our financial house in order."

Most serious of all, a sustained inflation is almost certain to be followed by a serious recession, perhaps a depression. This would be catastrophic in an interdependent society with an annual income of nearly $1.3 trillion, an affluence that has induced companies and in-dividuals to make financial commitments that could not be met in a period of recession or depression. A depression worse than that of the 1930s, while not likely, would not be impossible.

Closely related to the problem of inflation has been that of holding down total federal costs and determining priorities in federal spending. No nation can undertake at one time all that needs to be done. Countries with private competitive-enterprise systems and those with totally socialized economies know this from bitter experience. Determining what to do now and what to postpone is especially difficult when because of inflation severe restraints must be put on total expenditures.

President Nixon, correctly trying to hold down federal costs, arrived at judgments at variance with those of the Congress and most citizens. He favored a $4 billion increase in military costs, even when the war in Indochina was approaching an end and the possibility of mutual arms reductions by Eastern and Western powers seemed promising. With inflation continuing to be a problem of highest importance, and with growing sentiment in the Congress for reducing our overseas military commitments, it is difficult to fathom why Nixon felt a $4 billion increase in military expenditures to be advisable. Everyone is in favor of national security, but there is no such thing as absolute security through military preparedness, especially not in the atomic age. A healthy economy, overcoming human inequities in our society, achieving a firm degree of unity among the American people—these, too, have security value. Arriving at a balance in the military and human phases of national security is a delicate task of statesmanship. In my judgment President Nixon should have initiated a carefully calculated gradual reduction in military costs and thus provided some leeway in the budgetary process for modest increases in crime control, health, higher education, improved welfare, training, employment, anti-discrimination activities, and pollution control, *for the threat to the future of the American society is greater from forces at work internally than it is from any threat of a foreign power or combination of powers.* Every President from Truman to Nixon has agreed that in seeking a world of security the United States must negotiate from a position of strength, but the important addition to this statement is "balanced and total"— we must negotiate from a position of *balanced and total strength.* Indeed, if a choice for economic reasons must be made, it seems clear that in the American society unity of purpose, broad support of the nation's principal programs, dedication to the cardinal values of democracy, and happy agreement that genuine progress is being made in solving troublesome human and physical problems are even more important than a military posture which equals or surpasses that of any other power.

Nixon's 1972–73 reduction of non-military expenditures was achieved by impounding funds approved by the Congress. Patently the Senate and House had acted irresponsibly in appropriating far more funds than was wise in the face of an overheated economy with ruinous inflation. Indeed, not many representatives and senators knew the total of all appropriations, for the Congress had passed 160 separate funding measures with little or no thought given to the consequences of massive deficit financing. So the President had to act. His impounding program infuriated members of Congress who disagreed vehemently with his priorities and charged that he acted unconstitutionally in defying the legislative branch of the government by refusing to spend funds precisely as mandated. I believe the Congress was right in disagreeing with Nixon's priorities, but it was on shaky ground in objecting to his effort to overcome the irresponsible appropriation spree in which the Senate and House had engaged. Perhaps the President did act unconstitutionally, as several lower courts subsequently ruled. This is debatable; a ruling by the Supreme Court is needed. Had each appropriation carried a directive that all funds be spent, then clearly presidential impoundment would have been unconstitutional. Often in the past, with no such directive in appropriations bills, Presidents had impounded portions of congressional appropriations, but never on the scale Nixon used in 1972. Fortunately, as I have said, the President's action caused the Congress to institute reforms that promise to restore to it full control of the appropriations processes and to make impossible future presidential impoundments.

Much of the legislative-executive irritation in this highly publicized incident could have been avoided had the President maintained better relations with leaders of both parties in the Congress. He had withdrawn from them into splendid isolation, as had most of his principal counselors. Unable to reach those who seemingly were powerful in helping the President in decision making, some members of the Congress demanded that certain presidential aides, then enjoying executive privilege, be subject to Senate confirmation and to call by congressional committees for evidence and discussion. Fateful decisions were being made by an enlarged palace guard, all members of which were unavailable to the Congress.

The palace guard had seriously downgraded the importance of Cabinet members, who are, of course, normally available for congressional testimony. Congressional committees concerned with foreign policy could summon the Secretary of State, the Secretary of Defense, the head of the United States Information Agency, the head of CIA, and the Secretaries of Agriculture, Labor, and Commerce, but they knew that the combined testimony of these high-ranking officials was not as relevant as could be offered by Dr. Henry Kissinger, who, in his White House post, helped the President synthesize facts and ideas coming to the President from as many as forty federal agencies. Similarly, congressional committees could summon numerous department heads concerned with domestic economic activity, but their testimony would not be as complete or balanced as that of John Ehrlichman, then the President's domestic counselor.

Even before a series of charges involving high federal officials stunned the nation, the Congress became critical of the powerful men in the White House who wielded such enormous power with no accountability to the Congress or the people—except through the President himself. Initially, persons close to the President, such as Bryce Harlow and Robert H. Finch, were respected on the Hill and had friendly relations with scores of senators and representatives. Harlow left in 1971 and Finch either disappeared from the scene or was so remote from the power center in the White House that he became ineffective. It soon became apparent that the four intimate confidants of the President were Attorney General John Mitchell, H. R. Haldeman, John Ehrlichman, and Henry Kissinger.

Of the four, only Kissinger maintained helpful relations with key members of the Congress and with the media. He was always available to those who wished to consult him, even to those intelligent Republicans, such as Senator Percy and Senator Mathias, who were anathema to the President and his other chief counselors.

Mitchell, former law partner of the President and head of the 1968 presidential campaign, retained Nixon's confidence but was thoroughly disliked and distrusted, not only on the Hill but in many of the executive agencies.

Haldeman and Ehrlichman, abrupt, domineering, and intoxicated with power, isolated the President from the very leaders he should have seen regularly and, worst of all, refused to make themselves available informally to senators and congressmen who could have been helpful in keeping policies, programs, and attitudes on a better course.

I can only conclude that President Nixon wanted to be isolated, that he deliberately assumed the "monarchial" pose and enjoyed the isolation that comes from Reedy's warning: "The other [method of isolating a man] is simply to be certain that everybody in his vicinity is his servant." He maintained almost no direct contact with the press, avoided congressional leaders and distinguished citizens who might have given him points of view other than his own, and retreated in seclusion to Camp David or one of his other vacation homes at every opportunity.

It was in this milieu that banner headlines reported alleged governmental privileges to the International Telephone and Telegraph Company, the Watergate break-in and subsequent cover-up with its apparent interference in judicial processes, extravagant expenditure of public funds on the private properties of the President, misrepresentations of United States military actions in Cambodia and Laos, and alleged favors to the dairy industry in return for campaign contributions. Critical editorials, cutting cartoons, and the pungent punditry of columnists monopolized prime space and prime time in the media.

Through the summer of 1973 charges, invariably labeled "scandals," became the main topics of conversation wherever people came together. Fact, unsupported allegation, and rumor were constantly blended. Guilt by association or sheer assertion attributed to a "high authority," the crime of the McCarthy era, threatened to become rampant. As one startling revelation followed another, and as some officials confessed their guilt, the Senate Watergate Committee, the mass media, and many citizens began to ask: Had the President personally been a party to illegal actions? Had he, perhaps, though suspicious, remained aloof, hoping that the danger would fade away? Had he gradually become aware of the facts but was loath to see persons close to him exposed, humiliated, perhaps incarcerated? Or had he simply trusted the wrong persons while he was absorbed in other major issues of state? Regardless of the nature or extent of his involvement, if any, could he, in the light of all that had happened, govern effectively for the remainder of his second term? Should he resign? Should he be impeached by the House and tried by the Senate?

It was clear that the President had no intention of resigning. He would fight back, a fight that might require months. He denounced the Senate investigation as a witch hunt aimed at him. He accepted the resignations of Haldeman and Ehrlichman but ranked them among the finest of public servants. He appointed Elliot Richardson, who had served him with distinction in a variety of Cabinet positions, to replace

Attorney General Kleindienst, and he authorized Richardson to appoint an independent Special Prosecutor to pursue the entire matter legally. He wanted the "cover-up" confined to the courts, and he wanted those guilty of interfering with judicial processes brought to justice, while he proceeded with more important aspects of the "people's business." But initially he refused to make available to the Special Prosecutor, certainly not to the Senate Watergate Committee, the tapes which recorded his own relevant conversations with Haldeman, Mitchell, Dean, and others. To do so, he contended, would be incompatible with the doctrine of separation of powers and the need for the confidentiality of presidential discussions.

As a layman with knowledge of previous Supreme Court decisions involving the President and the separation of powers, I believe Nixon was on solid ground in refusing to give the tapes to the Senate committee. But his declining to present them to the court or the Special Prosecutor may have been unconstitutional. Nixon offered a compromise: he would provide a summary of the tapes and let Senator John Stennis listen to them to verify the accuracy of the summary. Prosecutor Archibald Cox rejected this plan and said he would keep pursuing the matter in the court.

The President then stunned the nation on Saturday, October 20, 1973, when, no doubt in anger, he ordered Attorney General Richardson to fire Special Prosecutor Cox. Richardson chose to resign instead. The White House then gave the same order to Acting Attorney General William D. Ruckelshaus, and, when he also refused, he was fired. Finally the Solicitor General Robert Bork became Acting Attorney General and dismissed Prosecutor Cox.

As the nation reacted in anger and disbelief, several congressmen announced that they would move for impeachment proceedings when the Congress returned after the long weekend. Early the next week Charles Alan Wright, one of the President's lawyers and an expert in constitutional law, announced that the President would release the controversial tapes to Judge John Sirica.

Nixon's verification of Wright's offer to release the tapes to the court temporarily offset the furor caused by the resignation of Richardson and the precipitous firing of Ruckelshaus and Cox. But a few days later the credulity of the American people was again severely tested when it became known that two key tapes—one of a conversation with Mitchell and the other of a meeting with Dean—did not exist.

As I bring the writing of this book to a close in mid-November 1973 it has not yet been established whether President Nixon was actually involved in the Watergate cover-up or whether he had been victimized by associates and by aggressive and willful newsmen. Many now contend that the truth has become almost irrelevant, for the tide of distrust, suspicion, loss of faith in government, and ironic disbelief in the credibility of chosen leaders has raised serious questions about the President's ability to govern effectively for the next three years.

But of course the truth must become known, and the action ultimately taken must be determined in the light of the truth.

It must be admitted, however, that even if the President is exonerated his administration will be scarred by the ITT case, the disgrace of the Vice-President, the use of taxpayers' funds to improve his private property, his own income tax problems, the indictment of key Cabinet members and close aides, the unjustified dismissal of Richardson, Ruckelshaus, and Cox, and lingering doubts about Watergate, even when the facts are known to all who wish to understand.

In an attempt to regain some degree of prestige for the White House, the President, over a period of months, took various actions: he saw to it that Mitchell, Haldeman, Ehrlichman, Dean, Stans, and many others were no longer identified with his administration. He induced men of integrity to join his staff. Bryce Harlow, at great sacrifice to himself, returned as a major counselor to the President. Former Secretary of Defense Melvin Laird took Ehrlichman's former post. Kissinger's right-hand man, General Alexander Haig, assumed Haldeman's old position. Finally the President ventured out of his isolation. On several occasions he met with the press in give-and-take sessions. He called for a "truce" of sorts, pleading with the nation to leave the scandals to the courts so that he and his associates could concentrate on the "people's business." The plea seemingly fell on deaf ears. The mass media tenaciously kept the scandals in the banner headlines, even when startling news about energy shortages, congressional efforts to curb presidential powers, and the unprecedented desertion of the United States by our European allies at a critical moment justified top billing.

Gone is the skillful way President Nixon dealt with the press early in his first administration. Now he makes no effort to conceal his distrust of some of the news media and of specific newspaper and television personnel.

I understand his distrust, even his bitterness. Never before have I seen representatives of the media display such rudeness and hurl such loaded questions at a President, "questions" which clearly indicate that they have already passed judgment. Even if one does not respect the President he should respect the presidency; rudeness and questions which imply guilt are unacceptable to the American people.

Often the mass media have been blatantly unfair: a two-column story in most newspapers said that the President had directed the Attorney General to drop a case against ITT, but at the end of the story, on an inner page, it was acknowledged that the President had changed his mind and authorized the investigation to go forward when he came in possession of the full facts. Again: the sale of grain to the Soviet Union was misrepresented, either maliciously or because reporters and commentators did not understand the facts. For years we had been paying billions of dollars to export price-depressing farm surpluses. Negotiations for the sale of the grain to the Soviet Union had been going on for many months. When agreement was reached it appeared to be a significant achievement, one that would greatly reduce government costs and improve farm income. It was a disastrous coincidence that world shortages of crop production caused farm prices everywhere to skyrocket. But the media blamed the difficulty on the Nixon administration. The one truly unfortunate aspect of the grain episode was that a single Assistant Secretary of Agriculture, who had nothing to do with negotiating the agreement with the Soviet Union, had resigned and joined a grain company which handled a portion of the sale to the Soviet Union. This was needlessly made into a scandal, especially by one television network which brutally distorted the facts. These two examples could be multiplied tenfold. Still, I have often said that the only thing worse than a free press, when it is in one of its periods of notable irresponsibility, is a controlled press. In my world travels I have lived for months with censored news. I accept completely the freedom of the press, even in its worst moments.

But I must also say that I think the President has been his own worst enemy in all the scandals of 1972 and 1973. Had he, within a few days after the Watergate break-in, condemned that stupid action and promised that he would discharge from the federal service all who had any part in it, the problem would then have been solved with the conviction of a relatively few persons. There would have been no cover-up. Further, throughout the whole sordid period White House spokesmen have often sought to obfuscate the facts, tactics that backfired. Some around the President have conveyed their conviction that somehow the press was really responsible for what had happened because reporters needlessly kept "digging" until they uncovered critical parts of the total bag of allegations.

One of the most pointed condemnations of the lack of integrity in government came in August 1973, not from newspaper or television personnel but from the National Advisory Commission on Criminal Justice, formed originally at the suggestion of Attorney General Mitchell because he did not like the Eisenhower report on the causes and prevention of violence. The Mitchell commission, headed by Russell W. Peterson, former governor of Delaware, repeated many of the recommendations of the Eisenhower commission, including one calling for the confiscation of concealable handguns. The commission then added a special section which declared that official corruption was flourishing and that this caused much of the public to perceive the war against crime as pitting the powerful against the powerless, and that "law and order" had become a hypocritical rallying cry. "Equal justice under the law" was an empty phrase. The commission stated its conviction that citizens generally believe that there is widespread corruption among federal, state, and local officials, that this corruption results in staggering costs to American taxpayers, and that corruption "breeds further crime by providing a model of lawlessness that undermines an acceptable rule of law."

Ironically, the new Special Prosecutor to take Cox's place, appointed just as I am completing the writing of this volume, is Leon Jaworski of Texas, former president of the American Bar Association, and one of my esteemed colleagues on the President's Commission on the Causes and Prevention of Violence, whose conclusions so provoked Attorney General Mitchell that he established the group that has condemned the character of the Nixon administration in language stronger than I have used.

I earnestly want to believe that President Nixon's worst sin is that he chose, trusted, and—with a Trumanesque loyalty—for too long stood by the wrong persons. Even that would be a terrible condemnation of his administration.

CHAPTER 27

An unheard appeal for reform has a way of
becoming a cry for revolution; a political
system which cannot adapt to the needs of
the future has no future.

"MEN OF ORDINARY physique and discretion," Wood-
row Wilson once said, "cannot be President and live, if the strain be
not somehow relieved."

Walter Lippmann, noting the burdens early in Wilson's administration, wrote in *Preface to Politics*,[37] "Surely the task of statesmanship
is more difficult today than ever before in history."

In 1936, when he was involved literally day and night in dealing
with problems of the depression, President Roosevelt said to Congress,
"The President cannot adequately handle his responsibilities; he is
overworked. It is humanly impossible to carry out his duties . . . because he is overwhelmed with minor details and needless contacts."

Clinton Rossiter in his book, *The American Presidency*,[32] says, "If
there is any one thing about [the President] that strikes the eye immediately, it is the staggering burden he bears for all of us." Eight years
earlier, Rossiter asserted that the limits of the presidency as a one-man
job had been reached if not passed.

Robert Gray, secretary of the Cabinet in the Eisenhower administration, says in his book, *Eighteen Acres Under Glass*,[34] that President Eisenhower had to sign as many as thirty to forty thousand letters
and documents a year. That required more than a hundred signatures
each working day. (Malcolm Moos, in an article in the Fall 1959 edition
of the *Kentucky Law Journal*, said that Franklin Roosevelt signed his
name two hundred times a day, that Truman by his own count signed
six hundred times a day, and that Eisenhower averaged several hundred

signatures a day. I once signed twelve hundred university diplomas, but it took me eight days to do so!)

William Lawrence, in his book,[12] declared that the burdens of the presidency are so great in modern times that "prolonged tenure inevitably shortens the longevity of any incumbent. There is a myth in politics that though the President is the pinnacle of American life, he must somehow prove his democratic credentials. This leads to open-air campaigning, and shaking of thousands upon thousands of hands—an open invitation to assassins."

Norman Cousins, in the *Saturday Review* of April 13, 1968, expressed his judgment that the presidency may no longer be manageable by any single individual, however wise or resourceful. "No one can stand up against that kind of pounding, or deal with such powerful cross-currents, or have the emotional and physical resiliency to cope with the demands of the office. . . . The most bruising single factor today has to do with the prodigious increase in the potency and number of pressure points from within and without the government."

George E. Reedy, press secretary to President Johnson, says in *The Twilight of the Presidency*,[38] that the presidency has taken on all the regalia of monarchy and that "The White House does not provide an atmosphere in which idealism and devotion can flourish. . . . There is no evidence that wisdom is being applied effectively to the overwhelming problems that beset us. . . . We may be witnessing the first lengthening shadows that will become the twilight of the presidency."

In the smooth change-over from the Eisenhower administration to the Kennedy administration, the President-elect called on President Eisenhower and in the course of their discussion Eisenhower said, "There are no easy matters that will come to you as President. If they are easy, they will be settled at a lower level." Theodore Sorensen, who was present, said three years later: "If I were to name one quality which characterizes most issues likely to be brought to the President, I would say it would be conflict—conflict between departments, between the views of advisers, between administration and the Congress, between groups with the country . . . or states versus the nation."[19]

Aside from President Calvin Coolidge, whose administration was calm and unruffled, all Presidents I have known, as well as President Wilson, have not been able to redeem adequately all the responsibilities devolving upon them by the Constitution, laws, and tradition, though each lived in constant tension and worked to the point of physical collapse.

Despite enormous efforts by the President, many things he ought to do are in fact not done. Time limits us all, even the President. In his book, *The Man in the White House*,[39] Wilfred E. Binkley quotes the remarks of an observer of Franklin Roosevelt as saying: "It is a mystery to me how every morning he selects the few things he *can* do from the thousands he *should* do."

If a President is struggling to find the formula for peace in Vietnam, it is ridiculous for him to have to take time to settle a quarrel between federal agencies, sign or veto private relief and private immigration bills, determine whether Pan American Airways should fly the central Pacific or great northern route to Japan, or sign military commissions, presidential appointments, foreign service appointments, proclamations, scores of letters to influential political persons, and rules governing affairs in the Panama Canal Zone. When he is struggling with the complex problems of imbalances in international payments, inflation and unemployment, he should not have to interrupt his thoughts by stepping into the Rose Garden to greet contingents of 4-H Clubs, League of Women Voters, Future Farmers of America, the AFL-CIO, the Association of American Alfalfa Driers, the Turkey Growers Association, the American Medical Association, the Republican Women of Salisbury, Maryland, foreign students at American University, and a host of others—for each of which he is frantically briefed for a few seconds by a staff member so that he may say something appropriate. It is even questionable that we should expect him to make speeches in all parts of the country on matters of importance, when by television he can reach all the people of the United States who care to listen.

One morning in 1960, I was sitting across the desk from President Eisenhower in his oval office. We had had breakfast at seven-thirty and had come to his office at eight. I was reading a newspaper and he was studying a document on the top of a huge stack of mail on his desk.

He looked up and growled, "I wonder what I did wrong last week?" I said nothing but looked at him inquiringly. He handed me a document and pointed to a particular column. The document was a statistical summary—he received one each week—of the general purport of the fifteen thousand letters sent to him the previous week. The column to which he pointed was headed: "Threats on the Life of the President."

"The number is double that of last week," he commented. "I really don't know what I did to stimulate so many nuts to threaten me."

In a normal week, of the fifteen thousand or more letters coming to his office, between three and four hundred would be abusive, obscene, or openly threatening. The Secret Service investigated the most menacing of these.

President Eisenhower's daily schedule was cruel. It is not surprising that in eight years he had several illnesses, none of which he suffered when he carried the horrendous burdens as Supreme Commander of Allied Forces in World War II. The difference was not just a matter of age. It was also a difference in complexity, fragmentation, frustration, recurring crises, conflict, and constant tension.

Normally President Eisenhower was up by six-thirty in the morning. Sergeant Moaney would bring him the newspapers, usually the New York *Times*, the New York *Herald Tribune*, the Baltimore *Sun*, and sometimes the *Christian Science Monitor*. By seven-thirty he had breakfast on a tray in his bedroom unless he was entertaining congressional leaders or others at an eight o'clock breakfast in the family dining room.

By eight-fifteen he would be in his office. He dictated letters and other documents to Mrs. Ann Whitman, his excellent secretary, until about nine-thirty, when appointments would begin. Certain appointments were scheduled on a regular basis each week, normally for about two hours each. These involved conferences with his own top White House staff, military and economic advisers, the National Security Council, the Cabinet, the weekly press conference, and legislative leaders. These regular meetings, interspersed with appointments with individuals or groups, and the inevitable interruptions to greet organizations or leaders of specialized groups in the Rose Garden, normally kept the day filled until about five or later in the afternoon. It was then that he would work on speeches, messages to Congress, or other state papers. In this work he punished himself to achieve precision of meaning. He might leave the official office at six, sometimes later. Then he often would have a conference on the second floor with an individual whom he wished to see in an atmosphere more relaxed than existed in the official office in the West Wing. Secretary of State Dulles was a frequent visitor at these informal sessions in the family rooms. Others included American ambassadors just home from abroad, a few personal friends, occasionally a legislative leader, and sometimes the Vice-President.

As often as he could, the President would take off his coat as soon as his guest had departed, put on a paint-smeared smock, and bring out an uncompleted oil on which he would work for half an hour. He nearly always had half a dozen uncompleted portraits, landscapes, and still lifes available; he would work on whichever one suited his mood at the moment. I often sat in that small studio with him, and sometimes painted a bit myself, but we never talked then, for he found relaxation by becoming completely absorbed in the sheer business of applying color to canvas.

At about seven forty-five he would have a drink, usually a weak scotch and water. If the President and Mrs. Eisenhower were not entertaining, they would have dinner on trays in the family rooms upstairs. Then the President would retire either to his bedroom or oval study to work for as much as four hours on a document sent to him in the field of economic policy, welfare, transportation, or national security. If the President and Mrs. Eisenhower were entertaining informally, they would usually take their guests to the theater on the ground floor after dinner to see a motion picture; usually the President would leave within ten minutes and retire to his room for work. When entertaining formally he could not escape. Not until the visiting dignitary and his wife had left could he leave, usually at about eleven o'clock.

As strenuous as I found the Eisenhower schedule to be, I saw later at first hand that President Johnson, then President Nixon, fortunately younger men, had to work even harder.

Today, because of serious intellectual and emotional divisions in our country, the threatening situation in the Middle East, corruption and dishonesty in high places, and a host of other problems, the President's mail has become mountainous. It now requires an army of clerks to open and classify the mail, make a statistical analysis of the contents, refer most letters and telegrams to others for handling, and select the few that seemingly must go to the President personally. It must be amusing to a modern President to realize that President Lincoln received about thirty-five letters a day which he opened and answered himself, and that President Cleveland personally answered the White House telephone! Recently a good friend of mine in New York sought to wire the White House his approval of a presidential decision but was notified that the congestion of messages to the White House was such that it would be forty-eight hours before his telegram could be sent.

In my experience with eight Presidents of the United States I have been impressed by the anxieties and frustrations of six of them in trying to redeem their responsibilities as:

(a) Head of state

(b) Chief Executive

(c) Commander-in-Chief of the armed forces

(d) Leader of a political party

(e) Director of foreign affairs

(f) Moral leader of the nation

(g) Spokesman for the free world

(h) Principal proposer and fighter for legislation

Not all of these duties are specified in the Constitution, which says: "The executive power shall be vested in a president of the United States. . . . The president shall be commander in chief of the army and navy. . . . He shall have power, by and with the advice and consent of the senate, to make treaties, provided two-thirds of the senators present concur . . . shall appoint ambassadors, other public ministers and consuls, judges of the supreme court, and all other officers of the United States, whose appointments are not herein otherwise provided for. . . . He shall from time to time give to the Congress information of the state of the union, and recommend to their consideration such measures as he shall deem necessary. . . . He may, on extraordinary occasions, convene both houses, or either of them . . . *he shall take care that the laws be faithfully executed,** and shall commission all the officers of the United States."

The most important clause in this constitutional prescription is the mandate for the President to take care that the laws enacted by the Congress are faithfully executed. While the President may recommend to the Congress such measures as he deems necessary, the framers

* Emphasis supplied.

516

of the Constitution contemplated that most laws would originate in the legislative branch and then be administered by the President. The authority for the President to be Commander-in-Chief of the army and navy was intended to keep the military forces under civilian control. The responsibility of the President in foreign affairs was limited to making treaties, subject to Senate approval, and the appointment of ambassadors and consuls.

The manifold duties and powers of the President, as they now exist, many of them not foreseen by the framers of the Constitution, have accrued over a period of years, many of them within my lifetime.

The sheer size and complexity of the federal establishment are two causes of this. When I was a youngster the total annual federal appropriation was about five hundred and fifty million dollars. Now, late in 1973, the annual budget is more than a quarter of a trillion dollars, and the end of expanding costs is not in sight. When I witnessed the Abilene flood of 1903—my first memory—no one in my home town was aware of a single federal employee, other than our senators and congressmen. Now more than five and a half million persons (including military personnel) work for the President—more than the population of the United States when George Washington was President—and Abilene and its environs have their quota of these—meat inspectors, a farm agent, a soil conservation agent, a Bureau of Internal Revenue representative, committees of the Agricultural Conservation Service, a Rural Electrification representative, and others, but no rat-control expert, so far as I am aware.

The unprecedented expansion of the central government has been neither capricious nor unplanned. Inexorable changes, domestic and foreign, are the primary causes and in the past half century have forced the presidency to evolve from an impossible position to a preposterous one.

Domestically and to some extent internationally, at the core of change are science and technology, in which developments are so rapid as to confound all but the most sophisticated.

In my youth there was not a single industrial research laboratory in the United States and fundamental research in our universities was in its swaddling clothes. Now our lives are essentially dominated by scientific and technological developments. Ninety per cent of all scientists who ever lived are alive today. Their achievements are monumental. Human knowledge doubles every ten years. In a single year biological and physical scientists alone publish nearly 1,400,000 monographs, technical articles, and books, and much of the new knowledge is put into use almost instantly. Thus eighty per cent of the drugs administered in our hospitals today were unknown fifteen years ago, and half the products of some of our leading industries have been conceived in industrial research laboratories in the past fifteen years. But the most dramatic example is in the field of national security. For thousands of years a weapons system was valid for five hundred years. In the latter part of the nineteenth century a system was good for fifty years. Now major elements of a weapons system are essentially obsolete before they are fully operational.

Science and technology are changing how we work, organize, think, and live. They are profoundly affecting our relations with other free nations, dominating our relations with the center of international Communism, and insistingly posing the critical question of our time: Will expanding knowledge and powerful new instruments lead us to the Golden Age which has eluded man since creation, or to mutual annihilation?

Science, with all its wonders, does not supply the answer. Science tells us what is *possible*, not what is right. Science tells us what we *can* do, not what we *should* do. The answer lies not with scientific man but with social man—with all of us.

Of all technological changes none has had greater impact on our lives than rapid transportation and world-wide instantaneous satellite and cable communication. These have shrunk the earth and brought peoples closer together than ever before. They have enhanced economic interdependence, so much so that the plants in our great industrial empire would cease to belch smoke, and millions would be out of work, if we could not import vital primary commodities from many nations in all the continents, and in payment could not ship to them and others vast quantities of food, fiber, and manufactured goods.

Economic interdependence has made essential solid and dependable political and human relations. But here is the rub: the imperative has seemingly come too soon. It has preceded mental preparation for it. Most of the peoples of the world, despite all our efforts toward correction, still misunderstand the United States—its social structure, its philosophy, its purposes. And our conceptions of others are not much more valid than theirs of us. So decisions, profoundly important decisions, too often are made by us and other nations not on the basis of what *is* but on the basis of what, in prejudice and ignorance, people *think* it is.

Concurrently with these measurable changes, and partly because of them—all within my lifetime—the seeds of a massive and unprecedented human revolution have taken root. This is what has come to be called the revolution in the "Third World" and it will for many years to come confound and haunt us. We are most familiar with the moral conflict between East and West. But in Latin America, where for centuries a few lived with fabulous riches, while oceans of illiterates lived in squalor, there is at this moment the certainty of revolution, peaceful or bloody. Radio and television, modest products of the scientific revolution, have reached the minds of the masses who cannot read but can see and hear. They have therefore come to understand that human degradation is neither universal nor inevitable. After a long sleep, giants of Latin America—and Africa, the Middle East, and Far East, too—are awake, angrily shaking the archaic social structures that have oppressed them. In the blink of an eye, as history is measured, they have all but eliminated imperialism in the free world, thus reversing several hundred years of history. Unfortunately this change in the free world, meriting enthusiastic approval, has been paralleled by the development of a new vicious imperialism in Eastern Europe and the Far East, involving a third of the three and a half billion people who inhabit the earth.

In the United States the scientific and technological revolution, the swelling of population, economic interdependence—both domestically and internationally—have caused us to cast aside isolationism for internationalism, and the concept of individualism for welfarism and dependence on government for nearly every aspect of life. Population growth and efficiency in production have had two significant consequences. When the Constitution was adopted, ninety-five per cent of all our people were engaged in farming; when Abraham Lincoln was President, half of our people were in farming; when I was young the percentage had dropped to twenty-five per cent. Now five per cent of our population of more than two hundred million produces so much that we have had to try to export the surplus, often at a large loss.

Sprawling urbanization is one unhappy consequence of this shift in productive employment. Today, more than seventy per cent of our people are in the metropolitan centers and their suburbs, and the number will surely grow, for despite a declining birth rate our population will reach three hundred million early in the next century. And as urbanization grows, so will the related problems of crime, insufficient tax base, slums, traffic congestion, pollution, depersonalization, to name a few.

We became an industrialized, urbanized, interdependent society almost before we realized. We were suddenly confronted with problems for which we had no solutions and on which an individual citizen seemingly could have no influence. So individuals have organized, and our nation is now the most organized society in the world. Many of these organizations have become pressure groups, some of which, majestically housed in marble structures near the nation's Capitol, are extremely powerful and bring enormous pressures to bear upon the Chief Executive and the Congress. Some of these pressure groups are strong enough to prevent the passage of legislation, as witness the National Rifle Association's long success in killing or watering down gun laws. Others, such as the Teamsters Union, could if they wished literally wreck the economy. Still others, in the industrial-military complex, can nudge the nation toward war.

These problems along with profound world problems must be solved. They can only be solved, however, when men are prepared to cast out prejudice and reason together in mutual understanding and respect. I see little evidence that men have reached that point.

As I struggle with these issues in my own mind, I honestly at times would welcome a return to the isolation, the individualism, the contentment, and certainties of my youth. Of course I know the futility of such passing thoughts. The essence of nostalgia is an awareness that what has been will never be again. So I try to marshal my thoughts and consider things as they are now. It must be obvious to all that the time is here when we should reappraise our domestic policies, programs, priorities, and our posture and methods in the world.

Our domestic and foreign situations are inseparable, but for clarity's sake I view them separately.

Domestically, we are like a nation cut adrift from its moorings. Age-old concepts of morality are collapsing all around us. Individualism yields to collectivism. The work ethic has been eroded. Crime and drug addiction are growing scourges. Economic welfare, no longer determined by the individual or even a single community, is primarily vested in the government. Each pressure group in Washington seeks to gain or preserve benefits for itself but generally opposes benefits for others. Sterile defense expenditures (and overexpenditures) make it difficult for a deficit-financed government adequately to solve the problems we have inherited from our own reckless history.

How foolish and naïve it is to expect the man in the White House, whoever he may be, to solve problems we do not fully understand and cannot agree on. If there was ever a time when critical study, a sober consideration of facts and alternative lines of action, and genuine statesmanship were imperative, it is now. Sheer political partisanship must be subordinated. Re-election to office must not be the criterion of senators, congressmen, and the President. A tremendous leap forward in planning and leadership must be the clarion call of the American people.

The international situation calls for the same dedicated and intelligent leadership. Since World War II four national administrations adhered to the policy of opposing, by force when necessary, the coercive spread of power, and the present Administration modified this policy only slightly. (The change is called the "Nixon Doctrine," though it scarcely merits such an impressive name.) In a strictly moral sense the Truman containment doctrine was right, for all peoples of the earth should have the inalienable right of free choice. But I fear the postwar policy is doomed to failure unless other free nations of the world—hopefully, in time, all nations—join us in every critical situation in the application of this policy. The achievement of a dependable alliance, confederation, or transnational compact is now the most important single obligation upon our statesmen.

We have worked feverishly to achieve better understanding among the world's peoples and governments. We have formed the United Nations and a host of affiliated organizations, set up world organizations for making loans and controlling currency relationships, held as many as six hundred regional and international conferences annually, and burdened the President with streams of visiting dignitaries from every continent. We have fostered freer trade relationships, stationed military forces around the world (NATO forces alone costing seventeen billion dollars a year), become mired in an apparently insoluble problem of imbalances in international payments, increased our foreign representation beyond reason (twenty-five different United States agencies report to our ambassador in Greece, thirty to our ambassador in the United Kingdom), and given generously of our resources to Europe, Greece, Turkey, and the developing nations. In spite of all this, wars and the possibility of new wars, even a world war, continue on our agenda.

With respect to foreign aid, I am persuaded that as we have conceived and practiced it for thirty years it is in most situations little more than a palliative at best, self-defeating at worst. But, given consistent concerted action by all nations and especially by the industrial nations, I can foresee a type of foreign aid, multilaterally financed and administered, that will help the peoples of the less advanced nations gradually improve their well-being and to some degree help lead us to a world of security.

Highest priority, in any reappraisal of our international posture and methods, must in my judgment begin with power. Peace, wherever it exists—in Abilene, Baltimore, the United States, or in the larger world around us—is partly the product of power. No one nation possesses sufficient power to enforce peace, nor would its exercise by a single power, even if possessed in abundance, be acceptable to others. Indeed, it would, as now, exacerbate competitive power. So we must, as I have argued previously, moderate preconceptions about absolute sovereignty and address ourselves to methods by which nations, all believing in mutuality in human relations and the free choice of peoples, may pool their power, or create new power, to enforce global peace. This has been achieved to a limited extent in NATO and to a lesser degree by the United Nations. The need now is to expand the NATO concept, which is transnational rather than supranational, to all free nations and eventually to every country of the world.

This negative approach—for that is obviously what it is—could yield us the time so desperately needed by governments and peoples everywhere to triple efforts to foster education and genuine mutual understanding; to improve health and increase productivity, especially in the developing nations; to develop more enlightened trade, aid, and credit relationships; to do all the multitude of things which must be done to build the positive peace that will give peoples everywhere the assurance of a better life with dignity, justice, and equality. At this moment there is reason to be mildly optimistic about some aspects of this awesome task. Better relations with the Chinese People's Republic and the Soviet Union, arms-reduction talks, and the European security conference are favorable signs.

This is, one statesman has said, the century of the common man. The valid aspirations of the oceans of common peoples of all nationalities, colors, religions, and circumstances can be achieved only in a world of peace. The common peoples of East and West, of the advanced and developing nations, instinctively want to live in a world free of conflict. To permit the people to gain their aspirations, governments can no longer cling to the historic and outmoded strategy of competitive power. Competitive power—a balance of power—has always failed and always will. Adherence to it dangerously postpones acceptance of the modern imperative.

There is a frightening irony at work here. The very scientific and technological revolution that has created the modern imperative—that has provided mankind with the means to a Golden Age of peace and plenty—is at the same time the greatest obstacle to our achieving the great objective.

Unfortunately individual citizens find it increasingly difficult to understand and cope with the incredibly complex problems that onrushing change creates. How can the individual be expected to understand the important facts, circumstances, and complexities of such vital issues as the disarray of the Atlantic Alliance, the details of the first agreements emanating from the SALT talks, the possibilities of increasing trade with the Soviet Union, the delicate problem of developing relations with Communist China without diminishing chances of better relations with the Soviet Union, the conflicts caused by divided nations, the population explosion and its consequences, the dangers of catastrophic war born of sheer religious differences, air pollution, imbalances in international payments, civil rights, the depersonalization of automation, crime, and the divisive bitterness of two internal societies, one white, one black?

We have no real precedents for dealing with these new and profound forces.

The modern situation can easily lead to apathy and a sense of despair. Several years ago I wrote: "There is a dangerous myth abroad in this land that the ordinary citizen can do nothing to influence the destiny of his country and the world. I have not decided whether this is a rationalization or an epitaph."[22]

Now I see that there is some substance to that myth. Perhaps the *ordinary* citizen is a political anachronism in this perilous and complicated age. Perhaps the hope of the future lies in our ability to produce more *extraordinary* citizens, a new breed of Americans who will devote as much time and energy to being broad-gauged, thoughtful, analytical citizens as they do to being good physicists or good doctors or good engineers.

Certainly in the Congress and in the presidency we need extraordinary citizens, with outstanding leadership ability, but we also need to create the conditions that will permit their wisdom to flourish and achieve constructive results.

The growth of presidential power has been a direct consequence of rapid and sometimes thoughtless national development, growing complexity of issues, and exacting domestic and international interdependence. So the duties of the President, so succinctly set forth in the Constitution, now seem almost naïve, for the responsibilities have become awesome, beyond the capacity of a single individual. They may be categorized, as I have said, under eight headings:

Head of State: This once indicated the purely ceremonial duties of the President, similar to those of the Queen of England, the Governor-General of Canada, or the President of the Party-governmental complex of the Soviet Union. To demonstrate the common touch which seemingly is expected in a democratic society, the President must greet hundreds of groups for no substantial reason; give large and tiresome dinners for members of the Supreme Court, the diplomatic corps, selected members of the Congress, and of course for all visiting dignitaries. He must telephone each group of astronauts as they complete their amazing flights, invite them to dinner, and confer medals upon them. Cutting ribbons to open a new bridge, issuing proclamations to designate weeks for health drives, and lighting the annual Christmas tree near the Washington Monument in bitter cold weather are traditional requirements.

The duties as head of state, however, are now a blend of ceremony and serious business. We are one of the few developed nations in the world that combines in one leader the duties of head of state and Chief Executive. We have no one in world protocol who ranks with a prime minister. So the President must personally be host not only to kings, queens, and presidents but also to prime ministers who come to the United States in increasing numbers. It is not unusual for the President to be burdened for one, two, or three months each year with this high duty. Official negotiations involved in these meetings—whether they be here or abroad—are usually critical, as they were with Chancellor Adenauer, President de Gaulle, Prime Minister Macmillan, President Lopez Mateos, and dozens of others in the Eisenhower administration and as they were with Chairman Brezhnev and Chairman Mao and Prime Minister Chou En-lai in the Nixon administration. For these sessions the President must be completely informed, alert, skillful and persuasive in negotiating, and always poised and fresh-looking, even when he is desperately tired.

As head of state the President has been referred to as "elected king" and as a "monarch." These designations are inaccurate, unless the President withdraws and stands aloof from the responsibilities we expect him to fulfill. But even as ceremonial head of American affairs the duties are so prescribed in protocol and tradition that they are terribly tiring to the President and the First Lady.

A ceremonial duty to which I object is the practice of the President's traveling about the country, making speeches, and shaking hands with hundreds in the audience as a means of demonstrating his democratic credentials. This not only sets his nerves on edge and saps his physical strength but, much more important, it subjects the President to possible assassination.

From President Lincoln to President Nixon, every third President has been assassinated or has been the target of an assassin. President Truman escaped the bullets of the assassins, as did candidate Franklin Roosevelt, but all Presidents and candidates are constantly in danger when they expose themselves to large crowds, as Governor George Wallace can testify. Every society has criminogenic individuals, and we have our share. In some countries presidents have been shot for political reasons—to cause a government to fall as in the Dominican Republic. In the United States there has been no such pragmatic political motivation for assassination or attempts at assassinations; obviously, if a

President is killed it does not overthrow the government or change government policy to any measurable degree. Assassins in our history have been deranged individuals rather than political opportunists. Our experience is sufficiently sobering, however, that we should change tradition. There are other ways to demonstrate adherence to democracy, such as being sensitive to public opinion, working to change laws to meet changing conditions, keeping the American people adequately and accurately informed, working constantly and openly with the people's elected representatives in Congress, and upholding the dignity and credibility of the presidential office.

Chief Executive: In this capacity the presidential duties are endless. Upon taking office, he must appoint several thousand officers who have important policy and program duties and they must carry out their responsibilities for the Chief Executive through a civilian army of permanent federal employees, many of whom may not be in sympathy with the President's policies. While the spoils system of the past surely was filled with shortcomings, cronyism, and corruption, the entrenched, often unresponsive civil service can often be as bad in fostering bureaucracy, insensitivity, and mediocrity. A rule of many civil servants is never to "rock the boat," for if one adheres to routine no one will notice. But no matter where a failure or accident in the executive branch of the government may occur, the President personally is held responsible by the people. The U-2 incident is a significant example, the unhappy mistake of the Secretary of the Air Force in handling a private matter on official stationery is a moderate one (it caused his dismissal), and the failure of the President's personal assistant to clear a political appointment with the appropriate party leaders is a minor one.

If the President accepts the advice of the Attorney General regarding an appointment to the Supreme Court, and a Senate committee finds that the candidate is unfit for the office—half his decisions having been reversed by a higher court—the President is blamed for nominating an unsuitable person. The President is praised or severely criticized for successes or failures in fighting crime, maintaining high employment, checking inflation, controlling riots, preventing pollution, promoting research, more help for the aged, and on and on, ad infinitum.

Consider how frustrating it is to a President who makes an important decision in the field of civil rights only to find that the vast and faceless bureaucracy does not carry out his decision. One agency may do its best, another may procrastinate and debate, and still another may do nothing.

Only the President can grant paroles or reprieves in cases involving federal laws, such as security acts. This is sometimes a tedious and worrisome task. However the President decides a particular case, he will be criticized, for normally the appeal would not have been placed before him unless it was controversial, supported by a pressure group, subject to possible alleviating action, and widely publicized.

Each President has his own method of trying to redeem his all but impossible task as Chief Executive. As I have said, President Eisenhower regularly used the Cabinet, the National Security Council, the Operations Coordinating Board, and individual conferences with department and agency heads as his main method of redeeming his responsibility in this area. Presidents Kennedy, Johnson, and Nixon added more and more personnel to the Executive Office of the President, an office which encompasses the Office of Management and Budget, the Council of Economic Advisers, many other presidential commissions and agencies, and a small army of counselors and personal assistants. Thus, of the 2,236 persons in the Executive Office, nearly 100 work for the President's personal assistant on foreign and security affairs, the specialists on the staff duplicating comparable personnel in several departments, especially the Department of State. Others work for his assistant who seeks to co-ordinate domestic policies and programs. Administrative direction by the palace guard is inefficient, demeaning to Cabinet members and agency heads, and tainted with undue efforts to protect or enhance the reputation of the "Chief." Some of this became apparent in the Watergate investigation of the key White House aides serving President Nixon.

Sheer size of the executive branch has become a major problem for the President in faithfully executing the laws as required by the Constitution. Agricultural programs until this year required an appropriation ten times as large as the total cost of all three branches of the federal government when I was a youngster. The Secretary of Agriculture, the Under Secretary, several Assistant Secretaries, and a score of bureau chiefs cannot overcome all the program conflicts in this one department, any more than I could report significant success when I was given the specific duty in the late thirties and early forties to eliminate the conflicts that were making the President and Congress uneasy. The Secretary of Defense, mindful of the need to economize in view of the public's resentment of an eighty-billion-dollar defense budget, cannot prevent enormous waste and extravagance, even in Vietnam, as was amply demonstrated during the war in Southeast Asia. There is a contagion to extravagance in large departments. If one two-star general is given use of a jet plane, a special chauffeur-driven car presumably for official use only, and a handsome and expensive intercommunication system to his subordinates, within a month all major generals have the same prerogatives. If public criticism develops, the President is the target.

When the President makes a decision that affects many agencies, he must wonder to what extent his order will be obeyed. This is especially frustrating in foreign affairs. With the approval of the Secretary of State, I once proposed to the President a program for Bolivia which I thought would enable that country to become self-sufficient in food production; co-operation by the State Department, what is now called the Agency for International Development, the Development Loan Fund, the Export-Import Bank, and the International Bank was required. The President approved. Little happened. Bolivia is still a deficit country in food and when the price of tin ore declines on the world market great numbers of persons, always on the verge of starvation, actually die.

Commander-in-Chief: The President's responsibility as Commander-in-Chief of the armed forces is arduous in peacetime, unbelievably demanding and exhausting in wartime, as Lincoln, Franklin Roosevelt, and Johnson learned. The President and no one else is held responsible by the nation for military preparedness so that the nation can meet any situation affecting our national interest and in which our armed forces might be engaged. The Secretary of Defense, the Joint Chiefs of Staff, and the National Security Council may give advice, but the President must make final decisions. These decisions must take into account not only sheer military needs but their cost in relation to other high-priority requirements.

In war the President is exclusively responsible for handling the political phases of the conflict, such as proclaiming the goal of unconditional surrender in World War II and deciding upon the division and governance of Germany after the war; he must approve major strategies and often even logistical and tactical ones. All Presidents have been involved in the peacetime duties of the Commander-in-Chief. In this century Presidents Wilson, Roosevelt, Truman, Kennedy, Johnson, and Nixon have had to meet the burdensome responsibility of making fateful decisions regarding the strategic and tactical use of armed might; obviously it was President Johnson who made the final decision to escalate the war in Vietnam and to bomb North Vietnam, and it was President Nixon who personally decided to attack the so-called sanctuaries in Cambodia and to continue to participate in the Cambodian war after the cease-fire agreement for Vietnam was signed.

The President's duty as Commander-in-Chief is not separable from his responsibility for maintaining a healthy economy with a minimum of inflation, and certainly it is not separable from his duties as principal authority, save for restrictions placed upon him by the Congress, for foreign policy decisions.

Under the war powers of the President, he can create new agencies, promote or demote military leaders, assume control of industries, break strikes, and do many other things which in peacetime would be unconstitutional. Thus, in World War II, when President Roosevelt by executive order decreed that Japanese Americans should be removed from the Pacific coast and that I, as head of the War Relocation Authority, could in fact move 120,000 persons, set up evacuee camps, determine wages to be paid, establish courts and schools, and make the evacuee camps largely self-governing, he was acting under his war powers, subsequently upheld by the Supreme Court.

It is frightening to contemplate the possibility of atomic war, but if such a horrible thing ever happened the President of the United States under the war powers would have to take control of essentially every activity in the United States. He would be a dictator with more power than that ever assumed by a dictator of a Latin American nation and equal to that of Mao and Brezhnev.

Head of a Political Party: His duties in this area are not easily categorized. Franklin Roosevelt was the master in political management and manipulation, especially in his first two terms when James Farley was chairman of the Democratic Committee. He solidified a coalition of labor, blacks, the underprivileged, and the urban liberals. The task of the President is to co-operate with party leaders, help improve the party, persuade intelligent and personable individuals to run for state and federal offices, yet, while carrying out this partisan chore, rise above the party itself, seek to unite the people of the United States, and foster legislation that benefits not only the party but the people generally. In a Jackson Day Dinner speech on January 8, 1940, Roosevelt said, "But the future lies with those wise political leaders who realize that the great public is more interested in government than in politics."

The Vietnam War made a shambles of party loyalty. Some of President Johnson's bitterest critics were Democrats—Eugene McCarthy, McGovern, Fulbright, and others. For a different reason President Eisenhower, in peacetime, had great difficulty with Republican leaders in the Congress during his first two years in the White House. Many believe that it is not possible to separate party leadership from the presidency. I do not agree. The practice began with Jefferson and since then some Presidents have all but ignored the duty while others have considered it a high and essential responsibility. My view is that the President, once he is elected, is responsible to all the people, not just the members of his party. Statesmanship requires that he serve all interests in an unbiased, non-partisan way. A single six-year term for the President would foster this impartiality. Some other prominent official might better be the active leader of the party. Most scholars in the field of political science will not agree with me, for they see political party leadership as a means of a President's jamming his program through the Congress. My view is that the President's real power comes from the people.

Director of Foreign Relations: Dr. Francis O. Wilcox, dean emeritus of The Johns Hopkins School of Advanced International Studies, former Assistant Secretary of State and former chief of staff of the Senate Foreign Relations Committee, recently wrote[40] that some forty agencies of the United States have something to do with the foreign policy of our country. So the President, as "the sole organ of the nation in external relations and its sole representative with foreign nations," according to Chief Justice John Marshall, cannot deal only with the State Department. If trade with the Soviet Union is on the agenda he must work with the State, Treasury, Defense, Justice, Commerce, Transportation, Agriculture, and other departments, and perhaps directly with the Export-Import Bank and indirectly with the International Bank. In our modern world foreign and security affairs are inseparable. So on almost any problem that arises in this area the President must work, hopefully through the National Security Council, with the Departments of State and Defense, the CIA, the United States Information Agency, the Atomic Energy Commission, and often with the Departments of Treasury, Agriculture, Labor, Commerce, the Agency for International Development, and others.

He must appoint all ambassadors and, through the Secretary of State and a multitude of ambassadors in all parts of the world, carry on consultations on a multitude of critical subjects. On any one day as many as a thousand or more classified telecommunications go from the State Department to ambassadors in the field and all must be harmonious with major decisions of the President. If an error is made in foreign affairs the President is held responsible.

The Constitution places important restrictions on the President in foreign relations. The Senate must approve treaties by a two-thirds vote. Congress must provide essential funds, and approve the appointment of major foreign service personnel. Theoretically only the Congress can declare war—save by a delegated authority as in the Tonkin Gulf Resolution and now by a curious legislative enactment which, seeking to curb the President's power, actually acknowledges his right to engage in war for sixty days, sometimes ninety days, without congressional approval. In recent years there have been other efforts by the Congress either by separate legislation or riders to place legislative restrictions in foreign affairs upon him. This requires the President personally to spend many hours each month with legislative leaders; it also makes it necessary for him to send the Secretary of State and often Under and Assistant Secretaries and even country-desk heads to deal with congressional committees on specific problems.

Moral Leader of the Nation: When Franklin Roosevelt said that the President's responsibility for moral leadership transcended his other duties, his model might well have been Thomas Jefferson, who in the words of Henry Steele Commager was a "representative figure of the American Enlightenment, faithfully reflecting its virtues, its optimisms, its faiths, its limitations." Clinton Rossiter called the President the "Voice of the people . . . moral spokesman for all. . . . [He] must be the symbol of our sovereignty, continuity, and grandeur."

The President's life and his family's must be exemplary. They must personify the idealism, selflessness, and noble purposes of the nation.

What they do must not only *be* morally and legally right; it must *appear* to be right to the American people.

When the presidential family attends church or holds ecumenical services in the Gold Room of the White House, it is not showmanship. It is a recognition that the cardinal concepts of a democratic society are drawn from the Judeo-Christian imperatives of human dignity, mutuality in human relations, and consecrated intelligence. Democracy cannot be explained or justified in any other way. In view of the pluralistic nature of society, comprised of individuals of varied talents, faiths, national origins, colors, and abilities in leadership and followership, one could argue in sheer logic that a benevolent dictatorship would function better in eradicating the evils of society; but this would violate the fundamental belief in the sonship of man, which compels us to maintain institutions and methods that protect above all the dignity and rights of each individual citizen.

Most aspects of life are competitive. The President, more than any other individual, group, or association, is in the supreme position to be the unifying force in this competitive milieu. This requires that he be of sterling character, integrity, and credibility. He must be poised, reassuring, and forthright in dealing with all situations. He must keep the people truthfully informed in detail on current problems, negotiations, and potential developments. The people must believe in him. They must trust him. If they do, they will listen to him when he offers creative compromises to apparently insoluble conflicts.

Presidents Washington, Jefferson, Lincoln (for the North), Franklin Roosevelt, Eisenhower, and, I think, Kennedy reached the minds and hearts of the people, even those who disagreed with some of their policies and programs. Each was a unifying force. Each fostered pride in the presidency itself, in the government, and in the nation and its purposes. They thus focused the minds of the people on issues, opportunities, and goals greater than their individual or group competitive, selfish interests.

If this quality in the President is lacking, debilitating divisions develop, respect for and faith in government decline, many begin to question the basic concepts on which our society is built, and a feeling of insecurity encompasses the land.

Moral leadership is not exercised in isolation. It permeates everything the President says and does in all his roles.

While all the manifold duties of the President make it necessary for him to be intimately in touch with changing views and conditions, that of moral leadership especially requires this. He cannot unify unless he knows the cause of intellectual divisions, the depth of bitterness. It is, then, the responsibility of all who work closely with the President to keep him intimately aware of major differences in public thought, of alternatives they see to proposals he is making. The President can read newspapers, magazines, commentaries, and books, but there is no substitute for his keeping regularly and personally in touch with elected leaders who understand the views of their constituents. His associates should not shield him from elective leaders, especially those who disagree with the President, for it is from them he can learn most and reevaluate decisions developed in isolation.

In the Nixon administration the White House staff became notorious for denying leading but dissenting senators and representatives, even of his own party, access to the oval office. The black list or enemy list was an ominous inducement to leadership failure. It injured his influence in the Congress, and it cost him dearly in his ability to symbolize to all the people the concern the President must have for the views of the masses. For many reasons the majesty of the presidency reached a low ebb, and at the heart of this disaster was the protective wall that surrounded and shielded him from the currents of American thought.

The power of the presidency resides not primarily in the Constitution or laws or tradition but in the people—in their support of his decisions, in their faith in him. The Constitution, laws, and tradition only give the President authority to transform popular will into power employed for creative action.

Spokesman for the Free World: The task of the President as spokesman for the free world is a consequence of our having two great modern power centers—the United States and the Soviet Union. As leader of the great power of the West he cannot escape this role. It requires constant collaboration with the leaders of the United Kingdom, France, Germany, and Japan at the minimum, but often also with all NATO powers (which includes Canada) and with the members of the Organization of American States, SEATO, and CENTO. These negotiations may be by letter, coded telegram, telephone, or face-to-face discussions. Personal negotiation has become the dominant method.

President Eisenhower devoted two months in one year to negotiations with other heads of state and premiers, President Kennedy frantically met with numerous Western leaders in his first seven months in office, prior to conferring with Khrushchev in Vienna, and President Nixon found it desirable, after minimum discussions with our allies, to go personally to China and the Soviet Union in 1972. Most of these direct negotiations, however, take place in Washington where, sometimes as often as once a week, the head of a foreign government comes for serious discussions.

As spokesman for the free world the President has enormous power. His role is much more than that of rhetorician. Franklin Roosevelt's Four Freedoms speech did much to shape the course of World War II, which involved numerous free nations, and his insistence upon unconditional surrender of the Axis powers, a declaration in which he persuaded Churchill to join, unquestionably prolonged the war. When England, France, and Israel attacked Egypt in 1956, the United States had no authority, save through the use of its military forces, to stop the conflict, but the voice of President Eisenhower did just that; mindful of our commitment to the United Nations Charter, he was convinced that we had to live up to its principles. The ability of the President to be spokesman rests, of course, not only upon the superior power of the United States but upon the President's keeping constantly in touch with other free world leaders. When he forgets this, as Kennedy did in negotiating with Macmillan on a multilateral atomic force for NATO, the President's voice is muted, and tragedy can follow, as exemplified by De Gaulle's intransigence thereafter.

Proposer of Legislation: The President's duty as proposer of legislation and subsequently of approving or vetoing acts of Congress is inseparable from all his other tasks from Chief Executive and principal diplomat to Commander-in-Chief and head of a political party. Historically most legislation originated in the Congress, as did the McNary-Haugen bills in the Coolidge administration, but as problems became more complex and numerous, a high percentage of legislation considered by the House and Senate originated with the President. This became especially evident in the Woodrow Wilson administration and became the rule under Franklin Roosevelt and later Presidents. In January 1955, President Eisenhower took the initiative in asking Congress for higher salaries in the federal government, lower tariffs, flexible farm

534

price supports to replace the rigid supports established during World War II, changes in the Taft-Hartley Act, reducing the voting age to eighteen, increased public housing, higher minimum wages, lower draft calls, increased aid to medical schools, an expanded program of health insurance, assistance for public schools, and special aid to low-income farmers.

A single proposal to the Congress may have been in preparation for a year or more. Certainly each one requires the President to spend many hours in studying documents, consulting with others, and writing a message to the Congress or revising, often rewriting, a message proposed by one of his staff.

In each session of the Congress the President must also study with care, again with the help of personal assistants, members of the Cabinet, and the Legislative Clearance Division of the Office of Management and Budget, a horde of important bills, some of which, such as a massive "pork barrel bill," ought never to have been considered in the legislative branch of the government, passed, and sent to the President. The President must build, with the help of the Director of Management and Budget, the immense annual budget, containing both administrative and trust fund estimates, submit it to the Congress, and then call upon an army of aides to defend each part of it before committees of the Congress. On the basis of a document tentatively prepared for him by the Council of Economic Advisers, he must study, revise, and master what it is he wishes to report to the Congress in the field of domestic and foreign economic development, wages, prices, inflation, and potential employment, production, and economic trends.

Early in his second term President Cleveland, operating scrupulously within the presidential powers set forth in the Constitution, said: "I am suffering many perplexities and troubles and this term of the presidency has cost me so much health and vigor that I have sometimes doubted if I could carry the burden to the end."

Every President since must have read that with amusement but with a touch of envy. For, as I have pointed out, in most of these administrations and with increasing relevance, the imperative, inescapable, and undelegable responsibilities of the President of the United States have to do with war or peace, prosperity or depression, moral leadership, and new social programs or changes in the existing programs to meet the rapidly changing conditions of the American and world society. These transcendent duties involve all eight of the President's functions I have briefly described.

Changes, normally embroiled in controversy, require the President to study so many documents that eyesight is temporarily strained; Theodore Sorensen in a lecture at Columbia University said that all modern Presidents have complained about their "reading pile," and few have been able to cope with it. They make it necessary for the President to confer with numerous officials of the executive establishment, hold long conferences with legislative leaders (preferably of both major parties), *and still have time for quiet reflection, careful consideration of alternatives, and finally making sound decisions.* Thereafter, with regard to each serious situation or decision, he normally must hold a press conference and probably speak to the nation by radio and television. Hopefully, it will become the practice for the President to appear regularly before the Congress to discuss matters of high importance.

At various points in this book I have suggested that:

●improvements in the selection of delegates to national conventions and radical reforms of the conventions themselves would likely lead to highly qualified persons of experience, knowledge, judgment, and integrity becoming candidates of the major parties for the highest office in the United States;

●a single term of six years for the President and limited terms for representatives and senators would probably induce these officials to be motivated largely by national needs rather than by partisan advantage and the inevitable desire to be re-elected; these changes might, probably should, transfer the duties of head of a political party from the President to a member of the Senate, the chairman of a national committee, or to some other individual;

●presidential commissions can become a useful method for impartial analysis and planning with respect to complex problems, provided we adopt a system similar to the royal commission-white paper legal requirement in Great Britain, thus requiring the President to send commission reports with his own recommendations to the Congress within a stated period of time;

●elimination of private relief and private immigration bills—a nuisance to the Congress and the President—by assigning responsibility in these areas to the Court of Claims and an administrative court in the Immigration Service—would yield some improvement in congressional action and save the President considerable time;

●a sharp reduction in the foreign service, especially in the number of non-State Department personnel stationed in foreign countries, would improve the quality of the daily conduct of foreign affairs, probably would induce better-qualified persons to serve as ambassadors, and would improve the President's ability to redeem his constitutional duty in this vast area;

●the development of transnational power to enforce peace—a negative approach to the problem—would yield the time needed to build the elements of a positive peace, a step probably not unwelcome in the Congress but requiring long negotiations with other nations;

●line-veto authority for the President to disapprove unrelated riders on legislation the President is now compelled to approve would restore the President's constitutional authority in approving or vetoing bills and would save him time and anguish;

●Congress must reassert its primacy in appropriations matters by adopting in each session a resolution establishing a predetermined ceiling on total appropriations and determining priorities in making reductions if the ceiling is broken, the final act of priorities carrying a mandate that the President cannot impound funds;

●the President should have permanent, broader authority to make essential organizational changes in the executive establishment, subject to veto by the Congress by a constitutional majority vote of both houses;

●the Office of Management and Budget should become the Office of Executive Management, the purpose being to have the many responsibilities of the office, from organizational planning and legislative clearance to personnel management and investigations, become coordinate with, not dominated by, the budget function—a modest change, largely of psychological though also of substantive importance;

●high priority in all foreign affairs should be to achieve an international flow of information among all nations and peoples, free of censorship, quotas, and other restrictions, thus making possible a substantial reduction in direct government and governmentally financed information activities, and enhancing the probability of better co-operation between nations and of détente between Eastern and Western powers; and

●legislation should be enacted to transfer all mandated responsibilities now vested in subordinate officials to Cabinet members and heads of independent agencies, thus placing responsibility on those with whom the President deals.

These changes in the Constitution, in laws, and in procedures and practices would constitute steps forward. But they would not, in my judgment, deal adequately with the present crisis. Our task is not only to develop laws, constitutional amendments, and procedures that maximize the probability of having talented leaders occupy all legislative and executive positions, and that relieve the President of lesser duties, including much trivial activity, without in any way decreasing his responsibility for effective government and moral leadership. We must go still further. So, finally, I propose a change that would eliminate what we now sarcastically call "the palace guard," would enhance the prestige and responsibility of Cabinet members, and would improve relations between the executive and legislative branches of government. This final change will seem radical to many and will surely elicit expert disapproval from as many citizens as now seemingly know the answers to the problems that have baffled the rest of us. I am proposing the creation of two additional Vice-Presidents.

CHAPTER 28

We must face the fact that the burdens of the presidency have become so enormous that no man can redeem them. The power and responsibility of the President would not be diminished through wise delegation.

PRESIDENT HERBERT HOOVER, after heading two special presidential commissions that analyzed the structure and functioning of the executive branch of government, recommended to the Senate the creation of an Administrative Vice-President in the White House complex. President Eisenhower at the end of eight years of experience suggested to the Congress that there should be created a supra-Cabinet post: First Secretary of Government (for Foreign Affairs).

I am convinced that two supra-Cabinet positions are needed, and needed at once. These should be Executive Vice-Presidents, and each should be occupied by an outstanding person appointed by the President, subject to Senate confirmation, *and each should be removable by the President.* These positions can be established by constitutional amendment, and their incumbents would relieve the President of many of his ministerial, executive, planning, and co-ordinating duties—*at his pleasure.* I feel certain that this can be accomplished without making the President assume the role of monarch and without relieving him of his final responsibility for domestic and foreign affairs.

One of the Executive Vice-Presidents should deal with domestic matters and the other with international affairs, both under the general direction of and in close collaboration with the President. They should rank next to the President in the executive branch and in world protocol should be of the level of prime ministers. I prefer the titles Executive Vice-President for Domestic Affairs and Executive Vice-President for International Affairs, but among friends with whom I have discussed this proposal the titles seem to be confusing. Why cannot the elected Vice-President occupy one of these positions? they ask. Would one of the appointed persons succeed to the presidency in the event of the incapacity or death of the President?

The elected Vice-President is not a member of the executive branch. The Constitution, in addition to indicating the method of his election, provides in the Twenty-fifth Amendment only that "In case of removal of the President from office or of his death or resignation, the Vice President shall become President." It then provides that, in the event the President specifies or "the Vice President and a majority of either the principal officers of the executive departments or of such body as Congress may by law provide" indicate to the Senate and House of Representatives by written declaration that the President is unable to discharge the powers and duties of his office, "the Vice President shall immediately assume the powers and duties of the office as *Acting President*." The amendment spells out in detail how a determination shall be made in the event that the President seems able to resume his responsibilities.

The provision that the Vice-President should succeed the President in office, either as President or Acting President, should not be changed, for he is the only individual, other than the Chief Executive, who is elected by the eligible voters of the United States. Obviously the appointed Executive Vice-Presidents, if such should be their titles, would not be in the line of succession, following the elected Vice-President, unless by legislation it should be so ordered, and it is highly unlikely that this would occur.

Several cogent reasons dictate that the elected Vice-President should not occupy either of the new positions I have suggested. He is not, as I have said, a member of the executive establishment. Even though he normally is suggested to a convention by the presidential nominee as a running mate, there is no guarantee that he will be in agreement with the President; there is no legal bar to his openly disagreeing with the President. Vice-Presidents have often disagreed with Chief Executives. Vice-President Dawes frequently and openly advocated the passage of legislation which President Coolidge denounced and vetoed. Most important of all, the President cannot discharge the elected Vice-President. This point is critical. In any organization delegation of authority is workable only if the chief executive has absolute confidence in the individual to whom he delegates some of his own duties, and this confidence exists only if there is mutual trust, a shared philosophy, and a recognition by the subordinate that final authority always rests with the chief; should directives of the President be unacceptable to the appointed Executive Vice-President, and he felt that he could not loyally do what was expected of him, he would have to resign or be removed by the President.

The elected Vice-President presides over the Senate when he so chooses, and in the event of a tie vote he may cast the deciding vote. He may also, if he opts to do so, accept special assignments from the President, but he is not required to do this. Presidents Eisenhower and Johnson assigned special duties to their Vice-Presidents, who carried out the assignments faithfully.

I do not wish to obscure the principal issue by quibbling about titles. More than semantics are involved, however. My reason for preferring the title Executive Vice-President is that it would be recognized globally as implying great responsibility and would enhance the chances of the officer's being ranked with prime ministers, which is important, especially for the Executive Vice-President for International Affairs.

The title First Secretary of the Government, as proposed by President Eisenhower, might be acceptable if there were only one such post. President Hoover's suggestion, "Administrative Vice-President," does not appeal to me, for it implies that the occupant of the post would not have policy, planning, and related responsibilities; the title usually encompasses, as in the United Nations, budgetary, accounting, personnel, physical development, and similar activities.

President Nixon, cognizant of the need for the type of assistance I propose, made two efforts to find a solution. The second of these never became fully operative. He directed that the Secretary of the Treasury become essentially a presidential co-ordinator of economic planning and policy, the Secretary of Agriculture the co-ordinator of plans, policies, and programs in the field of natural resources, the Secretary of Health, Education and Welfare to have similar responsibilities for human resources, and the Secretary of Housing and Urban Development to have these tasks for community development. This arrangement could not function effectively for two principal reasons. Each Cabinet member has a full-time task in working with the President in his single field of competence, administering the affairs of his own department, and testifying frequently, often for many days at a time, before committees of the Congress. The help the President needs is constant and not schedulable. The one to whom he delegates high authority must be a few steps from the oval office. Moreover, co-ordination in policy, planning, and progress development by one Cabinet member with others of equal rank is not the best arrangement one can devise; it becomes planning and co-ordination by committee rather than by higher-ranking leadership by delegation from the President.

The earlier and continuing effort made by the President involved his assigning authority for policy, planning, and co-ordination in domestic and international affairs to two counselors to the President. The two tasks are very different and therefore require separate explanation.

By Reorganization Plan No. 2, on March 12, 1970, President Nixon created a Cabinet-level Domestic Council, as a counterpart of the Security Council, with the President as chairman and a counselor to the President as executive director. Appointed as members of the council were the Vice-President, nine members of the Cabinet, two other counselors to the President, and the director of the Office of Management and Budget. The function of the Domestic Council included assessing national needs and defining goals, identifying alternative ways of achieving the goals, providing rapid responses to the President's need for policy guidance on pressing domestic issues, setting national priorities for the allocation of available resources, and maintaining a continuous review of the conduct of ongoing programs and proposing changes as needed. The council established a series of ad hoc project committees to deal with specific program areas and problems.

Patently, if the President personally served as chairman of all meetings of the council, this system would work, but the task is so continuous that his other pressing duties cannot possibly permit him to preside very often. So the major responsibility for the functioning of the council fell on the executive director, a counselor to the President, who ranks below all members of the council save the director of the Office of Management and Budget.

One must understand the rigid pecking order in Washington to comprehend the significance of this. An assistant or counselor to the

President cannot command the presence of Cabinet members. Pride, prestige, protocol—all forbid it. Hence much of the work done by the Domestic Council, when the President does not personally preside, especially when conferences are required, must be conducted either by the White House staff (the palace guard) or with assistant secretaries of departments and even assistants to Cabinet members. Conclusions reached may or may not be in harmony with the judgments of the relevant Cabinet members. Yet the Cabinet must, in my judgment, remain the President's principal advisory body. It would cause untold confusion and disarray in the executive branch if important policy and program decisions were approved by the President over the opposition of those who must carry out the decisions.

A further difficulty with this arrangement is that the President cannot delegate any of his own constitutional or legal duties to a counselor, but such delegation is imperative if the President's task is to be made viable.

If, however, the President had an associate with the title and legal status of Executive Vice-President for Domestic Affairs, that officer could become Deputy Chairman of the Domestic Council. His supra-Cabinet status would enable him to deal in conference or by other methods directly with department and agency heads and conclusions reached normally would not be challenged, save perhaps by the President himself, when recommendations were submitted to him. The Executive Vice-President for Domestic Affairs could not only supervise all the activities designed to meet the responsibilities set forth in Reorganization Plan No. 2 and keep the President informed of evolving thinking and potential policies and programs, but the President could delegate to him some of the final decisions which now by constitutional provision and law must be made by the President himself.

This would require a constitutional amendment. The amendment should establish in the White House the position of Executive Vice-President for Domestic Affairs, to be filled by presidential appointment subject to Senate confirmation, and provide that the President may delegate to him decision-authority as specified by congressional enactment or reorganization order, subject of course to veto by the Congress. The Congress would not object to the President's delegating to this officer decision making on manifold problems of interagency coordination, for this is delegable by the President now. The point is important, however. Some sixty-five departments, agencies, boards, and commissions report directly to the President. Conflicts among them are constantly arising. The need for effective help is self-evident. A problem may deal with transportation, involving consultations with the Departments of Transportation and Commerce, the Post Office, the Civil Aeronautics Board, and the Maritime Commission. A problem in water conservation and development may require co-ordination between the Departments of Agriculture, Interior, Army, and the Office of Management and Budget. Planning for a public works program to reduce unemployment may involve ten or more agencies. Preparing for the President the best thought of the departments and agencies on domestic economic affairs would involve the Office of Management and Budget, the Council of Economic Advisers, the Departments of Defense, Commerce, Treasury, Transportation, Agriculture, and Labor. In most of these tasks unanimity of judgment would usually be achieved. If conflicts persisted the President's decision would have to be obtained.

An Executive Vice-President for Domestic Affairs, to retain the confidence of the President, would keep the Chief Executive informed of major decisions being reached.

Delegations of a different character by the President to the Executive Vice-President for Domestic Affairs would be possible, and I would expect them to be made. I have pointed out that existing law permits the President to delegate legislatively mandated duties to Cabinet members if individual laws do not forbid this. He cannot delegate to a Cabinet member, however, a decision which affects several, perhaps numerous, departments and agencies. He could, however, authorize the Executive Vice-President for Domestic Affairs to make final decisions, for example, in cases dealing with routes to be followed by American air carriers abroad, a problem that involves the State Department, the Civil Aeronautics Board, the Defense Department, the Department of Commerce, the Post Office Authority, and sometimes other agencies. A single case in this area reaches the White House in a document that may run to four hundred pages or more. I once studied all decisions of this type made by President Truman and found that he reversed about half the time the recommendations of the Civil Aeronautics Board, which held the essential hearings and made the initial findings, and I concluded that the President was right. Evidence from other departments, such as the Department of Commerce, which then had to pay subsidies to the airlines if competitive flights made profits impossible, or the Post Office Department, which objected because of problems created in the distribution of air mail to foreign countries, or the State Department, which had to negotiate agreements with foreign countries, showed that the Civil Aeronautics Board had been wrong. This particular task, while assigned to the Executive Vice-President for Domestic Affairs, would obviously call for co-operation with the Executive Vice-President for International Affairs.

When the presidential study commission on an Isthmian sea-level canal, on which I served, reported to President Nixon in 1970 it placed before him a problem that involves the State, Defense, Transportation, Treasury, and Justice departments, the Panama Canal Company, and other agencies. The commission had worked for five years in arriving at its recommendations and its warning that the President would have to decide in about 1975 what he wished to do about the Canal problem. If the President personally held the conferences necessary at the White House level to arrive at a sound judgment, I estimate that he would hold as many as a dozen three-hour conferences with the appropriate federal officials of the executive establishment and with numerous members of the Congress. On the other hand, he could depend upon the Executive Vice-President for Domestic Affairs, with occasional consultation with the Executive Vice-President for International Affairs, to handle most of these negotiations; here especially the Executive Vice-President would keep the President informed on cardinal points. Similarly, if the President ultimately decided to place a workable crime-control program before the Congress—a program that recognized the social causes of crime and the multitude of things that must be done to reduce the incidence of crime—he could depend upon the Executive Vice-President for Domestic Affairs to hold the long and numerous conferences that would be required—conferences involving the top people of HEW, Justice, Housing, Civil Rights Commission, Office of Management and Budget, and consultation with the heads of appropriate House and Senate committees. In this and all similar matters the President *would remain the responsible official.*

While the President would continue to issue reorganization orders on problems of major consequence, such as possibly transferring the United States Information Agency back into the State Department where it belongs, he could delegate to the supra-Cabinet officer for domestic affairs routine orders in this field. This type of delegation would have to be authorized under the constitutional amendment I have suggested. Normally the basic studies would be made by the appropriate division of the Office of Executive Management (proposed successor to the Office of Management and Budget); if the proposal involved the transfer of a minor transportation activity in Commerce to the Department of Transportation, the domestic Executive Vice-President would sign the order, which would still have to escape a congressional veto. These minor changes are numerous, necessary, and ceaseless.

The most troublesome problem to which no one knows the answer involves what is often and properly referred to as the fourth branch of government. Over the years, as the Congress found it impossible to legislate details on matters within its cognizance, it created regulatory commissions which possess quasi-legislative, executive, and even judicial powers. The Interstate Commerce Commission, the Securities and Exchange Commission, the Federal Communications Commission, the Federal Trade Commission, and the Labor Relations Board are examples. They are not answerable to the President and do not have to abide by his policies. The Congress cannot supervise their work; indeed, the Congress has no executive ability. The President appoints commission members but cannot remove them. He can review and change their annual appropriation requests, but they are free to induce the Congress to change the President's decisions. A fourth branch of government is not provided in the Constitution; and the founding fathers did not foresee such a development.

What these agencies do, however, may have a profound effect on the general program of the President. In planning and carrying out a national economic policy, the President has not only a right but a duty to be concerned about decisions of the Interstate Commerce Commission on freight rates, and decisions on the discontinuance of non-profitable branch lines, as well as decisions of the Federal Communications Commission on interstate telephone rates. He is legitimately concerned about decisions of the Securities and Exchange Commission and the Commodities Exchange Commission.

The only agency in a wholly different category is the Federal Reserve Board. It is and should be independent, though the chairman of the Board should sit in on economic policy councils and be as helpful as possible.

I believe that the Executive Vice-President for Domestic Affairs should as a minimum have authority to summon the heads of all regulatory agencies into planning conferences, have them help in such planning, indicate to them what actions they have taken or contemplate that may affect the President's program, and advise the President, who in turn should *report to the Congress evidence of any intransigence or harmful actions taken by these agencies.* In each, too, are certain obvious administrative, not regulatory functions, which should by reorganization order be transferred to administrative agencies under the President's control; thus safety programs now handled by the Interstate Commerce Commission might well be transferred to the Department of Transportation.

Should the President have not only the appointive but also the removal power with respect to members of regulatory bodies? How can the regulatory commissions fulfill their legitimate duties, from determining what applicants may own and operate television stations to what railroads may merge, and still be brought under reasonable presidential control, thus avoiding the concept of a fourth branch of government?

Presidents Franklin Roosevelt, Truman, and Kennedy sought to achieve some control over the fourth branch of government. With some variations in their suggestions, they felt that the President should appoint the chairmen of the various commissions, to serve at the pleasure of the President and have broad general supervision over the commissions' work, and a staff member in the White House should have authority to co-ordinate commission activities in such fields as transportation and communications. The Congress did not agree.

Edward S. Corwin, in his scholarly book, *The President*,[18] points out that the Supreme Court has ruled that the duties of the regulatory commissions are "performed without executive leave and in contemplation of the statute must be free from executive control." A presidential commission appointed by President Franklin Roosevelt said: "The President is held responsible for the wise and efficient management of the Executive Branch of the Government. The people look to him for leadership. And yet we whittle away the effective control essential to that leadership by parceling out to a dozen or more irresponsible regulatory agencies important powers and administration. . . . As they grow in number [the President's] stature is bound to diminish."

The bankruptcy of the Penn Central Railroad brought the problem of regulatory commissions into public consciousness. Scholars in the field of transportation had insisted for years that if each form of transportation—railroads, airplanes, ships, regulated truck lines, unregulated private trucks, and private cars—were permitted to perform the service it could handle most efficiently, each could be moderately profitable and the transportation cost to consumers could be reduced by two billion dollars a year.

Their warnings went unheeded. Laws, written when the railroads had a monopoly, were not changed even though the competition among all forms of transportation had become a guarantee of bankruptcy in some areas. Most railroads in the Northeast and the vast Penn Central system are now not only in receivership but a threat of discontinuance of service is imminent. But the Interstate Commerce Commission, which regulates the railroads and trucks, and takes from six months to a year to make a simple decision, stubbornly refuses to permit the Penn Central to discontinue short branch lines which constantly operate at a serious deficit; this branch-line traffic should be handled by trucks and buses.

Ridiculous things have happened in the wake of railroad failures. The Interstate Commerce Commission, for example, ordered all other railroads to which the Penn Central owed large sums of money, primarily for demurrage charges, to cancel their claims, but the Internal Revenue Service would give no assurance that this drastic loss by marginally profitable railroads could be written off. In 1973 federal officials suggested that the government subsidize the bankrupt railroads, an action that would harm those railroads that are still able to operate without public aid. The fact is that the United States does not have a transportation policy, the President cannot by fiat promulgate one, and the President cannot even call in the regulatory agency heads, along with the Secretaries of Transportation and Commerce, and reason with them to take co-ordinated action that would hold promise of at least a modicum of success.

The Congress should give the President the authority he needs to keep the regulatory agencies operating in harmony with his total program and the President should delegate to the Executive Vice-

President for Domestic Affairs authority to hold conferences with heads of regulatory agencies, seek by general consent to bring them into harmony with other economic programs, and report as necessary to the President on successes and failures. Failures should be explained by the President to the Congress, a procedure which over a period of time could lead to further remedial legislation. This is a problem which must be dealt with delicately, patiently, and on a progressive basis, for otherwise a beginning will never be made.

The federal government has become the nation's largest monopoly. The government does and should regulate *private* monopolies, but who is to regulate this massive *public* monopoly?

Concentrated power, wherever it exists, possesses the potential of evil.

When I was a young man I became convinced, as I explained in an earlier chapter, that for much of our history too much power had been concentrated in the hands of capitalists. I had read about the robber barons, their ability to dictate the selection and election of candidates, their power to rig the stock market and make fortunes at the expense of naïve investors, and their practice of keeping labor essentially in servitude. No wonder many persons became aghast; no group in our society should have been permitted to possess such influence.

I had applauded measures which broke much of this power—child labor laws and anti-trust legislation, for example. Later had come broad labor laws, minimum wage legislation, security and exchange legislation, welfare and unemployment acts and many other liberal enactments. Today, in most corporations, greater authority resides with management, with directors who have only minimum stockholdings, stockholders, and even with the general public than with a few capitalists. The situation is not perfect, but it is correct to say that today "big business" holds not a fraction of the power attributed to it by its sharpest critics; further, most industries have developed a social conscience and work for the general welfare as well as for the benefit of their stockholders.

Anti-trust legislation did not and does not today, however, apply to labor. Now frightening power is concentrated in the hands of large unions. They can, if they wish, wreck the economy of the United States. They could close down the automobile industry which, because it is a massive employer and a major purchaser from a hundred other enterprises, would throw millions of persons out of work and cause a major depression. This concentration of power is undesirable. It is not, in my judgment, in the interest of unions themselves. Today public opinion is turning against labor, for from 1967 to 1971 and again in 1973 the cost-push aspect of inflation was obviously in large part due to wage levels rising much faster than productivity. An aroused public could in time insist upon action that would be detrimental to labor. A thoughtful solution, prior to a citizen revolt, would be preferable.

But the largest concentration of power today is in the federal government. Its power grows like weeds in an untended garden. In our free society, retaining, in principle at least, the basic social power in the hands of all citizens, any concentration of power, especially that now existing in a gargantuan federal government, must be considered a threat to the democratic system.

I recall again the conversation I had in 1946 with Chester Bowles, who said that the federal government was becoming so large, so bureaucratized, that it was difficult to get a decision made or an action taken, and the recent similar statement of Kenneth Galbraith with respect to the foreign service. Everyone, of course, wants *government of the several levels to perform those essential functions that people cannot perform for themselves.* But I object strenuously to the reasoning that the mere existence of a problem, even national in scope, automatically calls for public action. I also object to the philosophy that a federal policy must necessarily be carried out in its entirety by entrenched public employees, rather than by appropriate private constituents of our society. And certainly the mere existence of a national problem does not make the solution a *federal* rather than *state* or *local* responsibility.

Rat infestation is a problem in most urban centers. The federal government, therefore, developed in September 1967 a rat control program and appropriated $40 million to initiate it. It is ridiculously inefficient, but we nonetheless have a federal program. To eliminate rats, every household, every yard, must be kept clean every day. Should this be a federal responsibility? Once cleanliness exists, poison and traps will eliminate rats. One would think that this is a problem for private initiative. If government *must* enter the situation, on the ground that some householders will co-operate, while others will not, the problem surely should be handled by each municipality; if some householders do not meet acceptable standards of cleanliness the city should take remedial action and charge the cost to the property; this is now the rule in snow removal.

There exist today two agricultural programs offering advice and guidance to farmers: one is federal, the other is a federal-state-local co-operative effort. One began in 1914, the other thirty years later. Both have agents who work with individual farmers. Does this make sense? They should be consolidated, with the federal government making grants to the states, which should be matched by state and local government revenues.

Many activities of the federal government should be transferred to state and local governments. Such transfers would have to be accompanied either by federal grants or by federal tax reductions and commensurate increases in state and local taxes.

Some federal activities might better be administered by private institutions. Training, retraining, expanded employment, and other programs affecting individuals might better be privately administered with partial subventions from government. Today, for example, private agencies, Blue Cross and Blue Shield, administer important phases of the federal Medicare program. Many private institutions have the trained personnel and the management expertise to manage selected public programs more effectively and at lower unit costs than can new federal employees.

Years ago I read many of the writings of Justice Brandeis. Always in my mind has been his praise of the American system, including the system of private competitive enterprise, for he saw the competitive element in our economic system as making government intervention to obtain fairness unnecessary. The system decentralizes decisions which in a socialized economy must be centralized. This decentralization enables vastly more individuals to carry genuine responsibility and most normal individuals thrive and grow under responsibility. They become more productive. They become better citizens.

The Executive Vice-President for Domestic Affairs, with support of the President, should establish in the Executive Office an ad hoc commission of not more than seven persons to consider every conceivable method that might be used to minimize the monopolistic position of the federal government. Of these seven, one should be an experienced federal specialist; one should be the best former state governor available; and the third should be an outstanding former mayor; a tax expert, a former senator, an academic political scientist, and a noted philosopher might constitute the other four members of the commission. All others involved should be temporary consultants. The ad hoc commission should not have more than three years, preferably two, in which to complete its work. It should have subpoena power and a congressional appropriation which would enable it to meet its own expenses and hire research assistants. The President should be required in a congressional enactment to transmit the study, with his comments, to the Congress within six months after he receives it.

A reduction in the power and responsibility of the federal government would contribute to the viability of the presidency, would strengthen state and local governments, and would be harmonious with the basic citizen-control principle of representative government. President Franklin Roosevelt, in a fireside chat in mid-April 1938, said: "The only living bulwark of continuing liberty is a government strong enough to protect the interests of the people, *and a people strong enough and well enough informed to maintain its sovereign control over its government.*" The American concept has always been that government should be as close as possible to the people, for this enhances their "sovereign control" over governmental actions. Carelessness, apathy, and to some extent the failure of town, city, county, and state governments to meet their responsibilities have led to the present undue centralization of power in the federal establishment—to the monopolistic public power we now have.

I emphasize that the activities of a supra-Cabinet officer for domestic affairs *would not reduce the responsibility of the President of the United States* for all that occurs in domestic matters; it would reduce substantially the effort he must now devote to them. The conflict of responsibility and time is found in every human organization, and the solution to it is in general practice. The president of a university, for example, may delegate significant duties for educational development and interschool co-ordination to a provost, and thus reduce the time he must personally spend on this important campus problem, but the president is still held responsible for results by the trustees, faculty, students, alumni, and the public at large. The same holds true in industrial and financial institutions where executive vice-presidents, vice-presidents, and assistant vice-presidents carry substantial burdens within established policies. The president of the organization, however, is held ultimately responsible by the board of directors, stockholders, and the general public.

The second supra-Cabinet position should help the President in the international field. Helping the President form and implement a consistent foreign policy in recent years has been the responsibility of the National Security Council and the Assistant to the President for National Security Affairs. The Secretary of State was once the sole authority, under the President, for foreign affairs. This was true through the Roosevelt administration and to a considerable extent through the Truman and Eisenhower administrations, though for the latter two the National Security Council functioned fairly well.

Since then, with men like McGeorge Bundy, Walt Rostow, and Henry Kissinger, supported by very large staffs, helping co-ordinate and shape foreign policy, the Secretary of State for all practical purposes has been mainly the director of the diplomatic service. Since forty other departments and agencies having some aspects of international affairs as their business report directly to the President, his assistant for international affairs has necessarily become his constant adviser and co-ordinator.

It will be interesting to see what develops in this regard now that President Nixon has named Dr. Kissinger Secretary of State while keeping him also as foreign policy co-ordinator in the White House. This may restore to the position of Secretary of State some of the responsibilities and powers once inherent in that office, but I do not believe the dual assignment will work to anyone's satisfaction, any more than does the effort to have the Treasury Secretary co-ordinate at the presidential level all economic affairs. Both the tasks of Secretary of State and assistant to the President on foreign affairs require full-time leadership. One will be neglected, and that is likely to be the foreign policy post in the White House, a situation the President could not tolerate.

The Executive Vice-President for International Affairs, like his domestic counterpart, should be ranked above the Cabinet, just below the President, and equal to the rank of prime minister in other countries. He may then deal with the heads of all departments and agencies concerned. He should be the vice-chairman of the National Security Council.

By no means should the operation of this high officer be the same as was developed in the White House, where Dr. Kissinger ran a second but smaller State Department. The Executive Vice-President for International Affairs *should have only a very small staff*, for most of his research data, foreign intelligence, and recommendations should come from Cabinet members and agency heads and the personnel responsible to these officers. Here the volume of work in our modern world is massive, complex, and time-consuming.

The existence of this office would not reduce the President's *specific constitutional duty of handling the foreign relations of the United States*. But here there is a persuasive reason for the change, in addition to those discussed for domestic matters.

The Secretary of State and other Cabinet members concerned with foreign affairs must today travel a good deal. The President, on the other hand, must have constantly at his side one who comprehends the totality of current, impending, and potential foreign problems.

Further, the Executive Vice-President for International Affairs could relieve the President of an immense amount of work when foreign dignitaries come almost in lock-step parade to the United States. The President would still have to be the host for other heads of state (kings, queens, presidents), but the Executive Vice-President for International Affairs could help him with this chore in numerous ways. He could be host for chiefs of governments (prime ministers), carrying out most of the negotiations within the President's policies, with the President giving an appropriate amount of time to the negotiations, but less than now, especially in handling the inevitable social aspects of all such visits.

I am impressed, as most members of Congress and citizens generally must be, by the amazing success of Dr. Henry Kissinger in carrying out many difficult and sensitive tasks, especially in the People's Republic of China, the Soviet Union, Vietnam, and the Middle East. He has been received by Brezhnev, Mao, Sadat, prime ministers, and others as the alter ego of the President. He, not Secretary of State Rogers, was at the right hand of the President in critical negotiations which have given hope of eventual détente between the two great power centers of the modern world. This is truly extraordinary. His influence would be still greater, however, if he were the Executive Vice-President for International Affairs and an intelligent diplomat were Secretary of State.

But the issue involved transcends even this important consideration. The critical problem involves the difference between decisions made by the palace guard, by an army of presidential assistants and assistants to assistants, all having executive privilege and thus unavailable to the Congress, rather than by collaboration with the Cabinet members and agency heads to whom the President entrusts the management of programs involving more than five million persons. I shall deal in a moment with this larger problem which involves both of the supra-Cabinet posts.

Many of the onerous ministerial duties now devolving upon the President could be handled by the Executive Vice-Presidents. They could, under the general guidance of the President, relieve him of less important matters, prepare co-ordinated plans for his consideration, sign appointment papers, proclamations, and other documents—thus greatly reducing the need of the President to sign his name forty thousand times a year!—and in other ways make the presidency of the United States an office in which the incumbent could have time to deal intelligently with the supreme issues of our time. And the President would have greater opportunity to reflect and to make the office what President Franklin Roosevelt thought it should be: "primarily a place of moral leadership."

Since both Executive Vice-Presidents, with only small staffs of their own, would work primarily through department and agency heads, *the personnel of the Executive Office could be reduced drastically,* and the persons reporting directly to the President could also be reduced to manageable numbers. Further, *the responsibilities of the Cabinet members could be restored to what they once were.* I consider this point to be the most important of all.

The House Committee on the Post Office and Civil Service, using professional help, including Howard Stone, who had a distinguished career in the Bureau of the Budget, studied the White House problem; the chairman of the committee, Congressman Morris K. Udall, in a letter dated April 24, 1972, transmitting the committee report to the House, said:

> The . . . personal entourage of the President, responsible to no one except [the President] has become in effect this country's equivalent of a Palace Guard.

(Between 1955 and 1972 the personnel in the Executive Office of the President increased from 1,403 to 2,236.)

> Certainly no . . . American would begrudge any President the expertise or manpower needed to cope with the pressing problems of the nation and the world. But a serious problem arises when the White House staff begins to replace both the functions of the Cabinet and the career civil service. . . . The personal staff . . . with its overwhelming size, shadowy functions and influence has undermined the traditional decision-making rules and inter-relationships of the other branches of government. Not only has this affected the powers of Congress (because White House personnel cannot be summoned before Congressional Committees) but it has unquestionably eroded the responsibilities of the Cabinet. . . . The President's major administrators and advisors—the Cabinet—have always been properly questioned by Congress about their administration of public laws. . . . The origin of much of the present day conflict comes from the fact that on many vital issues . . . decisions are no longer made by Cabinet members. Instead, men little known to the public at large, never confirmed by the Senate, hired outside civil service requirements, make daily calls . . . in the name of the President. . . . Yet these anonymous men wielding enormous public power claim to be immune from any public accountability. . . . [They] have balked at testifying before Congress.
>
> The Constitution envisaged a President assisted by a Cabinet made up of his principal consultants and advisers. . . . [Now] the . . . Cabinet has been downgraded to a dangerous degree. . . . The plain fact today is that on most matters Cabinet members tend to deal with underlings who have far more influence on the President than the Cabinet members. Most major policy formulation is now made by a kind of medieval court where the king's favorites struggle for power, owing no allegiance except to their master.

Congressman Udall directed his criticisms mainly at the Nixon administration. I have deleted partisan statements, for the problem of White House-Cabinet-agency-head relationships has been developing steadily over a period of years. There were nearly 1,700 persons in the

Executive Office of the President when President Nixon took office. The practice of depending on assistants to the President, rather than on the Cabinet, was rife in the Franklin Roosevelt administration, began again in the Kennedy administration, increased substantially in the Johnson administration, and is much greater now. In my judgment the President's personal staff, including the two Executive Vice-Presidents, *should enhance the prestige and responsibility of the Cabinet* and lead to greater reliance on studies and evidence presented through normal department channels. Reducing the President's work load, as I have analyzed the possibilities, would not conflict with this desirable change—it would enhance it.

About a year before he resigned as Secretary of State, due to ill health, I broached the idea of a supra-Cabinet position in international affairs with Secretary Dulles. His instinctive reaction was negative. He was the third generation of his family to be immersed in foreign policy and he thought of himself as the sole foreign policy adviser to the President; once the President established a policy, it was incumbent upon all other agencies to carry it out. About a month later we chatted again. He said he had been thinking of changed conditions. He had tried to place himself in the presidential chair and then consider what he would need to arrive at wise decisions and take all actions needed to meet the varying and rapidly changing conditions throughout the world. He recognized that in his absence the President would see the Secretary of Defense about a problem in Israel, the head of CIA about a problem in Iran, the head of AID about developments in Taiwan, the head of the U. S. Information Agency about policies governing information to the Soviet Union, and the Secretary of Agriculture about food shipments to Bolivia and other nations. The President had to make decisions consistent with his total foreign policy objectives. He, Dulles, wished he could help the President on all these and scores of other problems. His own responsibilities took him away from Washington about thirty per cent or more of his time. In addition to his frequent absences, he had to supervise a world-wide department—a mighty task; as many as six hundred regional and international conferences a year, long consultations with his staff and ambassadors, a multitude of cables each day to our embassies around the world, and speeches before important groups such as the Foreign Policy Association, AFL-CIO, and the National Council of Churches prevented him from being available to the

President much of the time. Further, he had thought especially about the President's task in the National Security Council of receiving reports and urgent suggestions from many agencies that paralleled the State Department in foreign affairs. He had therefore come to the conclusion that my suggestion was valid and he would so report to the President.

I did not discuss with him the possibility of a comparable officer for domestic affairs, so he and the President arrived at the title First Secretary of the Government, which President Eisenhower mentioned in his final message to the Congress.

I could not persuade myself that this was sufficient, and so said to President Eisenhower. Through two new positions and with the use of procedures I have suggested we would witness, I feel certain, a return to a dependence on the officers heading major departments and agencies in policy and program formation, and in the execution of those policies and programs. The temptation to make the Executive Office of the President self-sufficient would disappear.

My brother once argued that the creation of two such positions would downgrade the Cabinet: "It's hard enough now to persuade the best people of the United States to make sacrifices and come to Washington to perform a public service. If we lower the standing of Cabinet members, the difficulty might be increased." My view is that if we restored confidence in and dependence on the regular departments of the government, instead of transferring their functions to the Executive Office, the top positions would have enhanced dignity and appeal to those the President wishes to have occupy them. We now have one classic and successful example of a pyramidal organization: the Defense Department, which has control of the three military departments. Presidents have had no difficulty in inducing able and dedicated persons to serve as Secretaries of the Departments of Army, Navy, and Air Force.

One of the problems every student of the presidency recognizes is the difficulty of having presidential decisions carried out by the personnel of the vast bureaucracy that now constitutes the executive branch of government. I have explained how President Eisenhower sought to solve this problem by creating an Operations Coordinating Board; it dealt primarily with foreign and security policies and programs. Each of the Executive Vice-Presidents I have suggested could (and should) be given authority by the President to monitor observances and discrepancies in policy and program execution, and through department and agency heads should strive to achieve correction, where that is needed, and keep the President informed of their failures, for only failures would require the President to take action.

One of the first questions to arise in Congress about having an Executive Vice-President for Domestic Affairs and an Executive Vice-President for International Affairs would be whether these officers could be required to testify before congressional committees or whether they would claim executive privilege. Committees of the House and Senate with responsibility in foreign affairs, for example, would point out that they may summon the Secretary of State, Secretary of Defense, and all other departments and agency personnel working in international relations for questioning and, patently, for expressing their dissatisfaction. Traditionally the President has not claimed executive privilege for Cabinet members. Since no one of these officers is any longer responsible for the totality of international relations, however, the committees would feel that they should be able to have evidence from the Executive Vice-President for International Affairs. The same would hold true for committees of Congress concerned with transportation, communications, development of water resources, and manifold other problems that cut across department and agency lines and would be subject to the co-ordinating authority of the Executive Vice-President for Domestic Affairs.

On this delicate and controversial question many will suffer an ambivalence.

Executive privilege is inherent in the basic concept of the separation of powers into three (unfortunately now four) branches of government. The President cannot command the presence of members of the Congress or of the Supreme Court. Neither may the Court or the Congress command the presence of the President or his personal staff. Further, in the White House new policies and programs or revisions of existing ones are constantly under study, and until the President has made decisions and announced them, confidentiality is normally important, often imperative.

This is of first importance in the conduct of foreign relations. When President Kennedy was working with his brother Robert and others to determine how to meet the missile threat in Cuba it could have been fatal if a staff member had been forced to appear before the Senate Foreign Relations Committee and compelled to reveal the alternatives under consideration. One of the successful techniques used by President Eisenhower in maintaining peace in the China Straits was never to disclose what his action might be if the Chinese People's Republic attacked Quemoy and Matsu as a preliminary to an attack on Formosa. On many troublesome international problems, telephone and coded cable messages flow between the President of the United States and, for example, the President of France or the Prime Minister of Great Britain; premature disclosure of negotiations and discussion of what the ultimate decision might be would be disastrous; the character of international intercourse would change, and not for the better.

When the President's study commission on a new Isthmian canal was in the midst of its work we had before us tentative proposals which if disclosed could have made a treaty with Colombia or Panama impossible. Neither the Congress nor the public would have benefited by premature disclosure of tentative, sometimes worthless documents which the commission itself ultimately discarded. The final report of the commission was made public. Most preliminary papers were then of no value. (Incidentally, as has happened to so many other presidential commission reports, President Nixon has never commented on the five-year canal study placed before him in 1970.) Since the President properly has executive privilege, it follows that those intimately associated with him ought to possess it too.

On the other hand, the Congress has a legitimate complaint in pointing out that it no longer has the privilege of obtaining testimony from the federal officials who comprehend all aspects of foreign or domestic affairs. Here is the dilemma, the cause of a possible ambivalence.

I believe it is possible to work out a carefully designed understanding between the Chief Executive and the Congress which would permit the Executive Vice-Presidents to appear before congressional committees on matters that have been determined, approved by the President, and publicized, but to retain executive privilege on matters in the development stage and on which the President has not made a decision. Even at present, this difference is observed to a limited extent. Since it was the Assistant to the President for National Security Affairs, not the Secretary of State, who was the confidant of the President in negotiations with Communist China and the Soviet Union, many congressional members were invited to the White House and there a thorough briefing by Dr. Kissinger took place, a briefing which elicited praise from those who were present.

Having suggested a possible agreement, I must add a caveat: often the relationship between what has been approved by the President and what is currently under consideration in domestic and foreign affairs is intricately intertwined. This was the situation when the first cease-fire in Vietnam was published and further tedious and exasperating negotiations were under way in Paris. Later, when Dr. Kissinger went to Moscow shortly before Brezhnev came to the United States, it was obvious that the President had decided what he hoped could be accomplished. The communiqués subsequently issued in Washington by Nixon and Brezhnev constituted essentially a ceremonial act, for the major decisions had been made by the Soviet leader and Kissinger, operating as the President's alter ego and under presidential orders. It would have been discourteous, to say the least, and difficult and fatal at worst, for Kissinger to have testified on these matters before the Senate Foreign Relations Committee prior to the formal issuance of the communiqués.

The Congress would have to rely on the judgment, tact, and integrity of the two Executive Vice-Presidents in Senate and House hearings as they determined what could and could not be discussed at a particular time. The rule should be maximum disclosure consistent with the need for confidentiality in manifold situations. Executive sessions of congressional committees on sensitive matters may seem to be a possibility, but unfortunately nothing appears to be withheld from the mass media on Capitol Hill. The only two certainties about this issue of executive privilege versus congressional testimony are that it will be difficult for the President and the Congress to resolve it, and that the two supra-Cabinet positions will never be approved unless an acceptable answer is found.

No one is sufficiently knowledgeable or wise to suggest with confidence the final answers to the major problems I have sought to illuminate in this book. I am acutely conscious of the fact that my views have been developed on the basis of practical experience with eight Presidents, which may be a record, but that alone does not make my judgments infallible. Years of scholarly research on a single problem, such as that of giving the President some degree of control over the regulatory agencies, would be a desirable test of what one has observed and learned by experience. Similar research is desirable on each of the main suggestions for change I have made. But we cannot wait. The presidency has become an impossible post. That changes are needed at once to make it an effective position of leadership in the face of modern complexity and enormity of government no one can deny. Nor should anyone doubt that we should so arrange the structure and responsibilities of the federal executive establishment that the President, in dealing with the paramount issues of the nation, has time for study, conferences, and serious contemplation of all possible alternatives. As Pericles said, "Wait for the wisest of all counselors, Time."

I hope what I have written will stimulate debate. More to the point, I hope that in the near future the President will appoint a special study commission, comprised of about seven highly competent persons who have had broad experience in federal management, to consider the total problem in depth and recommend the constitutional amendments, laws, and executive orders that are deemed to be needed. Citizens should have general comprehension of the nature and dimensions of the problem, but it is not one on which they can shape informed and detailed decisions. If the task is left solely to Congress, nothing will happen. The President is far too burdened with day-to-day decision making to carry out the essential studies. Some small and experienced group must bring all the facts and alternatives into a consistent whole and seek the President's approval. If he is satisfied that the commission has found a workable plan, he should appear personally before a joint session of the Congress, explain the proposals, and then work strenuously for their approval. Should he not agree with the commission's findings, he should forward the report to the Congress and explain his specific disagreements.

CHAPTER 29

The only thing worse than an irresponsible
free press is a controlled press; the people
have a *right* to know, the press a *duty* to
inform.

IBEGAN THIS BOOK by describing an evening at my home
in Baltimore with some Johns Hopkins students in June of 1968—the
dark and dismal day after Senator Robert Kennedy had died from an
assassin's bullet—the night that President Lyndon Johnson persuaded
me, against my better judgment, to serve as chairman of the Commission on the Causes and Prevention of Violence.

I now complete the circle by describing two other evenings with
student friends more than five years later, the first of these on Saturday
evening, October 20, 1973. That was another dismal day, an extraordinary Saturday on which a beleaguered President Nixon fired Special
Prosecutor Archibald Cox at the expense of two of his administration's
most talented and esteemed members—Elliot Richardson and William
Ruckelshaus.

Relaxing and chatting in my study that evening were six young
men: two undergraduates and four graduate students. We missed the
first news bulletin, which we later learned was transmitted by breathless
commentators on the White House lawn. But a friend called to alert
me that an incredible story was breaking, so I turned on the television,
with the sound lowered, and we soon had an up-to-date report on developments, unbelievable developments.

For the remainder of the evening we talked mainly about the crisis
in the White House—Watergate, cover-up, indictments, resignations,
tapes—the whole series of bizarre events.

The students who had visited me after Senator Kennedy's death
had been filled with despair and frustration. They were overcome by

a sense of helplessness and bewilderment that the insane and random act of a twisted and sick individual could have so altered an important historic process.

In contrast, the students in my study five years later were angry, disillusioned, and frightened.

They were angry over what they believed was the hypocrisy they had witnessed during the preceding months. High government officials had posed as moralizers, champions of law and order, and had condemned university students and "peaceniks" for criticizing presidential decisions, thus "undermining the democratic system." But these very men and others in the top councils of government had been forced to resign in disgrace, implicated in sordid scandals.

The students were disillusioned with politics and to some extent with government generally. It appeared to them, as they felt it did to millions of Americans, that politics is a dirty business and that many politicians are inherently dishonest. How could it be, they wondered in disbelief, that such things as had been revealed in the Watergate hearings could occur in our society? How could men attain high positions and become so arrogant and contemptuous not only of the American people but of the very laws on which our system is based?

And these young men were frightened—or perhaps it is more accurate to say that they were deeply apprehensive. In a few short months they had seen the national Administration virtually disintegrate. Could the President survive the loss of confidence in him and his associates?

The students reasoned that the nation faced an awful dilemma—that we were in a "no win" situation.

Impeachment would surely be a dangerous and painful course. The investigation by the House and the trial by the Senate might drag on for months, leaving the country virtually leaderless at a time in history when a misstep or failure to act promptly and effectively could result in serious global difficulty. The psychological and emotional trauma could be immensely debilitating for the country. Even if the President emerged from a trial the victor (and it was clear that no crime had yet been proven against him), he and the country would have paid a heavy toll.

Further, if President Nixon were exonerated, especially by a narrow margin, there unfortunately was grave danger that he could not regain the support and trust of the American people and the Congress. This would result, they believed, in a kind of paralysis of leadership and a lack of progress at a time when decisive action was needed to cope with severe economic problems, urgent social and energy issues, and delicate, constantly changing international situations. If the President were convicted, the country would have a caretaker President for the next three years.

This entire crisis, a graduate student contended, had been one consequence of the President's having too much power. It was an intoxication induced by power that caused the President to isolate himself from the Congress, the people, the critics. He felt that he and his trusted associates could do no wrong. He did not seem to feel that he was answerable to anyone but himself. Had he used some of his power in the right way immediately after the Watergate break-in, all subsequent history would have been different. Power bred arrogance. Hence, was not the real need to reduce presidential power?

The conversation that evening was fast-paced and intense. I could not begin to re-create it here. When the students left—the hour was late—I think they felt, as I did, a sense of incompleteness. As I brooded about the session for several days, I distilled from that troubled talk some thought-provoking observations which I decided were relevant to much that I have tried to convey in this book. An epilogue seemed a convenient place to put them. But before I could reduce my thoughts to paper the students came back to my home—exactly a week later, on Saturday evening, October 27.

They now were concerned about the "ready alert" of our military forces which President Nixon had ordered two days before, in response to the alleged preparation of Soviet forces to move into the Middle East in support of the Arab armies and air forces.

One of the young undergraduates heatedly argued that the President's action was unconstitutional. Only the Congress could declare war. Yet the "ready alert" clearly implied that the President would send our military forces into the Middle East conflict if the Soviet Union did in fact participate directly in the war. This would mean that the United States and Israel would be opposing the Arab countries and the Soviet Union, and this could lead to NATO and Warsaw powers becoming involved. World War III would be a reality, even though there would have been no declaration of war by the Congress of the United States.

The President, as one student had suggested the previous week, had too much power. It was one thing for Brezhnev, Mao, and dictators elsewhere to act without the consent of the people. But in our democracy it was mandatory for the President to abide by the Constitution. The people had said in the Constitution that only Congress could declare war. The members of the Congress represented the people. The people would have to do the fighting. They and they alone, speaking through their representatives, should make the fatal decision.

"But we live in the atomic age," a graduate student said. "If the Soviet Union unleashed intercontinental ballistic missiles toward the United States the President would have to make a decision in minutes. He wouldn't have time to ride up Pennsylvania Avenue to the Hill and ask the Congress to declare war. He would have to push a button that would send retaliatory missiles against the Soviet Union."

He paused and then added with emphasis: "*Our greatest guarantee that we will not be attacked by atomic bombs is the universal knowledge that we can retaliate without waiting for action by the Congress.*"

Another student pointed out that Congress was at that very time giving consideration to the problem of presidential authority to use our military forces. The Senate had passed a bill which would limit to thirty days the President's right to have our military forces engage in active combat unless in that period the Congress gave its approval to the President's action. The House of Representatives amended the bill to limit the permissive period to ninety days. In conference, the two houses compromised on a period of sixty days, plus an additional thirty days if the President determined that the extra time was needed to extricate our troops with minimum loss. It was assumed that the President would veto even this compromise on the basis that it would weaken his ability to conduct the foreign affairs of the United States.

"I think we need to distinguish sharply between a detected atomic attack and all other circumstances that could involve us in military action," the younger man argued. "We should never have been in Vietnam, for example. Atomic bombs were not involved. Our forces were sent there by Kennedy in 1961 and 1962 with no approval by the Congress. The Gulf of Tonkin Resolution gave a certain legitimacy to what

Johnson did, but war was never declared. Are we not abrogating a major provision of the Constitution?"

I had sat quietly in my favorite chair as this discussion, provocative at times, proceeded.

Now the students turned to me.

"You are writing a book on the presidency," one said. "You are familiar with conditions in the White House and with the relations of Presidents with the Congress. How do you feel about this?"

I felt strangely unwilling to speak. I had not yet had an opportunity to put in draft form the troubled thoughts about presidential power, presidential responsibility, balance of power, and the resilience of the American system which had been much on my mind all the previous week.

So I merely commented that we now lived in a time when the President had to be in a position to make quick judgments under certain circumstances, and I saw no way to draft laws or constitutional provisions which would define exactly when, if war threatened, he could act on his own authority or when he had to obtain the consent of the Congress. I did not like the bill which the Congress was about to enact, for while seeming to limit the President's warmaking authority it actually legitimized his right to engage in warfare anywhere in the world for a period of sixty, possibly ninety, days, unless the Congress took action to stop him. The whole situation emphasized to me the transcendent importance of having in the White House a man of great wisdom, free of arrogance; a man of patience, but not a procrastinator; a man of courage without truculence, and a man of moral character and integrity, free of a messianic complex. As never before in our history, constant cooperation of the Chief Executive and the Congress was imperative.

In the briefest possible way, I told the students of the basic arguments I have made in this book: "We need to change some of our traditional practices so as to maximize the probability of placing in the presidency a truly capable leader whom the people can respect, whose credibility never comes into question; we then must make it possible for the President to have time for study and reflection before he makes fateful decisions. While it is true that we are a nation of laws, not of men, nonetheless laws are administered by men. Further, it is not possible to write laws that deal with every contingency that might arise.

567

Hence the character and wisdom of the men who execute the laws are of supreme importance."

The students were not satisfied. Three of them had fought in Vietnam. One had been given conscientious objector status. Two had been too young to be drafted. All hated war. The time was here, they felt, that we either had to achieve peace without qualification or face the grave possibility of annihilating civilization.

I suggested that when, in a relaxed mood, I reflected on the long history of mankind—no period had been free of brutal conflict—I really felt we might now be closer to finding the solution to peace than had any earlier generation. The absolute destructiveness of atomic and hydrogen missiles had created a common enemy to all people wherever they lived. *No other force or circumstance was so conducive to agreement among men as a common enemy.* Men found it possible to subordinate their lesser differences and even their selfishness when they were threatened by a force that could be defeated only by a unified people. That force just possibly might be atomic power.

The millennium would not be here soon, but mankind faced the possibility of threading his way through the forces that had seen people killing one another since the dawn of civilization into a period of resurrection. But this slim possibility could be kept alive only if all nations, and especially those with the greatest power, had leaders capable of wisdom and with their time so ordered that wisdom could truly prevail.

Silence followed these remarks. I broke it by asking the students to excuse me, for suddenly I felt the need to put on paper the thoughts that had been nagging at my mind since our conversation the week before. As they stood to leave, I jokingly suggested that they would have to read my new book to learn what thoughts they had inspired.

To anyone, including a student friend, who has reached this point in my long memoir, it is apparent that I am essentially an idealist. I do not apologize for that. Indeed, I am convinced that, had there been more idealism among our political leaders and those of us who elected them, our nation would not now face its present plight. More importantly, I believe the United States will regain its own self-confidence and the respect of the world only if we are courageous enough to set high national ideals and stretch with all of our collective energy to reach them.

Events of the past year—indeed of the past decade—have raised grave doubts in the minds of many, particularly the young, about the strength and viability of our political system. These are not members of the cult of the nihilists, but good citizens who are now worried and uncertain.

My own faith in our system of representative government is as strong as it was when as a youngster I worshiped at the shrine of Woodrow Wilson.

The troubles of this period can dissolve into the achievements—or even possibly into wholly new problems—of tomorrow. Our nation has faced many crises in its history. So resilient is our system that we have always been able to find methods of recovery and increased strength.

History is not a sure guide, for present conditions are different from those of the past. My student friends were worried about the power residing in the President, but it must be recognized that *all branches of our government*—legislative, judicial, executive—*now have increased power*, partly because we expect government to do more and also because the problems we must deal with tend to increase geometrically in complexity.

The genius of our representative form of government lies in the separation and balance of powers. This is our automatic pilot, our self-correcting mechanism. Historically power has shifted among the branches of government in a cyclical way. One branch has been dominant for a period, even to the point of exceeding its constitutional authority. Then the public begins to react. Pressures build. One or both of the other two branches reassert their authority. The self-correcting mechanism, slow at times, really functions and a reasonable degree of balance is restored.

In his first term President Franklin Roosevelt used the power of his office to its fullest in his effort to cope with the depression not only of the economy but of the spirit of millions of our citizens. For a time the public approved, and the Congress and the courts acceded to executive authority. In Roosevelt's second term, however, the Supreme Court time and again functioned as a counterbalance and checked the excesses of the presidency and the indolence of Congress.

In the early fifties the Supreme Court moved into a partial vacuum made evident by a sluggish Congress, especially in the area of civil rights, but by the late fifties and early sixties the Court reached the point where it was legislating rather than adjudicating. This stimulated both the Chief Executive and the Congress to hasten reforms and to legislate with greater precision, thus reducing the danger of judicial encroachment. The self-correcting mechanism worked once again.

From 1962 to 1973 presidential power again expanded enormously. Our military involvement in Vietnam, Cambodia, and Laos, the President's impoundment of appropriated funds, and the President's decision to put our military forces on a world-wide "ready alert" late in 1973 illustrated dramatically the unilateral decision-making power of the presidency.

So new pressure has been building to curb what Arthur Schlesinger, Jr., has called the "runaway presidency." After a too long delay the self-correcting mechanism has begun to function again. Congress stopped the fighting in Cambodia and Laos over the objections of the President. Congress is again taking full control over appropriations. Congress rightly or wrongly overrode President Nixon's veto of the bill limiting the President's warmaking powers.

Even the Watergate mess may have made a positive contribution in that it sensitized the nation quickly and emphatically to the problems of separation of powers and the need for balance among the branches of government. Congress, having yielded some of its constitutional authority mainly by shirking its own obligations, is obviously well on the way to reasserting its own powers and restoring the delicate and shifting balance essential in our political system.

The press plays a crucial role in this process. In a democracy the ultimate social power rests with the people. If they are to decide wisely on complex issues and among candidates for office, they must have a free flow of accurate and untainted information. That is why the Constitution provides for the freedom of the press. It must be noted, however, that this is the only freedom assured by our Constitution that the people cannot exercise for themselves. From the citizen's point of view, the more important consideration is *his* or *her right to know*. I have often thought we should add this to the list of constitutional guarantees. This would not violate what is already provided—freedom of the press—but it would place upon the mass media, educational institutions, the government, and other agencies the positive obligation of seeing to it that the people's right to know is fulfilled.

Tension has always existed between the press and the President. This is inevitable, I suppose, and up to a point it is healthy for the Republic. In recent years this tension has become severe, and both sides are to blame. Attempts by the executive establishment to "manage the news" have motivated the media to dig and push harder for the facts. In its zeal the media have frequently compromised objectivity, distorted facts, and publicized unsubstantiated allegations and rumors. This situation jogs my memory, and I recall again the trauma I experienced during the notorious bullfrog charges in the Hoover administration. That experience taught me always to rush into print with true accounts of all activities within my area of responsibility; otherwise they would be ferreted out, most likely misinterpreted, and sometimes built into a major issue. Perhaps all federal government officials should suffer the humiliation I did. They would then never forget that government has a solemn obligation to conduct the people's business as openly as possible, and to provide full information to the nation, adhering scrupulously to demonstrable truth. With or without my "right to know" amendment to the Constitution, the men of the media have the obligation to transmit fully and accurately what government does and fails to do.

What of the office of the presidency? Has the presidency itself been permanently damaged by the charges and countercharges of the last year, as some have contended? Will the current erosion of public confidence leave permanent scars?

I simply do not believe any lasting damage is in prospect.

Our system, including the presidency, is tough, flexible, and durable. The office of the presidency is inseparable from the man who holds it. If the incumbent has the public's approval his powers reflect that support. If he earns the public's disapproval his ability to act is constrained. Public approval is not something that can be transferred with the office from one President to the next. Our concern, then, should be not only with the institution of the presidency but even more with the individuals we place in that high office.

Because I believe this, I am convinced that the nature and outcome of the election of 1976 will be decisive in determining the immediate future of our country. The democratic philosophy and our representative form of government are indeed strong and durable, but they must not be strained too much or for too long a time. Faith in personal, political, and economic freedom and in the ability of the people wisely to exercise social power through honest and responsible leaders must be restored. That is why I say the election of 1976 will be decisive.

Both political parties, recognizing this, should put aside natural partisan ambitions, traditional "balancing of the ticket," normal emotional appeals and misrepresentations in the 1976 campaign. Each party should nominate for President and Vice-President persons who clearly possess keen intelligence, broad knowledge of crucial problems, *absolute integrity, moral and executive leadership, and a determination to restore faith in the American system of representative government.* I even dare to hope that both parties will be less concerned about victory for themselves, more concerned about victory for the nation. The outcome must be such that the perilous situation we now face will be overcome. That, I frankly acknowledge, is idealistic, almost to the point of naïveté. But in this case it is an idealism that is shared by the overwhelming majority of Americans.

Many changes in conditions and in potential candidates will occur between now and the nominating conventions in 1976. Whatever the changes, however, we shall need a President, regardless of party, who can unite this nation, galvanize its great energy and imagination, set it on a sure and steady course.

The year 1976 will mark the bicentennial of the Republic. What an appropriate time to demonstrate to ourselves and to the world that we have the intellectual and moral determination to do what needs to be done to make a modern reality of those high ideals which ennobled the great adventure initiated two hundred years ago.

BOOKS CITED

1. George, Alexander L. and Juliette L. *Woodrow Wilson and Colonel House* (John Day Co., 1956).

2. Lyons, Eugene. *Herbert Hoover, a Biography* (Doubleday & Co., 1964).

3. Conn, Stetson. *Guarding the United States and Its Outposts* (U. S. Army's Official History of World War II, 1964).

4. Hosokawa, Bill. *Nisei: The Quiet Americans* (William Morrow & Co., 1969).

5. Grodzins, Morton. *Americans Betrayed* (University of Chicago Press, 1949).

6. Biddle, Francis B. *In Brief Authority* (Doubleday & Co., 1962).

7. Stimson, Henry L. *On Active Service in Peace and War* (Harper & Row, 1968).

8. Blum, John Morton. *From the Morgenthau Diaries*, Vol. 3, *Years of War* (Houghton Mifflin, 1959–67).

9. Smith, Merriman. *Thank You, Mr. President* (Harper & Bros., 1946).

10. Rollins, Alfred B., Jr. *Roosevelt and Howe* (Alfred A. Knopf, 1962).

11. Anderson, Patrick. *The President's Men* (Doubleday & Co., 1968).

12. Lawrence, William. *Six Presidents, Too Many Wars* (Saturday Review Press, 1972).

13. Truman, Margaret. *Harry S. Truman* (William Morrow & Co., 1973).

14. Byrnes, James F. *Speaking Frankly* (Harper & Bros., 1947).

15. Druks, Herbert. *Harry S. Truman and the Russians* (Robert Speller & Sons, 1963).

16. Khrushchev, Nikita. *Khrushchev Remembers* (Little, Brown & Co., 1970).

17. Schlesinger, Arthur, Jr. *A Thousand Days* (Houghton Mifflin, 1965).

18. Corwin, Edward S. *The President: Office and Powers* (New York University Press, 1957).

19. Sorensen, Theodore. *Decision Making in the White House* (Columbia University Press, 1963).

20. Wicker, Tom. *JFK–LBJ: The Influence of Personality on Politics* (William Morrow & Co., 1968).

21. Eisenhower, Dwight D. *Waging Peace* (Doubleday & Co., 1965).

22. Eisenhower, Milton S. *The Wine Is Bitter* (Doubleday & Co., 1963).

23. Briggs, Ellis A. *Farewell to Foggy Bottom* (David McKay Co., 1964).

24. Donovan, Robert J. *The Inside Story* (Harper & Bros., 1956).

25. Eisenhower, Dwight D. *Mandate for Change* (Doubleday & Co., 1963).

26. Nixon, Richard M. *Six Crises* (Doubleday & Co., 1962).

27. Ambrose, Stephen E. *Rise to Globalism* (The Penguin Press, 1971).

28. Salinger, Pierre. *With Kennedy* (Doubleday & Co., 1966).

29. Sorensen, Theodore. *Kennedy* (Harper & Row, 1965).

30. De Toledano, Ralph. *The Man Who Would Be President* (New American Library, 1967).

31. Thimmesch, Nick, and Johnson, W. O. *Robert Kennedy at 40* (W. W. Norton & Co., 1965).

32. Rossiter, Clinton. *The American Presidency* (Harcourt, Brace & World, 1956).

33. Robinson, James Harvey. *The Human Comedy* (Harper & Bros., 1937).

34. Gray, Robert. *Eighteen Acres Under Glass* (Doubleday & Co., 1962).

35. Reedy, George E. *The Presidency in Flux* (Columbia University Press, 1972).

36. Zweig, Stefan. *Erasmus of Rotterdam* (Viking Press, 1956).

37. Lippmann, Walter. *Preface to Politics* (University of Michigan Press, 1962).

38. Reedy, George E. *The Twilight of the Presidency* (World Publishing Co., 1970).

39. Binkley, Wilfred E. *The Man in the White House* (The Johns Hopkins Press, 1958).

40. Wilcox, Francis O. *Congress, the Executive, and Foreign Policy* (Harper & Row, 1971).

ADDITIONAL BIBLIOGRAPHY

Abels, Jules. *In the Time of Silent Cal* (G. P. Putnam's Sons, 1969).

Bailey, Thomas A. *Presidential Greatness: The Image and the Man, from Washington to the Present* (Appleton-Century-Crofts, 1966).

Barber, James David. *The Presidential Character* (Prentice-Hall, 1972).

Burns, James MacGregor. *Roosevelt: The Lion and the Fox* (Harcourt, Brace & World, 1956).

Cunliffe, Marcus. *Presidents and the Presidency* (American Heritage Press, 1972).

Goldman, Eric F. *The Tragedy of Lyndon Johnson* (Alfred A. Knopf, 1969).

Gunther, John. *Roosevelt in Retrospect* (Harper & Bros., 1950).

Hinshaw, David. *Herbert Hoover, American Quaker* (Farrar, Straus & Co., 1950).

James, Dorothy Buckton. *The Contemporary Presidency* (Pegasus Press, 1969).

Japanese American Citizens League, The. "The Case for the Nisei," 1946 (a pamphlet).

Koenig, Louis W. *The Chief Executive* (Harcourt, Brace & World, Inc., 1968).

Krock, Arthur. *The Consent of the Governed and Other Deceits* (Little, Brown & Co., 1971).

McCoy, Donald R. *Calvin Coolidge: The Quiet President* (The Macmillan Co., 1967).

McPherson, Henry. *A Political Education* (Little, Brown & Co., 1972).

Mazo, Earl, and Hess, Stephen. *Nixon: A Political Portrait* (Harper & Row, 1969).

Moran, Philip R. *Calvin Coolidge, 1872–1933* (Chronology, Documents, and Bibliographical Aids) (Oceana Publications, Inc., 1970).

Neustadt, Richard E. *Presidential Power* (New American Library, 1964).

Parmet, Herbert S. *Eisenhower and the American Crusades* (The Macmillan Co., 1972).

Phillips, Cabell. *The Truman Presidency* (The Macmillan Co., 1966).

577

Quint, Howard H., and Ferrell, Robert H. *The Talkative President: The Off-the-Record Press Conferences of Calvin Coolidge* (The University of Massachusetts Press, 1964).

Rosenau, James N., ed. *The Roosevelt Treasury* (Doubleday & Co., 1951).

Rosenman, Samuel T. *Working with Roosevelt* (Harper & Bros., 1952).

Rourke, Francis. *Bureaucratic Power in National Politics* (Little, Brown & Co., 1965).

Sidey, Hugh. *A Very Personal Presidency* (Atheneum Publishers, 1968).

Vinyard, Dale. *The Presidency* (Charles Scribner's Sons, 1971).

Wharton, Don, ed. *The Roosevelt Omnibus* (Alfred A. Knopf, 1934).

White, Theodore H. *The Making of the President, 1964* (Atheneum Publishers, 1965).

INDEX

tion, 197; on conquerors, 201–3; on international understanding, 204; on power, 205, 549–50, 552; on Communism, 207–9; on Western world, 207–9; on building peace, 212; on Truman, 218, 221, 231; on limiting congressional terms, 236; on seniority system in Congress, 239; president of Penn State, 247; at Ike's inauguration, 253–54; work with PACGO, 255, 260; on Reorganization Act, 278–79; on single-subject legislation, 281; on Congress, 281–84; recommends line-veto authority, 282–84; on U.S. Latin policy, 286; on Latin population policy, 299; official travels, 302–3; on U.S. foreign service, 303–7; on bureaucracy, 304; negotiates space-flight cooperation with Mexico, 304–5; on diplomacy, 306; confidant to Ike, 308, 312–16, 348; on nepotism, 308, 367–68; at White House during Ike's presidency, 309; press conferences, 311; criticism of, 312; middle-roader, 316; on Ike's syntax, 321–22; on Nixon, 326–35; on Russian spy system, 335; with Khrushchev in U.S., 336–37; on St. Lawrence Seaway, 338; represents President, 339; on entertaining Presidents, 340–42; opposed to second term for Ike, 343–46; and Ted Kennedy, 369; and Shriver, 369; on JFK, 370; on committee to free Bay of Pigs prisoners, 372; becomes chairman of Republican Critical Issues Council, 385; delegate at 1964 convention, 388, 391–94; on political conventions, 395–404, 536; on primary elections, 399, 402; on political debates, 404; on campaign financing, 407–8; meets

LBJ, 412; studies canal site, 416; on South Vietnam invasion, 418; on Dominican crisis, 421–22; consulted by LBJ on Vietnam, 423; opposed Vietnam War, 423; on educational TV, 430; on gun control, 453–54; on running mate for Nixon, 461; friendship with Nixon family, 464, 484; in Soviet Union, 466–74; on radio commission, 475; on Cambodia bombing, 487–88; on media, 509, 570; on science and technology, 518; on industrialization, 520; on morality, 520–21; on foreign aid, 522; on presidential commissions, 536; on foreign service reduction, 537; on "palace guard," 538; supra-Cabinet proposal, 539–42, 552–53; proposals for Vice-Presidency changes, 539–41, 554; Domestic Council proposal, 542–44; on railroads, 548; on agriculture, 551; on executive privilege, 559; on impeachment, 564; on Watergate scandal, 570
Eisenhower, Roy, 187
Elections, primary, 399, 402
Elizabeth II, Queen of England, 269
El Salvador: sewage disposal system, 295; industrial production of, 297; population increases in, 298
Emergency Banking Relief Act, 71
Emergency Relief Administration, Federal, 159
Ennis, Edward, 109
Erasmus of Rotterdam (Zweig), 489
European Recovery Program, 211
Executive privilege, 559
Export-Import Bank, 75, 302

Fair Deal, 226
Famine Emergency Relief Committee, 179

P